THE CONTRACTUAL NATURE OF
THE OPTIONAL CLAUSE

The International Law Commission's Guiding Principles for Unilateral Declarations and its Guide to Practice on Reservations to Treaties are among the recent developments in international law. These developments support a new assessment on how optional clauses (eg Article 62(1) of the American Convention on Human Rights) and especially the Optional Clause (Article 36(2) of the Statute of the International Court of Justice (ICJ)) can be characterised and treated. The question is in how far optional clauses and the respective declarations can be considered a multilateral treaty or a bundle of unilateral declarations and to what extent one of the corresponding regimes applies.

Based, inter alia, on the jurisprudence of the Permanent Court of International Justice and the ICJ on the Optional Clause, but also on the relevant jurisprudence of the Inter-American Court of Human Rights and the European Court of Human Rights and the General Comments of the United Nations Human Rights Committee, this book provides a comprehensive assessment of all legal issues regarding the Optional Clause and also optional clauses in general. The book deals with the making of Optional Clause declarations, the interpretation of such declarations and reservations made to the declarations as well as the withdrawal or amendment of declarations.

Volume 54 in the series Studies in International Law

Studies in International Law

Recent titles in this series

The Politics of International Criminal Justice: A Spotlight on Germany
Ronen Steinke

Fighting Corruption in Public Procurement: A Comparative Analysis of
Disqualification or Debarment Measures
Sope Williams-Elegbe

The Interception of Vessels on the High Seas: Contemporary Challenges
to the Legal Order of the Oceans
Efthymios Papastavridis

Integration at the Border: The Dutch Act on Integration Abroad and
International Immigration Law
Karin de Vries

An Equitable Framework for Humanitarian Intervention
Ciarán Burke

Democratic Statehood in International Law: The Emergence of New
States in Post-Cold War Practice
Jure Vidmar

International Law and the Construction of the Liberal Peace
Russell Buchan

The OIC, the UN, and Counter-Terrorism Law-Making: Conflicting or
Cooperative Legal Orders?
Katja Samuel

Statelessness: The Enigma of the International Community
William E Conklin

The Reception of Asylum Seekers under International Law: Between
Sovereignty and Equality
Lieneke Slingenberg

International Law and Child Soldiers
Gus Waschefort

**For the complete list of titles in this series, see 'Studies in International
Law' link at www.hartpub.co.uk/books/series.asp**

The Contractual Nature of the Optional Clause

Gunnar Törber

·HART·
PUBLISHING

OXFORD AND PORTLAND, OREGON
2017

Hart Publishing

An imprint of Bloomsbury Publishing Plc

Hart Publishing Ltd   Bloomsbury Publishing Plc
Kemp House   50 Bedford Square
Chawley Park   London
Cumnor Hill   WC1B 3DP
Oxford OX2 9PH   UK
UK

www.hartpub.co.uk
www.bloomsbury.com

Published in North America (US and Canada) by
Hart Publishing
c/o International Specialized Book Services
920 NE 58th Avenue, Suite 300
Portland, OR 97213-3786
USA

www.isbs.com

**HART PUBLISHING, the Hart/Stag logo, BLOOMSBURY and the
Diana logo are trademarks of Bloomsbury Publishing Plc**

First published in hardback, 2015
Paperback edition, 2017

British Library Cataloguing-in-Publication Data
A catalogue record for this book is available from the British Library.

ISBN: PB: 978-1-50991-768-6
HB: 978-1-84946-866-4

Typeset by Compuscript Ltd, Shannon
Printed and bound in Great Britain by
Lightning Source UK Ltd

To find out more about our authors and books visit www.hartpublishing.co.uk. Here you will
find extracts, author information, details of forthcoming events and the option to sign up for our
newsletters.

Erster Berichterstatter: Prof Dr Christian Walter
Zweiter Berichterstatter: Prof Dr Andreas von Arnauld
Dekan: Prof Dr Thomas Hoeren
Tag der mündlichen Prüfung: 09.07.2013

D 6

Zugl: Münster (Westf), Univ, Diss der Rechtswissenschaftlichen Fakultät, 2013.

Acknowledgements

This book is based on my doctoral thesis which has been accepted by the Faculty of Law of the University of Münster in 2013. Thanks to the flexibility of Hart Publishing, the current version of the book contains all recent developments up to the new Optional Clause declarations of Italy (25 November 2014) and the United Kingdom of Great Britain and Northern Ireland (31 December 2014).

My thesis has been supervised by Prof Dr Christian Walter whom I thank very much for his great support. He has always been available for discussion during the whole production of the manuscript and has provided helpful suggestions as well as sufficient scientific latitude. Furthermore, I have been honoured by having Prof Dr Andreas von Arnauld as second reviewer. He has also provided impulses for the later revision which I was happy to implement.

This book has furthermore largely benefited from the help of some dear friends of mine: many thanks go to Adrian Hoppe, Daniel Scholz, Sönke Sievers, Jonas Takors, Kristin Vorbeck and Andreas Weiss. They have provided valuable support, either through discussions during the time of writing or by commenting on the draft manuscript. I also want to thank Bill Asquith from Hart Publishing for the fruitful collaboration.

Furthermore, cordial thanks are due to my family, especially to my brother Ragnar Törber for his unconditional companionship and to Jürgen Böse for decades of backing.

Gunnar Törber,
Berlin, 2015

Summary of Contents

Detailed Table of Contents

List of Abbreviations

ACHR	American Convention on Human Rights
CCPR	International Covenant on Civil and Political Rights
CERD	International Convention on the Elimination of All Forms of Racial Discrimination
CESCR	International Covenant on Economic, Social and Cultural Rights
Convention against Torture	United Nations Convention against Torture and Other Cruel, Inhuman or Degrading Treatment or Punishment
Covenant	Covenant of the League of Nations
CRC	Convention on the Rights of the Child
ECHR	European Convention on Human Rights
ECJ	European Court of Justice
EComHR	European Commission of Human Rights
ECtHR	European Court of Human Rights
EMRK	Europäische Menschenrechtskonvention
ETS	European Treaty Series
European Convention	European Convention for the Peaceful Settlement of Disputes
FAO	Food and Agriculture Organization
General Act	General Act for the Pacific Settlement of International Disputes
Genocide Convention	Convention on the Prevention and Punishment of the Crime of Genocide
GPRT	Guide to Practice on Reservations to Treaties
GPUD	Guiding Principles for Unilateral Declarations (Guiding Principles applicable to unilateral declarations of States capable of creating legal obligations)
IACtHR	Inter-American Court of Human Rights
ICAO	International Civil Aviation Organization
ICJ/Court	International Court of Justice

ICSID	International Centre for the Settlement of Investment Disputes
ILA	International Law Association
ILC	International Law Commission
IRRC	International Review of the Red Cross
NATO	North Atlantic Treaty Organisation
OAS	Organization of American State
Pact of Bogotá	American Treaty on Pacific Settlement
PCIJ/Permanent Court	Permanent Court of International Justice
Revised General Act	Revised General Act for the Pacific Settlement of International Disputes
RIAA	Reports of International Arbitral Awards
Secretary-General	Secretary-General of the United Nations
UNCIO	United Nations Conference on International Organization
UNCHR	United Nations Committee on Human Rights
UNTS	United Nations Treaty Series
VCCR	Vienna Convention on Consular Relations
VCLT	Vienna Convention on the Law of Treaties
WHO	World Health Organisation

List of Cases

European Court of Justice

ECJ, *A Racke GmbH & Co v Hauptzollamt Mainz* (Case C-162/96) [1998] ECR I-3688

European Commission of Human Rights

EComHR, *Chrysostomos ao v Turkey* (App no 15299/89) ao [1991]
EComHR, *France ao v Turkey (Admissibility)* (App No 9940–9944/82) [1983]
EComHR, *Temeltasch v Switzerland* (App no 9116/80) [1983]
EComHR, *Austria v Italy* (App no 788/60) [1961]

European Court of Human Rights

ECtHR, *Loizidou v Turkey* (Preliminary Objections, Series A No 310) [1995]
ECtHR, *Chorherr v Austria* (Series A No 266-B) [1993]
ECtHR, *Weber v Switzerland* (Series A no 177) [1990]
ECtHR, *Belilos v Switzerland* (Series A no 132) [1988]
ECtHR, *Ireland v United Kingdom* (Series A no 25) [1978]

Inter-American Court of Human Rights

IACtHR, *Hilaire v Trinidad and Tobago* (Preliminary Objections) [2001] IACtHR
 Series C No 80
IACtHR, *Constitutional Court v Peru* (Competence) [1999] IACtHR Series C No 55
IACtHR, *Ivcher Bronstein v Peru* (Competence) [1999] IACtHR Series C No 54
IACtHR, *Restrictions to the Death Penalty (Arts 4(2) and (4) American Convention on
 Human Rights)* (Advisory Opinion) [1983] IACtHR Series A No 3
IACtHR, *The Effect of Reservations on the Entry Into Force of the American Convention on
 Human Rights (Arts 74 and 75)* (Advisory Opinion) [1982] IACtHR Series A No 2

International Court of Justice

ICJ, *Questions relating to the Seizure and Detention of Certain Documents and Data
 (Timor-Leste v Australia)* (Provisional Measures) [2014] http://www.icj-cij.org/
 docket/files/156/18078.pdf (last visit on 19 January 2015)
ICJ, *Whaling in the Antarctic (Australia v Japan; New Zealand intervening)* (Merits)
 [2014] http://www.icj-cij.org/docket/files/148/18136.pdf (last visit on 19
 January 2015)
ICJ, *Application of the International Convention on the Elimination of all Forms of Racial
 Discrimination (Georgia v Russian Federation)* (Preliminary Objections) [2011] ICJ
 Rep 70
ICJ, *Certain Activities Carried out by Nicaragua in the Border Area (Costa Rica v
 Nicaragua)* (Provisional Measures) [2011] ICJ Rep 6
ICJ, *Dispute Regarding Navigational and Related Rights (Costa Rica v Nicaragua)*
 (Judgment) [2009] ICJ Rep 13

International Centre for the Settlement of Investment Disputes

ICSID, *Gas Natural SDG, S.A. v Argentina* (Case No ARB/03/10) [2005]

Permanent Court of International Justice

PCIJ, *Electricity Company of Sofia and Bulgaria (Belgium v Bulgaria)* (Preliminary Objection) [1939] PCIJ Series A/B No 77 63

PCIJ, *Phosphates in Morocco (Italy v France)* (Preliminary Objections) [1938] PCIJ Series A/B No 74 9

PCIJ, *Free Zones of Upper Savoy and the District of Gex (France v Switzerland)* (Judgment) [1932] PCIJ Series A/B No 46 95

PCIJ, *Legal Status of the South-Eastern Territory of Greenland (Norway v Denmark)* (Interim Measures of Protection) [1932] PCIJ Series A/B No 48 276

PCIJ, *Customs Régime between Germany and Austria* (Advisory Opinion) [1931] PCIJ Series A/B No 41 37

PCIJ, *Brazilian Loans case (France v Brazil)* (Judgment) [1929] PCIJ Series A No 21 93

PCIJ, *Free Zones of Upper Savoy and the District of Gex (France v Switzerland)* (Order) [1929] PCIJ Series A No 22 4

PCIJ, *Case concerning the Factory at Chorzów (Germany v Poland)* (Jurisdiction) [1927] PCIJ Series A No 9 3

PCIJ, *The Case of the S. S. Lotus (France v Turkey)* (Judgment) [1927] PCIJ Series A No 10 3

PCIJ, *Exchange of Greek and Turkish Populations* (Advisory Opinion) [1925] PCIJ Series B No 10 5

PCIJ, *Polish Postal Service in Danzig* (Advisory Opinion) [1925] PCIJ Series B No 11 5

PCIJ, *Mavrommatis Palestine Concessions (Greece v United Kingdom)* (Jurisdiction) [1924] PCIJ Series A No 2 5

PCIJ, *S. S. Wimbledon Case (United Kingdom, France, Italy and Japan v Germany)* (Judgment) [1923] PCIJ Series A No 1 15

PCIJ, *Status of Eastern Carelia* (Advisory Opinion) [1923] PCIJ Series B No 5 7

Permanent Court of Arbitration

Permanent Court of Arbitration, *Award of the Arbitral Tribunal in the First Stage of the Proceedings between Eritrea v Yemen (Territorial Sovereignty and Scope of the Dispute)* [1998] RIAA 209

Permanent Court of Arbitration, *Delimitation of the Continental Shelf between the United Kingdom of Great Britain and Northern Ireland, and the French Republic (United Kingdom v France)* [1977] RIAA 3

United Nations Committee on Human Rights

UNCHR, *Manuel Wackenheim v France* (Communication No 854/1999) (2002) CCPR/C/75/D/854/1999

UNCHR, *Rawle Kennedy v Trinidad and Tobago* (Communication No 845/1999) (1999) CCPR/C/67/D/845/1999

Table of Dissenting Opinions, Separate Opinions and Declarations

Table of Miscellaneous Documents

Australia, *Current Notes on International Affairs, Vol 25* (Canberra, 1954) cited as 'Australia, Current Notes'

Council of Europe, Recommendation of the Committee of Ministers to member states on the acceptance of the jurisdiction of the International Court of Justice (2008) CM/Rec(2008)8

El Salvador, 'Declaration by El Salvador relating to the objection notified by the Government of Honduras on 3 July 1974' (1974) 948 *United Nations Treaty Series* 531 cited as 'El Salvador, Declaration'

ILA, Report of the Sixty Ninth Conference, London (2000) http://www.ila-hq.org/en/committees/index.cfm/cid/30 (last visit on 19 January 2015)

ILA, Report of the Fifty-First Conference, Tokyo (London, 1965)

Institut de Droit International, Compulsory Jurisdiction of International Courts and Tribunals (1959) http://www.idi-iil.org/idiE/navig_chon1953.html (last visit on 19 January 2015)

Institut de Droit International, Signature de la clause facultative de la Cour permanente de Justice internationale (1921) http://www.idi-iil.org/idiF/navig_chron1913.html (last visit on 19 January 2015)

League of Nations, Procès-verbaux des sessions XLVIII A LII du conseil (1929) League of Nations Official Journal Supplément Spécial No 72

League of Nations, Actes de la neuvième session ordinaire de l'Assemblée, Séances plénières (1928) League of Nations Official Journal Supplément Spécial No 64

League of Nations, Minutes of the Conference of States Signatories of the Protocol of Signature of the Statute of the Permanent Court of International Justice (1926) http://www.icj-cij.org/pcij/other-documents.php?p1=9&p2=8 (last visit on 19 January 2015)

League of Nations, Actes de la cinquième Assemblée, Séances de commissions, Procès-verbaux de la première commission (Questions constitutionnelles) (1924) League of Nations Official Journal Supplément Spécial No 24

League of Nations, Actes de la cinquième Assemblée, Séances plénières, Compte rendu de débats (1924) League of Nations Official Journal Supplément Spécial No 23

League of Nations, Protocol for the Pacific Settlement of International Disputes (1924) International Conciliation, Volume 205

League of Nations, Documents Concerning the Action Taken by the Council of the League of Nations under Article 14 of the Covenant and the Adoption by the Assembly of the Statute of the Permanent Court (1921) http://www.icj-cij.org/pcij/other-documents.php?p1=9&p2=8 (last visit on 19 January 2015)

League of Nations, Advisory Committee of Jurists, Documents Presented to the Committee Relating to Existing Plans for the Establishment of a Permanent Court of International Justice (1920) http://www.icj-cij.org/pcij/other-documents.php?p1=9&p2=8 (last visit on 19 January 2015)

League of Nations, *Records of the First Assembly, Meetings of the Committees* (Geneva, League of Nations, 1920) cited as 'League of Nations, *Records of the First Assembly, Meetings of the Committees*'

League of Nations, *Records of the First Assembly, Plenary Meetings* (Geneva, League of Nations, 1920) cited as 'League of Nations, *Records of the First Assembly, Plenary Meetings*'

Ministère des Affaires Étrangères, La Deuxième Conférence Internationale de la Paix—Actes et Documents, Tome Premier—Séances Plénières de la Conférence (La Haye, Imprimerie Nationale, 1907)

Ministère des Affaires Étrangères, La Deuxième Conférence Internationale de la Paix—Actes et Documents, Tome Deux—Première Commission (La Haye, Imprimerie Nationale, 1907)

PCIJ, Collection of Texts Governing the Jurisdiction of the Court (PCIJ Series D No 6) (1932)

UNCHR, General Comment No 26 (61) on issues relating to the continuity of obligations to the International Covenant on Civil and Political Rights (1997) CCPR/C/21/Rev.1/Add.8/Rev.1

UNCHR, General Comment No 24 (52) on issues relating to reservations made upon ratification or accession to the Covenant to the Optional Protocols thereto, or in relation to declarations under article 41 of the Covenant (1994) CCPR/C/21/Rev.1/Add.6

UNGA, Fifty-first Session, Report of the Human Rights Committee (1996) UN Doc A/51/40

UNGA, Peaceful settlement of international disputes (1974) UN Doc A/Res/3283 (XXIX)

UNGA, Review of the role of the International Court of Justice (1974) UN Doc A/Res/3232 (XXIX)

UNGA, Official Records of the Twenty-First Session, Third Committee, 1438th Meeting (1966) UN Doc A/C.3/SR.1438

UNGA, Official Records of the Twenty-First Session, Third Committee, 1439th Meeting (1966) UN Doc A/C.3/SR.1439

UNGA, Official Records of the Twenty-First Session, Third Committee, 1440th Meeting (1966) UN Doc A/C.3/SR.1440

UNGA, Resolution on the International Covenant on Economic, Social and Cultural Rights, the International Covenant on Civil and Political Rights and the Optional Protocol to the International Covenant on Civil and Political Rights (1966) UN Doc A/RES/2200 (XXI)

UNGA, Official Records of the Second Session of the General Assembly, Resolutions (1948) UN Doc A/519

United Kingdom, 'Observations by the United Kingdom on General Comment No 24 (52)' (1995) 16 *Human Rights Law Journal* 424 cited as 'United Kingdom, Observations'

United Nations, Official Records of the United Nations Conference on the Law of Treaties, First and Second Session, Documents of the Conference (1971) A/CONF.39/1 1/Add.2

United Nations, Official Records of the United Nations Conference on the Law of Treaties, Second Session, 9 April–22 May 1969 (1970) A/CONF.39/ll/Add.l

United Nations, *UNCIO I* (London, United Nations Information Organizations, 1945) cited as 'United Nations, *Conference on International Organization, Volume I—General*'

United Nations, *UNCIO XIII* (London, United Nations Information Organizations, 1945) cited as 'United Nations, *Conference on International Organization, Volume XIII—Commission IV, Judicial Organization*'

United Nations, *UNCIO XIV* (London, United Nations Information Organizations, 1945) cited as 'United Nations, *Conference on International Organization, Volume XIV—United Nations Committee of Jurists*'

United States of America, 'Memorandum Regarding Article XIII of the International Convention for the Prevention of Pollution of the Sea by Oil, May 23, 1960' (1960) 54 American Journal of International Law 941 cited as 'United States of America, Memorandum'

United States of America, Congressional Record (1946)

UNSC, Resolution of 15 October 1946 (1946) UN Doc S/Res/9(1946)

Introduction

The Optional Clause is provided for in Article 36(2) of the Statute. It reads as follows:

> The states parties to the present Statute may at any time declare that they recognize as compulsory ipso facto and without special agreement, in relation to any other state accepting the same obligation, the jurisdiction of the Court in all legal disputes concerning:
>
> a. the interpretation of a treaty;
> b. any question of international law;
> c. the existence of any fact which, if established, would constitute a breach of an international obligation;
> d. the nature or extent of the reparation to be made for the breach of an international obligation.

The Optional Clause is one means amongst others to establish the jurisdiction of the International Court of Justice (ICJ). Among these means it is, at least according to its drafters, an outstanding one. It was created in 1920 after the League of Nations had already been established and the elaboration of the Statute of the Permanent Court was one of the remaining projects to complete it. The majority of states wanted a court with compulsory jurisdiction for all disputes among them. Especially the smaller powers considered such a court as an instrument ensuring legal equality between them and the major powers. For the smaller states it was part of a bargain. They wanted a court with compulsory jurisdiction in return for their acceptance of the Council of the League, which increased the power of the major states as its permanent members. However, during the drafting of the Statute of the Permanent Court it became clear that at least some members of the already established Council of the League were unwilling to join a statute which would have provided compulsory jurisdiction itself. They ultimately refused and told the other states that, to use the words of United Kingdom's delegate Balfour in the General Assembly of the League of Nations, 'natura non fecit saltus' and that 'the true path of progress is the path of gradual, steady, wise and wholesome development'.[1] As medium for this development, the Optional Clause was designed.[2]

---

[1] League of Nations, *Records of the First Assembly, Plenary Meetings* 487, 489.
[2] For more on the Optional Clause's genesis see sub-s II A ii of ch 1 at 24 and sub-s II B of ch 2 at 55.

I. THE REASONS FOR THIS WORK

Eighty-seven years later, in November 2007, Simma aptly addressed the current situation of this Optional Clause. He concluded that it had enjoyed a certain success so far but also held that the high hopes connected to it still remained unfulfilled.[3]

Today, out of the United Nation's 193 Member States only 71 have made an Optional Clause declaration. The only permanent member of the UN Security Council with a valid Optional Clause declaration is the United Kingdom and many declarations are of limited value only as they contain substantial reservations.[4]

One strong factor for the limited success of the Optional Clause is the political problems surrounding it. States have to bind themselves, at least to a certain degree, to one means of peaceful dispute settlement. Therefore, many states would still be reluctant to join the Optional Clause even if it were a legally perfect, transparent and secure means to carry their intent. However, sometimes it seems that the Optional Clause is not even that. Even though Article 36(2) of the Statute has been subject to many scholarly articles, court rulings and even several theses,[5] there remain some unsettled issues and imbalances in the system as it is commonly understood today. This, the Optional Clause's current legal status, is likely to impair its success and the achievement of its objective pronounced in 1920. Despite all political reasons the states should at least not have legal insecurity as a reason not to join the Optional Clause.

Starting with the imbalances, the first is sometimes referred to as the 'sitting duck' problem.[6] States which have not made an Optional Clause declaration are in the position to opportunistically submit a declaration anytime and to immediately institute proceedings against a 'sitting duck' state with a long standing declaration whenever it is appropriate.[7] The second questionable phenomenon is the reservations which allow states to totally or partially withdraw their Optional Clause declarations with immediate effect. Because of these reservations states can reduce their commitment under the Optional Clause as soon as a dispute is likely to be brought before the Court. Therefore, these reservations hang like a Sword

---

[3] B Simma, 'Article 36 (2) of the ICJ Statute' 455–59.

[4] All the current declarations and their reservations can be found under http://www.icj-cij.org/jurisdiction/index.php?p1=5&p2=1&p3=3 (last visit on 19 January 2015) or in the Court's Yearbook. The declarations are also published in the UNTS under 'Treaties and international agreements' when they appear.

[5] For the latter see SA Alexandrov, *Declarations*; AN Farmanfarma, *Declarations*; B Maus, *Réserves*; F Wittmann, *Obligatorium*; H Wundram, *Fakultativklausel*.

[6] cp SA Alexandrov, 'Reservations' 105–08; A D'Amato, 'Modifying' 387 and also CHM Waldock, 'Decline' 280–83.

[7] For more on this issue see sub-s III A of ch 3 at 95.

of Damocles over other ways of peaceful dispute settlement. States facing another state which has made a declaration with such a reservation have to file an application before that state can withdraw its declaration. Thereby the reservations encourage a premature filing of applications.[8] The result has already been called a 'race to The Hague' between the notice of withdrawal and the application.[9] Unfortunately, the current jurisprudence of the Court further encourages states to include such reservations allowing them to withdraw without a period of notice. It has decided that reservations like these cannot be applied reciprocally.[10] States have to include them themselves if they do not want to grant other states a one-sided advantage.[11] The question is whether this really is the law.

It seems as if particularly the freedom to make reservations, which is said to be unlimited, has encouraged state practice which, at least regarding certain issues, is inconsistent with the original intention behind the Optional Clause. The resulting question is whether states have already established customary law or whether the Court could be stricter with those states and impede at least some of the destructive tactics like those referred to above. The recent developments in the field of human rights treaties, like for example the United Nations Commission on Human Rights' (UNCHR) more restrictive approach for reservations, could be a guideline.[12]

This idea, however, leads to the aforementioned problem that not all legal issues concerning the Optional Clause have been settled. Foremost, it is not clear which law to apply to the Optional Clause. Possible candidates are the rules for unilateral declarations and the law of treaties. The Optional Clause has been excluded from the codification of both. In the appendum to his ninth report on unilateral acts of states the International Law Commission's (ILC) Special Rapporteur Rodríguez-Cedeño described the scope of application of what became the Guiding Principles for Unilateral Declarations (GPUD). He wrote that 'excluded are declarations of acceptance of the compulsory jurisdiction of the International Court of Justice, which, although they are also unilateral as to their form, fall under the Vienna regime on the law of treaties'.[13] However, during the

---

[8] cp eg Waldock (n 6) 266.

[9] Notion from IR Cohn, 'Pre-Seisin Reciprocity' 699. For more on this issue see sub-ss III B iii c and iv–vii of ch 5 at 216 to 252.

[10] *Military and Paramilitary Activities in and against Nicaragua (Nicaragua v United States of America)* (Jurisdiction and Admissibility) [1984] ICJ Rep 392, para 62.

[11] For more on this issue see sub-s II C of ch 5 at 181.

[12] C Walter, 'Rechtsschutz' para 45.

[13] ILC 'Ninth Report on Unilateral Acts of States—Addendum' (6 April 2006) UN Doc A/CN.4/569/Add.1 para 130 (Rodríguez Cedeño). See also ILC 'Documents of the 50th Session' (1998) UN Doc A/CN.4/SER.A/1998/Add.1 (Part 1) 330–33, paras 96, 115–18 (Rodríguez Cedeño); ILC 'Documents of the 54th Session' (2002) UN Doc A/CN.4/SER.A/2002/Add.1 (Part 1) 101, para 73 (Rodríguez Cedeño); ILC 'Report of the International

drafting of the Vienna Convention on the Law of Treaties (VCLT) every reference to the Optional Clause was deleted.[14] And, as the ILC recently drafted the Guide to Practice on Reservations to Treaties (GPRT), it likewise excluded the Optional Clause from the scope of application of these guidelines. Guideline 1.5.3(2) GPRT expressly provides:

> A restriction or condition contained in a statement by which a State or an international organization accepts, by virtue of a clause in a treaty, an obligation that is not otherwise imposed by the treaty does not constitute a reservation.[15]

On the other hand case law concerning Optional Clause declarations has been used both in the establishment of the law for unilateral declarations and in the establishment of the law of treaties. Principle 7 GPUD concerning the interpretation of unilateral declarations is, for example, drafted with reference to the Court's interpretation of the Iranian Optional Clause declaration in the *Anglo-Iranian Oil Co* case and the interpretation of the Canadian Optional Clause declaration in the *Fisheries Jurisdiction* case between Spain and Canada.[16] The principle for the termination of unilateral acts is, at least to some degree, based on the Court's judgment concerning the United States' attempt to withdraw its Optional Clause declaration in the *Nicaragua* case.[17]

For the law of treaties the ILC referred to the 'analogous situation of the deposit of instruments of acceptance of the optional clause under Article 36, paragraph 2 of the Statute of the Court' and the judgment of the Court in the *Right of Passage* case as it drafted what finally became Article 16 VCLT.[18] Furthermore, state practice under the Optional Clause

---

Law Commission on the Work of Its 58th Session' (1 May–9 June and 3 July–11 August 2006) UN Doc A/61/10 378, fn 970 supported by ILC 'Summary Records of the Meetings of the 53rd Session' (23 April–1 June and 2 July–10 August 2001) UN Doc A/CN.4/SER.A/2001 189 f, para 33 (Herdocia Sacasa).

[14] ILC 'Summary Records of the 40th Session' (24 April–29 June 1962) UN Doc A/CN.4/Ser.A/1962 265, paras 135, 141. For more on this issue see s VI of ch 2 at 83.

[15] ILC 'Report of the International Law Commission on the Work of Its 63rd Session' (26 April–3 June and 4 July–12 August 2011) UN Doc A/66/10/Add.1 4. See also ILC 'Report of the International Law Commission on the Work of Its 62nd Session' (3 May–4 June and 5 July–6 August 2010) UN Doc A/65/10 40 and ILC 'Report of the Commission to the General Assembly on the Work of Its 52nd Session' (1 May–9 June and 10 July–18 August 2000) UN Doc A/CN.4/SER.A/2000/Add.1 (Part 2)/Rev.1 112–14.

[16] ILC 'Documents of the 53rd Session' (2001) UN Doc A/CN.4/SER.A/2001/Add.1 (Part 1) 130–33, paras 117, 121 f, 127, 135 f (Rodriguez Cedeño); ILC 'Report of the International Law Commission on the Work of Its 58th Session' (n 13) 377 (Note that draft principle 11 became Principle 7 GPUD). For similar reasoning in prior legal literature see eg G Schwarzenberger, *International Law* 555–58. Compare also the reasoning of Austria during the drafting process of the GPUD (ILC 'Documents of the 52nd Session' (2000) UN Doc A/CN.4/SER.A/2000/Add.1 (Part 1) 279).

[17] ILC 'Ninth Report on Unilateral Acts of States—Addendum' (n 13) para 87 (Rodríguez Cedeño).

[18] ILC 'Documents of the Second Part of the 17th Session and of the 18th Session Including the Reports of the Commission to the General Assembly' (1966) UN Doc A/CN.4/SER.A/1966/Add.1 201, para 3. See also O Elias and C Lim, 'Right of Passage Doctrine' 239.

has been used to support the draft article concerning the termination of treaties without corresponding provision,[19] and the jurisprudence concerning the Optional Clause declarations has been considered in relation to Article 41 VCLT and to the provision which became Article 44 VCLT.[20] Commentators on Article 56 VCLT refer inter alia to the Court's judgment in the *Nicaragua* case to prove the general customary nature of that article.[21] The same holds true for Article 44 VCLT,[22] and as the ILC recently drafted the GPRT, it again referred to Optional Clause declarations.[23] Especially the new Guideline 4.2.6 GPRT on the interpretation of reservations is based on the Court's jurisprudence on Optional Clause declarations.[24]

It becomes obvious that so far the Optional Clause has been considered as being somewhere in between the law of unilateral declarations and the law of treaties. In this context it would be interesting to know how far the Optional Clause can be treated like other optional clauses and how far optional clauses can generally be handled like treaties.[25] In the case of the Optional Clause, many of its aspects have been discussed in depth before the Court and in literature. Nevertheless, some of those topics have not really been settled yet. The withdrawing of Optional Clause declarations has been considered lengthily since the *Nicaragua* case. However, as the pleadings before the Court concerning the *Territorial and Maritime Dispute* between Nicaragua and Colombia show, it remains an open question. The Court refrained from addressing the issue for the *Territorial and Maritime Dispute* as it already had jurisdiction due to the Pact of Bogotá.[26]

Another issue which has been discussed very little is the hitherto unique Spanish reservation which links the period of notice for a withdrawal of the Spanish declaration to the period of notice of other declarations.[27]

---

[19] ILC 'Documents of the 15th Session Including the Report of the Commission to the General Assembly' (1963) UN Doc A/CN.4/SER.A/1963 68, para 18 (Waldock). See also the response of Verdross (ILC 'Summary Records of the 15th Session' (6 May–12 July 1963) UN Doc A/CN.4/SER.A/1963 101 f).

[20] ILC 'Documents of the 15th Session Including the Report of the Commission to the General Assembly' (ibid) 91 f, paras 6–8 (Waldock); ILC 'Documents of the Second Part of the 17th Session and of the 18th Session Including the Reports of the Commission to the General Assembly' (n 18) 238, para 1.

[21] T Christakis, 'Article 56 (2006)' paras 17 f; T Giegerich, 'Article 56 VCLT' paras 42, 53.

[22] cp K Odendahl, 'Article 44' paras 6, 9, fn 16, 29.

[23] See eg ILC 'Report of the International Law Commission on the Work of Its 62nd Session' (n 15) 142, 170 f, 200 f.

[24] ILC 'Report of the International Law Commission on the Work of Its 63rd Session' (n 15) 468, 470 f, paras 3, 5, 9, 13.

[25] See also K Oellers-Frahm, 'Der Rücktritt der USA' 566: 'Zwar ist auch auf einseitige Unterwerfungserklärungen Vertragsrecht grundsätzlich entsprechend anwendbar; fraglich ist jedoch, wo im Einzelnen die Gleichbehandlung von Verträgen und Unterwerfungserklärungen endet'.

[26] *Territorial and Maritime Dispute (Nicaragua v Colombia)* (Preliminary Objections) [2007] ICJ Rep 832, paras 138–40. For more on this issue see s II of ch 6 at 279.

[27] For more on this reservation see sub-ss II C iii b and v of ch 5 at 189 and 198.

As this reservation presumes that the states can shape their relationships under the Optional Clause also *inter partes* the question is to what extent the Optional Clause can be 'bilateralised'. This might also be relevant to answer the question of what role objections under the Optional Clause play. In January 2002, Costa Rica, for example, objected to a new reservation which Nicaragua had made to its Optional Clause in October 2001.[28]

II. THE COURSE OF THIS WORK

After all that has been said above, the main question of the present work is to what extent the Optional Clause is like a treaty and to what extent treaty law can be applied to it. In this regard, recent achievements in international law like the ILC's GPUD and its GPRT or maybe even the recent developments in human rights treaty law could be a help for further clarification.

The first necessary step to answer the central question will be an assessment of the obligations under Article 36(2) of the Statute. This is important as there have been two positions which influence the general perspective on the Optional Clause. Firstly, it has been said that the Optional Clause or, respectively, the Optional Clause declarations contained no obligations before the seisin of the Court for a particular case. Secondly, it has been said that an Optional Clause declaration established a relationship between the submitting state and the Court and not between the submitting state and other states. These issues are to a certain degree related and a clear answer in this regard is indispensable for any further assessment of the Optional Clause. They will be the subject of the first chapter which will also include a comparison to other optional clauses. The chapter will show that Optional Clause declarations establish horizontal rights and obligations between the states and that these rights and obligations exist already before the seisin of the Court for a particular case.

Based on the result of the first chapter the following chapter will address the unilateral origin of the Optional Clause declarations and assess to what extent the Optional Clause can be considered a treaty. It will not only refer to the GPUD but also to the wording and the genesis of Article 36 of the Statute, the other means to establish the Court's jurisdiction, state practice and the Court's jurisprudence. In the process, the

---

[28] This communication is attached to Nicaragua's Optional Clause declaration on the Court's homepage: http://www.icj-cij.org/jurisdiction/index.php?p1=5&p2=1&p3=3& code=NI (last visit on 19 January 2015). For more on objections to reservations see s V of ch 5 at 263. For more on the communication between Nicaragua and Costa Rice see sub-s II C i e of ch 6 at 299. For more on mutual amendments to Optional Clause declarations see sub-s III B of ch 6 at 316.

chapter will not address the practical consequences of the Optional Clause's legal nature. The questions concerning the rules for reservations and for withdrawals for example will be the subject of the later chapters. The result of the second chapter will be that the structure of the Optional Clause is similar to that of an optional protocol and that the Optional Clause can best be considered as an additional treaty to the Statute.

The third chapter will be the first one dealing with a practical aspect and will discuss the creation of obligations under the Optional Clause. Its subject will be the difference between the Optional Clause and treaties when it comes to issues like ratification for example. A main part of this chapter will be the question whether Article 36(4) of the Statute or another provision requires that an Optional Clause declaration has to be received by another state before it can have an effect. In relation to this the afore-mentioned 'sitting duck' problem will also be considered. The chapter will show that Optional Clause declarations are like accessions to a multilateral treaty and enter into force immediately when they are deposited with the Secretary-General.

According to many authors a difference between the Optional Clause and treaties is the way Optional Clause declarations are interpreted. The fourth chapter will address this question and ask whether such a difference really exists. As with most other chapters, this one will start with a short application of treaty law to the Optional Clause and then compare the result with state practice and jurisprudence. Taking into consideration the new developments in treaty law, the fourth chapter will show that Optional Clause declarations and their reservations have been interpreted like declarations of accession to a multilateral treaty and their reservations.

The fifth chapter will be the longest as it will assess the regime for reservations under the Optional Clause which many authors also consider to be different to the one for treaties. The question here will be to what extent the Articles 19 to 23 VCLT can be applied to the Optional Clause and again whether the Optional Clause is different from a treaty in this aspect. Subject of this assessment will be the effect of reservations, the objective permissibility of reservations and the role of objections to reservations. Thereby, this chapter will also answer the question whether the tendencies in the practice of human rights treaty bodies can be transferred to the Optional Clause. Moreover, this chapter will be the major place where the possibility of bilateralised relations under the Optional Clause will be taken into consideration. The result of this chapter will be that the regime for reservations under the Optional Clause is not different from the regime provided for by Articles 19 to 23 VCLT. However, the tendencies in the practice of human rights treaty bodies cannot be transferred.

The withdrawal of Optional Clause declarations will be subject of the sixth and last chapter. Also in this regard it is controversial to what extent the Optional Clause is like a treaty. The cases in which a withdrawal cannot be based on a reservation will be most interesting. The question is whether states can invoke the principle of *clausula rebus sic stantibus*, Article 56 VCLT or even the violation of the obligations under the Optional Clause by another state. Furthermore, this chapter will deal with amendments of the Optional Clause or of Optional Clause declarations by consent. With this foundation the sixth chapter will also address the relation of the Optional Clause and treaties establishing the jurisdiction under Article 36(1) of the Statute and treaties providing other means of dispute settlement. Based primarily on state practice and jurisprudence, this chapter will show that the rules for withdrawing Optional Clause declarations are those also provided by general treaty law.

A conclusion will sum up the results of this work.

III. TERMINOLOGY

The term 'Optional Clause' will refer to Article 36(2) of the Statute itself. This is how it is commonly used by the Court[29] and in literature.[30] An 'Optional Clause declaration' is a declaration made according to the Optional Clause.[31]

The term 'reservation' will refer to all conditions, exclusions, exceptions and limitations made by states to define their Optional Clause declarations.[32] The term has been considered as inappropriate by authors who wanted to emphasise the difference between Optional Clause declarations and a multilateral treaty.[33] Yet, the term 'reservation' has become dominant in the context of the Optional Clause.[34] It has also been used by the drafters of the two Statutes.[35] So, it will likewise be used here and it will also cover what some call 'formal conditions' and what they

---

[29] See eg *Case concerning the Right of Passage over Indian Territory (Portugal v India)* (Preliminary Objections) [1957] ICJ Rep 125, 143: 'object and purpose of the Optional Clause' and 'system of the Optional Clause'.

[30] cp DJ Ende, 'Reaccepting the Compulsory Jurisdiction' 1149, fn 26; JHW Verzijl, 'Optional Clause' 585; 'Fakultativklausel' (German, see eg R Bernhardt, 'Vorbehalte' 378), 'disposition facultative' (French, see eg S Dreyfus, 'Les déclarations souscrites par la France' 258; CG Ténékidès, 'Les actes concurrents' 721), 'clausula facultativa' (Spanish, see eg FJ Garcia, *Jurisdicción Obligataria* 311).

[31] See also M Fitzmaurice, 'Interpretation' 128. The Court also used the term 'Declarations of Acceptance of the Optional Clause' (cp RP Anand, *Compulsory Jurisdiction* 142, fn 1; *Portugal v India* (n 29) 144). For the terminology in French see JHW Verzijl, 'Certains emprunts norvégiens' 383, fn 1.

[32] cp HW Briggs, 'Reservations' 230.

[33] V Lamm, 'Reservations to Declarations' 120; Maus (n 5) 94 f.

[34] cp Fitzmaurice (n 31) 128 and also Lamm, ibid 120.

[35] See sub-s II A ii of ch 2 at 54.

see as an *aliud*.[36] Here, these conditions will be treated as a subclass of the broad term 'reservation'.[37]

A 'withdrawal' will be the ending of the treaty relations under a multilateral treaty for only one state.[38] In line with the VCLT 'amendments' will be used for every amendment of a treaty or a declaration *erga omnes*.[39] Concerning the Optional Clause the term 'amendment' will be used for the introduction of a new reservation to the declarations. As these 'amendments' are, however, nothing else than partial withdrawals, a right to withdraw an Optional Clause declaration will generally likewise be understood as including a right to amend an Optional Clause declaration by introducing a new reservation.[40]

[36] For the latter see eg Garcia (n 30) 315; S Rosenne and Y Ronen, *Practice 1920–2005* 740; R Szafarz, *Compulsory Jurisdiction* 46 f.

[37] cp Briggs (n 32) 230. For a further discussion and the application of Art 2(1)(d) VCLT see sub-s I A of ch 5 at 166.

[38] cp A Aust, 'Termination' para 1; A Aust, *Treaty Law* 245; T Giegerich, 'Article 54 VCLT' para 23. The term 'termination', which will sometimes appear in quotations, covers also withdrawals (Aust, 'Termination' para 1; Giegerich, ibid para 20).

[39] cp K Odendahl, 'Article 39' para 1; A Rigaux and others, 'Article 41' para 9; K Zemanek, 'Revision' 981.

[40] See s I of ch 6 at 275.

1

The Structure of Obligations Under the Optional Clause

A S ALREADY STATED above, the first chapter will deal with two related questions. It will first assess whether the Optional Clause declarations establish obligations before an application is filed. If this first question is answered in the affirmative the second question will be towards whom this obligation is established.

I. AN OBLIGATION PRE SEISIN?

Many authors have distinguished between the relations of the states under the Optional Clause before and after the seisin of the Court. Anand wrote that the Optional Clause declarations established consensual bonds which change into bilateral agreements when an application is submitted to the Court.[1] Likewise Shihata argued that before an application there were only vague relations between the states. For him the '"bilateral element" … becomes particularly important only after the seisin of the Court of a given case'.[2] In his latest work Rosenne wrote: 'There is, as yet, no element of direct engagement between any of the States making a declaration. The engagement will only come into existence when a legal dispute is submitted to the Court by the filing of an application'.[3] Similarly, Alexandrov wrote that 'obligations assumed by a unilateral declaration under the Optional Clause arise only when a specific case is presented before the Court'. According to him this distinguished the Optional Clause declarations from treaties as in the case of treaties the obligations were determined independently of a specific case.[4]

However, against this latter point it can already be said that, at least technically, it is equally possible to determine the scope of the accepted

---

[1] RP Anand, *Compulsory Jurisdiction* 147.
[2] IFI Shihata, *Compétence de la Compétence* 167.
[3] S Rosenne and Y Ronen, *Practice 1920–2005* 795. See already S Rosenne, *Essay* 318 supported in *Military and Paramilitary Activities in and against Nicaragua (Nicaragua v United States of America)* (Jurisdiction and Admissibility) Counter-Memorial (United States of America) para 383.
[4] SA Alexandrov, *Declarations* 16.

obligations from the moment at which the states have made their Optional Clause declarations. From that moment on states are obliged as far as they have mutually accepted the Optional Clause.[5] It could therefore also be said that obligations already arise when the Optional Clause declarations enter into force. A first argument for this latter opinion could come from the wording of the Optional Clause itself.

A. The 'Obligation' in Article 36(2) of the Statute

As already quoted at the beginning of this work, Article 36(2) of the Statute provides:

> The states parties to the present Statute may at any time declare that they recognize as compulsory ipso facto and without special agreement, in relation to any other state accepting the same obligation, the jurisdiction of the Court in all legal disputes ...

As the wording of the paragraph shows, the 'obligation' is the recognition of the 'jurisdiction of the Court' as 'compulsory'. The words of the paragraph suggest that this obligation is accepted with the making of a declaration. Nowhere does the paragraph refer to the moment at which an application is filed.

With regard to the words 'compulsory' and 'jurisdiction' this also makes sense. In relation to these words the Court already held in the *Nottebohm* case:

> The characteristic of this compulsory jurisdiction is that it results from a previous agreement which makes it possible to seise the Court of a dispute without a Special Agreement, and that in respect of disputes subject to it, the Court may be seised by means of an Application by one of the parties.[6]

This judgment underlines firstly that 'compulsory jurisdiction' results directly from the prior agreement and not from the filing of the application. Necessarily, the named 'possib[ility] to seise the Court' precedes the seising of the Court. Furthermore, the Court's statement suggests that the obligation established by an Optional Clause declaration exists even before a certain dispute arises. The word 'previous' in the judgment means that the agreement is made previous to the moment a certain dispute arises. This is in line with the common understanding that 'compulsory jurisdiction' provides jurisdiction which exists independently of a

---

[5] For the determination of the 'common ground' see sub-s II B of ch 5 at 168.

[6] *Nottebohm Case (Liechtenstein v Guatemala)* (Preliminary Objection) [1953] ICJ Rep 111, 122. See also HW Briggs, 'Incidental Jurisdiction' 87. For the meaning of the term 'special agreement' see sub-s I C iii of ch 1 at 17.

certain dispute and independently of a state's later willingness to appear
before the Court.[7]

All in all, the fact that, according to its wording, the Optional Clause
provides 'compulsory jurisdiction' and that the declarations bind states
to join future proceedings before the Court independently of the question
of whether they want these proceedings or not, implies that the Optional
Clause declarations provide an obligation to join later proceedings before
the Court. This implies that states are obliged before the dispute arises and
necessarily also before an application is filed.

B. The Genesis of the 'Obligation' in Article 36(2) of the Statute

The question is if this first impression can be confirmed with the genesis
of Article 36 of the Statute.[8]

Before the creation of the Permanent Court of International Justice (PCIJ),
international judiciary was based on international arbitration. Many treaties providing mandatory arbitration contained clauses excluding disputes affecting the nations' vital interests, independence and national
honour.[9] As these matters had been basically inaccessible to an objective
determination they strongly undermined the treaties. Those treaties have
therefore been understood to provide only a '[t]hou shalt ... if you wilt'[10]
and contained no real mandatory dispute settlement procedure. Compulsory jurisdiction executed by a permanent judicial institution had been
discussed but never established.[11] At the Peace Conference in The Hague
in 1907 the states had problems in agreeing on the separation of legal and
political disputes and the groups of disputes suitable for compulsory
judicial settlement.[12] Furthermore, the German delegate Marschall von

---

[7] For a detailed analysis of the meaning of the words 'compulsory jurisdiction' see
F Wittmann, *Obligatorium* 49–57, 104. cp also Briggs (n 6) 87–89, 95; M Dubisson, *La cour* 189;
AN Farmanfarma, *Declarations* 15, 100; GG Fitzmaurice, 'Jurisdiction, Competence and
Procedure' 73; R Kolb, *ICJ* 448; AP Llamazon, 'Compliance' fn 9; RC Lawson, 'Compul-
sory Jurisdiction' 222; K Oellers-Frahm, 'Obligatorische Gerichtsbarkeit' 443 f; R Szafarz,
Compulsory Jurisdiction 3. For a comparison to ad hoc jurisdiction see sub-s I C iii of ch 1 at 17.
[8] For the use of *travaux préparatoires* as a confirmative means of interpretation see eg
O Dörr, 'Article 32' paras 29–32 with reference to the practice in inter alia *Case concerning
Kasikili/Sedudu Island (Botswana/Namibia)* (Judgment) [1999] ICJ Rep 1045, para 46; *Territorial
Dispute (Libyan Arab Jamahiriya/Chad)* (Judgment) [1994] ICJ Rep 6, para 55.
[9] See eg Ministère des Affaires Étrangères 'La Deuxième Conférence Internationale de la
Paix—Actes et Documents' (1907) Tome Premier—Séances Plénières de la Conférence 529,
537 and also H Wundram, *Fakultativklausel* 34–40.
[10] E Gordon, 'Legal Disputes' 209–11. See also below sub-s III B iv b 1 of ch 5 at 227.
[11] M Vogiatzi, 'Historical Evolution' 45. cp also Wittmann (n 7) 560–64.
[12] Wittmann (n 7) 563; Wundram (n 9) 34–37. cp also Ministère des Affaires Étrangères
(n 9) 474–82, 498–502; Ministère des Affaires Étrangères 'La Deuxième Conférence Internationale de la Paix—Actes et Documents' (1907) Tome Deux—Première Commission 462, 464
(Marschall de Bieberstein).

Bieberstein in particular argued consistently that 'la question n'est pas mûre'.[13] Nonetheless, it can be seen that already in these days compulsory jurisdiction had been understood as providing jurisdiction for future disputes by a prior consensus.[14]

In 1920 the states drafted the Statute of the Permanent Court. At an early moment, the Portuguese delegate Costa referred to the state of international law as described in the previous paragraph and consequentially emphasised what he considered to be the task of the committee he worked in. He said that the mandate of the drafting committee, contained in Article 14 of the Covenant, demanded an obligation to have recourse to the Court because otherwise the new court would merely be another court of arbitration.[15] Later, the Romanian delegate Negulesco, too, contrasted the previous situation with the situation which for him would prevail under the Permanent Court as for the latter the states would be obliged to accept its jurisdiction.[16]

During the drafting of what became Article 36 of the Statute of the Permanent Court, the Swiss delegate Huber said that the choice of means of peaceful dispute settlement, then provided in Article 12 of the Covenant, ended 'as soon as [the states] had agreed to have recourse to a tribunal, or the case had been brought before the Council'.[17] This was also the position of the committee members Busatti, Fernandes, and Hagerup.[18] Busatti especially had emphasised the distinction between voluntary and compulsory jurisdiction earlier on.[19]

The fact that the whole Committee considered the obligation as being pre seisin becomes obvious in the draft it presented to the General Assembly. That draft contained an explanation for the suppression of an earlier suggested Article 36 *bis*. That explanation had been provided for by the sub-committee to the Committee and referred to the different grounds of jurisdiction. It named them either a 'special Convention of the Parties or [a] *pre-existing obligation* under a Treaty'.[20] As the 'special convention' referred to ad hoc jurisdiction for a certain dispute which had already arisen before, it becomes obvious that the other titles of jurisdiction were considered to contain an obligation existing before the dispute. Necessarily, the obligation therefore has to exist before the seisin of the Court. This shows that the drafters of the Statute of the Permanent Court

[13] ibid 464, 466 f (Marschall de Bieberstein).
[14] cp also Wittmann (n 7) 561.
[15] League of Nations, *Records of the First Assembly, Meetings of the Committees* 288 f (Costa).
[16] League of Nations, *Records of the First Assembly, Plenary Meetings* 453 f (Negulesco).
[17] League of Nations, *Records of the First Assembly, Meetings of the Committees* 384 (Huber).
[18] ibid 383 f (Busatti, Fernandes, Hagerup).
[19] ibid 383 (Busatti).
[20] ibid 534 f; League of Nations, *Records of the First Assembly, Plenary Meetings* 464 (emphasis added). For the suggested article see League of Nations, *Records of the First Assembly, Meetings of the Committees* 489.

considered also the Optional Clause, which was in any case no 'special convention',[21] as containing obligations pre seisin.

As this core part of the Optional Clause has not been changed during the creation of the current Statute in 1945, the result found for the Statute of the Permanent Court is still valid. Furthermore, the Committee of Jurists drafting the Statute for later deliberations described the Optional Clause in its report as 'permitting the states to accept *in advance* the compulsory jurisdiction of the Court'.[22]

C. The 'Obligation' in the Context with Other Sources of Jurisdiction

The difference between the Optional Clause and ad hoc jurisdiction has already been mentioned but deserves more consideration. The following sub-section will go on and highlight the similarities and the differences between the Optional Clause and other sources of the Court's jurisdiction. As Judge Oda wrote in 1989, 'all concerned jurists should, at every opportunity, emphasise the fact that the Optional Clause is not the only source of jurisdiction of the Court'.[23]

i. The Sources of Jurisdiction Provided for by Article 36(1) of the Statute

The other sources of jurisdiction of the Court are provided for in Article 36(1) of the Statute which reads as follows: 'The jurisdiction of the Court comprises all cases which the parties refer to it and all matters specially provided for in the Charter of the United Nations or in treaties and conventions in force'.

The 'matters specially provided for in the Charter of the United Nations' are few at best.[24] Therefore, the means provided for in the paragraph are basically four:

1. States can conclude treaties with compromissory clauses which provide compulsory jurisdiction for disputes about the content of the treaty.
2. States can conclude treaties whose only object and purpose is to provide compulsory jurisdiction for some or all disputes between them.
3. In case of a dispute states can provide the Court ad hoc with jurisdiction for that dispute by making a special agreement.

---

[21] See also the following sub-s C.

[22] United Nations, *Conference on International Organization, Volume XIV—United Nations Committee of Jurists* 667, 840 (emphasis added).

[23] S Oda, 'Reservations in the Declarations' 23. cp also FL Morrison, 'Potential Revisions' 62.

[24] cp Rosenne and Ronen (n 3) 640, 669–72; C Tomuschat, 'Article 36 of the Statute' para 46; MM Whiteman, *Digest* 1268. On Art 36(3) of the Charter see eg Whiteman, ibid 1287 f; Wittmann (n 7) 106–08.

4. In case of a dispute one state can apply to the Court without the prior consent of the other state and the other state can give its consent afterwards (*forum prorogatum*).[25]

These means have already been those provided for in Article 36(1) of the Statute of the Permanent Court. As that article was discussed again in 1945 the Chinese delegate Wang stated that the first paragraph of Article 36 of the Statute has no relation to the second.[26] From the context of his words, however, it becomes clear that they do not preclude drawing conclusions from the relation between the different sources. The means provided for in Article 36(1) of the Statute could cast some light on how the drafters saw the Optional Clause. It is unlikely that they wanted to make the second paragraph completely redundant in relation to the first one.[27] At the present stage of the work, the jurisdiction based on *forum prorogatum* and the ad hoc jurisdiction are relevant in this regard.

ii. Agreements Pre Seisin and the Forum Prorogatum

Jurisdiction provided for by a *forum prorogatum* is based on consent post seisin. In such cases the application is 'unrelated to any previous acceptance of the jurisdiction of the Court'.[28]

Article 38(5) of the Rules of the Court therefore provides:

> When the applicant State proposes to found the jurisdiction of the Court upon a consent thereto yet to be given or manifested by the State against which such application is made, the application shall be transmitted to that State. It shall not however be entered in the General List, nor any action be taken in the proceedings, unless and until the State against which such application is made consents to the Court's jurisdiction for the purposes of the case.[29]

This consent is also considered as given if the respondent does not invoke the otherwise lacking jurisdiction and starts to argue on the merits.[30]

---

[25] This fourth method has been disputed in the past but is now considered as being established (see eg Kolb (n 7) 160 f; S Oda, 'From the Bench' 45 f, para 43; Rosenne and Ronen (n 3) 672–96; Tomuschat (n 24) para 40).

[26] United Nations (n 22) 204 (Wang). He refers to 'jurisdiction by consent' under Art 36(1) of the Statute in contrast to the Optional Clause. It is, however, common opinion that all jurisdiction of the Court has to be based on consent. For that see also s I of ch 3 at 86.

[27] cp the argumentation of *Land and Maritime Boundary between Cameroon and Nigeria (Cameroon v Nigeria: Equatorial Guinea intervening)* (Preliminary Objections) Oral Proceedings (CR 1998/6) (Cameroon) 17 f, para 7 (Sinclair); *Nicaragua v United States of America* (n 3) para 340.

[28] Separate opinion of Judge H Lauterpacht, *ICJ Rep 1957*, 64. See also Kolb (n 7) 160 f; Morrison (n 23) 38; *Interhandel Case (Switzerland v United States of America)* (Preliminary Objections) Observations and Submissions (Switzerland) 411, para 8; Wittmann (n 7) 64.

[29] For the article's genesis see Oda (n 25) 45 f, para 43.

[30] *Haya de la Torre Case (Colombia v Peru)* (Judgment) [1951] ICJ Rep 71, 78; Rosenne and Ronen (n 3) 690–96.

It becomes clear that the *forum prorogatum* cannot be compared to the ad hoc jurisdiction and the consent established by treaties. The latter two are 'legal grounds upon which the jurisdiction of the Court is said to be based' which, according to Article 38(2) of the Rules of the Court, have to be specified as far as possible in the application already.[31] Therefore, in these cases there is necessarily a pre seisin relationship as the respondent has declared its consent before the application is filed.[32] After the application Article 30 of the Statute provides the ongoing of the jurisdiction. It does not matter if the means which has established the Court's jurisdiction later perishes. This has also been decided by the Court in the already mentioned *Nottebohm* case,[33] and is considered as being settled.[34] As Shihata put it, 'seisin establishes the crucial date for the efficacy of jurisdictional titles'.[35]

The Optional Clause is one of the 'legal grounds' as referred to by Article 38 of the Rules of the Court.[36] Like states concluding a treaty which provides jurisdiction under Article 36(1) of the Statute, states making Optional Clause declarations have already given their consent before an application is filed.[37] As treaties establish relationships before the application is filed, the same has to hold true for the Optional Clause. No matter if they conclude a treaty, adhere to a treaty or make an Optional Clause declaration, states are afterwards obliged to take part in later proceedings before the Court as long as their treaties or their Optional Clause declarations remain valid. It could be said against this that the Optional Clause is 'optional' to such an extent that only the current consent is crucial and states do not have to take part in later proceedings if they do not want.[38] However, this would render the Optional Clause completely redundant to the *forum prorogatum* and, therefore, such an interpretation cannot be maintained. Only the making of the Optional Clause declaration is optional.[39] From then on it provides obligations.[40]

---

[31] cp Rosenne and Ronen (n 3) 903 f; HWA Thirlway, 'International Court, 2014' 597 f.

[32] cp Briggs (n 6) 88. cp also Shihata (n 2) 134, 139.

[33] *Nottebohm Case* (n 6) 120–23 without any dissenting opinions on this point; supported by *Military and Paramilitary Activities in and against Nicaragua (Nicaragua v United States of America)* (Jurisdiction and Admissibility) [1984] ICJ Rep 392, para 54; SA Alexandrov, 'Reservations' 103–05; Thirlway (n 31) 1084 f; Tomuschat (n 24) para 77.

[34] Shihata (n 2) 164.

[35] Shihata (n 2) 152. See also Kolb (n 7) 216; Rosenne and Ronen (n 3) 549.

[36] Rosenne and Ronen (n 3) 904; Thirlway (n 31) 598.

[37] cp Briggs (n 6) 88; Farmanfarma (n 7) 25.

[38] For a discussion of this issue see E McWhinney, 'Jurisdiction and Justiciability' 87–92.

[39] For that see s I of ch 3 at 86. For the use of the word 'optional' in this context cp also Kolb (n 7) 376 f; Wittmann (n 7) 51 and for the French equivalent Dubisson (n 7) 154 f.

[40] cp also JHW Verzijl, 'Certains emprunts norvégiens' 383, fn 1; Wittmann (n 7) 114 f. cp furthermore E Hambro, 'Compulsory Jurisdiction' 135: '[I]t seems strange to refer to such acceptance as optional as if the optional character of undertaking this particular obligation were different from other instruments whereby states accept international obligations'.

iii. Comparison of the Optional Clause to Ad Hoc Jurisdiction

Ad hoc jurisdiction (sometimes also referred to as 'voluntary jurisdiction') is based on a consent which has been given after a dispute has arisen between states.[41] For such agreements ad hoc the term 'special agreement' has been used from the drafting of the Statute until today.[42]

The disadvantage of ad hoc jurisdiction is that states are unlikely to provide this kind of jurisdiction in a hostile atmosphere or for great political conflicts.[43] This holds true especially in cases in which one party of the dispute has violated international law intentionally and it is very likely that this state will lose the case on the merits. Therefore, the more obvious the violation of law the less likely will it be that the necessary consent to submit the case to the Court ad hoc will be given. Hence, the method of special agreements is commonly used for frontier disputes between states which have generally friendly relations.[44] Especially in those cases the decision on the merits is generally hard to predict and all involved states have a motivation to have judgment providing legal certainty concerning the shape of the frontier. It could further be domestically opportune to have a third party decision rather than a solution of the dispute based on consent.[45] In such cases in which all parties of the dispute are motivated to consent to the judicial settlement of the dispute the ad hoc jurisdiction of Article 36(1) of the Statute is an appropriate means. Nonetheless, it can be said that ad hoc jurisdiction fails where there is a heavy dispute and a judicial decision would actually be most helpful.

In such a case in which there is no current consent to submit the specific case to the Court only prior consent can be a remedy. This consent can either be provided by earlier treaties or, as referred to above, by the Optional Clause. These then provide 'compulsory jurisdiction' that requires no current consent.[46] This is based on the idea that states have already accepted the jurisdiction of the Court for the dispute when a dispute arises. As Judge Oda has put it, 'jurisdiction may be conferred upon the Court by an *ad hoc* agreement between the States for the submission of a particular dispute or

---

[41] Farmanfarma (n 7) 15; H Lauterpacht and L Oppenheim, *Treatise* 58; Oellers-Frahm (n 7) 442 f; HWA Thirlway, 'Compromis' para 4; Wittmann (n 7) 60, 595.

[42] cp League of Nations, *Records of the First Assembly, Meetings of the Committees* 533; A Aust, *Treaty Law* 312; Rosenne and Ronen (n 3) 638, 643 f; Thirlway (n 31) 597; Whiteman (n 24) 1268 f.

[43] cp Tomuschat (n 24) para 41.

[44] P Tomka, 'Special Agreement' 556. cp also JA Frowein, 'International Court' 159 f; Oda (n 25) 33 f, paras 17 f.

[45] cp Tomuschat (n 24) para 39.

[46] For the Optional Clause see s I A of ch 1 at 11. See further Fitzmaurice (n 7) 73; separate opinion of Judge M Shahabuddeen, *ICJ Rep 1988*, 138; Shihata (n 2) 139 who explained that the term 'compulsory jurisdiction' cannot only be used for Art 36(2) of the Statute but also for treaties falling under Art 36(1) of the Statute. cp also HW Briggs (n 6) 87 f, 95; Llamazon (n 7) fn 9; Thirlway (n 31) 595, 597 f.

by an *obligation* that they may have entered into, whether on a bilateral or multilateral basis, *prior* to the submission of the said dispute'.[47]

Similarly Sinclair pleaded in the recent *Bakassi Peninsula* case for Cameroon:

> [C]onsent can be given through the negotiation of a special agreement or through the operation of a clause in a treaty in force providing for the reference of specified types of dispute to the Court. This is the clear object and purpose of paragraph 1 of Article 36. Paragraph 2 of Article 36, which incorporates the Optional Clause system, serves a quite different purpose. It provides for the *advance*, I repeat *advance*, acceptance by States, through the operation of the system, of the jurisdiction of the Court ... To blur the distinction between the two would be to undermine the specific functioning of the Optional Clause system. It would tend to transform that system into a variant of the special agreement for which provision is made in paragraph 1 of Article 36.[48]

Having regard to this argumentation, the result already found regarding the wording of Article 36(2) of the Statute can be underlined further with a comparison to the ad hoc jurisdiction provided for in Article 36(1) of the Statute: if the Optional Clause declarations contained no obligation pre seisin and required any form of confirmation before a certain dispute could be submitted, Article 36(2) of the Statute would be redundant besides the ad hoc jurisdiction provided for in Article 36(1) of the Statute.[49]

Therefore, the existence of ad hoc jurisdiction under the latter paragraph strongly supports the impression that the Optional Clause shall provide jurisdiction especially in those cases in which there is no present consent to submit the dispute to the Court.[50] Like treaties with compromissory clauses the Optional Clause declarations shall generally provide jurisdiction in an abstract manner without relation to a present situation.[51] This necessarily requires an obligation pre seisin as the dispute is also necessarily pre seisin.

iv. Result

The jurisdiction based on an Optional Clause is different from ad hoc jurisdiction and especially the *forum prorogatum*. A comparison of these

---

[47] Oda (n 25) 31, para 13 (second and third italics added as emphasis). See also Kolb (n 7) 375 f; Wittmann (n 7) 70 f, 104, 595 and Dubisson (n 7) 189 referring to 'la condition d'antériorité du consentement par rapport à la date de survenance de différend, qui fonde la juridiction obligatoire de la Cour'.

[48] *Cameroon v Nigeria: Equatorial Guinea intervening* (n 27) 17 f, para 7 (Sinclair). See also the pleading of Simma presented in sub-s III B iv c 1 of ch 5 at 230 and Kolb (n 7) 448.

[49] cp also Gordon (n 10) 222.

[50] See also Briggs (n 6) 88 f; JA Frowein, 'Optional Clauses' 407; Lawson (n 7) 221, 233.

[51] Wundram (n 9) 28. cp also the dissenting opinion of Judge AG Koroma, *ICJ Rep 1998*, 381: 'the object and purpose of the Optional Clause system is to ensure advance acceptance of the jurisdiction of the Court'. cp also Thirlway (n 41) para 26; UNSC 'Resolution of 15 October 1946' (15.10.1946) UN Doc S/Res/9(1946) paras 1 f.

latter means, which come under Article 36(1) of the Statute and the compulsory jurisdiction provided for by Article 36(2) of the Statute supports the idea that in the case of Article 36(2) of the Statute the states have already accepted the jurisdiction of the Court when a dispute arises.[52] In this regard the jurisdiction based on the Optional Clause is the same as the one established by a treaty which provides compulsory jurisdiction under Article 36(1) of the Statute.[53] This heavily argues for the assumption that Optional Clause declarations provide obligations pre seisin.

D. State Practice and the Jurisprudence of the Two Courts

The question is to what extent this result can be corroborated by state practice and the jurisprudence of the two Courts.[54]

In the *Phosphates in Morocco* case the question of whether Optional Clause declarations provide an obligation pre seisin has been touched implicitly. Basically, France wanted only to invoke a reservation excluding disputes which arose prior to the ratification of its own declaration. However, France's arguments did not relate merely to the reservation, they were more general. France maintained that in relation to Italy the reservation excluded disputes prior to 7 September 1931, which was the date the latter Italian declaration had entered into force. France supported this by saying that this latter moment was the one in which the French declaration became operative in relation to Italy. For France, 'le moment où la juridiction obligatoire de la Cour commence à exister dans les rapports des deux États, est intervenue le 7 septembre 1931'.[55] Against this,

---

[52] This does, however, not necessarily exclude that the Optional Clause is *also* applied to disputes which arose before a state has accepted compulsory jurisdiction (for that see sub-s III A of ch 3 at 95).

[53] cp Oda (Oda (n 25) 36, para 23) who wrote that all the instruments may be regarded as 'functionally equivalent'. See also Lawson (n 7) 223. For the importance of the Optional Clause besides Art 36(1) of the Statute see sub-s II C of ch 2 at 65.

[54] For the use of state practice to corroborate results found in another way see *Case concerning Kasikili/Sedudu Island* (n 8) para 80; R Kolb, *Interprétation* 482. For more on the use of subsequent state practice as a means of interpretation or as basis for derogating customary law see sub-s III D of ch 3 at 108. For the use of judicial decisions as 'as subsidiary means for the determination of rules of law' according to Art 38(1)(d) of the Statute see eg A Pellet, 'Article 38 of the Statute' paras 307–16.

[55] *Phosphates in Morocco (Italy v France)* (Documents of the Written Proceedings) PCIJ Series C No 84 (France) 223–25, 714; *Phosphates in Morocco (Italy v France)* (Public Sittings and Pleadings) PCIJ Series C No 85 (France) 1022 f (Basdevant). See also the presentation of the French position in *Interhandel Case (Switzerland v United States of America)* (Preliminary Objections) Memorial (United States of America) 314 f.

Italy only maintained that the reservation still referred to the moment of the ratification of the French declaration. Italy argued:

> [C]'est la date de la ratification italienne qui marque le moment initial de la compétence de la Cour pour ce qui tient à la naissance du différend, tandis que c'est la date de la ratification française qui est décisive pour ce qui concerne l'existence des situations et des faits donnant lieu au différend.[56]

The Permanent Court did not decide this issue as it denied having jurisdiction for another reason.[57] However, in the opinion of both states, Italy and France, the moment their declarations became operative vis-à-vis each other and started to provide the Permanent Court's competence for their applications was the moment the second declaration was made.[58]

This, however, seems to contradict the Court's position in the later *Nottebohm* case. In this case the Court maintained that 'the filing of the Application is merely the condition required to enable the clause of compulsory jurisdiction to produce its effects in respect of the claim advanced in the Application. Once this condition has been satisfied, the Court must deal with the claim; it has jurisdiction to deal with all its aspects'.[59] Regarding these words it could be said that the 'condition required to enable the clause of compulsory jurisdiction to produce its effects' is also the condition required for the obligations under the Optional Clause to arise as these obligations are the effect of the Optional Clause. However, regarding the context of the *Nottebohm* case, it could better be said that the Court referred only to the requirements which are necessary to maintain a particular proceeding before the Court and not to the obligations accepted with Optional Clause declarations in general. In line with this latter understanding it could be said that, regarding these obligations, the particular proceedings are just a second step and that, by appearing before the Court, a state merely fulfills an obligation—an obligation which the state already accepted in the moment it made its declaration.

Yet, this latter position could be considered as contradicting the position which the United States presented in the *Nicaragua* case. In that case the United States emphasised that before the seisin of the Court the commitments under the Optional Clause had a variable and unilateral character. The commitment became only fixed as soon as an application was filed.[60] The Court followed this reasoning to a certain degree and

---

[56] *Phosphates in Morocco (Italy v France)* (Written Statements) PCIJ Series C No 84 (Italy) 482 f.
[57] *Phosphates in Morocco (Italy v France)* (Preliminary Objections) PCIJ Series A/B No 74 9, 25.
[58] For more on the moment the Optional Clause declarations enter into force see s III of ch 3 at 94.
[59] *Nottebohm Case* (n 6) 123.
[60] *Nicaragua v United States of America* (n 3) para 383.

spoke of obligations which were 'in a state of flux' until the moment an application is filed.[61] However, with regard to its context it can be said that the expression 'state of flux' only referred to the invocation of other states' reservations and the possibilities to withdraw an Optional Clause declaration.[62] Furthermore, it can very well be added that the statement that the obligations are in a flux necessarily implies that there were obligations. It seems as if, even though the obligations can arise, vary and end before seisin, they nonetheless exist before seisin.

This latter conclusion would also be in line with the states' and the Court's positions in the earlier *Right of Passage* case. In this case India had argued: 'States which adhere to the Optional Clause are entitled to expect a reasonable degree of certainty in regard to the obligations imposed on them by the Declarations of other States'. Furthermore, India had referred to the Portuguese possibility to alter obligations under the Optional Clause before the seisin of the Court.[63] Also this implies that there are obligations before the Court and that they arise with the making of the declarations. Similarly, Portugal had maintained:

> [L]es déclarations faites sur pied de l'article 36, paragraphe 2, entrent en vigueur automatiquement dès leur dépôt au Secrétariat. A partir de cet instant, l'État déclarant peut exercer le droit que le système lui confère, d'introduire devant la Cour un différend par la voie d'une requête unilatérale contre tout État 'acceptant la même obligation'.[64]

As the 'right' to which Pakistan had referred arises with the corresponding obligation it becomes clear that Pakistan, too, regarded the obligation as existing pre seisin.[65] In line with the positions of the two states the Court then decided that already the making of two Optional Clause declarations establishes a 'consensual bond, which is the basis of the Optional Clause'. Even more clearly the Court considered that

> by the deposit of its Declaration of Acceptance with the Secretary-General, the accepting State becomes a Party to the system of the Optional Clause in relation to the other declarant States, with all the rights and obligations deriving from Article 36.[66]

---

[61] *Nicaragua v United States of America* (n 33) para 64.

[62] For the reciprocal invocation of 'formal conditions' see sub-s II C of ch 5 at 181. For the withdrawal of Optional Clause declarations see s II of ch 6 at 279.

[63] *Case concerning the Right of Passage over Indian Territory (Portugal v India)* (Preliminary Objections) Memorial (India) 111, para 32.

[64] *Case concerning the Right of Passage over Indian Territory (Portugal v India)* (Preliminary Objections) Observations and Submissions (Portugal) 605, para 83.

[65] For more on the question whether the Optional Clause establishes rights for states see s II of ch 1 at 22.

[66] *Case concerning the Right of Passage over Indian Territory (Portugal v India)* (Preliminary Objections) [1957] ICJ Rep 125, 146; repeated in *Land and Maritime Boundary between Cameroon and Nigeria (Cameroon v Nigeria: Equatorial Guinea intervening)* (Preliminary Objections) [1998] ICJ Rep 275, para 25.

Although the main question in that part of the case had been whether a state needs to receive another state's declaration to let it enter into force,[67] the words of the Court were clear and furthermore clearer than those used in the earlier *Nottebohm* case. They show that also in the opinion of the Court the obligations under the Optional Clause arise when the declarations are made.

With regard to state practice and jurisprudence it can therefore be concluded that, while the states' opinions vary, the Court said that the obligations arising from the Optional Clause exist pre seisin.

E. Result

The wording of Article 36(2) of the Statute implies that the Optional Clause declarations establish obligations before seisin. The genesis of the Optional Clause supports this assumption as does the comparison between the Optional Clause and the means to establish the jurisdiction of the Court under Article 36(1) of the Statute. Lastly, also the Court seems to back this approach. In conclusion, it can therefore very well be said that the obligations under the Optional Clause already exist pre seisin.[68] They do not change when an application is filed. The participation in a certain proceeding before the Court can rather be considered as being the fulfilment of the obligation.

II. AN OBLIGATION TOWARDS OTHER STATES?

The question now arises whether the obligations existing under the Optional Clause pre seisin correspond to reciprocal rights of other states.

In one of the early volumes of his works on the Court, Rosenne wrote that the result of the deposit of an Optional Clause declaration 'is, at most, an engagement, in extremely vague terms, between the State making the declaration and the *United Nations*, regarding the facility of using the Court'. For him it was erroneous to think that the Optional Clause declarations establish series of bilateral obligations between the states.[69] His last work does not contain that part anymore.[70] As referred to above, he only

---

[67] For the entry into force of Optional Clause declarations in detail see s III of ch 3 at 94.

[68] JLI Buigues, 'Les déclarations d'acception' 273–75; G Enriques, 'Acceptation sans réciprocité' 853; M Kawano, 'Optional Clause' 428–31; Lawson (n 7) 221–23. cp also JG Merrills, 'Clause Revisited' 244; Wittmann (n 7) 59–61, 70 f, 162 f. For the minimal scope of the obligation and the permissibility of the Connally Reservation see sub-ss III B iii b, iii d and iv–vii of ch 5 at 214 to 252.

[69] Rosenne (n 3) 317 (emphasis added). See also Anand (n 1) 146.

[70] cp Rosenne and Ronen (n 3) 789–96.

wrote that '[t]here is, as yet, no element of direct engagement between any of the States making a declaration' before the filing of the application.[71] Similarly, in the early days of the Statute Vulcan spoke of an 'obligation envers la nouvelle Cour'.[72] Addressing jurisdiction established with the help of Article 36(5) of the Statute, Conac referred to the Court's 'propres droits de successeur de la Cour permanente de Justice'.[73] In the *Anglo-Iranian Oil Co* case Iran maintained that the Optional Clause declarations 'engagent chacun des États intéressés *vis-à-vis de la Cour*'.[74] In the *Fisheries Jurisdiction* case between Spain and Canada Judge Bedjaoui spoke of an 'obligation vis-à-vis the Optional Clause "system"' including the other states *and* the Court.[75]

The question is to what extent this could be seen otherwise. Under Article 36(2) of the Statute the obligation of one state results in the possibility for another state to file an application against the former state. It is the latter states' choice whether it wants to use this possibility while the Court has no influence on this. It seems as if the beneficiaries of the obligations provided by the Optional Clause are furthermore only the individual other states as the Optional Clause allows them to enforce their own substantive rights. Therefore, it also seems possible to maintain that the making of an Optional Clause declaration results directly in reciprocal rights for the submitting state and the other states which have already made a declaration.

A. Article 36 of the Statute

The first question is to what extent a decision on these different opinions can be found with a reference to the Statute itself.

i. *Article 36(2) of the Statute: 'In Relation to Any Other State Accepting the Same Obligation'*

As deduced from the wording of Article 36(2) of the Statute,[76] the 'obligation' in the Optional Clause is the recognition of the jurisdiction of the Court as compulsory. Rosenne wrote that 'jurisdiction' means the Court's power 'to do justice' between the litigating states. Later he referred to the

---

[71] Rosenne and Ronen (n 3) 795. See also above the introduction to s I of ch 1 at 10.

[72] C Vulcan, 'La Clause Facultative' 43 f. Compare also the earlier positions of Ténékidès and Wundram who considered the Optional Clause as a 'traité-loi' and not as a 'traité-contrat' (CG Ténékidès, 'Les actes concurrents' 729–33; Wundram (n 9) 14).

[73] G Conac, 'L'incident aérien' 736. For more on Art 36(5) of the Statute see sub-s II B iii of ch 2 at 62.

[74] *Anglo-Iranian Oil Co case (United Kingdom v Iran)* (Preliminary Objections) Observations (Iran) para 17. For more on this statement see sub-s II B of ch 1 at 26.

[75] Dissenting opinion of Judge M Bedjaoui, *ICJ Rep 1998*, para 46.

[76] See s I A of ch 1 at 11.

term also as 'the capacity of the Court to decide a particular case with final and binding force'.[77] In the *Corfu Channel* case, Judge Daxner wrote that the word jurisdiction is used, inter alia, 'to determine the competence of the Court, ie, to invest the Court with the *right to solve concrete cases*'.[78] This could be used to argue that the states are obliged towards the Court to follow its judgment.

The words 'in relation to any other state accepting the same obligation' in Article 36(2) of the Statute, however, seem to suggest something different. They would not if these words only meant that both states accept the same obligation. With this meaning it could still be assumed that the states accept the same obligations towards a third party. Yet, Article 36(2) of the Statute clearly speaks of the recognition of the compulsory jurisdiction in relation to another state. This seems to refer to the states as beneficiaries of the obligation accepted.[79]

ii. The Genesis of the Optional Clause: A Right for Smaller States

During the drafting of the PCIJ's statute the states expressed different views on what the future world court should look like. As mentioned in the Introduction,[80] especially the smaller states favoured a court with compulsory jurisdiction over all disputes as they saw the compulsory jurisdiction as a compensation for the supremacy of the Great Powers within the Council of the League of Nations.[81] Out of 12 early draft schemes six contained a possibility for the states to unilaterally summon other states without prior agreement.[82] The draft of Germany even expressly referred to a 'right to bring here a complaint which must be answered by the opposite party'.[83] It becomes obvious that at least these states regarded the

---

[77] Rosenne (n 3) 253; Rosenne and Ronen (n 3) 524. cp also DJ Ende, 'Reaccepting the Compulsory Jurisdiction' fn 16; Szafarz (n 7) 1; Tomuschat (n 24) para 7; Wittmann (n 7) 38 f.

[78] Dissenting opinion of Judge I Daxner, *ICJ Rep 1948*, 39 (emphasis added). For more on the notion 'jurisdiction' see Wittmann (n 7) 37–41.

[79] cp also B Maus, *Réserves* 60 and CHM Waldock, 'Decline' 251: '[The Optional Clause] declarations undoubtedly constitute "international engagements" binding on the State concerned in relation to any other State also making a declaration under the Optional Clause'. For the following considerations of Waldock, to which also Maus (Maus, ibis 60) seemed to refer to, related to the question how these 'engagements' are created and whether the Optional Clause declarations are really unilateral declarations. For these questions see s I of ch 2 at 40 and s III of ch 3 at 94.

[80] See Introduction at 1.

[81] cp League of Nations, *Records of the First Assembly, Plenary Meetings* 450 f; Kolb (n 7) 448 f; Vogiatzi (n 11) 70.

[82] Vogiatzi (n 11) 50. cp League of Nations, 'Advisory Committee of Jurists, Documents Presented to the Committee Relating to Existing Plans for the Establishment of a Permanent Court of International Justice' (1920) 123 (Art 22(b)), 127 (Art 30), 131 (Art 12), 265 (Art 37), 308 (Art 21), 335 f (Art 2).

[83] ibid 127 (Art 30).

establishment of compulsory jurisdiction as granting them an individual right to file applications against other states. This last position was also prominent in the last speech of the Brazilian delegate Fernandes in the General Assembly immediately before the Statute of the Permanent Court was adopted. Concerning the powerful positions granted to some states in the Council of the League and the desired compulsory jurisdiction he said: 'We have entered into mutual undertakings, not only with obligations on one side and rights on the other; rights and obligations are reciprocal'.[84]

The same delegate was also the one who had introduced the Optional Clause. Concerning the Optional Clause in particular, Fernandes had already said before that 'it was inadmissible for a State to accept the principle of compulsory jurisdiction without knowing exactly towards whom it accepted such obligation'.[85] It is obvious that here Fernandes considered the Optional Clause as providing obligations towards other states.

iii. In Light of Article 36(1) of the Statute: Treaties Establishing Reciprocal Rights and Obligations

This can be further supported with a comparison of the Optional Clause and the treaties establishing the jurisdiction of the Court under Article 36(1) of the Statute. Those are also considered as establishing reciprocal rights and obligations between the parties.[86]

For example in the General Act for the Pacific Settlement of International Disputes of 1928 the states are able to accede only for certain chapters of the treaty which provide conciliation, judicial settlement or arbitration. In this situation Article 38 of the General Act provides: 'The Contracting Parties may benefit by the accessions of other parties only in so far as they have themselves assumed the same obligations'. Likewise, Article 34(2) of the European Convention supports the result found so far. It provides: 'A High Contracting Party may only benefit from those provisions of this Convention by which it is itself bound'. Of course, these treaties did not only provide the jurisdiction of the Court,[87] but at least in the case of the General Act the provisions for the judicial settlement of disputes were among the options to choose. This suggests that also the provisions for the judicial settlement of disputes have been regarded as containing individual, to use the words of two treaties, 'benefits' for the Member States. There seems to be no reason to consider jurisdiction provided by the Optional Clause as something else.

[84] League of Nations, *Records of the First Assembly, Plenary Meetings* 451 (Fernandes).
[85] League of Nations, *Records of the First Assembly, Meetings of the Committees* 312 (Fernandes). See also Vogiatzi (n 11) 68.
[86] See eg the presentation in WW Bishop Jr and DP Myers, 'Connally-Amendment' 142 f.
[87] For more comparison between the Optional Clause and these treaties see sub-s III B of ch 2 at 71.

B. State Practice: The Optional Clause as a Source for the Right to File an Application

Yet, the legal opinions of the individual states seem to be diverse. As has already been referred to in the introduction, in the *Anglo-Iranian Oil Co* case Iran maintained that the Optional Clause declarations resulted in obligations towards the Court. For Iran, '[l]a situation des différents États signataires est semblable à celle d'individus soumis à la même loi, sans que la moindre discussion ou la moindre entente soit intervenue entre eux pour créer la situation juridique objective dans laquelle ils se trouvent'.[88] For the United Kingdom on the other hand it was 'clear that [by making its Optional Clause declaration] Persia was placing herself under an obligation towards other States'.[89]

This latter position was in line with the position of the parties of the later *Right of Passage* case. Referring to the right which corresponds to the obligation accepted with an Optional Clause declaration Portugal spoke of a 'droit que le système lui confère, d'introduire devant la Cour un différend par la voie d'une requête unilatéral'.[90] Similarly India addressed the 'right to bring a dispute before the Court by unilateral Application'.[91] These statements suggest that the majority of the states consider the states as beneficiaries of the obligations arising under the Optional Clause declarations.

Furthermore, the actual behaviour of states also argues for the United Kingdom's position and seems to be even more revealing. In at least four cases it was obvious that states made their Optional Clause declaration not in order to bind themselves towards the Court but to be able to institute proceedings in a certain dispute. One notorious example is the Portuguese application against India in the aforementioned *Right of Passage* case. In this case Portugal had filed that application on 22 December 1955 after it had made its Optional Clause declaration, on which the jurisdiction for that case was based, on 19 December 1955.[92] Another such case was

---

[88] *Anglo-Iranian Oil Co case* (n 74) para 17. See also the quotation reproduced above in the introduction to s II of ch 1 at 23. cp also *Electricity Company of Sofia and Bulgaria (Belgium v Bulgaria)* (Public Sittings and Pleadings) PCIJ Series C No 88 (Bulgaria) 436 (Altinoff) and *Border and Transborder Armed Actions (Nicaragua v Honduras)* (Jurisdiction and Admissibility) Oral Proceedings (CR 1988) (Honduras) 16 (Bowett).

[89] *Anglo-Iranian Oil Co case (United Kingdom v Iran)* (Preliminary Objections) Observations and Submissions (United Kingdom) para 16. cp also *Military and Paramilitary Activities in and against Nicaragua (Nicaragua v United States of America)* (Provisional Measures) Oral Proceedings (CR 1984) (Nicaragua) 70 f (Brownlie). See also United States of America 'Congressional Record' (1946) 10706 (Report of the Committee on Foreign Relations): 'The United States would acquire the right and duty to sue or be sued in respect to other states'.

[90] *Portugal v India* (n 64) 605. See also sub-s I D of ch 1 at 19.

[91] *Case concerning the Right of Passage over Indian Territory (Portugal v India)* (Preliminary Objections) Oral Proceedings (CR 1957) (India) 46 f (Waldock); *Portugal v India* (n 64) 605.

[92] *Portugal v India* (n 66) 127, 141.

the one concerning the *Bakassi Peninsula*. Therein Cameroon successfully based the jurisdiction of the Court for its application from 29 March 1994 on its Optional Clause declaration submitted on 3 March 1994.[93] Yugoslavia acted likewise in the 10 *Use of Force* cases it instituted. It wanted to base the jurisdiction of the Court for its applications and its requests for provisional measures inter alia on the Optional Clause declaration it had submitted on 26 April 1999. Here, too, this was done just three days before the seisin of the Court on 29 April 1999.[94]

Recently Timor-Leste and the Marshall Islands made Optional Clause declarations which were used for proceedings shortly afterwards. The Marshall Islands for example deposited its Optional Clause declaration on 24 April 2013 and submitted its application against inter alia the United Kingdom on 24 April 2014.[95] The amount of time between the deposition of the declaration and the application corresponded exactly to the United Kingdom's Anti Ambush Clause.[96]

Regarding these cases it becomes obvious that these states did not regard the Optional Clause declarations primarily as an instrument to establish the Court's jurisdiction in general. The close temporal connection to the proceedings instituted almost immediately afterwards shows that they regarded their Optional Clause declarations primarily as means to attain the possibility to file an application against other states which had already made a declaration. Yugoslavia itself expressed this clearly in the *Use of Force* cases. It asked: 'What was Yugoslavia's purpose in depositing this declaration?' And answered: 'What is in any event clear is that, initially, Yugoslavia wished to secure a judicial settlement of the disputes relating to the armed conflict then—and indeed still—in progress between Yugoslavia and the respondent States'.[97]

It becomes clear that in these states' perspective Optional Clause declarations provide not only an obligation but also a right directly for them. From this perspective the states are obliged towards each other.

---

[93] *Cameroon v Nigeria: Equatorial Guinea intervening* (n 66) paras 1, 22.

[94] cp eg *Legality of Use of Force (Yugoslavia v Spain)* (Provisional Measures) [1999] ICJ Rep 761, paras 9, 21. Another example, even though with a slightly longer period between the new declaration and the application, is the *Arbitral Award of 31 July 1989* case. In this case, Guinea-Bissau submitted its declaration on 7 August 1989 and filed its application against Senegal on 23 August 1989 (*Arbitral Award of 31 July 1989 (Guinea-Bissau v Senegal)* (Judgment) [1991] ICJ Rep 53, paras 1, 22; Rosenne and Ronen (n 3) 728). Furthermore, the Optional Clause declaration of Nauru is considered to have been made only to institute certain proceedings against Australia (Tomuschat (n 24) para 87).

[95] *Obligations concerning Negotiations relating to Cessation of the Nuclear Arms Race and to Nuclear Disarmament (Marshall Islands v United Kingdom)* (Provisional Measures) Application (Marshall Islands) para 114.

[96] For these clauses see below sub-ss III D and F of ch 3 at 109 f and 116.

[97] *Legality of Use of Force (Serbia and Montenegro v Canada)* (Provisional Measures) Oral Proceedings (CR 1999/25) (Yugoslavia) 45 f (Corten). For Portugal cp *Portugal v India* (n 91) 147 (Bourquin). For more on Yugoslavia's position see sub-s II B vi of ch 4 at 142.

C. Jurisprudence: 'Rights and Obligations Deriving from Article 36'

The picture drawn by the Court's jurisprudence seems, however, to be ambiguous.

In his often quoted individual opinion in the *Anglo-Iranian Oil Co* case Judge McNair for example wrote that the Optional Clause was 'a standing invitation made on behalf of the Court'.[98] According to Shihata, he thereby suggested that the declarations established bilateral relationships between the states and the Court.[99]

On the other hand, in the *Nicaragua* case the Court said that by making an Optional Clause declaration 'the United States entered into an obligation which is binding upon it *vis-à-vis* other States parties to the Optional-Clause system'. The Court then came to the conclusion that there was an 'obligation of the United States to submit to the compulsory jurisdiction of the Court *vis-à-vis* Nicaragua, a State accepting the same obligation'.[100] The aforementioned Court's ruling in the *Right of Passage* case sounds similar. The Court wrote there that by making the declaration 'the accepting State becomes a Party to the system of the Optional Clause in relation to the other declarant States, with all the rights and obligations deriving from Article 36'.[101] The Court explicitly refers to rights for the states deriving from the Optional Clause. In the recent *Bakassi Peninsula* case the Court furthermore said that the withdrawal of a declaration took an 'accrued right' from another state.[102] This seems to imply that the declaration also established that right for the other state. Judge Oda further clarified this in the recent *Use of Force* cases. He said: 'The making of a declaration is a unilateral act, which, far from being in the nature of a concession, is in fact to the State's advantage, in that it confers a right of action against States in a similar position'.[103] This corresponds to Judge Torres Bernárdez's dissenting opinion in the *Fisheries Jurisdiction* case between Spain and Canada. He held that 'through the deposit of a declaration, a State, acting freely and of its own deliberate choice, assumes solemn legal obligations vis-à-vis other declarant States'.[104]

Furthermore, it is obvious that the Court does not invoke titles of jurisdiction for itself.[105] In the *Norwegian Loans* case the Court had no jurisdiction

[98] Individual opinion of Judge AD McNair, *ICJ Rep 1952*, 116.
[99] Shihata (n 2) 145.
[100] *Nicaragua v United States of America* (n 33) paras 61, 65.
[101] *Portugal v India* (n 66) 146.
[102] (*Cameroon v Nigeria: Equatorial Guinea intervening* (n 66) para 34). See also Judge Weeramantry (dissenting opinion of Judge CG Weeramantry, *ICJ Rep 1998*, 362) who reflected about the moment in which the 'right to bring another declarant to Court' was established and Judge Koroma (dissenting opinion of Judge AG Koroma, *ICJ Rep 1998*, 390) who spoke of 'such a right' to invoke the jurisdiction of the Court.
[103] Separate opinion of Judge S Oda, *ICJ Rep 1999*, para 12.
[104] Dissenting opinion of Judge S Torres Bernárdez, *ICJ Rep 1998*, para 145.
[105] For that see also Tomuschat (n 24) para 31.

under the Optional Clause but nonetheless it did not invoke either the Franco-Norwegian Arbitration Convention of 1904 or the General Act of 1928 as title of jurisdiction because the parties did not ask it to do so. The Court wrote: 'If the French Government had intended to proceed upon that basis it would expressly have so stated'.[106] It becomes clear that the Court regards titles of jurisdiction as basis to proceed for the parties and not for itself. There is no reason why the obligations under normal treaties with compromissory clauses should be different to the Optional Clause in this respect. Furthermore, the Court considered as crucial the way in which the states understood their obligations. Concerning the French declaration in the *Norwegian Loans* case it said that it 'has before it a provision which both Parties to the dispute regard as constituting an expression of their common will relating to the competence of the Court'.[107] According to Maus, this is the proof that states do not engage with the Court but with each other and that the Optional Clause declarations establish only relations *inter se*.[108]

However, the first aspect of the latter judgment was criticised by Verzijl and Judge Basdevant in his dissenting opinion. As far as Judge Basdevant maintained that France had indeed invoked the General Act,[109] this dissent does not contradict the result found so far. However, he also wrote that the Court had to ascertain whether it had jurisdiction by all means when its jurisdiction raised objections.[110] This is similar to the position of Verzijl who pointed at the principle *iura novit curia* and maintained that no legal consideration barred the Court from referring to the convention and the General Act.[111] It seems as if Judge Basdevant and Verzijl wanted the Court to address the not invoked titles of jurisdiction *proprio motu*. This, however, does not necessarily mean that the Court would have invoked them in its own interest. It would not have been its choice to do so.[112] That the Court would have acted in the interest of the states shows also another part of Verzijl's work where he presented the position of Judge Basdevant. There Verzijl referred to Norway as 'obligée vis-à-vis de la France'.[113]

D. Comparison to Other Optional Clauses

Up to now it appears that the obligations established under the Optional Clause are obligations among states. The question is whether that assumption

---

[106] *Case of Certain Norwegian Loans (France v Norway)* (Judgment) [1957] ICJ Rep 9, 25.
[107] ibid 27.
[108] Maus (n 79) 61.
[109] Dissenting opinion of Judge J Basdevant, *ICJ Rep 1957*, 74.
[110] ibid 74.
[111] Verzijl (n 40) 395 f.
[112] cp also *Nicaragua v United States of America* (n 89) 115 (Pellet).
[113] Verzijl (n 40) 397.

can be supported by a comparison with other provisions establishing an obligation to accept a kind of compulsory third party dispute settlement. Especially the optional clauses to human rights treaties are of value as under these the way the obligations are structured is extensively discussed. Furthermore, in this discussion the Optional Clause has often been addressed and taken into consideration.

This sub-section will focus on the inter-state procedures under the American Convention on Human Rights (ACHR), the International Covenant on Civil and Political Rights (CCPR) and the old version of the European Convention on Human Rights (ECHR). The procedures for individuals are of lesser value as they are less comparable to the Optional Clause for obvious reasons. Therefore, the provisions for the procedures involving individuals will be taken into consideration only occasionally.

i. Article 45 and Article 62 ACHR

Article 62(1) ACHR is similar to the Optional Clause and provides:

> A State Party may, upon depositing its instrument of ratification or accession to this Convention, or at any subsequent time, declare that it recognizes as binding, ipso facto, and not requiring special agreement, the jurisdiction of the Court on all matters relating to the interpretation or application of this Convention.

This seems to be a difference to the Optional Clause as the declaration under Article 62(1) ACHR works not only 'in relation to any other state accepting the same obligation' as the declarations under Article 36(2) of the Statute do. However, Article 62(3) ACHR provides:

> The jurisdiction of the Court shall comprise all cases concerning the interpretation and application of the provisions of this Convention that are submitted to it, provided that the States Parties to the case recognize or have recognized such jurisdiction, whether by special declaration pursuant to the preceding paragraphs, or by a special agreement.

Article 61(1) ACHR speaks of the 'right to submit a case to the Court' which the commission and the state parties have.

Before the Inter-American Court of Human Rights (IACtHR) can hear a case there must have been a procedure before a commission (Article 61(2) ACHR).[114] For that procedure Article 45(1) ACHR provides a separate optional clause. Article 45(2) ACHR contains the rule that only those communications 'presented by a State Party that has made a declaration recognizing the aforementioned competence of the Commission' will be considered by the commission. In this respect both optional clauses are very similar to the Optional Clause.

---

[114] See also GL Neuman, 'IACtHR' para 16.

Therefore, it might shed a different light on the Optional Clause that the IACtHR said the optional clause of the ACHR includes the '*Court's right* to settle any controversy relative to its jurisdiction'.[115] Of course this remark related only to the Court's competence to decide upon the scope of its jurisdiction, but also in other situations it became obvious that the IACtHR does not regard the rights contained in the ACHR as being reciprocal rights and obligations among states. The court has frequently emphasised that the obligations under the American Convention of Human Rights are objective and 'independent of any criteria based exclusively on the principle of reciprocity'.[116] It said:

> In concluding these human rights treaties, the States can be deemed to submit themselves to a legal order within which they, for the common good, assume various obligations, not in relation to other States, but towards all individuals within their jurisdiction.[117]

This conviction is based on the idea that human rights treaties do not fit in the regular pattern of reciprocal treaties anymore. They have taken up a community interest and in some areas left the inter-state level.[118] The rights in human rights treaties are not granted for the sake of other states. The beneficiaries are individuals.[119] Therefore, some authors even maintained that human rights treaties are 'objective treaties' which are not governed by the same law as common treaties.[120] Simma said that the treaties of human rights law contain reciprocal rights and obligations like other treaties. Their only particularity is that the states themselves do not directly benefit from their rights.[121] However, he also said that the bilateral

---

[115] *Ivcher Bronstein v Peru* (Competence) IACtHR Series C No 54 (1999) para 34: '*derecho de la Corte* a resolver cualquier controversia relativa a su jurisdicción' (emphasis added).

[116] *The Effect of Reservations on the Entry Into Force of the American Convention on Human Rights (Arts 74 and 75)*, Advisory Opinion, IACtHR Series A No 2 (1982) para 29. cp also *Hilaire v Trinidad and Tobago* (Preliminary Objections) IACtHR Series C No 80 (2001) para 95. See further A Úbeda de Torres, 'Contentious Jurisdiction' 11.

[117] *The Effect of Reservations on the Entry Into Force of the American Convention on Human Rights (Arts. 74 and 75)*, ibid para 29; supported by Pellet in ILC 'Documents of the 48th Session' (1996) UN Doc A/CN.4/SER.A/1996/Add.1 (Part 1) 65, para 152.

[118] cp B Simma, 'Reservations' 679 f. Especially for the ACHR see AAC Trindade, 'IACtHR' 135 f.

[119] R Bernhardt, 'Gegenseitigkeitsprinzip' 626; T Giegerich, 'Reservations 2012' para 31; B Simma, 'Community Interest' 364 f; UNCHR 'General Comment No 24 (52) on issues relating to reservations made upon ratification or accession to the Covenant to the Optional Protocols thereto, or in relation to declarations under article 41 of the Covenant' (1994) CCPR/C/21/Rev.1/Add.6 para 8; C Walter, 'Article 21' para 22. See also ILC 'Documents of the 48th Session' (1996) UN Doc A/CN.4/SER.A/1996/Add.1 (Part 1) 65, paras 149–52 (Pellet) and Art 2(1) CCPR.

[120] cp B Hofmann, *Beendigung* 64–75; B Simma, *Reziprozitätselement* 176–81. See eg Gerald G Fitzmaurice (ILC 'Documents of the 9th Session Including the Report of the Commission to the General Assembly' (1957) UN Doc A/CN.4/SER.A/1957/Add.l 54, paras 125 f (Fitzmaurice)) speaking of obligations which had 'an absolute rather than a reciprocal character'.

[121] Simma (n 119) 364 f, 370–73; B Simma, 'Reciprocity' para 6.

structures and the reciprocity in human rights treaties are only of a purely formal character.[122]

The position of the IACtHR referred to above is therefore to be seen in light of this particularity of human rights law. Yet, the question is whether the statements and the rationale presented also refer to the optional clauses of the ACHR. On the one hand the statements are only of a general character and do not explicitly refer to the optional clauses. On the other hand it could be said that the states' option to bring a case to a supervisory human rights body is not for their own benefit and cannot be considered as a right towards other states either. In this respect they could be different from the Optional Clause. As Úbeda de Torres already remarked the terms of Article 62(1) ACHR 'are clearly an echo of those used in Article 36(2) of the Statute of the International Court of Justice'. But as he added these two optional clauses are fundamentally different as one concerns inter-state litigation and the other human rights.[123]

This is also the position of the IACtHR which maintained that 'the contracting States do not have any individual advantages or disadvantages nor interests of their own, but merely a common interest; hence the Convention's raison d'être is to accomplish its purposes'.[124] For the IACtHR this likewise holds true for the optional clause in Article 62(1) ACHR because, 'when a State consents to that clause, it binds itself to the whole of the Convention and is fully committed to guaranteeing the international protection of human rights that the Convention embodies'. The court went on saying that '[n]o analogy can be drawn between the State practice detailed under Article 36.2 of the Statute of the International Court of Justice and acceptance of the optional clause concerning recognition of the binding jurisdiction of this Court, given the particular nature and the object and purpose of the American Convention'. The IACtHR emphasised that unlike the declaration according to its Article 62(1) ACHR the Optional Clause concerned 'interstate litigation'.[125] In finding so the IACtHR referred inter alia to a decision of the European Court of Human Rights (ECtHR),[126] which might further illuminate the question at hand.

---

[122] Simma (n 118) 663. cp also Simma (n 119) 370. For the fact that treaties are neither only normative nor only reciprocal see eg M Fitzmaurice, 'Treaties' para 8; Simma (n 119) 335 f.

[123] Úbeda de Torres (n 116) 10.

[124] *Constitutional Court v Peru* (Competence) IACtHR Series C No 55 (1999) para 43 referring to *Reservations to the Convention on the Prevention and Punishment of the Crime of Genocide* (Advisory Opinion) [1951] ICJ Rep 15, 12. See also *The Effect of Reservations on the Entry Into Force of the American Convention on Human Rights (Arts 74 and 75)* (n 116) para 29.

[125] *Constitutional Court v Peru*, ibid paras 41–48. See also *Ivcher Bronstein v Peru* (Competence) IACtHR Series C No 54 (1999) para 48.

[126] *Constitutional Court v Peru* (n 124) para 46 referring to *Loizidou v Turkey* (Preliminary Objections) Series A No 310 (1995) para 84.

ii. Articles 25 and 46 ECHR (old)

As the ECtHR has emphasised, too, the optional clauses of the old version of the ECHR[127] have been modelled according to the Optional Clause.[128] The system of inter-state disputes under this version of the ECHR was similar to that of the current ACHR, as referred to above, but shows some differences.

Article 46(1) ECHR (old) provided the jurisdiction of the ECtHR and read as follows:

> Any of the High Contracting Parties may at any time declare that it recognizes as compulsory 'ipso facto' and without special agreement the jurisdiction of the Court in all matters concerning the interpretation and application of the present Convention.

Article 48 ECHR (old) provided:

> The following may bring a case before the Court, provided that the High Contracting Party concerned, if there is only one, or the High Contracting Parties concerned, if there is more than one, are subject to the compulsory jurisdiction of the Court, or failing that, with the consent of the High Contracting Party concerned, if there is only one, or of the High Contracting Parties concerned if there is more than one:
>
> (a)   the Commission;
> (b)   a High Contracting Party whose national is alleged to be a victim;
> (c)   a High Contracting Party which referred the case to the Commission;
> (d)   a High Contracting Party against which the complaint has been lodged.

From that last article it becomes clear that states which have not taken part in the corresponding previous procedure before the European Commission of Human Rights (EComHR) have only been able to bring a case before the ECtHR if, according to Article 48(b) ECHR (old) one of their nationals was a victim of the violation.[129] From this perspective the possibility to institute proceedings under Article 48 ECHR (old) could be regarded as a possibility for the states to enforce the rights of their own nationals and the optional clause declarations under Article 46(1) ECHR (old) as establishing reciprocal rights between the states.

Article 48(b) ECHR (old) has, however, never played an essential role. The practice focused on procedures which were brought before the EComHR and then the ECtHR by the same state[130] or the commission.[131]

---

[127] 'Old version' of the ECHR means the ECHR up to its 11th additional protocol which entered into force on 1 November 1998 (cp http://conventions.coe.int/Treaty/Commun/QueVoulezVous.asp?NT=155&CM=8&DF=19/01/2015&CL=ENG (last visit on 19 January 2015)).

[128] *Loizidou v Turkey* (n 126) para 83. See also J A Frowein and W Peukert, *EMRK-Kommentar, 1996* Art 46, para 1; Giegerich (n 119) 973 f.

[129] See also Frowein (n 50) 399.

[130] See eg *Ireland v United Kingdom* Series A no 25 (1978) para 1.

[131] cp Frowein (n 50) 399.

The first step, the procedure before the EComHR under Article 24 ECHR (old), did not require that a state had an own special interest in the enforcement of the right in question.[132] And the same then held true for the later procedure before the Court under Article 48(c) ECHR (old).[133] Therefore, the states did not necessarily enforce their own rights or the rights of their nationals respectively.

Concerning the obligations arising from the ECHR in general the ECtHR itself has already 'clarif[ied] the nature of the engagements placed under its supervision'. It said:

> Unlike international treaties of the classic kind, the Convention comprises more than mere reciprocal engagements between contracting States. It creates, over and above a network of mutual, bilateral undertakings, objective obligations which, in the words of the Preamble, benefit from a 'collective enforcement'.[134]

Furthermore, the EComHR has already made clear that this also holds true for the supervisory machinery of the convention. The objective character of the obligations 'also appears in the machinery provided in the Convention for its collective enforcement—"being designed rather to protect the fundamental rights of individual human beings from infringement by any of the High Contracting Parties than to create subjective and reciprocal rights for the High Contracting Parties themselves"'.[135]

All this supports the impression that states acting under Article 46 ECHR (old) as well as those acting under its successor Article 33 ECHR do not enforce their own rights but that they are acting to protect the European *ordre public*.[136] Furthermore, it can be said that Article 46 ECHR (old) and Article 33 ECHR provide the possibility for what is at least meant to be an *actio popularis*.[137]

Comparing this to the Optional Clause the ECtHR has additionally already expressed that

> in the first place, the context within which the International Court of Justice operates is quite distinct from that of the Convention institutions. The International

---

[132] *Ireland v United Kingdom* (n 130) para 239; Frowein and Peukert (n 128) Art 24, para 1.

[133] *Loizidou v Turkey* (n 126) para 70; JA Frowein and W Peukert, *EMRK-Kommentar, 2009* Art 33, para 1. cp *Ireland v United Kingdom* (n 130) para 239.

[134] *Ireland v United Kingdom* (n 130) para 239 repeated in *Temeltasch v Switzerland* (App no 9116/80) [1983] para 64; *Loizidou v Turkey* (n 126) para 70. See also *France ao v Turkey (Admissibility)* (App No 9940-9944/82) [1983] para 39; Frowein (n 50) 405.

[135] *Chrysostomos ao v Turkey* (App no 15299/89 ao) [1991] para 20 referring to *Austria v Italy* (App no 788/60) [1961] 19. cp also *Temeltasch v Switzerland* (n 134) para 63; *France ao v Turkey (Admissibility)* (n 134) para 40. In the case of *France ao v Italy* the EComHR further 'observe[d], in this respect, that the Convention clearly indicates where, as regards a right of action under it, a question of reciprocity may exceptionally arise. This is the case in Article 46, para 2, concerning recognition of the Court's jurisdiction- but not in Article 24, which contains no such indication' (ibid para 41). Article 46(2) ECHR, however, is modelled according to Art 36(3) of the Statute. For the impact of this 'condition of reciprocity' see n 38 of ch 5.

[136] Frowein and Peukert (n 133) Art 31, para 1. cp also Frowein and Peukert (n 128) Art 25, para 1.

[137] cp C Grabenwarter and K Pabel, *EMRK* 46 f, para 2.

Court is called on inter alia to examine any legal dispute between States that might occur in any part of the globe with reference to principles of international law. The subject-matter of a dispute may relate to any area of international law. In the second place, unlike the Convention institutions, the role of the International Court is not exclusively limited to direct supervisory functions in respect of a law-making treaty such as the Convention.[138]

Therefore, it seems as if the ECtHR does at least not fully distinguish between the substantive human rights and the supervisory possibility for states to file an application. It uses similar argumentations for both.[139] These argumentations do not apply to the Optional Clause. As Bernhardt, who took part in the judgment on the *Loizidou* case, wrote, the wording of the Optional Clause and the optional clause of the ECHR may have been the same but the obligations under them are different.[140]

Another comparison of an old ECHR optional clause to the Optional Clause was made by the EComHR as it considered the optional clause in Article 25 ECHR (old) which provided for petitions by individuals. The EComHR clearly said that

the character of the Convention, as a constitutional instrument of European public order in the field of human rights, excludes application by analogy, as suggested by the respondent Government, of the State practice under Article 36 para.3 of the Statute of the International Court of Justice. Declarations under this clause create mere reciprocal agreements between contracting States. The Commission notes that Article 36 para.3 of the Statute does not, like Article 25 (Art 25) of the European Convention on Human Rights, concern petitions brought by individuals but applications by States.[141]

All in all it becomes clear that in the opinion of the ECtHR and the EComHR and in contrast to the optional clauses of the old ECHR the Optional Clause provides reciprocal obligations between the states.

iii. Article 41 CCPR

The question is whether the same can be said concerning the optional clause of the CCPR and the position of the UNCHR. The optional clause can be found in Article 41(1) CCPR which provides:

A State Party to the present Covenant may at any time declare under this article that it recognizes the competence of the Committee to receive and consider communications to the effect that a State Party claims that another State Party is not fulfilling its obligations under the present Covenant. Communications under

---

[138] *Loizidou v Turkey* (n 126) para 84. As referred to in the previous section this was maintained by the IACtHR (n 124) paras 46 f; *Hilaire v Trinidad and Tobago* (n 116) para 16.

[139] cp Frowein (n 50) 404 f and below sub-s III B ii b of ch 5 at 208.

[140] R Bernhardt, 'Vorbehalte' 381 f.

[141] *Chrysostomos ao v Turkey* (n 135) para 22. According to Frowein the EComHR considered the agreements under the Optional Clause only as being 'semi-reciprocal' (Frowein (n 50) 404 f).

this article may be received and considered only if submitted by a State Party which has made a declaration recognizing in regard to itself the competence of the Committee. No communication shall be received by the Committee if it concerns a State Party which has not made such a declaration.

This is similar to the inter-state procedure which had been provided for by Articles 46 and 48 ECHR (old).[142] Article 41 CCPR has been considered as operating on the basis of reciprocity as it allows communications only if both states involved have made a declaration.[143] Concerning this latter provision the UNCHR has, however, adopted a more differentiated approach. Basically, the UNCHR, too, wrote that there is a difference between 'treaties that are mere exchanges of obligations between the states' and 'human rights treaties which are for the benefit of persons within their jurisdiction'.[144] In saying that, the committee primarily referred to the human rights themselves, but it equally emphasised the importance of the supportive guarantees 'on national [and] international level'. The committee also considered its own monitoring rule role as an 'essential element in the design of the Covenant, which is also directed to securing the enjoyment of the rights'.[145] However, the UNCHR further said that under the CCPR and its protocols '[t]he principle of inter-State reciprocity has no place, save perhaps in the limited context of reservations to the competence to the Committee under article 41'.[146] In this respect it left open whether it considers the obligations arising under Article 41 CCPR as being different from the other obligations under the CCPR.

The decision of this latter question makes no substantial difference for the understanding of the Optional Clause, though. If Article 41 CCPR were considered as being like the other provisions of the CCPR because it only provides the possibility for a states' *actio popularis* and ultimately serves the interests of individuals,[147] this would not apply to the Optional Clause as the latter is limited to the enforcement of the states' own rights and serves the states' own interests. Under the Optional Clause applications enforcing other than the submitting states' rights are impermissible.[148]

---

[142] See also E Schwelb, 'Measures of Implementation' 848.

[143] M Nowak, *CCPR Commentary* Art 41, para 13; E Schwelb, 'Legislative History' 288; Schwelb (n 142) 847.

[144] UNCHR 'General Comment No 24 (52) on issues relating to reservations made upon ratification or accession to the Covenant to the Optional Protocols thereto, or in relation to declarations under article 41 of the Covenant' (1994) CCPR/C/21/Rev.1/Add.6 paras 8, 17.

[145] ibid para 11.

[146] ibid para 17. See also the United Kingdom's position in United Kingdom, 'Observations' 424, para 5.

[147] cp M Lippman, 'Human Rights Revisited' 257; Nowak (n 143) Art 41, para 17; Schwelb (n 142) 847 f.

[148] *South West Africa (Ethiopia and Liberia v South Africa)* (Second Phase) [1966] ICJ Rep 6, paras 88, 99 f; *Barcelona Traction, Light and Power Company, Limited (Belgium v Spain) (New Application: 1962)* (Second Phase) [1970] ICJ Rep 3, paras 101, 103; dissenting opinion of Judge B Winiarski, *ICJ Rep 1962*, 452, 455; Oda (n 25) 50, para 54. cp also Whiteman (n 24) 1363.

If, on the other hand, the obligations arising under Article 41 CCPR were considered as reciprocal obligations because the corresponding declarations grant states the possibility to institute proceedings, this would hold true for the Optional Clause, too, under which states have the possibility to institute proceedings and do this for their own benefit.

iv. Result

The question the human rights treaty bodies had and have to decide is whether the obligations arising under the abovementioned optional clauses are like other obligations arising under the human rights treaties or whether they are reciprocal obligations among states. For the present thesis the comparisons with the Optional Clause made by the ECHR bodies and the IACtHR are most revealing. It becomes clear that they regarded the Optional Clause as establishing reciprocal rights and obligations among the states. In no instance the establishment of judicial review in general is considered as a common good or as a part of the common *ordre public*. All considerations are based on the effectiveness of human rights and the *actio popularis* for the benefit of the individuals. With good reasons the Optional Clause has been considered as something different as it primarily allows states to enforce their own rights only.[149] As far as the UNCHR considers Article 41 CCPR as establishing reciprocal rights this must hold true for the Optional Clause, too.

E. Conclusion

While the wording of Article 36(2) of the Statute provides no clear answer, the *travaux préparatoires*, state practice and jurisprudence support the assumption that the Optional Clause declarations establish horizontal rights and obligations between the states which have made an Optional Clause declaration.[150] Not only is the establishment of the relationships based on a pure *do ut des* between the states. Moreover the content of the relationships established can be considered as a possibility for states to file applications against each other to enforce their own substantive rights.[151]

---

[149] The question whether the regime for reservations in human rights law treaties can be applied to the Optional Clause nonetheless will be addressed in sub-s III B ii b of ch 5 at 203.

[150] cp Buigues (n 68) 275; IR Cohn, 'Pre-Seisin Reciprocity' 700; J Crawford, 'Automatic Reservations' 76; Enriques (n 68) 838 f, 843; Farmanfarma (n 7) 87, 160; F Rigaldies, 'L'acte unilatéral' 432; Waldock (n 79) 251; EB Weiss, 'Reciprocity' 96; Wittmann (n 7) 150, 163, 172. cp also Maus (n 79) 55: 'droits et … certaines obligations'. See also United States of America 'Congressional Record' (1946) 10706 (Report of the Committee on Foreign Relations).

[151] Enriques (n 68) 853 f: 'droit d'action'; Oda (n 25) 40, para 29: 'right of action'; United States of America 'Congressional Record' (1946) 10706 (Report of the Committee on Foreign Relations): 'right … to sue'; Tomuschat (n 24) para 28: 'right to sue'. cp also Farmanfarma (n 7) 87; A Yankov, 'Les réserves' 588 f.

This result leads to some other conclusions. First it becomes clear that the substance of the commitment accepted by a state under the Optional Clause generally depends on the declarations of other states. These declarations do not only add further possible adversaries as is the case of the optional clauses in the human rights treaties. Under the Optional Clause the material subjected to judicial review covered by a declaration, too, enlarges with every new declaration made as new disputes are then covered. Under the optional clauses of human rights treaties the quantity of covered relations, which are primarily those between the particular state and its citizens, remain the same independent of the number of states able to file an application.

Second, with regard to the opinion states have of the Optional Clause, it should be underlined that each Optional Clause declaration also establishes rights for the submitting state.[152] Maus wrote that certain states tend to see themselves only in the role of a respondent.[153] Considering the equal offensive potential of the Optional Clause, as especially shown in the state practice referred to above,[154] their perception seems to be wrong. As Oda, Tomuschat and Weil have already emphasised, Optional Clause declarations are no sacrifice.[155] They are a sovereign choice for one mode of peaceful dispute settlement and because of the general equilibrium of rights and obligations they are as much a burden as they are a benefit.[156]

The third and last conclusion is a more theoretical reflection about the Optional Clause. As hinted at above, there is a certain tendency in public international law away from inter-state reciprocity. Especially in the early stages of the development of legal systems they are generally based on direct reciprocity but in their further development institutions often emerge and take charge of policies which are common concern.[157] The institutions substitute direct reciprocity or pitch in where common concerns or third party interests have to be protected. Where reciprocity does not prevail it must be substituted by an objective order with subordination.[158] Nonetheless, today reciprocity is still a force with an importance 'which can hardly be overestimated'.[159] After all that has been said this latter remark of Simma holds true especially in the case of the Optional Clause. In particular state practice shows that an objective order with compulsory jurisdiction of the Court as common good has not or at least has not yet been established.

---

[152] See also Oda (n 25) 40, para 29.
[153] Maus (n 79) 195.
[154] Sub-s II B of ch 1 at 26.
[155] Oda (n 25) 40, para 29; Tomuschat (n 24) para 35; P Weil, *Écrits* 111. cp also A D'Amato, 'Modifying' 386, 395 f; Morrison (n 23) 60; LB Sohn, 'Compulsory Jurisdiction' 14 f.
[156] For the 'sitting duck' problem see sub-s III A of ch 3 at 95.
[157] cp Simma (n 121) para 1. cp also Simma (n 119) 230–35.
[158] Bernhardt (n 119) 626 f.
[159] Simma (n 121) para 1. cp also Simma (n 119) 230.

2

The Nature of the Optional Clause

SINCE THE OPTIONAL Clause has been created, its nature has been discussed extensively. It has been said that the Optional Clause declarations are unilateral declarations without contractual element,[1] that they establish a series of bilateral relations,[2] and that they are part of a multilateral treaty.[3] Furthermore, the Optional Clause declarations have been described as unilateral declarations giving rise to contractual relationships.[4] Waldock introduced the idea that the Optional Clause declarations established consensual relations *sui generis*.[5] Similarly, the declarations have been called a 'unique type of legal instrument,'[6] which consequently makes any legal deduction from the Optional Clause's character almost impossible and is not beneficial for legal clarity. In 2002,

---

[1] ILC 'Summary Records of the Meetings of the 53rd Session' (23 April–1 June and 2 July–10 August 2001) UN Doc A/CN.4/SER.A/2001 176, para 39 (Rodriguez Cedeño); RP Anand, *Compulsory Jurisdiction* 147 (agreement only after application); C Rousseau, *Droit* 420 f; M Rotter, 'Art 36 Abs 2 des Statuts' 645–48. Compare also Zemanek, according to whom the Optional Clause declarations belong to a group of unilateral declarations which 'are regulated, at least in part, by the sub-system to which they belong' (K Zemanek, 'Unilateral Acts' 212) and furthermore AP Rubin, 'Unilateral Declarations' 12: 'no basis is stated for characterizing the [Optional Clause] declarations as something like cross-offers and cross-acceptances'.

[2] Dissenting opinion of Judge BA Ajibola, *ICJ Rep 1998*, 395 f; K Holloway, *Modern Trends* 653; H Kelsen, *Fundamental Problems* 521. See also Wittmann (F Wittmann, *Obligatorium* 161–66, 185 f, 326 f, 599) who calculated that the 37 Optional Clause declarations of his time resulted into 666 bilateral treaties. See also HWA Thirlway, 'International Court, 2014' 600: 'a complex network of bilateral relationships'.

[3] H Lauterpacht, 'British Reservations' 170; DP Myers, 'Treaties' 592. For more see below n 275.

[4] See eg G Schwarzenberger, *International Law* 550; PC Ulimubenshi, *Domaine réservé* 120. According to Gerald G Fitzmaurice, the declarations are no treaties but 'give rise to a quasi-treaty situation' (GG Fitzmaurice, 'Jurisdiction, Competence and Procedure' 75). See also V Lamm, *Jurisdiction* 95: 'The states parties to the optional clause system undertake, by accession to that system, a unilateral commitment regarding the Court's jurisdiction, which could create a bilateral legal relationship at a later stage. This is activated when concrete disputes are referred to the Court'.

[5] CHM Waldock, 'Decline' 254. See also R Kolb, *ICJ* 375, 454–56, 488; S Rosenne and Y Ronen, *Practice 1920–2005* 796. See furthermore CG Ténékidès, 'Les actes concurrents' 721: 'un acte d'adhésion *sui generis*' and see also N Kebbon, 'Optional Clause' 261: 'The Optional Clause system exhibits unilateral, bilateral and multilateral features'. Rosenne's position, as far as it concerned reservations, was also supported in ILC 'Report of the Commission to the General Assembly on the Work of Its 52nd Session' (1 May–9 June and 10 July–18 August 2000) UN Doc A/CN.4/SER.A/2000/Add.1 (Part 2)/Rev.1 114, para 10.

[6] JHW Verzijl, 'Optional Clause' 603.

Gharbi remarked that neither the courts nor literature had ever clearly given their opinion about the nature of Optional Clause declarations and that there was merely a tendency to emphasise their unilateral origin and to add contractual elements where the declarations cohere.[7]

The following assessment will re-examine the issue in light of the result of chapter one and also in light of the International Law Commission's (ILC) work on the Guiding Principles for Unilateral Declarations (GPUD). It will refer to the Statute, state practice and the Court's jurisprudence and also address the question of whether the Optional Clause is an integral part of the Statute.

I. UNILATERAL DECLARATIONS, BILATERAL AND MULTILATERAL TREATIES

First some general arguments relating to the abstract nature of unilateral declarations and treaties merit consideration.

A. Pure and 'False' Unilateral Declarations

It has been argued that the Optional Clause had particular unilateral elements as there were no negotiations.[8] Rosenne wrote that 'the characteristic feature of the system of Article 36, paragraph 2' was 'that the declarations are unilateral acts of the individual States, the product of unilateral drafting'.[9] For him the lack of negotiations spoke against the assumption of a treaty.[10] Tomuschat, too, emphasised that, unlike Optional Clause declarations, multilateral treaties were negotiated and finely tuned. Unlike the Optional Clause, only multilateral treaties established an equilibrium which reservations disturbed.[11] Likewise Bernhardt wrote that Optional Clause declarations might have a contractual basis, Article 36(2) of the Statute, but that each of them nonetheless remained a separate unilateral proclamation with its own individual restrictions.[12] For Oda the declarations themselves were mere applications. According to Oda the analogy to treaty law was misleading. Making an Optional Clause declaration was for him different to the accession to a treaty.[13]

Conversely it could be said that also under other multilateral treaties the accession is a unilateral act. Such an accession to an open treaty is

---

[7] F Gharbi, 'Déclarations d'acceptation' 247, 251.
[8] SA Alexandrov, *Declarations* 13. cp also B Maus, *Réserves* 60.
[9] Rosenne and Ronen (n 5) 733. See also M Fitzmaurice, 'Optional Clause' para 6.
[10] Rosenne and Ronen, ibid 793. See also F Gharbi, 'Le déclin' 435; Gharbi (n 7) 272.
[11] C Tomuschat, 'Article 36 of the Statute' para 99.
[12] R Bernhardt, 'Vorbehalte' 370.
[13] S Oda, 'Reservations in the Declarations' 17 f.

likewise not necessarily accompanied by negotiations.[14] Furthermore, it could be said that the unilateral origin of the Optional Clause declarations cannot play an essential role for the determination of the nature of the Optional Clause as the declarations result in reciprocal obligations and rights among the states.[15] In total, the Optional Clause declarations could be merely as unilateral as those instruments which have been discussed under the notion of 'false unilateral declarations'.

These points require more assessment as they are essential to answer the question of how far the Optional Clause can be regarded as a treaty and of how far treaty law can be applied.

i. Optional Clause Declarations cannot be Purely Unilateral Declarations

The law of unilateral declarations is a complex and heterogeneous field of law.[16] Special Rapporteur Rodríguez Cedeño defined unilateral acts in his ninth report on the GPUD as follows: 'A unilateral act of a State means a unilateral declaration formulated by a State with the intent of producing certain legal effects under international law'.[17] In this definition he refers to the two main characteristics of purely unilateral acts: their autonomy and the state's intent.[18] For many authors the main characteristic of unilateral declarations is that they are independent of other states' reactions.[19] This is what distinguishes them from bi- and multilateral acts.[20]

---

[14] cp J Marchi, 'Article 15' paras 1, 13.

[15] For the latter point see s II of ch 1 at 22.

[16] cp ILC 'Summary Records of the Meetings of the 53rd Session' (n 1) 187, para 8 (Goco), 189, para 28 (Herdocia Sacasa); ILC 'Summary Records of the Meetings of the 54th Session' (29 April–7 June and 22 July–16 August 2002) UN Doc A/CN.4/SER.A/2002 63, para 54 (Rodriguez Cedeño); V Rodríguez Cedeño and MI Torres Cazorla, 'Unilateral Acts' paras 6–9.

[17] ILC 'Ninth Report on Unilateral Acts of States' (6 April 2006) UN Doc A/CN.4/569 1 (Rodriguez Cedeño). cp also Rodríguez Cedeño and Torres Cazorla, ibid paras 1 f. In the final GPUD this definition appears in the introduction (ILC 'Report of the International Law Commission on the Work of Its 58th Session' (1 May–9 June and 3 July–11 August 2006) UN Doc A/61/10 370).

[18] ILC 'Summary Records of the Meetings of the 53rd Session' (n 1) 198, para 36 (Kamto).

[19] *Nuclear Tests (Australia v France)* (Judgment) [1974] ICJ Rep 253, para 44; ILC 'Documents of the 53rd Session' (2001) UN Doc A/CN.4/SER.A/2001/Add.1 (Part 1) 122, para 47 (Rodriguez Cedeño); ILC 'Documents of the 52nd Session' (2000) UN Doc A/CN.4/SER.A/2000/Add.1 (Part 1) 255, paras 62–68 (Rodriguez Cedeño); A Cassese, *International Law* 185; A Gigante, 'Unilateral State Acts' 344 f, 352 f; F Rigaldies, 'L'acte unilatéral' 428; J Sicault, 'Engagements unilatéraux' 673 f. But see Principle 3 GPUD which provides: 'To determine the legal effects of such declarations, it is necessary to take account of ... the reactions to which they gave rise' (ILC 'Report of the International Law Commission on the Work of Its 58th Session' (n 17) 371). And see also Brownlie who said: 'Everything depended on the conduct, both of the precipitating State and of other States'. (ILC 'Summary Records of the Meetings of the 53rd Session' (n 1) 197, para 27 (Brownlie)). See further ILC 'Summary Record of the 2913th Meeting' (1 November 2006) UN Doc A/CN.4/SR.2913 11 (Economides). These statements, however, relate basically only to the cognisance of the other states and not to an acceptance of the act (cp the commentary to Principle 3 GPUD (ILC 'Report of the International Law Commission on the Work of Its 58th Session' (n 17) 371 f)).

[20] ILC 'Summary Records of the Meetings of the 53rd Session' (n 1) 198, para 36 (Kamto); Rigaldies, ibid 450; Sicault, ibid 641.

However, unilateral declarations, too, establish a relationship between the submitting state and the addressee or addressees even though this relationship is not like a relationship under a treaty.[21] Some authors argued that unilateral acts are not really unilateral acts because from a wider perspective they are made in reciprocal relationships and therefore can be considered treaties in a broader sense.[22] Yet, with such an understanding the notion of a treaty would be overstressed.[23] Therefore, unilateral declarations are a proper source of law.[24]

The unilateral act, however, is not among the sources of law enumerated in Article 38 of the Statute. Nonetheless, the Court and literature treat them as legal acts.[25] According to Principle 1(2) GPUD, 'the binding character of such declarations is based on good faith'.[26] This is also the position of the Court as voiced in the *Nuclear Tests* cases. It referred to the principle *pacta sunt servanda* which governs the law of treaties and is based on the principle of good faith. According to the Court, the same principle of good faith gives unilateral declarations their binding force. To support its position the Court emphasised 'the security of the international intercourse' and the importance of 'confidence and trust for the relations among States'.[27]

Nevertheless, autonomous unilateral declarations can impose no obligations onto other states. Declarations which try to bind other states without these states' consent would generally be void and without any legal effect.[28] Principle 9 GPUD clearly provides:

> No obligation may result for other States from the unilateral declaration of a State. However, the other State or States concerned may incur obligations

---

[21] ILC 'Ninth Report on Unilateral Acts of States—Addendum' (6 April 2006) UN Doc A/CN.4/569/Add.1 para 128 (Rodriguez Cedeño).

[22] E Suy, *Actes unilatéraux* 126.

[23] W Fiedler, 'Einseitige Versprechen' 51–55.

[24] cp Sicault (n 19) 643; Zemanek (n 1) 218.

[25] *Frontier Dispute (Burkina Faso/Republic of Mali)* (Judgment) [1986] ICJ Rep 554, paras 39 f; *Nuclear Tests (New Zealand v France)* (Judgment) [1974] ICJ Rep 457, para 51; *Nuclear Tests (Australia v France)* (n 19) para 43; Cassese (n 19) 184; W Fiedler, 'Unilateral Acts' 1018; GG Fitzmaurice, 'Treaty Interpretation and Other Treaty Points' 230; Gigante (n 19) 334, 337–41, 355; Rigaldies (n 19) 424, 427; Rousseau (n 1) 417 f; Sicault, ibid 646 f; W Wengler, *Völkerrecht* 306 f; Zemanek (n 1) 211 f, 218.

[26] ILC 'Report of the International Law Commission on the Work of Its 58th Session' (n 17) 370.

[27] *Nuclear Tests (Australia v France)* (n 19) paras 46, 51; confirmed in *Military and Paramilitary Activities in and against Nicaragua (Nicaragua v United States of America)* (Jurisdiction and Admissibility) [1984] ICJ Rep 392, para 60. See also Rigaldies (n 19) 428 and furthermore Escarameia (ILC 'Summary Record of the 2887th Meeting' (13 July 2006) UN Doc A/CN.4/SR.2887 4 (Escarameia)) who wanted to add the expectations of third states as a basis for the binding force of unilateral declarations. See, however, also the critical position of Rubin (n 1) 8–28.

[28] ILC 'Documents of the 54th Session' (2002) UN Doc A/CN.4/SER.A/2002/Add.1 (Part 1) 99 f, para 60 (Rodriguez Cedeño); Fiedler (n 25) 1021; Rigaldies, ibid 425; Rousseau (n 1) 423. Zemanek wrote that unilateral acts could create rights and/or obligations but in the context it becomes obvious that he refers also to unilateral declarations which require a kind of reaction of the other state and which are therefore not purely unilateral (Zemanek (n 1) 212).

in relation to such a unilateral declaration to the extent that they clearly accepted such a declaration.[29]

According to the ILC's commentary on that article its rationale is similar to Article 34 Vienna Convention on the Law of Treaties (VCLT)[30] and well established in international law.[31]

Maus, discussing the Optional Clause, also emphasised that unilateral declarations can only result in obligations for other states if a treaty or customary law provides so.[32] For him Article 36(2) to (5) of the Statute is such a treaty.[33] This, however, hardly seems accordant with the assumption that Optional Clause declarations are unilateral declarations. As it has been emphasised their main characteristic is that they themselves are a source of law without other state's reactions.[34] And as established above,[35] together with other Optional Clause declarations, each Optional Clause declaration results in obligations *and* *rights* for the submitting state. Therefore, *per definitionem* they do not fit into the scheme of purely unilateral declarations. Maus is right that they nonetheless have their legal effects because of the prior drafted Optional Clause, but in this respect the Optional Clause declarations are similar to all other accessions to other multilateral treaties. When the Optional Clause declarations are called unilateral declarations they must be considered as what have been named 'false unilateral declarations'.

ii. 'False Unilateral Declarations'

As even Rosenne, who did not consider the Optional Clause itself a treaty, said: 'The unilateral character of the act of making the declaration is not in itself decisive, since interlocked unilateral acts undoubtedly can constitute a form of international treaty'.[36]

---

[29] ILC 'Report of the International Law Commission on the Work of Its 58th Session' (n 17) 379. See also Rodríguez Cedeño and Torres Cazorla (n 16) para 23.

[30] Art 34 VCLT provides: 'A treaty does not create either obligations or rights for a third State without its consent'.

[31] ILC 'Report of the International Law Commission on the Work of Its 58th Session' (n 17) 379.

[32] Maus (n 8) 54.

[33] ibid 55. cp also Rubin (n 1) 11 (see also 13); Wittmann (n 2) 163 f.

[34] See also eg K Schmalenbach, 'Article 2' para 16: 'The fundamental characteristic of a unilateral declaration (or act) is its emanation from a single side. No previous participation and/or subsequent acceptance of a third party is required in order to create a legal obligation for the author'.

[35] s II of ch 1 at 22.

[36] Rosenne and Ronen (n 5) 792. See also AN Farmanfarma, *Declarations* 87: '[I]t is difficult to agree that such an acceptance, though unilateral, lacked the character of a treaty'.

This is based on the idea that there are certain unilateral declarations which form part of an engagement between two or more states.[37] These declarations then 'stand on the same footing as the Treaty itself'.[38] Offers and acceptances or accessions to a multilateral treaty, for example, are basically unilateral.[39] They are, however, not really unilateral declarations in the sense of the previous sub-section because they require counteraction or response to become binding.[40] These declarations are generally considered as treaty instruments and for example have to be interpreted as such.[41] According to Gigante, the essential difference in the intention to conclude a treaty and to submit a unilateral declaration was that in the former case the state wanted to secure the reciprocal obligations and rights emerging from that treaty.[42]

Because of this relation to a prior consent Rigaldies identified such unilateral declarations as 'faux actes unilatéraux'.[43] These 'false' unilateral acts can also bind other states because they are based on the consent of the other states.[44] Ratifications,[45] reservations,[46] accessions[47] and terminations are examples of such 'false unilateral declarations'.[48] Therefore, the fact that states draft their reservations unilaterally is not a special aspect of the Optional Clause. It is the same for all multilateral treaties.[49] Article 2(1)(d) VCLT expressly defines every reservation as a 'unilateral statement'.

Gerald Fitzmaurice classified Optional Clause declarations as declarations which are unilateral in form but not in substance. He attached weight to the interaction of the declarations with other declarations and the common ground established by the corresponding declarations.[50] Also

---

[37] cp Sicault (n 19) 637. See also Fomba who said: 'Unilateral acts f[a]ll into two categories: those whose fate was linked to that of treaties—whose legal regime should logically be aligned with that of treaties; and those that were autonomous, whose fate was not linked to that of treaties'. (ILC 'Summary Record of the 2887th Meeting' (n 27) 14 (Fomba)).

[38] *Status of Eastern Carelia* (Advisory Opinion) PCIJ Series B No 5 7, 26.

[39] A Verdross, 'Règles générales' 427 f: '[T]oute acte bilatéral supposant un accord de volontés enter deux ou plusieurs Etats se compose ainsi de deux ou plusieurs déclarations unilatérales'. J Klabbers, *Introduction* 75: 'Normally, when a state accedes to a treaty concluded between others, the accession is a unilateral act' (for cases in which no positive decision by an organ of the organisation is required).

[40] cp Rubin (n 1) 5 and Fitzmaurice (n 25) 229 f.

[41] Fitzmaurice, ibid 229 f.

[42] Gigante (n 19) 340 f.

[43] Rigaldies (n 19) 432.

[44] ibid 432. cp also J Dehaussy, 'Actes unilatéraux' 58; ILC 'Summary Record of the 2913th Meeting' (n 19) 11 (Economides).

[45] F Hoffmeister, 'Article 14' para 9.

[46] ILC 'Summary Records of the Meetings of the 53rd Session' (n 1) 191 f, para 47 (Al-Baharna). On the discussion whether reservations are uni-, bi- or multilateral acts see JM Ruda, 'Reservations' 103–05.

[47] J Dehaussy (n 44) 58, fn 36.

[48] cp ILC 'Ninth Report on Unilateral Acts of States—Addendum' (n 21) para 128 (Rodriguez Cedeño); Rigaldies (n 19) 432.

[49] cp Maus (n 8) 69, para 1.

[50] Fitzmaurice (n 25) 229–31.

Kelsen had already written that Optional Clause declarations together form an agreement.[51] All in all, if the Optional Clause declarations are referred to as unilateral this can only be understood as meaning 'false unilateral' declarations.[52] In line with this the ILC decided, although after some discussion, that the Optional Clause declarations are not covered by the GPUD.[53] According to the ILC, the Optional Clause declarations are 'false unilateral declarations' and therefore, at least in principle, governed by the law of treaties.[54]

iii. Result

The Optional Clause declarations cannot be regarded as purely unilateral declarations. Any rule deduced from such an assumption is unlikely to hold true for the Optional Clause declarations which provide rights and obligations for the submitting state and whose legal effectiveness is therefore necessarily based on the declarations of the other states.[55] At least at the present stage, there is no reason why they cannot be regarded as 'false unilateral declarations' establishing or related to a treaty.[56]

B. Bi- and Multilateral Treaties

According to Article 2(1)(a) VCLT, '"treaty" means an international agreement concluded between States in written form and governed by international law, whether embodied in a single instrument or in two or more related instruments and whatever its particular designation'.

---

[51] Kelsen (n 2) 521.

[52] cp also Rigaldies (n 19) 432; Rodríguez Cedeño and Torres Cazorla (n 16) para 12; Wittmann (n 2) 149 f, 161.

[53] ILC 'Report of the International Law Commission on the Work of Its 58th Session' (n 17) 378, fn 970; Rodríguez Cedeño and Torres Cazorla, ibid paras 12, 14. For the discussion see ILC 'Summary Records of the Meetings of the 53rd Session' (n 1) 194, para 1 (Lukashuk) against ibid 192, paras 49 f (Al-Baharna). The latter criticised the Special Rapporteur's approach as too narrow and wanted to include Optional Clause declarations as a separate category. Brownlie suggested excluding the Optional Clause declarations as they were discrete and only superficially resembled unilateral acts (ibid 193, paras 56 f (Brownlie)). But see also Pellet who wanted to include non-autonomous 'hetero-normative' unilateral declarations into the drafting process of law of unilateral declarations, too (ibid 186, para 1 (Pellet)). Herdocia Sacasa understood the Court's judgment in the *Fisheries jurisdiction* case between Spain and Canada as broadening the notion of unilateral declarations so that it covered also eg countermeasures (ibid 190, para 39 (Herdocia Sacasa)).

[54] cp the references in n 13 and also Rodríguez Cedeño and Torres Cazorla (n 16) paras 12, 23.

[55] cp also the IACtHR's position: 'A unilateral juridical act carried out in the context of purely interstate relations (for example recognition, promise, protest, renunciation) and independently self-consummated, can hardly be compared with a unilateral juridical act carried out within the framework of treaty law, such as acceptance of an optional clause recognizing the binding jurisdiction of an international court' (*Constitutional Court v Peru* (Competence) IACtHR Series C No 55 (1999) para 48).

[56] Compare also Anand (n 1) 145 f; Suy (n 22) 147.

The earlier version of that article had been more detailed as it named all the 'instruments' in brackets. That part contained the words 'treaty, convention, protocol, covenant, charter, statute, act, *declaration*, concordat, exchange of notes, agreed minute, memorandum of agreement, *modus vivendi* or any other appellation'.[57] The part had been based on the judgment of the Permanent Court of International Justice (PCIJ) stated in the *Austro-German Customs Union* case.[58] In this case the Permanent Court said: 'From the standpoint of the obligatory character of international engagements, it is well known that such engagements may be taken in the form of treaties, conventions, declarations, agreements, protocols, or exchange of notes'.[59] This part of the earlier definition was erased because it has been considered unnecessary.[60] Nonetheless, treaties within the meaning of the VCLT may be based on relating unilateral declarations.[61]

Therefore, the Optional Clause could also be considered as falling under the definition of Article 2(1)(a) VCLT. In commenting on the definition of 'treaty' in the VCLT Gautier even referred to the Optional Clause declarations as he discussed the declarations covered by the article.[62] However, the question of whether the Optional Clause really is a treaty requires a further assessment of the clause and all its particularities.

Corresponding to the question to what extent the Optional Clause has bi- and multilateral elements, the question remains whether the Optional Clause, if it is a treaty, is a multilateral treaty to which all states accede by a declaration or whether each pair of declarations results in a bilateral treaty. In the latter case the declarations have to be split into acceptances corresponding to each offer made in the earlier Optional Clause declarations and into offers made towards every state which has not yet made a declaration.[63]

In his early definitions Waldock referred to 'bilateral treaty' as 'a treaty participation in which is limited to two parties and no more'. A 'multilateral treaty' he considered

> a treaty which, by its terms or by the terms of a related instrument, has either been made open to participation by any State without restriction, or has been made open to participation by a considerable number of parties and either purports to

[57] ILC 'Summary Records of the First Part of the 17th Session' (3 May–9 July 1965) UN Doc A/CN.4/SER.A/1965 9 f (first italics added as emphasis).

[58] ibid 33.

[59] *Customs Régime between Germany and Austria* (Advisory Opinion) PCIJ Series A/B No 41 37, 47. See also M Fitzmaurice, 'Treaties' para 5; H Lauterpacht, *Development* 345.

[60] ILC 'Documents of the First Part of the 17th Session Including the Report of the Commission to the General Assembly' (1965) UN Doc A/CN.4/SER.A/1965/Add.l 12.

[61] See also P Gautier, 'Article 2' paras 7–12. See further Huber's presentation of 'abstract treaties' in M Huber, 'Gemeinschaftsrecht' 836–44. For more on Huber's position see sub-s II A i b 2 of ch 2 at 52.

[62] Gautier, ibid para 10.

[63] cp eg Lauterpacht (n 3) 147 f or the position of Judge Badawi in the *Right of Passage* case (below sub-s IV B of ch 2 at 76).

lay down general norms of international law or to deal in a general manner with matters of general concern to other States as well as to the parties to the treaty.[64]

With regard to these definitions the Optional Clause seems to be rather a multilateral treaty as it is open to 'states parties to the present Statute' and deals with the jurisdiction of the Court, a matter of general concern. However, these definitions were dropped later.[65] Furthermore, the clear distinction between bi- and multilateral treaties was blurred by the fact that multilateral treaties too can be 'bilateralised' to a certain degree.[66]

Therefore, also the question of to what extent the Optional Clause has bi- and multilateral elements cannot be answered by purely theoretical considerations at this point.

II. ARTICLE 36 OF THE STATUTE

An answer on the nature of the Optional Clause might come from the following assessment of the Statute and especially its genesis.

A. The Wording of Article 36 of the Statute

Again the starting point will be the wording of Article 36 of the Statute.

i. *Article 36(2) of the Statute*

First it might be helpful to recall the wording of its paragraph two once more:

> The states parties to the present Statute may at any time declare that they recognize as compulsory ipso facto and without special agreement, in relation to any other state accepting the same obligation, the jurisdiction of the Court in all legal disputes ...

a. The Reference to the 'Special Agreement'

One argument to say that the Optional Clause declarations form a kind of treaty could be the words 'without special agreement'. As said above, the term 'special agreement' refers to agreements which have been concluded

---

[64] For both definitions see ILC 'Documents of the 14th Session Including the Report of the Commission to the General Assembly' (1962) UN Doc A/CN.4/SER.A/1962/Add.l 31.

[65] cp Gautier (n 61) para 8.

[66] cp Fitzmaurice (n 59) para 57; Schmalenbach (n 34) para 9. Whether the relations under the Optional Clause as a multilateral treaty can be bilateralised will especially be discussed below at sub-s II C iv c of ch 5 at 195.

ad hoc for a certain dispute.[67] As the 'special agreements' are treaties,[68] it could be argued that similarly the Optional Clause also is a treaty. As Judge Badawi already emphasised the Optional Clause establishes the Court's jurisdiction without a *special* agreement. He seemed to use this to support the idea that what he calls the Optional Clause 'system' has a conventional character.[69] The reference to the 'special agreement' alone is not sufficient for a reliable conclusion, though. It only provides that no further treaty is necessary. This does not necessarily mean that also the Optional Clause itself is a treaty. It only makes another treaty redundant.

b. The Fact that States 'May Declare'

A better argument, however, is the beginning of the paragraph saying that '[t]he states parties to the present Statute may … declare'. This has two consequences.

The fact that the states 'may declare' means that Article 36(2) of the Statute itself provides no obligations at all if the states make no declarations. In other words, all obligations arising from the Optional Clause require the making of Optional Clause declarations.[70] In line with this already Wittmann wrote that, unlike the other provisions of the Statute, Article 36(2) of the Statute and the following paragraphs have no proper normative character themselves and require the Optional Clause declarations for substance.[71]

With regard to this structure it can be said that the Optional Clause and the Statute provide different obligations for two different groups of states.[72] The Statute provides obligations for states having acceded to the Statute and the Optional Clause provides obligations for states having acceded to the Optional Clause. Concerning these two groups Article 36(2) of the Statute provides that only 'parties to the present Statute' can accept the additional obligations.[73] This gives the Optional Clause a kind of secondary character to the Statute.

---

[67] cp sub-s I C iii of ch 1 at 17.

[68] cp A Aust, *Treaty Law* 312; HWA Thirlway, 'Compromis' para 6.

[69] Dissenting opinion of Judge AH Badawi, *ICJ Rep 1957*, 157. See also the interpretation in Holloway (n 2) 674.

[70] Farmanfarma (n 36) 44 f; C Schachor-Landau, 'Aerial Incident Case' 286. cp also *Case concerning the Aerial Incident of July 27th, 1955 (Israel v Bulgaria)* (Preliminary Objections) [1959] ICJ Rep 127, 139; G Enriques, 'Acceptation sans réciprocité' 841.

[71] Wittmann (n 2) 146.

[72] cp Farmanfarma (n 36) 53; Suy (n 22) 147.

[73] Farmanfarma, ibid 23. For the Optional Clause of the Statute of the Permanent Court see MO Hudson, *Permanent Court* 451; Wittmann (n 2) 111 f. As today almost all states are parties of the United Nations and Member States of the Statute this work will not discuss the position of non-member states. For that see eg J Crawford, 'Automatic Reservations' 84 f; Farmanfarma, ibid 31–35, 51–55; Hudson, ibid 450; Rosenne and Ronen (n 5) 711 f and especially UNSC 'Resolution of 15 October 1946' (15.10.1946) UN Doc S/Res/9(1946) para 2.

1. Optional Protocols and Optional Clauses are Treaties

Having regard to this relationship between the Optional Clause and the Statute, there seems to be no difference between the Optional Clause and optional protocols made to other treaties. Also in the case of optional protocols there are two different sets of obligations: those provided for by the major treaty and those provided for in the optional protocol. The first optional protocol to the International Covenant on Civil and Political Rights (CCPR), for example, has been separated from the CCPR to allow states to adopt the CCPR without necessarily adopting the obligations provided for in the optional protocol.[74] As its genesis will show this reasoning is very similar to the Optional Clause.[75]

Therefore, what the United Nations Commission of Human Rights (UNCHR) said concerning the optional protocol to the CCPR might also hold true for the Optional Clause. According to the UNCHR 'the first Optional Protocol is itself a treaty, distinct from the Covenant but closely related to it'.[76] The CCPR and its optional protocol are related because only members of the CCPR can accede to the optional protocol and they are distinct because their drafters had the intention to separate their contents.[77] Concerning this latter point, especially the fact that some optional protocols even contain a proper provision for withdrawals, emphasises that they remain separate from the major treaty even after a state has acceded to both.[78] In addition a withdrawal from an optional protocol has no influence on the membership in the major treaty.[79] This supports the idea to consider a major treaty, like the CCPR, and its optional protocol as two treaties.[80]

---

[74] cp MJ Bossuyt, *Guide* 640, 798.

[75] See sub-s II B i of ch 2 at 55.

[76] UNCHR 'General Comment No 24 (52) on issues relating to reservations made upon ratification or accession to the Covenant to the Optional Protocols thereto, or in relation to declarations under article 41 of the Covenant' (1994) CCPR/C/21/Rev.1/Add.6 para 13. cp also M Lippman, 'Human Rights Revisited' fn 154; E Schwelb, 'Measures of Implementation' 861.

[77] For the latter aspect see also T Giegerich, 'Article 56 VCLT' para 45.

[78] cp eg the possibility to withdraw according to Art 12 of the optional protocol to the CCPR to the missing possibility to withdraw from the CCPR itself (UNCHR 'General Comment No 26 (61) on issues relating to the continuity of obligations to the International Covenant on Civil and Political Rights' (1997) CCPR/C/21/Rev.1/Add.8/Rev.1 para 2; M Nowak, *CCPR Commentary* introduction, paras 32–36. For the opposite approach concerning the optional protocol to the VCCR see K Oellers-Frahm, 'Der Rücktritt der USA' 569, 580 f. For the opposite approach concerning the optional clause declarations under Art 62(1) ACHR see *Ivcher Bronstein v Peru* (Competence) IACtHR Series C No 54 (1999) paras 40, 46, 50. For more on these latter approaches see the introduction to s II of ch 6 at 280.

[79] Dissenting opinion of Judges N Ando, PN Bhagwati, E Klein and D Kretzmer, *CCPR/C/67/D/845/1999 1999*, para 3.

[80] For this result see Aust (n 68) 23 f; dissenting opinion of Judges N Ando, PN Bhagwati, E Klein and D Kretzmer, *CCPR/C/67/D/845/1999 1999*, para 3; C Stahn, 'Vorbehalte' 610.

However, it could be said that this conclusion does not necessarily apply to optional clauses, too. Like annexes and unlike optional protocols, optional clauses are generally considered as an integral part of the treaty they belong to.[81] The question is whether this, assuming it is true, has legal consequences.

During the drafting of the CCPR, an optional clause (Article 41 *bis*) for the right of petition had been suggested and considered.[82] At the end the delegates argued on whether that right shall be provided for in an optional clause in the covenant or in an optional protocol.[83] In their debate there were almost no arguments relating to the legal difference between the two means,[84] and the Iraqi delegate Afnan even expressly acknowledged that there was none.[85] The Nigerian delegate Mohammed who had introduced one of the proposals for the clause said that he had simply favoured an optional clause to an additional protocol because in his opinion the delegates had no time to draft a preamble and a final clause for the latter.[86] In line with this the Uruguayan delegate Gros-Espiell remarked that 'the end result would be the same as with an additional protocol, since ratification of the Covenant would not automatically entail recognition of the human rights committee's competence'.[87]

For the optional protocol to VCCR jurisdiction see also Oellers-Frahm (n 78) 566 f. Especially for protocols providing the jurisdiction of the Court see Aust, ibid 314. For the additional protocol to the African Charter on Human and Peoples' Rights see also Behnsen (A Behnsen, *Vorbehaltsrecht* 82 f).

[81] cp UNGA 'Official Records of the Twenty-First Session, Third Committee, 1438th Meeting' (29.11.1966) UN Doc A/C.3/SR.1438 para 3 (Mohammed), para 50 (Dombo). For the named difference of annexes and optional protocols see Aust (n 61) 23 f, 383 f.

[82] See the discussions in UNGA 'Official Records of the Twenty-First Session, Third Committee, 1438th Meeting' (29.11.1966) UN Doc A/C.3/SR.1438; UNGA 'Official Records of the Twenty-First Session, Third Committee, 1439th Meeting' (30.11.1996) UN Doc A/C.3/SR.1439; UNGA 'Official Records of the Twenty-First Session, Third Committee, 1440th Meeting' (30.11.1966) UN Doc A/C.3/SR.1440. For a reproduction of this discussion and the proposals see Bossuyt (n 74) 796–99.

[83] cp UNGA 'Official Records of the Twenty-First Session, Third Committee, 1440th Meeting' (30.11.1966) UN Doc A/C.3/SR.1440.

[84] The only argument of this kind came from the Madagascan delegate Ramaholimihaso who argued that an additional protocol was unlike an optional clause as accessions to it were subject to ratification and the protocol contained precise obligations (UNGA 'Official Records of the Twenty-First Session, Third Committee, 1438th Meeting' (29.11.1966) UN Doc A/C.3/SR.1438 27). For the first argument see s II of ch 3 at 87. For the second argument see s I of ch 1 at 10.

[85] UNGA 'Official Records of the Twenty-First Session, Third Committee, 1439th Meeting' (30.11.1996) UN Doc A/C.3/SR.1439 para 21 (Afnan). See also the presentation of the discussion in Bossuyt (n 74) 798 f.

[86] UNGA 'Official Records of the Twenty-First Session, Third Committee, 1438th Meeting' (29.11.1966) UN Doc A/C.3/SR.1438 para 3 (Mohammed).

[87] ibid para 41 (Gros Espiell). See also Schwelb (n 76) 846.

The point which made the debate nonetheless so controversial was a question of principle. As the Dutch delegate Schaapveld said, the whole debate focused on the question whether 'the principle of the right of petition [is] to be incorporated in the Covenant'.[88] In particular the delegates Paolini and MacDonald argued for an optional clause to include the principle of individual petition in the covenant.[89] Against this especially the delegates Bultrikova, Groza and Lukyanovich argued that international law still was essentially law between states and that individuals could not act in their own capacity on this level.[90] The Polish delegate Resich emphasised that with an optional clause the states ratifying the covenant 'would contract moral obligations' which were able to prevent some states from ratifying the covenant.[91]

Finally, the delegates chose an optional protocol instead of an optional clause with 41 to 39 votes.[92] From a procedural point of view, the General Assembly adopted the CCPR and its optional protocol separately, but not the optional clause for interstate disputes which has already been mentioned above.[93] Yet, as Schwelb has rightly remarked and as the debate presented in the previous paragraphs shows, the legal effects of

---

[88] UNGA 'Official Records of the Twenty-First Session, Third Committee, 1440th Meeting' (30.11.1966) UN Doc A/C.3/SR.1440 para 45 (Schaapveld). cp also Schwelb (n 76) 862; Lippman (n 76) 263.

[89] UNGA 'Official Records of the Twenty-First Session, Third Committee, 1438th Meeting' (29.11.1966) UN Doc A/C.3/SR.1438 para 51 (Paolini); UNGA 'Official Records of the Twenty-First Session, Third Committee, 1439th Meeting' (30.11.1996) UN Doc A/C.3/SR.1439 para 46 (MacDonald). cp also ibid paras 44 f (Jativa); UNGA 'Official Records of the Twenty-First Session, Third Committee, 1440th Meeting' (30.11.1966) UN Doc A/C.3/SR.1440 para 5 (Caprio) and furthermore Katigbak (ibid para 6 (Katigbak)) who remarked vaguely that the covenant would be 'weaker' if the right to petition was attached in an additional protocol.

[90] UNGA 'Official Records of the Twenty-First Session, Third Committee, 1438th Meeting' (29.11.1966) UN Doc A/C.3/SR.1438 para 37 (Lukyanovich); UNGA 'Official Records of the Twenty-First Session, Third Committee, 1439th Meeting' (30.11.1996) UN Doc A/C.3/SR.1439 paras 34–36 (Bultrikova); UNGA 'Official Records of the Twenty-First Session, Third Committee, 1440th Meeting' (30.11.1966) UN Doc A/C.3/SR.1440 para 7 (Groza). cp also the reproduction of the discussion in Bossuyt (n 74) 797–99 and furthermore Nowak (n 78) Preamble First OP, para 4; Schwelb (n 76) 861 f.

[91] UNGA 'Official Records of the Twenty-First Session, Third Committee, 1438th Meeting' (29.11.1966) UN Doc A/C.3/SR.1438 para 20 (Resich).

[92] UNGA 'Official Records of the Twenty-First Session, Third Committee, 1440th Meeting' (30.11.1966) UN Doc A/C.3/SR.1440 para 52. cp also Nowak (n 78) Preamble First OP, para 4; Schwelb (n 76) 861.

[93] UNGA 'Resolution on the International Covenant on Economic, Social and Cultural Rights, the International Covenant on Civil and Political Rights and the Optional Protocol to the International Covenant on Civil and Political Rights' (16.12.1966) UN Doc A/RES/2200 (XXI); E Schwelb, 'Legislative History' 287. For more on Art 41 CCPR see sub-s II D iii of ch 1 at 35. For more on the authentication of a treaty and its optional clause see sub-s II A of ch 3 at 88.

the optional protocol to the CCPR and those of an optional clause in it would have been the same.[94] Schwelb's following statement can be fully maintained:

> Apart from the implied theoretical recognition of the principle of the right of petition by states supporting a treaty providing for such a right on an optional basis, there is no difference in law between the insertion of an optional clause in the body of a treaty and the establishment of a separate protocol.[95]

All this supports the impression that the choice between an optional clause and an additional protocol is at most the choice whether or not to make a declaration on a certain principle. Besides this choice the distinction between a clause and a protocol is purely formalistic.[96] Additional protocols and optional clauses likewise provide an option for a group of Member States of the major treaty which wants to go a step further. The words 'may declare' in the case of an optional clause are just one way to make clear that the accession to the major treaty does not result in the obligations provided in the clause. In the case of an additional protocol the same result is achieved by the fact that the protocol is placed behind the place for the signature of the major treaty or placed in an additional document. This seems to be the only difference between an optional clause and an additional protocol. So if additional protocols are considered as treaties there seems to be no reason to treat optional clauses otherwise.

2. *The Optional Clause is not Different in this Regard*

The Optional Clause does not seem to be different in this regard.

In 1911, Huber commented on the Optional Clause's predecessor which Switzerland had proposed at the Second Hague Conference. Huber wrote that it was an 'abstract treaty' which allowed states to accede only for matters they choose and emphasised that the abstract treaty when it was drafted contained no obligations for the states itself and required further unilateral steps. For him such a treaty was a remedy in situations where a treaty had a content which could be divided and which states only wanted to adopt to a certain degree or in certain cases. In such a situation an abstract treaty was flexible enough to allow states to shape their accession to the degree they want.[97] Regarding the similarities between

---

[94] Schwelb (n 76) 846, 862. See also Yokota who spoke of an 'optional clause in a protocol' in one of the ILC's meetings (ILC 'Documents of the 10th Session Including the Report of the Commission to the General Assembly' (1958) UN Doc A/CN.4/SER.A/1958/Add.1 190, para 24 (Yokota)).

[95] Schwelb, ibid 862.

[96] cp Oellers-Frahm (n 78) 572: 'unerheblich und reine Formsache'. See further Fuchs (E Fuchs, 'Optional Provision') who did not distinguish between the different 'optional provisions'.

[97] Huber (n 61) 836–44.

the Swiss proposal, which was also incorporated in an article of a major treaty, and the current Optional Clause,[98] it becomes clear that the treaty he described fully corresponds to the current Optional Clause. With the position of Huber both can be considered as treaties.

This approach can be further supported with the comparison of the Optional Clause and a corresponding additional protocol. As for the CCPR's first optional protocol, it can be very well maintained that the Optional Clause's legal content would not have been different if it had been drafted as an optional protocol.

Supposing that the Optional Clause had been drafted as an optional protocol, Article 36(2) of the Statute would have been Article 1 of that protocol. The words '[t]he states parties to the present Statute may' would have been substituted for '[t]he states parties to this protocol declare'. As said above, this is an equal way to show that the following terms require an additional affirmative action by the states to become binding. To clarify that only '[t]he states parties to the present Statute' can join the optional protocol a corresponding Article 2 could have been added. Article 36(3) and Article 36(4) of the Statute would have been Article 3 and Article 4 of the optional protocol. In line with the terminology for treaties, the word 'declaration' could have been substituted for the word 'accession'.[99] In total, the so constructed hypothetical optional protocol could have read as follows:

Article 1. The states parties to this protocol declare that they recognize as compulsory ipso facto and without special agreement, in relation to any other state accepting the same obligation, the jurisdiction of the Court in all legal disputes concerning:

a.   the interpretation of a treaty;
b.   any question of international law;
c.   the existence of any fact which, if established, would constitute a breach of an international obligation;
d.   the nature or extent of the reparation to be made for the breach of an international obligation.

Article 2. The present Protocol shall be open to accession by any state party to the Statute of the International Court of Justice.

Article 3. Accessions may be made unconditionally or on condition of reciprocity on the part of several or certain states, or for a certain time.

---

[98] cp Ministère des Affaires Étrangères 'La Deuxième Conférence Internationale de la Paix—Actes et Documents' (1907) Tome Deux—Première Commission 888 f (Annexe 27). See also Huber, (n 61) 837, fn 1. See furthermore the second edition of the proposal in Ministère des Affaires Étrangères 'La Deuxième Conférence Internationale de la Paix—Actes et Documents' (1907) Tome Deux—Première Commission 889 f (Annexe 28) with the introduction of Carlin (ibid 467 (Carlin)).

[99] For the fact that states making an Optional Clause declaration hereby accede to the Optional Clause see below sub-s II B iv of ch 3 at 93.

> Article 4. Accessions shall be deposited with the Secretary-General of the United Nations, who shall transmit copies thereof to the parties to the Statute and to the Registrar of the Court.

Despite the mentioned purely formal changes this optional protocol is equivalent to the Optional Clause. Regarding the substance of clause and protocol, they are both completely equal. In line with this the General Assembly of the League of Nations referred to the Optional Clause as 'the special protocol provided for in the said Article'.[100]

So if the UNCHR considers the first optional protocol to the CCPR as a treaty, there seems to be absolutely no reason to treat the Optional Clause otherwise.[101] That the Optional Clause has been placed and labelled differently than an optional protocol cannot make a difference. According to Article 2(1)(a) VCLT a treaty is a treaty 'whatever its particular designation'.[102]

ii. Article 36(3) of the Statute

Article 36(3) of the Statute provides: 'The declarations referred to above may be made unconditionally or on condition of reciprocity on the part of several or certain states, or for a certain time'.

With regard to these words it could be emphasised that Article 36(3) of the Statute uses the term 'condition' and not the term 'reservation' which would have been common in the case of multilateral treaties.[103] This could be used to argue that the drafters of the Statute therefore did not conceive the Optional Clause as a multilateral treaty.

However, going to the genesis of this paragraph, it can be said that the drafters of the Statute have not been precise here. It does not seem as if they used the term 'condition' with a certain purpose. At least the drafters of the current Statute very clearly preferred the term 'reservations'.[104] As the subcommittee considered paragraph 3 it expressly referred to '[t]he

---

[100] League of Nations 'Protocol for the Pacific Settlement of International Disputes' (1924) International Conciliation, Volume 205 532 (Art 3). See also ibid 549 (Politis): 'States only have to declare their intention through the special Protocol annexed to the Statute'. cp furthermore Suy (n 22) 147.

[101] cp also ILC 'Summary Records of the 40th Session' (24 April–29 June 1962) UN Doc A/CN.4/Ser.A/1962 56, para 71 (Liang).

[102] For that see also Aust (n 61) 20–27; Gautier (n 61) paras 11–13. For a corresponding statement prior to the VCLT see Myers (Myers (n 3) 574–77) whose table concerning the names of treaties also included an entry named 'optional clause' which referred to one treaty for the years 1920–1945.

[103] For the latter part cp V Lamm, 'Reservations to Declarations' 120; Maus (n 8) 94 f.

[104] See eg United Nations, *Conference on International Organization, Volume XIII—Commission IV, Judicial Organization* 390–92, 559; United Nations, *Conference on International Organization, Volume XIV—United Nations Committee of Jurists* 208, 235, 302, 416.

question of reservations' and 'the right of states to make ... reservations'.[105] In this regard they used the terminology for multilateral treaties.[106]

Furthermore, the paragraph itself points to the character of the Optional Clause as a separate multilateral treaty. As said in the previous sub-section, the optional protocol to the CCPR provides its own provision for withdrawals. For the Optional Clause Article 36(3) of the Statute likewise provided, at least initially,[107] a proper rule for reservations which was separate from the rules for reservations to the Statute. No reservations have been allowed to the latter. As Crawford said this 'reinforces the distinction between the obligations imposed by a declaration and the "obligations contained in" the Statute as incorporated in the Charter'.[108] This underlines the impression that just as an optional protocol the Optional Clause is a treaty separated from the Statute.

B. The Genesis of the Optional Clause

The genesis of Article 36(2) of the Statute might further strengthen the impression that the Optional Clause can be regarded as a separate treaty.

i. The Drafting of the Statute of the Permanent Court: The Necessity for an Additional Treaty

The Statute of the Permanent Court was a treaty with a protocol of signature. The states accepted the Statute by signing the protocol which was also subject to ratification.[109] Besides the protocol of signature there was an additional protocol termed 'Optional Clause'. It read as follows:

> The undersigned, being duly authorised thereto, further declare on behalf of their Government, that, from this date, they accept as compulsory 'ipso facto' and without special Convention, the jurisdiction of the Court in conformity with Article 36, paragraph 2, of the Statute of the Court, under the following conditions:[110]

---

[105] United Nations, *Conference on International Organization, Volume XIII—Commission IV, Judicial Organization* 559.

[106] See also the terminology used by the two General Assemblies (League of Nations 'Protocol for the Pacific Settlement of International Disputes' (1924) International Conciliation, Volume 205 532, Art 3; League of Nations 'Actes de la neuvième session ordinaire de l'Assemblée, Séances plénières' (1928) League of Nations Official Journal Supplément Spécial No 64 183; UNGA 'Official Records of the Second Session of the General Assembly, Resolutions' (8.1.1948) UN Doc A/519 104; UNGA 'Review of the role of the International Court of Justice' (12.11.1974) UN Doc A/Res/3232 (XXIX); UNGA 'Peaceful settlement of international disputes' (12.12.1974) UN Doc A/Res/3283 (XXIX).

[107] For the interpretation of Art 36(3) of the Statute see sub-s III A of ch 5 at 200.

[108] Crawford (n 73) 79 f, fn 8.

[109] cp League of Nations, *Records of the First Assembly, Plenary Meetings* 468.

[110] ibid 468.

This is astonishing in so far as generally an optional clause is understood as being an article in the major treaty.[111] Following this idea, one could assume that the additional protocol was only a subsidiary instrument to Article 36(2) of the Statute, the Optional Clause itself, which was then as it basically is today. Hudson for example said that the additional protocol 'was a subsidiary, not an independent instrument. It was designed to serve only as a text for the declarations referred to in paragraph 2 of Article 36 of the Statute [of the Permanent Court]'.[112] Similarly, Enriques wrote that there has been a 'protocole spécial pour l'acceptation de la clause facultative'.[113] For Rosenne on the other hand, the additional protocol itself was the Optional Clause and, as the additional protocol had been dropped in 1945 and there was only Article 36(2) of the Statute remaining, he even suggested not using the term Optional Clause anymore.[114] The Institut de Droit International asked the states to sign 'le Protocole visé en l'article 36 du Statut'.[115] Thus far it can be said that there was Article 36(2) of the Statute and a protocol termed 'clause'. Leaving aside the question of which instrument was decisive there remains the fact that there had been both, a clause and a protocol. This duplication puzzled and led to confusion.[116] It demands another excursion into the genesis of the Optional Clause.

From 16 June to 24 July 1920 an Advisory Committee of Jurists charged by the Council of the League of Nations elaborated a draft for the Statute of the Permanent Court. The committee's final draft contained an article providing compulsory jurisdiction between the state parties of the Statute.[117] The Council of the League of Nations considered the provisions of that

---

[111] See Bernhardt (n 12) 369; JA Frowein, 'Optional Clauses' 397 and sub-s II A i b 1 at 50. But see Judge Jennings who said with regard to the extra protocol that 'there was an *actual* "Optional Clause", which parties could sign' (dissenting opinion of Judge RY Jennings, *ICJ Rep 1984*, 535) and seems thereby to suggest that he considered such a protocol to be a typical optional clause.

[112] Hudson (n 73) 453 f. cp also Anand (n 1) 141 f; V Lamm, 'Declarations' 31.

[113] Enriques (n 70) 859 f, fn 23.

[114] S Rosenne, *Essay* 303, fn 4: 'The optional clause was part B of the Protocol of Signature of the [old] Statute'. cp also RC Lawson, 'Compulsory Jurisdiction' 230; Wittmann (n 2) 598.

[115] Institut de Droit International, 'Signature de la clause facultative de la Cour permanente de Justice internationale' (1921).

[116] cp eg the letter from Registrar of the Court López-Oliván to Judge Hudson reproduced in *Military and Paramilitary Activities in and against Nicaragua (Nicaragua v United States of America)* (Jurisdiction and Admissibility) Counter-Memorial (United States of America) Annex 35). See also the different perspective of the organs of the League of Nations: In 1922, the council referred to the '"optional clause" provided for by the additional protocol of December 16th, 1920' (PCIJ, Series E No 1, 143). In 1924, the General Assembly of the League of Nations referred to 'the special protocol provided for in the said Article' (League of Nations 'Protocol for the Pacific Settlement of International Disputes' (1924) International Conciliation, Volume 205 532 (Art 3)).

[117] League of Nations, *Records of the First Assembly, Meetings of the Committees* 447–49. cp also League of Nations, *Records of the First Assembly, Plenary Meetings* 443–45, 456; L Lloyd, 'Britain's Role' 31; M Vogiatzi, 'Historical Evolution' 59; MM Whiteman, *Digest* 1278; Wittmann (n 2) 597; H Wundram, *Fakultativklausel* 5–7.

draft which established a court with compulsory jurisdiction as an 'equivalent to a Convention giving to the Court of Justice a compulsory jurisdiction in matters mentioned in Article 34 of the draft scheme'.[118] However, it opposed the introduction of compulsory jurisdiction. According to the council, compulsory jurisdiction in the Statute of the Permanent Court was contrary to Article 12 and Article 13 of the Covenant. Those articles left the choice of means for peaceful settlement to the states and summoned the world court only for cases submitted by parties. According to the council, compulsory jurisdiction in the Statute of the Court therefore required an amendment of the Covenant. For the council such an amendment was not recommendable as it would also open the discussion for other provisions of the Covenant. Furthermore, the council indicated the danger that some states might not have approved such an amendment. Therefore, the council unanimously suggested dropping the compulsory jurisdiction in the Statute of the Permanent Court.[119]

In the Committee of the General Assembly of the League which then had to draft the Statute, the Panamanian delegate Arias said that the position of the council imperilled the Permanent Court as it was against the public opinion which demanded compulsory jurisdiction.[120] However, the council's amendment was in line with what especially the great powers favoured. They preferred the means which were provided for in Article 36(1) of the Statute of the Permanent Court. They wanted the competence of the Court to be based on further agreements between the states and to let the PCIJ evolve through practice and the gaining of confidence through time.[121] According to the British delegate Hurst to introduce states to conclude mutual treaties was '[t]he true solution'.[122] Against this the Belgian delegate Lafontaine stressed how few treaties for compulsory jurisdiction the states had made since 1907. He emphasised that several hundred bilateral treaties would be necessary to establish compulsory jurisdiction between the states with bilateral means. For him the lack of such treaties was exactly why there was a demand for a general treaty.[123]

In line with this idea, the Brazilian delegate Fernandes proposed using two different versions of the Statute so that the states could choose whether they wanted compulsory jurisdiction by adopting the corresponding text.

---

[118] League of Nations, 'Documents Concerning the Action Taken by the Council of the League of Nations under Article 14 of the Covenant and the Adoption by the Assembly of the Statute of the Permanent Court' (1921) 46.

[119] ibid 46 f. cp League of Nations, *Records of the First Assembly, Plenary Meetings* 442, 445; Kolb (n 5) 450; Vogiatzi (n 117) 60–62; Wundram (n 117) 7 f.

[120] League of Nations, *Records of the First Assembly, Meetings of the Committees* 281 (Arias).

[121] cp League of Nations, *Records of the First Assembly, Plenary Meetings* 442, 445, 487–89; Waldock (n 5) 244.

[122] League of Nations, *Records of the First Assembly, Meetings of the Committees* 294 (Hurst).

[123] ibid 294 (Lafontaine).

He explained the necessity of creating an additional 'stipulation' providing compulsory jurisdiction. For him the provisions of the Covenant could bar such a stipulation being established together with the Statute. Therefore such an addition for compulsory jurisdiction needed to be based on an additional ratification.[124] According to Waldock the version with the compulsory jurisdiction would have created an ordinary treaty obligation between the states.[125] Similarly to Fernandes, the Italian delegate Busatti made the proposal 'to insert the provisions concerning compulsory jurisdiction in a special agreement'.[126] The Swiss delegate Huber declared that he might submit to the General Assembly a 'convention for compulsory arbitration between such members of the League as would be willing to sign it'.[127] This is also similar to a proposal made by the British and the Italian Governments and by a Swedish and Norwegian Committee prior to discussion in the General Assembly's Committee. They suggested a 'separate Convention binding between the contracting parties' establishing compulsory jurisdiction.[128]

Concerning Fernandes' proposal the Norwegian delegate Hagerup suggested 'a provision which the States might accept at the moment of the ratification of the Court statute' instead of drafting two different statutes.[129] This was the additional paragraph to Article 36 of the draft Statute.[130] Fernandes agreed as reciprocity had been sufficiently secured.[131] For the Swiss delegate Huber 'the effect of the additional paragraph to Article 36' was 'to make possible a universal agreement on compulsory jurisdiction'.[132]

Later the Dutch delegate Loder referred to that new 'scheme' as allowing states to accept compulsory jurisdiction by mutual agreement when ratifying.[133] The Swiss delegate Motta referred to an announcement 'by means of a protocol'.[134] Hagerup said that states would be able to extend

---

[124] ibid 302 (Fernandes). cp also Lloyd (n 117) 41.

[125] Waldock (n 5) 251.

[126] League of Nations, *Records of the First Assembly, Meetings of the Committees* 380 (Busatti). He, however, withdrew his proposal due to the decision of the Council of the League of Nations. Note furthermore that Busatti departed from the normal meaning of the term 'special agreement'. For that cp sub-s I C iii of ch 1 at 17.

[127] League of Nations, *Records of the First Assembly, Meetings of the Committees* 381 (Huber).

[128] ibid 496. 498 f. The proposed text was: 'Every State signing the present Act is considered as agreeing to submit to the Permanent Court of International Justice, in conformity with the provision regarding the establishment of the Court, any dispute mentioned in Article 34 of the above provisions and arising between the State and another signatory State'.

[129] ibid 312 (Hagerup).

[130] See also the draft submitted by the sub-committee (ibid 166 (Annex 14)).

[131] ibid 313 (Fernandes).

[132] ibid 313 (Huber).

[133] League of Nations, *Records of the First Assembly, Plenary Meetings* 445 (Loder).

[134] ibid 490 (Motta).

the scope of compulsory jurisdiction 'by means of a simple declaration',[135] but as said above,[136] the accession to a multilateral treaty, too, is a simple declaration. The French delegate Bourgeois referred to an 'opportunity, given to those who are prepared to conclude, as it were, a private Covenant, entailing compulsory recourse to the Court of Justice, to sign an agreement, recognising at the same time that they have the right to make what conditions they please, and to decide with what states they are prepared to bind themselves reciprocally'.[137]

Considering the genesis of the Optional Clause it is clear that also its drafters understood the additional provision as a treaty. The whole development of the Optional Clause was based on the idea that the Covenant did not allow a provision for compulsory jurisdiction in the Statute and required an additional treaty for that. The proposals of the drafters concerned the form and the content of that treaty. The Optional Clause was one of these proposals. According to Waldock what the drafters finally preferred was 'a single text of the jurisdiction Article, voluntary in form, and in a special clause to provide what was really an additional Protocol of Compulsory Jurisdiction to which States could separately adhere by an independent and unilateral act'.[138] The fact that at the end the Statute of the Permanent Court contained an optional clause and an optional protocol further underlines this. All this together strongly strengthens the impression that the Optional Clause is nothing other than an additional treaty to the Statute.

What also became obvious is that during most of their time the drafters of what became the Optional Clause were focused on other issues. Until the end their main concerns were whether compulsory jurisdiction should be introduced at all and whether this was contrary to the Covenant. The drafting of the actual Optional Clause happened in a rather short period and was almost devoid of profound legal considerations. This might be the reason for what Hudson rightly remarked. He said that the form of the Optional Clause in the Statute of the Permanent Court was 'far from satisfactory, and … has resulted in much confusion in references to the Clause'.[139]

ii. The Drafting of the Statute of the Court: No Major Changes

The question is whether the drafters of the current Statute changed something in this regard as they created the current Court along with the United Nations in San Francisco in 1945.

---

[135] ibid 492 (Hagerup).
[136] Sub-s I A ii of ch 2 at 43 and sub-s I B of ch 2 at 45.
[137] League of Nations, *Records of the First Assembly, Plenary Meetings* 445 (Loder) 495 (Bourgeois).
[138] Waldock (n 5) 251.
[139] Hudson (n 73) 451.

What can be said in any case is that the discussion concerning compulsory jurisdiction was dominated by the same opposing ideas like the creation of the PCIJ about 25 years earlier. China, as the only major power, and several smaller powers supported the idea of a post-war international court with compulsory jurisdiction.[140] Again the smaller states regarded compulsory jurisdiction as a compensation for the dominance of the major powers in the political organ, the Security Council.[141] The Soviet Union and the United States stood once more against them. The latter provided a proposal for the Committee of Jurists which prepared a draft of the Statute for the San Francisco Conference. The United States' proposal was largely based on the Statute of the Permanent Court and contained no compulsory jurisdiction. The committee, however, provided an alternative Article 36 providing compulsory jurisdiction.[142]

Together with the Soviet Union, the United States nonetheless still opposed the compulsory jurisdiction. It made it clear that it would not join the United Nations if the Court had compulsory jurisdiction for disputes between all the Member States. According to the United States it therefore was better to keep the system of voluntary step-by-step accession to let the jurisdiction grow concurrently with the confidence of the states.[143] Even though the majority of the states favoured compulsory jurisdiction, until the end the United States and the Soviet Union spoke out against it.[144] As the membership of the Statute was linked to the membership of the United Nations, insisting on compulsory jurisdiction would have excluded these two major powers from the organisation.[145] Many States were afraid that their efforts in San Francisco might be in vain and therefore accepted to maintain the Optional Clause.[146] At the end, the

---

[140] Vogiatzi (n 117) 78; H Steinberger, 'International Court' 195. For China see United Nations, *Conference on International Organization, Volume XIII—Commission IV, Judicial Organization* 225; United Nations, *Conference on International Organization, Volume XIV—United Nations Committee of Jurists* 147 f (Wang), 300. For especially the Latin American states but also Australia, Belgium and the Netherlands see ibid 418–35.

[141] Vogiatzi (n 117) 84. See eg the clear statement of the Mexican delegate (United Nations, *Conference on International Organization, Volume XIII—Commission IV, Judicial Organization* 227; Whiteman (n 117) 1283).

[142] Vogiatzi, ibid 79. cp United Nations, *Conference on International Organization, Volume XIV—United Nations Committee of Jurists* 338, 668–70, 841–43.

[143] cp United Nations, *Conference on International Organization, Volume XIII—Commission IV, Judicial Organization* 226; United Nations, *Conference on International Organization, Volume XIV—United Nations Committee of Jurists* 151, 163–65. cp also Vogiatzi, ibid 80–81, 85; MO Hudson, 'Twenty-Fourth Year' 32 f.

[144] L Preuss, 'Connally Amendment' 662. cp United Nations, *Conference on International Organization, Volume XIII—Commission IV, Judicial Organization* 56, 224–27, 246–51, 390 f, 557; Whiteman (n 117) 1282 f. See also Fitzmaurice (n 9) para 4; H Lauterpacht and L Oppenheim, *Treatise* 59.

[145] Waldock (n 5) 245.

[146] cp United Nations, *Conference on International Organization, Volume XIII—Commission IV, Judicial Organization* 56, 247 (Canada and New Zealand). See also Steinberger (n 140) 195 f.

first draft, which is mentioned above, was basically also the final draft presented to the San Francisco Conference on 25 June 1945.[147] There, it was unanimously accepted.[148]

There were only minor amendments to the Optional Clause. The coexistence of the Optional Clause and additional protocol ended. The additional protocol no longer exists and there is also no protocol of signature anymore.[149] According to Article 93(1) of the Charter the membership of the Statute is now basically linked to the membership of the United Nations and does not any longer require a separate signature or ratification. A proposal concerning a new additional protocol besides Article 36(2) of the Statute made by the Iranian delegation has not been adopted.[150] Another amendment has been the introduction of Article 36(4) of the Statute and the dropping of the words 'or any of the classes of' in the second paragraph.[151] For the transfer of the accessions to the Optional Clause of the Statute of the Permanent Court the drafters provided Article 36(5) of the Statute. The basic wording of the Optional Clause, its structure and the obligations arising from it, the drafters of 1945, however, left untouched. Therefore, the position of Wittmann does not convince. With regard to the deletion of the additional protocol he wrote that at least from then on the Optional Clause could be no longer considered as an open multilateral treaty.[152] Yet, no substantial meaning can be attached to this deletion. Article 36(2) of the Statute basically provides exactly the same as Article 36(2) of the Statute of the Permanent Court and the additional protocol had provided before.

Furthermore, some of the delegates in 1945 again made remarks which underline that they considered the Optional Clause as being a separate treaty even though they scarcely discussed the Optional Clause itself. The British delegate Gerald Fitzmaurice and the Yugoslavian delegate Gavrilovic both expressly called the Optional Clause a 'document separate from the Statute'.[153] The Yugoslavian delegate Gavrilovic further described how the Optional Clause had been accompanied by reservations and that, if compulsory jurisdiction was placed in the Statute, the Statute

---

[147] cp also Vogiatzi (n 117) 87.

[148] United Nations, *Conference on International Organization, Volume I—General* 629–31.

[149] DJ Ende, 'Reaccepting the Compulsory Jurisdiction' 1149, fn 26. For Anand, there was therefore no 'Optional Clause' under the new Statute anymore (Anand (n 1) 142). For the same reason Rosenne suggested not to use the term 'optional clause' anymore (Rosenne (n 114) 303, fn 4).

[150] United Nations, *Conference on International Organization, Volume XIII—Commission IV, Judicial Organization* 276 f, 284.

[151] For Art 36(4) of the Statute see sub-s III C of ch 3 at 102 and for meaning of the deletion of the words in Art 36(2) of the Statute see sub-s III B iv b 2 of ch 5 at 228.

[152] Wittmann (n 2) 161, 599.

[153] United Nations, *Conference on International Organization, Volume XIV—United Nations Committee of Jurists* 153 (Fitzmaurice), 154 (Gavrilovic).

would have been subject to these.[154] This suggests that he regarded the Optional Clause and the Statute as being equal, as being a treaty. Gerald Fitzmaurice also made a further remark in this direction: as if he spoke about a treaty he said that the United Kingdom 'had signed the Optional Clause with … reservations'.[155]

iii. The Preservation of Prior Optional Clause Declarations and Compromissory Clauses

As the time of the Permanent Court ended and the new Court was established the Optional Clause declarations made to the Statute of the Permanent Court were transferred by Article 36(5) of the Statute, which was already mentioned in the previous sub-section. Article 36(5) has clearly been drafted to preserve these old declarations.[156] The question is whether the provision and the transfer of the declarations can further illuminate the character of the Optional Clause.

Article 36(5) of the Statute reads as follows:

> Declarations made under Article 36 of the Statute of the Permanent Court of International Justice and which are still in force shall be deemed, as between the parties to the present Statute, to be acceptances of the compulsory jurisdiction of the International Court of Justice for the period which they still have to run and in accordance with their terms.

Interestingly Article 37 of the Statute contains a similar provision for treaties which had provided jurisdiction of the Permanent Court. It provides:

> Whenever a treaty or convention in force provides for reference of a matter to a tribunal to have been instituted by the League of Nations, or to the Permanent Court of International Justice, the matter shall, as between the parties to the present Statute, be referred to the International Court of Justice.

Article 37 of the Statute was made to redirect the treaties containing compromissory clauses for the old court and thereby to preserve them as a source of jurisdiction.[157] Article 36(5) and Article 37 of the Statute therefore have the same purpose.[158] As Article 37 of the Statute clearly refers

---

[154] ibid 154 (Gavrilovic).

[155] ibid 153 (Fitzmaurice).

[156] United Nations, *Conference on International Organization, Volume XIII—Commission IV, Judicial Organization* 63. See also *Case concerning the Aerial Incident of July 27th, 1955 (Israel v Bulgaria)* (n 70) 145; *Military and Paramilitary Activities in and against Nicaragua (Nicaragua v United States of America)* (n 27) paras 32–34; G Conac, 'L'incident aérien' 725; Kolb (n 5) 57 f and furthermore Maus (n 8) 64: 'conserver la juridiction acquise par la Cour Permanente de Justice Internationale au profit de la nouvelle Cour'.

[157] United Nations, *Conference on International Organization, Volume XIV—United Nations Committee of Jurists* 170, 186 f, 669 f; Rosenne and Ronen (n 5) 657–69.

[158] IFI Shihata, *Compétence de la Compétence* 154. cp also the joint dissenting opinion of Judges H Lauterpacht, VK Wellington Koo and PC Spender, *ICJ Rep 1959*, 166.

to treaties the question is why the drafters also provided Article 36(5) of the Statute if the Optional Clause can be considered as a treaty, too. The answer in line with the result found so far would be that the drafters of the new Statute provided a new additional treaty by making a new Optional Clause. As some states had already acceded to the old Optional Clause they just acceded to the new Optional Clause as far as they had acceded to the old Optional Clause. Especially for these accessions the drafters provided Article 36(5) of the Statute. In this regard the Optional Clause was unlike the treaties covered by Article 37 of the Statute. Those treaties remained the same. Due to what happened in San Francisco in 1945 no new treaties have been concluded and no old treaties of this kind ceased to exist. The old treaties just had to be redirected.

The Court has already had to decide upon both articles. In the case concerning the *Aerial Incident of 1955* it decided that Bulgaria's Optional Clause declaration was not transferred according to Article 36(5) of the Statute as Bulgaria had not been among the original signatory states of the Charter and the Statute, but joined the United Nations later.[159] For Article 37 of the Statute on the other hand the Court decided in the *Barcelona Traction* case that it does not matter whether the states involved had been founding members of the United Nations or joined later. It distinguished the latter from the former case by referring to the former as being *sui generis*.[160]

To find this *sui generis* it is worth considering why in the first case the Court decided that the Optional Clause declaration of Bulgaria was no longer in force. According to the Court:

> The acceptance set out in that Declaration of the compulsory jurisdiction of the Permanent Court of Justice was [after the dissolution of that court] devoid of object since that Court was no longer in existence. The legal basis for that acceptance in Art 36, paragraph 2, of the Statute ceased to exist with the disappearance of that Statute.[161]

According to the Court,'[i]mmediate preservation of the declaration was necessary in order to save it from the lapsing by which it was threatened by the imminent dissolution of the Permanent Court which was then in contemplation'.[162]

The Court therefore held that the declarations of states which did not take part in the drafting of the Statute and did not immediately accede to the new Statute perished with the dissolution of the PCIJ. Article 36(5) of

[159] *Case concerning the Aerial Incident of July 27th, 1955 (Israel v Bulgaria)* (n 70) 136–45. See also Conac (n 156) 718 f.
[160] *Barcelona Traction, Light and Power Company, Limited (Belgium v Spain) (New Application: 1962)* (Preliminary Objections) [1964] ICJ Rep 6, 28–30. See also Whiteman (n 117) 1272–78.
[161] *Case concerning the Aerial Incident of July 27th, 1955 (Israel v Bulgaria)* (n 70) 143.
[162] ibid 137.

the Statute 'could not maintain them in being' as it would have imposed an obligation upon Bulgaria without its consent. For the Court the states present in San Francisco only wanted and were only able to transfer their own Optional Clause declarations of the new Court.[163]

The argument 'devoid of object' needs to be treated carefully here. As the Judges Lauterpacht, Koo and Spender wrote in their joint dissenting opinion, this also applies to treaties which had established the Permanent Court's jurisdiction. Although they considered Article 37 of the Statute to cover 'a different sphere',[164] they wrote that if the dissolution of the PCIJ had resulted in the lapse of the Optional Clause declarations the same would have to apply to treaties falling under Article 37 of the Statute.[165] But as the genesis of the Statute shows, Article 37 of the Statute also applies to treaties of states which later accede to the Statute. The drafters expressly feared that treaties of states which did not take part in San Francisco would have to be renegotiated and therefore made the provision.[166] As it is also implied in the Court's judgment in the *Barcelona Traction* case, the treaties and clauses providing the Permanent Court's jurisdiction did not lapse.

Therefore, the *sui generis* of the *Aerial Incident of 1955* case must be something else. As already mentioned above the Court also said: 'The legal basis for that acceptance in Article 36, paragraph 2, of the Statute of the Permant Court of International Justice, ceased to exist with the disappearance of that Statute'.[167] This fits well in the scheme presented above. The old Optional Clause was a treaty itself. According to its wording it was open for '[t]he Members of the League of Nations and the States mentioned in the Annex to the Covenant' which had joined the Statute of the Permanent Court. As the League of Nations and the Permanent Court ceased to exist, there were no more states which could be member of the old Optional Clause and no states which were able to join it anymore.[168] Therefore, it made no sense to redirect the old Optional Clause to the

---

[163] ibid 136–45. As Shihata summarised the Court's arguments the old Optional Clause declaration of Bulgaria became 'dead' or 'devoid of object' with the dissolution of the Court and was not open to later resurrection (Shihata (n 158) 156). For a different interpretation of Art 36(5) of the Statute see eg the joint dissenting opinion of Judges H Lauterpacht, VK Wellington Koo and PC Spender, *ICJ Rep 1959*, 174–86; Schachor-Landau (n 70) 280–89.

[164] Joint dissenting opinion of Judges H Lauterpacht, VK Wellington Koo and PC Spender, *ICJ Rep 1959*, 171.

[165] ibid 163.

[166] United Nations, *Conference on International Organization, Volume XIV—United Nations Committee of Jurists* 235.

[167] *Case concerning the Aerial Incident of July 27th, 1955 (Israel v Bulgaria)* (n 70) 143. See also Conac (n 156) 725 f. On how the League of Nations and the Permanent Court ceased to exist see LC Caflish, 'Aerial Incident' 858 f; Whiteman (n 117) 1161–69.

[168] For the interdependence of the membership of the Optional Clause and the membership to the Statute of the Permanent Court see also the dissenting opinion of Judge SM Schwebel, *ICJ Rep 1984*, paras 6 f. For the similar situation under the current Statute see also Wittmann (n 2) 191 f. cp also the dissenting opinion of Judge EC Armand-Ugon, *ICJ Rep 1959*, 91.

Court as it happened for treaties under Article 37 of the Statute. The drafters of the current Statute provided a new Optional Clause with new Member States. With Article 36(5) of the Statute they made a provision which made them Member States of that new Optional Clause as far as they had already been Member States of the old Optional Clause.

iv. Result

This sub-section shows that the drafters of the two Statutes regarded the two Optional Clauses themselves as multilateral treaties. Also the coexistence of Article 36(5) and Article 37 of the Statute along with the corresponding court's rulings can be explained best when the Optional Clause is considered as a separate treaty. This can be underlined by the fact that under the Statute of the Permanent Court there had even been a clause and a protocol. This confirms the result which has also been found in the analysis of the wording of the Statute.

C. The Role of the Optional Clause Besides Other Treaties Establishing Jurisdiction

However, with regard to the Statute there remains one question. As said above,[169] it is at least unlikely that Article 36(2) of the Statute is intended to be redundant to the first paragraph. Article 36(1) of the Statute has been drafted to cover bi- as well as multilateral treaties.[170] Furthermore, as it has been discussed in chapter one, treaties falling under Article 36(1) of the Statute can establish compulsory jurisdiction like the Optional Clause.[171] So the question is whether there is the difference between the Optional Clause and the treaties under Article 36(1) of the Statute if the Optional Clause is understood as a treaty.

Today, there are 296 international treaties which contain compromissory clauses and provide jurisdiction under Article 36(1) of the Statute.[172] They cover such a wide area of international law that in the preparation of the German Optional Clause declaration it has been discussed whether there is actually a need to make an Optional Clause declaration besides all the treaties.[173] However, in general the compromissory clauses in the treaties

---

[169] See sub-s I C i of ch 1 at 14.
[170] cp United Nations, *Conference on International Organization, Volume XIV—United Nations Committee of Jurists* 415.
[171] See sub-s I C of ch 1 at 14 and there especially n 46.
[172] http://www.icj-cij.org/jurisdiction/index.php?p1=5&p2=1&p3=4 (last visit on 19 January 2015).
[173] cp C Eick, 'Anerkennung' 765.

are always limited to the contracting states and the content of the treaty.[174] Such treaties therefore only provide jurisdiction which is limited *ratione personae* and *ratione materiae*. All they do is to provide spots of jurisdiction. Even though these spots have become many and cover various different areas, there are still gaps between them. For example, disputes on whether behaviour violates the principle of the non-use of force are generally not covered by treaties.[175] The international public law's core question of war and peace is therefore generally not open to a judicial settlement and remains in the political sphere.[176] Furthermore, there are new areas like international environmental law, where new international law emerges and which are not covered by compromissory clauses.[177] Insofar, there is still need for the compulsory jurisdiction provided by Optional Clause declarations.[178] This corresponds to the statement the drafting committee made as it presented its draft to the General Assembly of the League of Nations. There it named the Optional Clause as a possibility for states 'to accept compulsory jurisdiction in a larger measure than provided for in the first paragraph of the article.[179]

This is, however, not necessarily true as all states could theoretically also draft a treaty among them which covers all disputes between them.[180] Oda considered such treaties as 'functional equivalents' to the Optional Clause.[181] So the maximum scope of the compulsory jurisdiction does not distinguish Article 36(1) and Article 36(2) of the Statute.[182]

Vicuña wrote that Article 36(2) of the Statute was created to overcome difficulties which had emerged in relation to bilateral treaties and that therefore the result of the unilateral Optional Clause declarations cannot be considered a treaty.[183] Rotter emphasised that it is the unilateral character of the Optional Clause declarations which distinguishes Article 36(1) of the Statute from Article 36(2) of the Statute. Therefore, according to him,

---

[174] Tomuschat (n 11) para 56; Rosenne and Ronen (n 5) 559, fn 128, pp 648 f; Kolb (n 5) 451. According to Rosenne only the treaty law itself could be applied while Tomuschat also wanted to consider the other sources of law relating to the matters covered by the treaty.

[175] Tomuschat, ibid para 55.

[176] Of course also Optional Clause declarations, like eg the current German one which excludes 'any dispute which ... relates to, arises from or is connected with the deployment of armed forces abroad, involvement in such deployments or decisions thereon', do not change this situation. Whether such a change is desirable or might hamper the recent developments in that field of law cannot be discussed here. For the debate in Germany see eg Eick (n 173) 771 f; M Bothe and E Klein, 'Anerkennung der Gerichtsbarkeit' 836–38; CJ Tams and A Zimmermann, 'German Optional Clause Declaration' 410 f.

[177] A Zimmermann, 'Die obligatorische Gerichtsbarkeit' 250.

[178] Bothe and Klein (n 176) 839.

[179] League of Nations, *Records of the First Assembly, Plenary Meetings* 467.

[180] For the treaties which have already been drafted see sub-s III B of ch 2 at 71.

[181] S Oda, 'From the Bench' para 23.

[182] This holds especially true as there is no practical difference between the notions 'cases' and 'matters' in Art 36(1) of the Statute and the notion 'legal disputes' in paragraph two anymore (Tomuschat (n 11) para 13).

[183] FO Vicuña, 'Legal Nature' 466.

the Optional Clause is devoid of any consensual element.[184] These two positions are both right to a certain degree. In general, it is right to say that Article 36(2) of the Statute provides a possibility for the states to accept the jurisdiction of the Court in advance for an undefined number of future legal disputes by depositing a unilateral declaration.[185] In this regard the Optional Clause can be considered as being a procedural facilitation compared to the later drafting of a corresponding multilateral treaty.[186] As already Rosenne wrote Article 36(1) of the Statute and Article 36(2) of the Statute are distinct as under the latter there is no 'phase of negotiation'.[187] As said above,[188] this does, however, not necessarily mean that there is no consensual element in the 'Optional Clause system' as Rotter wrote. All of what has been said also holds true if the Optional Clause is considered as a treaty. It is merely an already drafted treaty to which states may easily accede. From this perspective it became what the Council of the League of Nations suggested in 1920: '[I]t is difficult to see why this agreement [making the Court competent] should not be established by a general Convention after discussion by the League of Nations, instead of by a special Convention arrived at by two or more Parties'.[189] With regard to Article 36(1) of the Statute it can therefore be well maintained what Crawford wrote. For him Article 36(2) of the Statute is no method of seising the Court distinct from treaty. The Optional Clause is, to a certain degree, a sub-class of Article 36(1) of the Statute.[190]

---

[184] M Rotter (n 1) 646 f.

[185] Vogiatzi (n 117) 41. cp also Huber (n 61) 838–44.

[186] cp also Farmanfarma (n 36) 25; Hudson (n 73) 450. Relating to the corresponding Swiss Proposal of 1907 see Ministère des Affaires Étrangères 'La Deuxième Conférence Internationale de la Paix—Actes et Documents' (1907) Tome Deux—Première Commission 463 f, 467 (Carlin).

[187] Rosenne and Ronen (n 5) 710, fn 23.

[188] See sub-s I A ii of ch 2 at 43.

[189] League of Nations, 'Documents Concerning the Action Taken by the Council of the League of Nations under Article 14 of the Covenant and the Adoption by the Assembly of the Statute of the Permanent Court' (1921) 46. With this statement the Council referred to an earlier draft for the Statute of the Permanent Court providing compulsory jurisdiction. However, the rationale is the same.

[190] Crawford (n 73) 83. See also sub-s I C iii of ch 1 at 17 where it was shown that both, the treaties under Art 36(1) of the Statute and the Optional Clause, provide compulsory jurisdiction. Optional Clause declarations which are expressly made *erga omnes* and not only in relation to any other state accepting the same obligation establish jurisdiction as unilateral declarations under Art 36(1) of the Statute as far as there is no corresponding Optional Clause declaration (cp Wundram (n 117) 48 even though he reduces the effect of such unilateral declarations to states having made an Optional Clause declarations). For a similar result in general treaty law see Ruda (n 46) 107. For another solution under the Optional Clause see Enriques who spoke of an 'accord' with the states not having an Optional Clause declaration (Enriques (n 70) 847, 850–55 followed by Farmanfarma (n 36) 54). See also the solution of HWA Thirlway, 'Reciprocity' 108. However, there have not been any Optional Clause declarations *erga omnes* yet. The declarations, like the one of Nicaragua, which were made 'unconditionally' have to be regarded in light of Art 36(3) of the Statute. These declarations only emphasise that none of the reservations as provided for in that paragraph are made (Shihata (n 158) 149 f; Waldock (n 5) 255).

Besides being a treaty ready for accession, the Optional Clause might have yet another function. Oda referred to it as an 'option which would exist even in the absence of the provision' but also remarks that the Optional Clause provides a certain exhortation or stimulus.[191] According to Hudson, Article 36(2) of the Statute was also made to encourage the states to submit themselves to compulsory jurisdiction.[192] As mentioned above,[193] in the case of the CCPR an optional protocol was preferred to an optional clause to avoid making a declaration in principle by all the signatory states of the treaty.

In line with this, it seems as if the Optional Clause contains this declaration in principle. The Optional Clause functioned like an assurance to the majority of the states which had wanted compulsory jurisdiction but were disappointed.[194] These states were told that with the Statute compulsory jurisdiction was just a question of time. The drafters of 1945 presented Article 36 of the Statute as 'the way open for substantial advance towards the goal of universal jurisdiction'.[195] They said:

> The judicial process will have a central place in the plans of the United Nations for the settlement of international disputes by peaceful means. An adequate tribunal will exist for the exercise of the judicial function, and it will rank as a principal organ of the Organization. It is confidently anticipated that the jurisdiction of this tribunal will be extended as time goes on.[196]

The drafters even provided a special statement which they attached to the Statute and which recommended to all states to make the Optional Clause declarations as soon as possible. This statement was unanimously adopted along with the Statute.[197]

In total it can be said that, even though Article 36(1) of the Statute already covers all treaties providing jurisdiction, Article 36(2) of the Statute can be considered a treaty without being redundant. As a ready drafted multilateral treaty allowing states simply to accede, it is a procedural facilitation in relation to a corresponding multilateral treaty which the states would otherwise have to draft themselves. Furthermore, the Optional Clause contains a certain statement proclaiming universal compulsory jurisdiction as a common aim.[198]

---

[191]   Oda (n 181) para 27. cp also Wittmann (n 2) 163.
[192]   Hudson (n 73) 450.
[193]   See sub-s II A i b 1 of ch 2 at 51.
[194]   For that part of the genesis see sub-s II B i of ch 2 at 55.
[195]   United Nations, *Conference on International Organization, Volume XIII—Commission IV, Judicial Organization* 391.
[196]   ibid 393.
[197]   United Nations, *Conference on International Organization, Volume I—General* 627; United Nations, *Conference on International Organization, Volume XIII—Commission IV, Judicial Organization* 60–64.
[198]   cp C Walter, 'Rechtsschutz' para 40: 'Zielbestimmung'.

III. THE NATURE OF THE OPTIONAL CLAUSE AS SEEN BY STATES

The question is to what extent the states, too, understood the Optional Clause as being a treaty.[199]

A. Ambiguous General Remarks

General expressions on the nature of the Optional Clause independent of a certain case are, however, few. Some states only expressed rather casually that they 'adhered' to the Optional Clause.[200] Even though its relation to the term 'accession' was not yet clear in those days the word 'adherence' has been used for multilateral treaties.[201]

On the other hand as the ILC made an inquiry for the GPUD, the Netherlands answered:

> Unilateral statements concerning the acceptance of the jurisdiction of the Court on the basis of the optional clause are in a category of their own, although, as noted above, these statements would be excluded from the definition of unilateral acts on the basis of the Special Rapporteur's and the ILC Working Group's criteria.[202]

This 'category of their own' speaks against the assumption that the Optional Clause is a treaty.

Before the Court, states made a big variety of statements. In the *Anglo-Iranian Oil Co* case Iran presented it as unacceptable to understand the Optional Clause declarations in question as having a 'caractère contractuel' or as establishing a treaty,[203] while the United Kingdom contrarily emphasised the 'consensual nature' of the declarations.[204] In 1974, in a correspondence with Honduras, El Salvador referred to the prior jurisprudence of the Court and held that Optional Clause declarations were unilateral declarations with a consensual bond which is only established through the reciprocal application of the reservations. El Salvador further emphasised that there had been no negotiations accompanying

---

[199] For the use of state practice as source of customary international law or means of interpretation see below sub-s III D of ch 3 at 108.

[200] Hudson (n 73) 453. cp eg PCIJ, Series E No 1, 362 (France); PCIJ, Series E No 16, 363 (Canada).

[201] cp Marchi (n 14) paras 6–8. See also United Nations, *Conference on International Organization, Volume XIII—Commission IV, Judicial Organization* 153 (Fitzmaurice): 'adhere to the Statute'.

[202] ILC 'Documents of the 52nd Session' (n 19) 276.

[203] *Anglo-Iranian Oil Co case (United Kingdom v Iran)* (Preliminary Objections) Observations (Iran) para 17.

[204] *Anglo-Iranian Oil Co case (United Kingdom v Iran)* (Preliminary Objections) Observations and Submissions (United Kingdom) para 19.

the making of Optional Clause declarations.[205] In the *Nicaragua* case the United States similarly argued that the Optional Clause declarations were declarations *sui generis* which were not determined by the law of treaties.[206] It emphasised the unilateral character of the declarations before the seisin of the Court.[207] Furthermore, it maintained that the declarations formed no treaty as they would otherwise be redundant with Article 36(1) of the Statute.[208] Nicaragua on the other hand considered the result of the Optional Clause declarations as being a consensual bond between the states.[209] This latter position was close to the position of India in the earlier *Right of Passage* case. There, India had even argued that the Optional Clause system was at its core a multilateral treaty. According to India, state practice had changed the Optional Clause system and made it necessary to apply treaty law.[210] Another example comes from the more recent *Aerial Incident of 1999* case where Pakistan called the result of the Optional Clause declarations a 'treaty relationship'.[211] In the *Whaling in the Antarctic* case it was Australia calling the Optional Clause again *sui generis*. According to Australia, Optional Clause declarations 'are unilateral declarations while simultaneously giving rise to consensual relations between States. They are not treaties'.[212]

These examples show how different the perception of the Optional Clause among the states is. While the United Kingdom, Nicaragua, India and Pakistan emphasised the consensual treaty character of the obligation under the Optional Clause, Australia, Iran, the United States and El Salvador argued against it.

---

[205] El Salvador, 'Declaration' 537 f. See also S Rosenne, *Documents* 365 f. For more on El Salvador's correspondence with Honduras see sub-s II C i b of ch 6 at 295.

[206] *Military and Paramilitary Activities in and against Nicaragua (Nicaragua v United States of America)* (n 116) paras 338–51. See also *Fisheries Jurisdiction (Spain v Canada)* (Jurisdiction) Counter-Memorial (Canada) 67 f, 72–75.

[207] *Military and Paramilitary Activities in and against Nicaragua (Nicaragua v United States of America)* (n 116) paras 342 f, 351, 383. For more on the importance of the moment of seisin see s I of ch 1 at 10.

[208] *Military and Paramilitary Activities in and against Nicaragua (Nicaragua v United States of America)* (n 116) para 340. For that argument see the previous section (sub-s II C of ch 2 at 65).

[209] *Military and Paramilitary Activities in and against Nicaragua (Nicaragua v United States of America)* (Jurisdiction and Admissibility) Memorial (Nicaragua) paras 106–14.

[210] *Case concerning the Right of Passage over Indian Territory (Portugal v India)* (Preliminary Objections) Oral Proceedings (CR 1957) (India) 48 (Waldock).

[211] *Aerial Incident of 10 August 1999 (Pakistan v India)* (Jurisdiction) Oral Proceedings (CR 2000/1) (Pakistan) 13, para 5 (E Lauterpacht).

[212] *Whaling in the Antarctic (Australia v Japan; New Zealand intervening)* (Judgment) Oral Proceedings (CR 2013/11) (Australia) 43, para 14 (Burmester).

B. The Reasons for Concluding the General Treaties Besides the Optional Clause

Another issue of state practice, which to a certain degree also involves the practice of the organs of the League of Nations and of the United Nations, are the multilateral treaties providing the Court's jurisdiction, especially the two General Acts of 1928 and 1949. The question is why these multilateral treaties have been drafted when there had already been the Optional Clause as a multilateral treaty with the same target. It would argue against the assumption that the states consider the Optional Clause a treaty if they later draft identical and therefore unnecessary treaties.

In 1928, the General Assembly adopted the General Act whose second chapter deals with the judicial settlement of disputes.[213] Comprehensively, Article 17 of the General Act provides:

> All disputes with regard to which the parties are in conflict as to their respective rights shall subject to any reservations which may be made under Article 39, be submitted for the decision to the Permanent Court of International Justice, unless the parties agree, in the manner hereinafter provided, to have resort to an arbitral tribunal. It is understood that the disputes referred to above include in particular those mentioned in Article 36 of the Statute of the Permanent Court of International Justice.

According to Article 19 of the General Act the parties may bring the dispute before the PCIJ by unilateral application with three months' notice if they fail to agree upon an arbitral tribunal. As the General Act also aims at universality (Article 43 (2) of the General Act) it could be said that it duplicates the Optional Clause.

Judge De Castro raised this issue in one of the *Nuclear Tests* cases and answered that in his view Article 36(2) of the Statute and Article 17 of the General Act 'certainly coincide both in objects and means, but they are independent provisions which each have their own individual life'.[214] He pointed at an article of Gallus where the latter analysed whether the General Act is useful and assessed the difference between the two instruments. Gallus wrote that the General Act provides a stricter regime for withdrawals as all states are bound for five years and have to actively withdraw when they do not want to be bound for another five years. Optional Clause declarations of that time did just expire. Furthermore,

---

[213] It is disputed whether the General Act is still valid today (for several cases before the Court see JG Merrills, 'General Act' 137, 141–48, 150–52). In the *Nuclear Tests* cases France argued that the General Act lapsed as it was closely linked to the judicial system of the League of Nations (*Nuclear Tests (Australia v France)* Correspondence (France) 349–54). Compare also sub-s II B iii of ch 2 at 62 for other effects of the dissolution of the League and the Permanent Court.

[214] Dissenting opinion of Judge F De Castro, *ICJ Rep 1974*, 378.

Article 39 of the General Act contains an exhaustive list of allowed reservations which does not exist for the Optional Clause. Additionally, Gallus pointed at the states' choice between the Permanent Court and an arbitral tribunal which Articles 18 and 19 of the General Act provide and emphasise. At the end he came to the conclusion that the General Act is not redundant besides the Optional Clause.[215]

Furthermore, in Articles 1 to 16 the General Act provides a method of conciliation for 'disputes of any kind'. This procedure of conciliation applies where the General Act establishes no compulsory judicial settlement or where the parties agree so (Articles 20(1) and (2) of the General Act). In Articles 21 to 28 the General Act also provides rules for arbitration. Therefore, the General Act has a broader scope than only establishing compulsory jurisdiction of the PCIJ. It shall arrange all the means of peaceful dispute settlement. Even if, according to Article 38 of the General Act, states only accede to certain chapters of it according to that article they cannot accede to chapter II with the compulsory jurisdiction alone. Therefore, the General Act necessarily has a larger content than the Optional Clause, even if the latter is understood as a multilateral treaty, as the Optional Clause only provides plain compulsory jurisdiction. Furthermore, at least at the time the General Act had been drafted Article 36(2) of the Statute was maybe also considered as a more restricted treaty in comparison to the General Act which, coming under Article 36(1) of the Statute, had not been limited to 'judicial disputes'.[216]

In 1949, the United Nations General Assembly issued a Revised General Act which has eight Member States up to now.[217] As the provisions mentioned above remained as they were, the same conclusion may be drawn.

In addition to those two universal acts there are regional multilateral treaties like the Pact of Bogotá from 1948 and the European Convention from 1957. Article XXXI of the Pact of Bogotá provides:

> In conformity with Article 36, paragraph 2, of the Statute of the International Court of Justice, the High Contracting Parties declare that they recognize, in relation to any other American State, the jurisdiction of the Court as compulsory ipso facto, without the necessity of any special agreement so long as the present Treaty is in force, in all disputes of a juridical nature that arise among them ...

---

[215] Gallus, 'L'acte général' 391 f; supported by the dissenting opinion of Judge F De Castro, *ICJ Rep 1974*, 378. Gallus furthermore wrote that the possible circle of member states is bigger under the General Act and that it is therefore more universal (Gallus, ibid 390). For the possible circle of member states see also Ténékidès (n 5) 731. See also the interesting position on the General Act by Judge Oda who held that the General Act itself did not provide jurisdiction (separate opinion of Judge S Oda, *ICJ Rep 2000*, paras 11–17).

[216] cp Enriques (n 70) 856, fn 20; Ténékidès (n 5) 735.

[217] http://treaties.un.org/pages/ViewDetails.aspx?src=IND&mtdsg_no=II-1&chapter=2&lang =en (last visit on 19 January 2015). The most recent accession was made by Estonia which acceded in 1991.

Article 1 of the said European Convention reads as follows: 'The High Contracting Parties shall submit to the judgement of the International Court of Justice all international legal disputes which may arise between them'.

The first interesting issue here is the mentioning of Article 36(2) of the Statute in the Pact of Bogotá. According to Judge Parra-Aranguren the Member States of the pact made new declarations and thereby each state 'necessarily replaced the first one in their reciprocal relations'.[218] There are, however, also good arguments to consider Article XXXI of the Pact of Bogotá as providing an alternative source of jurisdiction besides the Optional Clause. Despite its wording the said article can very well be considered as establishing jurisdiction under Article 36(1) of the Statute like other treaties.[219] Be that as it may, the Pact of Bogotá, too, provides not only compulsory jurisdiction. It arranges several methods of peaceful dispute settlement and does not focus on compulsory jurisdiction alone. In this regard also the Pact of Bogotá has a meaning besides the Optional Clause if the latter is perceived as a treaty.

The European Convention, however, is different. In Article 34 it allows states to accept only the chapter providing the compulsory jurisdiction of the Court. However, it is not redundant besides the Optional Clause, as according to its Article 41(1)(1) it is a special treaty only for members of the Council of Europe. It aims at enforcing the peaceful settlement of disputes on a regional level. Of course, if states would have only aimed at such enforcement they could have legally also made corresponding Optional Clause declarations referring to disputes with each other. But such a solution would, however, have been complicated, as with every new member states would have had to enlarge their individual declaration and states would furthermore have to exclude all other non-regional states

---

[218] Declaration of Judge G Parra-Aranguren, *ICJ Rep 2007*, 892. See also Judge Oda (separate opinion of Judge S Oda, *ICJ Rep 1988*, 109) for whom Art XXXI of the Pact of Bogotá itself provided no jurisdiction at all. See also the pleading of Honduras in the *Border and Transborder Armed Actions* case (*Border and Transborder Armed Actions (Nicaragua v Honduras)* (Jurisdiction and Admissibility) Memorial (Honduras) 55, 57; *Border and Transborder Armed Actions (Nicaragua v Honduras)* (Jurisdiction and Admissibility) Oral Proceedings (CR 1988) (Honduras) 15–17 (Bowett)). For more on Honduras' and the Judges' position see sub-ss III B ii and iii of ch 6 at 322 f and 325.

[219] Lamm (n 112) 34–37; Rosenne and Ronen (n 5) 529, fn 61. cp also the position of Nicaragua in the *Border and Transborder Armed Actions* case (*Border and Transborder Armed Actions (Nicaragua v Honduras)* (Jurisdiction and Admissibility) Counter-Memorial (Nicaragua) paras 107–09). In that case the Court did not expressly decide whether the jurisdiction provided for by the Pact of Bogotá falls under Art 36(1) or Art 36(2) of the Statute but held that the pact 'is an autonomous commitment, independent of any other which the parties may have undertaken or may undertake by depositing with the United Nations Secretary-General a declaration of acceptance of compulsory jurisdiction under Article 36, paragraphs 2 and 4, of the Statute' (*Border and Transborder Armed Actions (Nicaragua v Honduras)* (Jurisdiction and Admissibility) [1988] ICJ Rep 69, paras 34, 36). For more on this very controversial issue see sub-s III B of ch 6 at 316.

which might be politically difficult. Additionally, like the corresponding provisions of the General Act, Article 40 of the European Convention provides a stricter regime for withdrawals and Article 35 of the European Convention regulates the use of reservations. In relation to this here the result of Gallus presented above also applies.

All these assessments show that, even if the Optional Clause is understood as a comprehensive additional treaty to the Statute providing the Court's jurisdiction, the other multilateral treaties are not redundant. The practice to draft such treaties does therefore not suggest that their drafters have a different perception of the Optional Clause.

IV. THE NATURE OF THE OPTIONAL CLAUSE IN JURISPRUDENCE

The last question on this issue is which position the two Courts have taken.[220]

A. The Jurisprudence of the Permanent Court: No Clear Picture

The general remarks of the Permanent Court can be considered as ambiguous. In the case concerning the *Legal Status of the South-Eastern Territory of Greenland* it wrote that with their declarations Denmark and Norway had '*acceded* to the optional clause of Article 36, paragraph 2, of the Statute of the Court'.[221] With these words the Permanent Court seems to suggest that the Optional Clause is a treaty. In the *Phosphates in Morocco* case, on the other hand, the Permanent Court emphasised the unilateral nature of the declaration and stated that 'the ... declaration is a unilateral act with which the government has accepted the jurisdiction of the Court'.[222]

In the case concerning the *Electricity Company of Sofia and Bulgaria* the Permanent Court then treated the Bulgarian and the Belgian declaration as one single instrument.[223] It referred to the Optional Clause as an 'agreement,' named the Optional Clause declarations 'declarations of

---

[220] As said in s II of the introduction at 6 f, this chapter will only address the Court's general remarks on the Optional Clause. The findings of the Court concerning the particular subjects like the permissibility of reservations or the withdrawal of Optional Clause declarations will be discussed below in the corresponding chapters.

[221] *Legal Status of the South-Eastern Territory of Greenland (Norway v Denmark)* (Interim Measures of Protection) PCIJ Series A/B No 48 276, 270 (emphasis added).

[222] *Phosphates in Morocco (Italy v France)* (Preliminary Objections) PCIJ Series A/B No 74 9, 23 f. See also Wittmann (n 2) 148 f.

[223] Thirlway (n 190) 111. cp *Electricity Company of Sofia and Bulgaria (Belgium v Bulgaria)* (Preliminary Objection) PCIJ Series A/B No 77 63, 81 f.

adherence' and spoke of the 'adherence' to the Optional Clause.[224] As Waldock wrote these phrases argued for the 'contractual nature of the obligation resulting from the declarations'.[225] The dissenting opinion of Judge
Anzilotti in the same case points at a more bilateral basis. For him two
Optional Clause declarations established an 'agreement ... between the
two states'. With the submission of the second declaration a reciprocal relation was established. However, he also wrote that both the declarations
and the Statute formed the basis of the Court's jurisdiction.[226] Similarly to
Judge Anzilotti, Judge Hudson spoke of a relation *inter se*.[227]

The dissenting opinion of Judge Urrutia Olano requires deeper consideration. He referred to the 'declarations of adherence ... to the optional
clause'. Furthermore, he wrote that two declarations under Article 36(2)
of the Statute were an equivalent to 'an international agreement' between
the states 'within the limits fixed by the reservations'. According to Judge
Urrutia Olano, '[t]he Undertaking could be modified either by extending
or restricting the obligations, or by supplementary provisions embodied
in some later agreement'.[228] Crawford understood that view as pointing at a difference between the Optional Clause and normal treaties. For
Crawford Judge Urrutia Olano suggested that for a treaty there is a treaty
text from which reservations derogate while for reservations to Optional
Clause declarations there is no such treaty text. Crawford added that as
under the Optional Clause reservations can be made without limitation,
there is no prior agreement and that the reservations are an 'integral part
of the act which constitutes the agreement'.[229]

With regard to his few sentences it cannot be said for sure whether
Judge Urrutia Olano really implied this. He was focused on the relation
between Optional Clause declarations and later treaties.[230] Furthermore,
Crawford's deduction seems to overemphasise the quality of the reservations' influence. The degree to which reservations are allowed is a
particular feature of every treaty. Even treaties which are generous with
reservations still remain treaties.[231] Even if Article 36(2) to (4) of the Statute
provides little, it is possible to consider their content as the basis for a
treaty. The states only need to make short declarations to accede to it and
these declarations can be made without any reservation at all. They also

---

[224] ibid 76, 80.

[225] Waldock (n 5) 252.

[226] Separate opinion of Judge D Anzilotti, *PCIJ Series A/B No 77 1939*, 63, 86 f. See also
Waldock (n 5) 252.

[227] Dissenting opinion of Judge MO Hudson, *PCIJ Series A/B No 77 1939*, 118, 121.

[228] Dissenting opinion of Judge FJ Urrutia Olano, *PCIJ Series A/B No 77 1939*, 101, 103 f.

[229] Crawford (n 73) 77. See also *Fisheries Jurisdiction (Spain v Canada)* (Jurisdiction) Counter-
Memorial (Canada) para 74; Holloway (n 2) 653.

[230] For more on this see sub-s III B of ch 6 at 316.

[231] For the regime for reservations under the Optional Clause see ch 5 (140).

need not reproduce the text already provided for in Article 36(2) of the Statute. All that is necessary is that a state shows the intent to be bound under the Optional Clause.[232] An example may be the original Nicaraguan declaration of 1929: 'On behalf of the Republic of Nicaragua I recognize as compulsory unconditionally the jurisdiction of the Permanent Court of International Justice'. The freedom to make reservations to Optional Clause declarations does not distinguish it from other treaties. Furthermore, it seems as if reservations are as much an integral part of Optional Clause declarations as they are an integral part of other declarations of accession.[233]

In total it can be held that the jurisprudence of the Permanent Court provides no clear picture. Especially the remarks in the *Electricity Company of Sofia and Bulgaria* case pointing at a treaty relation seem to contradict the remarks made in the *Phosphates in Morocco* case emphasising the unilateral origin of the declarations. However, the position of the Permanent Court in the latter cases does not fully preclude the assumption that the Optional Clause is a multilateral treaty. The court wrote that an Optional Clause declaration was unilateral and that the court could not exceed the consent expressed therein.[234] This does, however, also apply for accessions to multilateral treaties which are at their basis unilateral and for which the expressed consent is, at least in general, likewise the limit of the obligation of the acceding state.[235]

B. The Court's *Sui Generis* Approach

One of the most prominent statements the Court made was pronounced in its early case concerning the *Anglo-Iranian Oil Co*. There it said that 'the text of the Iranian Declaration is not a treaty text resulting from negotiations between two or more states. It is the result of a unilateral drafting'.[236] As Hersch Lauterpacht and Debbasch already remarked it is not clear what the Court wanted to say with this. The statement could either be directed against the treaty character of the Optional Clause declarations

---

[232] M Dubisson, *La cour* 191; *Temple of Preah Vihear (Cambodia v Thailand)* (Preliminary Objections) [1961] ICJ Rep 17, 32–34; *Military and Paramilitary Activities in and against Nicaragua (Nicaragua v United States of America)* (n 27) para 45; Lamm (n 112) 33; Rosenne and Ronen (n 5) 723 f; Whiteman (n 117) 1338; Wittmann (n 2) 150 f. See also the separate opinion of Judge PC Spender, *ICJ Rep 1961*, 40: 'No requirements of form are called for by paragraph (2) of Article 36. If consent to recognize this Court's jurisdiction in terms of that paragraph is clearly manifested, it matters not in what form the declaration containing that consent is cast'.
[233] For the question whether reservations and declarations can be separated see s IV of ch 5 at 254.
[234] *Phosphates in Morocco (Italy v France)* (n 222) 23 f.
[235] For the special case of impermissible reservations see s IV of ch 5 at 254.
[236] *Nuclear Tests (Australia v France)* (n 19) 105.

or the fact that there have been no negotiations.[237] However, even if the Court meant all its words as it wrote them, this does not preclude that the Optional Clause declarations are accessions to the Optional Clause, because all accessions and their reservations are drafted unilaterally and are not accompanied by negotiations. In this regard the texts of Optional Clause declarations are not different from the texts of other declarations of accession.

The separate opinion of Judge Alvarez also points into this direction. He wrote that the Optional Clause declaration is a 'multilateral act of a special character' and that 'it is the basis of a treaty made by Iran with the States which had already acceded and with those which would consequently accede'.[238] In line with the conclusion above, Judge Read wrote:

> Admittedly it was drafted unilaterally. On the other hand, it was related, in express terms, to Article 36 of the Statute, and to the declarations of other States which had already deposited, or which might in the future deposit, reciprocal declarations. It was intended to establish legal relationships with such States, consensual in their character, within the regime established by the provisions of Article 36.[239]

Less clearly Judge McNair described the Optional Clause as a 'machinery ... of "contracting in", not of "contracting out"'.[240]

In the *Norwegian Loans* case, the Court made clear that its jurisdiction is based on both Article 36(2) of the Statute and the unilateral Optional Clause declarations. The Court emphasised that it has jurisdiction only as far as the two unilateral declarations coincide.[241] Rosenne used this statement of the Court as well as similar ones in the *Right of Passage* case and in the case concerning the *Aerial Incident of 1955* to show how the Court emphasises Article 36(2) of the Statute as a 'constituent element' of the states' obligations.[242] This is true but does not mean that the Optional Clause is not a treaty as with this argument the texts of all multilateral treaties can be considered as a 'constituent elements', too. Another interesting aspect of the judgment in the *Norwegian Loans* case was how the Court treated the French declaration and the position of the involved states concerning the French Connally Reservation.[243] It referred to the states' 'common will relating to the competence of the Court'.[244] This seems to point towards

---

[237] C Debbasch, 'La compétence' 233, fn 5; Lauterpacht (n 59) 345.

[238] Dissenting opinion of Judge A Alvarez, *ICJ Rep 1952*, 125.

[239] Dissenting opinion of Judge JE Read, *ICJ Rep 1952*, 142.

[240] Individual opinion of Judge AD McNair, *ICJ Rep 1952*, 116.

[241] *Case of Certain Norwegian Loans (France v Norway)* (Judgment) [1957] ICJ Rep 9, 23.

[242] Rosenne and Ronen (n 5) 791 also referring to *Case concerning the Right of Passage over Indian Territory (Portugal v India)* (Preliminary Objections) [1957] ICJ Rep 125, 145 and *Case concerning the Aerial Incident of July 27th, 1955 (Israel v Bulgaria)* (n 70) 143.

[243] For more on this reservation see especially s V of ch 4 at 160.

[244] *Case of Certain Norwegian Loans (France v Norway)* (n 241) 23.

a bilateral relationship between France and Norway.[245] In the aforementioned judgment in the *Right of Passage* case of the same year the Court similarly spoke of the 'contractual relation' between the states from which the jurisdiction of the Court emerges.[246]

The judgments concerning the *Norwegian Loans* case and the *Right of Passage* case were accompanied by very different opinions of individual judges. In his separate opinion Judge Lauterpacht for example compared the submission of an Optional Clause declaration to the accession to a text prepared by the General Assembly. At the end, however, he did not decide whether treaty law had to be applied.[247] Judge Guerrero referred to the parties' 'declarations of accession to paragraph 2 of Article 36'.[248] Concerning the *Right of Passage* case Judge Badawi strongly argued for a bilateral and conventional relationship among the states as result of the declarations which he strictly considered as bilateral offer and acceptance. For him there was no 'contract by accession in which the dual elements of offer and acceptance become merged'. Unlike Optional Clause declarations, such contracts' essential features were their uniformity as for single states it was impossible to discuss the terms of the contract. They were 'obliged to contract and [to give their] accession to the all powerful will of the other'.[249] Yet, with such a view on all accessions the phenomenon of reservations can hardly be explained. What Judge Badawi seems to say is that the Optional Clause is no closed multilateral treaty which has special requirements for the admission of a further Member State or requires negotiations of the whole relation.[250] In this regard the position of Judge Badawi can well be supported as the Optional Clause allows all 'states parties to the present Statute' to join and can in so far be considered as an 'open' treaty. This does, however, not mean at all that the Optional Clause declarations establish strictly bilateral relations.

In the two combined cases concerning *South West Africa* the Judges Spender and Fitzmaurice maintained that the interaction of the declarations conferred upon them a bi- or multilateral aspect. Nonetheless, for them the Optional Clause declarations did not result in a treaty because otherwise it was redundant to Article 36(1) of the Statute.[251] In the *Barcelona Traction* case the Court again emphasised the unilateral origin of

---

[245] cp Crawford (n 73) 82 f.

[246] *Case concerning the Right of Passage over Indian Territory (Portugal v India)* (n 242) 146. See also Maus (n 8) 61 f.

[247] Separate opinion of Judge H Lauterpacht, *ICJ Rep 1957*, 48.

[248] Dissenting opinion of Judge JG Guerrero, *ICJ Rep 1957*, 70.

[249] Dissenting opinion of Judge AH Badawi, *ICJ Rep 1957*, 157 f.

[250] For the distinction between closed, semi-closed and open treaties see Marchi (n 14) paras 29–33. cp also Fitzmaurice (n 59) para 27; F Hoffmeister, 'Article 15' paras 2–6, 12–19, 25–29.

[251] Joint dissenting opinion of Judges PC Spender and GG Fitzmaurice, *ICJ Rep 1962*, 476. The latter argument has already been considered in sub-s II C of ch 2 at 65.

the Optional Clause declarations.[252] Judge Armand-Ugon, however, went further and said:

> It is true that the declarations were unilateral undertakings. But as those undertakings were addressed to other States, which had accepted the same obligation, they gave rise to agreements of a treaty character concerning jurisdiction which were legally equivalent to the jurisdictional clause embodied in a treaty or convention.[253]

In 1984, the Court made its second prominent statement. In the *Nicaragua* case it seemed to refer to the Optional Clause as being everything. It said:

> [T]he declarations, even though they are *unilateral acts*, establish a series of *bilateral engagements* with other States accepting the same obligation of compulsory jurisdiction, in which the conditions, reservations and time-limit clauses are taken into consideration. In the establishment of this *network of engagements*, which constitutes the Optional-Clause system, the principle of good faith plays an important role.[254]

Furthermore, the Court referred to its judgment in the *Nuclear Tests* cases in which it had established the binding force of unilateral declarations.[255] From the principle of good faith the Court then also deduced that the Optional Clause declarations should be treated by analogy according to the law of treaties.[256] Concerning the first statements it could still again be said that accessions to multilateral treaties are also basically unilateral. Yet, the latter points allow no conclusion which is in line with the idea that the Court considers the Optional Clause a treaty. If the Court had understood the Optional Clause as a multilateral treaty, the reference to the precedent of the *Nuclear Tests* cases would not have been necessary and also treaty law could have been applied directly and not only by analogy. The 'engagements' referred to by the Court could also be those which likewise result from a purely unilateral declaration.[257]

The United States' position mentioned above,[258] was largely taken up by Judge Jennings who referred to the Optional Clause as a treaty *sui generis*. He wrote:

> The declarations are statements of intention; and statements of intention made in a quite formal way. Obviously, however, they do not amount to treaties or contracts; or, at least, if one says they are treaties, or contracts, one immediately

---

[252] cp *Barcelona Traction, Light and Power Company, Limited (Belgium v Spain) (New Application: 1962)* (n 160) 29.

[253] Dissenting opinion of Judge EC Armand-Ugon, *ICJ Rep 1964*, 135.

[254] *Military and Paramilitary Activities in and against Nicaragua (Nicaragua v United States of America)* (n 27) para 60 (emphasis added).

[255] ibid para 60.

[256] ibid para 63. For criticism see eg Ende (n 149) 1161, fn 109.

[257] See sub-s I A i of ch 2 at 41.

[258] See sub-s III A of ch 2 at 69.

has to go on to say they are a special kind of treaty, or contract, partaking only of some of the rules normally applicable to such matters. Thus, however one starts, one ends by treating them as more or less *sui generis*.[259]

The Court adopted this *sui generis* approach in its more recent cases. In the *Bakassi Peninsula* case, the Court reiterated its finding in the *Right of Passage* case and furthermore wrote:

> Any State party to the Statute, in adhering to the jurisdiction of the Court in accordance with Article 36, paragraph 2, accepts jurisdiction in its relations with States previously having adhered to that clause. At the same time, it makes a standing offer to the other States party to the Statute which have not yet deposited a declaration of acceptance. The day one of those states accepts that offer by depositing in its turn its declaration of acceptance, the consensual bond is established ... [260]

This terminology comes at least close to the terminology used for treaties. However, the Court only spoke of an 'adherence' to its jurisdiction and not to the Optional Clause. Furthermore, at the end it referred to its finding in the *Nicaragua* case and wrote again that treaty law can only be applied by analogy.[261] As the Court also referred to Article 36(4) of the Statute in this regard it could still be said the reason for the special character of the Optional Clause here has been seen in that paragraph four.

However, this is not convincing in light of the judgment in the *Fisheries Jurisdiction* case which the Court delivered in the same year. In this judgment it made a clear statement saying generally that the Optional Clause is *sui generis*. The Court first emphasised the unilateral origin of Optional Clause declarations and wrote that 'a declaration of acceptance of the compulsory jurisdiction of the Court, whether there are specified limits set to that acceptance or not, is a unilateral act of State sovereignty'. Then it went on by considering the declarations as establishing consensual bonds and being furthermore a standing offer for other states. It ended by concluding that the 'acceptances' of the Optional Clause have *sui generis* character and that the rules of the VCLT were only applicable as far as they are in accordance with that character.[262] Later the Court contrasted the terms of Optional Clause declarations with the terms of 'contractual provisions'.[263]

The perception that the Optional Clause declarations are no accessions to a multilateral treaty can furthermore be found in the dissenting

---

[259] Separate opinion of Judge RY Jennings, *ICJ Rep 1984*, 547.

[260] *Land and Maritime Boundary between Cameroon and Nigeria (Cameroon v Nigeria: Equatorial Guinea intervening)* (Preliminary Objections) [1998] ICJ Rep 275, para 25. This quote was used as description of the nature of Optional Clause declarations in Thirlway (n 2) 1082.

[261] *Land and Maritime Boundary between Cameroon and Nigeria (Cameroon v Nigeria: Equatorial Guinea intervening)*, ibid paras 25, 30.

[262] *Fisheries Jurisdiction (Spain v Canada)* (Jurisdiction) [1998] ICJ Rep 432, para 30.

[263] ibid para 46.

opinion of Judge Koroma who wrote: 'The point is not that declarations are treaties, which they are not as such, but even as unilateral acts, they establish a series of bilateral engagements with other States accepting the same obligation of compulsory jurisdiction'.[264]

In total the Court's position on the nature of the Optional Clause and the declarations is ambiguous.[265] On the one hand, it emphasised the unilateral origin of the Optional Clause declarations. While the judgment in the *Anglo-Iranian Oil Co* case would still have allowed the conclusion that the Court considered the Optional Clause as a treaty,[266] this does not seem to work for the judgment in the *Nicaragua* case.[267] On the other hand, the Court referred to the 'contractual relation' established by the Optional Clause and used terms like 'offer', 'acceptance' and 'adhering'.[268] In line with these positions the Court came to the result that the Optional Clause is *sui generis*. The idea, to interpret this *sui generis* of the Court as being basically as uni-, bi- and multilateral as the accession to a multilateral treaty, seems to be furthermore barred by the fact that so far the Court has applied treaty law only via analogy.

C. Result Concerning the Jurisprudence

The position of both Courts has moved between the unilateral origin of the Optional Clause declarations and the relationship created by them. At least so far the Court, like its predecessor, has never referred to Article 36(2) of the Statute as a multilateral treaty and to the Optional Clause declarations as being the corresponding declarations of accession. In relation to all the judgments, however, directly opposing statements are also rare. The fact that the Court neither refuses to apply treaty law nor applies it consistently supports the impression of an approach which can be considered rather ambiguous so far.[269] Taking into consideration that the Optional Clause has now existed for over ninety years this can be due to the fact that treaty law developed simultaneously and especially the

---

[264] Dissenting opinion of Judge AG Koroma, *ICJ Rep 1998*, 383.

[265] See also M Fitzmaurice, 'Interpretation' 128.

[266] For the judgment in the *Anglo-Iranian Oil Co* case and the interpretation of the Optional Clause declarations in this case see below, sub-s III B of ch 4 at 146.

[267] See also Gharbi according to whom 'la jurisprudence des deux cours de La Haye n'a pas bien développé l'idée de l'élaboration d'un accord international par l'ensemble des déclarations d'acceptation'(Gharbi (n 7) 251).

[268] For Weiss the jurisprudence of both Courts points towards a bilateral contractual obligation between the states (EB Weiss, 'Reciprocity' 96). Also for Alexandrov the jurisprudence leads to the conclusion that there are consensual and contractual relations between the states having made an Optional Clause declaration (SA Alexandrov, *Declarations* 12 f).

[269] See also the criticism of Weiss, ibid 97.

law concerning the accession to a multilateral treaty with reservations has really been clarified only recently.[270] Klabbers already wrote that labelling of the Optional Clause as 'sui generis' is 'reminiscent' of a past in which multilateral treaties have been 'couched' in the form of related and almost identical bilateral treaties.[271] The same might hold for emphasising the unilateral origin of the Optional Clause declarations.

Be this as it may, it may be recalled that, according to Article 38(1)(d) of the Statute, judicial decisions are, just as 'the teachings of the most highly qualified publicists of the various nations', only a subsidiary means for determining rules of law. Of course, international courts have to develop and establish law to a certain degree.[272] Yet, unlike the states the Court is not a legislative body in international law and has no power to derogate law established by the states.[273] Furthermore, the Court is not bound by its prior judgments and is free to depart from them if there is a reason to do so.[274] So even if the previous jurisprudence might at some points suggest that the Optional Clause is not a treaty this could not persist if the states have drafted the Optional Clause as a treaty and there is no derogating customary law. This leads to the conclusion of this chapter.

V. CONCLUSION

As an Optional Clause declaration, together with other Optional Clause declarations, establishes also rights for the submitting state, it cannot be regarded as a purely unilateral act. With regard to its relation to the Statute, the Optional Clause can best be considered as an additional treaty to it. Like an optional protocol the Optional Clause allows Member States of the Statute to undertake an additional commitment which does not come from the membership of the Statute itself. The genesis of the Optional Clause supports this result as the Optional Clause was born out of the idea to provide the compulsory jurisdiction of the Permanent Court in an additional treaty to its statute. Even though there is no clear supporting state practice in this regard there is also no clear derogating state practice. Therefore,

---

[270] See eg the GPRT which the ILC has just completed in 2011 (cp ILC 'Report of the International Law Commission on the Work of Its 63rd Session' (26 April–3 June and 4 July–12 August 2011) UN Doc A/66/10 12-47 and A Pellet, 'Article 19 VCLT' paras 63–69).
[271] J Klabbers, *Treaty* 44, fn 43. For the mentioned development in international law see also Fitzmaurice (n 59) para 10; P Reuter, *Introduction* 2 f; B Simma, 'Community Interest' 323, 336.
[272] cp R Bernhardt, 'Rechtsfortbildung' 11.
[273] cp *South West Africa (Ethiopia and Liberia v South Africa)* (Second Phase) [1966] ICJ Rep 6, paras 89 f; Rosenne and Ronen (n 5) 574.
[274] *Land and Maritime Boundary between Cameroon and Nigeria (Cameroon v Nigeria: Equatorial Guinea intervening)* (n 260) para 28; G Acquaviva and F Pocar, 'Stare Decisis' paras 10–13.

it can very well be said that the Optional Clause is a multilateral treaty and that the Optional Clause declarations are declarations of accession to it.[275]

Yet, as pointed out above,[276] this result is up to now only based on rather theoretical considerations and general statements. The following chapters have to show whether practical aspects like the interpretation of Optional Clause declarations and the Optional Clause's regime for reservations support or rebut the finding of this chapter.

VI. EXCURSUS: THE APPLICABILITY OF THE VCLT

Today, treaty law is basically provided by customary international law and the VCLT.[277] In general, there seems to be no reason not to apply treaty law to the Optional Clause after it has been established that the latter is a treaty. It cannot be maintained that treaty law cannot be applied to the Optional Clause because, for example, a 'treaty link' is missing among Optional Clause declarations.[278] The question which nonetheless arises and which will be the last one of this chapter is whether the VCLT can be applied to the Optional Clause.

Article 1 VCLT simply provides: 'The present Convention applies to treaties between States'. As established above, the Optional Clause is a treaty among the states as defined by Article 2(1)(a) VCLT. Therefore, the Optional Clause is generally covered by the VCLT's area of application.

Furthermore, also according to the ILC's drafting committee for the VCLT, the Optional Clause should have been regulated by the VCLT.[279]

---

[275] See also Lauterpacht (n 3) 170: 'The Optional Clause ... is the most comprehensive multilateral arbitration convention in existence'. See furthermore Farmanfarma (n 36) 156 with exactly the same wording. Later, Lauterpacht also wrote that Optional Clause declarations 'are not in all respects like a treaty. But they are essentially a treaty'. Nonetheless, he still considered the making of an Optional Clause declaration to be like the accession to a treaty (Lauterpacht (n 59) 345 f For this see also ILC 'Summary Records of the 40th Session' (n 101) para 43 (Waldock)). cp also Klabbers (n 271) 44 who referred to the Optional Clause declarations as he discussed unilateral ways to create agreements. cp furthermore Kolb (n 5) 448; Myers (n 3) 592; Suy (n 22) 147 and also Verzijl (Verzijl (n 6) 586) according to whom the system of the Optional Clause 'consists of a series of engagements with varying contents, much the same as in the case of a multilateral arbitration or jurisdiction treaty accompanied by individual reservations, such as Pact of Bogotá of 1948'. For a similar position concerning the Optional Clause of the Statute of the Permanent Court see Ténékidès (n 5) 729–33; Wittmann (n 2) 161; Wundram (n 117) 13 f.

[276] See s II of the introduction at 6 f.

[277] For the current importance and frame of customary international law see A Watts, 'Customary International Law' 251.

[278] For this argumentation see DW Bowett, 'Reservations' 76.

[279] cp ILC 'Summary Records of the 40th Session' (n 101) p 265, para 135. cp also ILC 'Documents of the 11th Session Including the Report of the Commission to the General Assembly' (1959) UN Doc A/CN.4/Ser.A/1959/Add.l 92, 94, fn 28.

However, as addressed above,[280] as the ILC considered that draft the reference to the Optional Clause in the commentary was deleted.[281] Later, Rosenne, who had proposed this deletion, referred to this fact as he argued that the law applicable on the Optional Clause is different from the law of treaties.[282] This is, however, not the only way to read the deletion. Concerning Rosenne's proposal Waldock expressly said that

> [h]e had no objection to the deletion proposed by Mr Rosenne but the question had been discussed before and some members had seemed to want the declaration to be treated on that basis, but there was no need to make any reference to it.[283]

On this base the proposal was accepted.

In the earlier discussion, there had been a strong position for including Optional Clause declarations into the scope of the VCLT. Ado had maintained that '[d]eclarations under article 36(2) of the Statute of the International Court of Justice were certainly covered by the draft articles'.[284] And Liang had emphasised that '[i]t was important to make it clear that the rules relating to such matters as the interpretation and the termination of treaties applied to declarations under article 36(2) of the Statute'. For him, '[t]here was no reason to treat declarations under article 36 (2) of the Statute differently from declarations under the Vienna Protocol [concerning the Compulsory Settlement of Disputes]'.[285]

Therefore, the Optional Clause is not necessarily excluded from the VCLT's scope of application. With regard to the presented positions of the drafters of the VCLT it can even be said that the Optional Clause shall fall under its scope. This would also be in line with what has been established in the current chapter.

Nonetheless, many states are not Member States of the VCLT and for them the rules of the VCLT can only be applied as far as they are customary law.[286] The definition of a 'treaty' in Article 2(1)(a) VCLT which has already been used above is customary law.[287] Furthermore, according to its Article 4 the VCLT is only applicable to treaties 'concluded' after 27 January 1980. It is still not settled whether conclusion here refers to

---

[280] See s II of the introduction at 3 f.

[281] ILC 'Summary Records of the 40th Session' (n 101) p 265 paras 135, 141. See also ILC 'Documents of the 14th Session Including the Report of the Commission to the General Assembly' (n 64) 35 para 2.

[282] S Rosenne, *Law and Practice* 410 f; Rosenne and Ronen (n 5) 791 f. See also Greig's position on Rosenne's reference to the deletion (DW Greig, 'Confrontation' 178).

[283] ILC 'Summary Records of the 40th Session' (n 101) p 265, para 141 (Waldock).

[284] ibid 57, para 79 (Ado).

[285] ibid 56, paras 71 f (Liang).

[286] ILC 'Ninth Report on Unilateral Acts of States—Addendum' (n 21) para 115; A Aust, 'Article 24' para 1; M Falkowska, M Bedjaoui and T Leidgens, 'Article 44' para 13; T Giegerich, 'Article 54 VCLT' para 6; W Graf Vitzthum, 'Rechtsquellen' para 115.

[287] A Aust, 'Vienna Convention' para 13; Gautier (n 61) paras 1, 29; Klabbers (n 271) 41, 46.

the end of the drafting or the entry into force of the treaty.[288] If it was understood as emphasising the last expression of will, it could be said to apply also to treaties whose text has been drafted before that date but to which states accede later.[289] From this perspective the VCLT could at least apply directly in cases where the states involved have made their Optional Clause declarations after 1980.[290] Of course and in both cases, the rules of the VCLT apply anyway as far as they correspond to customary international law.[291]

Taking into account these limitations it can be said that in general the VCLT can be applied to the Optional Clause.[292] This would also concur with examples from other optional clauses. Concerning the optional clause of the ACHR Úbeda de Torres emphasised that the VCLT's rules for interpretation have been applied to the ACHR. For him they were 'therefore clearly applicable to the interpretation of the optional clause of Article 62(1) of the American Convention of Human Rights'.[293] The UNCHR, which generally does not want to apply the VCLT's regime for reservations on the CCPR, suggested that there might be an exception for its optional clause in Article 41 CCPR since, at least to a certain degree, there was room for the principle of inter-state reciprocity under that Article.[294] Considering the structure of obligations under the Optional Clause,[295] the UNCHR's reasoning must *a fortiori* hold for the Optional Clause.

---

[288] F Dopagne, 'Article 4' paras 7 f. For the controversial debate among the VCLT's drafters see PV McDade, 'Effect of Article 4' 507 f.

[289] cp Dopagne, ibid paras 7 f; McDade, ibid 506–10; K Schmalenbach, 'Article 4' para 14.

[290] For the position that the VCLT does not require that all states of a multilateral treaty have acceded to it see McDade, ibid 505 f.

[291] Aust (n 287) para 13; McDade, ibid 502. cp also the position in UNCHR 'General Comment No 24 (52) on issues relating to reservations made upon ratification or accession to the Covenant to the Optional Protocols thereto, or in relation to declarations under article 41 of the Covenant' (n 76) fn 2. For the high degree of correspondence of VCLT and customary law and the high practical impact of the VCLT even among non-member states see Aust, ibid paras 14–18; McDade, ibid 502–05.

[292] cp also Rodríguez Cedeño and Torres Cazorla (n 16) para 12.

[293] A Úbeda de Torres, 'Contentious Jurisdiction' 11.

[294] UNCHR 'General Comment No 24 (52) on issues relating to reservations made upon ratification or accession to the Covenant to the Optional Protocols thereto, or in relation to declarations under article 41 of the Covenant' (n 76) para 17. For Art 41 CCPR see also sub-s II D iii of ch 1 at 35 and below sub-s III B ii b of ch 5 at 208.

[295] See above s II of ch 1 at 22.

3

The Creation of Obligations Under the Optional Clause

T HE FOLLOWING CHAPTER will be the first one to discuss whether the result found in the second chapter can be rebutted or further supported with a practical aspect of the Optional Clause. It will discuss how the Optional Clause declarations 'enter into force' and especially when obligations and rights start to emerge from them. Some authors have referred to the creation of obligations under the Optional Clause to maintain that the Optional Clause or optional clauses in general are different from treaties or that treaty law cannot be applied to the Optional Clause. This chapter will show that Optional Clause declarations are like declarations of accession to a multilateral treaty and treaty law can be applied.

I. FREEDOM TO JOIN OR TO ABSTAIN

Tomuschat argued against the application of treaty law on the Optional Clause that, according to Article 33(1) of the Charter, there was no obligation to accept judicial settlement and that states were free to stay aloof from it.[1] He used this argument to support a generous regime for reservations which according to Tomuschat was essentially different from that of the Vienna Convention on the Law of Treaties (VCLT).[2] In the *Nicaragua* case the Court made the statement:

> Declarations of acceptance of the compulsory jurisdiction of the Court are facultative, unilateral engagements, that States are absolutely free to make or not to make. In making the declaration a State is equally free either to do so unconditionally and without limit of time for its duration, or to qualify it with conditions or reservations.[3]

---

[1] C Tomuschat, 'Article 36 of the Statute' para 99.

[2] ibid paras 83, 99. cp also E Jiménez De Aréchaga, 'International Law' 154; *Military and Paramilitary Activities in and against Nicaragua (Nicaragua v United States of America)* (Jurisdiction and Admissibility) Counter-Memorial (United States of America) para 344: '*in plus stat minus*'. For the regime on reservations under the Optional Clause see ch 5 at 165.

[3] *Military and Paramilitary Activities in and against Nicaragua (Nicaragua v United States of America)* (Jurisdiction and Admissibility) [1984] ICJ Rep 392, para 59; repeated in *Aerial Incident of 10 August 1999 (Pakistan v India)* (Jurisdiction) [2000] ICJ Rep 12, 29, para 36. See also *Temple of Preah Vihear (Cambodia v Thailand)* (Preliminary Objections) [1961] ICJ Rep 17, 33.

Similarly, Gharbi wrote that 'comme tout acte rédigé unilatéralement, la déclaration est soumise au régime de la souveraineté et de la compétence discrétionnaire des États'.[4]

These statements are right in so far as states are free not to accede to the Optional Clause.[5] There is also no kind of constraint to submit disputes to the Court. The states are free to choose their means of peaceful settlement and the Court only has jurisdiction when each state has consented.[6] Article 33(1) of the Charter leaves the choice of means to the states.[7] And also Article 36(3) of the Charter makes no difference in this regard. It simply suggests referring disputes to the Court but contains no duty to do so even if the Security Council recommends this.[8] Furthermore, Article 36(2) of the Statute contains no such obligation and clearly says that states 'may' make an Optional Clause declaration.[9]

This freedom, however, is no difference to other multilateral treaties. There is no obligation to join those either.[10] Even after a signature there is no obligation to ratify a treaty.[11] In this regard there is no difference between the Optional Clause and other treaties and no reason to conclude that the Optional Clause is no treaty.[12]

II. ACCESSION, SIGNATURE, RATIFICATION AND DEPOSITION

Discussing the Optional Clause, Gharbi wrote: 'Ce type d'accord se fait au moyen d'une procédure simple et dépourvue de la solennité inhérente

---

[4] F Gharbi, 'Le déclin' 471.

[5] ibid 458; R Kolb, *ICJ* 370–73; H Lauterpacht, *Development* 65; WM Reisman, 'Termination' 80 f; Verzijl (n 5) 383, fn 1; C Walter, 'Rechtsschutz' paras 31, 40, 45.

[6] *Case concerning the Factory at Chorzów (Germany v Poland)* (Jurisdiction) PCIJ Series A No 9 3, 32; *Case of the Monetary Gold Removed from Rome in 1943 (Italy v France, United Kingdom of Great Britain and Northern Ireland and United States of America)* (Preliminary Question) [1954] ICJ Rep 19, 32; *Military and Paramilitary Activities in and against Nicaragua (Nicaragua v United States of America)* (n 3) para 59; *Armed Activities on the Territory of the Congo (New Application: 2002) (Democratic Republic of the Congo v Rwanda)* (Jurisdiction and Admissibility) [2006] ICJ Rep 6, paras 68, 127; SA Alexandrov, *Declarations* 1 f; V Lamm, 'Reciprocity' 45 f; Oellers-Frahm (n 6) 247; *Military and Paramilitary Activities in and against Nicaragua v United States of America)* (n 2) paras 249 f; CG Ténékidès, 'Les actes concurrents' 720; P Weil, *Écrits* 111; F Wittmann, *Obligatorium* 26–28, 46; Tomuschat (n 1) para 19.

[7] C Tomuschat, 'Article 33 UN Charter' paras 22, 35.

[8] T Giegerich, 'Article 36 UN Charter' para 56.

[9] cp also United Nations, *Conference on International Organization, Volume XIV—United Nations Committee of Jurists* 668, 841: 'an option which each state [is] free to take or not to take'.

[10] See also *SS Wimbledon Case (United Kingdom, France, Italy and Japan v Germany)* (Judgment) PCIJ Series A No 1 15, 25; *Exchange of Greek and Turkish Populations* (Advisory Opinion) PCIJ Series B No 10 5, 21; AN Farmanfarma, *Declarations* 38; Walter (n 5) para 45.

[11] A Aust, *Treaty Law* 98.

[12] Walter (n 5) para 45. For an application of Art 45 VCLT on an Optional Clause declaration see Declaration of Judge P Tomka, *ICJ Rep 2007*, paras 10 f.

aux traités classiques'.[13] He maintained: 'Le mécanisme de la clause facultative dans le système de la CIJ se distingue nettement, puisque les États formulent unilatéralement leurs déclarations d'acceptation de la juridiction obligatoire de cette Cour'.[14] Concerning the point that states formulate the Optional Clause declarations unilaterally it can again be said that other accessions with reservations are also formulated unilaterally.[15]

However, the point that the Optional Clause provides a procedure which is simpler than the one for other treaties sounds similar to what Schwelb said concerning optional clauses in general. For him the difference between an optional clause and an optional protocol was that to the former only a single acceptance was possible while for the latter there was the possibility to sign it first and to ratify it later. States could thus express their intent to be bound in a way which was not possible for an optional clause.[16] This section will show that the Optional Clause declarations are like declarations of accession to a multilateral treaty and that they do not require ratification.

A. Accessions, Signature and Ratification in General Treaty Law

Schwelb is right as far as normally treaties are signed and later ratified. Normally, they have to be ratified to enter into force.[17] However, according to Rosenne, 'there is no absolute rule in international law requiring that a treaty should be subject to ratification'.[18] Article 14 VCLT makes it very clear that it depends on the intention of the states whether ratification is required.[19] Article 110 of the Charter for example provides: 'The present Charter shall be ratified by the signatory states in accordance with their respective constitutional processes'.

Generally, for the states this depends on whether the drafting and signing states' organs still have to fulfil internal requirements to be allowed to bind their state. As Marchi points out, where a treaty text has already been established such a two-step procedure is not necessary. Therefore, a later accession is not subject to ratification as in such cases the states have sufficient time to fulfil internal requirements.[20] Hence it can be said that

---

[13]   F Gharbi, 'Déclarations d'acceptation' 262.
[14]   Gharbi (n 4) 472. cp also UNGA 'Official Records of the Twenty-First Session, Third Committee, 1438th Meeting' (29.11.1966) UN Doc A/C.3/SR.1438 27 (Ramaholimihaso).
[15]   See sub-s I A ii of ch 2 at 43.
[16]   E Schwelb, 'Measures of Implementation' 862.
[17]   B Maus, *Réserves* 107, fn 2.
[18]   S Rosenne, 'Conclusion of Treaties' 934.
[19]   F Hoffmeister, 'Article 14' para 1.
[20]   J Marchi, 'Article 15' para 3. See also Rosenne (n 18) 933; Wittmann (n 6) 154.

accession replaces signature and ratification.[21] However, there have also been accessions 'subject to ratification' in the history of treaties.[22] These cannot be considered as accessions in the sense of Article 15 VCLT and do not have the consequences of an accession.[23] According to Hoffmeister they are based on a misunderstanding by the states involved.[24] At most, such accessions can be considered a letter of intent.[25]

For optional clauses which are generally made for later accession there is basically no need for a two step system. Nonetheless, there seems to be no reason why a state should be unable to sign an optional clause and to ratify it later. For example, many states likewise signed the first optional protocol to the International Covenant on Civil and Political Rights (CCPR) before they later expressed their final intention to become bound by it while others simply acceded.[26] The situation is similar for optional clauses. As for optional protocols it cannot be said that the signature or the ratification of the major treaty has an influence on the rights and obligations which shall be established with an optional clause. All that can be said is that the text of the optional clause is necessarily authenticated along with the text of the corresponding multilateral treaty.[27]

Furthermore, even if the Optional Clause is not open to signature and only allows the single act of accession this does still not necessarily mean that it is not a treaty. There are also treaties which are likewise not signed and only subject to a later expression of consent to be bound.[28] Article 11 VCLT clearly provides: 'The consent of a State to be bound by a treaty may be expressed by signature, exchange of instruments constituting a treaty, ratification, acceptance, approval or accession, or by any other means if so agreed'. Even if it does not require a separate signature, a treaty is a treaty. This corresponds with the general decline of form in state practice.[29]

B. The Way Optional Clause Declarations are Made

The question is what the Optional Clause provides in this regard. As there might be a difference between the old and the current Statute here, these two will be considered separately.

---

[21] M Nowak, *CCPR Commentary* Art 48, para 3.
[22] Marchi (n 20) paras 17 f.
[23] F Hoffmeister, 'Article 15' para 10; Marchi (n 20) para 18.
[24] Hoffmeister, ibid, para 10.
[25] cp Marchi (n 20) para 18.
[26] For the state practice under Art 8 of the first optional protocol to the CCPR see M Nowak, *CCPR Commentary* Art 8 First OP, para 1.
[27] For the requirements and legal effects of the authentication of the text of a treaty see M Fitzmaurice, 'Treaties' para 37; F Hoffmeister, 'Article 10' paras 1 f, 6–13.
[28] cp Aust (n 11) 21 for the 'acceptance' of treaties adopted by the FAO conference. See also W Karl, 'Article 69' para 25.
[29] cp F Hoffmeister, 'Article 11' para 22; S Szurek, 'Article 11' para 30.

i. The Statute of the Permanent Court: Providing Two Protocols

The original 'Optional Clause' of the Statute of the Permanent Court only stated that states shall sign it.[30] Unlike the protocol of signature to the Statute of the Permanent Court it did not mention ratification. Yet, it could be emphasised that the Optional Clause had by some drafters been expected to be accepted together with the ratification of the Statute of the Permanent Court.[31] Therefore it could be argued that in such cases the ratification covered both, the protocol of signature of the Statute and the Optional Clause.[32] Nonetheless, the old Optional Clause had also been open for later acceptances. Article 36(2) of the old Statute clearly had allowed states to accept it 'either when signing or ratifying the Protocol to which the present Statute is adjoined, or at a later moment'. From the wording of the additional protocol and Article 36(2) of the Statute it cannot be surely inferred whether in the latter cases both signature and ratification were necessary.[33]

The genesis of the Optional Clause allows no clear result either, but it seems to suggest that accessions by a simple declaration are also possible. The drafters spoke of 'ratifying' the Optional Clause declarations but that has to be seen from a different perspective. As said above,[34] Fernandes suggested what became the Optional Clause mostly because he thought that, unlike the Statute, a provision for compulsory jurisdiction would require a separate ratification. Still in the last discussion of the Statute of the Permanent Court Negulesco maintained that only the Optional Clause and not the Statute required ratification. Also he based this assumption on the idea that compulsory jurisdiction would go beyond the provisions of the Covenant and would therefore require a separate ratification while the Statute could have been adopted by a resolution of the General Assembly.[35] In this context the term 'ratification' that they used has to be understood. It seems to express only that separate consent has to be given by the states and does not really say how it has to be expressed. This impression can furthermore be supported with the words of delegate Hagerup who said that states would be able accept the compulsory jurisdiction 'by means of a simple declaration'.[36] This sounds like the possibility to accede to the Optional Clause.

---

[30] League of Nations, *Records of the First Assembly, Plenary Meetings* 468.
[31] cp ibid 445; League of Nations, *Records of the First Assembly, Meetings of the Committees* 312.
[32] cp H Wundram, *Fakultativklausel* 14.
[33] G Enriques, 'Acceptation sans réciprocité' 836, fn 1 seems to suggest that all Optional Clause declarations require ratification.
[34] See sub-s II B i of ch 2 at 55.
[35] League of Nations, *Records of the First Assembly, Plenary Meetings* 454 (Negulesco).
[36] See sub-s II B i of ch 2 at 55.

ii. Diverse State Practice Under the Statute of the Permanent Court

The later state practice provides no clear picture in this regard. Some states like the Dominican Republic made their declarations explicitly 'subject to ratification'.[37] Others ratified their Optional Clause declarations even without having provided this requirement in the declaration.[38] Some states just deposited their declarations without ratification.[39] They regarded this as sufficient.[40] The Court acknowledged this latter practice in 1984 in the *Nicaragua* case when it considered Nicaragua's Optional declaration of 1929. This case was special as Nicaragua had ratified neither its signature of the Statute of the Permanent Court nor its Optional Clause declaration. In 1984 the United States argued that therefore Nicaragua's declaration had not been 'in force' as it entered the United Nations and hence was not subject to Article 36(5) of the Statute.[41] The Court followed this reasoning to a certain degree. It said that the Optional Clause declaration only had a 'certain potential effect' and 'has not yet taken the concrete form of a commitment having binding force'. For the Court the declaration had had no binding force yet as the Statute had not been ratified and Nicaragua had hence not been one of its Member States. Concerning the declaration itself the Court expressly said that it was not 'subject to ratification'. The ratification of the Statute of the Permanent Court would have been sufficient to let it enter into force.[42]

---

[37] See eg the still valid Optional Clause declaration of the Dominican Republic from 1924 and the declarations of Yugoslavia and Albania in PCIJ Series D No 6, 51–54. For a complete list see Alexandrov (n 6) 144.

[38] V Lamm, 'Declarations' 38; Wittmann (n 6) 179. See eg the declaration of Panama (ICJ Yearbook 1955–1956, 195).

[39] See eg the still valid declarations of Uruguay and of Panama from 1921 and of Nicaragua from 1929. For more see Wundram (n 32) 20.

[40] cp *Military and Paramilitary Activities in and against Nicaragua (Nicaragua v United States of America)* (n 3) para 27. Interestingly though, Nicaragua's Senate and Chamber of Deputies had decided that both 'Statute and protocol' of the Permanent Court should be ratified. Later Nicaragua informed the General Secretary of the League of Nations that the instrument of ratification for statute and protocol were forwarded (cp *Military and Paramilitary Activities in and against Nicaragua (Nicaragua v United States of America)* (Jurisdiction and Admissibility) Memorial (Nicaragua) paras 76 f; *Military and Paramilitary Activities in and against Nicaragua (Nicaragua v United States of America)* (n 2) para 50). The term 'protocol' here has to be understood, however, as referring to the protocol of signature of the statute and not the other additional protocol (cp *Military and Paramilitary Activities in and against Nicaragua (Nicaragua v United States of America)* (Provisional Measures) [1984] ICJ Rep 169, paras 14, 17; *Military and Paramilitary Activities in and against Nicaragua (Nicaragua v United States of America)* (n 3) paras 25–27; *Military and Paramilitary Activities in and against Nicaragua (Nicaragua v United States of America)* (n 40) para 83; *Military and Paramilitary Activities in and against Nicaragua (Nicaragua v United States of America)* (n 2) paras 51, 55 and especially Annex 35).

[41] *Military and Paramilitary Activities in and against Nicaragua (Nicaragua v United States of America)* (n 2) paras 50–57. 150.

[42] *Military and Paramilitary Activities in and against Nicaragua (Nicaragua v United States of America)* (n 3) paras 25–27, 34. Likewise MO Hudson, *Permanent Court* 452. See also the later position of Oda who considered the Nicaraguan declaration as invalid because Nicaragua had not ratified 'the Protocol of Signature of the Statute' (S Oda, 'Reservations in the Declarations' 9 f).

It becomes clear that according to the Court only the ratification of the Statute was missing and not the ratification of the declaration. As for other accessions such ratifications are only required when an Optional Clause declaration itself provides so.[43] Having in mind what has been said on accessions made subject to ratification in general,[44] such Optional Clause declarations can likewise be regarded as a letter of intent while the other declarations are themselves sufficient to trigger the legal consequences.[45]

iii. The Current Statute and the Now Consistent State Practice

The new Optional Clause is not different in this respect. As it seems that the coexistence of the additional protocol and Article 36(2) of the Statute had no influence on the question at hand anyway, the disappearance of the two protocols does not change the result found so far.[46] That Article 36(4) of the Statute now contains a provision for the deposition and the further transmission of Optional Clause declarations does not influence the result that states can simply accede to the Optional Clause by a simple declaration either. Also in ensuing state practice almost no state anymore included a reservation concerning ratification into their Optional Clause.[47] The vast majority of states simply made one single declaration and never ratified it. Similarly, the Court held that everything that is required is a clear manifestation of the intention to recognise as compulsory the jurisdiction of the Court under the terms of the Optional Clause.[48] At least today it is therefore common opinion that the ratification of an Optional Clause declaration is not necessary.[49]

---

[43] cp also Farmanfarma (n 10) 67; Hudson (n 42) 452; ICJ Yearbook 1946–1947, 207, fn 2; ICJ Yearbook 1971–1972, 61, fn 1; ICJ Yearbook 2002–2003, 159, fn 1; PCIJ, Series E No 1, 359, fn 1; Wundram (n 32) 15. Whether Nicaragua agreed to accede to the new Optional Clause via Art 36(5) of the Statute as it joined the United Nations is another question. For that see eg: *Military and Paramilitary Activities in and against Nicaragua (Nicaragua v United States of America)* (n 3) paras 28–35; separate opinion of Judge RY Jennings, *ICJ Rep 1984*, 536–40; *Military and Paramilitary Activities in and against Nicaragua (Nicaragua v United States of America)* (n 40) paras 10–27, 178; *Military and Paramilitary Activities in and against Nicaragua (Nicaragua v United States of America)* (n 2) paras 58–94; Lamm (n 38) 39 f; Oellers-Frahm (n 6) 245; Reisman (n 5) 131 f.

[44] See sub-s II A of ch 3 at 88.

[45] cp also Hudson (n 42) 452; JHW Verzijl, 'Optional Clause' 603 f. In line with this states were able to withdraw from the Optional Clause until the ratification of their declarations if the declaration required it. For more on this see sub-s II C i a of ch 6 at 292.

[46] For the disappearance of the protocols see sub-s II B ii of ch 2 at 59.

[47] cp Alexandrov (n 6) 144; Lamm (n 38) 37.

[48] See the references in n 232 of ch 2.

[49] See eg Alexandrov (n 6) 144; Farmanfarma (n 10) 66; F Gharbi (n 4) 262, 472; Kolb (n 5) 456–59; Maus (n 17) 63, 107; Verzijl (n 45) 603 f; Wittmann (n 6) 154.

iv. Result

Schwelb is right in saying that one single declaration is sufficient to become bound. But there is no difference to accessions to a multilateral treaty. As far as it is possible to make accessions subject to ratification to show a state's intention under these treaties, the same is also possible under the Optional Clause. Anyway, it seems as if Optional Clause declarations subject to ratification disappear as accessions subject to ratification disappear in general treaty law.[50]

C. The Deposition of the Optional Clause Declarations

The subsequent question is whether the deposition and the registration of the Optional Clause declarations are somehow particular. Since the creation of the Optional Clause the declarations have been deposited with the General Secretary of the League of Nations, respectively the Secretary-General.[51]

Even though there seem to have been no problems in this regard before,[52] the drafters of the Statute provided a rule for the deposition of Optional Clause declarations in the newly introduced Article 36(4) of the Statute. The *travaux préparatoires* contain no debate on this amendment and simply say that it was adopted.[53] The new paragraph provides that Optional Clause declarations 'shall be deposited with the Secretary-General of the United Nations who shall transmit copies thereof ... to the Registrar of the Court'.

Optional Clause declarations therefore have to be deposited with the Secretary-General to make them effective.[54] The Secretary-General registers them like treaties and international agreements according to

---

[50] For the latter see Hoffmeister (n 23) para 10.

[51] Alexandrov (n 6) 12; RP Anand, *Compulsory Jurisdiction* 143; Maus (n 17) 60; CHM Waldock, 'Decline' 251 f.

[52] S Rosenne and Y Ronen, *Practice 1920–2005* 724 f. The General Secretary of the League of Nations published the Optional Clause declarations according to Art 18 of the Covenant as belonging to the category of 'international engagement or acts by which nations or their governments intend to establish legal obligations between them and another State, nation or government' (see eg LNTS, Volume 1 (1920) 8). Hudson's position that there have been problems will be considered with regard to the second part of Art 36(4) of the Statute (sub-s III C ii of ch 3 at 104).

[53] United Nations, *Conference on International Organization, Volume XIII—Commission IV, Judicial Organization* 276, 284.

[54] *Case concerning the Right of Passage over Indian Territory (Portugal v India)* (Preliminary Objections) [1957] ICJ Rep 125, 146; Farmanfarma (n 10) 67 f; E Hambro, 'Compulsory Jurisdiction' 141; Rosenne and Ronen (n 52) 725; R Szafarz, *Compulsory Jurisdiction* 65; F Wittmann (n 6) 137.

Article 102(1) of the Charter.[55] Furthermore, the declarations are published in the daily *Journal of the United Nations*.[56] In total it can be said that the procedure including the Secretary-General is similar to that for other treaties.[57]

In the second step provided for by Article 36(4) of the Statute the declarations are forwarded to the Registrar of the Court. Then they are also published in the Court's Yearbook.[58] There is no difficulty with that part of Article 36(4) of the Statute. The most debated and also the central issue of this chapter is whether Optional Clause declarations additionally have to be forwarded to the states in order to become effective. This issue will be examined more closely in the following sub-section.

III. THE MOMENT DECLARATIONS ENTER INTO FORCE

Alexandrov wrote that the Optional Clause system was unlike a treaty because states having submitted an Optional Clause declaration were in a different position than states having acceded to a treaty. For him states having made an Optional Clause declaration were in a much more vulnerable and insecure position as they did not know which other states would also submit a declaration and thereby enable themselves to file an application against the state. Under the Optional Clause the declarations enabled the declaring state to file an application immediately after it had submitted it. The Member States of a treaty on the other hand already knew who

[55] Alexandrov (n 6) 12; Anand (n 51) 143; HW Briggs, 'Reservations' 245; Waldock (n 51) 252. See eg UNTS, Volume 1 (1946–1947) 3–13; UNTS, Volume 1581 (1990) 167–71. The fact that inside the UNTS the Optional Clause declarations are not published in the annexes which contain inter alia 'ratifications' and 'accessions' has no consequences as the United Nation's Secretariat clearly states that the registration of an instrument 'does not imply a judgment by the Secretariat on the nature of the instrument' (see eg UNTS, Volume 1581 (1990) XIV and also R Caddell, 'Registration' para 11). Interestingly though, unlike the Optional Clause declarations, their withdrawals are registered in the annexes (cp UNTS, Volume 265 (1957) XIV, 391; UNTS, Volume 257 (1957) 360).

[56] Rosenne and Ronen (n 52) 730. These publications are no means of general distribution because they are only used as day work programmes for the United Nations headquarters in New York (ibid 730). According to Judge Weeramantry states could not be required to observe all the journals because this task surmounted the capacities of some states' missions (Dissenting opinion of Judge CG Weeramantry, *ICJ Rep 1998*, 363). However, the Court took the publication of the declarations in the Journal of the United Nations into consideration as it considered Cameroon's knowledge and the issue of good faith in the *Bakassi Peninsula* case (*Land and Maritime Boundary between Cameroon and Nigeria (Cameroon v Nigeria: Equatorial Guinea intervening)* (Preliminary Objections) [1998] ICJ Rep 275, para 40). Judge Koroma questioned this approach because the Court did, among other things, not make clear what the influence of the journal was (dissenting opinion of Judge AG Koroma, *ICJ Rep 1998*, 386).

[57] Alexandrov (n 6) 12 f; Briggs (n 55) 245; Lamm (n 38) 46; Waldock (n 51) 251 f. But nonetheless at least one unilateral declaration has already been registered under Art 102 of the Charter (see the Egyptian declaration of April 24, 1957 in UNTS, Volume 265 (1957) 299).

[58] Lamm (n 38) 26. See eg ICJ Yearbook 1959–1960, 233.

the other party or parties of their treaty were.[59] The question is whether such a difference exists.

The problem that states cannot foresee how their relationships to other states will develop exists under the Optional Clause as it exists under other treaties. The argument that there is particular insecurity can therefore only be based on the way new states can accede to the Optional Clause by making a new Optional Clause declaration. The majority of judges in the Court and the majority of authors held that under the Optional Clause states can immediately file an application after they deposited their declaration.[60] The following sub-section will support this position. It will, however, also show that the rules for the Optional Clause are not different to the law regarding declarations of accession to a multilateral treaty.

Under the Optional Clause, the discussion of this subject is closely related to the discussion of what is called the 'sitting duck' problem, which is why it will also be dealt with here.

A. The 'Sitting Duck' Problem and the Retroactivity of Optional Clause Declarations

The already mentioned 'sitting duck' problem is the name of a certain phenomenon under the Optional Clause which is largely considered negative.[61] The Legal Adviser of the United States' Department of State Sofaer, for example, named it as one reason for the withdrawal of the United States' Optional Clause declaration in 1985. He considered it as 'one of the principle disadvantages to the system of compulsory jurisdiction under article 36(2)'.[62]

The problem is based on the simple and undisputed fact that states which have made an Optional Clause declaration cannot file an application against states which have not made such a declaration while the latter can make their declaration—with the words of Article 36(2) of the Statute—'at any time' and thereby create the opportunity to file application as soon as it is appropriate for them and they want to file an application. Those states therefore have the possibility to enter the Optional Clause ad hoc for opportunistic reasons.[63] Gharbi argued against this that this possibility carries no weight as bad faith cannot be presumed.[64]

---

[59] Alexandrov (n 6) 14 f. cp also SA Alexandrov, 'Reservations' 105–08.
[60] See eg Farmanfarma (n 10) 67 f; Gharbi (n 13) 257; JG Merrills, 'Optional Clause Today' 101; Tomuschat (n 1) paras 78 f. For the jurisprudence see sub-s III E of ch 3 at 113.
[61] The 'sitting duck problem' has already been mentioned in s I of the introduction at 2.
[62] AC Arend, *Compulsory Jurisdiction* 220 (Sofaer). See also Reisman (n 5) 94.
[63] cp A D'Amato, 'Modifying' 387; H de Fumel, *Les réserves* 13; Maus (n 17) 148; FL Morrison, 'Potential Revisions' 57; Waldock (n 51) 280–82.
[64] Gharbi (n 4) 450.

However, state practice already showed that at least in four cases Optional Clause declarations have been made to be able to file an application shortly afterwards.[65] Therefore, the problem is also of practical importance.[66]

The problem would not exist if the Optional Clause declarations did not work retroactively and could not cover disputes prior to their entry into force. In the early days of the Optional Clause this was disputed. According to Farmanfarma for example the Optional Clause declarations generally do not cover prior disputes. Only those which are made 'unconditionally' did so. He supported this with a reference to the *Mavrommatis* case.[67] There the Permanent Court said that in case of doubt jurisdiction based on an international agreement only covers 'all disputes referred to it after its establishment'.[68] However, there are different aspects which may not be confused.[69] There is one time frame relating to the moment the dispute arises and another time frame for the moment an application can be filed. Regarding what the Permanent Court also said it seems much more likely that the limitation 'after its establishment' relates only to the moment the application is filed and not the moment in which the dispute arises. Concerning the latter aspect the Court made especially clear that earlier disputes, too, are covered in cases of doubt. It emphasised that states make limitations where they want to exclude this rule and considers this as a confirmation of the rule found.[70] This corresponds to state practice under the Optional Clause as many states made reservations excluding the retrospective application of their Optional Clause declarations.[71] Furthermore, the presumed retroactivity is also supported by the jurisprudence of the Court. The Court affirmed its jurisdiction in cases in which the reservations excluding prior disputes did not apply.[72] Today it is therefore common opinion that Optional Clause declarations work retroactively if the declaring state uses no reservation.[73] To a certain degree this is contrary to the presumption of non-retroactivity in Article 28 VCLT. However, there is no difference to other treaties establishing the jurisdiction of the Court.[74]

---

[65] See sub-s II B of ch 1 at 26.

[66] But see Tomuschat (n 1) para 79.

[67] Farmanfarma (n 10) 71.

[68] *Mavrommatis Palestine Concessions (Greece v United Kingdom)* (Jurisdiction) PCIJ Series A No 2 5, 35.

[69] cp A Mahiou, 'Article 24' para 18; Rosenne and Ronen (n 52) 562–67, 751–53; A Yankov, 'Les réserves' 591.

[70] cp *Mavrommatis Palestine Concessions (Greece v United Kingdom)* (n 68) 5, 35.

[71] cp Alexandrov (n 6) 142 f; M Rotter, 'Art 36 Abs 2 des Statuts' 635. For the problem with this argumentation in general see sub-s III D ii of ch 3 at 111.

[72] See eg *Interhandel Case (Switzerland v United States of America)* (Preliminary Objections) [1959] ICJ Rep 6, 20–23, 29 f.

[73] Alexandrov (n 6) 40; R Bernhardt, 'Gegenseitigkeitsprinzip' 623; C Debbasch, 'La compétence' 242 f; de Fumel (n 63) 8, 10; Maus (n 17) 82; Ténékidès (n 6) 724; HWA Thirlway, 'Reciprocity' 121–25; C Vulcan, 'La Clause Facultative' 36; Yankov (n 69) 591.

[74] See the already mentioned judgment in the *Mavrommatis* case (*Mavrommatis Palestine Concessions (Greece v United Kingdom)* (n 68) 5, 35 f). cp also Rosenne and Ronen (n 52) 563 f.

Nonetheless, due to the general retroactivity of Optional Clause declarations the 'sitting duck' problem exists and it can be said that it is no good advertisement for the Optional Clause.[75] If the making of an Optional Clause declaration puts the declaring states into a weaker position in relation to those states not having made such a declaration it obviously reduces the motivation to make long lasting declarations. Even though the possibility to bring an application against a 'sitting duck' is also an incentive to make a declaration, in the long run such an approach leads to a situation in which all states, in the language of treaties, want to accept but not to offer. This holds especially true when newcomer states can file their applications immediately after they have made their Optional Clause declaration. Between the Member States of the Optional Clause it is no problem if states are able to file applications against each other whenever they want to because it is a right they grant each other. All states alike profit from their choice and the legal security their declarations grant them. States not having made an Optional Clause declaration or only a very restricted one do not grant other states such a possibility. In this regard, states without an Optional Clause declaration are in a particularly advantageous position.

B. The Accession to a Multilateral Treaty in General Treaty Law

The question is how general treaty law handles this problem and what it normally provides for the entry into force of accessions submitted to a depositary.

i. Articles 16, 24 and 78 VCLT

Today, basically Article 78 VCLT deals with the time period between the reception of notice by the depositary and the reception of the depositary's notice by other states and establishes certain principles.[76] In general, declarations are not considered as received by another state if they are only received by the depositary,[77] as depositaries can generally not

---

[75] cp Maus (n 17) 196.

[76] R Daoudi, 'Article 78' para 6. The problem with the time between the deposit of the declaration with the Secretary-General and the reception by a state may, however, minimise if the secretary continues to send emails on the day he receives a new declaration or treaty (cp Aust (n 11) 140; Tomuschat (n 1) para 79). In the *Bakassi Peninsula* case, however, it took 11.5 months between the deposition of an Optional Clause and the reception of the Secretary-General's notice by Nigeria (see sub-s III F of ch 3 at 116).

[77] ILC 'Documents of the Second Part of the 17th Session and of the 18th Session Including the Reports of the Commission to the General Assembly' (1966) UN Doc A/CN.4/SER.A/1966/Add.l 270 f, paras 3 f; Daoudi (n 76) para 6.

be considered as the agents of states.[78] According to Article 78(c) VCLT declarations only become effective after other states have received it.[79] However, as the article establishes only principles it only applies '[e]xcept as the treaty or the present Convention otherwise provide'.

For declarations establishing consent between the states Article 16 VCLT provides three ways by which the consent to be bound to a treaty may be expressed. It is therefore *lex specialis* for Article 78 VCLT.[80] According to Article 16(b) VCLT, 'instruments of ratification, acceptance, approval or accession establish the consent of a State to be bound by a treaty upon ... their deposit with the depositary'. Article 24(3) VCLT adds: 'When the consent of a State to be bound by a treaty is established on a date after the treaty has come into force, the treaty enters into force for that State on that date'. The reception of the declaration establishing consent by another state is not necessary under these provisions.[81] Concerning this provision the ILC expressly stated:

> [T]he act of deposit will be sufficient by itself to establish a legal nexus between the depositing State and any other State which has expressed its consent to be bound by the treaty. The depositary has the duty to inform the other States of the deposit but the notification, under existing practice, is not a substantive part of the transaction by which the depositing State establishes legal relations with them under the treaty.[82]

---

[78] ILC 'Documents of the Second Part of the 17th Session and of the 18th Session Including the Reports of the Commission to the General Assembly', ibid 271, para 4. For a construction based on such an assumption see Kolb (n 5) fn 1145.

[79] cp also O Elias and C Lim, 'Right of Passage Doctrine' 239.

[80] Daoudi (n 76) paras 12 f; F Horchani and Y Ben Hammadi, 'Article 16' para 17. cp also ILC 'Documents of the Second Part of the 17th Session and of the 18th Session Including the Reports of the Commission to the General Assembly' (n 77) 271, para 7. See especially the clear ruling by the Court in *Bakassi Peninsula* case (*Land and Maritime Boundary between Cameroon and Nigeria (Cameroon v Nigeria: Equatorial Guinea intervening)* (n 56) 293. cp also Lamm (n 38) 44). Art 102(1) of the Charter has no influence in this regard as it only removes the bar imposed on an agreement by Art 102(2) of the Charter and does not refer to other requirements (*Land and Maritime Boundary between Cameroon and Nigeria (Cameroon v Nigeria: Equatorial Guinea intervening)* (Preliminary Objections) Oral Proceedings (CR 1998/5) (Nigeria) 19 f (Watts) against *Land and Maritime Boundary between Cameroon and Nigeria (Cameroon v Nigeria: Equatorial Guinea intervening)* (Preliminary Objections) Oral Proceedings (CR 1998/3) (Cameroon) 36–38, paras 13–17 (Simma)).

[81] Elias and Lim (n 79) 239; Daoudi (n 76) para 13; F Hoffmeister, 'Article 16' para 10; Horchani and Ben Hammadi, ibid, paras 18, 22. See also the proposed change by Rosenne which had not been adopted (ILC 'Documents of the First Part of the 17th Session Including the Report of the Commission to the General Assembly' (1965) UN Doc A/CN.4/ SER.A/1965/Add.l 73).

[82] ILC 'Documents of the Second Part of the 17th Session and of the 18th Session Including the Reports of the Commission to the General Assembly' (n 77) 271, para 7. cp also ibid 201, para 3: '[T]he existing general rule clearly [was] that the act of deposit by itself establishes the legal nexus'.

The International Law Commission (ILC) elaborated this inter alia from the judgment concerning the Optional Clause in the *Right of Passage* case.[83] The rule can be supported with the position that, as the declaring state does not have to concern itself with the question of whether the depositary fulfils its duties, the state's position may not depend on the action or the inaction of the depositary.[84]

According to Judge Koroma there is a development in treaty law towards the idea that a certain amount of time is required before a treaty becomes effective.[85] Indeed especially treaties establishing international organisations and human rights treaties contain corresponding provisions.[86] Such a tendency has, however, already been recognised by the ILC in 1966. It nonetheless

> concluded that it would be inappropriate to introduce *de lege ferenda* the concept of such a time-lag into the article as a general rule, and that it should be left to the negotiating States to insert it in the treaty as and when they deemed it necessary.[87]

As Article 16 VCLT makes clear at its beginning it is up to the states to provide otherwise in their treaties. With such flexibility Article 16 VCLT is still today considered as being customary law.[88]

ii. The Entry Into Force of an Accession Accompanied by a Reservation

The formulation of reservations, however, might make a difference. In general, it is common opinion that even ratifications with reservations count immediately as a full ratification if a treaty requires a minimum number of ratifications to enter into force.[89] The question is if this is also true for the effectiveness of the individual ratification or accession. Article 23(1) VCLT clearly provides: 'A reservation, an express acceptance of a reservation and an objection to a reservation must be formulated in writing and communicated to the contracting States and other States entitled

---

[83] Hoffmeister (n 81) para 5. cp ILC 'Documents of the Second Part of the 17th Session and of the 18th Session Including the Reports of the Commission to the General Assembly' (n 77) 201, para 3. For more on this judgment see also sub-s III E of ch 3 at 113.

[84] cp also F Ouguergouz, S Villalpando and J Morgan-Foster, 'Article 77' para 10.

[85] Dissenting opinion of Judge AG Koroma, *ICJ Rep* 1998, 380, 384. See also Elias and Lim (n 79) fn 35.

[86] Horchani and Ben Hammadi (n 80) paras 36, 39. See eg Art 9(1) of the optional protocol to the CCPR ('three months').

[87] ILC 'Documents of the Second Part of the 17th Session and of the 18th Session Including the Reports of the Commission to the General Assembly' (n 77) 210, para 5.

[88] cp Hoffmeister (n 81) para 5; Horchani and Ben Hammadi (n 80) paras 4–6, 39.

[89] ILC 'Report of the International Law Commission on the Work of Its 62nd Session' (3 May–4 June and 5 July–6 August 2010) UN Doc A/65/10 127–29; Aust (n 11) 140, 153 f.

to become parties to the treaty'.[90] For Ruda, 'the procedure regarding reservations should necessarily be analogous to the procedure for the conclusion of treaties'.[91] According to Ben Hammadi and Horchani, declarations containing a reservation only enter into force after at least one other state has accepted the reservation or at least not objected within the time period specified by Article 20(5) VCLT. Only declarations without a reservation enter into force immediately according to Article 16(b) VCLT.[92]

One of the early versions of the VCLT provided that reservations and objections must be notified to the depositary if there is one.[93] These provisions have, however, later been omitted as the issue of the depositary was settled in Articles 76 to 78 VCLT.[94] With reference to the genesis of the articles Pellet and Schabas showed that it is 'beyond question that where there is a depositary, it is the initial recipient of communications by States concerning reservations. The depository bears the responsibility to notify other interested states'.[95] Nonetheless, for them the reservation has no effect until it is received by the state.[96]

Recently, the ILC addressed this issue in the Guide to Practice on Reservations to Treaties (GPRT). In Guideline 4.2.1 GPRT the ILC provided that the author of a reservation becomes a contracting state as soon as its reservation is established in accordance with Guidelines 4.1 to 4.1.3.[97] According to the mentioned Guideline 4.1 GPRT:

> A reservation formulated by a State … is established with regard to a contracting State … if it is permissible and was formulated in accordance with the required form and procedures, and if that contracting State … has accepted it.[98]

---

[90] This also corresponds to the new ILC's guideline 2.1.5 (cp ILC 'Report of the International Law Commission on the Work of Its 63rd Session' (26 April–3 June and 4 July–12 August 2011) UN Doc A/66/10/Add.1 6). See also C Walter, 'Article 23' para 8: 'It is evident that a reservation, once it has been formulated, needs to be transmitted to those that might be affected by the reservation'.

[91] JM Ruda, 'Reservations' 193.

[92] Horchani and Ben Hammadi (n 80) paras 27, 29. cp also Elias and Lim (n 79) 240.

[93] ILC 'Documents of the First Part of the 17th Session Including the Report of the Commission to the General Assembly' (n 81) 53.

[94] A Pellet and W Schabas, 'Article 23' para 63; Walter (n 90) paras 8, 18. cp also Daoudi (n 76) para 7.

[95] Pellet and Schabas, ibid para 64.

[96] ibid para 65. cp ILC 'Documents of the Second Part of the 17th Session and of the 18th Session Including the Reports of the Commission to the General Assembly' (n 77) 270 f, paras 4, 6.

[97] cp ILC 'Report of the International Law Commission on the Work of Its 63rd Session' (n 90) 22. Guideline 4.2.3 further makes clear that this rule also applies as far as the entry into force *inter partes* is concerned (ibid 23: 'The establishment of a reservation constitutes its author a party to the treaty in relation to contracting States and contracting organizations in respect of which the reservation is established if and when the treaty is in force'.).

[98] ibid 21.

Guideline 4.1.1 GPRT adds:

> A reservation expressly authorized by a treaty does not require any subsequent acceptance by the other contracting States ..., unless the treaty so provides. A reservation expressly authorized by a treaty is established with regard to the other contracting States ... if it was formulated in accordance with the required form and procedures.[99]

Therefore, the entry into force of an accession with a reservation also depends on whether that reservation is expressly authorised by the treaty. If it is not authorised the state becomes a party of the treaty only after at least one other state has accepted its reservation or one year has passed without an objection.[100] This makes sense as the reservation can be considered as an offer to the other states which they still have to accept.[101] However, if the reservation is authorised, the acceptance of the other state is not required anymore and therefore these reservations are established at the moment they are made.[102] They only need to be formulated to become established and as soon as they are established the author becomes a party of the treaty.[103] For these reservations the status of being 'formulated' immediately results in the status of being 'made'.[104] For the other cases a certain delay is justified as it is the states' own decision to make the reservation. Furthermore, it can be also backed with Article 20(4)(c) VCLT according to which a declaration with a reservation requires the reservation's acceptance to become effective.[105] According to the Inter-American Court of Human Rights (IACtHR) this is different for treaties which do not establish reciprocal rights and obligations. Such treaties, as for example human rights treaties, entered into force immediately even though they were made with reservations and other states still had to decide upon them.[106] However, as the Optional Clause establishes reciprocal rights

---

[99] ibid 22. This guideline, however, does not refer to implicitly authorised reservations (ILC 'Report of the International Law Commission on the Work of Its 62nd Session' (n 89) 117). For more on expressly authorised reservations and the Optional Clause see sub-s V B ii of ch 5 at 266.

[100] ILC 'Report of the International Law Commission on the Work of Its 62nd Session' (n 89) 129 f; C Walter, 'Article 20' paras 44–46. cp also *The Effect of Reservations on the Entry Into Force of the American Convention on Human Rights (Arts 74 and 75)*, Advisory Opinion, IACtHR Series A No 2 (1982) para 34.

[101] For the latter see Pellet and Schabas (n 94) para 93. cp also Walter, ibid paras 7 f and see furthermore ILC 'Report of the International Law Commission on the Work of Its 62nd Session' (n 89) 114: 'Consent to the reservation is therefore a *sine qua non* for the reservation to be considered established and to produce its effects'.

[102] ILC 'Report of the International Law Commission on the Work of Its 62nd Session' (n 89) 116 f.

[103] ibid 130.

[104] ibid 117, fn 508.

[105] ibid 129 f; Walter (n 100) para 46.

[106] *The Effect of Reservations on the Entry Into Force of the American Convention on Human Rights (Arts 74 and 75)* (n 100) paras 33 f. See also R Bernhardt, 'Vorbehalte' 375; Horchani and Ben Hammadi (n 80) para 28.

and obligations,[107] this argumentation of the IACtHR needs no further consideration here.

If all this is applied to the Optional Clause, the Optional Clause declarations enter into force immediately if they contain no reservations or only those which have been expressly accepted earlier. Only if other states still have to accept a reservation, these states have to receive the Optional Clause declaration and it might take up to twelve months until it enters into force.[108]

Regarding the protection of 'sitting ducks' in general treaty law it becomes obvious that treaty law itself provides no period to protect states against new accessions. Like for expressly permissible reservations, treaty law seems to emphasise that states have previously allowed the new state to accede. Treaty law requires the drafters of a treaty to provide otherwise in the treaty itself if they want to change this and to protect the states which have acceded.[109]

C. Article 36 of the Statute

So it is crucial what the Optional Clause itself provides.

i. The Wording of Article 36(2) and Article 36(4) of the Statute

According to Article 36(2) of the Statute the states 'may at any time declare that they recognize as compulsory ipso facto and without special agreement … the jurisdiction of the Court'.

The 'at any time' clearly indicates that states are free to choose the moment they make their Optional Clause declaration. From this perspective there seems to be nothing wrong when they choose a moment which is advantageous for them. However, this 'at any time' only refers to the moment a declaration can be made and does not refer to the moment an Optional Clause declaration becomes effective.

However, the words 'ipso facto' could make a difference in this regard. Tomuschat argued that these words implied that no other steps than the making of the Optional Clause declaration are required and that it is therefore sufficient if the declaration is deposited with the Secretary-General.[110]

---

[107] See s II of ch 1 at 22.

[108] On the question whether the reservations under the Optional Clause still have to be accepted or have been accepted previously see s V of ch 5 at 263.

[109] The Arts 16, 24 and 78 of the VCLT only apply as far as the treaty does not provide otherwise (cp ILC 'Documents of the Second Part of the 17th Session and of the 18th Session Including the Reports of the Commission to the General Assembly' (n 77) 201, paras 2–4, 209 f, paras 1–3, 270 f, paras 2, 7; Hoffmeister (n 23) para 9; Horchani and Ben Hammadi (n 80) paras 7, 28 f, 34–39; A Aust, 'Article 24' para 4; Daoudi (n 76) para 11).

[110] Tomuschat (n 1) para 79. See also Kolb (n 5) 517.

Also the Court emphasised the words 'ipso facto' and held that every state having submitted a declaration had to be aware that at any time another state could submit a new declaration and invoke the jurisdiction of the Court under the Optional Clause.[111] Conversely, the Judges Chagla, Weeramantry and Badawi read the 'ipso facto' in Article 36(2) of the Statute in relation to the closely following words 'and without special agreement'.[112] This interpretation has the disadvantage that it would render the words 'ipso facto' meaningless besides the named following words and normally in case of doubt legal texts shall be read in a way that makes no part of it superfluous.[113] However, the question whether other states have to receive the Optional Clause declaration is like the question whether the declaration has to be deposited with the Secretary-General and both relate to the making of the declaration. In this regard it could be said that only if a declaration is made this results in the 'ipso facto' situation. Therefore, it is decisive to understand what 'declare' in Article 36(2) of the Statute means and requires.

The aforementioned Article 36(4) of the Statute could provide an answer to this. According to this paragraph the Optional Clause declarations 'shall be deposited with the Secretary-General of the United Nations, who shall transmit copies thereof to the parties to the Statute'.

This part of Article 36(4) of the Statute describes the common procedure for the accession to a multilateral treaty. The declarations are transmitted to the depositary who sends a notice to the state parties.[114] As established above, the first part of Article 36(4) of the Statute is constitutive for the entry into force of an Optional Clause declaration.[115] Therefore, it could be said that the second part of the paragraph, too, is mandatory and that a declaration only becomes effective when the Secretary-General has transmitted a copy to the parties of the Statute and the registrar of the Court.[116] There seems to be no reason to treat the two parts of Article 36(4) of the

---

[111] *Case concerning the Right of Passage over Indian Territory (Portugal v India)* (n 54) 146 f; maintained in *Land and Maritime Boundary between Cameroon and Nigeria (Cameroon v Nigeria: Equatorial Guinea intervening)* (n 56) 291. For the whole position of the Court see sub-s III E of ch 3 at 113.

[112] Dissenting opinion of Judge AH Badawi, *ICJ Rep 1957*, 170; dissenting opinion of Judge MAC Chagla, *ICJ Rep 1957*, 157; dissenting opinion of Judge CG Weeramantry, *ICJ Rep 1998*, 366 f.

[113] For the latter see sub-s I D of ch 4 at 133.

[114] For the common procedure see Horchani and Ben Hammadi (n 80) para 23.

[115] See sub-s II C of ch 3 at 93 and see especially Hambro who maintained that the requirement derived from Art 36(4) of the Statute and not from another source (Hambro (n 54) 141, fn 1). For this cp also *Case concerning the Right of Passage over Indian Territory (Portugal v India)* (n 54) 146; *Temple of Preah Vihear (Cambodia v Thailand)* (n 3) 31.

[116] cp dissenting opinion of Judge MAC Chagla, *ICJ Rep 1957*, 170: 'It is difficult to understand why, if the first part of Art 36(2) of the Statute is mandatory, the second part is not equally mandatory'. See also the dissenting opinion of Judge BA Ajibola, *ICJ Rep 1998*, 364 f; dissenting opinion of Judge CG Weeramantry, *ICJ Rep 1998*, 366 f.

Statute differently.[117] Of course Article 36(4) of the Statute puts the transfer of the copies in the hand of the Secretary-General who is no agent of the submitting state. But likewise he is no agent of the receiving state either and therefore the argument that no state should have a disadvantage from its inactivity works both ways.[118]

This suggests that Article 36(4) of the Statute contains two requirements for the entry into force of Optional Clause declarations and that the other states have to receive a new declaration before it can enter into force.[119]

ii. The Genesis of Article 36(2) and (4) of the Statute Allows No Clear Conclusion

The drafters of the Statute of the Permanent Court did not consider the introduction of a period of time to pass before an accession becomes effective. To a certain degree this is astonishing as they often referred to the 1907 The Hague Convention for the Pacific Settlement of International Disputes. Its Article 95 provided:

> The present Convention shall take effect, in the case of the Powers which were not a party to the first deposit of ratifications, sixty days after the date of the procès-verbal of this deposit, and, in the case of the Powers which ratify subsequently or which adhere, sixty days after the notification of their ratification or of their adhesion has been received by the Netherlands Government.

Regarding this precedent it seems as if the drafters deliberately omitted such a provision for the Optional Clause.

On the other hand, as mentioned above,[120] the drafters had only little time and focused mainly on the principle of compulsory jurisdiction and less on the Optional Clause's legal details. Nonetheless, it seems as if the drafters would have included a provision if they had known about it. When the Optional Clause was created delegate Fernandes emphasised that it was 'inadmissible for a State to accept the principle of compulsory jurisdiction without knowing exactly towards whom it accepted such obligation'.[121] As delegate Hagerup made clear the objection raised in this respect 'could easily be met'.[122] The final result of this exchange was only the 'condition of reciprocity' in Article 36(3) of the Statute. However,

---

[117] Dissenting opinion of Judge BA Ajibola, *ICJ Rep 1998*, 396 f, 402; dissenting opinion of Judge CG Weeramantry, *ICJ Rep 1998*, 364 f.

[118] For the General-Secretary not being an agent for one of the states see sub-s III B i of ch 3 at 97.

[119] cp also the dissenting opinion of Judge AH Badawi, *ICJ Rep 1957*, 157; dissenting opinion of Judge CG Weeramantry, *ICJ Rep 1998*, 366 f.

[120] See sub-s II B i of ch 2 at 55.

[121] See above n 85 of ch 1. See also Thirlway (n 73) 103; M Vogiatzi, 'Historical Evolution' 68.

[122] League of Nations, *Records of the First Assembly, Meetings of the Committees* 313 (Hagerup).

having in mind the words of Fernandes it seems as if the situation, where a state can never know whether in a particular moment it is already bound towards a new state with a new declaration, is contrary to the intention expressed by Fernandes and supported by Hagerup.

During the drafting of the Statute in 1945 the new Article 36(4) of the Statute which had been submitted by the Iranian delegation was discussed and approved but the discussion has not been reproduced.[123] Only shortly before the Iranian delegate had remarked that 'the Committee had not yet specified the organ to which accessions to the Statute should be addressed'.[124] He was not addressing the Optional Clause directly here but the Iranian proposal for the Optional Clause arrived only four days after that remark.[125] From this perspective it could be said that the Iranian delegate introduced Article 36(4) of the Statute to settle the question which organ should receive the declarations and not the question whether the states also have to receive them.

However, the subsequent proposal also included the transfer of copies to the states.[126] The decision of the whole Committee might show that this was at least not a totally irrelevant part as the Committee favoured the Iranian proposal to the second one submitted by the French delegation at the same instance as the Iranian delegation.[127] The French proposal was an additional phrase added to paragraph 3 which provided: 'This declaration shall be deposited with the Secretary-General of the United Nations'.[128] In this situation the Committee then voted for the Iranian amendment. At that stage the Committee already worked with high speed and there is no information on whether there was even a short debate.[129] In this regard it seems that little can be inferred from this. As the Court has already pointed out:

> The fact that a particular proposal is not adopted by an international organ does not necessarily carry with it the inference that a collective pronouncement is made in a sense opposite to that proposed. There can be many reasons determining rejection or non-approval.[130]

According to Judge Chagla however, there must have been a reason for the introduction of Article 36(4) of the Statute and the obvious reason is that some time should elapse between the making of the Declaration and the

---

[123] See the reference in n 53 of this ch. cp also Rosenne and Ronen (n 52) 724.
[124] United Nations, *Conference on International Organization, Volume XIII—Commission IV, Judicial Organization* 251.
[125] cp ibid 246, 251, 276.
[126] ibid 276.
[127] ibid 270, 279, 283 f.
[128] ibid 485.
[129] cp ibid 282.
[130] *Legal Consequences for States of the Continued Presence of South Africa in Namibia (South West Africa) notwithstanding Security Council Resolution 276 (1970)* (Advisory Opinion) [1971] ICJ Rep 16, para 69. See also O Dörr, 'Article 32' para 37.

filing of an application.[131] On the other hand and as mentioned above,[132] according to Hudson the introduction of the paragraph was 'only a detail of housekeeping' to dispel the uncertainties as to the formalities which had arisen under the Permanent Court.[133] Hudson does, however, not name these uncertainties. According to Rosenne he might have referred to Nicaragua's ratification of the Statute of the Permanent Court which had disappeared after it had passed the necessary national process.[134] This, however, does not seem to be something that the new Article 36(4) of the Statute could have prevented as Nicaragua, too, had already intended to send the document to the General Secretary of the League of Nations.[135] Furthermore, the uncertainty created by the coexistence of clause and additional protocol which might have required 'housekeeping' ended anyway. For Anand, Hudson's position 'seems to convey too narrow a conception of the effect of that provision because it also prescribes an essential step to be followed in the making of the declaration'.[136] Yet this, too, cannot be surely maintained as the little documentation of the drafting procedure in this regard does likewise not allow the certain conclusion that the new paragraph was not just a 'detail of housekeeping'.

What can, however, be said is that the drafters had not yet known of the states' later 'ambushes' as the first one happened roughly ten years later.[137] If they had known they might have provided another rule or would have attached another meaning to Article 36(4) of the Statute, if they had really intended it as Hudson maintained. But what the drafters were able to know about was the General Act of 1928. Article 44 (2) of the General Act provided that accessions only enter into force after a period of ninety days since the reception by the General Secretary of the League of Nations. That the drafters of the Optional Clause again did not adopt a corresponding provision strengthens the impression that they did not want such a period for it.

All in all, the genesis allows no clear conclusion for whether the Optional Clause declarations need to be forwarded to the states to become effective. Having in mind the words of Fernandes there is at most a slight support for the position demanding that the states receive it. In any case, there is no basis to argue that the drafters of the Optional Clause wanted to provide a fixed amount of time to pass before the declaration becomes effective.

---

[131] Dissenting opinion of Judge MAC Chagla, *ICJ Rep 1957*, 170.

[132] Sub-s II C of ch 3 at 93.

[133] MO Hudson, 'Twenty-Fourth Year' 34.

[134] Rosenne and Ronen (n 52) 725, fn 60.

[135] cp *Military and Paramilitary Activities in and against Nicaragua (Nicaragua v United States of America)* (n 2) paras 50–52.

[136] Anand (n 51) 151 f. cp also Hambro who maintained a similar position with regard to the first part of Art 36(4) of the Statute (Hambro (n 54) 141, fn 1).

[137] See sub-s II B of ch 1 at 26.

iii. Systematic Approach: Ad Hoc Jurisdiction is Already Provided
   by Article 36(1) of the Statute

As said above, Article 36(2) of the Statute is not supposed to be redundant to the first paragraph and unlike the jurisdiction ad hoc it shall provide long-term jurisdiction and not just jurisdiction for a particular dispute.[138]

This function of Article 36(2) of the Statute collides, at least to a certain degree, with the practice of states to accept the Optional Clause in the face of a certain dispute. Of course, it could be argued that even Optional Clause declarations which are made for a certain proceeding before the Court remain in force afterwards and continue being a source for long-term compulsory jurisdiction. But as Waldock has already rightly remarked it is possible that states make their Optional Clause declaration for such a short period that they lapse again before other states even have a chance to file an application.[139] This is even independent of the question whether states can make reservations which allow immediate withdrawals,[140] as the same result can be achieved with an Optional Clause declaration made for a fixed period of a few days. Such tactics seem to lack good faith. But up to now the Court has never denied its jurisdiction due to bad faith and there would also be no need to rely on such a vague principle if the Optional Clause is understood as not allowing states to establish jurisdiction ad hoc.

The result found so far does not support the conclusion that the Optional Clause provides a period of time to pass before a new declaration can enter into force. Even if for the establishment of such a rule the object and purpose of the treaty also have to be taken into consideration,[141] there is no sign for such a rule in either the wording or in the genesis of the Optional Clause. Nonetheless, hit-and-run tactics as presented in the previous paragraph would be altogether impossible if states had to receive a copy of an Optional Clause declaration before it could enter into force. With such an approach the otherwise only responding other state would know about the declaration and would at least be able to likewise file an application against the newcomer if the latter had not completely limited its declaration *ratione materiae* to the one issue presented by it. But even in such cases the possibility to provide ad hoc jurisdiction with an Optional Clause declaration would at least be limited by requiring the state with the new declaration to wait until the other state is informed. This approach is not barred by the result found above for the wording and the genesis of the Optional Clause.

---

[138] See sub-s I C iii of ch 1 at 17.
[139] Waldock (n 51) 281.
[140] On this issue see sub-ss III B iii c and iv–vii of ch 5 at 216 to 252.
[141] For that possibility see Horchani and Ben Hammadi (n 80) para 34.

iv. Result

Especially with this latter comparison to the ad hoc jurisdiction provided for under Article 36(1) of the Statute all in all it can be reasonably maintained that the Statute provides that states have to receive the declaration before it can enter into force.

D. State Practice

The result of the previous sub-section does, however, not need to be the final result. Among the law provided by treaties and customary law, there is no hierarchy.[142] Later customary law can derogate earlier treaty law.[143]

Furthermore, subsequent state practice can influence the interpretation of a treaty according to Article 31(3)(b) VCLT. Article 31(3) VCLT is customary international law.[144] 'Subsequent' according to Article 31(3) VCLT means that the practice is linked to the prior treaty and follows the moment in which the treaty text has been established.[145] The difference between interpretation according to Article 31(3)(b) VCLT and derogating customary law is that the latter leaves the border of possible results reached by interpretation.[146] The threshold for derogating customary law is therefore higher.[147] The elements of state practice taken into consideration are however the same.[148] For Article 31(3)(b) VCLT as well as for derogating customary law it is not necessary that all state parties of a treaty are actively involved in the practice.[149]

---

[142] HWA Thirlway, 'Sources' 109 f; W Graf Vitzthum, 'Rechtsquellen' paras 154 f. cp also ILC 'First Report on Formation and Evidence of Customary International Law' (17 May 2013) UN Doc A/CN.4/663 paras 34 f (Wood).

[143] ILC 'Report of the International Law Commission on the Work of Its 64th Session' (7 May–1 June and 2 July–3 August 2012) UN Doc A/67/10 126; ILC 'Formation and Evidence of Customary International Law (Memorandum by the Secretariat)' (14 March 2013) UN Doc A/CN.4/659 34; A Aust, 'Vienna Convention' para 20; J Klabbers, 'Amendment' para 16; Thirlway, ibid 110; ME Villiger, *Customary International Law* paras 309–13, 323–26, 354.

[144] ILC 'Report of the International Law Commission on the Work of Its 65th Session' (6 May–7 June and 8 July–9 August 2013) UN Doc A/68/10 14. For Art 31 and 32 VCLT in general see also the references in n 7 of ch 4.

[145] ILC 'Report of the International Law Commission on the Work of Its 65th Session', ibid 24 f; ILC 'First Report on Subsequent Agreements and Subsequent Practice in Relation to Treaty Interpretation' (19 March 2013) UN Doc A/CN.4/660 34 f (Nolte); G Hafner, 'Subsequent Agreements and Practice' 114, 119. cp also O Dörr, 'Article 31' para 80.

[146] Hafner, ibid 114–17. Left open in G Nolte, 'Introductory Report' 207.

[147] Hafner, ibid 114–17.

[148] Dörr (n 145) para 78.

[149] ILC 'Second Report on Subsequent Agreements and Subsequent Practice in Relation to Treaty Interpretation' (26 March 2014) UN Doc A/CN.4/671 59–70 (Nolte); ILC 'Report of the International Law Commission on the Work of Its 64th Session' (n 143) 125; Nolte (n 146) 192–95; Dörr (n 145) paras 83, 86 f; Villiger (n 143) paras 48–53.

It is sufficient that the passive parties are aware of the practice and accept it.[150]

Even if state practice does not meet either the threshold of customary law or of Article 31(3)(b) VCLT, it can still be considered as supplementary means of interpretation under Article 32 VCLT.[151]

i. State Practice Concerning the Entry into Force of Optional Clause Declarations

Under the Optional Clause, some states such as Cote d'Ivoire have expressly provided that their Optional Clause declarations become effective immediately when received by the Secretary-General. This could argue for the assumption that Optional Clause declarations without such a provision enter into force at a later moment.

However, there are also other appearances in state practice which suggest otherwise. In the history of the Optional Clause, there have been three applications which followed immediately after the deposit of an Optional Clause declaration.[152] As the relating pleadings before the Court showed, the behaviour of the three applicants had been accompanied by a corresponding *opinio iuris*.[153] Even the first applicant, Portugal, had been convinced that '[c]onformément à ce système, les déclarations faites sur pied de l'article 36, paragraphe 2, entrent en vigueur automatiquement dès leur dépôt au Secrétariat'.[154] Of the respondents only India and later Nigeria rejected the idea that they had already been obliged because of the new Optional Clause declaration. In 1957 Waldock argued for India that, even if it was the drafters' intention to let Optional Clause declarations enter into force immediately, then contemporary state practice required otherwise.[155]

---

[150] *Case concerning Kasikili/Sedudu Island (Botswana/Namibia)* (Judgment) [1999] ICJ Rep 1045, para 74; ILC 'Second Report on Subsequent Agreements and Subsequent Practice in Relation to Treaty Interpretation', ibid 55 (Nolte); Dörr (n 145) para 88; ME Villiger, *Commentary* para 22.

[151] ILC 'Subsequent Agreements and Subsequent Practice in Relation to Treaty Interpretation, Draft Conclusions 1–5' (24 May 2013) UN Doc A/CN.4/L.813 1; Nolte (n 146) 189; Villiger, ibid para 22.

[152] cp sub-s II B of ch 1 at 26.

[153] cp *Case concerning the Right of Passage over Indian Territory (Portugal v India)* (Preliminary Objections) Observations and Submissions (Portugal) paras 77–83; *Land and Maritime Boundary between Cameroon and Nigeria (Cameroon v Nigeria: Equatorial Guinea intervening)* (Preliminary Objections) Observations (Cameroon) paras 1.06–1.77. Yugoslavia did not need to address this issue as the respondents did not raise it anymore (for the latter see below in this section).

[154] *Case concerning the Right of Passage over Indian Territory (Portugal v India)*, ibid para 83.

[155] *Case concerning the Right of Passage over Indian Territory (Portugal v India)* (Preliminary Objections) Oral Proceedings (CR 1957) (India) 39 (Waldock). Shortly before, Waldock had emphasised that many states had used the term 'vis-à-vis de tout autre état' in the French originals of their Optional Clause declarations. For him this suggested that these states directed their declaration rather towards other states than to the Court (Waldock (n 51) 251. cp also EB Weiss, 'Reciprocity' 96).

However, with the exception of the position of Nigeria,[156] at least after Portugal's *Right of Passage* case state practice clearly argues against Waldock's position. In the year 2000 none of the states rejected the Court's jurisdiction in the *Use of Force* cases due to the short period of time having passed between the deposit of Yugoslavia's declaration and the filing of the application.[157] Only the states which had made a reservation to prevent such an application invoked these reservations.[158]

These latter reservations seem to be a strong reflection of an *opinio iuris* among the states. Since the *Right of Passage* case many states have adopted a reservation which protects them against such applications.[159] The standard form of such an Anti Ambush Clause excludes

> any dispute in respect of which any other Party to the dispute has accepted the compulsory jurisdiction of the International Court of Justice only in relation to or for the purpose of the dispute; or where the acceptance of the Court's compulsory jurisdiction on behalf of any other Party to the dispute was deposited or ratified less than twelve months prior to the filing of the application bringing the dispute before the Court.[160]

There have been slightly different alternatives to this standard clause. In its old Optional Clause declaration of 1988 Cyprus required that a corresponding declaration had to be made six months prior to the filing of the application.[161] Furthermore, there also existed a 'French version' of the clause which excluded disputes with states which had not yet made an Optional Clause declaration as the dispute arose.[162] In the history of the Optional Clause, 22 states have so far made an Optional Clause

---

[156] Nigeria's position will be further discussed with the jurisprudence at sub-s III E of ch 3 at 113.

[157] *Legality of Use of Force (Serbia and Montenegro v Belgium)* (Preliminary Objections) Memorial (Belgium) paras 235–314; *Legality of Use of Force (Serbia and Montenegro v Canada)* (Preliminary Objections) Memorial (Canada) paras 61–100; *Legality of Use of Force (Serbia and Montenegro v Netherlands)* (Preliminary Objections) Memorial (Netherlands) paras 4.1–4.13; *Legality of Use of Force (Serbia and Montenegro v Portugal)* (Preliminary Objections) Memorial (Portugal) paras 69–95.

[158] *Legality of Use of Force (Serbia and Montenegro v United Kingdom)* (Preliminary Objections) Memorial (United Kingdom) paras 4.1–4.48. For Spain cp *Legality of Use of Force (Yugoslavia v Spain)* (Provisional Measures) [1999] ICJ Rep 761, para 23.

[159] See also V Lamm, 'Reservations to Declarations' 127; Tomuschat (n 1) para 94.

[160] This example has been taken from the United Kingdom's and Northern Ireland's declaration of 5 July 2004. In this book only the second part containing the twelve months requirement will be referred to as the Anti Ambush Clause since the first part has never played a role yet (see furthermore the declaration of Poland which contains only the second part).

[161] ICJ Yearbook 1994–1995, 87. See also Alexandrov (n 6) 153, 164; JG Merrills, 'Clause Revisited' 220.

[162] Alexandrov (n 6) 153, 164; C Vignes, 'La nouvelle déclaration française' 71. Interestingly, Art 39(2)(a) of the General Act of 1928 already allowed states to exclude '[d]isputes arising out of facts prior to the accession of either to the Party making the reservation or of any other Party with whom the said Party may have a dispute'. See also the previous proposal by Waldock (n 51) 282.

declaration with an Anti Ambush Clause or a similar reservation protecting them against 'ambushes'.[163]

ii. In Light of the Requirements for Customary Law

The question, however, is if the named practice is sufficient to establish customary law under the Optional Clause.

This necessarily includes the question of who can establish customary law under the Optional Clause. Normally, states can create customary law relating to the application of a treaty among them. It is important for such derogation that the derogating countries are the countries which would be also empowered to expressly change the treaty.[164] It is no problem that basically only the states having made an Optional Clause declaration are the ones who establish customary law as they are generally also the states which could amend the Optional Clause.[165] Furthermore, according to Article 23(1) VCLT the reservations and the objections to reservations have to be communicated to the states entitled to become parties to the treaty as well.[166] These then also have the possibility to make objections which they have to confirm when they accede to the treaty in question.[167] And as already mentioned above, it is not necessary for customary law that all states actively participated in the practice. Their acquiescence is sufficient.[168]

The next question is the threshold for customary law. It may be recalled that the allegation of customary law contains the allegation that states are bound to rules to which they have not expressly consented. Therefore, customary international law may not be assumed too generously. The two constituent elements of customary law may neither be considered improperly nor be ignored.[169] Customary law may also not be established by selecting the behaviour of some actors of international law only. Customary law thus found is based on mere fiction.[170]

---

[163] See Annex 5. cp also Alexandrov (n 6) 153, 164.

[164] B Hofmann, *Beendigung* 108–10; Thirlway (n 142) 110. cp also Fitzmaurice (n 27) para 70.

[165] For this and the participation of the General Assembly see sub-s III A of ch 6 at 310.

[166] States which can accede have to be determined by reference to the treaty in question (Pellet and Schabas (n 94) para 53; Walter (n 90) para 10). With regard to Art 36(2) of the Statute these are all 'states parties to the present Statute'.

[167] cp Guidelines 2.6.3(2) and 2.6.11 GPRT (ILC 'Report of the International Law Commission on the Work of Its 63rd Session' (n 90) 12 f). cp also *Reservations to the Convention on the Prevention and Punishment of the Crime of Genocide* (Advisory Opinion) [1951] ICJ Rep 15, 30; Pellet and Schabas (n 94) paras 92–99; Walter (n 100) para 23. See also the consideration of this subject in ILC 'Report of the International Law Commission on the Work of Its 60th Session' (5 May–6 June and 7 July–8 August 2008) UN Doc A/63/10 189–93, paras 3–10.

[168] See references in fn 149 and fn 150.

[169] B Simma, 'Ungeschriebenes Völkerrecht' 96–102.

[170] M Herdegen, 'Dynamik des Völkerrechts' 905 f. For the ongoing discussion on the threshold for customary international law see ILC 'First Report on Formation and Evidence of Customary International Law' (n 142) paras 94–101.

Furthermore, in international law reservations sometimes establish provisions which already exist otherwise. This has to be taken into account when evaluating the relevance of state practice. Especially under the Optional Clause states have made reservations even if it had already been common opinion that they were unnecessary. Such reservations are, for example, all formulations expressing that the Optional Clause declaration shall only apply as far as other states have accepted the same obligation, because this is already provided for in the Statute.[171] Furthermore, many states have adopted a reservation protecting the field which is by international law their domestic jurisdiction even though it has been common opinion for a long time that these reservations are legally superfluous.[172] These two phenomena show that just the incorporation of a reservation into a declaration alone does not necessarily mean that the substance of the reservation would not exist without it.[173] This can also be the case for the Anti Ambush Clauses or those declarations providing for their immediate entry into force.

The prior paragraph underlines the importance of the establishment of the *opinio iuris* besides state practice.[174] The *opinio iuris* for the current issue can inter alia be established with the pleadings of the states before the Court presented in the previous sub-section. Pleadings of states are an expression of their legal opinion and can be used as one pillar of customary law.[175] To use the words of Brownlie, 'pleadings before the

---

[171] Alexandrov (n 59) 99 f; JA Frowein, 'Optional Clauses' 398; Gharbi (n 4) 445 f; Hudson (n 42) 465; Kolb (n 5) 461; Lamm (n 6) 51; Maus (n 17) 109–11; IFI Shihata, *Compétence de la Compétence* 149; Vulcan (n 73) fn 21; Waldock (n 51) 255; Wittmann (n 6) 600. Against this Enriques considered declarations without this reservation as being made *erga omnes* (Enriques (n 33) 835–37, supported by Farmanfarma (n 10) 49 f). Judge Ajibola furthermore distinguished between 'statutory reciprocity' and reciprocity named in Optional Clause declarations (Dissenting opinion of Judge BA Ajibola, *ICJ Rep 1998*, 394. See also the prior pleading in *Land and Maritime Boundary between Cameroon and Nigeria (Cameroon v Nigeria: Equatorial Guinea intervening)* (Preliminary Objections) Oral Proceedings (CR 1998/5) (Nigeria) 22 (Watts)).

[172] Alexandrov (n 6) 67 f; R Arnold, 'Fakultativklausel' 16–18; de Fumel (n 63) 15; JA Frowein, 'International Court' 162; Gharbi (n 4) 447 f; P Guggenheim, 'Der automatische Vorbehalt' 121; L Preuss, 'Connally Amendment' 660; Tomuschat (n 1) para 95; PC Ulimubenshi, *Domaine réservé* 110–13, 305 f; Verzijl (n 5) 400, 402; Walter (n 5) para 43. There are several opinions how to reach this result. One is eg that Art 2(VII) of the Charter already prohibits all United Nations' organs and therefore also the Court to interfere into domestic affairs.

[173] Gharbi and Kebbon even considered the reservations for other methods of peaceful settlement as superfluous (Gharbi (n 4) 446 f; N Kebbon, 'Optional Clause' 267). Kolb did the same for some 'reservation[s] of "recognition"' (Kolb (n 5) 471). cp also the inclusion of prior disputes in Suriname's Optional Clause declaration of 1987 and sub-s III A of ch 3 at 95.

[174] See also ILC 'Formation and Evidence of Customary International Law (Memorandum by the Secretariat)' (n 143) para 28 naming different reasons why state practice is not necessarily carried by a corresponding *opinio iuris*.

[175] ILC 'Second Report on Formation and Evidence of Customary International Law' (22 May 2014) UN Doc A/CN.4/672 para 75; ILA, Report of the Sixty Ninth Conference, London 14; J Henckaerts, 'Customary Humanitarian Law' 179; P Sands and J Peel, *Principles* 112. See also A Roberts, 'Power and Persuasion' 217–19 arguing for the use of pleadings as subsequent practice. Against the use of pleadings with regard to Art 31(3)(b) VCLT see *Gas Natural SDG, SA v Argentina* (Case No ARB/03/10) [2005] para 47, fn 12.

Court ... have value as comprehensive statements of the opinions of particular states on legal questions'.[176]

Therefore, the mentioned reactions of the defendant states in the *Use of Force* cases are also of relevance for the entry into force of Optional Clause declarations. As mentioned above, in these cases none of the ten defendant states argued that Optional Clause declarations submitted to the Secretary-General require some time or further receipt by other states before they enter into force. The eight states which were unable to invoke an Anti Ambush Clause simply accepted this aspect of the Court's jurisdiction. And also the two states which invoked their Anti Ambush Clauses did not present any further argumentation on this point. Taken together with the mentioned positions of the applicant states in the *Right of Passage* case, the *Bakassi Peninsula* case and the *Use of Force* cases, these reactions support the strong impression that at least today the states consider the Optional Clause declarations as entering into force immediately when received by the Secretary-General.

iii. Result

In total it can therefore be very well maintained that there is state practice and a corresponding *opinio iuris* which are able to change the result found above for the provisions of the Statute. If states make no reservations providing otherwise, new Optional Clause declarations are immediately applicable. The corresponding provision in the Optional Clause declaration of for example Cote d'Ivoire is therefore unnecessary.

E. The Jurisprudence in the *Right of Passage* and the *Bakassi Peninsula* Case

This result is also accordant with the Court's jurisprudence.[177] Already in its first judgment on this issue, in the *Right of Passage* case, the Court expressly maintained that Portugal's declaration became effective as soon as it had been deposited with the Secretary-General. According to the Court Article 36(4) did not require that the states receive a copy by the Secretary-General to let the Optional Clause declaration enter into force. For the Court only the first part of Article 36(4) of the Statute concerned the state and the legal effect of the declaration did not depend on

---

[176] I Brownlie, *Principles* 24. cp also HWA Thirlway, 'Law and Procedure' 43 saying with regard to pleadings: '... which means no more than that is the opinion of that State that such is the legal situation'.

[177] The Court's and some judges' positions on how to interpret the Statute have already been mentioned above (sub-s III C i of ch 3 at 102).

subsequent action or inaction of the Secretary-General. Neither did the Statute require that a declaration reached the other state to let it become effective, nor did it demand a certain amount of time to pass after the deposition.[178] According to the Court such a requirement introduced an element of uncertainty into the Optional Clause system.[179] This judgment has been widely supported or at least accepted in literature[180] and repeated by the Court as obiter dicta in the *Temple of Preah Vihear* and the *Nicaragua* case.[181] It has, however, also received the aforementioned criticism by the Judges Chagla, Weeramantry and Badawi.[182]

In the later *Bakassi Peninsula* case the Court had to decide on the issue again.[183] In this case the Court had to treat Nigeria's new argument that the law of treaties and especially its Article 78(c) had to be applied.[184] The Court noted that

> the regime for depositing and transmitting declarations of acceptance of compulsory jurisdiction laid down in Article 36, paragraph 4, of the Statute of the Court is distinct from the regime envisaged for treaties by the Vienna Convention. Thus the provisions of that Convention may only be applied to declarations by analogy.[185]

The Court continued and rejected Nigeria's argument 'in any event' because Articles 16 and 24 VCLT which had adopted the rationale of the

---

[178] *Case concerning the Right of Passage over Indian Territory (Portugal v India)* (n 54) 146 f. See also the summary in Lamm (n 38) 41 f.

[179] *Case concerning the Right of Passage over Indian Territory (Portugal v India)* (n 54) 146 f. See also *Land and Maritime Boundary between Cameroon and Nigeria (Cameroon v Nigeria: Equatorial Guinea intervening)* (Preliminary Objections) Oral Proceedings (CR 1998/6) (Cameroon) 19, para 9 (Sinclair).

[180] Alexandrov (n 6) 53; Lamm (n 38) 47 f; Maus (n 17) 56 f, 78, 82 f; Merrills (n 60) 101; Tomuschat (n 1) paras 78 f.

[181] *Temple of Preah Vihear (Cambodia v Thailand)* (n 3) 31; *Military and Paramilitary Activities in and against Nicaragua (Nicaragua v United States of America)* (n 3) para 25.

[182] Dissenting opinion of Judge AH Badawi, *ICJ Rep 1957*, 170; dissenting opinion of Judge MAC Chagla, *ICJ Rep 1957*, 157; dissenting opinion of Judge CG Weeramantry, *ICJ Rep 1998*, 366 f. See sub-s III C i of ch 3 at 102.

[183] This issue has not been addressed by the Court in the *Use of Forces* cases even though the former Yugoslavia filed its application only three days after the deposition of the Optional Clause declaration. The applications and the requests for interim measures have been dismissed for other reasons. See eg *Legality of Use of Force (Yugoslavia v Spain)* (n 158) paras 21–25; *Legality of Use of Force (Serbia and Montenegro v Belgium)* (Provisional Measures) [1999] ICJ Rep 124, paras 22–29 and cp Lamm (n 38) 45 f. Only Judge Oda addressed the 'ambush' by Yugoslavia and wanted to deny jurisdiction also for those cases in which the states had no Anti Ambush Clause as he thought it should make no difference that states have failed to include such a reservation. He based this on bad faith of Yugoslavia (separate opinion of Judge S Oda, *ICJ Rep 1999*, paras 8–16).

[184] *Land and Maritime Boundary between Cameroon and Nigeria (Cameroon v Nigeria: Equatorial Guinea intervening)* (Preliminary Objections) Oral Proceedings (CR 1998/1) (Nigeria) 23 (Watts); *Land and Maritime Boundary between Cameroon and Nigeria (Cameroon v Nigeria: Equatorial Guinea intervening)* (Preliminary Objections) Oral Proceedings (CR 1998/5) (Nigeria) 24 f (Watts). For Art 78 VCLT see sub-s III B of ch 3 at 97.

[185] *Land and Maritime Boundary between Cameroon and Nigeria (Cameroon v Nigeria: Equatorial Guinea intervening)* (n 56) para 30.

judgment of the *Right of Passage* case would have been applicable.[186] In the earlier pleadings, Simma had argued for Cameroon that the rationale of the Court's judgment in the *Right of Passage* case was 'a 'cornerstone' of the Optional Clause system and that it is essential that states cannot reconsider their position if another state files an application against them'.[187] On the other side, Watts argued for Nigeria:

> Cameroon upholds the merits of a system which allows for, and even encourages, the 'surprise' institution of proceedings before this Court against unsuspecting States; Nigeria upholds a system which allows for a genuine consensual approach to the Optional Clause system. Nigeria submits that there can be no doubt that it is the latter which has the better claim to represent the 'cornerstone' of the system.[188]

This latter argumentation by Watts has been supported by Judge Weeramantry according to whom such a solution 'would also give to States making such declarations the confidence that they will not be taken by surprise, thereby reinforcing their willingness to accept the Court's optional jurisdiction'.[189] In line with what has already been said above,[190] Judge Weeramantry did furthermore 'not think such results were within the contemplation of those who drafted the Statute of the Court, especially having regard to their particular concern with the question of communication, as reflected in the wording of the Article itself'.[191] As the other dissenting Judges Koroma and Ajibola, too, he additionally addressed the insecurity which was Cameroon's argument in the current case and the Court's argument in the *Right of Passage* case. For Judge Weeramantry, Cameroon and the Court had considered the insecurity only from the perspective of the states which submit a new declaration. For these states the early moment of the deposition provided a clear point of reference.[192] States already having made an Optional Clause declaration, on the other hand, always had to be insecure whether there was a new Optional Clause declaration which was effective and allowed other states to file an application.[193]

---

[186] *Land and Maritime Boundary between Cameroon and Nigeria (Cameroon v Nigeria: Equatorial Guinea intervening)* (n 56) paras 30 f.

[187] *Land and Maritime Boundary between Cameroon and Nigeria (Cameroon v Nigeria: Equatorial Guinea intervening)* (Preliminary Objections) Oral Proceedings (CR 1998/3) (Cameroon) 40, 43 f, para 42 (Simma).

[188] *Land and Maritime Boundary between Cameroon and Nigeria (Cameroon v Nigeria: Equatorial Guinea intervening)* (Preliminary Objections) Oral Proceedings (CR 1998/5) (Nigeria) 23 (Watts).

[189] Dissenting opinion of Judge CG Weeramantry, *ICJ Rep 1998*, 374.

[190] See sub-s III C ii of ch 3 at 104.

[191] Dissenting opinion of Judge CG Weeramantry, *ICJ Rep 1998*, 362.

[192] cp see also *Land and Maritime Boundary between Cameroon and Nigeria (Cameroon v Nigeria: Equatorial Guinea intervening)* (Preliminary Objections) Oral Proceedings (CR 1998/6) (Cameroon) 19, para 9 (Sinclair).

[193] Dissenting opinion of Judge AG Koroma, *ICJ Rep 1998*, 382, 388; dissenting opinion of Judge CG Weeramantry, *ICJ Rep 1998*, 375.

The states which submitted a new declaration knew about the ongoing process and could inquire when the copy of the declaration has already been transmitted.[194] The other states did not even know about the process.[195]

However, even though the dissenting judges presented some good arguments,[196] it has to be said that the Court has already ruled otherwise twice.[197] It has to be noted that for the Court the Optional Clause declarations enter into force already when they are deposited with the Secretary-General.

F. The Security Provided by Anti Ambush Clauses

The resulting question is whether this means that under the Optional Clause there really is a degree of uncertainty which distinguishes it from other treaties. As established above the Optional Clause does not provide any protection against 'ambushes' for states having made a declaration. The remedy seems to be the Anti Ambush Clauses which some states have already adopted and which even the Court promoted in the *Bakassi Peninsula* case.[198]

Regarding Alexandrov's position presented above,[199] the question is therefore to what extent states having made an Optional Clause declaration with an Anti Ambush Clause are still in a particularly vulnerable position and whether Anti Ambush Clauses can offer efficient 'protection' at all. Protection here is understood as allowing states with an Optional Clause declaration to evade disputes for which a newcomer state wants to use the Optional Clause as a source of jurisdiction ad hoc. Therefore, the protection granted by an Anti Ambush Clause essentially depends on

---

[194] Dissenting opinion of Judge BA Ajibola, *ICJ Rep 1998*, 397 f.

[195] For this position it can be added that with the position of the dissenting judges the delay caused by the transmission by the Secretary-General would be a disadvantage for the state which submits the new Optional Clause declaration. Thereby, the disadvantage is on the side of the state that is responsible for the fact that there has been no declaration before. Of course, according to Art 33(1) of the Charter states are free to choose their peaceful means of dispute settlement, but if they want to refer their disputes to the Court by using the Optional Clause, they should show a commitment which corresponds to that of the states which have already made an Optional Clause declaration.

[196] See also Elias and Lim (n 79) 234–44.

[197] cp also ILC 'Report of the International Law Commission on the Work of Its 55th Session' (5 May–6 June and 7 July–8 August 2003) UN Doc A/58/10 238.

[198] For the latter see *Land and Maritime Boundary between Cameroon and Nigeria (Cameroon v Nigeria: Equatorial Guinea intervening)* (n 56) para 45; *Land and Maritime Boundary between Cameroon and Nigeria (Cameroon v Nigeria: Equatorial Guinea intervening)* (Preliminary Objections) Oral Proceedings (CR 1998/3) (Cameroon) 39 f, paras 26–28 (Simma); *Land and Maritime Boundary between Cameroon and Nigeria (Cameroon v Nigeria: Equatorial Guinea intervening)* (Preliminary Objections) Oral Proceedings (CR 1998/6) (Cameroon) 19–22, paras 10–12, 16 (Sinclair). cp also Kolb (n 5) 518.

[199] See the introduction to s III of ch 3 at 94.

whether a state has the opportunity to withdraw its Optional Clause declaration in the face of the new declaration and the coming application.[200] Without this possibility the Anti Ambush Clause could just postpone the application.[201] The newcomer state could still adjust the wording and the timing of its declaration to establish compulsory jurisdiction for a certain chosen case. The state would just have to wait some months until it files its application.

In the *Bakassi Peninsula* case Judge Koroma wrote that even with 'a lapse of a reasonable time' between the deposition of the declaration and its entry into force states could not protect themselves due to the rationale of the *Nottebohm* case.[202] However, this depends on whether a state learns about the new Optional Clause declaration before the application is filed as the named rationale renders withdrawals ineffective only for proceedings which have already been instituted.[203] If a state has sufficient time to effect a withdrawal before proceedings can be instituted it can protect itself. The time which the Anti Ambush Clause needs to provide for effective protection therefore depends on the amount of time a notification by the Secretary-General generally takes and how long the period of notice for a withdrawal is.[204] The length of the first period, however, is mutable and can be as long as eleven and a half months as the *Bakassi Peninsula* case has shown.[205] Hence, a more secure way might be to attach the starting of the period provided not to the deposition of the declaration but to the reception of the notice by the reserving state.

However, the protection would still be incomplete if the Anti Ambush Clauses did not apply to cases where a state enlarges its obligations not by making a new declaration but by withdrawing a reservation.[206] Also this technique can be used by states to create ad hoc jurisdiction for a particular conflict. Malta for example withdrew a reservation in January 1981 to make sure that its Optional Clause declaration contains the dispute which was the object of the *Continental Shelf* case between Tunisia and Libya.[207] Similarly to the situation in which Malta had no Optional Clause declaration at all, up to that moment Tunisia and Libya had not been

---

[200] For that question see sub-ss III B iii c and vii of ch 5 at 216 and 252 and s II of ch 6 at 279.

[201] cp Merrills (n 161) 220 f; JA Pastor Ridruejo, 'The Spanish Declaration' 29 f, 31 f. See also sub-s III A of ch 3 above at 95.

[202] Dissenting opinion of Judge AG Koroma, *ICJ Rep 1998*, 390.

[203] cp *Nottebohm Case (Liechtenstein v Guatemala)* (Preliminary Objection) [1953] ICJ Rep 111, 122 f and above sub-s I C ii of ch 1 at 15.

[204] cp D'Amato (n 63) 388 f; Merrills (n 161) 220 f.

[205] *Land and Maritime Boundary between Cameroon and Nigeria (Cameroon v Nigeria: Equatorial Guinea intervening)* (n 56) para 22.

[206] For such withdrawals see s IV of ch 3 at 120.

[207] *Continental Shelf (Tunisia/Libyan Arab Jamahiriya)* (Application for Permission to Intervene) Application (Malta) para 25. cp ICJ Yearbook 1981–1982, 78 f and see also Merrills (n 161) 235 f.

able to file a corresponding application against Malta under the Optional Clause. It was in this respect also here Malta's choice whether the Court has compulsory jurisdiction.

Regarding the wording of the Anti Ambush Clauses so far only Portugal has drafted a clause also including 'amendments' while other states only referred to new declarations.[208] Maus wrote that the reservations of the latter cover no amendments as otherwise they would have been drafted like that.[209] Such a strict interpretation seems, however, to be contrary to the obvious intention of states to protect themselves against 'ambushes'.[210] For the reserving states it makes no difference whether a state makes a new Optional Clause declaration or just enlarges a previously made one.[211] In both cases the state with the broader commitment is likewise a 'sitting duck'. In light of this, all Anti Ambush Clauses therefore have to be interpreted as including also withdrawals of reservations.[212]

Hence, Anti Ambush Clauses allow states to protect themselves against any 'ambushes'. States only have to make sure that the period provided by their Anti Ambush Clause is sufficient to let them exclude the dispute in question in time from their Optional Clause declaration. After all that has been said it becomes clear that these reservations are not regrettable at all. They provide equality between states with and without an Optional Clause. With them there is no 'sitting duck' problem.[213] They even have an additional positive side effect as they have the potential to reduce the fluctuation of Optional Clause declarations. They are a small incentive for states not to reduce or withdraw their Optional Clause declaration because afterwards the state in question would have to wait until the periods of time in the other states' Anti Ambush Clauses have lapsed. Additionally, as D'Amato wrote, the clauses encourage states to 'file their declarations well in advance of a given dispute'.[214]

---

[208] See Portugal's 2005 reservation excluding 'any dispute with any State that has deposited or ratified the acceptance of the Court's compulsory jurisdiction *or an amendment thereto so that the dispute became included in its scope* less than twelve months prior to the filing of the application bringing the dispute before the Court' (emphasis added).

[209] Maus (n 17) 147 f. For Maus it also made a difference whether a state withdrew its declaration to submit a new one containing another reservation or whether that states just added the new reservation to its old declaration (ibid 186). According to Maus the Anti Ambush Clauses applied to the first case. See, however, the following n 212.

[210] ibid 148.

[211] For that see s IV of ch 3 at 120.

[212] FJ Garcia, *Jurisdicción Obligataria* 313. See also Merrills (n 161) 221 for declarations made by 'existing parties'. For the object and purpose of the Anti Ambush Clauses there is no need to apply them in the case where a state has reduced its commitment. This also holds in cases in which a state has withdrawn a declaration to immediately reintroduce it with a new reservation (but see FJ Garcia, ibid 313 f).

[213] For the 'sitting duck' problem see sub-s III A of ch 3 at 95.

[214] D'Amato (n 63) 387 f.

Conversely the criticism on the Anti Ambush Clauses hardly convinces. Gharbi regarded them as 'redoutable' as they reduce the scope covered by Optional Clause declarations.[215] Kebbon considered the possibility of states to react to new declarations as a 'serious impediment to the realisation of a comprehensive system for compulsory jurisdiction'. States should not 'be able to foresee and to control which disputes go to the Court'.[216]

Concerning this latter point it can already be said the Optional Clause itself necessarily allows all states which have not yet made an Optional Clause declaration to foresee and to control which disputes go to the Court. With the words of Article 36(2) of the Statute they can make their Optional Clause declarations at 'any time' and thereby choose times in which they want to bring a case for the Court. To allow states having made an Optional Clause to react to those new Optional Clause declarations simply provides those two groups with the same footing. As referred to above,[217] allowing states to use the Optional Clause for jurisdiction ad hoc can hardly be considered as accordable with a system of compulsory jurisdiction either. Additionally, allowing states to react to new Optional Clause declarations does furthermore not anticipate the question whether they can do so in cases where both states have already accepted compulsory jurisdiction.[218] Concerning the position of Gharbi it can be said that the alternative to the reduction of the scope of the Optional Clause declarations would be inequality between the states with and without Optional Clause declaration. This inequality incites states not to make an Optional Clause declaration, so that there might be even less compulsory jurisdiction because states do not make a declaration at all.[219]

G. Result

The above arguments suggest that the Optional Clause had originally required that states receive the notification provided for in Article 36(4) of the Statute. However, after the judgment of the Court in the *Right of Passage* case a new *opinio iuris* rose among the states and their practice changed. Today and especially after the behaviour of the states in the *Use of Force* cases, there is customary law providing that Optional Clause declarations enter into force immediately when they are deposited with the

---

[215] Gharbi (n 4) 471. See also the dissenting opinion of Judge CG Weeramantry, *ICJ Rep 1998*, 367 f.

[216] Kebbon (n 173) 267. cp also the position of Simma pleading for Cameroon (sub-s III E of ch 3 at 113).

[217] See sub-s III C iii of ch 3 at 107.

[218] For that see sub-ss III B iii c and iv–vii of ch 5 at 216 to 252 and s II of ch 6 at 279.

[219] For a similar argumentation concerning the reciprocal application of reservations see sub-s II C iv b of ch 5 at 194.

Secretary-General. Furthermore, the Optional Clause provides no period which has to lapse between the deposition and the entry into force of the Optional Clause declaration.[220] States have to provide such a period in their declarations themselves.

However, this does not distinguish the Optional Clause from other treaties. As referred to above, the general rules for treaties are even based on the Court's jurisprudence on the Optional Clause. To a large degree Article 16 VCLT was established on the Court's judgment in the *Right of Passage* case.[221] Moreover, authors who comment on Articles 16, 24, 77 or 78 VCLT also refer to the judgments which the Court made in relation to the Optional Clause.[222] Also with regard to these close ties between the law of treaties and the Optional Clause, it can be said that the subject of this sub-section heavily argues for the assumption that the Optional Clause is nothing else than a treaty.

Additionally, there is no higher insecurity or vulnerability under the Optional Clause than there is under other multilateral treaties. The residual rules of Articles 16(b) and 24(3) VCLT put states under multilateral treaties in the same position as states under the Optional Clause. In both cases states have to provide the regime they want in the treaty or in their reservations. Under the Optional Clause Anti Ambush Clauses can provide a comprehensive protection.

IV. THE WITHDRAWAL OF RESERVATIONS

The last point of this chapter which has already been briefly touched in the previous sub-section is that rights and obligations can be created by withdrawing a reservation, too.

If a state withdraws a reservation it can afterwards file applications in more cases but it can likewise be brought before the Court in more cases. For Maus it was an open question whether the law governing the withdrawal of reservations to Optional Clause declarations was similar to that of treaties. According to him under treaty law reservations could be withdrawn immediately. He contrasted this with the situation of the Optional Clause where such a withdrawal could be considered as a new

[220] This holds also for cases in which states make reservations. Normally, the entry into force of a declaration with a reservation requires that the other states receive the declaration and expressly or tacitly accept the reservation (see sub-s III B ii of ch 3 at 99). But like also for all other treaties this is not necessary for the Optional Clause as far as the Optional Clause does not provide the possibility to object against reservations (for that see s V of ch 5 at 263).

[221] See above section I of the introduction at 4 f and especially the references in n 18.

[222] Daoudi (n 76) paras 14 f; Hoffmeister (n 81) paras 5, 10; Horchani and Ben Hammadi (n 80) paras 6, 16 f, 26; Mahiou (n 69) para 10; Ouguergouz, Villalpando and Morgan-Foster (n 84) para 10.

declaration.[223] Unfortunately, he did not make clear where he saw the difference between the making of a new declaration and a withdrawal of a reservation in treaty law.

For the Optional Clause there is no difference in substance. The withdrawal of a reservation basically has the same effect as the making of a new Optional Clause declaration. However, this is not different from treaty law. According to the ILC's Guideline 2.5.7(1) GPRT:

> The withdrawal of a reservation entails the application as a whole of the provisions on which the reservation had been made in the relations between the State or international organization which withdraws the reservation and all the other parties, whether they had accepted the reservation or objected to it.[224]

Maus is right as treaty law allows the immediate withdrawal of reservations.[225] Today's Article 22(1) VCLT provides that 'a reservation may be withdrawn at any time and the consent of a State which has accepted the reservation is not required for its withdrawal'.[226] The ILC's recent Guideline 2.5.1 GPRT reads likewise:

> Unless the treaty otherwise provides, a reservation may be withdrawn at any time and the consent of a State or of an international organization which has accepted the reservation is not required for its withdrawal.[227]

These two provisions additionally make clear that the withdrawing state does not require other states' consent.[228] Independent of the question whether the withdrawal of an Optional Clause declaration is considered as the making of a new Optional Clause declaration, it becomes clear that there is no difference to treaty law. If considered as a new Optional Clause declaration such a declaration could also be made 'at any time' and would not require any state's consent. And as the withdrawal of a reservation to another treaty may be only partial,[229] also Optional Clause declarations can be shaped correspondingly.[230]

---

[223] Maus (n 17) 94.

[224] ILC 'Report of the International Law Commission on the Work of Its 63rd Session' (n 90) 10. See also C Walter, 'Article 22' paras 14, 30–34: 'Given the fact that the withdrawal of a reservation enlarges the commitment of the respective State to a treaty in question, it has consequences which are similar to those of entering a treaty obligation'.

[225] See also League of Nations 'Actes de la neuvième session ordinaire de l'Assemblée, Séances plénières' (1928) League of Nations Official Journal Supplément Spécial No 64 169 (Politis).

[226] See also ILC 'Documents of the Second Part of the 17th Session and of the 18th Session Including the Reports of the Commission to the General Assembly' (n 77) 209, para 1; A Pellet, 'Article 22 VCLT' paras 13–19, 26 f.

[227] ILC 'Report of the International Law Commission on the Work of Its 63rd Session' (n 90) 9.

[228] See also A Pellet (n 226) paras 6–19; Ruda (n 91) 201; Walter (n 224) paras 1, 4.

[229] Aust (n 11) 139; Walter, ibid paras 5 f.

[230] For the latter see also League of Nations 'Actes de la neuvième session ordinaire de l'Assemblée, Séances plénières' (1928) League of Nations Official Journal Supplément Spécial No 64 169 (Politis) and Kolb (n 5) 463.

One last interesting aspect, in which there could be a difference between the Optional Clause and multilateral treaties, is the entry into force of the withdrawal. Article 22(3)(a) VCLT provides:

> Unless the treaty otherwise provides, or it is otherwise agreed ... the withdrawal of a reservation becomes operative in relation to another contracting State only when notice of it has been received by that State.[231]

Even if the accession to a treaty becomes effective as soon as the depositary has received the declaration,[232] a withdrawal of a reservation which has a similar effect requires the notification to the other states.[233] This distinction has been made to prevent the other states from unknowingly violating the newly applicable provision.[234] The provision is, however, only residual and states can provide otherwise in the treaty.[235] Article 36(2) of the Statute does not expressly do so and it seems as if neither in 1920 nor in 1945 the drafters considered such a detail. However, the old Optional Clause allowed states to accede to the Optional Clause 'in all or any of the classes of legal disputes'. This wording seemed to allow them to likewise widen their Optional Clause declaration for additional groups of disputes with the same procedure later.[236] As it will be further addressed below the choice of reservations has later substituted the choice of groups of disputes.[237] It makes no difference whether a state widens its commitment

---

[231] Likewise, Guideline 2.5.8 GPRT provides: 'Unless the treaty otherwise provides, or it is otherwise agreed, the withdrawal of a reservation becomes operative in relation to a contracting State or a contracting organization only when notice of it has been received by that State or that organization' (ILC 'Report of the International Law Commission on the Work of Its 63rd Session' (n 90) 11). So also Aust (n 11) 139; Pellet (n 226) paras 31–40; Ruda (n 91) 202; Walter (n 224) para 22. See also ILC 'Report of the International Law Commission on the Work of Its 55th Session' (n 197) 237 where also the difficulties for the withdrawing state were emphasised. This state does generally not know when each of the other states will receive the notice.

[232] For that see s III of ch 3 at 94.

[233] ILC 'Report of the International Law Commission on the Work of Its 55th Session' (n 197) 237; Pellet (n 226) para 33; Walter (n 224) para 22.

[234] ILC 'Documents of the 14th Session Including the Report of the Commission to the General Assembly' (1962) UN Doc A/CN.4/SER.A/1962/Add.l 182, para 2; ILC 'Documents of the Second Part of the 17th Session and of the 18th Session Including the Reports of the Commission to the General Assembly' (n 77) 209, para 2. See also ILC 'Report of the International Law Commission on the Work of Its 55th Session' (n 197) 238; Pellet (n 226) para 40; Walter (n 224) para 22.

[235] Pellet (n 226) paras 37–39; Walter (n 224) para 2. See also the model clauses which had been provided for by the ILC (ILC 'Report of the International Law Commission on the Work of Its 62nd Session' (n 89) 49) and should have been moved to the commentary (ILC, 'Oral report by the Chairman of the Working Group on Reservations to Treaties, Mr Marcelo Vázquez Bermúdez' (2011) 5).

[236] This can be well supported with the similar situation under the two General Acts. Art 40 of the General Act provided that a state may extent its accession at any time by opting for another chapter of the act or by abandoning all or a part of its reservations. According to Art 44(2)(2) of the General Act the procedure for these 'additional declarations' is the same as for a new accession.

[237] See sub-s II B i of ch 5 at 175.

by choosing another group of disputes or by withdrawing a reservation.[238] Both actions have identical results. Therefore, in line with what has been said in the previous sub-section, in both cases only the depositary has to be notified. Under the Optional Clause this also makes sense as the other state cannot unknowingly violate an obligation arising from it as it will be informed of the filing of the application anyway.[239] All this supports the impression that, even though there is almost no practice under the Optional Clause in this regard,[240] the Optional Clause provides otherwise in the sense of Article 22(3)(a) VCLT. In any way the Optional Clause is not different from other treaties in this regard.[241]

In total it can be said that the withdrawal of a reservation can be made at any time without the consent of other states and enters into force when the Secretary-General receives it. It is therefore, as Maus wrote, like the making of a new Optional Clause declaration. Nonetheless this does not distinguish the Optional Clause from other treaties.[242]

V. RESULT

The way, how obligations under the Optional Clause declarations are created, confirms the impression that they are nothing else but the declarations of accession to a treaty. States are completely free to make or not to make Optional Clause declarations as they are free to accede or not to accede to any other treaty. Like other declarations of accession the Optional Clause declarations do not have to be ratified. As far as it is possible for other accessions to declare them 'subject to ratification' this is also possible under the Optional Clause. The entry into force of Optional Clause declarations has—to a large degree—been the model for the

---

[238] cp Art 40 of the two General Acts and Art 36 of the European Convention which provide likewise for both.

[239] For the other state's protection with an Anti Ambush Clause see sub-s III F of ch 3 at 116.

[240] As Malta widened its Optional Clause declaration to make it cover the subject of the *Continental Shelf* case between Tunisia and Libya (see sub-s III F of ch 3 at 116), it seems as if it was natural that a withdrawal made on the 2.1.1981 was already effective on the 28.1.1981 (*Continental Shelf (Tunisia/Libyan Arab Jamahiriya)* (Application for Permission to Intervene) Application (Malta) 25, 27). Unfortunately, it is not clear whether the other two states had already received the notice of the withdrawal by that date.

[241] Kolb (n 5) 463. For corresponding treaty practice see eg Art 32(3)(2) of the European Convention on Transfrontier Television (ETS, Volume 132 (1989) 12) which has also been used in ILC 'Report of the International Law Commission on the Work of Its 63rd Session' (n 90) 222 f, para 10.

[242] cp also Art LIV of the Pact of Bogotá: 'Any American State which is not a signatory to the present Treaty, or which has made reservations thereto, may adhere to it, or may withdraw its reservations in whole or in part, by transmitting an official instrument to the Pan American Union, which shall notify the other High Contracting Parties in the manner herein established'.

corresponding law in the VCLT. The declarations enter into force as soon as the depositary receives them. Additionally, the commitment undertaken with an Optional Clause can be enlarged by the withdrawal of a reservation just like under other multilateral treaties. There is furthermore no particular insecurity for the states having made an Optional Clause declaration which could distinguish the Optional Clause from other multilateral treaties. In all cases the states have to provide protection against unpredictable events in the treaty itself or with reservations. Under the Optional Clause states can do this with Anti Ambush Clauses in their declarations.

4

Interpretation of the Optional Clause Declarations

THE COURT ESPECIALLY seems to see a difference between the interpretation of Optional Clause declarations and the interpretation of treaties. In its recent judgment on the *Fisheries Jurisdiction* case between Spain and Canada the Court expressly said: 'The regime relating to the interpretation of declarations made under Article 36 of the Statute is not identical with that established for the interpretation of treaties by the Vienna Convention on the Law of Treaties'.[1] Alexandrov wrote that due to the unilateral character of Optional Clause declarations the Court had to disregard some principles for the interpretation of treaties. The Court had to pay special attention not to exceed the states' consent and interpreted Optional Clause declarations restrictively. For Alexandrov this was a 'specific' feature of Optional Clause declarations.[2] Also emphasising the unilateral origin of Optional Clause declarations, Maus wrote that Optional Clause declarations had to be interpreted restrictively in case of doubt.[3] Similarly, Wittmann maintained that the declarations had to be interpreted restrictively in case of doubt even though in general they could be interpreted as treaties.[4] Kolb saw the difference in the fact that Optional Clause declarations are to be interpreted 'in light of the declaring State's wishes and intentions'.[5]

---

[1] *Fisheries Jurisdiction (Spain v Canada)* (Jurisdiction) [1998] ICJ Rep 432, para 46. For more on this judgment see sub-s III E of ch 4 at 154. See also M Fitzmaurice, 'Optional Clause' paras 10–15; PC Ulimubenshi, *Domaine réservé* 122 f and furthermore M Dubisson, *La cour* 193 f: 'Les règles d'interprétation qui s'appliquent généralement en matière de traites doivent … être écartées'.

[2] SA Alexandrov, *Declarations* 13; SA Alexandrov, 'Reservations' 94. cp also Shihata (IFI Shihata, *Compétence de la Compétence* 147) who wrote that the unilateral element of the Optional Clause declarations must be especially taken into consideration when they are interpreted.

[3] B Maus, *Réserves* 55, 57.

[4] F Wittmann, *Obligatorium* 167–71, 599 f.

[5] R Kolb, *ICJ* 456, 489, 491–94. On the other hand Kolb also wrote: 'In treaty interpretation, the text prevails over the non-expressed will of the treaty parties … The position with regard to optional declarations is very similar. In this respect, their "bilateralisation" or "conventionalisation" is carried quite far' (ibid 489).

Hersch Lauterpacht on the other hand stated that the Optional Clause is potentially the most important source of the Court's jurisdiction and that the Optional Clause declarations should not be reduced to unilateral declarations which are subject to a restrictive interpretation.[6] This emphasis of the potential of the Optional Clause seems to oppose the cautious approach by some of the other authors named above.

With these different perspectives in mind the next questions shall be how Optional Clause declarations have been interpreted so far and whether they have been interpreted differently from accessions to multilateral treaties. For the comparison the first sub-section will assess how the Optional Clause declarations would be interpreted if the rules for the interpretation of treaties and reservations were applied. Especially the International Law Commission's (ILC) new Guideline 4.2.6 GPRT (Guide to Practice on Reservations to Treaties) for the interpretation of reservations will lead to the overall conclusion that states and courts have interpreted Optional Clause declarations not like treaties but like declarations of accession to multilateral treaties.

I. THE RULES FOR TREATY INTERPRETATION APPLIED TO THE OPTIONAL CLAUSE

The basic rule of treaty interpretation is provided for in Article 31(1) VCLT which reads: 'A treaty shall be interpreted in good faith in accordance with the ordinary meaning to be given to the terms of the treaty in their context and in light of its object and purpose'.[7] Article 31(1) VCLT provides one rule for the interpretation of a treaty and names three elements which shall be taken into consideration: the treaty's wording, its context and its object and purpose.[8]

This sub-section will not consider all rules of treaty interpretation and will focus on those which are relevant for the assessment of the Optional Clause with regard to crucial state practice and jurisprudence.

---

[6] H Lauterpacht, *Development* 346.

[7] Today, Art 31 VCLT, like Art 32 VCLT, is mostly considered as being customary law (*Dispute Regarding Navigational and Related Rights (Costa Rica v Nicaragua)* (n 7) 13, para 47; *Arbitral Award of 31 July 1989 (Guinea-Bissau v Senegal)* (Judgment) [1991] ICJ Rep 53, para 48; dissenting opinion of Judge S Torres Bernárdez, *ICJ Rep 1998*, para 154; ILC 'Subsequent Agreements and Subsequent Practice in Relation to Treaty Interpretation, Draft Conclusions 1–5' (24 May 2013) UN Doc A/CN.4/L.813 1; ILC 'Documents of the 53rd Session' (2001) UN Doc A/CN.4/SER.A/2001/Add.1 (Part 1) 131, para 124 (Rodriguez Cedeño); O Dörr, 'Article 31' paras 6 f. But see also ME Villiger, *Commentary* Art 31 VCLT, paras 37–39).

[8] A Aust, *Treaty Law* 208.

A. Internal *Travaux Préparatoires* and Circumstances
of Making a Declaration

For Optional Clause declarations the first relevant question is to what extent they can be or even have to be interpreted in light of the domestic *travaux préparatoires* and the circumstances of their formulation.

In general the recourse to *travaux préparatoires* of a treaty has been given a secondary place among the means of treaty interpretation.[9] Article 32 VCLT provides:

> Recourse may be had to supplementary means of interpretation, including the preparatory work of the treaty and the circumstances of its conclusion, in order to confirm the meaning resulting from the application of article 31, or to determine the meaning when the interpretation according to article 31 ... leaves the meaning ambiguous or obscure; or ... leads to a result which is manifestly absurd or unreasonable.

Resort to extraneous material is therefore only made where the interpretation of a text with regard to the natural and ordinary meaning leads to an unreasonable result or where the text is ambiguous.[10] Also the Permanent Court of International Justice (PCIJ) and the International Court of Justice (ICJ) confirmed that there is no recourse to preparatory work if the expressed will is sufficiently clear.[11]

A further question is to what extent the *travaux préparatoires* can also be used to interpret declarations of accession and reservations. The problem seems to be that they are drafted unilaterally and that the submitting state has more information on the reservation than the other states. For the latter it might be difficult to obtain the material they need for interpretation. The ILC provided no answer for this issue in the GPRT until 2011. In that year the ILC presented the new Guideline 4.2.6 GPRT which reads as follows:

> A reservation is to be interpreted in good faith, taking into account the intention of its author as reflected primarily in the text of the reservation, as well as the object and purpose of the treaty and the circumstances in which the reservation was formulated.[12]

According to the corresponding ILC's commentary this guideline is based on the fact that reservations are both unilateral declarations and acts

---

[9] cp ibid 217 f; JLI Buigues, 'Les déclarations d'acception' 278.

[10] J Klabbers, *Introduction* 86 f; GG Fitzmaurice, *Law and Procedure* 345. See also G Conac, 'L'incident aérien' 730 f; M Fitzmaurice, 'Law of Treaties' 181 f.

[11] *The Case of the SS Lotus (France v Turkey)* (Judgment) PCIJ Series A No 10 3, 16; *Conditions of Admission of a State to Membership in the United Nations (Article 4 of the Charter)* (Advisory Opinion) [1948] ICJ Rep 57, 63; cp ILC 'Documents of the 53rd Session' (n 7) 34, para 146 (Rodriguez Cedeño).

[12] ILC 'Report of the International Law Commission on the Work of Its 63rd Session' (26 April–3 June and 4 July–12 August 2011) UN Doc A/66/10/Add.1 23.

attached to a treaty.[13] Concerning the recourse to domestic material the ILC especially referred to the *Aegean Sea Continental Shelf* case in which the Court had to consider a reservation made to the General Act by Greece. According to the Court, '[r]egard must be paid to the intention of the Greek Government at the time when it deposited its instrument of accession to the General Act'. To establish this intention the Court considered, amongst others, a letter sent by the Greek lawyer and diplomat Politis to the Greek Foreign Minister.[14] The ILC concluded:

> Other elements should be taken into consideration for the purposes of determining the intention of the author of the reservation, including in particular the texts accompanying the formulation of the reservation, especially those explaining the reasons for the reservation, and possibly circumstances of its formulation (or, in the words of the International Court of Justice, 'circumstances of its preparation') that may clarify the meaning of the reservation.[15]

Similar to Guideline 4.2.6 GPRT is the Principle 7(3) of the Guiding Principles for Unilateral Declarations (GPUD) which provides:

> In interpreting the content of such obligations, weight shall be given first and foremost to the text of the declaration, together with the context and the circumstances in which it was formulated.[16]

Concerning the reference to domestic material also the corresponding debate in the ILC is fruitful. Special Rapporteur Rodríguez-Cedeño noted that domestic preparatory work was hard to find and to analyse, but nonetheless he wanted to allow states to refer to those domestic sources to demonstrate their intention.[17] With reference to the judgment of the Permanent Court of Arbitration in the *Eritrea/Yemen* case, he said that the weight of these sources should depend on each individual case.[18] Pellet emphasised that in the case of unilateral declarations internal sources were even less accessible than in the case of treaties. This could lead to inequality between the author and the addressee.[19] Gaja answered that this problem can be reduced by limiting the recourse to sources which are reasonably accessible to other states.[20]

---

[13] ibid 467 f, para 2.

[14] *Aegean Sea Continental Shelf (Greece v Turkey)* (Jurisdiction) [1978] ICJ Rep 3, para 69.

[15] ILC 'Report of the International Law Commission on the Work of Its 63rd Session' (n 12) 470 para 9 (footnotes omitted).

[16] ILC 'Report of the International Law Commission on the Work of Its 58th Session' (1 May–9 June and 3 July–11 August 2006) UN Doc A/61/10 377.

[17] ILC 'Documents of the 53rd Session' (n 7) 134 f, paras 147 f (Rodriguez Cedeño).

[18] ibid 135, para 148 (Rodriguez Cedeño) referring to *Award of the Arbitral Tribunal in the First Stage of the Proceedings between Eritrea v Yemen (Territorial Sovereignty and Scope of the Dispute)* (1998) XXII RIAA 235 f, para 94.

[19] ILC 'Summary Records of the Meetings of the 53rd Session' (23 April–1 June and 2 July–10 August 2001) UN Doc A/CN.4/SER.A/2001 186 f, para 6 (Pellet). See also Wittmann (n 4) 171.

[20] ILC 'Summary Records of the Meetings of the 53rd Session', ibid 188, para 16 (Gaja). cp also ILC 'Documents of the 53rd Session' (n 7) 134, para 147 (Rodriguez Cedeño).

This approach can be supported with the Court's jurisprudence. In the case concerning the *Oil Platforms* the Court had to interpret a treaty between the United States and Iran and referred to domestic material produced by the United States to assess which meaning the United States gave to a certain provision. It considered a message from the United States Department of State to a United States embassy and a message from the Department of State to the United States Senate. The Court did not refer to Iranian domestic material as none had been submitted by either party.[21] This supports the impression that the rules for the interpretation of treaties allow the reference to domestic material.[22]

This holds likewise for the reference to the circumstances which had accompanied the making of the instrument in question. Under treaty law these circumstances include the historical background of the treaty. This background is supposed to have been in the mind of those who concluded it.[23] Even for purely unilateral declarations the relevant historical situation with all its judicial and political relations has to be taken into consideration to assess the intention of the submitting state.[24] In the *Nuclear Tests* cases the Court emphasised the necessity to assess the circumstances of the making of the declarations to establish their impacts.[25] Likewise in the case concerning the *Frontier Dispute* between Burkina Faso and Mali, the Court stated that all the factual circumstances must be taken into account in order to assess the intention of the author of a unilateral act.[26] In line with the ILC's Guideline 4.2.6 GPRT this must also hold for 'false unilateral declarations' such as declarations of accession with reservations and Optional Clause declarations.

B. Restrictive Interpretation (*In Dubio Mutius*)

As it has already been mentioned in the introduction to this chapter, some authors maintained that the Optional Clause declarations have to be interpreted restrictively.

---

[21] *Oil Platforms (Islamic Republic of Iran v United States of America)* (Preliminary Objection) [1996] ICJ Rep 803, para 29.

[22] cp also O Dörr, 'Article 32' para 14; Klabbers (n 10) 86. For the question in how far the material must have been accessible see the different opinions in Aust (n 8) 218 f; Dörr, ibid para 14; C Grabenwarter and K Pabel, *EMRK* 32, para 6.

[23] Dörr, ibid para 21.

[24] V Rodríguez Cedeño and MI Torres Cazorla, 'Unilateral Acts' paras 25–27. See also ILC 'Summary Records of the Meetings of the 53rd Session' (n 19) 189, para 26 (Simma).

[25] *Nuclear Tests (Australia v France)* (Judgment) [1974] ICJ Rep 253, para 51.

[26] *Frontier Dispute (Burkina Faso/Republic of Mali)* (Judgment) [1986] ICJ Rep 554, para 40.

i. No Rule of Restrictive Interpretation in General

In treaty law, there is, however, no such general rule which requires that in case of doubt a treaty has to be interpreted restrictively.[27] Only the Permanent Court made rulings in this direction in the *Free Zones* and the *Wimbledon* case,[28] while the current Court never adopted such an approach. In the recent case concerning *Navigational and Related Rights* the Court maintained:

> While it is certainly true that limitations of the sovereignty of a State over its territory are not to be presumed, this does not mean that treaty provisions establishing such limitations, such as those that are in issue in the present case, should for this reason be interpreted *a priori* in a restrictive way. A treaty provision which has the purpose of limiting the sovereign powers of a State must be interpreted like any other provision of a treaty, i.e. in accordance with the intentions of its authors as reflected by the text of the treaty and the other relevant factors in terms of interpretation.[29]

ii. Restrictive Interpretation of Instruments with Unilateral Origin?

Yet, the question is whether the unilateral origin of the terms of Optional Clause declarations makes a difference. For purely unilateral declarations it is debated whether they have to be interpreted restrictively in case of doubt.[30] At the end of its deliberations the ILC presented Principle 7(2) GPUD which provides: 'In the case of doubt as to the scope of the obligations resulting from such a [unilateral] declaration, such obligations must be interpreted in a restrictive manner'.[31] Also according to Maus a restrictive interpretation should be preferred for unilateral declarations in case

---

[27] Dörr (n 7) para 34; M Leibiger, *Auslegung* 355–57; C Tomuschat, 'Article 36 of the Statute' paras 35, 72.

[28] *SS Wimbledon Case (United Kingdom, France, Italy and Japan v Germany)* (Judgment) PCIJ Series A No 1 15, 24; *Free Zones of Upper Savoy and the District of Gex (France v Switzerland)* (Judgment) PCIJ Series A/B No 46 95, 167. cp also K Schmid, *Rechtsprechung* 107.

[29] *Dispute Regarding Navigational and Related Rights (Costa Rica v Nicaragua)* (n 7) para 48.

[30] For a rather restrictive interpretation see *Nuclear Tests (Australia v France)* (n 25) para 44; ILC 'Summary Records of the Meetings of the 53rd Session' (n 19) 189, para 25 (Momtaz) 191, para 44 (Simma), 200, para 55 (Economides); ILC 'Documents of the 53rd Session' (n 7) 132, 135, paras 126, 153 (Rodriguez Cedeño). Rather against a restrictive interpretation have been: P Cahier, 'Le comportement des états' 255; GG Fitzmaurice, 'Treaty Interpretation and Other Treaty Points' 230; G Schwarzenberger, *International Law* 551. cp also the positions voiced by states during the drafting of the GPUD (ILC 'Documents of the 52nd Session' (2000) UN Doc A/CN.4/SER.A/2000/Add.1 (Part 1) 270, 279 f (Finland and Netherlands against Israel)).

[31] ILC 'Report of the International Law Commission on the Work of Its 58th Session' (n 16) 377.

of doubt.[32] For reservations however, the ILC held that for these there is no general rule of restrictive interpretation.[33]

This latter position seems also to be the right one for Optional Clause declarations. As Maus also put it the reason for the restrictive interpretation of unilateral declarations is that they only result in a disadvantage for the declaring state.[34] This does not apply to Optional Clause declarations. As in any case in which reservations to declarations are applied reciprocally, the Optional Clause declarations' terms define the rights and obligations for the submitting state and for every other state in relation to that state.[35] As Tomuschat already emphasised the reciprocal acceptance of jurisdiction is no one-sided sacrifice and the normal rules of interpretation shall apply.[36]

iii. Restrictive Interpretation for Titles of Jurisdiction?

Another reason for the restrictive interpretation of Optional Clause declarations is said to be the fact that they establish the jurisdiction of the Court and that in this regard the Court has to be especially cautious. In the aforementioned *Free Zones* case, the Permanent Court interpreted a compromissory clause restrictively.[37] In 1936 Ténékidès wrote that in this regard the Permanent Court might not exceed its power and that the compromissory clauses therefore had to be interpreted restrictively. For him the Permanent Court had to consider itself without jurisdiction in case of doubt.[38] However, the Permanent Court's decision and Ténékidès' statement have to be seen in light of contemporary law. The Court never addressed a rule according to which instruments providing its jurisdiction have to be interpreted restrictively in case of doubt. Already in 1949, Hersch Lauterpacht wrote with regard to jurisprudence that '[t]here is no trace in all these pronouncements or, what is more important, in the unambiguous instances of assumption of jurisdiction, of any restrictive interpretation of jurisdictional clauses'.[39] In the later *Aegean Sea Continental Shelf* case the Court made no statement in this regard although it had the opportunity.[40]

---

[32] Maus (n 3) 55, 57.
[33] ILC 'Report of the International Law Commission on the Work of Its 63rd Session' (n 12) 471, para 13.
[34] Maus (n 3) 55.
[35] For the reciprocal application of reservations see s II of ch 5 at 172.
[36] Tomuschat (n 27) para 35. See also sub-s II E of ch 1 at 37.
[37] *Free Zones of Upper Savoy and the District of Gex (France v Switzerland)* (Order) PCIJ Series A No 22 4, 138 f. See also Lauterpacht (n 6) 339 f; Wittmann (n 4) 36. cp also *Case concerning the Factory at Chorzów (Germany v Poland)* (Jurisdiction) PCIJ Series A No 9 3, 32.
[38] CG Ténékidès, 'Les actes concurrents' 720.
[39] H Lauterpacht, 'Interpretation' 66.
[40] cp *Aegean Sea Continental Shelf (Greece v Turkey)* (n 14) 69–76. For the Optional Clause declarations see the *Fisheries Jurisdiction* case below in sub-s III E of ch 4 at 154.

As Tomuschat rightly wrote, today there is no such restrictive interpretation anymore. That doctrine did not 'survive' the coming into force of the
VCLT.[41]

iv. Result

In total, general treaty law provides no reason to interpret Optional Clause
declarations restrictively.

C. The Rule *Contra Proferentem*: Not for Reservations

The rule *contra proferentem* has been originally applied in cases where the
terms of a treaty had been dictated by one of the parties involved.[42] In
such a case unclear terms were to be interpreted to the disadvantage of the
responsible dictating state.[43] The Permanent Court also applied this rule
in a case where a government had issued a prospectus. It referred to the
rule as the 'familiar rule for the construction of instruments that, where
they are found to be ambiguous, they should be taken *contra proferentem*'.[44]

Yet, it is not clear what, besides ambiguity, the requirement for the rule
to apply is. Some authors argued that the rule applies in all cases where
one party has introduced the terms of a treaty.[45] They based this on the
idea that the drafting state is responsible for the drafting and that therefore
vagueness shall be to its disadvantage.[46] For Optional Clause declarations
this would mean that in case of doubt the terms of a reservation made to
the Optional Clause declaration would be interpreted to the disadvantage
of the submitting state.

However, the interpretation *contra proferentem* of treaty terms which
are not dictated but only suggested by a party is disputed.[47] Against the
rule Dörr argued that normally the terms of a treaty are the result of a
common effort and of negotiations and that therefore there is no special
responsibility of one party.[48] Leibiger similarly maintained that it is up to
the states consenting to the provision introduced to protect their interests
themselves.[49] This approach is in line with the ILC's Guideline 4.2.6 GPRT

---

[41] Tomuschat (n 27) para 35. cp also S Rosenne and Y Ronen, *Practice 1920–2005* 645.
[42] cp Leibiger (n 27) 384–86.
[43] See also Lauterpacht (n 39) 56 f, 63.
[44] *Brazilian Loans case (France v Brazil)* (Judgment) PCIJ Series A No 21 93, 114.
[45] Leibiger (n 27) 386.
[46] cp also ibid 386 f.
[47] Dörr (n 7) para 37; Leibiger (n 27) 387. See also Lauterpacht (n 39) 64.
[48] Dörr, ibid para 37. cp also Lauterpacht ibid 64; Leibiger, ibid 387.
[49] ibid 387.

which does not provide that a reservation has to be interpreted to the disadvantage of the state which has formulated it.[50]

If this is applied to the Optional Clause, also the terms of Optional Clause declarations are not to be interpreted *contra proferentem*.[51]

D. Principle of Effectiveness (*Ut Res Magis Valeat Quam Pereat*)

The last general question is to what extent there exists a principle of effectiveness in general treaty law which can influence the interpretation of Optional Clause declarations.

In general, this principle states that treaty provisions are to be interpreted so that they can fulfil their declared object and purpose.[52] This also includes that texts shall be generally interpreted so that a reason and a meaning can be attributed to every part of them.[53] The principle of effectiveness is closely linked to the object and purpose of the treaty and the principle of good faith.[54] The Court considered it as being part of international law. In the *Corfu Channel* case the Court already made clear that '[i]t would … be incompatible with the generally accepted rules of interpretation to admit that a provision of this sort occurring in a special agreement should be devoid of purport or effect'.[55] In its recent judgment in the *CERD* case between Georgia and Russia the Court repeated this finding and referred to it as a 'well-established principle in treaty interpretation'. For the Court this principle included the 'principle that words should be given appropriate effect whenever possible' which the Court then applied to the provision in question.[56] According to Rodríguez-Cedeño the principle of effectiveness has furthermore been one of the relevant factors in

[50] cp ILC 'Report of the International Law Commission on the Work of Its 63rd Session' (n 12) 467–72.

[51] For the question whether the Optional Clause can be considered as being different from other treaties, because it is rather generous with reservations or because states cannot object reservations, see ss III and V of ch 5 at 199 and 263.

[52] Dörr (n 7) paras 11, 35; GG Fitzmaurice, *Law and Procedure* 345; M Fitzmaurice, 'Law of Treaties' 182. cp also Ulimubenshi (n 1) 114–18.

[53] Dörr, ibid para 35. See also *Whaling in the Antarctic (Australia v Japan; New Zealand intervening)* (Judgment) Counter-Memorial (Japan) para 1.19; GG Fitzmaurice, *Law and Procedure* 345; M Fitzmaurice, 'Interpretation' 139 f.

[54] ILC 'Documents of the Second Part of the 17th Session and of the 18th Session Including the Reports of the Commission to the General Assembly' (1966) UN Doc A/CN.4/SER.A/1966/Add.l 219, para 6. See also *Fisheries Jurisdiction (Spain v Canada)* (Jurisdiction) Counter-Memorial (Canada) para 69; Dörr, ibid para 35; J Sorel and VB Eveno, 'Article 31' para 28; Ulimubenshi (n 1) 116.

[55] *Corfu Channel Case (United Kingdom of Great Britain and Northern Ireland v Albania)* (Merits) [1949] ICJ Rep 4, 24. See also the later *Fisheries Jurisdiction (Spain v Canada)* (n 1) para 52.

[56] *Application of the International Convention on the Elimination of all Forms of Racial Discrimination (Georgia v Russian Federation)* (Preliminary Objections) [2011] ICJ Rep 70, paras 133 f. See also Dörr (n 7) para 35 and furthermore Ulimubenshi (n 1) 114 with additional references.

arbitration decisions for the interpretation for all legal texts including uni-lateral ones.[57] This must especially hold for the interpretation of accessions with reservations. As the ILC wrote concerning Guideline 4.2.6 GPRT:

> [T]he exogenous elements to consider in the interpretation of the reservation should include the object and purpose of the treaty, since the reservation is a non-autonomous unilateral act, which only produces an effect within the frame-work of the treaty.[58]

In this regard it also makes no difference whether a title of jurisdiction is involved as in the order concerning the aforementioned *Free Zones* case the Permanent Court already affirmed the applicability of the principle of effectiveness on a compromissory clause.[59]

For the Optional Clause declarations this would mean two things. On the one hand the Optional Clause declarations themselves have to be interpreted in such a way that the obvious intent of the declaring state to accept the compulsory jurisdiction is given effect. On the other hand the reservations attached to the Optional Clause declarations, too, have to be interpreted like that. They have to be interpreted so that they have an effect and that generally every word of the reservation has a meaning. Of course, there seems to be a conflict between the effectiveness of the decla-ration and the reservation but it should be kept in mind that effectiveness as understood here is only one means of interpretation besides several others. It is not an isolated goal or concept.[60]

II. THE STATUTE, THE CHARTER AND STATE PRACTICE

Article 36 of the Statute itself provides no particular rules for the interpre-tation of Optional Clause declarations.

A. Extensive Interpretation Due to Article 1 of the Statute and the Charter?

Yet, the rest of the Statute and the Charter also have to be taken into con-sideration as they are the context of the Optional Clause.

---

[57] ILC 'Documents of the 53rd Session' (n 7) 131, para 123 (Rodriguez Cedeño). During the drafting of the GPUD there was a debate on whether unilateral declarations have an object and purpose and whether the principle of effectiveness can be applied (for the members in favour see ILC 'Summary Records of the Meetings of the 53rd Session' (n 19) 187, para 13 (Gaja), 190, para 38 (Herdocia Sacasa), 194, para 4 (Lukashuk), 196, para 16 (Yamada)).

[58] ILC 'Report of the International Law Commission on the Work of Its 63rd Session' (n 12) para 10.

[59] *Free Zones of Upper Savoy and the District of Gex (France v Switzerland)* (n 37) 13. See also Ulimubenshi (n 1) 119.

[60] Dörr (n 7) para 35.

According to Article 1 of the Statute and Article 92(1) of the Charter, the Court shall be the 'principal judicial organ of the United Nations'. With reference to these words Judge Read wrote:

> [The Court] cannot ignore the Preamble of the Charter, and its statement of Purposes and Principles. It cannot overlook the fact that the acceptance of the compulsory jurisdiction of the Court is one of the most effective means whereby Members of the United Nations have sought to give practical effect to the Preamble and to the Purposes and Principles. I should be failing in my duty, as a judge, if I applied a rule of interpretation, designed to frustrate the efforts of the Members to achieve this object.[61]

With this statement Judge Read explained why for him Optional Clause declarations were not to be interpreted restrictively. Judge Alvarez even went further and emphasised the character of the Court as a court established by the Charter. He held that the Court was therefore able to develop the law and even had the task to do so. At the end he came to a result where Optional Clause declarations were not always necessary and the Court even had jurisdiction in some cases in which no Optional Clause declarations applied.[62] Without taking such a rather extreme position the argument presented by both judges could be used to support a more generous interpretation of Optional Clause declarations.[63]

This would, however, overemphasise the role of the judicial settlement of disputes in the Charter. It is the peaceful settlement of disputes in general which is the aim proclaimed in the Charter. It is not particularly the judicial way of settlement before the Court and there are also other means the states may choose. As referred to above, Article 33(1) and Article 36(3) of the Charter leave the choice of means to the states.[64] Because of this the judicial settlement by the Court is limited to the cases which the states transfer to it.[65] As long as the states do not consent to settle a dispute in a certain way, all means are equal. This allows no kind of extensive interpretation of Optional Clause declarations.[66]

---

[61] Dissenting opinion of Judge JE Read, *ICJ Rep 1952*, 143 f.

[62] Dissenting opinion of Judge A Alvarez, *ICJ Rep 1952*, 134 f. See also the presentation of this opinion in Wittmann (n 4) 105 f.

[63] cp the presentation of Judge Alvarez's and Judge Read's opinion in Rosenne and Ronen (n 41) 555.

[64] See s I of ch 3 at 86.

[65] See also eg *Case concerning the Factory at Chorzów (Germany v Poland)* (n 37) 32; *Phosphates in Morocco (Italy v France)* (Preliminary Objections) PCIJ Series A/B No 74 9, 23 f; *Fisheries Jurisdiction (Spain v Canada)* (n 1) para 44; *Aerial Incident of 10 August 1999 (Pakistan v India)* (Jurisdiction) [2000] ICJ Rep 12, para 36. For these judgments see s III of ch 4 at 145. cp also Wittmann (n 4) 105 f and furthermore M Hilf and S Hörmann, 'Effektivität' 932: 'begrenzte Einzelermächtigung'.

[66] See also Wittmann, ibid 36.

B. The Interpretation of Optional Clause Declarations in State Practice

State practice on the interpretation of Optional Clause declarations consists almost only of pleadings made before the Court.

i. The Austrian Statement: 'Much Higher Interpretative Significance to the Subjective Element'

An exception was the statement made by Austria in relation to the drafting of GPUD. Asked about the interpretation of unilateral declarations Austria answered with a reference to jurisprudence on Optional Clause declarations:

> [T]he intention of the State concerned could be deduced not only from the text of the relevant clause, but also from the context in which the clause is to be read, and an examination of evidence regarding the circumstances of its preparation and the purposes intended to be served. With respect to the interpretation of these unilateral acts, therefore, it appears that the Court attaches much higher interpretative significance to the subjective element than would be permissible under the rules of 'objective' treaty interpretation pursuant to articles 31 and 32 of the Vienna Convention on the Law of Treaties.[67]

Even though Austria is very cautious by making no decisive statement ('it appears') and only reiterates jurisprudence, this statement suggests that Austria considers Optional Clause declarations as something to be interpreted differently from treaties.[68]

ii. Pleadings of Iran and the United Kingdom in the Anglo-Iranian Oil Co *Case*

The first relevant argumentations by states before the Court in this regard have been made by the parties in the *Anglo-Iranian Oil Co* case.[69]

Iran, after having emphasised that Optional Clause declarations did not contain a contractual element, started with a grammatical interpretation of its reservation. In doing so it compared the wording of its reservation with the wording of similar reservations made by other states. It then referred to the special historical circumstances which had been the motivation to make the reservation.[70] The United Kingdom on the

---

[67] ILC 'Documents of the 52nd Session' (n 30) 279.

[68] Like the following arguments by other states, the argument presented by Austria will be discussed together with those presented by the Court in s III of ch 4 at 145.

[69] For the use of pleadings as legal argument and as states' *opinio iuris* see above sub-s III D ii of ch 3 at 111.

[70] *Anglo-Iranian Oil Co case (United Kingdom v Iran)* (Preliminary Objections) Observations (Iran) paras 17–19.

other hand supported an interpretation which was 'in accordance with the ordinary rules of interpretation'. It wanted to apply the principle of effectiveness and to interpret the Iranian declaration so that all its words had a meaning. With all this the United Kingdom aimed at establishing the intention of the Persian government in 1930. Additionally, the United Kingdom suggested interpreting the Iranian declaration *contra proferentem* as its ambiguity had been caused by the Persian government. It left open whether the Iranian argument concerning the historical circumstances was permissible and presented its own assessment of the circumstances which might have motivated the Persian government. For that assessment the United Kingdom referred inter alia to treaties Persia had signed with third states at the time it also made its Optional Clause declaration.[71]

It becomes clear that both states wanted to establish the original intention of Iran by referring to the wording of the declaration. While the United Kingdom wanted to apply principles of treaty interpretation, Iran focused more on the historical circumstances and the *travaux préparatoires* of the unclear declaration. Even though the United Kingdom was reluctant to refer to domestic material and Iran emphasised the unilateral origin of the declarations both ways of interpretation would have also been generally possible under treaty law.[72]

iii. Pleadings of Nicaragua and the United States in the Nicaragua Case

In the *Nicaragua* case it was especially Nicaragua which interpreted the United States' reservation allowing the withdrawal of the Optional Clause declaration with a period of notice of six months.[73] Nicaragua first referred to the jurisprudence of the Court and held: 'The general principles of treaty interpretation are applicable, though with some necessary modification in light of the unilateral nature of the individual instruments'. It then emphasised the original intent of the United States in 1946 and referred to a report of a committee of the United States Senate which read as follows: 'The provision for 6 months' notice of termination ... has the effect of a renunciation of any intention to withdraw our obligation in the face of a threatened legal proceeding'.[74]

---

[71] *Anglo-Iranian Oil Co case (United Kingdom v Iran)* (Preliminary Objections) Observations and Submissions (United Kingdom) paras 17–21.

[72] cp sub-ss I A, C and D of ch 4 at 127, 132 and 133 and see sub-s III B of ch 4 at 146.

[73] The United States did not present a different way to interpret the reservation. It only argued that state practice had changed the reservation (see sub-s III D of ch 4 at 151).

[74] *Military and Paramilitary Activities in and against Nicaragua (Nicaragua v United States of America)* (Jurisdiction and Admissibility) Memorial (Nicaragua) paras 117, 122–26. In para 122 Nicaragua furthermore referred to 'the normal principle of interpretation ... *expressio unius est exclusio alterius*'.

Nicaragua then also addressed the Vandenberg Reservation.[75] It emphasised the wording of the reservation and maintained that it only covered 'disputes arising under a multilateral treaty' and therefore did not cover the dispute as far as it arises under customary law, too. Additionally, Nicaragua considered the domestic material relating to the drafting of the reservation and referred to a hearing before a subcommittee of the Committee for Foreign Relations of the United States Senate.[76] Nicaragua maintained that this recourse to *travaux préparatoires* was necessary because the text of the reservation was confusing.[77] Concerning the Vandenberg Reservation the United States, too, presented its method of interpretation. Like Nicaragua it presented material from the Committee for Foreign Relations of the United States Senate to show that in 1946 the intention behind the reservation had been different. Thereby, the United States referred to its prior experience with an international tribunal, a debate before the United States Senate, bilateral treaties concluded by the United States before the making of the declaration and the United States' previous behaviour before the Permanent Court.[78] 'In light of this historical and legislative background' the United States then presented an argument that might be considered as referring to the object and purpose of the reservation. The United States maintained that the Vandenberg Reservation had been made to exclude multilateral disputes and not only the disputes arising under multilateral treaties. It emphasised that it had wanted to protect itself and third states from complex multiparty proceedings before the Court.[79] For the United States this intention of the original drafters of the reservations was also essential to determine the meaning of the words 'affected by the decision' which determined the scope of application of

[75] That reservation excludes '[d]isputes arising under a multilateral treaty, unless (1) all parties of the treaty affected by the decision are also parties to the case before the Court or (2) the United States of America specially agrees to jurisdiction' (UNTS, Volume 1 (1946–1947) 11 f; MM Whiteman, *Digest* 1304 f). It is also called 'multilateral treaty reservation' (cp *Military and Paramilitary Activities in and against Nicaragua (Nicaragua v United States of America)* (Jurisdiction and Admissibility) [1984] ICJ Rep 392, para 67; Kolb (n 5) 468; Tomuschat (n 27) para 97).

[76] *Military and Paramilitary Activities in and against Nicaragua (Nicaragua v United States of America)* (n 74) paras 259–64. See *Military and Paramilitary Activities in and against Nicaragua (Nicaragua v United States of America)* (n 75) para 70; *Military and Paramilitary Activities in and against Nicaragua (Nicaragua v United States of America)* (Merits) Memorial (Nicaragua) paras 357 f.

[77] *Military and Paramilitary Activities in and against Nicaragua (Nicaragua v United States of America)* (Jurisdiction and Admissibility) Oral Proceedings (CR 1984) (Nicaragua) 274 (Reichler).

[78] *Military and Paramilitary Activities in and against Nicaragua (Nicaragua v United States of America)* (Jurisdiction and Admissibility) Counter-Memorial (United States of America) paras 255–69. See also *Military and Paramilitary Activities in and against Nicaragua (Nicaragua v United States of America)* (n 77) (United States of America) 199–214 (Norton).

[79] *Military and Paramilitary Activities in and against Nicaragua (Nicaragua v United States of America)* (n 78) paras 270–78. See also *Military and Paramilitary Activities in and against Nicaragua (Nicaragua v United States of America)* (n 75) paras 68 f; SA Alexandrov, *Declarations* 114 f.

the reservation.[80] Additionally, the United States referred to the rules of treaty interpretation and emphasised that the Vandenberg Reservation cannot be interpreted as having no effect.[81] Concerning this latter argument Nicaragua reminded the United States of its position that treaty law cannot be applied on the Optional Clause. It then referred to the judgment of the Court in the *Anglo-Iranian Oil Co* case and held that the principle of effectiveness cannot be applied when another interpretation can be established from the domestic *travaux préparatoires*.[82]

It becomes clear that in this case no party presented arguments which would have been impossible under treaty law either.[83] Nicaragua only said that there are modifications due to the unilateral character of the instruments, but in the end it presented none.[84]

iv. Pleadings of Canada and Spain in the Fisheries Jurisdiction *Case*

In the *Fisheries Jurisdiction* case Spain demanded that the Court applied the rules of treaty interpretation to Canada's Optional Clause declaration. Spain said that even though the rules did generally not apply to unilateral declarations, the rules could be applied by analogy in the present case and emphasised that also reservations to treaties were unilateral acts. Alternatively, Spain suggested that the rules of interpretation for Optional Clause declarations and their reservations were simply similar to those of treaties. As other states relied on the terms of an Optional Clause declaration including the reservations they were to be interpreted objectively on the day an application was filed. Spain argued that for treaties as for declarations the intention of the author had to be established from the text of the instrument with due regard to its object and purpose and the context in which it has been made. For Spain, '[r]ien n'oblige sur ce point à distinguer l'interprétation des déclarations de celle des traités'.[85] Spain added that the rule *contra proferentem* also had to be applied and that

---

[80] *Military and Paramilitary Activities in and against Nicaragua (Nicaragua v United States of America)* (n 78) para 297. For the United States the reservation should have especially applied where the other states involved were not bound by the Court's decision due to Art 59 of the Statute.

[81] *Military and Paramilitary Activities in and against Nicaragua (Nicaragua v United States of America)* (n 77) (United States of America) 206 f (Norton).

[82] *Military and Paramilitary Activities in and against Nicaragua (Nicaragua v United States of America)* (n 77) (Nicaragua) 274 f (Reichler). See also the counter-argument of Norton who argued that Nicaragua had made a selective choice of legislative material (*Military and Paramilitary Activities in and against Nicaragua (Nicaragua v United States of America)* (n 77) (United States of America) 286 f (Norton)).

[83] cp sub-s I A of ch 4 at 127 and below sub-s III D of ch 4 at 151.

[84] For Nicaragua's argument in relation to the *Anglo-Iranian Oil Co* case see sub-s III B of ch 4 at 146.

[85] *Fisheries Jurisdiction (Spain v Canada)* (Jurisdiction) Memorial (Spain) paras 32–35. cp also *Fisheries Jurisdiction (Spain v Canada)* (n 1) para 40; P Weil, *Écrits* 137–39.

therefore the ambiguous wording of a Canadian reservation should be to the disadvantage of its drafter Canada. Spain again emphasised the unilateral character of Optional Clause declarations to argue for the application of this rule. Nonetheless Spain also wanted the Court to apply the principle of effectiveness and to give effect to Canada's intention to accept the Court's jurisdiction.[86] Furthermore, Spain demanded to interpret the Canadian reservation in light of prior declarations which had a similar purpose and in light of the lawfulness of the excluded behaviour.[87]

Conversely Canada maintained that even though general principles of treaty law might be applied, attention had to be paid to the unilateral character of Optional Clause declarations. As these were unilateral declarations *sui generis* the principle of good faith had to play an important role. Canada felt the need to emphasise that it did not suggest a subjective interpretation. According to its own terms it only wanted an objective interpretation taking into consideration the circumstances of the drafting. In total, for Canada Optional Clause declarations with their reservations were to be interpreted in a natural way, in context and with particular regard to the intention of the reserving state at the time it made its declaration.[88] Canada furthermore added that the principle of effectiveness, based on the principle of good faith and required by the respect for the object and purpose of an instrument, also had to be applied to its reservation.[89] In consequence it can be concluded for this case that while Spain clearly spoke out for an application of treaty law, Canada emphasised the *sui generis* character of Optional Clause declarations but nonetheless presented arguments which would also have been valid under treaty law.[90]

v. Pleadings of India and Pakistan in the Case Concerning
   the Aerial Incident of 1999

In the case concerning the *Aerial Incident of 1999* India invoked its Vandenberg and its Commonwealth reservation.[91] Concerning the former

---

[86]   *Fisheries Jurisdiction (Spain v Canada)* (n 85) paras 36 f.

[87]   ibid paras 38–42, 133–46. For the latter cp also *Fisheries Jurisdiction (Spain v Canada)* (n 1) para 53.

[88]   *Fisheries Jurisdiction (Spain v Canada)* (n 54) paras 54–68 referring inter alia to the *Nuclear Tests*, the *Anglo-Iranian Oil Co* and the *Aegean Sea Continental Shelf* case. See also the criticism Judge Torres Bernárdez who called Canada's way of interpretation 'a system of extreme subjectivity' (dissenting opinion of Judge S Torres Bernárdez, *ICJ Rep 1998*, para 150).

[89]   *Fisheries Jurisdiction (Spain v Canada)* (n 54) paras 69–71. See also Ulimubenshi (n 1) 125.

[90]   cp sub-ss I A and D of ch 4 at 127 and 133 and below sub-s III E of ch 4 at 154.

[91]   The Indian Commonwealth reservation excludes 'disputes with the government of any State which is or has been a Member of the Commonwealth of Nations'. Note that the Commonwealth reservations are not all identical. The one of Canada for example excludes 'disputes with the government of any other country which is a member of the Commonwealth, all of which disputes shall be settled in such manner as the parties have agreed or shall agree'.

reservation both parties, India and Pakistan, basically argued on the basis of the Court's judgment in the *Nicaragua* case and did not reopen the question of how the reservation was interpreted.[92]

India only mentioned that the wording of its reservation was a little different from that of the original Vandenberg Reservation as for India the passage 'all parties to the treaty affected by the decision' in the United States' version had been ambiguous.[93] Concerning the Commonwealth reservation Pakistan argued with regard to its object and purpose and maintained that the reservation had lost its substance because the dispute settlement mechanisms of the Commonwealth never came into being. Pakistan furthermore wanted to interpret the reservation in light of the Simla Accord of 1972 which referred to the principles of the UN Charter including the judicial settlement of disputes.[94] India on the other hand reiterated what it understood to be the position of the Court and maintained that Optional Clause declarations 'are *sui generis* by their very nature and in interpreting and examining their validity, principles of the Vienna Convention on the Law of Treaties are not applicable'.[95] Again with reference to the jurisprudence of the Court India then emphasised that a reservation should have an effect in harmony with the 'underlying intention of the declaring state at the relevant time'.[96] Lastly, India referred to the positions of, amongst others, Rosenne and Gerald Fitzmaurice who held that generally the principles of treaty law are applicable but the Court has to pay particular attention to the intention of the drafting state. India concluded saying that the Commonwealth reservation was 'a fundamental basis for interpreting the intention of India as a declarant state'.[97]

---

[92] *Aerial Incident of 10 August 1999 (Pakistan v India)* (Jurisdiction) Counter-Memorial (India) paras 79–83; *Aerial Incident of 10 August 1999 (Pakistan v India)* (Jurisdiction) Memorial (Pakistan) para H(1); *Aerial Incident of 10 August 1999 (Pakistan v India)* (Jurisdiction) Oral Proceedings (CR 2000/1) (Pakistan) 23 f, paras 50–55 (E Lauterpacht). For the named judgment see sub-s III D of ch 4 at 151.

[93] *Aerial Incident of 10 August 1999 (Pakistan v India)* (Jurisdiction) Counter-Memorial (India) para 82. The wording of India's reservation excludes 'disputes concerning the interpretation or application of a multilateral treaty unless *all the parties to the treaty* are also parties to the case before the Court or Government of India specially agree to jurisdiction' (emphasis added).

[94] *Aerial Incident of 10 August 1999 (Pakistan v India)* (Jurisdiction) Memorial (Pakistan) para E; *Aerial Incident of 10 August 1999 (Pakistan v India)* (Jurisdiction) Oral Proceedings (CR 2000/1) (Pakistan) 13 f, paras 2–6 (E Lauterpacht). cp also *Aerial Incident of 10 August 1999 (Pakistan v India)* (n 65) para 41. For the latter argument see sub-s II A of ch 4 at 134.

[95] *Aerial Incident of 10 August 1999 (Pakistan v India)* (Jurisdiction) Counter-Memorial (India) para 73 referring to the *Fisheries Jurisdiction* case between Spain and Canada (see sub-s III E of ch 4 at 154).

[96] *Aerial Incident of 10 August 1999 (Pakistan v India)* (Jurisdiction) Counter-Memorial (India) para 74 referring to the *Anglo-Iranian Oil Co* case (see sub-s III B of ch 4 at 146).

[97] *Aerial Incident of 10 August 1999 (Pakistan v India)* (Jurisdiction) Counter-Memorial (India) paras 75–77. For the position of the authors mentioned see also below sub-s III B of ch 4 at 146).

In this case both parties rather distanced themselves from the law of treaties. Even though Pakistan referred to the Simla Accord which was a source that might be considered as one of Article 31(3)(a) VCLT,[98] its complete disregard for the wording of the reservation is hardly in line with normal treaty interpretation. India's argumentation generally matched the principles of treaty interpretation but nonetheless India explicitly spoke out against their application to Optional Clause declarations.

vi.　*Pleadings of Canada and Yugoslavia in the* Use of Force *Cases*

The *Use of Force* cases are little mentioned in relation to the interpretation of Optional Clause declarations but they show interesting aspects in this regard.

As referred to above,[99] Yugoslavia had made an Optional Clause declaration precisely for its dispute with NATO Member States about their attacks on its territory which occurred during the time the declaration was made. Nonetheless, Yugoslavia limited the 'jurisdiction of the said Court [to] disputes arising or which may arise after the signature of the present Declaration, with regard to the situations or facts subsequent to this signature'. Canada as one of the respondents argued that all the attacks formed part of only one dispute which arose with the start of the attacks. For Canada it was clear that this 'utterly defeats the whole purpose of the so-called declaration' but maintained its first thesis nonetheless. It further emphasised that Yugoslavia had good reasons to exclude prior disputes, too, because it did not want those to be brought to the Court either. Canada seems to suggest that Yugoslavia therefore risked making an unusable declaration. Lastly, Canada referred to the earlier cases in which the Court had interpreted similar reservations.[100] Yugoslavia started by stating: 'The problem before the Court is that of interpreting a unilateral declaration of acceptance of its jurisdiction, and thus of ascertaining the meaning of the declaration on the basis of the intention of its author'. It based its position on the wording of the reservation and its understanding of the word 'dispute' and maintained that every attack after the making of the Optional Clause declaration was a single 'dispute'. Yugoslavia admitted, however, that the wording of its declaration was 'a little ambiguous on this point' but then pressed its second point, the 'real intention of the author of the

---

[98] Art 31(3)(a) VCLT reads as follows: 'There shall be taken into account, together with the context ... any subsequent agreement between the parties regarding the interpretation of the treaty or the application of its provisions'.

[99] See sub-s II B of ch 1 at 26.

[100] *Legality of Use of Force (Serbia and Montenegro v Canada)* (Provisional Measures) Oral Proceedings (CR 1999/16) (Canada) 10–12 (Kirsch). cp also *Legality of Use of Force (Serbia and Montenegro v Canada)* (Provisional Measures) Oral Proceedings (CR 1999/25) (Yugoslavia) 42 (Corten).

declaration'. It emphasised that it had made its Optional Clause declaration exactly for the disputes which were before the Court and argued that therefore it would be 'particularly and manifestly absurd and unreasonable' to understand its reservation as excluding disputes relating to the attacks on its territory. This 'would run entirely counter to the manifest and clear intention of Yugoslavia' as it had made its Optional Clause declaration especially for these cases.[101] To this Canada replied: 'The words "after" and "subsequent" permit no room for ambiguity, nor do they require this Court to enquire into the Federal Republic of Yugoslavia's purported intentions in order to be understood'.[102]

Especially taking into consideration this reply of Canada it becomes clear that the argument between Canada and Yugoslavia was at least very similar to an application of Article 32 VCLT. While Canada argued that the rule was unambiguous and no further reference to the circumstances of the drafting was necessary, Yugoslavia maintained that the wording was ambiguous and that therefore the special circumstances had to be taken into consideration.[103]

vii. Pleadings of Australia and Japan in the Whaling in the Antarctic *Case*

The last statements which will be discussed here are those which were made in the *Whaling in the Antarctic* case.

Japan invoked one of Australia's reservations and wanted to apply the principle of effectiveness to it. Similar to the United Kingdom in the *Anglo-Iranian Oil Co* case, Japan emphasised that every word of Australia's reservation had to have a meaning.[104] In the oral proceedings, Pellet pleading for Japan furthermore interpreted the wording of the reservation 'conformément aux intentions de l'Australie'. He referred inter alia to Australia's prior Optional Clause declaration, Australia's reservation to another treaty and Australia's external relations to establish its intention at the moment the Optional Clause declaration was submitted.[105]

Australia argued that the interpretation may not be purely grammatical and that 'the Court must clearly consider the text against the intention that

---

[101] *Legality of Use of Force (Serbia and Montenegro v Canada)* (Provisional Measures) Oral Proceedings (CR 1999/25) (Yugoslavia) 42–47 (Corten). cp also *Legality of Use of Force (Serbia and Montenegro v Belgium)* (Provisional Measures) [1999] ICJ Rep 124, para 25.

[102] *Legality of Use of Force (Serbia and Montenegro v Canada)* (Provisional Measures) Oral Proceedings (CR 1999/27) (Canada) 8 (Kirsch).

[103] cp sub-s I A of ch 4 at 127.

[104] *Whaling in the Antarctic (Australia v Japan; New Zealand intervening)* (n 53) para 1.19.

[105] *Whaling in the Antarctic (Australia v Japan; New Zealand intervening)* (Judgment) Oral Proceedings (CR 2013/12) (Japan) 27–35, paras 9–22 (Pellet). See also *Whaling in the Antarctic (Australia v Japan; New Zealand intervening)* (Judgment) Oral Proceedings (CR 2013/21) (Japan) 37, paras 12 f (Pellet).

lies behind it'. Burmester pleading for Australia emphasised the unilateral character of the Optional Clause declarations and maintained that 'it is not the mutual intention of the parties but that of the depositing State that is relevant'. He referred to a press release issued by its government and an analysis submitted by the government to a parliamentary committee to show Australia's original intention. Additionally, Burmester named negotiations with other countries as reason for the reservation to explain its meaning.[106] He then went on analysing the wording of the reservation.[107] Burmester criticised the Japanese interpretation as not being 'the natural or reasonable interpretation of the words in light of [Australia's] intent'.[108]

Even though Australia and Japan did not refer to Guideline 4.2.6 GPRT, their arguments followed at least the guideline's pattern: Australia and Japan interpreted the wording of Australia's reservation, as reflected primarily in its text, taking into account the intention of the reservation's author and the circumstances in which the reservation was formulated. Just like Australia, the guideline refers to the intention of the author of the reservation and not to the 'mutual intention of the parties' of the relevant treaty.[109]

viii. Result

With the exception of Austria, India and Pakistan, basically all states have presented arguments which could have been made under treaty law, too.[110] Defendant states invoking their own declarations, like Iran or Canada, tend to emphasise the unilateral origin of Optional Clause declarations and the attention which has to be paid to their original intention. It seems as if they try to benefit somehow from the slightly unclear jurisprudence of the two Courts on the character of Optional Clause and Optional Clause declarations.[111] Yet regarding the arguments actually presented by the states, all in all state practice provides no basis to maintain that the Optional Clause is not a treaty and that the treaty law for interpretation cannot be applied.

---

[106] *Whaling in the Antarctic (Australia v Japan; New Zealand intervening)* (Judgment) Oral Proceedings (CR 2013/11) (Australia) 43–46, paras 12–26 (Burmester). See also *Whaling in the Antarctic (Australia v Japan; New Zealand intervening)* (Judgment) Oral Proceedings (CR 2013/18) (Australia) 26 f, para 15 (Burmester).

[107] *Whaling in the Antarctic (Australia v Japan; New Zealand intervening)* (Judgment) Oral Proceedings (CR 2013/11) (Australia) 46–51, paras 27–44 (Burmester).

[108] *Whaling in the Antarctic (Australia v Japan; New Zealand intervening)* (Judgment) Oral Proceedings (CR 2013/18) (Australia) 22, para 3 (Burmester).

[109] For Guideline 4.2.6 GPRT and the reference to domestic material as a means of interpretation see above sub-s I A of ch 4 at 127.

[110] The compatibility of the presented arguments and treaty law will be further elaborated in the following assessment of the jurisprudence of the Court (see especially the assessment of the *Anglo-Iranian Oil Co* case in sub-s III B of ch 4 at 146).

[111] For that see s IV of ch 2 at 74.

III. JURISPRUDENCE ON THE INTERPRETATION OF OPTIONAL CLAUSE DECLARATIONS

With all the positions of the parties in mind, the Permanent Court's and Court's jurisprudence could provide further information on how the Optional Clause declarations have to be interpreted and whether there is a difference to other treaties.

A. The *Phosphates in Morocco* Case

A case yet neglected is the *Phosphates in Morocco* case which is the most prominent judgment of the Permanent Court regarding the interpretation of Optional Clause declarations.[112] In this case the Permanent Court had to interpret a reservation excluding the retroactive effect of an Optional Clause declaration and considered the terms and the intention of the drafting state to be clear. Therefore, the court said:

> In these circumstances, there is no occasion to resort to a restrictive interpreta-
> tion that, in case of doubt, might be advisable in regard to a clause which must
> on no account be interpreted in such a way as to exceed the intention of the
> States that subscribed to it.[113]

This seems to imply that where a declaration is not clear it will be inter-preted restrictively. Besides the aforementioned *Free Zones* case, this was the reason for Alexandrov's assumption that the Courts tended to inter-pret Optional Clause declarations restrictively in order not to exceed the state's consent.[114] Yet, as referred to above,[115] these two cases were based on general contemporary law which does not exist anymore. As also the following cases will show with regard to Optional clause declarations, the Court never made a similar ruling.[116]

One further aspect is that the Permanent Court also emphasised the unilateral character of Optional Clause declarations and said that it can 'on no account' exceed the intention of the declaring state. In line with this the court made clear that the jurisdiction transferred by Optional Clause declaration 'only [existed] within the limits within which it [had] been

---

[112] For the pleadings of the parties see *Phosphates in Morocco (Italy v France)* (n 65) 23 and above sub-s I D of ch 1 at 19.

[113] *Phosphates in Morocco (Italy v France)* (n 65) 22–24.

[114] SA Alexandrov, *Declarations* 13. See also above in the introduction of this chapter at 125.

[115] See sub-s I B of ch 4 at 129.

[116] See for the decline of the restrictive interpretation in general above sub-s I B of ch 4 at 129. For an early statement in this direction see also Lauterpacht (Lauterpacht (n 6) 339–41) who already emphasised the limited value of the obiter dicta suggesting restrictive interpre-tation for titles of jurisdiction.

accepted'.[117] These words have been repeated by the Court up until recent cases.[118] Gharbi considered this as being a particular feature of Optional Clause declarations.[119] Maus even wrote that this is a consequence of the unilateral character of Optional Clause declarations.[120] However, it seems as if this is no special feature of the Optional Clause and does not distinguish it from other treaties. In any treaty the consent expressed by a state is the limitation of its obligations arising from that treaty. It does not matter what the subject of the treaty is, in none should the Court transcend the states' consent. Judge Schwebel said in a later judgment that when the Court takes 'liberties not earlier taken the Court risks losing the support of those states which have created and sustained it'.[121] This is true but it is true for all treaties. Independent of the subject of the treaty it can be expected that where the Court takes 'liberties' it risks losing the states' support. The fact that the Permanent Court already ruled likewise for treaties establishing the jurisdiction of the Court under Article 36(1) of the Statute shows that the Optional Clause is at least not different to those.[122]

B. The *Anglo-Iranian Oil Co* Case

The Court's judgment in the case concerning the *Anglo-Iranian Oil Co* is often quoted. In this case the Court made the frequently repeated statement that it interprets Optional Clause declarations in 'a natural and reasonable way of reading the text, having due regard to the intention of the [state concerned] at the time when it accepted the compulsory jurisdiction of the Court'.[123] In the *Anglo-Iranian Oil Co* case the Court first came to the result that a purely grammatical interpretation could support the interpretation of both parties. It then compared the reservation in question to similar ones which had to be known to the government of Persia as it drafted its declaration. The Court then further referred to historical

---

[117] *Phosphates in Morocco (Italy v France)* (n 65) 23 f.

[118] See eg *Fisheries Jurisdiction (Spain v Canada)* (n 1) para 44; *Aerial Incident of 10 August 1999 (Pakistan v India)* (n 65) para 36.

[119] F Gharbi, 'Déclarations d'acceptation' 267. cp also Rosenne and Ronen (n 41) 780–82; SA Alexandrov, *Declarations* 13 f.

[120] Maus (n 3) 57.

[121] SM Schwebel, 'The Role' 1069. See also Weil's assessment of the judgment in the *Fisheries Jurisdiction* case between Spain and Canada, which he called one of the great judgments in international jurisprudence (Weil (n 85) 138 f).

[122] cp *Mavrommatis Palestine Concessions (Greece v United Kingdom)* (Jurisdiction) PCIJ Series A No 2 5, 16; *Case concerning the Factory at Chorzów (Germany v Poland)* (n 37) 32.

[123] *Anglo-Iranian Oil Co case (United Kingdom v Iran)* (Preliminary Objection) [1952] ICJ Rep 93, 104; repeated in *Fisheries Jurisdiction (Spain v Canada)* (n 1) para 49; *Aerial Incident of 10 August 1999 (Pakistan v India)* (n 65) para 42; *Whaling in the Antarctic (Australia v Japan; New Zealand intervening)* (Merits) [2014] para 36. cp also *Fisheries Jurisdiction (Spain v Canada)* (n 54) para 54.

circumstances which accompanied the making of a declaration and even considered Iranian law under which the Optional Clause declaration had been approved. This law had not been communicated to other states and had only been published in the Persian language and only inside Persia. The Court, however,

> was unable to see why it should be prevented from taking this piece of evidence into consideration. The law was published in the Corpus of Iranian laws voted and ratified during the period from January 15th, 1931, to January 15th, 1933. It has thus been available for the examination of other governments during a period of about twenty years.[124]

The Court explained the fact that the Persian government had shown a different intent in some bilateral treaties by pointing at the different relations Persia had maintained with these other states in those days. At the end the Court therefore supported the interpretation Iran had suggested.[125]

Judge Hackworth dissented and criticised that the domestic Iranian law was taken into consideration. For him states are not required to investigate into such material and for him such material can only be of value if it is attached to the declaration and thus publicised.[126] In line with this Malgosia Fitzmaurice argued that under treaties there would have been no such extensive recourse to extraneous matters to find the intent like in this case of Optional Clause declarations.[127] With regard to this case Rosenne similarly wrote that for treaties the interpretation seeks to elucidate the combined intent of the states involved but that 'with a declaration, the whole process is stamped by the particular quality of the declaration as a unilateral act, the product of unilateral drafting'. For Rosenne the Court therefore has to pay attention to the possibility that particular limiting factors have influenced a state when it made its declaration. In the present case for him, too, the Court 'ha[d] accepted as an indication of that Government's intentions extraneous evidence of a type not normally admissible, such as a contemporary domestic law'.[128] However, as established above also for treaties and reservations to treaties the Court refers to domestic material.[129] The material used in the *Anglo-Iranian Oil Co* case has no different quality than that used in the *Oil Platforms* and the *Aegean Sea Continental Shelf* case.[130] As it referred to Greek domestic

---

[124] *Anglo-Iranian Oil Co case (United Kingdom v Iran)* (n 123) 107.

[125] *Anglo-Iranian Oil Co case (United Kingdom v Iran)* (n 123) 104–06.

[126] Dissenting opinion of Judge GH Hackworth, *ICJ Rep 1952*, 136 f. See also A Gigante, 'Unilateral State Acts' 26.

[127] M Fitzmaurice, 'Interpretation' 139 f. For Lauterpacht (Lauterpacht (n 6) 346) this reference to Iranian domestic material gave the judgment an appearance of restrictive interpretation.

[128] Rosenne and Ronen (n 41) 771 f, 780–82. See also GG Fitzmaurice, *Law and Procedure* 503; Gharbi (n 119) 268 f; Lauterpacht (n 6) 346 f.

[129] See sub-s I A of ch 4 at 127.

[130] cp sub-s I A of ch 4 at 127.

material to establish the meaning of the Greek reservation in the *Aegean Sea Continental Shelf* case, the Court referred to Iranian domestic material to establish the meaning of the Iranian reservation in the *Anglo-Iranian Oil Co* case. The impression that there is no difference gains further support by the way the Court used the cases as reference. In the *Aegean Sea Continental Shelf* case concerning the reservation to the General Act the Court referred inter alia to the *Anglo-Iranian Oil Co* and the *Phosphates in Morocco* case and transferred the rationale without hesitation.[131]

However, it remains that the Court denied to apply the principle of effectiveness and emphasised the unilateral drafting of Optional Clause declarations. The Court wrote:

> It may be said that this principle should in general be applied when interpreting the text of a treaty. But the text of the Iranian Declaration is not a treaty text resulting from negotiations between two or more States. It is the result of unilateral drafting by the Government of Iran ...[132]

This could be read as a complete denial of the application of the principle of effectiveness on Optional Clause declarations.[133] However, the Court simultaneously stressed that the Government of Iran

> appears to have shown a particular degree of caution when drafting the text of the Declaration. It appears to have inserted, *ex abundanti cautela*, words which, strictly speaking, may seem to have been superfluous. This caution is explained by the special reasons which led the Government of Iran to draft the Declaration in a very restrictive manner.[134]

Taking this whole passage into consideration it may also be concluded that the Court did not deny the application of the principle of effectiveness on Optional Clause declarations in general. The Court could also not have applied the principle for the reason that it was able to infer the intention of the Persian government completely with the help of the historical circumstances accompanying the making of the declaration. There was then no room to apply the principle of effectiveness as it is only one way to assess the intent of the drafter of a text.[135] Insofar the beginning of the quoted passage could just be read as pointing towards the fact that the Court was able to establish the intent otherwise. This would also be in line with the fact that the Court presented no reason why the principle of effectiveness should not be applied to assess the intention of the drafter making

---

[131] *Aegean Sea Continental Shelf (Greece v Turkey)* (n 14) paras 55, 69 referring to *Anglo-Iranian Oil Co case (United Kingdom v Iran)* (n 123) 104 and *Phosphates in Morocco (Italy v France)* (n 65) 22–24.

[132] *Anglo-Iranian Oil Co case (United Kingdom v Iran)* (n 123) 105.

[133] So especially Ulimubenshi (n 1) 123 f.

[134] *Anglo-Iranian Oil Co case (United Kingdom v Iran)* (n 123) 105.

[135] For that cp sub-s I D of ch 4 at 133.

a declaration.[136] With such an understanding the Court did not deny the application of the principle on Optional Clause declarations in general.

With regard to the individual and dissenting opinions in particular the one of Judge Read is of interest here. He argued against a too generous interpretation of Optional Clause declarations. He wrote that he was 'unable to accept the contention that the principles of international law which govern the interpretation of treaties cannot be applied to the Persian Declaration, because it is unilateral'. Judge Read correctly maintained that the making of an Optional Clause declaration was a free exercise of state sovereignty and not just a limitation of state sovereignty. For him it was therefore only necessary to give effect to the intention of the state expressed by the words used. There was no need for a restrictive interpretation and for him the prior jurisprudence of the Court did not demand to act otherwise either.[137]

All in all, if understood as suggested in this sub-section, the Court's judgment in the *Anglo-Iranian Oil Co* case provides no argument that the Optional Clause is somehow different to a treaty. Especially the Court's reference to domestic material is completely accordant to its general approach towards interpretation.

C. The *Right of Passage* and the *Temple of Preah Vihear* Case

The impression that the Court did not deny the application of the principle of effectiveness as such can be further supported with the judgment of the Court in the *Right of Passage* case. The Court had to interpret the Portuguese reservation allowing Portugal to amend its declaration without a period of notice. India argued that the reservation also allowed Portugal to exclude disputes which were already subject of a proceeding before the Court.[138] Portugal argued that its reservation had no such retroactive effect.[139] The Court addressed this issue by first stating that it 'must determine the meaning and the effect of the Third Condition by reference to its actual wording and applicable principles of law'. For the Court the

---

[136] For the application of the principle of effectiveness on unilateral declarations in general see sub-s I D of ch 4 at 133.

[137] Dissenting opinion of Judge JE Read, *ICJ Rep 1952*, 142 f.

[138] *Case concerning the Right of Passage over Indian Territory (Portugal v India)* (Preliminary Objections) Memorial (India) para 33 referring to the Swedish letter of 23 February 1956 (see Annex 1). cp also *Case concerning the Right of Passage over Indian Territory (Portugal v India)* (Preliminary Objections) [1957] ICJ Rep 125, 142. See also Whiteman (n 75) 1339 f.

[139] *Case concerning the Right of Passage over Indian Territory (Portugal v India)* (Preliminary Objections) Observations and Submissions (Portugal) paras 9–11 referring to Portugal's letter of 5 July 1956 (see Annex 2). cp also *Case concerning the Right of Passage over Indian Territory (Portugal v India)* (n 138) 142.

ordinary sense of the wording of the reservation only allowed Portugal to exclude disputes before they were brought to Court. The Court then backed this result with a reference to the rationale of the *Nottebohm* case according to which the lapse of a title of jurisdiction has no influence on the proceedings already before the Court. For the Court this rationale was relevant as '[i]t is a rule of interpretation that a text emanating from a Government must, in principle, be interpreted as producing and as intended to produce effects in accordance with existing law and not in violation of it'.[140] Of course this is not exactly like the principle of effectiveness as presented above,[141] because in the present case the Court contrasted the situation of lawful and unlawful effects. But nonetheless this approach also includes, at its core, the general assumption that the declaration is intended to have an effect. For Gross it seemed in this regard 'obvious that the Court was applying, directly or by analogy, principles of treaty law'.[142]

This last impression can be supported with the judgment of the Court in the *Temple of Preah Vihear* case which followed shortly after the judgment in the *Right of Passage* case. In that judgment the Court had to interpret Thailand's Optional Clause declaration and according to the Court itself had to 'determine what is its real meaning and effect if that Declaration is read as a whole and in light of its known purpose'.[143] This seems to suggest an uncommonly strong emphasis on the purpose of the declaration but the Court went on by explaining:

> In so doing, the Court must apply its normal canons of interpretation, the first of which, according to the established jurisprudence of the Court, is that words are to be interpreted according to their natural and ordinary meaning in the context in which they occur.[144]

The fact that the Court went on saying that it can depart from a purely grammatical interpretation where this would lead to 'something unreasonable or absurd' further underlines how close the Court's interpretation of the Optional Clause declaration is to that of treaties which are interpreted likewise.[145] Additionally, the Court then maintained that in case of a contradiction in the wording of a declaration it is 'entitled to go outside

---

[140] *Case concerning the Right of Passage over Indian Territory (Portugal v India)* (n 138) 142. See also JG Merrills, 'Clause Revisited' 210 f; Whiteman (n 75) 1339 f.

[141] cp sub-s I D of ch 4 at 133.

[142] L Gross, 'Optional Clause' 32.

[143] *Temple of Preah Vihear (Cambodia v Thailand)* (Preliminary Objections) [1961] ICJ Rep 17, 32.

[144] ibid 32. On this page the Court furthermore emphasised that it must interpret Optional Clause declarations 'without any preconceptions of an *a priori* kind' which suggests that there is no kind of presumption for a restrictive interpretation. For more on this issue see the *Fisheries Jurisdiction* case in sub-s III E of ch 4 below at 154.

[145] For the similar rule for treaties in general see sub-s I A of ch 4 at 127.

the terms of the Declaration'. It continued by referring to the 'relevant circumstances' which included 'the history of Thailand's consistent attitude to the compulsory jurisdiction'.[146] In order to establish these rules the Court referred to the judgment in the case concerning the *Polish Postal Service in Danzig*,[147] in which the Permanent Court had interpreted a treaty (the Warsaw Agreement).[148] This heavily supports the assumption that also in the opinion of the Court there is no difference between the interpretation of Optional Clause declarations and treaties.

D. The *Nicaragua* Case

In the *Nicaragua* case the Court had to deal with two reservations made by the United States. First it assessed the reservation allowing the United States to withdraw its declaration with a period of notice of six months. Even though some states introduced such reservations without period of notice after the United States had made its declaration in 1946 the Court interpreted the United States' reservation strictly to its wording.[149] Facing the clear wording and the clear intention of the United States as they drafted their Optional Clause declaration the Court did not even address the United States' argument that changing state practice could have influenced its declaration.[150]

The Vandenberg Reservation, however, led to some more consideration. On the one hand the Court was concerned with establishing whether other states might be 'affected' by its decision and came to the result that El Salvador would be so.[151] In this regard the Court adopted more of the United States' position which was a more teleological approach.[152]

---

[146] *Temple of Preah Vihear (Cambodia v Thailand)* (n 143) 32–34.

[147] ibid 32 f referring to *Polish Postal Service in Danzig* (Advisory Opinion) PCIJ Series B No 11 5, 39. See also the similar approach which Judge Read had adopted for the Connally Reservation four years earlier (dissenting opinion of Judge JE Read, *ICJ Rep 1957*, 94 f).

[148] cp *Polish Postal Service in Danzig*, ibid 38 f.

[149] *Military and Paramilitary Activities in and against Nicaragua (Nicaragua v United States of America)* (n 75) paras 61 f, 65.

[150] For that argument see *Military and Paramilitary Activities in and against Nicaragua (Nicaragua v United States of America)* (n 78) paras 362–64, 399–401. As Oellers-Frahm rightly remarked the United States had had the opportunity to change its declaration in order to adjust it to recent state practice (K Oellers-Frahm, 'Obligatorische Gerichtsbarkeit' 251). If states want to change their Optional Clause declaration according to current state practice they have the possibility (see s II of ch 6 at 279) and also the responsibility to do so. Without adjustment other states can rely on the declaring state's original intent as it appears in the terms used in its declaration.

[151] *Military and Paramilitary Activities in and against Nicaragua (Nicaragua v United States of America)* (n 75) paras 72, 75; *Military and Paramilitary Activities in and against Nicaragua (Nicaragua v United States of America)* (Merits) [1986] ICJ Rep 14, paras 47–56; supported by Oellers-Frahm, ibid 254 f.

[152] See sub-s II B iii of ch 4 at 137. Criticised by eg Judge J Sette-Camara, *ICJ Rep 1986*, 193–98 and V Lamm, 'Multilateral Treaty Reservation' 344.

Concerning the question whether the reservation excludes multilateral disputes as such or only disputes as far as they relate to a multilateral treaty the Court referred only briefly to the wording of the reservation and to the position of the two parties including their reference to domestic material. It then rather suddenly concluded:

> It may first be noted that the multilateral treaty reservation could not bar adjudication by the Court of all Nicaragua's claims, because Nicaragua, in its Application, does not confine those claims only to violations of the four multilateral conventions referred to above.[153]

For the Court the customary law which was codified in the treaties remained applicable even though the Vandenberg Reservation applied. The Court took the object and purpose of the reservation, as presented by the United States,[154] into account but considered only that the Statute already protected the interests of third states. At the end the Court followed the presentation of Nicaragua, holding the United States to the words used in the declaration.[155]

Criticism of this interpretation came from the Judges Oda, Ruda and Schwebel.[156] Judge Ruda made use of the domestic material presented by the United States and Nicaragua and referred inter alia to a discussion in the United States Senate, a report of the Committee on Foreign Relations and a memorandum presented to the Committee.[157] From this material Judge Ruda established the intention behind the reservation. For him, '[t]he history of the proviso is well known and it is not of much help to find the intention of its authors, but that is the only source of interpretation available'. He then used his 'reading of this legislative history' to establish the objective of the reservation which for him was the protection of the United States in disputes with several parties. As the United States had a dispute with Nicaragua only and no other state—and as all other states also had a dispute with Nicaragua only—for Judge Ruda the reservation did therefore not apply.[158] Judge Schwebel criticised the Court's

---

[153] *Military and Paramilitary Activities in and against Nicaragua (Nicaragua v United States of America)* (n 75) para 73.

[154] See sub-s II B iii of ch 4 at 137.

[155] *Military and Paramilitary Activities in and against Nicaragua (Nicaragua v United States of America)* (n 75) paras 69, 72–75; *Military and Paramilitary Activities in and against Nicaragua (Nicaragua v United States of America)* (n 151) paras 56, 172, 182. cp *Military and Paramilitary Activities in and against Nicaragua (Nicaragua v United States of America)* (n 76) para 357 f and above sub-s II B iii of ch 4 at 137.

[156] Dissenting opinion of Judge S Oda, *ICJ Rep 1986*, paras 7–14; separate opinion of Judge JM Ruda, *ICJ Rep 1984*, paras 17–27; dissenting opinion of Judge SM Schwebel, *ICJ Rep 1984*, paras 71 f, 78, 87–90. See also Maus (n 3) 164 f.

[157] Separate opinion of Judge JM Ruda, *ICJ Rep 1984*, paras 17–20 referring inter alia to United States of America 'Congressional Record' (1946) 10618 (Thomas of Utah, Vandenberg), 10707 (Report of the Committee on Foreign Relations).

[158] Separate opinion of Judge JM Ruda, *ICJ Rep 1984*, paras 17–27. cp also the presentation in SA Alexandrov, 'Reservations' 114 f, fn 569.

treatment of the reservation for several reasons and emphasised inter alia that according to Article 32 VCLT the Court was not allowed to 'come to a result which is manifestly absurd or unreasonable'. For him this was the case as the Court's interpretation was inconsistent with another provision of the Statute (Article 62). Judge Schwebel referred to the domestic material and came to a result which led him to conclude that customary law is also excluded as far as it is similar to the treaty law in question.[159] Without reference to the domestic material Judge Oda came to the result that the reference to multilateral treaties in the Vandenberg Reservation is 'merely a means of drawing the boundaries' and that the reservation shall exclude the disputes in total and not just sources of law.[160] Judge Mosler, however, supported the interpretation of the Court. He mentioned the domestic material presented and referred to misunderstandings in the United States Senate but then clearly said: 'The basis of the interpretation is however the text itself'.[161]

Taking into consideration the positions of the Judges Mosler and Ruda it becomes clear that at the end the decision upon the effect of the Vandenberg Reservation had, to a certain degree, been the choice between an interpretation close to the wording of the reservation and an interpretation taking into consideration the domestic *travaux préparatoires*. The United States had the intention to exclude multilateral disputes but this did not appear in the wording.[162] If the Court had referred to domestic material in the *Nicaragua* case as it did in the *Anglo-Iranian Oil Co* case it would have been very likely that it would have interpreted the Vandenberg Reservation in another way. An explanation for the behaviour of the Court might have been that it considered 'disputes arising under a multilateral treaty' as sufficiently clear. In such cases Article 32 VCLT demands no recourse to *travaux préparatoires* or the circumstances of the drafting either.[163] All in all the Court's judgment in the *Nicaragua* case likewise provides no material

---

[159] Dissenting opinion of Judge SM Schwebel, *ICJ Rep 1984*, paras 71 f, 78, 87–90.

[160] Dissenting opinion of Judge S Oda, *ICJ Rep 1986*, paras 13 f. However, Judge Oda's emphasis on the facts that states accept the Optional Clause declarations voluntarily and that their reservations limit the consent given (ibid paras 11 f, 48 f) is less convincing. As said above (see s I of ch 3 at 86), the named facts hold true for all treaties and particular rules for the Optional Clause cannot be inferred from this.

[161] Separate opinion of Judge H Mosler, *ICJ Rep 1984*, 468.

[162] cp SA Alexandrov, *Declarations* 114 f, fn 569; Maus (n 3) 164 f. For the original intention see United States of America 'Congressional Record' (1946) 10618 (Vandenberg) and the memorandum of *Dulles* on this point (Whiteman (n 75) 1302 f).

[163] See sub-s I A of ch 4 at 127. Another question is whether the interpretation of the Court is accordable with Art 38 of the Statute (cp JHW Verzijl, 'Optional Clause' 599 and the argumentation by Pakistan in *Aerial Incident of 10 August 1999 (Pakistan v India)* (Jurisdiction) Memorial (Pakistan) para H(4)). If the answer is negative, the principle of effectiveness (sub-s I D of ch 4 at 133) as applied in the *Right of Passage* case (sub-s III C of ch 4 at 149) might demand a different interpretation.

which could support the assumption that the rules of interpretation for the Optional Clause are different from those for a treaty.

E. The *Fisheries Jurisdiction* Case Between Spain and Canada

The next relevant judgment on the interpretation of Optional Clause declarations is the one in the *Fisheries Jurisdiction* case between Spain and Canada. The Court's following statement has attained great attention: 'The régime relating to the interpretation of declarations made under Article 36 of the Statute is not identical with that established for the interpretation of treaties by the Vienna Convention on the Law of Treaties'. The Court made this statement after it repeated its perception of how the unilateral Optional Clause declarations together form consent. It came to the result that the rules of the VCLT may only apply as far as they are 'compatible with the *sui generis* character of the unilateral acceptance of the Court's jurisdiction'.[164] According to Pellet, the judgment was a 'warning' by the Court not to apply treaty law to Optional Clause declarations too eagerly.[165] It is, however, not obvious how exactly the two regimes differed from one another. As reference the Court points at a paragraph of its judgment in the *Bakassi Peninsula* case which was, however, not related to the interpretation of Optional Clause declarations at all.[166]

The difference mentioned by the Court could be the *contra proferentem* rule. For that rule the Court decided in the *Fisheries Jurisdiction* case:

> [It] may have a role to play in the interpretation of contractual provisions. However, it follows from the foregoing that the rule has no role to play in this case in interpreting the reservation contained in the unilateral declaration made by Canada under Article 36, paragraph 2, of the Statute.[167]

'[T]he foregoing' has to be understood as expressing the unilateral character of the Optional Clause declarations and the way they create consent.[168] However, having in mind what has been said concerning the rule of *contra proferentem* above,[169] there seems to be no difference from treaty law in this regard. Moreover, the way the Court treated the Optional Clause declaration is perfectly in line with what has been said there. As under the Optional Clause no state dictates the terms of an Optional Clause

---

[164] *Fisheries Jurisdiction (Spain v Canada)* (n 1) para 46. See also Rosenne and Ronen (n 41) 776 f; Ulimubenshi (n 1) 122 f.

[165] ILC 'Summary Records of the Meetings of the 53rd Session' (n 19) 186, para 3 (Pellet).

[166] *Fisheries Jurisdiction (Spain v Canada)* (n 1) para 46 referring to *Land and Maritime Boundary between Cameroon and Nigeria (Cameroon v Nigeria: Equatorial Guinea intervening)* (Preliminary Objections) [1998] ICJ Rep 275, para 30.

[167] *Fisheries Jurisdiction (Spain v Canada)* (n 1) para 51.

[168] ibid para 46.

[169] See above sub-s I C of ch 4 at 132.

declaration it is right that the rule cannot play a role here. The fact that the Court cautiously added that the rule *contra proferentem* 'may have a role to play in the interpretation of a contractual provision' does not change this result. Therefore, this rule of interpretation, too, provides no basis to argue that the Optional Clause is different from a treaty.

Another relevant aspect of this judgment is that the Court again used internal material to interpret the Canadian reservations. With reference to the *Anglo-Iranian Oil Co* case the Court said that since an Optional Clause declaration '[was] a unilaterally drafted instrument, the Court [had] not hesitated to place a certain emphasis on the intention of the depositing State'. The Court repeated that also 'the context' of an Optional Clause declaration and 'the evidence regarding the circumstances of its preparation and the purposes intended to be served' had to be taken into consideration. Therefore, the Court took into consideration 'Canadian ministerial statements, parliamentary debates, legislative proposals and press communiqués'.[170] As Gaya pointed out these materials were not easy to find for a state which wants to interpret the Canadian reservation.[171] In line with this Weil, too, noted that the Court interpreted the Optional Clause declarations with a strong emphasis on the intention of the parties and the *travaux préparatoires*.[172] Judge Torres Bernárdez called this a *'free interpretation* of Canada's purported "underlying intention"' which neglected the actual text of the declaration.[173] However, as said in relation to the *Anglo-Iranian Oil Co* case, there is no difference to the Court's jurisprudence for treaties and reservations to declarations of accession.[174]

Moreover, for the Court there seems to be no difference regarding the question whether there is a kind of restrictive interpretation. As Tomuschat analysed inter alia for the *Fisheries Jurisdiction* case between Spain and Canada, the Court held that there is no restrictive interpretation of Optional Clause declarations.[175] Expressly the Court only wrote: 'There

---

[170] *Fisheries Jurisdiction (Spain v Canada)* (n 1) paras 48 f, 60. The Court endorsed this approach also in the recent *Whaling in the Antarctic* case. In that case the Court followed Australia's arguments and considered 'a press release issued by the Attorney-General and the Minister for Foreign Affairs of Australia' and a 'National Interest Analysis submitted by the Attorney-General to Parliament' to determine the scope of Australia's reservation (*Whaling in the Antarctic (Australia v Japan; New Zealand intervening)* (Merits) [2014] paras 36, 38). Judge Abraham criticised the Court's interpretation of Australia's reservation but his criticism did not refer to the use of the named material (cp Declaration of Judge R Abraham, *2014*, paras 11–14).

[171] ILC 'Summary Records of the Meetings of the 53rd Session' (n 19) 187 f, para 15 (Gaya).

[172] Weil (n 85) 127–29. See also ILC 'Documents of the 52nd Session' (n 30) 279 (Austria).

[173] Dissenting opinion of Judge S Torres Bernárdez, *ICJ Rep 1998*, paras 150, 157–60.

[174] cp sub-s III B of ch 4 at 146.

[175] Tomuschat (n 27) para 35. See also Ulimubenshi (Ulimubenshi (n 1) 125) according to whom the Court spoke out for the application of the principle of effectiveness on the reservations attached to Optional Clause declarations.

is thus no reason to interpret [conditions or reservations] restrictively'. Yet, in the same paragraph the Court said, too, that all elements of an Optional Clause declaration 'are to be interpreted as a unity, applying the same legal principles of interpretation throughout'.[176] This suggests that the first quote also referred to the declaration as such. This position of the Court on the Optional Clause is therefore in line with what has been said concerning restrictive interpretation in general.[177]

All in all, also the Court's judgment in the *Fisheries Jurisdiction* case between Spain and Canada provides no basis to argue that the Court interprets the Optional Clause differently from other declarations of accession. Even though the Court reduced the application of treaty law to application by analogy, its interpretation of reservations made to the Optional Clause completely corresponds with its interpretation of reservations made to other treaties. As Judge Torres Bernárdez remarked, '[w]hen the Judgment invokes the *sui generis* character of declarations …, it does so not with reference to particular aspects of the application of one or more interpretative elements accepted by international law'.[178]

F. The *Use of Force* Cases

In the decision upon the request for provisional measures in the *Use of Force* cases the Court had to interpret the word 'dispute' in the Yugoslavian declaration.[179] The Court did so in line with the pleading of Canada and without referring to the circumstances in which Yugoslavia had made the declaration. The Court only maintained that all the attacks on Yugoslavia were to be considered as being all part of one dispute. This dispute therefore arose before the making of the declaration and was therefore excluded by its terms.[180] Similarly Judge Higgins approached the terms of the Yugoslavian declaration without considering how the drafter might

---

[176] *Fisheries Jurisdiction (Spain v Canada)* (n 1) para 44.

[177] See sub-s I B of ch 4 at 127. Another part of the judgment for which the Court deserves endorsement is the distinction between reservations to Optional Clause declarations and the compatibility of excluded acts with international law. The potential illegality of an excluded behaviour is no factor for the reservation's interpretation (*Fisheries Jurisdiction (Spain v Canada)* (n 1) paras 54 f. See also separate opinion of Judge SM Schwebel, *ICJ Rep 1998*, paras 4 f; Weil (n 85) 129–39. But see also the criticism by Judge CG Weeramantry, *ICJ Rep 1998*, paras 10, 24–28, 37–42, 69 and the criticism referred to in *Hilaire v Trinidad and Tobago* (Preliminary Objections) IACtHR Series C No 80 (2001) fn 24).

[178] Dissenting opinion of Judge S Torres Bernárdez, *ICJ Rep 1998*, para 155.

[179] In the later judgment the Court denied its jurisdiction for another reason (cp eg *Legality of Use of Force (Serbia and Montenegro v Belgium)* (Preliminary Objections) [2004] ICJ Rep 279, para 127).

[180] See eg *Legality of Use of Force (Serbia and Montenegro v Belgium)* (Provisional Measures) [1999] ICJ Rep 124, paras 22 f, 28 f; supported by Judge PH Kooijmans, *ICJ Rep 1999*, para 30.

have understood it. She interpreted the terms of the declaration in light of prior judgments of the Court on similar reservations and came to the same result as the Court.[181]

Judge Koroma on the other hand interpreted the term 'dispute' with reference to Article 25 of the ILC's Draft Articles on State Responsibility. He inferred from that article and its commentary that there had been a new dispute after the making of the declaration and that in this respect the Court therefore made a wrong decision.[182] Judge Weeramantry likewise referred to the said article to support his prior and rather long assessment of the word 'dispute'. Also addressing Yugoslavia's intention as it drafted its declaration he came to a result which is different from that of the Court.[183] Another dissenting opinion came from Judge Shi who similarly referred to the said Article 25. He further assessed the meaning of the Yugoslavian reservation in light of earlier jurisprudence and maintained inter alia that the prior dispute had been a dispute with the North Atlantic Treaty Organization (NATO) which, he emphasised, is not identical with the respondent state.[184] Lastly, Judge Vereshchetin, too, presented an interpretation different to that of the Court. For him the wording of the reservation in question was 'not without ambiguity'. He then assessed the meaning of the terms by referring to other judgments. Additionally, '[a]nother ground on which [he] disagree[d] with the majority [was] their complete disregard of the clear intention of Yugoslavia'. Judge Vereshchetin argued that it was 'absurd' to conclude that the reservation excluded the dispute in the present case due to Yugoslavia's obvious original intention.[185]

Regarding these opinions together with the judgment of the majority it becomes obvious that again there was a certain disharmony between the wording of the Optional Clause declaration and the intention of its drafter. The Court and Judge Higgins only referred to the wording of the declaration and not to the circumstances of the declaration's drafting. The Judges Weeramantry and Vereshchetin came to a different result by referring inter alia to these circumstances. Again this seems to be at least very similar to an application of Article 32 VCLT. While for the Court and Judge Higgins the result of their interpretation was not ambiguous and therefore no

---

[181] Separate opinion of Judge R Higgins, *ICJ Rep 1999*, paras 3–8. With reference to other judgments Judge Higgins nonetheless maintained that 'this particular jurisdictional problem, as any other, requires close attention to be given to the intention of the State issuing its declaration with limitations or reservations'.

[182] Declaration of Judge AG Koroma, *ICJ Rep 1999*, 142 f. See also the dissenting opinion of Judge M Kreća, *ICJ Rep 1999*, 246 f.

[183] Dissenting opinion of Judge CG Weeramantry, *ICJ Rep 1999*, 185–88.

[184] Dissenting opinion of Judge J Shi, *ICJ Rep 1999*, 205–07.

[185] Dissenting opinion of Judge VS Vereshchetin, *ICJ Rep 1999*, 210–12.

reference to the circumstances of the drafting was necessary,[186] especially for Judge Vereshchetin the wording of the declaration was not unambiguous and so he referred inter alia to the circumstances of the drafting of the declaration.

G. The Case Concerning the *Aerial Incident of 1999*

The last case presented here is the case concerning the *Aerial Incident of 1999* in which the Court had to decide upon India's Vandenberg and India's Commonwealth reservations. Starting with the latter the Court began by reiterating its prior findings on how to interpret Optional Clause declarations. It then added:

> While the historical reasons for the initial appearance of the Commonwealth reservation in the declarations of certain States under the optional clause may have changed or disappeared, such considerations cannot, however, prevail over the intention of a declarant State, as expressed in the actual text of its declaration … Whatever may have been the reasons for this limitation, the Court is bound to apply it.[187]

Concerning the Simla Accord the Court just said that it demands the peaceful settlement of disputes and has no influence on the invocation of the Commonwealth reservation.[188] The way the Court referred to the drafting state's original intention consequentially upholds the rationale of the judgment in the *Nicaragua* case.[189] If India had no longer wanted its reservation it would have had to adjust it. As it did not, India was still able to rely on it just like Pakistan would have also been. As the Commonwealth reservation therefore applied, the Court did not decide about the Vandenberg Reservation.[190]

H. Result

Taking into consideration all of the two Courts' jurisprudence there is not much left of the Court's statement that the regime concerning the

---

[186] cp sub-s I A of ch 4 at 127 and the similar situation in the *Anglo-Iranian Oil Co* case (sub-s III B of ch 4 at 146).

[187] *Aerial Incident of 10 August 1999 (Pakistan v India)* (n 65) paras 41–44. For criticism see Judge Pirzada (dissenting opinion of Judge SSU Pirzada, *ICJ Rep 2000*, paras 27–42) who considered the Commonwealth reservation as obsolete.

[188] *Aerial Incident of 10 August 1999 (Pakistan v India)* (n 65) para 45.

[189] See sub-s III D of ch 4 at 151.

[190] *Aerial Incident of 10 August 1999 (Pakistan v India)* (n 65) para 46. The Judges Al-Khasawneh and Pirzada who dealt with the Vandenberg Reservation in their dissenting opinions did not interpret it again and only applied it as it had been applied in the earlier *Nicaragua* judgment (dissenting opinion of Judge AS Al-Khasawneh, *ICJ Rep 2000*, para 7; dissenting opinion of Judge SSU Pirzada, *ICJ Rep 2000*, para 86).

interpretation of Optional Clause declarations is not identical to that established for the interpretation of declarations of accession in general treaty law.

As already maintained by Tomuschat, there is no restrictive interpretation of Optional Clause declarations just as there is no restrictive interpretation in general.[191] The same holds for the rule *contra proferentem* which the Court did not apply to the Optional Clause declarations.[192] The principle of effectiveness exists as it exists for treaties.[193] As far as the Court interprets Optional Clause declarations 'in harmony with a natural and reasonable way of reading the text, having due regard to the intention of the [declaring state] at the time when it accepted the compulsory jurisdiction of the Court,'[194] there is in fact not much difference to the interpretation of other treaties. In this regard Rosenne correctly wrote:

> For the canons of interpretation, the tendency of the Court is to approach a declaration in much the same way that it approaches all questions of textual interpretation, whether relating to a treaty, a unilateral statement or declaration, a resolution of an international organization or another document. It attempts to establish what the words used mean in their context. Its point of departure, for declarations as for all other texts, is the ordinary meaning of the words used in their context, provided that this will not lead to what the Permanent Court first called 'something unreasonable or absurd', or what the present Court—interpreting a compromissory clause in a treaty—has called a meaning 'incompatible with the spirit, purpose and context of the clause or instrument in which the words are contained'.[195]

In total, the difference between the interpretation of Optional Clause declarations and the law of treaties is therefore marginal at most also in the jurisprudence of the two Courts.[196] As Hersch Lauterpacht wrote the view that the general principle of interpretation cannot be applied to the Optional Clause declarations 'is not the view of the Court'.[197] For Gharbi the two Courts have basically applied the rules of interpretation for treaties. He wrote that their way of interpretation is 'pleinement compatible

---

[191] Tomuschat (n 27) paras 35, 72. cp also Kolb (n 5) 489 f; Lauterpacht (n 6) 338–41, 346 f; M Schröder, 'Streitbeilegung' para 92 and furthermore Rosenne and Ronen (n 41) 779–82: '[Passages of the Court's judgments] are far from supporting a view that the declarations *per se* have to be subjected to restrictive interpretation simply because they belong to a class of document which is automatically subject to restrictive interpretation'.

[192] cp above IV A 3.

[193] For the Optional Clause cp Ulimubenshi (n 1) 126.

[194] *Anglo-Iranian Oil Co case (United Kingdom v Iran)* (n 123) 104; *Fisheries Jurisdiction (Spain v Canada)* (n 1) para 47.

[195] Rosenne and Ronen (n 41) 779. For the fact that Rosenne, like Gerald G Fitzmaurice (GG Fitzmaurice, *Law and Procedure* 366), also emphasised that the Court had paid special attention to the intention of the drafting states see sub-s III B of ch 4 at 146.

[196] Tomuschat (n 27) para 72.

[197] Lauterpacht (n 6) 347.

avec l'esprit et les dispositions des articles 31 et 32 de la *Convention de Vienne sur le droit des traités*.[198]

IV. RESULT

The Optional Clause and the Optional Clause declarations have not been interpreted differently from other treaties and their declarations of accession with reservations.[199] Neither the Statute nor state practice demands a different treatment. Most states have interpreted the Optional Clause declarations as declarations of accession to a treaty. The jurisprudence of the Court provides no reason for a different interpretation, either. In this regard, the jurisprudence even provides many examples in which the Court treated the Optional Clause like a treaty. Also with regard to the ILC's new Guideline 4.2.6 GPRT on the interpretation of reservations there seems to be absolutely no difference between the law of treaties and the law applied to the Optional Clause at all. Without hesitation the ILC based this guideline on jurisprudence concerning Optional Clause declarations.[200] It seems as if the *sui generis* factor of the Optional Clause has never been more than the fact that under the Optional Clause the two Courts had to interpreted declarations of accession with reservations in times in which there have been no established rules for interpreting these.

V. EXCURSUS: INTERPRETATION OF THE CONNALLY RESERVATION

For a long time there has been a discussion under the Optional Clause whether there are reservations which allow subjective determination. The discussion focused on the Connally Reservation which in its original form excluded disputes 'with regard to matters which are essentially within the domestic jurisdiction of the United States of America as determined by the United States of America'.[201] A similar reservation was introduced by the United Kingdom in 1957. It excluded disputes 'relating to any question which, in the opinion of the Government of the United Kingdom, affects the national security of the United Kingdom or of any of its dependent

---

[198] Gharbi (n 119) 267, 270. As far as Gharbi saw certain particularities in the Courts' way of interpreting Optional Clause declarations (ibid 264, 267–71), these have been already addressed above (146 and 147).

[199] See also Buigues (n 9) 285 f; Tomuschat (n 27) paras 35, 72; ILC 'Summary Records of the 40th Session' (24 April–29 June 1962) UN Doc A/CN.4/Ser.A/1962 56, para 72 (Liang). For the ACHR cp A Úbeda de Torres, 'Contentious Jurisdiction' 11.

[200] ILC 'Report of the International Law Commission on the Work of Its 63rd Session' (n 12) 468–72.

[201] UNTS, Volume 1 (1946–1947). cp also the similar Mexican declaration of 1947 (UNTS, Volume 9 (1947)).

territories'.[202] Reservations relating to national constitutions are generally not considered as subjective. As already Wittmann wrote they refer to the constitution of the corresponding state in the moment the application is filed. A later change in the constitution does not influence proceedings which are already taking place. These reservations are therefore objective and can be determined by the Court.[203]

The question remains whether the Connally Reservation and the named British reservation really grant the submitting state a right to arbitrarily determine its scope. According to its wording the Connally Reservation clearly allows the submitting state to determine the scope of its national *domaine réservé* by itself.[204] Yet, understood like that, the reservation has received a lot of criticism and even renders the whole Optional Clause declaration invalid.[205] Bearing this consequence in mind, it could be emphasised that the states making an Optional Clause declaration with a Connally Reservation also have the intention to accept the compulsory jurisdiction of the Court. Taking further into consideration the principle of effectiveness, as it was also applied by the Court in the *Right of Passage* case, it could be argued that therefore the reservation has to be interpreted otherwise as it is unlikely that a state has the intention to make an invalid declaration.[206] There have been basically two other interpretations of the Connally Reservation.

The first of these would be to limit the state's freedom to determine the scope of its reservation by the principle of good faith and let the Court decide whether the state's decision violated that principle.[207] This approach could be supported by the original intent of the United States. The United States Senate referred to a number of certain situations and

---

[202] HW Briggs, 'Reservations' 302; J Crawford, 'Automatic Reservations' 67 f, fn 3; Maus (n 3) 162; C Stahn, 'Connally Reservation' para 2; Whiteman (n 75) 1334 f; Wittmann (n 4) 416 f. cp also UNTS, Volume 265 (1957) 224. According to Yankov, also the Vandenberg Reservation contained in fact a 'right to veto' and was therefore similar to the Connally Reservation (A Yankov, 'Les réserves' 595 f, see furthermore Lamm (n 152) 346). However, unlike the Connally Reservation, the scope of the Vandenberg Reservation can be determined objectively (see sub-s III D of ch 4 at 151), which makes it essentially different.

[203] Wittmann (n 4) 418–21. But see also the position of the IACtHR which stated that also reservations relating to national constitutions allowed a state 'to decide in each specific case the extent of its own acceptance of the Court's compulsory jurisdiction to the detriment of this Tribunal's compulsory functions' (*Hilaire v Trinidad and Tobago* (n 177) para 92).

[204] cp also H de Fumel, *Les réserves* 28; separate opinion of Judge PC Spender, *ICJ Rep 1959*, 58 f; CHM Waldock, 'Decline' 271 f.

[205] See sub-ss III B iii d and iv-viii of ch 5 at 219 to 252.

[206] cp DW Greig, 'Confrontation' 192, 213; dissenting opinion of Judge JE Read, *ICJ Rep 1957*, 94 f; Ulimubenshi (n 1) 141–45. See also sub-s I D of ch 4 at 133 and III C at 149.

[207] Maus (n 3) 158–63; Ulimubenshi, ibid 139–47. cp also Kolb (n 5) 513–17 ('perhaps preferable') and Norway's position in the *Norwegian Loans* case (*Case of Certain Norwegian Loans (France v Norway)* (Preliminary Objections) Memorial (Norway) para 26). On the latter see also RY Jennings, '"Automatic" Reservations' 355.

did not want to support misuse.[208] Wilcox, who assisted during the drafting of the United States' Optional Clause declaration,[209] spoke of a 'qualified veto' limited to matters which are not clearly international.[210] Initially, the approach was also adopted by the United States in the *Aerial Incident of 1955* case when it argued that Bulgaria invoked the reservation in bad faith.[211] In the *Norwegian Loans* case, Judge Read similarly suggested that the Court was able to decide upon whether the state's decision was 'genuine'.[212]

The second approach would be to treat the Connally Reservation like an objective domestic jurisdiction reservation and simply ignore the part of the reservation in which the reference to the submitting state is made.[213] Such an approach could find support in the judgment of the Court in the *Interhandel* case.[214] In this case, the Court had to decide upon the United States' invocation of the Connally Reservation against Switzerland's request for provisional measures. The Court found that the question concerning the validity of the reservation was too complex at this early stage of proceedings and then decided itself that the dispute in question was an international one which it could judge upon. The Court thereby ignored the opposing decision by the United States.[215]

Both approaches, however, cannot be maintained. Firstly, there are rather small arguments against each of them alone. Concerning the first approach Hersch Lauterpacht already remarked that there were no means and no thresholds to establish whether there was bad faith.[216] Furthermore, the United States withdrew its position in the *Aerial Incident of 1955* case referred to above. It expressly revoked its position that there

---

[208] See eg United States of America 'Congressional Record' (1946) 10615, 10622 (Thomas of Utah), 10624, 10695 (Connally). The senators wanted to exclude disputes relating to the Panama channel, immigration and customs tariffs. cp also MM Whiteman (n 75) 1309 (Macomber).

[209] cp United States of America 'Congressional Record' (1946) 10614 (Thomas of Utah).

[210] FO Wilcox, 'Compulsory Jurisdiction' 712. According to him the United States was bound in cases which clearly fell in one of the four categories of Art 36(2) of the Statute.

[211] *Case concerning the Aerial Incident of July 27th, 1955 (United States of America v Bulgaria)* (Preliminary Objections) Observations and Submissions (United States of America) 308; Whiteman (n 75) 1306. cp also K Holloway, *Modern Trends* 694.

[212] Dissenting opinion of Judge JE Read, ICJ Rep 1957, 94 f. cp also the dissenting opinion of Judge J Basdevant, ICJ Rep 1957, 72–74; Crawford (n 202) 67, fn 2.

[213] Briggs (n 202) 362 f; R Pinto, 'Interhandel' 60–72.

[214] cp C Walter, 'Rechtsschutz' para 43.

[215] *Interhandel Case (Switzerland v United States of America)* (Interim Measures of Protection) [1957] ICJ Rep 105, 110 f following the proposal of Guggenheim (*Interhandel Case (Switzerland v United States of America)* (Provisional Measures) Oral Proceedings (CR 1957) (Switzerland) 462 f (Guggenheim)). Unfortunately, in the following procedure the Court affirmed another preliminary objection and did not touch the current question anymore (*Interhandel Case (Switzerland v United States of America)* (Preliminary Objections) [1959] ICJ Rep 6, 25 f).

[216] Separate opinion of Judge H Lauterpacht, ICJ Rep 1957, 52–55. cp also Jennings (n 207) 861. But see also Kolb who suggested using the respective state's prior practice as criterion (Kolb (n 5) 515).

is a limit for the decision of the state under that reservation.[217] The second approach has the deficit that it would render the reservation meaningless, as the scope of the domestic jurisdiction is already excluded *per se* in every Optional Clause declaration.[218] This would be contrary to the principle that the text of a legal instrument generally has to be interpreted as producing legal effects. Furthermore, this approach gives no meaning to the words 'as determined by the United States of America' even though normally a text has to be interpreted so that every word has a meaning.[219]

Furthermore, both approaches are not in line with the very clear wording of the Connally Reservation and its *travaux préparatoires*. Even though the drafters had certain disputes in their minds as they drafted the Connally Reservation, they wanted a reservation which makes their government the ultimate judge upon the issue whether a dispute comes within the scope of domestic jurisdiction. They intentionally drafted the declaration in such a way that the Court could not decide about how far the domestic jurisdiction reaches.[220] Senator Connally said expressly that it would be up to the state to decide and that the Court would not be able to judge this decision. He emphasised: '[I]f we say that it is a domestic question, the International Court cannot take jurisdiction of it'.[221]

Of course this makes the point of reference (domestic jurisdiction) legally irrelevant because even a state's decision which completely disregards the scope of that reference would not be open to any judicial review. To interpret the Connally Reservation this way would therefore reduce the reservation to an exclusion of disputes 'as determined by the United States of America'.[222] Such an interpretation would therefore render the words 'with regard to matters which are essentially within the domestic

---

[217] *Case concerning the Aerial Incident of July 27th, 1955 (United States of America v Bulgaria)* Correspondence (United States of America) 676 f; Whiteman (n 75) 1307. See also Crawford (n 202) 67; Holloway (n 211) 695; Ulimubenshi (n 1) 136.

[218] See sub-s III D ii of ch 3 at 111.

[219] For both rules of interpretation see sub-s I D of ch 4 at 133.

[220] de Fumel (n 204) 27 f; L Preuss, 'Connally Amendment' 661; Crawford (n 202) 67; F Gharbi, 'Le déclin' 453, 457; dissenting opinion of Judge H Lauterpacht, *ICJ Rep 1959*, 101 f; separate opinion of Judge PC Spender, *ICJ Rep 1959*, 57 f; *Case concerning the Aerial Incident of July 27th, 1955 (United States of America v Bulgaria)* (n 217) 676 f; Waldock (n 204) 272, fn 3; Wittmann (n 4) 408–11. For more on the drafting process see Maus (n 3) 152 f. For the French reservation cp S Dreyfus, 'Les déclarations souscrites par la France' 268 f. For a different conclusion see Pinto (n 213) 64–68.

[221] United States of America 'Congressional Record' (1946) 10689 (Connally). See also ibid 10690 (Donnell): 'right to determine whether a matter is or is not essentially within the domestic jurisdiction of the United States'. See further ibid 10691 (Morse).

[222] cp also the following descriptions: Dissenting opinion of Judge H Lauterpacht, *ICJ Rep 1959*, 101: 'right to determine with finality'; Maus (n 3) 155: 'droit unilatéral de décider l'application de la réserve' and 'droit de décliner la compétence de la Cour'; C Vulcan, 'La Clause Facultative' 51: 'droit de veto'; Dubisson (n 1) 189: 'faculté de ... retirer discrétionnairement [n'importe quel différend]'; Waldock (n 204) 271 f: 'general power to veto'. cp also Crawford (n 202) 70; JHW Verzijl, 'Certains emprunts norvégiens' 388.

jurisdiction of the United States of America' meaningless. Yet, this seems to be the effect intended by the drafters of the declaration by adding the words 'as determined by the United States of America'. As also the United States Senator Morse put it, the reservation grants the 'right for a political veto in questions of judicial character'.[223]

Therefore, the Connally Reservation and the British reservation of 1975, too, will be understood as granting the submitting state a right to arbitrarily determine the scope of their Optional Clause declarations.[224]

---

[223] United States of America 'Congressional Record' (1946) 10684 (Morse). See also Preuss (n 220) 661.

[224] cp also SA Alexandrov, *Declarations* 96; Crawford (n 202) 67 f (especially fn 3), 70; C de Visscher, 'Interhandel' 418 f; Dubisson (n 1) 189; de Fumel (n 204) 27 f; Holloway (n 211) 691; N Kebbon, 'Optional Clause' 263; Kolb (n 5) 503; dissenting opinion of Judge H Lauterpacht, *ICJ Rep 1959*, 111; Maus (n 3) 153, 155; Preuss (n 220) 661; separate opinion of Judge PC Spender, *ICJ Rep 1959*, 59; C Vulcan, 'La Clause Facultative' 51; Waldock (n 204) 272 f. cp also the very clear position of the United States (*Interhandel Case (Switzerland v United States of America)* (Provisional Measures) Oral Proceedings (CR 1957) (United States of America) 452–54 (Becker); *Case concerning the Aerial Incident of July 27th, 1955 (United States of America v Bulgaria)* (n 217) 676 f and furthermore AC Arend, *Compulsory Jurisdiction* 219 (Sofaer)). cp furthermore the way the reservation has been understood by Norway and France in *Norwegian Loans* case (*Case of Certain Norwegian Loans (France v Norway)* (Judgment) [1957] ICJ Rep 9, 24, 27). For the British reservation see especially Jennings (n 207) 362.

5

Reservations Under the Optional Clause

B ESIDES THE ISSUE of interpretation—which has just been dealt with—many authors considered the rules for reservations as being different from those provided by general treaty law.

Rosenne wrote that 'the normative rules of the Vienna Convention are not followed for reservations in declarations accepting the compulsory jurisdiction. These have their own regime'.[1] Adhering to this position also the International Law Commission (ILC) excluded Optional Clause declarations from the scope of the Guide to Practice on Reservations to Treaties (GPRT).[2] Tomuschat maintained similarly that the regime for reservations under the Optional Clause was essentially different from the one which was provided for multilateral treaties by Articles 19 to 22 the Vienna Convention on the Law of Treaties (VCLT).[3] Also Bernhardt saw a difference between reservations to treaties and reservations to optional clauses like the Optional Clause of the Statute. While reservations to treaties were made to restrict the treaties' scope the reservations to optional clause declarations were made to the declarations. Bernhardt further maintained that while the rules for the reservations might be the same in some aspects they can be different in others.[4] Maus likewise wrote that there were several similarities between the law governing the reservations in Optional Clause declarations and those in multilateral treaties but also some differences.[5] According to Thirlway the prevailing view was 'that, since a state was free to decide to accept or to decide not to accept the Optional Clause, it was

---

[1] S Rosenne and Y Ronen, *Practice 1920–2005* 729, fn 68.

[2] cp the references in n 15 of the introduction.

[3] C Tomuschat, 'Article 36 of the Statute' para 99.

[4] R Bernhardt, 'Vorbehalte' 369 f: 'Die viel erörterten Vorbehalte zu völkerrechtlichen Verträgen betreffen Einschränkungen der Tragweite eines Vertrages, die ein Staat bei Unterzeichnung und/oder Ratifikation des Vertrages verkündet oder mitteilt. Vorbehalte zu einseitigen Unterwerfungserklärungen werden getrennt von etwaigen Vorbehalten zu einem Vertrag in Verbindung mit eben diesen Unterwerfungserklärungen ausgesprochen' (footnote omitted).

[5] B Maus, *Réserves* 93 f.

also free to accept it subject to whatever reservation it saw fit to make'. For him this was a 'principle' of the Optional Clause.[6]

Concerning the latter point it can again be said that the freedom to make an Optional Clause declaration is not different to the accession to other multilateral treaties. States are likewise free to abstain from these treaties.[7] This is the normal situation in which the rules of treaty law apply. In this regard there is no reason to treat the Optional Clause differently from other treaties. Also the other alleged differences can be explained with an application of the rules for treaties. The following sub-sections will show that the regime for reservations under the Optional Clause corresponds to the individual provisions of Article 2(1)(d) VCLT and Articles 19 to 21 VCLT. These articles represent, at least in their basics, customary law.[8] Each of them will be analysed in one sub-section of this chapter. One additional sub-section will address the question whether an impermissible reservation can be separated from the corresponding Optional Clause declaration.

I. THE NOTION 'RESERVATION' (ARTICLE 2(1)(D) VCLT)

The first sub-section will show that the reservations made to Optional Clause declarations are actually reservations and can also be referred to as reservations.

A. Are 'Reservations' to Optional Clause Declarations Reservations?

As referred to in the introduction, Guideline 1.5.3(2) GPRT provides:

> A restriction or condition contained in a statement by which a State or an international organization accepts, by virtue of a clause in a treaty, an obligation that is not otherwise imposed by the treaty does not constitute a reservation.[9]

And also Kühner, for example, considered such 'restrictions' as raising fundamentally different problems than the reservations normally made to treaties. For Kühner they were inter alia different as they were no

---

[6] HWA Thirlway, 'International Court, 2014' 600. cp also E Jiménez De Aréchaga, 'International Law' 154; H Kelsen, *Fundamental Problems* 525 f; R Kolb, *ICJ* 459; Tomuschat (n 3) paras 83, 99; *Military and Paramilitary Activities in and against Nicaragua (Nicaragua v United States of America)* (Jurisdiction and Admissibility) Oral Proceedings (CR 1984) (United States of America) 220 (McDougal); F Wittmann, *Obligatorium* 331.

[7] See s I of ch 3 at 86.

[8] J Crawford, 'Automatic Reservations' 79; C Walter, 'Article 19' para 133. For Art 2(1)(d) VCLT see T Giegerich, 'Reservations 2012' para 1; Walter, ibid para 1.

[9] See the references in n 15 of the introduction.

reduction of an obligation provided for in a treaty.[10] And Giegerich also referred to reservations made to optional clause declarations as 'restrictive statements', 'quasi-reservations' and 'conditions'.[11]

Article 2(1)(d) VCLT defines a reservation, however, as

> a unilateral statement, however phrased or named, made by a State, when signing, ratifying, accepting, approving or acceding to a treaty, whereby it purports to exclude or to modify the legal effect of certain provisions of the treaty in their application to that State.[12]

With regard to this definition, it can be said that basically all reservations made to Optional Clause declarations exclude the effect of the Optional Clause in certain cases:[13] Some reservations restrict the scope of disputes which opposing states can bring to Court while others limit the time frame in which states can file their applications. It seems as if reservations made to Optional Clause declarations limit the effect of the Optional Clause as reservations made to accessions to other treaties limit the effect of these treaties.[14] If the latter are called reservations, there is no reason to call the former otherwise.

Concerning general treaty law, Giegerich wrote that the 'conditions' made to an optional clause declaration have the same effect as reservations made to an accession to a treaty or an optional protocol. He further mentioned that the 'restrictive statements' or 'conditions' made to optional clause declarations raise similar problems like reservations and should be dealt with likewise.[15] However, if the two kinds of unilateral declarations are so identical, the question remains why they should be called different. As said above the drafters of the Statue used the term 'reservation',[16] and, in general, there seems to be no need to do otherwise.[17]

---

[10] R Kühner, *Vorbehalte* 51 f. cp also Crawford (n 8) 77; V Lamm, 'Reservations to Declarations' 130 f; R Szafarz, *Compulsory Jurisdiction* 47; Wittmann (n 6) 327 f, 602; United States of America 'Congressional Record' (1946) 10618 (Thomas of Utah) and ILC 'Report of the Commission to the General Assembly on the Work of Its 52nd Session' (1 May–9 June and 10 July–18 August 2000) UN Doc A/CN.4/SER.A/2000/Add.1 (Part 2)/Rev.1 112–14. For the reservations made to optional clause declarations under the old version of the ECHR see J Polakiewicz, 'Anmerkung zum Chrysostomos Fall' 148.

[11] See Giegerich (n 8) paras 4, 38 and the earlier version (T Giegerich, 'Reservations 1998' 973 f).

[12] cp also Guideline 1.1(1) GPRT (ILC 'Report of the International Law Commission on the Work of Its 63rd Session' (26 April–3 June and 4 July–12 August 2011) UN Doc A/66/10/Add.1 1) which also specifies the moment of time in which reservations can normally be made. For that part of the definition see ILC, 'Oral report by the Chairman of the Working Group on Reservations to Treaties, Mr Marcelo Vázquez Bermúdez' (2011) 3.

[13] For the only exception see the following section.

[14] For the effect of reservations and the classification of reservations see sub-s I C of ch 5 at 170 and s II of ch 5 at 172.

[15] See Giegerich (n 8) para 4; Giegerich (n 11) 974. See also Walter (n 8) para 45.

[16] See sub-s II A ii of ch 2 at 54.

[17] For a similar position on reservations made to optional clause declarations under the old version of the ECHR see W Kälin, 'Vorbehalte der Türkei' 424. See further United States of America 'Congressional Record' (1946) 10631 (Morse).

Even reservations allowing the withdrawal of Optional Clause declarations are not different from other reservations and can be subsumed under the common definition of reservations.[18] Although they still require a second notice, at the end they exclude the obligation accepted with an Optional Clause declaration. Also Giegerich's commentary on Article 54 VCLT includes reservations allowing states to withdraw and shows that they are no particular phenomenon of the Optional Clause.[19] This corresponds to the statement Lauterpacht made in 1930 as he discussed the United Kingdom's Optional Clause that had been made 'for a period of ten years and thereafter until such time as notice may be given to terminate the acceptance'. Addressing this part of the declaration Hersch Lauterpacht wrote: 'A time limit partakes logically of the nature of a reservation'.[20]

B. Optional Clause Declarations which are Made for a Certain Period of Time

The only exception could be Optional Clause declarations which are made for a certain period of time or provide that the declaration can be withdrawn with a period of notice which is longer than a 'reasonable' period of time.

As it will be shown in the last chapter, all Optional Clause declarations which contain no provision for withdrawals and which are not made for a certain period of time can be withdrawn with a reasonable period of notice.[21] Therefore, states which provide that their Optional Clause declarations are valid for a certain period of time or that they can be withdrawn with a period of, for example, three years effectively exclude their right to withdraw with a reasonable period of notice. Thereby, these states deepen the commitment which the Optional Clause contains for bare declarations.

According to the ILC, however, reservations can only reduce an obligation or 'discharge an obligation with an equivalent means'. A reservation cannot add anything to the treaty or extend the commitment the treaty provides.[22] Hence, the provisions which bind the declaring states for a

---

[18] But see Wittmann who wrote that especially 'formal conditions' cannot be considered as reservations (Wittmann (n 6) 336 f). For the definition and treatment of 'formal conditions' see sub-s II C of ch 5 at 181.

[19] T Giegerich, 'Article 54 VCLT' para 35. See also K Widdows, 'Unilateral Denunciation' 100 f and T Christakis, 'Article 56' paras 46–48 who referred to the reservation which the United States made to their accession to the WHO.

[20] H Lauterpacht, 'British Reservations' 144.

[21] See sub-s II F of ch 6 at 305.

[22] ILC 'Report of the International Law Commission on the Work of Its 63rd Session' (n 12) 45–48, 90, para 8.

certain period of time or which extend the period of notice for withdrawals cannot be called reservations according to the definition of the ILC.

Nonetheless, also these provisions can be treated like reservations. States can invoke them reciprocally as they can invoke reservations made to Optional Clause declarations. As mentioned in the previous sub-section, reservations allowing states to withdraw their declaration can generally be called reservations. Under the Optional Clause, also reservations allowing states to withdraw without period of notice or a period of notice of, for example, six month are reductions of commitment and also fulfil the ILC's definition for reservations. As it will be shown below, these reservations can be invoked reciprocally, too. States whose Optional Clause declaration can, for example, be withdrawn with a period of notice of six months can invoke the reservations of other states which allow them to withdraw immediately.[23] With the same ratio it makes sense that a state whose Optional Clause declaration can be withdrawn with a period of notice of, for example, three years can invoke the reservations of other states which allow them to withdraw with a period of notice of two years. There is no reason to treat these two cases differently. Furthermore, the same holds true for states which have excluded their right to withdraw and have bound themselves for a certain period of time. These states, too, can invoke other states' reservations allowing them to withdraw. On the other hand, the other states can likewise invoke the time limit and the state whose Optional Clause declaration contained the time limit can no longer file applications after that period of time has lapsed.

All in all, the content of this sub-section, too, provides no basis to argue that the Optional Clause is no treaty as there is no reason why a treaty should not be able to provide likewise. The fact that the Optional Clause provides that states can enlarge their commitment can be explained with Article 36(3) of the Statute which expressly provides this possibility. Additionally, when the Optional Clause was designed, it was not clear whether states could withdraw from it. It seems as if, at least for some of the Optional Clause's drafters, the Optional Clause declarations were of indefinite duration if they were not made for a certain period of time.[24] From this perspective also the provisions discussed in this sub-section would be a reduction of a larger commitment and therefore reservations according to the provision of the ILC.

Anyway, Optional Clause declarations with periods of notice for withdrawals which are longer than one year have not appeared in state practice yet.[25] Furthermore, Optional Clause declarations which are made for a certain period of time become less common. Therefore, this work will

---

[23] See s II of ch 5 at 172.
[24] See also sub-s II B of ch 6 at 290.
[25] SA Alexandrov, *Declarations* 158 f.

not address the issue presented in this sub-section again and refer to the reservations only.

C. Excursus: The Classification of Reservations

Generally, reservations are divided into reservations *ratione temporis*, *ratione materiae* and *ratione personae*. Under the Optional Clause the use of these notions is not consistent and some reservations are not consistently classified.

First, the definition of reservations *ratione temporis* is not clear. Many authors distinguish two types of reservations *ratione temporis*.[26] This is due to the two dimensions reservations *ratione temporis* may have. They can either relate to the dispute and exclude disputes by a time related criterion or they can relate to the declaration itself and the timeframe in which it is applicable.[27] The entire submitted amount of disputes could be regarded as belonging to the material scope of the declaration. With that argumentation every reservation reducing the amount of disputes would be a reservation *ratione materiae*. Also reservations which reduce the amount by a time related criterion would be *ratione materiae*. Reservations *ratione temporis* would then only be those relating to the validity of the declaration itself.[28] Some, however, consider especially these latter reservations as not belonging to the group of reservations *ratione temporis*.[29] Nicaragua, for example, considered reservations *ratione temporis* as being something different than reservations allowing withdrawals or 'time-limits set by States for the duration and termination of their declarations'.[30] Also the Court seems to consider only reservations limiting the scope of covered disputes via a certain time related criterion to be reservations *ratione temporis*.[31] Alexandrov treated all of the named reservations, whether relating to the disputes or to the declaration itself, in the chapter concerning reservations *ratione temporis*. Yet, at the end of his book he listed the reservations referring to the declarations itself nonetheless under the separate headings 'Duration of Declarations' and 'Others'.[32]

---

[26] M Rotter, 'Art 36 Abs 2 des Statuts' 634; IR Cohn, 'Pre-Seisin Reciprocity' 720 f; EB Weiss, 'Reciprocity' 88; A Yankov, 'Les réserves' 591.

[27] Rotter, ibid 634; Rosenne and Ronen (n 1) 563. cp also Kolb generally distinguishing between 'content' and 'container' (Kolb (n 6) 473).

[28] cp F Gharbi, 'Le déclin' 468, 470.

[29] JG Merrills, 'Clause Revisited' 203, 213; JA Pastor Ridruejo, 'The Spanish Declaration' 20, 30–32. cp also the definition of reservations *ratione temporis* in H de Fumel, *Les réserves* 9.

[30] *Military and Paramilitary Activities in and against Nicaragua (Nicaragua v United States of America)* (Jurisdiction and Admissibility) Memorial (Nicaragua) para 145.

[31] *Phosphates in Morocco (Italy v France)* (Preliminary Objections) PCIJ Series A/B No 74 9, 22–24. See also the dissenting opinion of Judge WJM Jonkheer van Eysinga, *PCIJ Series A/B No 77 1939*, 109. For the 'formal conditions' see sub-s II C of ch 5 at 181.

[32] Alexandrov (n 25) 40–66, 152–59.

A reservation not consistently classified is for example the Vandenberg Reservation which could be either *ratione materiae* or *ratione personae*.[33] As the Court understands it, it limits the scope of rules applied and is closest to the group of reservations *ratione materiae*.[34] Alexandrov listed the Anti Ambush Clause as 'others' while Kolb considered it being *ratione temporis*.[35] However, the reservation excludes all disputes with certain states and therefore it could also make sense to treat it as a reservation *ratione personae*.[36] Another example of inconsistency is the position of Maus who treated the reservation named by Article 36(3) of the Statute as 'condition of reciprocity on the part of several or certain states' as a reservation *ratione personae*.[37] This is contrary to the more common understanding that reservations *ratione personae* exclude certain other states from the scope of a declaration. The reservations provided for in Article 36(3) of the Statute affects, however, the entry into force of the Optional Clause declaration vis-à-vis all other states,[38] and can therefore be considered best as *ratione temporis* in relation to the declaration itself. One last example are the reservations excluding disputes 'arising out of events occurring during World War II'. Alexandrov seems to consider them as reservations *ratione temporis* and reservations *ratione materiae* at the same time.[39]

What becomes clear is that the classification of a reservation is sometimes only a question of perspective. As, however, the classification is without any judicial relevance, because under the Optional Clause all of these reservations are treated likewise,[40] this is rather a theoretical than a practical problem. The VCLT as well does not distinguish between the

---

[33] For *ratione materiae* see ibid 122; for *ratione personae* see L Gross, 'Optional Clause' 25; Yankov (n 26) 590, 596–97. cp also Weiss (n 26) 91.

[34] cp sub-s III D of ch 4 at 151.

[35] Alexandrov (n 25) 130; Kolb (n 6) 470.

[36] See also de Fumel (n 29) 13; JG Merrills, 'Optional Clause Today' 101 f. However, the French version of the Anti Ambush Clause (see sub-s III D i of ch 3 at 109) was different as it was *ratione temporis* and *ratione personae* (cp C Vignes, 'La nouvelle déclaration française' 71).

[37] B Maus, *Réserves* 75.

[38] For the today uncontested fact that the 'condition of reciprocity' in Art 36(3) of the Statute provides the possibility to make a 'suspensive condition' see JA Frowein, 'Optional Clauses' 398; Gharbi (n 28) 465; Kolb (n 6) 461; IFI Shihata, *Compétence de la Compétence* 148; HWA Thirlway, 'Reciprocity' 107 f; CHM Waldock, 'Decline' 255. For the fact that the Court has twice referred to Art 36(3) of the Statute as the source of the principle of reciprocity under the Optional Clause (*Case of Certain Norwegian Loans (France v Norway)* (Judgment) [1957] ICJ Rep 9, 24; *Military and Paramilitary Activities in and against Nicaragua (Nicaragua v United States of America)* (Jurisdiction and Admissibility) [1984] ICJ Rep 392, para 64) see the explanation of Briggs (HW Briggs, 'Reservations' 256) which holds for both judgments. In other cases the Court referred only to Art 36(2) of the Statute (cp *Electricity Company of Sofia and Bulgaria (Belgium v Bulgaria)* (Preliminary Objection) PCIJ Series A/B No 77 63, 81; *Case concerning the Right of Passage over Indian Territory (Portugal v India)* (Preliminary Objections) [1957] ICJ Rep 125, 144). For more on this principle of reciprocity in Art 36(2) of the Statute see sub-s II B of ch 5 at 175.

[39] Alexandrov (n 25) 41, 150 f, 153. See especially ibid 41, fn 166: 'Those reservations include a condition *ratione materiae*'.

[40] For the 'formal conditions' see sub-s II C of ch 5 at 181.

different groups of reservations and general treaty law attaches no legal meaning to them. The distinction only serves analytical purposes.[41]

II. THE EFFECTS OF RESERVATIONS UNDER THE OPTIONAL CLAUSE (ARTICLE 21 VCLT)

One of the most discussed issues under the Optional Clause is how to apply reservations. Especially the 'principle of reciprocity' and the creation of 'formal conditions' prompted a lot of debate.

A. The Effects of Reservations in General Treaty Law

Article 21(1) VCLT provides:

> A reservation established with regard to another party in accordance with articles 19, 20 and 23:
>
> (a) modifies for the reserving State in its relations with that other party the provisions of the treaty to which the reservation relates to the extent of the reservation; and
>
> (b) modifies those provisions to the same extent for that other party in its relations with the reserving State.[42]

This provision introduces the general principle of reciprocity into the law of reservations as the reservations thereby work equally for the parties

---

[41] For general treaty law see Walter (n 8) para 41.

[42] See also Guideline 4.2.4 GPRT which describes the possible effect of reservations:

1. A reservation established with regard to another party excludes or modifies for the reserving State or international organization in its relations with that other party the legal effect of the provisions of the treaty to which the reservation relates or of the treaty as a whole with respect to certain specific aspects, to the extent of the reservation.

2. To the extent that an established reservation excludes the legal effect of certain provisions of a treaty, the author of that reservation has neither rights nor obligations under those provisions in its relations with the other parties with regard to which the reservation is established. Those other parties shall likewise have neither rights nor obligations under those provisions in their relations with the author of the reservation.

3. To the extent that an established reservation modifies the legal effect of certain provisions of a treaty, the author of that reservation has rights and obligations under those provisions, as modified by the reservation, in its relations with the other parties with regard to which the reservation is established. Those other parties shall have rights and obligations under those provisions, as modified by the reservation, in their relations with the author of the reservation (ILC 'Report of the International Law Commission on the Work of Its 63rd Session' (n 12) 23).

involved.[43] This prevents a one-sided benefit of the reserving state and an imbalance under the treaty.[44] Furthermore, reservations and also the corresponding reactions by the other states only influence the relationship between each pair of states. As Article 21(2) VCLT provides: 'The reservation does not modify the provisions of the treaty for the other parties to the treaty inter se'.[45] This makes sense where the rights and obligations are reciprocal because then reservations and reactions work on the corresponding level.[46] Under treaty law generally all reservations are applied reciprocally and even reservations which modify the obligations under a treaty are no exception.[47]

This does, however, not mean that the principle of reciprocal application of reservations is absolute and that there are no exceptions at all. To use the words of the ILC:

> [The principle] cannot, in particular, find application in cases where a rebalancing between the obligations of the author of the reservation and the State or international organization with regard to which the reservation is established is unnecessary or proves impossible. This is the case essentially because of the nature of the obligation to which the reservation relates, the object and purpose of the treaty or the content of the reservation itself.[48]

Guideline 4.2.5 GPRT therefore provides:

> Insofar as the obligations under the provisions to which the reservation relates are not subject to reciprocal application in view of the nature of the obligations or the object and purpose of the treaty, the content of the obligations of the parties other than the author of the reservation remains unaffected. The content of the obligations of those parties likewise remains unaffected when reciprocal application is not possible because of the content of the reservation.[49]

---

[43] JM Ruda, 'Reservations' 196; Walter (n 8) para 19. cp also ILC 'Report of the International Law Commission on the Work of Its 62nd Session' (3 May–4 June and 5 July–6 August 2010) UN Doc A/65/10 141–44; A Aust, *Treaty Law* 129; C Tomuschat, 'Reservations' 466.

[44] A Behnsen, *Vorbehaltsrecht* 114. Behnsen also described the problem that the individual obligation might not have the same value for all states and so the provision can only establish formal but not material reciprocity. This material imbalance, however, is based on the consent of the states and is no particular problem of the regime for reservations (ibid 115 f).

[45] For the same result prior to the entry into force of the VCLT see Maus (n 37) 72.

[46] Behnsen (n 44) 113 f. cp also T Giegerich, 'Vorbehalte zu Menschenrechtsabkommen' 742.

[47] ILC 'Report of the International Law Commission on the Work of Its 62nd Session' (n 43) 137–41.

[48] ibid 144.

[49] ILC 'Report of the International Law Commission on the Work of Its 63rd Session' (n 12) 23. cp also ILC 'Documents of the 48th Session' (1996) UN Doc A/CN.4/SER.A/1996/Add.1 (Part 1) 65, para 155 (Pellet).

This latter point means that there are firstly some reservations which because of their specification cannot be applied reciprocally. These are, for example, reservations related to the territorial application of the treaty or reservations relating to a certain group of persons.[50] In such cases there is no corresponding item to which an obligation of another state relates. In line with this Wittmann argued that, also in the case of Optional Clause declarations, reservations relating to certain specific national characteristics, like for example the Commonwealth reservations, cannot be applied reciprocally.[51] Yet, this does not convince as the Optional Clause covers only disputes between states and not the specific matter itself. Even though a reservation might exclude disputes which are related to a nation specific matter, the parties of the dispute are always two or more states. Concerning the dispute both states are likewise obliged and there is always a corresponding obligation for both states. The dispute therefore cannot be so specifically linked to one state that the reservation cannot be applied reciprocally.[52]

The other exception named above is related to the obligation the reservation is attached to and applies as far as the obligations under a treaty are not reciprocal. In those cases also the effect of reservations is not reciprocal.[53] An example for this are the obligations under human rights treaties.[54] The European Commission of Human Rights (EComHR) for example has decided that France was able to institute proceedings against Turkey even though France had made a reservation to one of the rights in question. The EComHR emphasised that the European Convention on Human Rights (ECHR) is not based on reciprocity here.[55] As the obligations arising under the Optional Clause are reciprocal,[56] this exception does not apply for it.

The only remaining question is whether the object and purpose of the Optional Clause demands an exception.

---

[50] cp ibid 65, para 155 (Pellet); ILC 'Report of the International Law Commission on the Work of Its 62nd Session' (n 43) 146; P Imbert, *Les réserves* 258 f; B Simma, *Reziprozitätselement* 258; C Walter, 'Article 21' para 21.

[51] Wittmann (n 6) 246 f.

[52] For the proper treatment of Wittmann's examples see the following sections and for reservations *ratione personae* especially sub-s II B iv of ch 5 at 178.

[53] Behnsen (n 44) 129; Walter (n 50) paras 22 f. cp also Simma (n 50) 155.

[54] ILC 'Documents of the 48th Session' (n 49) 65, paras 154 f (Pellet); ILC 'Report of the International Law Commission on the Work of Its 62nd Session' (n 43) 144 f, paras 4, 6.

[55] *France ao v Turkey (Admissibility)* (App No 9940-9944/82) [1983] para 39: 'The Commission finds that the general principle of reciprocity in international law and the rule, stated in Article 21, para 1 of the Vienna Convention on the Law of Treaties, concerning bilateral relations under a multilateral treaty do not apply to the obligations under the European Convention on Human Rights, which are "essentially of an objective character …"'. cp also JA Frowein and W Peukert, *EMRK-Kommentar, 2009* Art 33, para 6.

[56] See s II of ch 1 at 22.

B. 'The Same Obligation' in Article 36(2) of the Statute

Under the Optional Clause the reciprocal application of reservations has been lengthily discussed. The dispute is linked to the notion 'the same obligation' in Article 36(2) of the Statute. For most authors these words are the basis for the reciprocal application of reservations to Optional Clause declarations.[57]

i. The Development of the 'Same Obligation'

In 1920, the words 'the same obligation' were designed to refer to the groups of disputes enumerated in Article 36(2) of the Statute of the Permanent Court. States were able to pick certain groups of disputes for which they accepted compulsory jurisdiction towards all other states which picked the same.[58] According to Thirlway,

> [w]hat was contemplated was a system equivalent to four distinct multilateral treaties of judicial settlement. The filing of a declaration accepting jurisdiction in one or more of the four classes of disputes was equivalent to acceding to one or more of the four treaties.[59]

This approach was similar to a concept of earlier arbitral agreements.[60] It dates back to the conference in The Hague in 1907 where it was common that states opt in for some classes of disputes and were only bound for disputes as far as another state opted in for the same class, too.[61] In the history of the Optional Clause, there has so far been only one state, though, that has referred to the classes of disputes. In the declaration of 1930 referred to above,[62] Persia accepted compulsory jurisdiction only 'à l'application des traités ou conventions acceptés par La Perse'.[63] Waldock considered this as being a limitation to the group of disputes named in Article 36(2)(a) of the Statute of the Permanent Court ('the interpretation of a treaty').[64]

---

[57] See eg Briggs (n 38) 242; Frowein (n 38) 397 f; Gharbi (n 28) 445, 465 f; Maus (n 37) 97; FL Morrison, 'Potential Revisions' 40; *Border and Transborder Armed Actions (Nicaragua v Honduras)* (Jurisdiction and Admissibility) Counter-Memorial (Nicaragua) para 123; Wittmann (n 6) 600. For the meaning of the 'condition of reciprocity' in Art 36(3) of the Statute see above n 38 of this ch.

[58] cp Waldock (n 38) 257; Weiss (n 26) 83; Thirlway (n 38) 104 f.

[59] Thirlway, ibid 104.

[60] cp E Gordon, 'Legal Disputes' 219–22.

[61] Waldock (n 38) 257; Weiss (n 26) 83. cp Ministère des Affaires Étrangères 'La Deuxième Conférence Internationale de la Paix—Actes et Documents' (1907) Tome Premier—Séances Plénières de la Conférence 541–43.

[62] sub-s III B of ch 4 at 146.

[63] PCIJ, Series D No 6, 53.

[64] Waldock (n 38) 247. See also Briggs (n 38) 234, fn 2.

Even though it can therefore be said that the drafters' approach has not found its way into state practice, the idea behind it is obvious. The obligations accepted under the Optional Clause shall face an according obligation by another state. As the Optional Clause with pre-defined groups to choose from turned out to be too inflexible for the states, it has been substituted for the possibility to choose the disputes by excluding other disputes with reservations.[65] In this way the states can frame their own groups. What has been the reciprocity for categories of disputes became the reciprocity of reservations.[66]

ii. The Approach to Look for the 'Common Ground'

Today it is common opinion that the Court therefore has to look for the 'common ground' of the declarations in question when states file their application.[67] The 'common ground' are all those disputes which none of the parties has excluded with a reservation. Reservations are therefore applied for both sides and states may invoke each other's reservations.[68] In this respect there is no difference to the application of Article 21(1) VCLT.[69] Under the Optional Clause there has, however, been a further discussion on whether the reservation remains as it is in the declaration which contains it or whether it adjusts to the other state when it is invoked via the principle of reciprocity.

An example would be a state A which has excluded all disputes relating to 'its ports'.[70] If state A now files an application against state B the question arises what content the reservation has when state B invokes it.

---

[65] See sub-s II B i of ch 5 at 175.

[66] See also E Decaux, *Réciprocité* 88.

[67] MO Hudson, *Permanent Court* 466; Rosenne and Ronen (n 1) 733; *Nuclear Tests (Australia v France)* (Judgment) [1974] ICJ Rep 253, 114; Waldock (n 38) 257–61. cp also Decaux, ibid 88; V Lamm, 'Reciprocity' 49; Tomuschat (n 3) para 29. For an earlier approach see eg Kelsen who considered it as sufficient that the applicant made an Optional Clause declaration. He did not take the applicant's reservations into consideration. On this way the reservations only worked for the states which had attached them to their declarations (Kelsen (n 6) 526 f; cp also E Hambro, 'The Jurisdiction' 186 f).

[68] *Electricity Company of Sofia and Bulgaria (Belgium v Bulgaria)* (n 38) 63, 81; *Case of Certain Norwegian Loans (France v Norway)* (n 38) 27; *Interhandel Case (Switzerland v United States of America)* (Preliminary Objections) [1959] ICJ Rep 6, 23; *Whaling in the Antarctic (Australia v Japan; New Zealand intervening)* (Merits) [2014] paras 32–41; *Case concerning the Right of Passage over Indian Territory (Portugal v India)* (Preliminary Objections) Oral Proceedings (CR 1957) (India) 41–45; *Whaling in the Antarctic (Australia v Japan; New Zealand intervening)* (Judgment) Counter-Memorial (Japan) paras 1.13 f; R Bernhardt, 'Gegenseitigkeitsprinzip' 621; Briggs (n 38) 245; Decaux, ibid 88; de Fumel (n 29) 5; JA Frowein, 'International Court' 162; Gharbi (n 28) 466; Hudson, ibid 465 f; N Kebbon, 'Optional Clause' 259; Kolb (n 6) 476 f; Rosenne and Ronen (n 1) 733; MM Whiteman, *Digest* 1296. cp also Art 39(3) of the General Act: 'If one of the parties to a dispute has made a reservation, the other parties may enforce the same reservation in regard to that party'.

[69] cp also ILC 'Report of the International Law Commission on the Work of Its 62nd Session' (n 43) 140.

[70] This example is taken from MO Hudson, *Cour Permanente* 472 and has also been used in Decaux (n 66) 89.

The reservation could either still refer to the ports of state A which is the reservation's meaning which it has in state A's declaration. On the other hand the reservation could also refer to state B's ports because this is the meaning the reservation would have in state B's declaration ('its ports'). The last approach would have the result that the specific object of the reservation changes depending on who files an application. If state B files an application state A can invoke its reservation and exclude disputes relating to ports in state A. If state A files an application, state B can invoke the same reservation to exclude disputes relating to ports in state B. Following the first approach the reservation would relate to ports in state A in both cases.

Confronted with this situation, one answer could be to maximise the impact of the reservation and to allow both states to exclude disputes relating to the ports of both states. Concerning this approach, Decaux asked whether state A could really bar state B from introducing procedures concerning disputes relating to ports in state B.[71] This seems wrong because the reservation of state A does not cover such disputes,[72] and there is no reservation of state B that state A could invoke. State A could only try to change the scope of its own reservation by reading it into state B's declaration and then invoking it reciprocally.[73]

iii. No 'Adjustment' of the Reservation if Invoked by Its Author

The Court had to deal with such an attempt in the *Interhandel* case. In that case, the United States had a declaration which covered only disputes arising 'hereafter' which meant that the declaration excluded prior disputes. The question was which declaration's date of entry into force was decisive. The dispute between Switzerland and the United States arose on 26 July 1948. The United States' declaration became effective on 26 July 1946 and therefore the reservation for prior disputes so far did not exclude the particular dispute. But Switzerland's declaration became effective on 28 July 1948 and therefore after the dispute arose. The United States now wanted the latter date to be decisive for its reservation and argued that if Switzerland could invoke the 'hereafter arising' it could defend itself against a similar application by the United States. The United States should therefore likewise be able to use the reservation against Switzerland's application in the current case.[74]

---

[71] Decaux (n 66) 89. cp also Hudson, ibid 472.
[72] Of course, this would be different if the reservation of state A excluded all disputes concerning all ports in all states.
[73] cp Decaux (n 66) 92 f: 'effet de boomerang'.
[74] *Interhandel Case (Switzerland v United States of America)* (Preliminary Objections) Memorial (United States of America) 310–15. See also *Interhandel Case (Switzerland v United States of America)* (n 68) 10 f, 22 f. cp also the reasoning of France in the *Phosphates in Morocco* case (*Phosphates in Morocco (Italy v France)*) (Documents of the Written Proceedings) PCIJ Series C No 84 (France) 714 and above in sub-s I D of ch 1 at 19).

The Court did not follow this reasoning. According to the Court the principle of reciprocity did not allow states to invoke a reservation which does not appear in another state's declaration.[75] With good reason this judgment found wide support in literature.[76] The United States' approach would lead to something like double reciprocity which is contradictive. It would require that the reservation if invoked by Switzerland would adjust to the Swiss declaration. It would further require that the United States can then invoke the reservation with the meaning it has got by the first reciprocal application and that this time the reservation would not adjust to the United States' declaration.[77] In this regard it can be concluded that a reservation always and only refers to its own declaration if the state with that declaration is the respondent. Using the example from above, this means that state A's reservation always refers to disputes about the ports in state A if state B files the application.[78]

iv. No 'Adjustment' of the Reservation if Invoked by Another State

The question remains to which declaration the reservation refers when state A files the application. For this question the rationale of the *Interhandel* case could be that the United States' declaration covers all disputes after 26 August 1946 while the declaration of Switzerland covers all disputes and no declaration excludes disputes before 28 July 1948. The 'common ground' of both declarations therefore refers to disputes after 26 August 1946.[79] This way, both states accept the 'same obligation' which would be an obligation relating to all disputes after 26 August 1946.

The Court adopted this approach in the orders concerning the *Use of Force* cases. Here, the applicant Yugoslavia had included only 'disputes arising or which may arise after the signature of the present Declaration, with regard to the situations or facts subsequent to this signature'. Yugoslavia had submitted its declaration on 26 April 1999 while for example the respondent Canada had submitted its declaration on 10 May 1994. As Canada invoked the Yugoslavian reservation via reciprocity it could be said that the 'present declaration' for Canada is the Canadian and that therefore 10 May 1994 is the decisive date. The Court, however, did not adjust the reservation to the Canadian declaration. Without comment it

---

[75] *Interhandel Case (Switzerland v United States of America)* (n 68) 23.

[76] See eg Alexandrov (n 25) 54 f; Briggs (n 38) 248 f; Decaux (n 66) 103–07; Lamm (n 67) 59. For the same conclusion drawn from the *Phosphates in Morocco* case see Waldock (n 38) 258 f.

[77] cp also Decaux, ibid 104; Lamm, ibid 59; G Perrin, 'Interhandel' 153–55; Thirlway (n 38) 124.

[78] cp also *Case concerning the Aerial Incident of July 27th, 1955 (Israel v Bulgaria)* (Preliminary Objections) Oral Proceeding (CR 1959/1) (Israel) 513 (Rosenne).

[79] cp also the similar position of *Phosphates in Morocco (Italy v France)* (n 74) (Italy) 840.

referred to 26 April 1999, the date of the Yugoslavian declaration.[80] With this approach the result for the port example would be that the reservation always refers to disputes relating to the ports of state A independently of who invokes it.[81]

It might be argued that this approach had not been followed by the Court in the earlier *Norwegian Loans* case. In this case Norway wanted to invoke the French Connally Reservation which excluded 'differences relating to matters which are essentially within the national jurisdiction as understood by the Government of the French Republic'. Following the reasoning from above, the reservation would refer to the French national jurisdiction no matter who invokes the reservation. The Court, however, decided that 'Norway, equally with France, is entitled to except from the compulsory jurisdiction of the Court disputes understood by Norway to be essentially within its national jurisdiction'.[82] '[I]ts jurisdiction' here seems to refer to the Norwegian national jurisdiction and not the French one.[83] For Minagawa, this leads to the conclusion that in the port example, state B could also exclude disputes relating to ports in state B when state B is sued by state A.[84] This would be a contradiction to the orders in the *Use of Force* cases as understood above. Yet, as said above the part of the Connally Reservation referring to the domestic jurisdiction is unimportant and the reservation grants a right to veto the Court's jurisdiction.[85] Therefore, the application of this reservation in the *Norwegian Loans* case does not contradict the result found so far in this sub-section. Norway, like France, was just entitled to veto the Court's proceedings.

v. Conclusion

With this it can be concluded that also in the Court's jurisprudence the 'common ground' is abstract and does not change according to who invokes it.[86]

---

[80] *International Status of South West Africa* (Advisory Opinion) [1950] ICJ Rep 128, paras 21–29.

[81] cp also *Case concerning the Aerial Incident of July 27th, 1955 (Israel v Bulgaria)* (n 78) (Israel) 504–14, 536 (Rosenne) and the pleading of Pellet in the *Whaling in the Antarctic* case: 'Pour répondre à la question de savoir si le présent différend relève ou non de la compétence de la Cour, il convient donc de se placer du point de vue de l'Australie et de se demander si celle-ci pourrait s'opposer avec succès au règlement du différend par la Cour dans l'hypothèse où elle serait défenderesse dans une affaire du même type que celle qu'elle vous a soumise' (*Whaling in the Antarctic (Australia v Japan; New Zealand intervening)* (Judgment) Oral Proceedings (CR 2013/12) (Japan) 28 para 12 (Pellet)).

[82] *Case of Certain Norwegian Loans (France v Norway)* (n 38) 24.

[83] So JHW Verzijl, 'Optional Clause' 590.

[84] T Minagawa, 'Reciprocity' 37, fn 21 (with the difference that Minagawa referred to continental shelves).

[85] See s V of ch 4 at 160.

[86] Thirlway (n 38) 113. See also Bernhardt (n 68) 623 f who only wants to switch the parties before the Court and leave the rest of the case untouched. And cp also the example in Verzijl (n 83) 590.

This is especially convincing in light of the genesis presented above. The groups of disputes as provided by the drafters of the Statute of the Permanent Court would likewise not have changed depending on who filed the application. With the reservations, applied as suggested here, also the group of disputes excluded by the reservation always remains the same. If in the port example the reservation of state A would adjust to state B if state A filed an application the amount of disputes covered by a declaration would suddenly change. The result would be that state A could file proceedings against state B for disputes concerning its own ports and state B could file proceedings against state A for disputes for its own ports while the same disputes would be excluded from the Optional Clause declarations if the other state filed that application. Such a concept of reciprocity would render all reservations into mutable elements which take forms different to the forms the introducing party gave them.[87]

Following the method presented here, reciprocity also provides satisfying results for reservations which are generally considered as being *ratione personae*.[88] In the case of Anti Ambush Clauses for example, the 'other party' in its text also refers to the newcomer state when the latter invokes the reservation via reciprocity.[89] If the reservation would adjust to that state's declaration 'the other state' would be the other state which might have made its Optional Clause declaration a long time ago. The Anti Ambush Clause would then not apply. With such an understanding the clauses would be a one-sided benefit and states could make such clauses with any period shorter than the period their Optional Clause declarations exist to be able to file applications against states and bar those states from doing the same. With the way suggested above on the other hand, the 'other party' in the Anti Ambush Clause remains the state which has not made the reservation. So in each constellation the clause hinders both states equally. Anti Ambush Clauses made in new declarations bar neither applications by the older states nor applications by the new state. Taking the object and purpose of these reservations to prevent 'ambushes' against the state making the reservation into account,[90] this result is convincing.

---

[87] cp *Case concerning the Aerial Incident of July 27th, 1955 (Israel v Bulgaria)* (n 78) (Israel) 504–14 (Rosenne).

[88] According to Weiss, in 1987, it was still an open question whether the principle of reciprocity applies on these reservations (Weiss (n 26) 91 f). Yet, she presented no reason why it should not. As it has been said above there is basically no meaning attached to the categories of disputes (see above sub-s I C of ch 5 (170)).

[89] For the same result see FJ Garcia, *Jurisdicción Obligataria* 312 f. For the opposite result see Maus who, however, did not present his reasoning in this regard (Maus (n 37) 147).

[90] See sub-s III D of ch 3 at 108 and F at 116.

C. 'Formal Conditions'

Due to its appearance in the Court's jurisprudence and in literature the notion of 'formal conditions' also has to be discussed here. Its underlying concept suggests that there is an exception for the reciprocal application for certain reservations made under the Optional Clause.

i. What are 'Formal Conditions'?

According to the Court, 'formal conditions' are reservations which concern the 'creation, duration or extinction' of declarations. The Court distinguished these conditions from reservations which for the Court concern the 'subject-matter' of the commitment entered into with an Optional Clause declaration.[91] According to the Court states can only invoke the latter reciprocally while the former only work for the state which included them in its declaration.[92]

Leaving the possible reasons for this distinction aside, firstly, the Court's broad definition of 'formal conditions' surprises. If 'creation, duration or extinction' would be interpreted broadly the definition would for example also cover suspensive reservations like that provided for in Article 36(3) of the Statute or reservations which limit the duration of a declaration for a period of time, like for example five years. Yet, this seems not to be the Court's position. The exclusion of these reservations from the reciprocal invocation of reservations would lead to the result that a state whose Optional Clause declaration has already expired or whose Optional Clause declaration has not yet entered into force could nonetheless invoke it to file applications against other states. It seems absurd if in such cases the respondents could not invoke the reservation in that state's declaration.

Of course, a state cannot argue that another state's declaration is only valid for a certain period of time and that therefore its own declaration should be valid for that period, too.[93] But as shown above,[94] this is just the result of the regular application of the principle of reciprocity: The reservation does not adjust to the declaration of the invoking state.

---

[91] *Military and Paramilitary Activities in and against Nicaragua (Nicaragua v United States of America)* (n 38) paras 62, 64. See also *Land and Maritime Boundary between Cameroon and Nigeria (Cameroon v Nigeria: Equatorial Guinea intervening)* (Preliminary Objections) [1998] ICJ Rep 275, para 43; DW Greig, 'Confrontation' 171; Weiss (n 26) 91 f; Wittmann (n 6) 146. Kolb introduced the distinction between 'content' and 'container' (Kolb (n 6) 473).

[92] *Military and Paramilitary Activities in and against Nicaragua (Nicaragua v United States of America)* (n 38) paras 62, 64. See also below sub-s II C iv a of ch 5 at 192.

[93] *Military and Paramilitary Activities in and against Nicaragua (Nicaragua v United States of America)* (n 30) para 149.

[94] See sub-s II B of ch 5 at 175.

If a reservation provides a fixed period of validity (eg 5 years) for the declaration it is declared with (eg in 1993), the end of that period depends on that declaration (here eg 1998). Another state cannot invoke that reservation for its own declaration (eg from 1991) to make it end earlier (here in 1996) if it normally runs longer (eg until 1998).[95] That latter declaration remains in force according to its own terms. In this respect the situation is similar to that for reservations excluding prior disputes as discussed above.[96] There is no difference between these reservations, as both are applied reciprocally.

Therefore, it seems as if the Court's definition of 'formal conditions' must be interpreted differently. It could be interpreted in light of the Court's further remarks on the principle of reciprocity. In the *Right of Passage* and the *Nicaragua* case, the Court has already presented its opinion on the period of time in which the principle of reciprocity applies. For the Court the principle of reciprocity only applied at the 'moment of the filing of an application instituting proceedings'. It wanted to determine 'the same obligations' only in that moment.[97] With that approach, time limits and suspensive reservations can all be applied reciprocally because in that crucial moment it is always possible to assess whether a declaration is not yet in force or has already expired.[98] With such an approach a state can, of course, also invoke that the other state's declaration has been withdrawn.[99]

The only reservations known so far which cannot be applied with such an approach are those allowing states to withdraw.[100] These have to be invoked before the seisin of the Court as withdrawals after that moment have no influence on the proceedings set in motion anymore.[101] For reservations allowing withdrawals it is therefore crucial whether there is 'pre-seisin reciprocity'.[102] On the other hand all other reservations including for example time limits, suspensive reservations and also the Connally Reservation can still be effectively invoked when the application is filed.

---

[95] cp also the result in *Military and Paramilitary Activities in and against Nicaragua (Nicaragua v United States of America)* (n 30) para 149 (with a similar example).

[96] cp sub-s II B of ch 5 at 175. Decaux wrote that the Court did not apply the principle of reciprocity on reservations *ratione temporis* (Decaux (n 66) 108; cp also Gharbi (n 28) 470). Yet, it becomes obvious from his explanation that Decaux referred to the fact that the Court had not adjusted the reservations in question to the respondent's declaration. For the latter point see sub-ss II B iii and iv of ch 5 at 177–79.

[97] *Case concerning the Right of Passage over Indian Territory (Portugal v India)* (n 38) 144; *Military and Paramilitary Activities in and against Nicaragua (Nicaragua v United States of America)* (n 38) para 64. See also the interpretation of these judgments in de Fumel (n 29) 6.

[98] cp C Debbasch, 'La compétence' 252.

[99] *Case concerning the Right of Passage over Indian Territory (Portugal v India)* (n 38) 144.

[100] cp Debbasch (n 98) 252–54.

[101] cp Briggs (n 38) 276 f and see the presentation of the *Nottebohm* case in sub-s I C ii of ch 1 at 15.

[102] The notion is taken from Cohn (n 26) 699. See also Kolb (n 6) 482, 483.

In light of this context it seems to be possible to interpret the broad wording used by the Court to describe 'formal conditions' more strictly. It seems as if the Court did not want to exclude all reservations relating to the 'creation, duration or extinction' of Optional Clause declarations from the reciprocal application. It only intended to exclude reservations allowing states to withdraw their declaration. Only these reservations have been relevant in the two cases concerning this question, the *Right of Passage* and the *Nicaragua* case.[103]

After this has been clarified, the question is whether reservations allowing withdrawals can be invoked pre seisin by other states. Like the Connally Reservation, the reservations allowing states to withdraw establish a right,[104] and they could likewise be invoked. According to the law of treaties there seems to be no problem with this. As said above, the reservations allowing withdrawals are generally nothing particular,[105] and the general exceptions concerning the reciprocal application of reservations law do not apply to the Optional Clause.[106]

ii. Article 36 of the Statute and the Drafters' Attitude on Reciprocity

As said above, the basis for the reciprocal invocation of reservations under the Optional Clause has been considered to be the 'the same obligation' part of Article 36(2) of the Statute which originally had been designed to refer to the groups of disputes named in the paragraph.[107] It could now be argued that, as the drafters provided reciprocity only in this regard, only reservations which relate directly to the amount of disputes covered by the declaration can be invoked reciprocally.[108] Reservations relating to the declaration itself would not be covered and could not be invoked reciprocally. This would support a kind of distinction as the Court's definition of 'formal conditions' suggested.[109]

On the other hand Article 36(3) of the Statute suggests two reservations which refer to the Optional Clause declarations as such.[110] These concern the entry into force of the declarations and their ending and work reciprocally as no state is able to invoke a declaration which has not yet entered into force or is not in force anymore.[111] As these two kinds of reservations

---

[103] For these see sub-s II C iv of ch 5 at 192.
[104] AN Farmanfarma, *Declarations* 77. For the Connally Reservation see s V of ch 4 at 160.
[105] See sub-s I A of ch 5 at 166.
[106] See sub-s II A of ch 5 at 172.
[107] See sub-s II B i of ch 5 at 175.
[108] cp Weiss (n 26) 86.
[109] See sub-s II C i of ch 5 at 181.
[110] For the interpretation of Art 36(3) of the Statute see sub-s III A of ch 5 at 200 and above n 38 of this ch.
[111] See sub-s II C i of ch 5 at 181.

and the choice of disputes in Article 36(2) of the Statute are every choice the Statute expressly allows, it can be very well maintained that every choice expressly allowed by the Statute works reciprocally. There is therefore not only reciprocity as far as it is provided for in Article 36(2) of the Statute. With this approach the reciprocal application of reservations is therefore not necessarily limited to reservations relating directly to the amount of disputes covered.

Unfortunately, the drafters' discussion of the issue of reciprocity has been rather short and has not even been completely reproduced.[112] Furthermore, they did not anticipate any other reservations to be made to Optional Clause declarations besides those named in Article 36(3) of the Statute of the Permanent Court.[113] In line with this Thirlway rightly remarked that the draftsmen of 1920 never contemplated on the reciprocal operation of reservations.[114] According to him the 'application of the criterion of the "same obligation" has to be determined without help from the intention of the draftsmen of the Statute'.[115] However, one thing could nonetheless be inferred from the delegates' debates. As the draft in discussion already contained the reciprocity as provided for with the words 'the same obligation', the delegates nevertheless discussed this subject as the delegate Fernandes wanted 'a more explicit statement concerning the conditions of reciprocity'.[116] Delegate Huber remarked that the draft already contained a reciprocity *ratione materiae*. What Fernandes suggested was for him a 'reciprocity *ratione personae*'. According to Huber they could combine those two things without difficulty.[117] Together the delegates drafted what today is the 'condition of reciprocity' in Article 36(3) of the Statute.[118] Even though this was all the delegates drafted in the short time, it can be said that reciprocity was important to them.[119] Concerning the League of Nations in general, Fernandes later said: '[W]e have entered into mutual undertakings, not only with obligations on one side and rights on the other; rights and obligations are reciprocal'.[120]

---

[112] League of Nations, *Records of the First Assembly, Meetings of the Committees* 313 ('after some discussion').

[113] See sub-s III B iv b 1 of ch 5 at 227.

[114] Thirlway (n 38) 112. See also Waldock (n 38) 257; Decaux (n 66) 85; Lamm (n 67) 52.

[115] Thirlway, ibid 134.

[116] League of Nations, *Records of the First Assembly, Meetings of the Committees* 313 (Fernandes).

[117] ibid 313 (Huber). According to the minutes of the debate the remark of Huber followed an earlier statement of Fernandes and not the one quoted in the text. It does, however, not seem as if Fernandes had changed his position between his two statements.

[118] cp ibid 313, 566 (annex 14). For the interpretation of that provision see above n 38 of this ch.

[119] cp Decaux (n 66) 109.

[120] League of Nations, *Records of the First Assembly, Plenary Meeting* 451 (Fernandes). See also sub-s II A ii of ch 1 at 24.

It seems therefore at least likely that, if they would have anticipated the use of reservations, they would have provided rules for the Optional Clause so that all reservations would be applied reciprocally.

This, the drafters' intention, would also be in line with the attitude that had generally dominated international law in those days. States have basically accepted deductions from their sovereignty only for similar concessions by other states.[121] As, for example, the states discussed compulsory jurisdiction at The Hague in 1907, the adopted declaration on this subject has been introduced with emphasis on the 'concessions réciproques' which prevailed at the conference.[122] Furthermore, in 1926, as the states signatories of the Statute of the Permanent Court debated about an offer by the United States to join the Statute of the Permanent Court under certain special conditions, they have been confronted with a reservation allowing the United States to withdraw their accession at any time. Even though one delegate demanded to be cautious not to discuss the general right to withdraw in public, they considered the United States' right to withdraw in light of their own right to withdraw. Concerning states signatories' right to withdraw, however, there has been no unanimous position.[123] The Norwegian delegate Castberg suggested granting the United States a one-sided benefit and especially justified this with the exceptional importance of the participation of this state.[124] As the Italian delegate Pilotti presented the final draft of the conference he said: 'In the general discussion in plenary session of the Conference, it was suggested that it would be natural to give a similar right to the other signatory States'. He said that the drafting committee adopted this idea.[125] The Romanian delegate Negulesco stated: 'The right which it gave to the Powers to denounce their acceptance of the United States reservations was designed to ensure equality of treatment between all the Powers'.[126] In line with this the Canadian delegate Foster argued: 'In any transaction between nations or people it was unreasonable and unjust—when a conditional arrangement was made—for one party to demand and obtain the right to withdraw, unless the same right were given to the other party'. Foster therefore held that 'there should be a reciprocal arrangement for withdrawal'.[127]

---

[121] B Simma, 'Reciprocity' para 7.

[122] Ministère des Affaires Étrangères 'La Deuxième Conférence Internationale de la Paix—Actes et Documents' (1907) Tome Premier—Séances Plénières de la Conférence 338 f.

[123] cp League of Nations, 'Minutes of the Conference of States Signatories of the Protocol of Signature of the Statute of the Permanent Court of International Justice' (1926) 12–15, 17–19.

[124] ibid 17 (Castberg). See also ibid 13 (Markovitch).

[125] ibid 53 (Pilotti).

[126] ibid 57 (Negulesco). New Zealand proposed to delete the corresponding parts from the draft because it considered the states signatories as not competent to decide such issues (cp ibid 55 f (Bell)).

[127] ibid 58 (Foster).

The delegates Hurst, Sjöborg and Zumeta supported Foster's position,[128] and at the end the delegates only argued on the scope of their right to withdraw and the appropriate procedure for their withdrawal vis-á-vis the United States.[129] All in all this debate clearly shows that, at that time, also the right to withdraw was considered as being granted only in case of reciprocal treatment.[130] This argues for the assumption that, already six years earlier, the states which took part in drafting the Statute, too, would have expressed a similar solution if they had considered the subject.[131]

The current Statute is not different in this regard. As said above, its drafters made no major changes in 1945.[132] They did not even discuss reciprocity.[133] However, as the drafters endorsed the use of reservations,[134] they knew that, according to the Permanent Court, these reservations held good for both states involved.[135]

From all this it might be concluded that Article 36 of the Statute in light of its *travaux préparatoires* argues rather for the reciprocal application of all reservations. In any case it does not argue against it.

iii. The Reciprocal Application of 'Formal Conditions' in State Practice

State practice, however, could provide arguments to exclude 'formal conditions' from the reciprocal application of reservations.

---

[128] ibid 58 f (Hurst, Sjöborg, Zumeta).

[129] ibid 58–60, 61–63.

[130] cp also Maus (n 37) 72, fn 13. The fact that the final act only allowed states to withdraw their acceptance to the United States' conditions and did not grant them a similar right to withdraw (cp League of Nations, 'Minutes of the Conference of States Signatories of the Protocol of Signature of the Statute of the Permanent Court of International Justice' (1926) 77, 83) is due to the special circumstance of the conference. With regard to the right of the United States to accede the delegates only considered them as competent to decide upon the conditions of the United States (cp eg ibid 56 f (Fromageot, Negulesco)).

[131] For the similar circle of participating states cp League of Nations, 'Minutes of the Conference of States Signatories of the Protocol of Signature of the Statute of the Permanent Court of International Justice' (1926) 5–7 to League of Nations, 'Documents Concerning the Action Taken by the Council of the League of Nations under Article 14 of the Covenant and the Adoption by the Assembly of the Statute of the Permanent Court' (1921) 83.

[132] See sub-s II B ii of ch 2 at 59.

[133] The proposal by the Egyptian delegate Moneim-Riad Bey might have brought a change. He suggested an opt-out-system for the compulsory jurisdiction of the Court. The interesting point of the draft was the second sentence of the proposed third paragraph which read: 'Reservations made by a State will benefit any other party to a dispute against which that State may have prevailed itself of the jurisdiction of the Court'. (United Nations, *Conference on International Organization, Volume XIV—United Nations Committee of Jurists* 302). This seems to limit the possibility to invoke other states' reservation to the situation of a dispute. However, with Moneim-Riad Bey's proposal there would have been no Optional Clause declarations anymore. Unfortunately, there has been no discussion about this proposal which had been quickly disapproved by the Committee of Jurists with ten to four votes (ibid 229).

[134] See sub-s III A of ch 5 at 200.

[135] See *Electricity Company of Sofia and Bulgaria (Belgium v Bulgaria)* (n 38) 63, 81.

a. The *Right of Passage* and the *Nicaragua* Case

As referred to above,[136] there have been two cases before the Court in which the reciprocal application of reservations allowing states to withdraw have been relevant and in which therefore also the parties involved presented their opinions. In the *Right of Passage* case Waldock argued in the name of India that Portugal had violated India's rights because Portugal filed its application before India had the possibility to invoke Portugal's reservation which allowed Portugal to add new reservations without period of notice.[137] He said:

> [T]he reciprocity provided for in the Optional Clause was clearly intended to be a general and continuing reciprocity governing the relations between the two States from the date of the establishment of the juridical bond between them until the date of its termination by the expiry of the Declaration of one of them.[138]

Portugal on the other hand referred to the *Nottebohm* case and stated that the Court had already made clear that the only decisive moment in this regard is the one of the seisin of the Court. All that was required from the Court was to decide whether in that moment the states had accepted the same obligation. According to Portugal the Court was not required to ask itself whether up to that moment one state had had the possibility to withdraw its declaration. Portugal also emphasised 'la fragilité et les dangers' the Indian approach resulted in and concluded that 'le principe de réciprocité énoncé à l'article 36, paragraphe 2, du Statut de la Cour ne s'applique pas en l'occurrence'. According to Portugal only new reservations introduced with Portugal's reservation could be invoked by India.[139]

In the *Nicaragua* case the United States basically repeated the position of India while Nicaragua argued as Portugal before. The United States considered itself as entitled to invoke the possibility to withdraw which the Nicaraguan declaration in their opinion provided. It emphasised that it thereby did not want to withdraw its declaration *erga omnes*. It only wanted to do so vis-à-vis Nicaragua. With good reason it emphasised that if it were bound stricter than Nicaragua this would have been 'intrinsically inequitable and contrary to the Statute's tenets of reciprocal and equal treatment'.[140] Additionally, the United States emphasised that, with regard to its own reservation allowing it to withdraw with a period of notice,

---

[136] sub-s II C i of ch 5 at 181.

[137] *Case concerning the Right of Passage over Indian Territory (Portugal v India)* (n 68) (India) 41–45 (Waldock).

[138] ibid 47 (Waldock). cp also Lamm (n 67) 61 f and further Decaux (Decaux (n 66) 100, 102) who spoke of 'India's liberal concept of reciprocity'.

[139] *Case concerning the Right of Passage over Indian Territory (Portugal v India)* (Preliminary Objections) Observations and Submissions (Portugal) paras 84–87.

[140] *Military and Paramilitary Activities in and against Nicaragua (Nicaragua v United States of America)* (n 57) (United States of America) para 405.

Nicaragua had not accepted 'the same obligation' and could therefore not invoke that period. The United States presented the importance of the reciprocal application of reservations furthermore in light of the making of reservations. As states had no possibility to object to other states' reservations under the Optional Clause,[141] it was especially necessary that they could invoke the other states' reservations. For the United States there was also no Court's decision which could have led to a different conclusion and to a reason to distinguish between time limits and other reservations.[142] Nicaragua on the other hand held that the Court had already ruled upon this issue in the *Right of Passage* case and relied on Briggs according to whom international law only allowed states to withdraw from engagements according to the terms of that engagement. Nicaragua inferred from this that '[i]t is the substantive content of the declaration at any particular time that is the subject of the régime of reciprocity and not the right to vary itself'.[143] Lastly, Nicaragua presented the example with the reciprocal application of time limits which has already been presented above.[144] Rightly Nicaragua, too, concluded that a state cannot invoke a time limit in another state's Optional Clause declaration to make its own Optional Clause declaration end earlier. However, Nicaragua inferred from this that 'durational provisions' cannot be applied reciprocally.[145]

Be this as it may, it becomes obvious that in both cases the applicants presented their opinion that the defendants were not able to invoke the terms of the applicant's declaration while the respondents maintained the opposite and were equally sure. In this respect the pleadings of the states before the Court provide an ambiguous picture of the states' opinion on the issue. However, as referred to above, to a certain degree, the later state reactions to a judgment by the Court can be considered as an expression of the states' legal opinion.[146] It could be emphasised that for example

[141] For that see s V of ch 5 at 263.

[142] *Military and Paramilitary Activities in and against Nicaragua (Nicaragua v United States of America)* (n 57) (United States of America) paras 411–20; *Military and Paramilitary Activities in and against Nicaragua (Nicaragua v United States of America)* (n 6) (United States of America) 225–27 (McDougal) referring inter alia to Waldock (n 38) 278 f.

[143] *Military and Paramilitary Activities in and against Nicaragua (Nicaragua v United States of America)* (n 30) paras 145–49; *Military and Paramilitary Activities in and against Nicaragua (Nicaragua v United States of America)* (n 6) (Nicaragua) 73–78 (Brownlie) inter alia referring to Briggs (m 38) 268, 277 f.

[144] See sub-s II C i of ch 5 at 181.

[145] *Military and Paramilitary Activities in and against Nicaragua (Nicaragua v United States of America)* (n 30) para 149. As already established above, what Nicaragua suggested would not have been the application of the principle of reciprocity as it is understood here in light of the *Norwegian Loans*, the *Interhandel* and the *Use of Force* cases (see sub-s II B of ch 5 at 175). In so far Nicaragua's assessment can be considered as misleading and not as offering an argument against the reciprocal application of reservations allowing the withdrawing of a declaration.

[146] cp sub-s III D of ch 3 at 108.

Honduras has introduced a new reservation allowing it to withdraw its declaration without a period of notice immediately after the Court's judgment in the *Nicaragua* case. As, however, the material collected by Alexandrov shows, the example of Honduras is only accompanied by the examples of Canada and Cyprus. Suriname on the other hand which had also made its new declaration closely after the judgment in the *Nicaragua* case made it for an initial period of five years and with a twelve month period of notice for withdrawals. Furthermore, many states reserved the possibility of immediate withdrawal even before the judgment and Barbados even did this shortly before the judgment was delivered. Therefore, there is no difference between state practice before and after the judgment in the *Nicaragua* case. Likewise, also the earlier judgment in the *Right of Passage* case had no influence in this regard. It triggered the introduction of Anti Ambush Clauses but had no particular influence on the states' practice concerning reservations allowing withdrawals.[147] It therefore cannot be said that the judgment has changed the states' legal opinion.

b. 'Clause[s] Unilatéral de Réciprocité'

There is, however, another aspect in state practice which might be relevant in this regard and has already been referred to in the introduction of this book. States seem to have tried to ensure reciprocity by the making of special reservations,[148] which, with the words of Debbasch, can be called 'clause[s] unilatéral de réciprocité'.[149] The appearance of such reservations could be considered as proof for the states' legal opinion that the reciprocity in this regard is not provided without these reservation.

The first reservation which could be considered as such a 'clause unilatéral de réciprocité' was the one introduced by France in 1959. That reservation required that the corresponding declaration was made for a period of time which was at least as long as the period of time provided for in the French declaration (three years).[150] As Vignes rightly wrote, it was a reservation *ratione personae* which excluded other certain states from the scope of the French Optional Clause declaration. According to him, the reservation accented the principle of reciprocity.[151] Also according

---

[147] cp Alexandrov (n 25) 156–59.

[148] See already the reference to the Spanish Clause in s I of the introduction at 5.

[149] Debbasch (n 98) 254 f. Debbasch used this term also for Anti Ambush Clauses. For him all these reservations promote a 'justice privée'. cp also Yankov (n 26) 593.

[150] The reservation excluded 'des différends avec un Etat qui, au moment où les faits ou situations donnant naissance au différend se sont produits, n'avait pas accepté la juridiction obligatoire de la Cour internationale de Justice pour une durée au moins égale à celle qui figure dans la présente déclaration' (UNTS, Volume 337 (1959) 66; J Feydy, 'La déclaration française' 161).

[151] Vignes (n 36) 71.

to Yankov, '[l]e but de réserves en que[st]ion est donc d'obtenir un certain équilibre en une matière où en règle générale la réciprocité ne joue point'.[152] For Feydy the reservation was made to protect France against hit-and-run tactics and could be viewed in the context of the 'traditional' Anti Ambush Clause.[153] Vignes emphasised that the reservation granted France time to file an application itself after it had been ambushed.[154] A difficulty of this reservation had been, however, the two questions of whether it applied to declarations without any clarification concerning the duration of the declaration and whether it applied to declarations allowing withdrawals.[155] Anyhow, it can be said that this reservation has nothing to do with the reciprocal invocation of other states' reservations. With or without this reservation, France was able to invoke that another states' declaration is not yet or not anymore in force. Even though the reservation seems to exclude other states' declarations with a right to withdraw, it does not relate anyhow to France's possibility to invoke those reservations. All the reservation does is to require a certain standard which the other declaration has to have. If that standard had not been met, both states had not been able to file applications against each other.[156]

A different issue could, however, be the Spanish Clause of 1990. It is an up to now unique reservation and reads:

> The withdrawal of the Declaration shall become effective after a period of six months has elapsed from the date of receipt by the Secretary-General of the United Nations of the relevant notification by the Spanish Government. However, in respect of States which have established a period of less than six months between notification of the withdrawal of their Declaration and its becoming effective, the withdrawal of the Spanish Declaration shall become effective after such shorter period has elapsed.[157]

This seems to argue clearly for the point that Spain considered the Optional Clause itself as not allowing the reciprocal invocation of the other states' reservation itself.

Unfortunately, literature has only rarely touched this reservation. Merrills wrote that the reservation was an attempt to apply the principle

---

[152] Yankov (n 26) 593.

[153] Feydy (n 150) 157 f.

[154] Vignes (n 36) 71. See also Feydy, ibid 157 f.

[155] Vignes, ibid 71–73.

[156] France dropped this reservation as it made a new declaration in 1966 (Decaux (n 66) 109; Feydy (n 150) 156).

[157] UNTS, Volume 1581 (1990) 171. The reservation is unique, but see the proposals for a new United States' declaration by the American legal scholars Sohn and D'Amato which they made after the United States had withdrawn its declaration due to the *Nicaragua* case (A D'Amato, 'New Declaration' 335 f; LB Sohn, 'Compulsory Jurisdiction' 16, 25). The 2003 Optional Clause declaration of Peru seems to be similar. It provides: 'This declaration shall apply to countries that have entered reservations or set conditions with respect to it, with the same restrictions as set by such countries in their respective declarations'. (ICJ Yearbook 2002–2003, 160 f). Unlike the Spanish declaration, the Peruvian declaration is immediately withdrawable itself.

of reciprocity to the right to withdraw and that it was 'the response to a perceived inequality'. For him it was a by-pass of the ruling in the *Nicaragua* case and 'has yet to be tested before the Court'.[158] According to Alexandrov a reservation like this could be used to 'even the odds' for states which did not want to include a reservation allowing immediate withdrawal themselves.[159] Lamm only wrote that the reservation contradicted the judgment of the Court in the *Nicaragua* case and that 'it would be of interest to know the position of the Court'.[160] According to Ende, the result of the *Nicaragua* case should also apply to such reservations like the Spanish Clause.[161] With regard to that judgment, García wrote that the principle of good faith and also the criterion of a 'reasonable delay' did not seem to bar a Spanish withdrawal from having effect on states with immediately withdrawable declarations. For García the reservation added an element of reciprocity to the Spanish reservation, but he also emphasised that the modification did not make the 'formal condition' a normal reservation. He referred to the Court's jurisprudence and pressed that the principle of reciprocity, as the court understood it, was related to the moment of seisin. The Spanish Clause did not modify this.[162]

Be this here as it may,[163] the Spanish Clause says nothing about the Spanish legal opinion. The Spanish declaration had initially been drafted by a group of Spanish experts which had been gathered by the Spanish International Legal Service of the Ministry of Foreign Affairs.[164] The draft of that group did not contain the Spanish Clause. It was added at a later stage by the 'Consejo de Estado'.[165] That council was not sure when a withdrawal of the Spanish declaration would become effective towards a state with a declaration containing a shorter period of notice than the Spanish (six months). In presenting its incertitude the council referred to the principle of reciprocity according to Article 36 of the Statute and the *Nicaragua* case. The council wanted to give the Court a 'guideline' for such a situation.[166] It becomes obvious that in this regard there was no certain legal opinion behind Spain's behaviour.[167] Having in mind that states normally adjust their behaviour to the Court's jurisprudence as the example

---

[158] Merrills (n 29) 207.

[159] Alexandrov (n 25) 66.

[160] Lamm (n 67) 64.

[161] DJ Ende, 'Reaccepting the Compulsory Jurisdiction' 1169, fn 168.

[162] Garcia (n 89) 315.

[163] For the final assessment of the reservation see sub-s II C v of ch 5 at 198.

[164] Pastor Ridruejo (n 29) 23.

[165] ibid 32; Garcia (n 89) 315. cp also the Spanish document in Annex 4.

[166] See Annex 4. cp also Pastor Ridruejo (n 29) 32.

[167] The same holds true for the still valid Mexican declaration which contains a 'condition of strict reciprocity'. According to Maus the Mexican declaration 'évite toute application différente du principe de la réciprocité' (Maus (n 37) 110). However, the real purpose of this reservation, which was drafted in 1947, remains vague.

of the Anti Ambush Clauses shows,[168] it could only be said that Spain doubted the correctness of the judgment in the *Nicaragua* case. This, however, depends on how the judgment has to be understood.

Concerning state practice it can be said that it allows no conclusion on whether the reciprocal invocation of reservations allowing withdrawals is possible or not.

iv. The Court's Position and Its Arguments Against the Reciprocal Application of 'Formal Conditions'

After the states' positions have been presented in the previous sub-section, it is now interesting to see how the Court decided in the named cases and what reasons the Court presented.

a. The Judgments in the *Right of Passage* and the *Nicaragua* Case

In the first judgment, the one concerning the *Right of Passage* case, the Court held that reciprocity and equality were no abstract concepts and had to 'be related to some provision of the Statute or of the Declarations'. The Court decided:

> It is not necessary that 'the same obligation' should be irrevocably defined at the time of the deposit of the Declaration of Acceptance for the entire period of its duration. That expression means no more than that, as between States acceding to the Optional Clause, each and all of them are bound by such identical obligations as may exist at any time during which the Acceptance is mutually binding.[169]

The Court felt the need to add: 'It is clear that any reservation notified by Portugal in pursuance of its Third Condition becomes automatically operative against it in relation to other Signatories of the Optional Clause'.[170]

As presented above, the United States argued that with this judgment the Court did not decide whether states could invoke other states' declarations to withdraw their own declarations and that the Court only repeated the *Nottebohm* case.[171] Nicaragua's position, however, is more convincing. Already in the *Right of Passage* case the Court reduced the reciprocal invocation of the Portuguese reservation reservations to the invocation of the reservations which might be introduced with the reservation. The

---

[168] See sub-s III D and E of ch 3 at 108 and 114.

[169] *Case concerning the Right of Passage over Indian Territory (Portugal v India)* (n 38) 144 f.

[170] ibid 144. See also de Fumel (n 29) 6.

[171] See *Military and Paramilitary Activities in and against Nicaragua (Nicaragua v United States of America)* (n 57) (United States of America) para 418 f and the United States in sub-s II C iii a of ch 5 at 187 and Maus (n 37) 101 f, 186.

Court thereby decided against the reciprocal application of Portuguese reservation itself.[172]

This understanding of the Court's position is also in line with its later judgment in the *Nicaragua* case. As referred to above,[173] it created the group of 'formal conditions' which are not covered by the principle of reciprocity. It wrote that it was irrelevant whether one state had a more generous right to withdraw than another. The Court linked the establishment of the 'same obligation' to the moment an application is submitted and thereby reduced the effect of the principle of reciprocity to the post seisin period. According to the Court, it was inappropriate and impossible 'to try to determine whether a State against which proceedings had not yet been instituted could rely on a provision in another State's declaration to terminate or modify its obligations before the Court was seized'. To support this argument the Court referred to 'previous cases' and named the *Right of Passage* case.[174]

Taking these two judgments together it becomes obvious that in the Court's opinion states were not able to invoke the other states' possibilities to withdraw their declaration.[175] This opinion has gained the support of several authors.[176] Some emphasised that the reciprocal invocation of reservations effectively doubled their impact and thereby reduced the jurisdiction of the Court.[177] It reduced the states' commitments to the lowest level established by the states with the most and the most comprehensive reservations. In the latter context, Decaux spoke about a 'généralisation abusive'.[178] According to him the Court tried to stabilise the effect of reservations and to reduce their negative impact with its handling

---

[172] See *Military and Paramilitary Activities in and against Nicaragua (Nicaragua v United States of America)* (n 30) paras 145–48 and Nicaragua in sub-s II C iii a of ch 5 at 187 and Alexandrov (n 25) 57 f; Briggs (n 38) 260; de Fumel (n 29) 6; Morrison (n 57) 40; Wittmann (n 6) 243.

[173] See sub-s II C i of ch 5 at 181.

[174] *Military and Paramilitary Activities in and against Nicaragua (Nicaragua v United States of America)* (n 38) paras 62–64.

[175] The wording of the judgments further shows that for the Court it makes no difference whether the state wants to invoke a reservation or the residual possibility to withdraw an Optional Clause declaration provided for a state by the Optional Clause itself (for the latter possibility see s II of ch 6 at 279). According to Cohn, however, the Court had not ruled upon the pre seisin application of 'substantive reservations of the right to modify' (Cohn (n 26) 715).

[176] Bernhardt (n 68) 624 f; Briggs (n 38) 249, 276; Decaux (n 66) 101–03; Kolb (n 6) 482–86; PH Kooijmans, 'Compulsory Jurisdiction' 78–80; K Oellers-Frahm, 'Obligatorische Gerichtsbarkeit' 252–54; Shihata (n 38) 152; Weiss (n 26) 86, 100; Wittmann (n 6) 601. See further Cohn, ibid 721 who addressed only the Court's 'failure to denounce categorically the application of reciprocity to any *type* of temporal limitation'.

[177] Weiss, ibid 95, 100. For this argument concerning the reciprocal application of reservations under the Optional Clause in general see Gharbi (n 28) 439, 458; E Hambro, 'Compulsory Jurisdiction' 151. For the similar situation under Art 64 ECHR see JA Frowein and W Peukert, *EMRK-Kommentar, 1996* Art 64, para 11.

[178] Decaux (n 66) 106.

of the notion of reciprocity.[179] Also Gharbi wrote that a limited use of reciprocity was good because this way the reservations did not double their effect.[180] Oellers-Frahm argued that the reciprocal invocation of reservations allowing withdrawals would introduce legal insecurity as it was not clear when other states could start to invoke the reservation.[181]

b. Criticism Concerning the Two Judgments

On the other hand both the Court's judgments have also received strong criticism. According to Judge Chagla for example, 'it cannot be disputed that India has the right to make use of the third condition as against Portugal as much as Portugal had the right as against India'.[182] In the *Nicaragua* case, the Judges Mosler, Oda and Schwebel argued for the reciprocal application of reservations allowing states to withdraw.[183]

The obvious but nonetheless good argument which is pressed by many is inequality. Everytime a reservation cannot be invoked by another state it leads to a one-sided benefit for the declaring state.[184] As also the United States had pointed to in its pleadings before the Court, equality in the application of reservations is especially important under the Optional Clause as states cannot object to reservations.[185]

The argument, that the reciprocal application of reservations pre seisin created insecurity because it was not sure from which moment on the other states could invoke other states' reservations, does not convince. The moment the two declarations face each other is a clear reference. From that moment on states are able to reciprocally file applications and therefore it would also make sense to consider them as being able to invoke other states' reservations from that moment on. In this respect there would be no insecurity.

---

[179]   ibid 98–108.

[180]   Gharbi (n 28) 470.

[181]   Oellers-Frahm (n 176) 252 f.

[182]   Dissenting opinion of Judge MAC Chagla, *ICJ Rep 1957*, 170 f. cp also Waldock (n 38) 278 f.

[183]   Separate opinion of Judge H Mosler, *ICJ Rep 1984*, 465 f; separate opinion of Judge S Oda, *ICJ Rep 1984*, 511–13; dissenting opinion of Judge SM Schwebel, *ICJ Rep 1984*, paras 109–16. See also S Oda, 'Reservations in the Declarations' 18–19.

[184]   cp also A D'Amato, 'Modifying' 390; RP Anand, *Compulsory Jurisdiction* 186; AP Fachiri, 'Repudiation' 56; K Holloway, *Modern Trends* 673 f; Maus (n 37) 196; Merrills (n 29) 206; S Oda, 'From the Bench' 43, para 38; dissenting opinion of Judge SM Schwebel, *ICJ Rep 1984*, para 113; *Military and Paramilitary Activities in and against Nicaragua (Nicaragua v United States of America)* (n 57) (United States of America) para 420; Waldock (n 38) 278 f; Weiss (n 26) 98; Yankov (n 26) 593; cp further (El Salvador, 'Declaration' 541). For the same position in general treaty law see ILC 'Report of the International Law Commission on the Work of Its 62nd Session' (n 43) 142.

[185]   cp sub-s II C iii a of ch 5 at 187.

Additionally, the argumentation that the reciprocal invocation doubled the negative impact of reservations and reduced the scope of the Court's compulsory jurisdiction deserves reconsideration. The result of this approach would be that some states still benefit from those reservations and others simply do not. It is like adding inequality to a destructive reservation. Giving one state a one-sided benefit does not help reducing the motivation for such reservations. Actually, states are even incited to adopt the strongest reservation as they do not benefit from other states' reservations.[186] Even though the judgments of the Court concerning the reciprocal application of reservations had no direct impact on state practice regarding the reservations allowing states to withdraw immediately,[187] the insecurity of the states on whether reservations are equally applied motivates to introduce those reservations without any period of notice to be safe. Of course, there might be other reasons and states might also adopt those reservations because they want such a possibility in any case for themselves, but it can be said that an unequal application could at least discourages them from raising their standard. As the example of the decline of the Connally Reservation shows,[188] if states realise that their reservations also work against them, they are motivated to withdraw them or to not use them in the first place.[189] Without such an incentive it is likely that at the end all states adopt the most comprehensive reservations. Therefore, it can very well be said that an unequal application of reservations supports a race to the bottom and that is even more destructive to the Optional Clause than the reciprocal application of the reservations. In the latter cases the states at least have an interest to reduce the impact of their reservations also for their own sake because their reservations similarly bar themselves from filing an application.[190]

An exception from the general reciprocal application of reservations, which has to be based on the object and purpose of the Optional Clause, therefore needs a very good reason.[191]

c. The 'Bilateralisation' of the Optional Clause

There have been, however, hardly any reasons given by the Court. Its statements like '[t]he coincidence or interrelation of those obligations thus

[186] cp Debbasch (n 98) 247; Morrison (n 57) 57; Oda (n 183) 22.
[187] See sub-s II C iii a of ch 5 at 187.
[188] For that see furthermore below sub-s III B v c of ch 5 at 238.
[189] Alexandrov (n 25) 124. See also Kolb (n 6) 477 and L Gross, 'Connally Amendment' 357: 'Boomerang effect'. For general treaty law cp ILC 'Report of the International Law Commission on the Work of Its 62nd Session' (n 43) 142 f.
[190] cp Cohn (n 26) 727; Debbasch (n 98) 258; Oda (n 183) 22.
[191] See also Maus (n 37) 98. cp for exceptions in general treaty law sub-s II A of ch 5 at 172.

remain in a state of flux until the moment of the filing of an application instituting proceedings' and 'the possibility that, prior to that moment, the one enjoyed a wider right to modify its obligation than did the other, is without incidence on the question' show the results of its decision but no reasons for it.[192] In the *Nicaragua* case, the Court only wrote that it was not convinced that the alternative was appropriate or possible.[193] The point 'not appropriate' can well be considered as rebutted after all that has been said in the previous sub-section. Concerning the point 'not possible' the Court might have meant what also Judge Schwebel referred to in his dissenting opinion. He wrote that the withdrawal vis-à-vis only one state might give rise to 'complications'.[194] Brownlie, pleading for Nicaragua, spoke of 'chaos'.[195] Kolb wrote that 'the reciprocity of the Statute in relation to reservations operates on an *inter partes* basis' and that

> it does not exist to create reciprocity *erga omnes* on an inchoate basis between all the States that are parties to the system of the optional clause, so as to permit a State to select, in advance, any declaration whatsoever so that, by way of reciprocity, that State achieves favourable terms to any question connected with the State's own declaration.[196]

These statements can be based on the right idea that the invocation of another states' declaration can only lead to a withdrawal effective vis-à-vis that state because a right emerging from an *inter partes* relationship shall not have consequences *erga omnes*.[197] To a certain degree, the United States acknowledged this as, in 1984, it wanted to withdraw its Optional Clause declaration only with effect towards Nicaragua.[198]

The result of this approach would, however, be that an Optional Clause would have more than one single shape. When withdrawals *inter partes* would be possible they might have several shapes depending on which *inter partes* relation is regarded. A state might even have fully withdrawn its Optional Clause declaration concerning one state or some states while the declaration is still valid for others. According to Decaux this would result in something like lists attached to the declarations which contain the *inter partes* withdrawals.[199] For Cohn the whole Optional Clause would be

---

[192] Both citations are taken from: *Military and Paramilitary Activities in and against Nicaragua (Nicaragua v United States of America)* (n 38) para 63.

[193] ibid para 64.

[194] Dissenting opinion of Judge SM Schwebel, *ICJ Rep 1984*, para 116. See also Cohn (n 26) 725 f.

[195] *Military and Paramilitary Activities in and against Nicaragua (Nicaragua v United States of America)* (n 6) (Nicaragua) 75 (Brownlie).

[196] Kolb (n 6) 483.

[197] cp Oellers-Frahm (n 176) 253 f; Waldock (n 38) 278 f.

[198] See especially *Military and Paramilitary Activities in and against Nicaragua (Nicaragua v United States of America)* (n 6) (United States of America) 225 (McDougal). See further *Military and Paramilitary Activities in and against Nicaragua (Nicaragua v United States of America)* (n 57) (United States of America) para 405.

[199] Decaux (n 66) 101, fn 64. cp also Wittmann (n 6) 244 f.

fractioned and there would be an 'overall confusion due to the inability to rely on a single version of a state's commitment *erga omnes*'.[200]

This leads to the last main question of this sub-section which is whether the Optional Clause allows individual bilateral relations.[201] As it can also happen under other multilateral treaties, the relations arising under the Optional Clause could be 'bilateralised',[202] so that there would be different bilateral relations among the states even though they were all bound by the same multilateral treaty. The answer of this question is essential to understand what kind of multilateral treaty the Optional Clause is if it is a treaty.

The wording of the Statute allows no clear results in this respect. And also state practice provides no clear guidance as, besides the attempt of the United States, there have not been any more attempts of such withdrawals *inter partes* yet.[203] However, it can be said that under the Optional Clause the 'common grounds' between the states are already individually shaped by the sum of the reservations in the corresponding declarations anyway.[204] Furthermore, states are free to combine reservations *ratione materiae* and *ratione personae* and to make special reservations for only one specific state.[205] Also without the possibility of withdrawals *inter partes*, states can 'fraction' the Optional Clause by excluding other single states or by making reservations like 'this declaration does not cover disputes concerning environmental issues with state X'. Pushed to the extreme, also without the possibility of withdrawals *inter partes* there could be 71 declarations each in 70 'versions' under the current Optional Clause. For the fragmentation of the Optional Clause withdrawals *inter partes* are therefore just one means among others. Following Judge Mosler it can very well be said that the allowance of withdrawals *inter partes* does not significantly raise the complexity of the system.[206] Therefore, there is, at most, little reason to prohibit the invocation of other states reservations allowing states to withdraw their declaration. And in any case, as already Waldock wrote, the additional fragmentation of the system is a price worth paying for equality.[207] So, as also Judge Schwebel held, 'there is no persuasive reason … to exclude temporal conditions from the reach of reciprocity'.[208]

---

[200] Cohn (n 26) 724–27. cp also Weiss (n 26) 95; Wittmann, ibid 244 f.
[201] Maus focused his whole similar discussion on that point (cp Maus (n 37) 101).
[202] For that notion K Zemanek, 'Object and Purpose' 336. cp also JLI Buigues, 'Les déclarations d'acception' 286 (la 'bilatéralisation des conventions multilatérales').
[203] For mutual interactions of states under the Optional Clause see sub-s III B of ch 6 at 316.
[204] cp Farmanfarma (n 104) 60.
[205] See s III of ch 5 at 199 and there especially B iii e at 220.
[206] cp separate opinion of Judge H Mosler, *ICJ Rep 1984*, 466.
[207] Waldock (n 38) 278 f. See also Anand (n 184) 186 and cp dissenting opinion of Judge SM Schwebel, *ICJ Rep 1984*, para 116.
[208] Dissenting opinion of Judge SM Schwebel, *ICJ Rep 1984*, para 109.

v. Result

All in all this sub-section supports the approach that states can invoke all other states' reservations including those allowing states to withdraw their declaration.[209] The opposite opinion can only be based upon two judgments of the Court which provide almost no arguments and are criticised with good reason. Unlike in the similar situation concerning the entry into force of the Optional Clause declarations the result of the jurisprudence of the Court concerning a limitation of the reciprocal application of reservations is not supported by state practice.[210] The genesis of the Optional Clause even argues rather for the reciprocal application of all reservations than against it. In this respect there is no reason not to apply Article 21(1)(b) VCLT to all reservations made to Optional Clause declarations. For the Spanish Clause this means that it is only a repetition of this general rule and not necessary.

D. Result

The practice under the Optional Clause is consistent with Article 21(1)(b) VCLT. Also under the Optional Clause states can invoke all other states' reservations. In this regard the Optional Clause is like the General Act whose Article 39(3) spells out: 'If one of the parties to a dispute has made a reservation, the other parties may enforce the same reservation in regard to that party'.[211] It does not surprise that the ILC referred, inter alia, to the jurisprudence of the Court on the Optional Clause as it established Guideline 4.2.4 GPRT which provides for the reciprocal application of reservations.[212]

Besides these provisions the 'principle of reciprocity' should not be used anymore as the basis for the reciprocal application of reservations under the Optional Clause. Even though many authors discussed the interaction of Optional Clause declarations and the effect of reservations thereto under the term of 'reciprocity' or the 'principle of reciprocity',[213]

---

[209] See also Anand (n 184) 180; separate opinion of Judge H Mosler, *ICJ Rep 1984*, 465 f; separate opinion of Judge S Oda, *ICJ Rep 1984*, 511; dissenting opinion of Judge SM Schwebel, *ICJ Rep 1984*, paras 109–16; *Military and Paramilitary Activities in and against Nicaragua (Nicaragua v United States of America)* (n 57) (United States of America) paras 411–20; Waldock (n 38) 278 f.

[210] cp sub-s III D and E of ch 3 at 108 and 113.

[211] Ténékidès already considered this provision as containing a general principle and applied it on the Optional Clause (CG Ténékidès, 'Les actes concurrents' 724. See also Maus (n 37) 97, fn 4). Today, this is, however, not necessary as Art 21(1)(b) VCLT already provides so.

[212] ILC 'Report of the International Law Commission on the Work of Its 62nd Session' (n 43) 142.

[213] See eg: Weiss (n 26) 82; Frowein (n 38) 397; Lamm (n 67) 45; Cohn (n 26) 699; Minagawa (n 84) 32 and the strong focus on reciprocity in Alexandrov (n 25).

the term is 'misleading'.[214] And also the Court has already decided that 'the notions of reciprocity and equality are not abstract conceptions. They must be related to some provision of the Statute or of the Declarations'.[215]

In any way, whether or not reference to the principle is made, the effect of reservations made to Optional Clause declarations is not different to the effect of reservations made to other accessions to a multilateral treaty.

III. THE PERMISSIBILITY OF RESERVATIONS (ARTICLE 19 VCLT)

As referred to above, some authors have considered the Optional Clause as being especially generous with reservations.[216] They emphasised the freedom to make declarations and used it to establish the freedom to make reservations. According to them, states which were free not to accept the Optional Clause at all were also free to accept it to a lesser degree.[217] Maus considered the reservations made to Optional Clause declarations to be different from reservations made to declarations of accessions to multi-lateral treaties. For him the difference was that under the Optional Clause all reservations were allowed as long as they were accordable with the Optional Clause and the rest of the Statute.[218]

Concerning this last point it can already be said that there is no differ-ence to the law of treaties in this regard. Also under multilateral treaties, reservations made to declarations of accession have to be accordable with the treaty. And with regard to the fact that reservations made to Optional Clause declarations have to be accordable with the Statute, it has to be said that also under general treaty law reservations made to the accession to one treaty cannot influence obligations which have already been accepted under another. Regarding the argument relating to the freedom to make Optional Clause declarations, it has already been established above that the free choice whether to make an Optional Clause declaration is not dif-ferent from the free choice whether to accede to a multilateral treaty.[219] Therefore, these aspects seem to be no basis to draw particular conclusions

---

[214] Thirlway (n 38) 97, 138.

[215] See sub-s II C iv a at 192.

[216] See the introduction to s III of ch 5 at 199.

[217] *Military and Paramilitary Activities in and against Nicaragua (Nicaragua v United States of America)* (n 6) (United States of America) 220 (McDougal); Kelsen (n 6) 525 f; Jiménez De Aréchaga (n 6) 154; Tomuschat (n 3) para 99; Wittmann (n 6) 331. See also the position of Senator Connally as he made the proposal for the Connally Reservation (United States of America 'Congressional Record' (1946) 10624 (Connally)). See further the position of Senator Morse (ibid 10690 (Morse)).

[218] Maus (n 37) 94.

[219] See s I of ch 3 at 86 and in the current context especially the dissenting opinion of Judge H Lauterpacht, *ICJ Rep 1959*, 105.

on the possibility to make reservations under the Optional Clause as these conclusions would also apply to any multilateral treaty.

For multilateral treaties the permissibility of reservations is determined by Article 19 VCLT. As the following sub-section will show the generous possibility to make reservations to Optional Clause declarations can be explained with a mere application of that article.

A. Article 19(b) VCLT Applied to the Optional Clause

According to Article 19(b) VCLT a reservation is impermissible if 'the treaty provides that only specified reservations, which do not include the reservation in question, may be made'.[220]

This could be applied to Article 36(3) of the Statute which reads: 'The declarations referred to above may be made unconditionally or on condition of reciprocity on the part of several or certain states, or for a certain time'. The clear wording of Article 36(3) of the Statute seems to forbid every reservation except those two expressly foreseen.[221] Under Article 19(b) VCLT a reservation is, however, only impermissible if interpretation of the provisions in question leads to the result that the naming of some reservations shall implicitly prohibit others,[222] and Article 36(3) of the Statute has never really been interpreted as opposing other reservations. Such an interpretation of that paragraph would have been contrary to state practice and the jurisprudence since the early years of the Permanent Court. As the Court was created, the drafters of the Statute decided not to change the paragraph because they knew that it was interpreted as not limiting the freedom to make reservations. They wanted to leave this situation as it was. They said:

> The question of reservations calls for an explanation. As is well known, the article has consistently been interpreted in the past as allowing states accepting the jurisdiction of the Court to subject their declarations to reservations. The sub-committee has considered such interpretation as being henceforth established. It has therefore been considered unnecessary to modify paragraph 3 in order to make express reference to the right of states to make such reservations.[223]

---

[220] See also Guideline 3.1(b) GPRT (ILC 'Report of the International Law Commission on the Work of Its 63rd Session' (n 12) 17).

[221] cp J Crawford (n 8) 79; Gharbi (n 28) 448 f. Vulcan and Alexander Higgins even wrote that in fact only the reservations mentioned in that paragraph were allowed (AP Higgins, *British Acceptance* 6; C Vulcan, 'La Clause Facultative' 41 f, 54). See also the dissenting opinion of Judge LF Carneiro, *ICJ Rep 1952*, 154.

[222] ME Villiger, *Commentary* Art 18, para 11; Walter (n 8) para 62.

[223] United Nations, *Conference on International Organization, Volume XIII—Commission IV, Judicial Organization* 391 f, 559.

According to the Egyptian delegate Ramadan Pacna, 'the third paragraph is practically useless'.[224]

This historical element was also what the Court referred to when it dealt with Pakistan's argumentation in the case concerning the *Aerial Incident of 1999*.[225] Pakistan had reintroduced the idea that Article 36(3) of the Statute is exhaustive and that India's Commonwealth reservation was therefore impermissible.[226] The Court did not follow this reasoning as it rightly regarded Pakistan's interpretation of Article 36(3) of the Statute as not being in accordance with the paragraph's genesis and state practice.[227]

Therefore, it can be said that at least Article 36(3) of the current Statute does not impede states from making reservations even if Article 19(b) VCLT is applied.

B. Article 19(c) VCLT Applied to the Optional Clause

More difficult than Article 19(b) VCLT is, however, Article 19(c) VCLT which provides that a state may not formulate a reservation if 'the reservation is incompatible with the object and purpose of the treaty'. Before it will be applied to the Optional Clause, there shall be a short introduction on how to apply that provision and an assessment of how far the Optional Clause could be treated like a human rights treaty in this regard.

i. Introduction: The Object and Purpose Test

The object and purpose test has been introduced by the Court in 1951.[228] This decision has been criticised, inter alia, because there are no reliable means to establish the 'object and purpose'.[229] Nonetheless, the object and

---

[224] United Nations, *Conference on International Organization, Volume XIV—United Nations Committee of Jurists* 155.

[225] *Aerial Incident of 10 August 1999 (Pakistan v India)* (Jurisdiction) [2000] ICJ Rep 12, para 37 referring to United Nations, *Conference on International Organization, Volume XIII— Commission IV, Judicial Organization* 559.

[226] *Aerial Incident of 10 August 1999 (Pakistan v India)* (Jurisdiction) Memorial (Pakistan) paras D(1), G.

[227] *Aerial Incident of 10 August 1999 (Pakistan v India)* (n 225) paras 35–39. cp also SA Alexandrov, 'Reservations' 99; Briggs (n 38) 232; *Aerial Incident of 10 August 1999 (Pakistan v India)* (Jurisdiction) Counter-Memorial (India) para 64; Kolb (n 6) 459 f; Oda (n 183) 4–6. According to Crawford this was a 'striking case of interpretative development of Article 36 by subsequent practice' (Crawford (n 8) 79). For state practice in detail see sub-s III B v of ch 5 at 233.

[228] *Reservations to the Convention on the Prevention and Punishment of the Crime of Genocide* (Advisory Opinion) [1951] ICJ Rep 15, 24. For the history of the decision and the earlier treaty law see eg C Redgwell, 'Reservations' 246–50.

[229] Dissenting opinion of Judges JG Guerrero, AD McNair, JE Read and H Mo, *ICJ Rep 1951*, 44. See also P Hilpold, 'Vorbehaltsregime' 412 f; L Lijnzaad, *Reservations* 404; Redgwell, ibid 251; Zemanek (n 202) 342 f.

purpose test later became Article 19(c) VCLT and for some authors even represents customary law today.[230] According to Pellet the regime established by the VCLT in this regard is the 'end of an evolution initiated long ago' which likewise facilitates the participation in multilateral treaties and protects their object and purpose.[231]

The question remains how to establish the object and purpose of a treaty. In 2006, Pellet as the ILC's Special Rapporteur suggested two possible definitions for the part of the treaty covered by Article 19(c) VCLT. According to alternative A, that part consisted of 'the essential rules, rights and obligations indispensable to the general architecture of the treaty, which constitute the *raison d'être* thereof and whose modification or exclusion could seriously disturb the balance of the treaty'. According to alternative B, a reservation was impermissible if 'it has a serious impact on the essential rules, rights or obligations indispensable to the general architecture of the treaty, thereby depriving it of its *raison d'être*'.[232] The Guideline 3.1.5 GPRT finally provided:

> A reservation is incompatible with the object and purpose of the treaty if it affects an essential element of the treaty that is necessary to its general thrust, in such a way that the reservation impairs the *raison d'être* of the treaty.[233]

According to Guideline 3.1.5.1 GPRT:

> The object and purpose of the treaty is to be determined in good faith, taking account of the terms of the treaty in their context. Recourse may also be had in particular to the title of the treaty, the preparatory work of the treaty and the circumstances of its conclusion and, where appropriate, the subsequent practice agreed upon by the parties.[234]

With regard to the content of the Optional Clause the question is how this applies to provisions or treaties establishing the jurisdiction of the Court or another dispute settlement body. For the Genocide Convention the

---

[230] For the latter see Hilpold, ibid 414; Lijnzaad, ibid 408; A Pellet, 'Article 19 VCLT' paras 55–62, 168. For the UNCHR the provisions of the VCLT concerning reservations are general international law as affirmed by the Court (UNCHR 'General Comment No 24 (52) on issues relating to reservations made upon ratification or accession to the Covenant to the Optional Protocols thereto, or in relation to declarations under article 41 of the Covenant' (1994) CCPR/C/21/Rev.1/Add.6 fn 2).

[231] Pellet, ibid para 64. See also Walter (n 8) para 72: 'While ... critical appraisals are without doubt correct, the problem remains that no better standard has been developed and that, in fact, in the absence of specific provisions dealing with reservations, nothing other than the 'object and purpose' of a treaty seems to be available in order to evaluate the permissibility of reservations'.

[232] ILC 'Report of the International Law Commission on the Work of Its 58th Session' (1 May–9 June and 3 July–11 August 2006) UN Doc A/61/10 296 (Pellet). For other definitions cp Tomuschat (n 43) 474.

[233] ILC 'Report of the International Law Commission on the Work of Its 63rd Session' (n 12) 18.

[234] ibid 18. cp also J Klabbers, 'Object and Purpose' paras 11, 14–16.

Court has already allowed a complete exclusion of the compulsory juris-diction normally provided for in its Article 9.[235] Also according to Walter there is no general principle prohibiting such reservations concerning the jurisdiction of a monitoring body.[236] This does, however, not contradict the finding of Pellet according to whom 'it is self-evident' that such a res-ervation excluding compulsory jurisdiction is impermissible in a treaty which shall establish that jurisdiction.[237]

ii. The Treatment of Reservations Under Human Rights Treaties as Guideline?

Especially in relation to human rights treaties this issue has been dis-cussed lengthily. With regard to the extensive use of reservations under the Optional Clause, the question has been raised whether the tendencies in human rights law could provide guidance in dealing with reserva-tions under the Optional Clause and whether the Court could treat the reservations similarly.[238]

Today, it seems to be the dominant opinion that the regime of the VCLT can also be applied to 'normative treaties' such as human rights treaties.[239] In their 'Preliminary Conclusions' for the project which led to the GPRT the ILC held that the general 'objectives apply equally in the case of reservations to normative treaties, including treaties in the area of human rights and that, consequently, the general rules enunciated in the above-mentioned Vienna Conventions govern reservations to such instruments'.[240] Consequently also the GPRT regulates normative treaties

---

[235] *Legality of Use of Force (Yugoslavia v Spain)* (Provisional Measures) [1999] ICJ Rep 761, paras 29–33; *Armed Activities on the Territory of the Congo (New Application: 2002) (Democratic Republic of the Congo v Rwanda)* (Provisional Measures) [2002] ICJ Rep 219, paras 69–72. See also ILC 'Report of the International Law Commission on the Work of Its 42nd Session' (7 May–5 June and 9 July–10 August 2007) UN Doc A/62/10 117 f, paras 1–3.

[236] cp Walter (n 8) para 78.

[237] Pellet (n 230) para 120.

[238] cp C Walter, 'Rechtsschutz' para 45. cp also C Tomuschat (n 3) para 83.

[239] See eg R Higgins, 'Introduction' xvii–xxii; B Hofmann, *Beendigung* 30–31; ILC 'Docu-ments of the 48th Session' (n 49) 65 f, paras 153–58 (Pellet); Pellet (n 230) paras 35–58; Redgwell (n 228) 280; Walter (n 8) para 82 and cp UNGA 'Fifty-first Session, Report of the Human Rights Committee' (16.9.1996) UN Doc A/51/40 118; ILC 'Report of the International Law Commis-sion on the Work of Its 42nd Session' (n 235) 113, para 1. For doubts concerning the appropri-ateness of the VCLT see eg Behnsen (n 44) 129; Giegerich (n 46) 742 f, 757; Lijnzaad (n 229) 400; B Simma, 'Reservations' 663; UNCHR 'General Comment No 24 (52) on issues relating to reser-vations made upon ratification or accession to the Covenant to the Optional Protocols thereto, or in relation to declarations under article 41 of the Covenant' (n 230) para 17.

[240] ILC 'Report of the Commission to the General Assembly on the Work of Its 49th Session' (12 May–18 July 1997) UN Doc A/CN.4/SER.A/1997/Add.l (Part 2) 57. See also the United Kingdom which emphasised that the current law of treaties in this area is based on the ICJ's advisory opinion concerning the Genocide Convention, which is a human rights treaty, too (United Kingdom, 'Observations' 424, para 4).

and especially human rights treaties together with other treaties. There was only one provision demanding to pay attention to their particularity. Guideline 3.1.12 GPRT provided:

> To assess the compatibility of a reservation with the object and purpose of a general treaty for the protection of human rights, account shall be taken of the indivisibility, interdependence and interrelatedness of the rights set out in the treaty as well as the importance that the right or provision which is the subject of the reservation has within the general thrust of the treaty, and the gravity of the impact the reservation has upon it.[241]

In relation to the provisions of the VCLT it can be said that at least Article 19(c) is generally considered as being applicable to human rights treaties.[242]

a. The Tendency Concerning the Treatment of Reservations in Human Rights Treaties

In general, also for the treaties concerning human rights reservations fulfil a practical task. They allow states to join a treaty even though one or more provisions collide with their national law and would otherwise bar them from joining the treaty.[243] Sometimes the goal to bind all states can only be achieved at the expense of the level of protection.[244] However, some bodies monitoring human rights treaties have shown a certain tendency to be strict to the states. They declared reservations as being impermissible and bound states even against the contradicting will which they had expressed in a reservation.[245]

1. The United Nations Commission on Human Rights (UNCHR)'s Position

The UNCHR addressed this issue in its famous General Comment No 24 in which it stated that it had the competence to decide upon the permissibility of reservations and to test them against the object and purpose of the

---

[241] For the redrafting of the Guideline see ILC, 'Oral report by the Chairman of the Working Group on Reservations to Treaties, Mr Marcelo Vázquez Bermúdez' (2011) 7. All other particularities of human rights treaties can be solved with the remaining guidelines of the GPRT which are sufficiently flexible. See eg Guideline 4.2.5 GPRT which is also treated above in sub-s II A of ch 5 at 172.

[242] M Bauer, *Vorbehalte* 78 f; ILC 'Documents of the 48th Session' (n 49) 66, para 158 (Pellet); M Nowak, *CCPR Commentary* introduction, para 22; Pellet (n 230) paras 35 f; MG Schmidt, 'Two Covenants' 20 f; Simma (n 239) 662; Walter (n 8) paras 82, 84. See also Art 75 ACHR.

[243] cp C Stahn, 'Vorbehalte' 610; UNCHR 'General Comment No 24 (52) on issues relating to reservations made upon ratification or accession to the Covenant to the Optional Protocols thereto, or in relation to declarations under article 41 of the Covenant' (n 230) para 4. cp also Pellet (n 230) paras 31–35.

[244] Lijnzaad (n 229) 398.

[245] M Herdegen, 'Dynamik des Völkerrechts' 907.

International Covenant on Civil and Political Rights (CCPR). The UNCHR held that, as the supervision by the Committee was essential to secure the human rights, 'a reservation that rejects the Committee's competence to interpret the requirements of any provisions of the Covenant would also be contrary to the object and purpose of that treaty'. This should hold also true for reservations to the first optional protocol to the CCPR which provides a right of submission of communications for individuals. Impermissible reservations should 'generally' be separated and states bound without them. The UNCHR furthermore made clear that it would also consider the overall effect of reservations together and make sure that the states accepted 'the Covenant as such' and not only single obligations.[246] As Higgins pointed out, this assessment of the permissibility of reservations was based on the test provided for in Article 19(c) VCLT.[247] In the *Kennedy v Trinidad and Tobago* case the UNCHR already declared a reservation to a substantive human right impermissible and the state bound without the reservation.[248] Concerning the optional protocol the UNCHR stated that only a very limited amount of reservations was allowed. According to the UNCHR the protocol only allowed states to restrict the retroactive application of their declaration of accession and to exclude cases which were already under consideration by a similar international body.[249] For the declarations according to Article 41 CCPR there is no practice as there has not been any such state to state communications as provided for by the article yet.[250]

2. The Position of the European Court of Human Rights (ECtHR) and the EComHR

Compared to this the situation under the ECHR is and was slightly different as it contains a provision expressly dealing with reservations. Article 57(1) ECHR (formerly Article 64(1)) provides:

> Any State may, when signing this Convention or when depositing its instrument of ratification, make a reservation in respect of any particular provision of

---

[246] UNCHR 'General Comment No 24 (52) on issues relating to reservations made upon ratification or accession to the Covenant to the Optional Protocols thereto, or in relation to declarations under article 41 of the Covenant' (n 230) paras 8 f, 11, 13, 18 f; maintained in *Rawle Kennedy v Trinidad and Tobago* (Communication No 845/1999) (1999) CCPR/C/67/D/845/1999 paras 6.1–7. and supported by Nowak (n 242) introduction, paras 26, 28. But see also the dissenting opinion (dissenting opinion of Judges N Ando, PN Bhagwati, E Klein and D Kretzmer, *CCPR/C/67/D/845/1999 1999*, paras 5 f, 14–16), the critical observations of the United States and the United Kingdom (United States of America, 'Observations' 422–24; United Kingdom, 'Observations' 424–26) and the criticism to certain points by Aust (n 43) 134 f; Stahn (n 243) 610, 611.

[247] Higgins (n 239) xvii. See also PR Ghandhi, *Human Rights Committee* 358; Giegerich (n 8) para 39.

[248] *Rawle Kennedy v Trinidad and Tobago* (n 246) para 6.7.

[249] UNCHR 'General Comment No 24 (52) on issues relating to reservations made upon ratification or accession to the Covenant to the Optional Protocols thereto, or in relation to declarations under article 41 of the Covenant' (n 230) para 14.

[250] G Cohen-Jonathan, 'Covenants' 920; C Tomuschat, 'ICCPR' para 35. For more on that article see sub-s II D iii of ch 1 at 35.

the Convention to the extent that any law then in force in its territory is not in conformity with the provision. Reservations of a general character shall not be permitted under this article.

In the *Temeltasch* case, the EComHR claimed the competence for deciding upon the conformity of reservations with the ECHR and based the competence on the system of the ECHR.[251] In the *Belilos* case, the ECtHR adopted this position, considered a reservation as invalid under Articles 64(1) and (2) ECHR (old) and Switzerland still as a party of the convention.[252] However, the main focus of this development is the competence to decide upon the validity and the consequences of the invalidity.[253] It was not the material validity of reservations which was of relevance.[254] The object and purpose of the convention has been mentioned by the responding government in the *Temeltasch* case but has been of no importance to the case as the Commission only measured the reservation against Article 64 ECHR (old).[255] Also in the *Belilos* case, the reservation in question violated Article 64 ECHR (old) and therefore no reference to the object and purpose test was necessary.[256] In this respect only Article 64 ECHR (old) had been the threshold for the permissibility of reservations and it was an open question whether reservations which fulfil the requirements there could be still impermissible according to Article 19(c) VCLT.[257]

Article 64 ECHR (old), however, referred to the substantive human rights provisions and not to the two optional clauses in Article 25 and Article 46 ECHR (old).[258] According to the EComHR in the *Chrysostomos and others* case, optional clause declarations under Article 25 ECHR (old) could only be made with reservations according to Article 25(2) ECHR (old). The EComHR emphasised the character of the ECHR as constitutional instrument and held that this provision had to be regarded as exhaustive.[259] For the optional clause declarations according to Article 46

---

[251] *Temeltasch v Switzerland* (App no 9116/80) [1983] paras 59–67. Switzerland had not expressly challenged the competence of the Commission (ibid para 59). For that see also S Marks, 'Three Treaties' 40.

[252] *Belilos v Switzerland* (Series A No 132) paras 50–60. Again, the Court also paid attention to the fact that his competence was undisputed (ibid para 50). See also Marks, ibid 40.

[253] cp the presentation in Bernhardt (n 4) 374 f; Giegerich (n 11) 973; J Klabbers, *Introduction* 77; Lijnzaad (n 229) 116–27; T Schilling, *Menschenrechtsschutz* para 98; Simma (n 239) 670 f.

[254] For the competence of the Court to decide upon the permissibility of reservations to Optional Clause declarations see sub-s V D of ch 5 at 271.

[255] cp *Temeltasch v Switzerland* (n 251) paras 37, 84–92. cp also *Chorherr v Austria* Series A No 266-B (1993) paras 17–21.

[256] cp *Belilos v Switzerland* (n 252) paras 55, 59. cp also *Weber v Switzerland* Series A no 177 (1990) para 38 (in which only Art 64(2) ECHR had been violated).

[257] Marks (n 251) 46–48, 61. For Art 64 ECHR (old) see Bauer (n 242) 79; Giegerich (n 46) 731. For Art 57(1) ECHR see Giegerich (n 8) para 33.

[258] Frowein and Peukert (n 177) Art 64, para 1. For these two optional clauses see s II D ii of ch 1 at 33.

[259] *Chrysostomos ao v Turkey* (App no 15299/89 ao) [1991] paras 17–22, 37–42; Polakiewicz (n 10) 145 f.

ECHR (old) the ECtHR took the same position in the *Loizidou* case. It empha-sised that provisions like Articles 25(2), 46(2) and 64 ECHR (old) allowed only particular reservations. With regard to the object and purpose of the ECHR 'as an instrument for the protection of individual human beings' and state practice the ECtHR regarded the named provisions as being exhaustive.[260] In this way, the reference to the object and purpose supported the exclusion of reservations not allowed by Article 46(2) ECHR (old). Like the new Article 57 ECHR,[261] this whole jurisprudence can therefore rather be considered as a case of Article 19(b) VCLT than Article 19(c) VCLT.

3. The Inter-American Court of Human Rights (IACtHR)'s Position

Article 75 ACHR (American Convention on Human Rights) expressly pro-vides: 'This Convention shall be subject to reservations only in conform-ity with the provisions of the Vienna Convention on the Law of Treaties signed on May 23, 1969'. Nonetheless, this seems to make no difference to the ECHR as the position of the IACtHR is again very similar to that of the ECtHR.[262] The IACtHR also established its own right to decide upon reservations.[263] Concerning the permissibility of reservations the IACtHR stated in 1983 that reservations relating to fundamental human rights were contrary to the object and purpose of the treaty. It allowed only reserva-tions which relate to a part of a particular human right and do not deny it in total.[264] In the case of *Hilaire against Trinidad and Tobago* the IACtHR then decided on the permissibility of a reservation which had been made to the acceptance of its jurisdiction under the optional clause in Article 62(1) ACHR.[265] The IACtHR referred to Article 62(2)(1) ACHR which provided: 'Such declaration may be made unconditionally, on the condition of reci-procity, for a specified period, or for specific cases'. For the reservation of Trinidad and Tobago the court ruled:

> It is general in scope, which completely subordinates the application of the Amer-ican Convention to the internal legislation of Trinidad and Tobago as decided by its courts. This implies that the instrument of acceptance is manifestly incompat-ible with the object and purpose of the Convention. As a result, the said article

---

[260] *Loizidou v Turkey* (Preliminary Objections) Series A No 310 (1995) paras 70–89. See also Frowein and Peukert (n 177) Art 46, para 1; Giegerich (n 11) 974 f.

[261] C Grabenwarter and K Pabel, *EMRK* 8, para 5.

[262] See sub-ss II D i and ii of ch 1 at 30 and 33.

[263] *The Effect of Reservations on the Entry Into Force of the American Convention on Human Rights (Arts 74 and 75)*, Advisory Opinion, IACtHR Series A No 2 (1982) paras 12 f. See also Klabbers (n 253) 77. Concerning the IACtHR's position concerning the entry into force of the declarations see sub-s III B of ch 3 at 97.

[264] *Restrictions to the Death Penalty (Arts 4(2) and (4) American Convention on Human Rights)*, Advisory Opinion, IACtHR Series A No 3 (1983) para 61; Giegerich (n 11) 973.

[265] For more on these optional clauses see also sub-s II D i of ch 1 at 30.

does not contain a provision that allows Trinidad and Tobago to formulate the 'restriction' it made.[266]

Also referring to the other parts of the ACHR, the IACtHR concluded, similar to the ECtHR, that Article 62(2)(1) ACHR is exhaustive and continued by assessing the merits of the case.[267] Regarding the considerations of the IACtHR and the strong influence of the prior decisions of the ECtHR,[268] it can also be held here that the reference of the IACtHR to the object and purpose of the ACHR has to be seen as part of the interpretation of Article 62(2)(1) ACHR. Also this decision is therefore rather a decision of Article 19(b) VCLT than Article 19(c) VCLT.

4. Conclusion

In relation to the question whether the tendency described here can be useful guidance for the treatment of the Optional Clause, at this point it already has to be said that some parts of the tendency could only be of limited use. Under the Optional Clause it is basically already clear that it is up to the Court to decide upon the permissibility of the reservations,[269] so that there is no need for guidance in this regard. Furthermore, there are no provisions like Articles 25(2), 46(2) and 64 ECHR (old) or Article 62(2)(1) ACHR for the Optional Clause. As said above, Article 36(3) of the Statute cannot be interpreted as prohibiting reservations under Article 19(b) VCLT.[270] But nonetheless, at least some parts of the jurisprudence under the human rights treaties might be transferable. An example is the UNCHR's proposal to assess also the overall effect of reservations together and to prohibit that states only accept single obligations as such. For the Optional Clause this could mean that an Optional Clause declaration has to result in an acceptance of compulsory jurisdiction with exceptions and not in the acceptance of compulsory jurisdiction for exceptional cases.[271]

b. Comparison to the Optional Clause

The question is, however, whether the reasons which have led the bodies of the human rights treaties to their decisions also apply to the Optional Clause.

---

[266] *Hilaire v Trinidad and Tobago* (Preliminary Objections) IACtHR Series C No 80 (2001) para 88.

[267] ibid paras 78–98 referring inter alia to *Ivcher Bronstein v Peru* (Competence) IACtHR Series C No 54 (1999) para 40 where the court had decided upon the possibility to withdraw an optional clause declaration. For that see the introduction to s II of ch 6 below at 280.

[268] cp *Hilaire v Trinidad and Tobago* (n 266) paras 96 f and the reference there to inter alia *Austria v Italy* (App no 788/60) [1961]; *Ireland v United Kingdom* Series A no 25 (1978); *Loizidou v Turkey* (n 260).

[269] See sub-s V D of ch 5 at 271.

[270] See sub-s III A of ch 5 at 200.

[271] The 'separability' of declarations and reservations will be discussed below in s IV of ch 5 at 254.

Firstly, it can be said that just like an Optional Clause declaration an accession to a human rights treaty brings political benefits with it.[272] Even if states are not really interested in the reciprocal obligations, they are motivated to accede to present themselves as law-abiding states or human rights ensuring states respectively. This contains the danger that they accede but formulate so many reservations that their declaration is an empty shell.[273] Furthermore, as under the Optional Clause, states seldom object to reservations and, if they object, they are generally not eager to let their objections have consequences.[274] Higgins even spoke of 'collusion' among states in this regard.[275] In both cases it is therefore necessary that a third party guards the treaty.[276] In these aspects, human rights treaties and the Optional Clause are similar.

Nonetheless, the differences between human rights treaties and the Optional Clause prevail. Concerning generally all provisions of human rights treaties, it can be said that states object so seldom to other states' reservations, because these reservations are at least not primarily their prejudice.[277] Due to the lacking reciprocity of obligations under human rights treaties, reservations made by one state do not harm other states. They are only a disadvantage for the individuals which would have otherwise benefited from the human rights.[278] The same holds true for reservations made to provisions for supervisory mechanisms as they are considered only as means to enforce the substantive human rights.[279]

It becomes clear that the considerations based on lacking reciprocity under human rights treaties do not apply to the Optional Clause as the obligations there are reciprocal.[280] Under the Optional Clause the reservations hold good for all state parties involved.[281] Under the Optional Clause there is therefore an additional factor regulating and limiting the

---

[272] For the Optional Clause see also Gharbi (n 28) 493; H Lauterpacht, *Development* 65.

[273] cp Simma (n 239) 659–61.

[274] UNCHR 'General Comment No 24 (52) on issues relating to reservations made upon ratification or accession to the Covenant to the Optional Protocols thereto, or in relation to declarations under article 41 of the Covenant' (n 230) para 17; Behnsen (n 44) 140 f; Simma, ibid 664. cp also Higgins (n 239) xxiv.

[275] R Higgins, 'The United Nations' 12. For a similar remark on the Optional Clause see Lamm (n 10) 132.

[276] Simma spoke of a 'certain correlation' between the lack of a system based on states' reactions and the desirability of the observance by a treaty body (Simma (n 239) 664). For the fact that under the Optional Clause states cannot object to reservations and that it is up to the Court to decide see s V of ch 5 at 263.

[277] cp *Reservations to the Convention on the Prevention and Punishment of the Crime of Genocide* (n 228) 23; Higgins (n 239) xxiv; Lijnzaad (n 229) 401, 406. cp also B Simma, 'Community Interest' 342–44.

[278] Higgins (n 275) 11 f. cp also sub-s II D i of ch 1 at 30 and sub-s II A of ch 5 at 172.

[279] cp also sub-s II D of ch 1 at 29.

[280] See s II of ch 1 at 22.

[281] See s II of ch 5 at 172.

use of reservations which human rights treaties do not have.[282] The consequences of this can be inferred directly from the statements of the UNCHR. The committee said that where there is place for reciprocity under CCPR, the rules of the VCLT apply.[283] It added that

> even if the nature of the obligation or the object and purpose of the treaty as a whole exclude the reciprocity of reservations, elements of reciprocity may nevertheless remain in the relations between the author of the reservation and the other parties to the treaty.[284]

Therefore, the UNCHR suggests that the optional clause of Article 41 CCPR could be treated according to treaty law because it is at least to a certain degree based on reciprocity. However, as discussed above,[285] this argument would hold even more for the Optional Clause.

That the approach adopted by the human rights treaty bodies cannot be applied to the Optional Clause can further be underlined with a reference to the decisions of the ECtHR. In the *Loizidou* case the ECtHR expressly distinguished the old ECHR's optional clause from the Optional Clause by the Statute. With reference to the reservations permissible under the Optional Clause it said that 'it does not follow that such restrictions to the acceptance of jurisdiction of the Commission and Court must also be permissible under the Convention'.[286] The ECtHR based this on the difference between the object of the compulsory jurisprudence. While it has to decide upon a 'law-making treaty' the Court has to decide upon disputes between states. The ECtHR therefore sees 'a fundamental different role and purpose' between itself and the Court.[287] In addition to this the ECtHR rightly referred to the inequality created by the reservations which under the human rights treaties are, even for provision concerning the interstate supervisory mechanism, not applied reciprocally.[288] Furthermore, the ECtHR emphasised that state practice under the ECHR

---

[282] For the Optional Clause cp Alexandrov (n 227) 123 f.

[283] UNCHR 'General Comment No 24 (52) on issues relating to reservations made upon ratification or accession to the Covenant to the Optional Protocols thereto, or in relation to declarations under article 41 of the Covenant' (n 230) para 17. Note that the UNCHR was of the opinion that the tendency described above is derogation from the VCLT and not according to the VCLT. For that issue see the introduction to sub-s III B ii of ch 5 at 203.

[284] UNCHR 'General Comment No 24 (52) on issues relating to reservations made upon ratification or accession to the Covenant to the Optional Protocols thereto, or in relation to declarations under article 41 of the Covenant' (n 230) para 17. See also ILC 'Report of the International Law Commission on the Work of Its 62nd Session' (n 43) 145.

[285] See sub-s II D iii of ch 1 at 35.

[286] *Loizidou v Turkey* (n 260) para 83.

[287] ibid paras 84 f. See also Simma who distinguished between 'the regime applying to (inadmissible) reservations at the inter-state level' and 'the role of human rights treaty bodies in light of the adequacy of these rules' (Simma (n 239) 979).

[288] *Loizidou v Turkey* (n 260) para 77. cp also Bauer (n 242) 55 f; Bernhardt (n 4) 381.

was different from that under the Optional Clause.[289] It was also this latter point to which the IACtHR referred. It rightly maintained:

> No analogy can be drawn between the State practice detailed under Article 36(2) of the Statute of the International Court of Justice and acceptance of the optional clause concerning recognition of the binding jurisdiction of this Court, given the particular nature and the object and purpose of the American Convention.

Beside that, the IACtHR reiterated the findings of the ECtHR and argued that unlike the Optional Clause their optional clauses are part of a law-making treaty.[290]

This last point emphasises what the Guideline 3.1.5.7 GPRT spells out, too. That guideline links the permissibility of the reservations to a provision for the judicial settlement to the substantial provisions of a treaty and reads:

> A reservation to a treaty provision concerning dispute settlement or the monitoring of the implementation of the treaty is not, in itself, incompatible with the object and purpose of the treaty, unless ... [t]he reservation purports to exclude or modify the legal effect of a provision of the treaty essential to its *raison d'être* ... [or t]he reservation has the effect of excluding the reserving State or international organization from a dispute settlement or treaty implementation monitoring mechanism with respect to a treaty provision that it has previously accepted, if the very purpose of the treaty is to put such a mechanism into effect.[291]

Interestingly, this guideline is, inter alia, based on the practice of the UNCHR which has likewise connected the impermissibility of reservations under the first optional protocol to the CCPR to the question whether the corresponding substantive rights are obligatory under the convention.[292] Especially with regard to this last part, it becomes clear that the special treatment of reservations by the bodies of human rights treaties is closely related to the human rights and therefore cannot be transferred to the Optional Clause.[293]

---

[289] *Loizidou v Turkey* (n 260) paras 79–82, 85. Supported also by Bernhardt, ibid 380; J Finke, *Streitbeilegungsmechanismen* 306 f. See also *Hilaire v Trinidad and Tobago* (n 266) para 16. For the state practice under the Optional Clause in this regard see sub-s III B v of ch 5 at 233 and s V of ch 5 at 263.

[290] *Constitutional Court v Peru* (Competence) IACtHR Series C No 55 (1999) para 46; *Ivcher Bronstein v Peru* (n 267) para 47; *Hilaire v Trinidad and Tobago* (n 266) para 97.

[291] ILC 'Report of the International Law Commission on the Work of Its 63rd Session' (n 12) 19. See also the commentary in ibid 387–90.

[292] UNCHR 'General Comment No 24 (52) on issues relating to reservations made upon ratification or accession to the Covenant to the Optional Protocols thereto, or in relation to declarations under article 41 of the Covenant' (n 230) paras 11, 13; ILC 'Report of the International Law Commission on the Work of Its 42nd Session' (n 235) 119 f, para 4. See also Nowak (n 242) introduction, para 29. cp also Giegerich (n 11) 969; Walter (n 8) para 79.

[293] cp also Bernhardt (n 4) 380 f. It has also been said that, from a political point of view, the ECtHR has been able to take its 'robust approach' because it could afford it and it was unlikely that states withdraw from the ECHR (Marks (n 251) 62 f). This does also not hold true for the Optional Clause.

iii. General Considerations on the Object and Purpose of the Optional Clause

As no analogy to the jurisprudence of the human rights treaty bodies is possible, a proper assessment on the object and purpose of the Optional Clause is necessary.

Maus rightly wrote: 'Il n'y a aucune raison d'interpréter la Clause facultative comme permettant de faire de réserves qui seraient contraires à son but, à son objet ou aux principes qui la gouvernent'.[294] In 1960, Minagawa similarly wrote that 'any reservation which has the effect of frustrating the very purpose of the optional clause should be regarded as null and void'.[295] For Szafarz on the other hand the application of the object and purpose test on the Optional Clause does not seem to be correct. She wrote:

> Unlike treaties, where it is easy to distinguish provisions with a certain degree of connection with the object and purpose of a given treaty, declarations concern only one provision—Article 36(2) of the ICJ Statute—which specifies a single obligation, namely, the submission of disputes to the compulsory jurisdiction of the ICJ. Therefore, only two conclusions are possible: either it is pointless to speak about the object and purpose of that obligation, or that every reservation restricting the Court's compulsory jurisdiction refers to the very object and purpose of that obligation, and yet such reservations are admissible.[296]

This argument of Szafarz can be supported as far as she says that reservations made to the Optional Clause declarations relate only to the one basic obligation provided for in Article 36(2) of the Statute. It is also right to say that it is not easy to assess the object and purpose of the Optional Clause. Kelsen already held so in 1966.[297] However, in this regard the Optional Clause is not different to other treaties. Also for these the object and purpose test has been heavily criticised for being particularly difficult if not impossible.[298] For the Optional Clause, the question remains whether there are really only two results for its object and purpose.

What can clearly be said is that the very basic object and purpose of the Optional Clause is to establish or enlarge the Court's jurisdiction.[299]

[294] Maus (n 37) 91: 'Les réserves doivent être compatibles avec le but et l'objet de la Clause facultative'. See also de Fumel (n 29) 3.
[295] Minagawa (n 84) 35.
[296] Szafarz (n 10) 48 f.
[297] H Kelsen and RW Tucker, *Principles* 538, fn 114 (Tucker). cp also Crawford (n 8) 81. Kelsen's remarks on the Connally Reservation can, however, not be maintained as he considered states as having *per se* the power to ultimately decide upon the scope their domestic jurisdiction (cp Kelsen (n 6) 527–29).
[298] cp the references in n 229 of this ch.
[299] cp Gharbi (n 28) 495; Merrills (n 29) 244. cp also the position of the UNCHR which said concerning its optional protocol: 'Its object and purpose is to recognize the competence of the Committee to receive and consider communications from individuals' (UNCHR 'General

There are, however, different means to establish the jurisdiction of the Court and the question is therefore what the particular object and purpose of the Optional Clause is and how it shall establish that jurisdiction. There are several considerations possible in this regard which influence the permissibility of reservations.

a. Universality: A Maximum Number of States Participating

The first part of the object and purpose of the Optional Clause could be universality. Especially since 1945 the state community has tried to enforce universal multilateral treaties and became more generous with reservations to achieve that universality.[300]

As Alexandrov wrote for the Optional Clause, 'the right to include in declarations a variety of reservations may in fact contribute to the wider acceptance of compulsory jurisdiction'.[301] Bernhardt doubted this and wrote that this cannot stand in light of state practice. He argued that while the ECHR with the restricted regime offered wide competence to the ECtHR the Optional Clause had only a relatively limited importance even though it was generous with reservations.[302] Against this comparison it can, however, be said that the motivations of states to join a particular treaty can be various and the possibility to make reservations is just one of them. The choice to accede to a regional human rights treaty can have completely different reasons than the accessions to a treaty which provides compulsory jurisdiction for the Court. In this regard the Optional Clause rather has to be compared to the General Acts. These have provided a stronger regime for reservations.[303] Article 39 of the Revised General Act only allows states to exclude prior disputes, disputes falling under domestic jurisdiction and disputes concerning clearly specified subject matters or categories. The number of accessions to those two treaties has been rather low.[304] But as even these treaties are not completely similar,[305] the different numbers of accessions can have various reasons.

Comment No 24 (52) on issues relating to reservations made upon ratification or accession to the Covenant to the Optional Protocols thereto, or in relation to declarations under article 41 of the Covenant' (n 230) para 13).

[300] Hilpold (n 229) 387.
[301] Alexandrov (n 25) x.
[302] Bernhardt (n 4) 381. See also Gharbi (n 28) 440 f.
[303] See sub-s III B of ch 2 at 71.
[304] Up to now there have been 22 accessions to the General Act (https://treaties.un.org/Pages/LONViewDetails.aspx?src=LON&id=567&chapter=30&lang=en (last visit on 19 January 2015)) and 8 accessions to the Revised General Act (see sub-s III B of ch 2 at 71).
[305] See sub-s III B of ch 2 at 71.

Therefore, it can be held that, just like in general international law, reservations allow states to adjust a multilateral treaty to their particular needs. In this respect the reservations are important to achieve universal participation and it can well be argued that they should therefore be allowed.[306] For the General Act, Gallus took this argument to the extreme as he wrote that the choice was basically limited to two alternatives. It was either giving the states enough freedom to form their declarations or to damn them to abstain. He came to the conclusion that an incomplete system was better than none.[307] For the Optional Clause this would mean that the Optional Clause's object and purpose should be interpreted rather generously in this regard. The reservations are the price to be paid for a high number of states making an Optional Clause declaration.[308] All in all it could be said that '[h]owever restrictive the scope of the undertaking may be, it will always be better than no undertaking at all'.[309]

b. A Minimum Amount of Substance?

Such an emphasis on the freedom of the states to make reservations and such a desire to achieve a high quantity of declarations have, however, led to a certain anarchy in the field of reservations.[310]

States started to make declarations containing almost no substantial commitment. According to Kooijmans, for example, some declarations are mere letters of intent as their reservations practically exclude every dispute.[311] Concerning the Vandenberg Reservation Yankov already wrote that it could be declared as invalid because it rendered the commitment of the declaration illusory.[312] Tomuschat wrote that no state which wanted to make a serious commitment declared this reservation.[313] Having in mind the high number of multilateral treaties today this reservation can have

---

[306] cp Alexandrov (n 25) 123. For the importance of the reservations in eg the German Optional Clause declaration see M Bothe and E Klein, 'Anerkennung der Gerichtsbarkeit' 832. See also Waldock who emphasised that 'criticism of these devices, however well-founded in theory, must also take account of the really indefensible advantage given by the Statute and Rules of the Court to States which prefer to stay outside the Optional Clause as against those which undertake its obligation' (Waldock (n 38) 246).

[307] Gallus, 'L'Acte General' 222. cp also Gross (n 33) 21.

[308] cp also C Tomuschat (n 3) para 74 and Kolb (n 6) 460.

[309] League of Nations 'Protocol for the Pacific Settlement of International Disputes' (1924) International Conciliation, Volume 205, 552. See also below sub-s III B v a of ch 5 at 233.

[310] cp Debbasch (n 98) 247, 255.

[311] Kooijmans (n 176) 85. cp also the criticism by C Eick, 'Anerkennung' 768; M Schröder, 'Streitbeilegung' para 92; Tomuschat (n 3) para 70; Yankov (n 26) 597. See also Vulcan who wrote that 'donner et retenir ne vaut pas' and spoke of an 'ombre d'un véritable compétence' (Vulcan (n 221) 53).

[312] Yankov, ibid 594, 595.

[313] Tomuschat (n 3) para 97.

the practical effect that Optional Clause declarations containing it almost run empty.[314] This holds especially true as it also bars disputes arising concerning the Charter.[315] Maus asked whether Optional Clause declarations were valid which were made for only one certain case. A state could thereby choose a dispute which it was likely to win. Maus pressed that such a state took the benefit of the Optional Clause without any risk.[316]

All this leads to the question of whether Optional Clause declarations have to have a certain minimum effect or have to cover a certain minimum amount of disputes.[317] In other words the question is again whether the states can accept the compulsory jurisdiction for exceptional cases only or whether they have to accept the compulsory jurisdiction with exceptions for particular cases.[318] The Institut de Droit International has already emphasised that the Optional Clause declarations 'aient un caractère effective et ne soient pas illusoires'.[319] In line with this Wittmann and Wundram argued that the Optional Clause should provide general jurisdiction for an indefinite number of cases. Therefore, for them states could make no declarations covering only one certain dispute.[320] According to Yankov it would have been better if states abstained from making an Optional Clause declaration than to accede with such reservations as the United States had done. For him there is a contradiction between the making of such a declaration and the reservations and the expressed attitudes are absolutely incompatible.[321] With regard to the position of Gallus, mentioned in the previous sub-section, it has to be asked whether it is not also in the interest of the states to accede to a system where reservations are at least somehow restricted. They might also have an interest in a stable and working Optional Clause where the use of reservations is limited where this is required.

One argument against Optional Clause declarations with huge numbers of reservations covering almost every possible dispute could be the general prohibition of a *venire contra factum proprium*.[322] Also under Article 36 of the Statute the idea behind this principle is not new. The establishment of the jurisdiction of the Court via a *forum prorogatum* is recognised today and is

---

[314] cp A D'Amato, 'General Discussion' 172; V Lamm, 'Multilateral Treaty Reservation' 345; Morrison (n 57) 54 f; Walter (n 238) para 44; Waldock (n 38) 275 and Maus (n 37) 196: 'excluant pratiquement tous les autres différends possibles'.

[315] cp Farmanfarma (n 104) 151 f.

[316] Maus (n 37) 148, fn 71.

[317] cp Walter (n 238) para 45.

[318] See sub-s III B ii a 1 of ch 5 at 204 for a similar position of the UNCHR.

[319] Institut de Droit International, 'Compulsory Jurisdiction of International Courts and Tribunals' (1959) para 2.

[320] Wittmann (n 6) 152; H Wundram, *Fakultativklausel* 28.

[321] Yankov (n 26) 597.

[322] cp C Walter (n 238) para 45.

based on the principles of *allegans contraria non audiendus est* and estoppel.[323] These are similar to *venire contra factum proprium*. As Judge Alfaro wrote, 'the legal effect of the principle is always the same: the party which by its recognition, its representation, its declaration, its conduct or its silence has maintained an attitude manifestly contrary to the right it is claiming before an international tribunal is precluded from claiming that right'.[324] It will therefore be necessary to establish whether a state making an Optional Clause declaration also declares that it makes a substantial commitment without reservations which make the declaration run empty.

c. The Unreliability of the Optional Clause and the Sword of Damocles

Additionally, another question, which has already been referred to in the introduction of this work, is whether it is compatible with the object and purpose of the Optional Clause to make reservations allowing states to withdraw their declaration without period of notice.

Many authors considered these reservations as being a general threat to the ideal of compulsory jurisdiction. Most clearly Fachiri and Kolb wrote that the whole object of the Optional Clause was to create an effective system of compulsory jurisdiction. According to them this object would be entirely defeated if the Optional Clause was open to withdrawals at will since the submission of any given dispute to the Court could always be prevented.[325] Also Maus wrote that these reservations were against the object and purpose of the Optional Clause which was to create compulsory jurisdiction.[326] Similarly, Merrills wrote that reservations allowing the withdrawal of declarations are a threat to the ideal of compulsory jurisdiction.[327] Waldock wrote that they tend to undermine the whole purpose of the Optional Clause.[328]

Some authors suggested a period of notice as remedy. Debbasch, for example, proposed a period for withdrawals of six months. According to him, the Court should declare such reservations without period of notice as invalid as they were against the Statute.[329] The Institut de Droit International

---

[323] cp Rosenne and Ronen (n 1) 672. See also the reference to the principle of estoppel in *Land and Maritime Boundary between Cameroon and Nigeria (Cameroon v Nigeria: Equatorial Guinea intervening)* (n 91) paras 57–60 and cp also *Aerial Incident of 10 August 1999 (Pakistan v India)* (n 226) para E.

[324] Separate opinion of Judge RJ Alfaro, *ICJ Rep 1962*, 40. cp also A Gigante, 'Unilateral State Acts' 347 f.

[325] Fachiri (n 184) 56; Kolb (n 6) 526.

[326] Maus (n 37) 80.

[327] Merrills (n 29) 209 f, 241.

[328] Waldock (n 38) 266. cp also the critical positions of Briggs (n 38) 285; Yankov (n 26) 593.

[329] Debbasch (n 98) 251, 258 f.

recommended Optional Clause declarations which are valid for five years and renew if they are not withdrawn twelve months before.[330] Vignes argued that even a little period of notice was sufficient to allow states to file an application themselves.[331] Gharbi, however, considered even a period of one year as being not long enough to sufficiently protect diplomatic means of dispute settlement. The periods of notice only reduced the uncertainty of the other states.[332]

These two last points mark the problems with reservations allowing immediate withdrawal or the withdrawal with a short period of notice respectively. The first problem is that states can use the reservations without period of notice to dodge judicial procedures by withdrawing or amending their declarations shortly before the application.[333] Secondly, but closely related, such reservations can therefore be like a Sword of Damocles for other ways of peaceful dispute settlement and encourage the premature filing of applications.[334] States that try to solve a dispute via diplomatic efforts may lose their possibility to base an application on the Optional Clause from one day to the other. They have to file an application before the other state withdraws a declaration. As Debbasch emphasised, the uncertainty resulting from the possibilities to withdraw leads to 'la saisine de la Cour alors qu'un différend n'est pas encore mûr'.[335] The result is likely to be described as a 'race to The Hague' between the application and the declaration of withdrawal.[336]

Unfortunately, this is not just a theoretical problem as the history of the Optional Clause contains several examples of states which withdrew their Optional Clause without a period of notice to avoid that a certain dispute was brought before the Court. In 1954, Australia withdrew its Optional Clause declaration due to a dispute with Japan. It submitted a new one which, unlike the old one, required an interim solution before the Court had jurisdiction over disputes concerning pearl fishery.[337] According to Maus, also the United Kingdom's 'national security' reservation had been

---

[330] Institut de Droit International, 'Compulsory Jurisdiction of International Courts and Tribunals' (1959) para 3. cp also Verzijl (n 83) 610.

[331] Vignes (n 36) 73.

[332] Gharbi (n 28) 478.

[333] ibid 437; Maus (n 37) 80, 197–99; Holloway (n 184) 670; Kebbon (n 68) 261 f; Kolb (n 6) 526; Merrills (n 29) 209 f; Oda (n 183) 8; Wittmann (n 6) 197 f. See also s I of the introduction at 2 f.

[334] cp Cohn (n 26) 724; Holloway, ibid 670, 676; Kolb, ibid 527; Waldock (n 38) 266; Wittmann, ibid 190 f. cp also J Sicault, 'Engagements unilatéraux' 653; Rosenne and Ronen (n 1) 694 f.

[335] Debbasch (n 98) 251.

[336] Notion from Cohn (n 26) 699. See sub-s III A of ch 3 at 95.

[337] cp Australia, *Current Notes* 134–37, 139 f, 347, 360 f (Casey, McEwen). See also Gharbi (n 28) 475; Holloway (n 184) 671, 672 f; Separate opinion of Judge RY Jennings, *ICJ Rep 1984*, 551; Maus (n 37) 179–81.

introduced to prevent a Japanese application linked to the British nuclear tests.[338] In 1955, the United Kingdom withdrew its only five months young declaration to submit a new one. The latter excluded disputes with states which had not submitted an Optional Clause declaration in the moment of the dispute. For some authors this was only done to evade a proceeding linked to the administration of Buraimi.[339] Iran's attempt in the *Anglo-Iranian Oil Co* case and the Indian attempt in the *Right of Passage* case were unsuccessful. These states submitted their withdrawals after the Court had already been seised by another state.[340] Maus suggested that in the *Right of Passage* case this was exactly what Portugal had intended. For him Portugal's 'ambush' was motivated by the Indian reservation which allowed India to withdraw without a period of notice. Portugal wanted to bar India from invoking that reservation.[341] In 1984, the United States submitted its notorious 'Shultz Letter' three days before Nicaragua filed its application and aimed at excluding exactly disputes like the one the United States had had with Nicaragua.[342] In 1986, and again shortly before Nicaragua filed an application, it was Honduras which made a new amended Optional Clause declaration. According to Nicaragua this happened to bar Nicaragua's application.[343] The most recent example is the withdrawal of the Colombian Optional Clause declaration just one day before Nicaragua filed its application. According to Nicaragua the current dispute was Colombia's only reason to withdraw its declaration.[344] Colombia objected to this presentation.[345]

The question which arises is whether a situation like this is accordable with the object and purpose of the Optional Clause.[346] If the Optional Clause shall provide jurisdiction which is abstract and truly independent of specific disputes, the possibility to withdraw in the face of a dispute is

---

[338]   Maus, ibid 162, fn 135.

[339]   Gharbi (n 28) 475; Holloway, ibid 671; Separate opinion of Judge RY Jennings, *ICJ Rep 1984*, 551; Maus, ibid 191, 198; Waldock (n 38) 268; Wittmann (n 6) 197, 372 f.

[340]   cp Waldock, ibid 268.

[341]   See also Maus (n 37) 184, 199 who referred to Portugal's behaviour as showing 'une certain précipitation'. For a withdrawal by India which might have prevented a proceeding before the Court see Oda (Oda (n 183) 8) according to whom India changed its Optional Clause declaration in 1974 to exclude disputes about maritime boundaries while it negotiated with Bangladesh.

[342]   cp Annex 3 and see also *Military and Paramilitary Activities in and against Nicaragua (Nicaragua v United States of America)* (n 38) para 13; Gharbi (n 28) 437, fn 9.

[343]   *Border and Transborder Armed Actions (Nicaragua v Honduras)* (Jurisdiction and Admissibility) Oral Proceedings (CR 1988) (Nicaragua) 78 f (Argüello Gomez).

[344]   *Territorial and Maritime Dispute (Nicaragua v Colombia)* (Preliminary Objections) Written Statement (Nicaragua) 129.

[345]   *Territorial and Maritime Dispute (Nicaragua v Colombia)* (Preliminary Objections) Oral Proceedings (CR 2007/16) (Colombia) 27 f (Watts). For more on this case see sub-s II C i e of ch 6 at 299.

[346]   cp Maus (n 37) 80; Gharbi (n 28) 478, 480 and also Kebbon (n 68) 261: 'undermines the purpose of the Optional Clause'.

hardly reconcilable with its object and purpose. In line with this idea at least some treaties providing jurisdiction under Article 36(1) of the Statute contain provisions which frustrate such behaviour as described in this sub-section. Article 35(4) of the European Convention provides that new reservations which exclude disputes cannot exclude prior disputes if they are submitted to the Court within one year. Article 40(2) of the European Convention contains a corresponding provision for withdrawals, additionally to the six month period of notice provided for in paragraph one of that article. Also the Pact of Bogotá contains a one year period of notice in Article LVI(1).[347] Even though the Optional Clause does not contain a similar rule its object and purpose could be understood as being a similar bar to withdrawals without period of notice. The reservations allowing states to withdraw without a period of notice would then be impermissible according to Article 19(c) VCLT.

d. Not Just Political Statements

It is, however, much more likely that the Optional Clause's object and purpose is not consistent with subjective reservations like the Connally Reservation which allow states to determine the scope of the reservation themselves.[348]

Since the introduction of these reservations there has been a lot of discussion about their permissibility. According to Rotter, the Connally Reservation is not different from other reservations.[349] Wittmann considered subjective reservations as permissible because declarations with these reservations provided jurisdiction at least in cases in which states do not invoke them.[350] According to Rosenne an Optional Clause declaration with such a reservation was something 'mid-way between a normal acceptance of the compulsory jurisdiction, and a unilateral invitation to accept the jurisdiction on basis of the *forum prorogatum*'.[351] Merrills left open whether such reservations were impermissible or just a 'serious deficiency' but wrote that they 'pose an obvious threat to the integrity of Article 36(2) [of the Statute]' anyway.[352] It is interesting in this regard

---

[347] See also Art 19(1) of the Optional Protocol of the CEDAW which provides a period of notice of six months and Art 12(1) of the Optional Protocol of the CCPR which provides a period of notice of three months. But see also Art 41(2)(3) CCPR and Art 14(3)(2) CERD which allow states to withdraw without period of notice. Discussing Art 41(2) CCPR, the drafters of the CCPR focused on the question whether states could withdraw with effect on proceedings already been installed (MJ Bossuyt, *Guide* 683 f; Nowak (n 242) Art 41, para 14).

[348] For the interpretation of these reservations see s V of ch 4 at 160.

[349] Rotter (n 26) 643.

[350] Wittmann (n 6) 412–15, 421.

[351] Rosenne and Ronen (n 1) 751.

[352] Merrills (n 29) 240.

that, as the reservation was introduced, even the United States Senate's Committee on Foreign Relations itself warned that the reservation tended to defeat the purpose of the United States' declaration.[353] Also according to United States Senator Pepper the reservation 'flies, first, into the very teeth of the purpose and concept of the Court, and in the second place, into violent conflict with sub-paragraph 6 of Article 36'.[354]

During the drafting of the VCLT Peru had suggested an Article 16(d) VCLT which would have prohibited reservations which render 'the treaty inoperative by making its application subject, in a general and indeterminate manner, to national law'.[355] It is not completely clear why this provision was not adopted but it seems as if the drafters considered the additional rule as unnecessary besides Article 16(c) VCLT that later became Article 19(c) VCLT.[356]

Be this as it may, the crucial question for the Optional Clause is whether its object and purpose requires that the states are obliged by their declarations. It seems as if a state which can still decide on the scope of its acceptance can hardly be considered as having accepted an obligation. This question which also decides upon the admissibility of subjective reservations will be central in the following assessment of Article 36 of the Statute, state practice and jurisprudence.

e. Other Considerations

There are, however, some other approaches to the object and purpose of the Optional Clause which will not be taken into further consideration because they can be dismissed with a few words.

If not all reservations could be invoked by the other states, it could be said that those which cannot be invoked reciprocally cause an inequality which renders the reservations in question impermissible under Article 19(c) VCLT, as inequality is against the object and purpose of the Optional Clause. In relation to the subjective reservations Holloway referred to the jurisprudence of the Court concerning 'formal conditions' and inferred that reservations allowing states to withdraw without period of notice were even more prejudicial to the Optional Clause than the Connally Reservation, as the latter can

[353] See the quote in sub-s III B vii of ch 5 at 253. See also R Pinto, 'Interhandel' 63; Rosenne and Ronen (n 1) 748.

[354] United States of America 'Congressional Record' (1946) 10692 (Pepper). cp also FO Wilcox, 'Compulsory Jurisdiction' 712.

[355] United Nations 'Official Records of the United Nations Conference on the Law of Treaties, First and Second Session, Documents of the Conference' (1971) A/CONF.39/11/Add.2 134, 137. See also ILC 'Report of the International Law Commission on the Work of Its 42nd Session' (n 235) 84, para 4.

[356] cp ILC 'Report of the International Law Commission on the Work of Its 42nd Session' (n 235) 84, fn 232.

at least be applied reciprocally.[357] Yet, as even reservations allowing with-drawals can be invoked reciprocally,[358] there are no reservations under the Optional Clause to which such a consideration could apply.

Furthermore, the Court has already rightly decided in the *Fisheries Juris-diction* case between Canada and Spain that the legality of the behaviour covered by a reservation does not have an effect on the latter. The consent to the jurisdiction of the Court and the merits of the case are two issues which have to be separated.[359] The object and purpose of the Optional Clause does not prohibit reservations made to cover illegal behaviour.[360] The same holds true for reservations covering matters falling under *jus cogens*.[361]

In the *Aerial Incident of 1999* case, Pakistan argued that the Indian Commonwealth reservation was only directed towards Pakistan. For Pakistan the reservation was discriminatory and India therefore unable to invoke it. Pakistan wanted to elaborate this principle from the 'principle of sovereign equality', the 'universality of rights and obligations of mem-bers of the United Nations' and the principle of 'good faith'.[362] In the early days of the Permanent Court, the United Kingdom had similarly main-tained that the Optional Clause was not flexible enough to let states shape their Optional Clause declarations according to the particularities of their different relations with different states.[363] In 1959, Maus considered this problem and emphasised that, according to the wording of Article 36(2) of the Statute, a state should accept the compulsory jurisdiction 'in rela-tion to any other state accepting the same obligation'. He considered the Commonwealth reservations as allowed nonetheless because these were not discriminatory.[364] In line with these statements it could be said that reservations which discriminate against a certain state could be impermis-sible according to Article 19(c) VCLT.[365] However, already in 1930, Hersch

---

[357] Holloway (n 184) 676.

[358] See sub-s II C of ch 5 at 181.

[359] cp sub-s III E of ch 4 at 154.

[360] Thirlway (n 6) 600. For the other opposite opinion cp the dissenting opinion of Judge M Bedjaoui, *ICJ Rep 1998*, paras 47–54.

[361] Kolb (n 6) 501 f.

[362] *Aerial Incident of 10 August 1999 (Pakistan v India)* (n 225) para 30; *Aerial Incident of 10 August 1999 (Pakistan v India)* (Jurisdiction) Oral Proceedings (CR 2000/1) (Pakistan) 14 f, paras 7 f (E Lauterpacht).

[363] League of Nations 'Procès-verbaux des sessions XLVIII A LII du conseil' (1929) League of Nations Official Journal Supplément Spécial No 72 697, para 15. See also the presentation by Lauterpacht (n 20) 148.

[364] Maus (n 37) 146.

[365] For discriminatory reservations in human rights law see *Rawle Kennedy v Trinidad and Tobago* (n 246) para 6.7. Also the UNCHR's members with the dissenting opinion seemed to have agreed on the basic reasoning and denied only that there was a discrimination (dissenting opinion of Judges N Ando, PN Bhagwati, E Klein and D Kretzmer, *CCPR/C/67/D/845/1999* 1999, paras 7–9). Stahn also referred to general prohibition of racial discrimination in interna-tional law (Stahn (n 243) 611) which, however, is different from the exclusion of a state from the scope of an Optional Clause declaration.

Lauterpacht argued conversely that nothing in the text or in the spirit of the Optional Clause could bar a state from limiting the scope of his reservation *ratione personae*.[366] And as also the Court decided in the *Aerial Incident of 1999* case against Pakistan's position, '[s]tates are in any event free to limit the scope *ratione personae* which they wish to give to their acceptance of the compulsory jurisdiction of the Court'.[367] With regard to this judgment, it can be said that states are free to exclude particular other states. Even 'discriminatory' reservations are therefore compatible with the object and purpose of the Optional Clause.

Likewise it is possible to exclude groups of states or to include only groups of states. The Anti Ambush Clause is one example. For Gharbi the latter are illicit as they are against the Statute and the judgment of the Court in the *Right of Passage* case. For him every declaration has to immediately result in the right of the declaring state to file its application.[368] This, however, can be doubted as in that judgment the Court only says that declaring states must be aware that other states can deposit a declaration and then immediately file an application. The Court did not say anything on the situation of states having made a declaration with an Anti Ambush Clause. In the later *Use of Force* cases the Court had no problem applying, for example, the Spanish Anti Ambush Clause.[369] The state practice described above supports this approach.[370] States clearly consider the Anti Ambush Clause to be permissible. And there seems to be no reason why they should not.

One last group of reservations are vague reservations. Hersch Lauterpacht contemplated whether 'sweeping and indefinite' reservations could be contrary to the object and purpose of the Optional Clause but did not decide the question.[371] General treaty law is likewise cautious in this regard. The ILC's final Draft Guideline 3.1.5.2 GPRT provides only: 'A reservation shall be worded in such a way as to allow its scope to be

---

[366] Lauterpacht (n 20) 147. Also supported by de Fumel (n 29) 11 f. Already the committee to the League of Nations' General Assembly which presented the draft of the Statute of the Permanent Court mentioned the possibility 'to specify the States ... in relation to which each Government is willing to agree to a more extended jurisdiction' (League of Nations, *Records of the First Assembly, Plenary Meetings* 467 and see also the speech of ibid 495 (Bourgeois)). However, as the Statute of the Permanent provided no such possibility (cp sub-s III B iv b 1 of ch 5 at 227) it might be a reference to the 'condition of reciprocity' in Art 36(3) of the Statute.

[367] *Aerial Incident of 10 August 1999 (Pakistan v India)* (n 225) para 40.

[368] Gharbi (n 28) 449–51.

[369] *Legality of Use of Force (Yugoslavia v Spain)* (n 235) para 25. For the limited value of the jurisprudence in this regard see sub-s III C vi a of ch 5 at 241.

[370] See sub-s III D of ch 3 at 108.

[371] Lauterpacht (n 20) 169.

determined, in order to assess in particular its compatibility with the object and purpose of the treaty'.[372] According to the ILC vague reservations

> raise particular problems. It would seem difficult, at the very outset, to maintain that they are invalid *ipso jure*: the main criticism that can be levelled against them is that they make it impossible to assess whether or not the conditions for their substantive validity have been fulfilled. For that reason, they should lend themselves particularly well to a 'reservations dialogue'.[373]

In Optional Clause declarations there have always been reservations which could be considered as being vague. The notion of national security in extinct reservations, for example, was hard to define.[374] And the same can be said for the already addressed Vandenberg Reservation.[375] However, not every vagueness has to raise the problems referred to by the ILC. Most, if not all, cases can and have to be solved through the means of interpretation. As Judge Jennings already remarked concerning the Vandenberg Reservation the difficulty interpreting them should not be exaggerated.[376] The way the Courts have already been able to define reservations excluding disputes relating to prior situations or facts shows how unclear reservations can be defined.[377]

f. Result

All in all, four questions concerning the object and purpose of the Optional Clause in regard to Article 19(c) VCLT remain. The first question is whether

[372] ILC 'Report of the International Law Commission on the Work of Its 63rd Session' (n 12) 18. See also Walter (n 8) paras 88–93.
[373] ILC 'Report of the International Law Commission on the Work of Its 42nd Session' (n 235) 88, para 11. See also the stronger position of the UNCHR (UNCHR 'General Comment No 24 (52) on issues relating to reservations made upon ratification or accession to the Covenant to the Optional Protocols thereto, or in relation to declarations under article 41 of the Covenant' (n 230) para 19; Schilling (n 253) para 97) and the criticism concerning the Maldivian reservation to the CEDAW in Simma (n 239) 661. The EComHR and the ECtHR have also been relatively strict when it comes to vague reservations but here this can be based on Art 57(1)(2) ECHR (Art 64(1)(2) ECHR (old)) (*Belilos v Switzerland* (n 252) 54 f; Marks (n 251) 41–43). See also Giegerich who considered vague reservations as incompatible with the object and purpose of a treaty if due to the vagueness no object and purpose test is possible (Giegerich (n 8) para 11).
[374] cp Alexandrov (n 25) 91; Briggs (n 38) 302 f; Morrison (n 57) 49. cp also D'Amato (n 314) 173.
[375] cp sub-ss II B iii and III D of ch 4 at 137 and 151. cp also Lamm (n 314) 341, 345; Waldock (n 38) 274 f.
[376] Separate opinion of Judge RY Jennings, *ICJ Rep 1984*, 554 f.
[377] For the interpretation of these reservations by the Courts see *Electricity Company of Sofia and Bulgaria (Belgium v Bulgaria)* (n 38) 63, 80–83; *Case concerning Right of Passage over Indian Territory (Portugal v India)* (Merits) [1960] ICJ Rep 6, 34 f; *Certain Property (Liechtenstein v Germany)* (Preliminary Objections) [2005] ICJ Rep 6, paras 34–46. cp also Farmanfarma (n 104) 74–77; de Fumel (n 29) 10 f; Walter (n 238) para 41; Waldock (n 38) 271. For an early presentation of these reservations' vagueness see Lauterpacht (n 20) 142–44.

reservations are allowed at all. If the answer is yes, the following subsections will assess whether the Optional Clause declarations have to have a certain minimum of content. Furthermore, they will discuss whether it is against the object and purpose of the Optional Clause when states have the possibility to withdraw immediately in the face of a dispute without period of notice. The last question will be whether the Optional Clause's object and purpose is to provide only obligations or whether the Optional Clause also allows the making of declarations which are actually not legally binding.

iv. Article 36 of the Statute

The first source for answers to these questions will be Article 36 of the Statute.

a. The Wording of Article 36(2), (3) and (6) of the Statute

The wording of the Statute seems to be mainly suitable to answer the last question of whether subjective reservations, like the Connally Reservation, are allowed.

1. Subjective Reservations: No 'Compulsory' Jurisdiction
   and No 'Obligation'

Some judges and authors maintained that Article 36(6) of the Statute argued against the permissibility of the Connally Reservation.[378] It provides: 'In the event of a dispute as to whether the Court has jurisdiction, the matter shall be settled by the decision of the Court'. According to the authors and judges that paragraph establishes the Court's competence to decide upon the scope of its jurisdiction. For them the paragraph is not accordable with a reservation allowing a state to actually decide itself. Against this, Maus and Kebbon wrote that a Connally Reservation only determined the scope of a declaration and that the Court nonetheless retained the position granted by Article 36(6) of the Statute. For them the reservation therefore denies the Court's jurisdiction like any other reservation, too.[379] With the same result Crawford wrote that where the Connally Reservation was invoked the Court could decide that there was no 'dispute' in the sense of Article 36(6) of the Statute.[380] With these constructions the wording of

---

[378] M Fitzmaurice, 'Optional Clause' para 7; Gharbi (n 28) 455; RC Lawson, 'Compulsory Jurisdiction' 238; PC Ulimubenshi, *Domaine réservé* 141–45; JHW Verzijl, 'Certains emprunts norvégiens' 399; Whiteman (n 68) 1311 f, 1320 (Herter, Rusk).
[379] Kebbon (n 68) 264; Maus (n 37) 156 ff. See also Crawford (n 8) 71 f; MO Hudson, 'America's Declaration' 836.
[380] Crawford, ibid 70 f. For criticism on this position see Anand (n 184) 207.

Article 36(6) of the Statute could be considered as not being violated by subjective reservations. But as also Waldock wrote the reservation might be reconciled with the 'letter' but not with the 'spirit' of Article 36(6) of the Statute.[381] Yet, to elaborate on this spirit it is worth reading Article 36(6) of the Statute together with Article 36(2) of the Statute.

Article 36(2) of the Statute provides that states shall 'recognize as compulsory … the jurisdiction of the Court'. Of course there is no compulsion as far as a state itself is free to decide ultimately whether it has accepted jurisdiction or not.[382] In light of this, subjective reservations seem to be clearly against the object and purpose of the Optional Clause. Crawford argued against this that even with a Connally Reservation at least the procedure before the Court was compulsory. The state was still obliged to come to the Court and to invoke the Connally Reservation. For him it was possible to give Article 36(2) of the Statute such a 'procedural, facultative nature'.[383] However, this is hardly accordable with the idea that the jurisdiction of the Court shall be compulsory. Having regard to what the jurisdiction of the Court is and that it includes inter alia the decision on the dispute with binding force,[384] 'recognize as compulsory … the jurisdiction of the Court' cannot be interpreted as Crawford did. As Senator Thomas of Utah said during the debate on the Connally Reservation, a reservation which gives a state a right to decide upon the question whether an issue belongs to its domestic jurisdiction is 'a contradiction of compulsory jurisdiction itself'.[385]

This can be furthermore supported with the word 'obligation' in Article 36(2) of the Statute which has already been discussed in the first chapter.[386] As Hersch Lauterpacht already said in 1930, the possibility of a state to decide upon the scope of its acceptance means to 'deny the essence of the obligation to arbitrate'.[387] A state making an Optional Clause declaration with such a reservation accepts in fact no obligation because it is not bound to anything. As Verzijl rightly wrote with regard to the Optional Clause, it is 'incompatible with the very essence of a judicial obligation to make it dependent upon a declaration of the person who contracts it

---

[381] Waldock (n 38) 272. cp also Kebbon (n 68) 265.

[382] M Dubisson, *La cour* 189; Farmanfarma (n 104) 100; Kebbon, ibid 264 f; Maus (n 37) 155 f; Waldock, ibid 273. cp also Gharbi (n 28) 458; Yankov (n 26) 594 f. cp also the IACtHR's judgment in the *Hilaire* case concerning a similar situation under the ACHR: '[The reservation] would give the State the discretional power to decide which matters the Court could hear, thus depriving the exercise of the Court's compulsory jurisdiction of all efficacy' (*Hilaire v Trinidad and Tobago* (n 266) para 92).

[383] Crawford (n 8) 75.

[384] See sub-s II A i of ch 1 at 23.

[385] United States of America 'Congressional Record' (1946) 10626 (Thomas of Utah).

[386] See s I A of ch 1 at 11.

[387] Lauterpacht (n 20) 154.

that it actually exists'.[388] This argues heavily against the permissibility of subjective reservations.

2. Article 36(3) of the Statute and Reservations Allowing States to Withdraw Without Period of Notice

Concerning the question whether the object and purpose of the Optional Clause admits reservations allowing states to withdraw without a period of notice, Article 36(3) of the Statute could provide an answer.[389]

As seen above,[390] the paragraph cannot be read as an exhaustive enumeration of permissible reservations but it nonetheless expressly provides that declarations can be made 'for a certain time'. For Waldock the question whether reservations allowing withdrawal were 'compatible with Article 36' depended on whether they fall 'within the authority given in paragraph 3 of Article 36 to make declarations "for a certain time"'.[391] With regard to these words already Briggs mentioned that declarations with reservations allowing states to withdraw were not made for a time which was 'certain'.[392] Vulcan made a distinction in this regard. He understood this term as covering reservations allowing states to withdraw with a period of notice but not those without such a period. In contrast to the latter, the former rendered the period at least 'determinable' and was therefore permissible.[393] Similarly, Holloway argued that reservations providing a period of notice of six months or one year for withdrawals were not literally made 'for a certain time' but were at least accordant to the spirit of Article 36(3) of the Statute. In this respect they were different from reservations without a period of notice.[394] Waldock argued conversely that the time was already 'certain' if the period could be determined ex post (*'id certum est quod certum reddi potest'*).[395] Following this argument also reservations providing no period of notice would be covered by the wording of Article 36(3) of the Statute. However, the wording

---

[388] Verzijl (n 83) 601. cp also Gharbi (n 28) 456; Kolb (n 6) 505; Maus (n 37) 155; C de Visscher, 'Interhandel' 418 and the illustration by Crawford (n 8) 74. In the United States Senate, Senator Pepper emphasised that 'no litigant shall decide his own case' (United States of America 'Congressional Record' (1946) 10694 (Pepper)).

[389] For Farmanfarma and Kolb, the right to immediately withdraw is not accordable with the principle of compulsory jurisdiction (Farmanfarma (n 104) 88; Kolb (n 6) 525–29). It could therefore be argued that already in light of Art 36(2) of the Statute reservations allowing immediate withdrawal are impermissible. That argument will be treated along with the comparison of Art 36(1) of the Statute and Art 36(2) of the Statute. For that see sub-s III B iv c 1 of ch 5 at 230.

[390] See sub-s III A of ch 5 at 200.

[391] Waldock (n 38) 270.

[392] Briggs (n 38) 278. See also Debbasch (n 98) 251.

[393] Vulcan (n 221) 40 f; supported by Maus (n 37) 81.

[394] Holloway (n 184) 670 f.

[395] Waldock (n 38) 270.

of Article 36(3) of the Statute seems to argue against Waldock. It suggests that the period of the Optional Clause declarations already has to be certain when the declaration is made.[396]

3. Result

Summing up, it can be said that, the wording of at least Article 36(2) of the Statute argues heavily against the permissibility of subjective reservations. The wording of Article 36(3) of the Statute at least suggests that reservations allowing states to withdraw their declaration are not accordable with the Optional Clause's object and purpose. Especially for this latter question, however, an assessment of the intention of the Optional Clause's drafters is required.

b. The Genesis of the Optional Clause

1. No Statement by the Drafters of the Optional Clause in 1920

As referred to above,[397] the drafters of Article 36 of the Statute of the Permanent Court provided certain options for the states.[398] As the drafting committee presented its draft of the Statute of the Permanent Court, it wrote that Article 36 of the Statute granted the power to choose among the four groups of disputes and to make the 'condition of reciprocity on the part of several or certain Members or States'.[399] Even though the committee omitted the possibility to make a declaration for a certain time it becomes, however, obvious what they expected the Optional Clause to be like. They expected that no other reservations would be made.[400]

Nonetheless, it can also be emphasised that the drafters did not consider the issue of reservations and that they made neither a positive nor a negative statement in this regard. Therefore, it cannot be said for sure whether the choice which the drafters provided was meant to be exhaustive.[401]

Regarding the reservations allowing withdrawals, for example, no clear result can be obtained by the reference to the Optional Clause's genesis. According to Farmanfarma it was as 'quite probable' that the drafters avoided providing a strict rule in this matter to make it possible for more states to join the Optional Clause.[402] Waldock on the other hand doubted that the instability caused by reservations allowing withdrawals was what

---

[396] Debbasch (n 98) 251.
[397] cp sub-ss II B i and C ii of ch 5 at 175 and 183.
[398] cp also Maus (n 37) 86.
[399] League of Nations, *Records of the First Assembly, Plenary Meetings* 467.
[400] Oda (n 183) 4. cp also the 'presumed intention' in Thirlway (n 38) 105.
[401] Thirlway, ibid 105 f.
[402] Farmanfarma (n 104) 78.

the drafters had hoped for.[403] Both positions are probable. It cannot be said for sure how the drafters would have decided in this affair if they had considered such reservations because they did not voice their opinions in this regard at all.

Concerning the question whether the Optional Clause shall provide obligations or whether it is open to declarations with subjective reservations it can be emphasised that also prior arbitration treaties have been open to such subjective determination by the states. In 1930 Hersch Lauterpacht wrote that it had been common in arbitration treaties that states decided upon the scope of general reservations. For him it was therefore 'difficult to maintain' that general principles of international law 'or the history of international arbitration exclude the right to a state to determine unilaterally whether a general reservation is applicable or not'.[404] Also Crawford referred to the prior practice to include 'vital interests' clauses in arbitration treaties. Like many other authors he considered the Connally Reservation as being the functional substitution of these clauses.[405] However, Crawford went on and doubted whether Article 36(2) of the Statute necessarily required to have a 'substantive obligation'. For him the word 'obligation' in that paragraph was 'more a description of what is recognized than a requirement of what should be'.[406] He emphasised that also the arbitration treaties had been considered as treaties and also as not being void.[407] However, this prior practice in international law does not necessarily mean that also drafters of the Statute of the Permanent Court adopted it. On the contrary it seems as if they wanted to do otherwise. The Romanian delegate Negulesco referred to the prior practice and concluded that in the past 'no constraint was possible'. He went on by saying that the vital interest and national honour reservations were no longer applicable and that in the future states would be obliged to settle their disputes without such escape.[408]

For the drafters of the Statute of the Permanent Court it can therefore be said that they did not articulate any thoughts on the permissibility of reservations besides those named in Article 36(3) of that Statute but that is unlikely that they would have allowed subjective reservations.

2. The Optional Clause's Drafters of 1945 Simply Endorsed the Prior Practice

The position of the drafters of the current Statute is much clearer in this regard. In San Francisco there were many proposals concerning the

---

[403] Waldock (n 38) 270.

[404] Lauterpacht (n 20) 152.

[405] Crawford (n 8) 70. Similar also Maus (n 37) 195 f; L Preuss, 'Connally Amendment' 662; Vulcan (n 221) 53.

[406] Crawford, ibid 75.

[407] ibid 70.

[408] League of Nations, *Records of the First Assembly, Plenary Meetings* 453 f (Negulesco).

treatment of reservations. Egypt suggested that the Court should have compulsory jurisdiction *ipso iure* but states would be free to reduce the jurisdiction by making reservations.[409] New Zealand proposed general compulsory jurisdiction with certain exceptions.[410] Australia suggested maintaining the status quo in general but to limit the range of possible reservations. It proposed to provide an exhaustive list of reservations and took Article 39 of the General Arbitration Act as guideline into consideration.[411] Canada, too, suggested limiting the use of reservations.[412]

However, all these new proposals have not been adopted. The proposal of New Zealand was dismissed with a majority of seven to five in the sub-committee. Those of Australia and Canada were dismissed six to three.[413] As said above,[414] the drafters of the Statute basically kept the old system. Instead of dealing with the issue of reservations actively, the drafters only referred to the prior practice to interpret Article 36 of the Statute as allowing reservations and endorsed it.[415]

The drafters only made a little amendment and changed Article 36(2) of the Statute so that Optional Clause declarations no longer refer to 'all or any of the classes of legal disputes' enumerated in the paragraph. In the current version, all declarations refer automatically to 'all legal disputes' falling in one of the four categories of disputes. There has been a discussion whether the freedom to make reservations has been reduced this way. Vulcan interpreted the deletion of the words 'or any of the classes of' as being a reduction of the freedom to shape the declaration.[416] However, having regard to the drafters' expressed endorsement of the prior practice on reservations, this cannot be maintained. It seems much more as if the drafters only wanted to point out that declarations without reservations automatically refer to all four categories.[417] In this regard it was just the official goodbye to the group-related approach as described above.[418]

---

[409] United Nations, *Conference on International Organization, Volume XIV—United Nations Committee of Jurists* 207 f, 235, 302, 667–69, 840–42.

[410] United Nations, *Conference on International Organization, Volume XIII—Commission IV, Judicial Organization* 225, 247, 487, 557.

[411] ibid 225, 558. cp Lamm (n 10) 125; M Vogiatzi, 'Historical Evolution' 85; Wittmann (n 6) 325. See also the proposal in United Nations, *Conference on International Organization, Volume XIV—United Nations Committee of Jurists* 668, 841.

[412] United Nations, *Conference on International Organization, Volume XIII—Commission IV, Judicial Organization* 226, 558. cp also Vogiatzi, ibid 85; Wittmann, ibid 325.

[413] United Nations, *Conference on International Organization, Volume XIII—Commission IV, Judicial Organization* 558. See also Wittmann, ibid 325.

[414] See sub-s II B ii of ch 2 at 59.

[415] See sub-s III A of ch 5 at 200. For state practice and jurisprudence of the Court see below sub-ss III B v and vi of ch 5 at 233 and 241.

[416] cp Vulcan who, however, argued on the basis that Art 36(3) of the Statute is exhaustive (Vulcan (n 221) 36 f).

[417] See also Lamm (n 10) 128; Wittmann (n 6) 113. cp United Nations, *Conference on International Organization, Volume XIII—Commission IV, Judicial Organization* 559.

[418] sub-s II B i of ch 5 at 175.

With regard to the questions presented at the end of the previous sub-section, it can be concluded that the drafters of the current Statute very much emphasised the aim of achieving universal acceptance of the Optional Clause as they expressly acknowledged the generous prior practice. Yet, as Judge Oda already emphasised, some of the far-reaching reservations have been introduced only after 1945.[419] This concerns especially the subjective reservations whose first one was the United States' Connally Reservation of 1946. In the same declaration also the Vandenberg Reservation has been introduced for the first time. With these reservations the drafters in San Francisco had not been confronted and it cannot be said for sure that they would have still endorsed the entire prior practice if they had known about these reservations. The same could also be said about the reservations allowing expressly the introduction of new reservations as the first of these reservations has been introduced by Portugal in 1955.[420] However, as it will be established below, there is no relevant difference between reservations allowing states to add new reservations and reservations allowing them to withdraw an Optional Clause declaration.[421] Such reservations were not new in 1945 as already in 1929 there had been the first declaration which contained a reservation allowing a withdrawal without period of notice after an initial period of ten years. Furthermore, in 1940 there was the first Optional Clause declaration which contained such a reservation and was not made with an initial period.[422] Therefore, it cannot be said that the drafters were unable to know these reservations and it is therefore more likely that they also endorsed them.

All in all this sub-section shows that the drafters of the Statute did not articulate their opinion on subjective reservations and the Vandenberg Reservation but considered all other reservations as being permissible.

c. The Object and Purpose of the Optional Clause
   with Regard to Article 36(1) of the Statute

The means to establish jurisdiction under Article 36(1) of the Statute could provide further answers regarding the object and purpose of the Optional Clause.

1. *Ad Hoc Jurisdiction and Reservations Allowing*
   Withdrawals Without Period of Notice

Concerning the reservations allowing states to withdraw without a period of notice a comparison to Article 36(1) of the Statute could again raise doubts.

---

[419] cp Oda (n 183) 7.
[420] cp also *Military and Paramilitary Activities in and against Nicaragua (Nicaragua v United States of America)* (n 57) (United States of America) 120 f, fn 2.
[421] See s I of ch 6 at 275.
[422] See sub-s III B v b of ch 5 at 236.

As said above,[423] in contrast to the ad hoc jurisdiction the Optional Clause shall provide abstract jurisdiction and not dispute related jurisdiction. As Judge Koroma already held in the *Bakassi Peninsula* case: 'The object and purpose of the Optional Clause system is to ensure advance acceptance of the jurisdiction of the Court'.[424] The possibility to withdraw when a dispute arises seems to thwart this aim. To allow states to withdraw their declaration immediately before a dispute is brought to Court would just shift the behaviour from accepting to not withdrawing. In both cases it would be the same state to decide and in both cases no abstract compulsory jurisdiction exists.[425] In this respect it could be said that the reservations allowing withdrawals without a period of notice are against the object and purpose of the Optional Clause.[426]

A very good expression of this argument can be found in the recent pleadings of Simma and Sinclair in the *Bakassi Peninsula* case. Simma argued for Cameroon:

> It is essential to such compulsory jurisdiction that States, once they have subjected themselves to the system, are not entitled to reconsider their acceptance of the Court's jurisdiction if another State files an application against them. The whole object and purpose of the system of the Optional Clause is to ensure an advance acceptance of the jurisdiction of the Court within the limits of the respective declarations of acceptance.[427]

For Simma states accepting compulsory jurisdiction 'renounce their former freedom to decide *ad hoc* against which States and in which disputes they are prepared to litigate before the Court'.[428] As already quoted above, Sinclair, too, emphasised the difference between the ad hoc jurisdiction and the Optional Clause as he pleaded for Cameroon. He said that it was the object and purpose of Article 36(1) of the Statute to provide the Court's jurisdiction for specified types of disputes while it was the object and purpose of the Optional Clause to provide 'advance ... acceptance' of the jurisdiction of the Court.[429] It becomes obvious that these two pleadings, too, provide a good argument against reservations allowing states to withdraw without a period of notice.[430]

---

[423] See sub-s I C iii of ch 1 at 17.

[424] Dissenting opinion of Judge AG Koroma, *ICJ Rep 1998*, 381.

[425] cp Maus (n 37) 80.

[426] cp Kebbon (n 68) 267; Kolb (n 6) 525 f.

[427] *Land and Maritime Boundary between Cameroon and Nigeria (Cameroon v Nigeria: Equatorial Guinea intervening)* (Preliminary Objections) Oral Proceedings (CR 1998/3) (Cameroon) 43, paras 39 f (Simma).

[428] ibid 43, paras 39 f (Simma).

[429] *Land and Maritime Boundary between Cameroon and Nigeria (Cameroon v Nigeria: Equatorial Guinea intervening)* (Preliminary Objections) Oral Proceedings (CR 1998/6) (Cameroon) 17 f, para 7 (Sinclair). For the full quotation see sub-s I C iii of ch 1 at 17.

[430] Nigeria defended against this argument by pointing at the Anti Ambush Clauses in state practice which allow states to reconsider their position vis-à-vis states making a new declaration (*Land and Maritime Boundary between Cameroon and Nigeria (Cameroon v Nigeria:*

Reservations which allow withdrawals but provide at least a small period of notice are, however, different in this regard. Of course, also the period of notice might not completely bar states from withdrawing their declaration in the face of a dispute but in such cases the other party at least has an opportunity to act if it receives the notice in time. It can still file its application based on the other state's Optional Clause declaration before it lapses. What is important is that the terms of the declarations do not generally allow states to evade the submission of any dispute to the Court.

2. Forum Prorogatum *and Subjective Reservations*

Concerning Optional Clause declarations with subjective reservations it can also be said that they provide no jurisdiction besides Article 36(1) of the Statute.[431] The jurisdiction that these declarations provide is already covered by jurisdiction based on a *forum prorogatum* because states that have made a declaration with a subjective reservation can frustrate any proceeding before the Court by invoking this reservation. This is similar to a situation in which a state has made no declaration at all. In this situation the state can frustrate any proceeding, which could otherwise be based on a *forum prorogatum*, by referring to the lacking title of jurisdiction.[432] The only disadvantage for a state invoking a Connally Reservation might be political as it has to declare that it considers a certain matter as being subject to its domestic jurisdiction. Yet, from a legal point of view there is no difference whether a state invokes a subjective reservation or the missing title of jurisdiction. Therefore, it can be very well maintained that Optional Clause declarations with subjective reservations are superfluous and that an Optional Clause allowing these reservations is very much redundant to the *forum prorogatum* covered by Article 36(1) of the Statute.

d. Result

The wording of the Optional Clause heavily argues against the permissibility of subjective reservations. Likewise does a systematic comparison of the Optional Clause to Article 36(1) of the Statute. The latter provides a good argument to consider reservations allowing states to withdraw without period of notice as impermissible, too. Besides that, all other reservations seem to be allowed and there is little basis to argue that Optional Clause declarations have to have a certain minimum of disputes covered.

Equatorial Guinea intervening) (Preliminary Objections) Oral Proceedings (CR 1998/5) (Nigeria) 23 (Watts)). For this aspect of the Optional Clause see sub-s III F of ch 3 at 116.

[431] R Arnold, 'Fakultativklausel' 10–13 (especially 13).
[432] See sub-s I C ii of ch 1 at 15.

v. Reservations in State Practice

The states' opinion as a whole is an important means to establish the object and purpose under Article 19(c) VCLT.[433] The following sub-section will address expressions of this opinion and the states' practice.

a. The Use of Reservations in General

The first reservation was made by the Netherlands in 1921 as they made an Optional Clause declaration with reservations for prior disputes and disputes allocated to another means of peaceful dispute settlement.[434] Nonetheless, states have not been sure to what extent they can make reservations to their Optional Clause declaration in those days.[435] As said above, the drafters of the Statute of the Permanent Court presented no decision upon this issue and provided only a limited possibility to shape Optional Clause declarations.[436]

In 1924, the United Kingdom's Prime Minister MacDonald therefore raised the issue at the General Assembly of the League of Nations. He emphasised that his country wanted to make a commitment like an Optional Clause declaration but had to be sure about the clause before.[437] On 2 October 1924, the General Assembly of the League of Nations made a resolution in which it acknowledged the freedom of states to make reservations not named in Article 36 of the Statute of the Permanent Court. The assembly considered the terms of Article 36(2) of the Statute to be sufficiently wide to allow states to adopt reservations which they regarded as indispensible.[438] This resolution was based on a report by the assembly's First Committee. In this report the committee had emphasised that every new undertaking, no matter how restricted, was always better than none.[439] Yet, the committee had inferred the possibility to make additional reservations from the choice provided for in Article 36(2) of the Statute: According to the committee states were able

---

[433] See sub-s V A of ch 5 at 264 and for the use of subsequent state practice as a means to assess the object and purpose of a treaty see ILC 'Second Report on Subsequent Agreements and Subsequent Practice in Relation to Treaty Interpretation' (26 March 2014) UN Doc A/CN.4/671 paras 27–29. For the use of subsequent state practice as a means of interpretation or basis for derogating customary law see sub-s III D of ch 3 at 108.

[434] Maus (n 37) 16; Waldock (n 38) 248; Wittmann (n 6) 334.

[435] Wundram (n 320) 30.

[436] sub-s III B iv b 1 of ch 5 at 227.

[437] League of Nations 'Actes de la cinquième Assemblée, Séances plénières, Compte rendu de débats' (1924) League of Nations Official Journal Supplément Spécial No 23 44. See also Maus (n 37) 16 f; Wittmann (n 6) 323.

[438] League of Nations, ibid 229. For this position in the prior debates see League of Nations 'Actes de la cinquième Assemblée, Séances de commissions, Procès-verbaux de la première commission (Questions constitutionnelles)' (1924) League of Nations Official Journal Supplément Spécial No 24 23 (Unden). See also Oda (n 183) 5; Wittmann (n 6) 324, 579.

[439] League of Nations (n 309) 552; Wittmann, ibid 618.

to reduce the scope of the four groups of disputes.[440] Therefore, it seems as if the committee had not referred to reservations relating to the period of validity of the Optional Clause declaration itself. These had also not been listed in the examples the committee gave.[441] At the same time, the assembly's First Committee also prepared a Draft Protocol for the Pacific Settlement of International Disputes. The draft's Article 3 on Article 36(2) of the Statute provided that states can 'make reservations compatible with the said clause'.[442] This suggests that there were limitations to the freedom to make reservations.[443] However, the drafters' 'analysis' on the draft only reproduced the committee's report to the General Assembly and contained no additional signs of limitations. Like the commission's report, the analysis emphasised: 'However restrictive the scope of the undertaking may be, it will always be better than no undertaking at all'.[444]

In 1928, four years later, the General Assembly of the League of Nations passed another resolution emphasising again the freedom to shape Optional Clause declarations. In that resolution the General Assembly expressed its concern that the resolution of 1924 had not produced the desired results. The assembly therefore wanted 'to facilitate effectively the acceptance of the clause' by diminishing 'the obstacles which [prevented] States from committing themselves'.[445] This suggests that this resolution should have gone further than the prior one.[446] Indeed, the second resolution also referred to reservations limiting the duration of the Optional Clause declarations and additionally emphasised the possibility to combine different types of reservations. Furthermore, the resolution of 1928 no longer emphasised that the states should only attach reservations which they regard as indispensible.[447]

These two resolutions had a strong impact and led to declarations of, for example, the United Kingdom (1929), France (1924, 1929) and Germany (1927).[448] The United Kingdom still justified the making of its reservations

---

[440] League of Nations (n 309) 550; Wittmann, ibid 616. See also Lamm (n 10) 123.

[441] League of Nations (n 309) 550 f; Wittmann, ibid 616.

[442] League of Nations (n 309) 532, Art 3. See also Oda (n 183) 5.

[443] See also Maus (Maus (n 37) 17 f) who additionally referred to the debates which had taken place in the First Committee.

[444] League of Nations (n 309) 552. See also League of Nations (n 438) 109 f.

[445] Oda (n 183) 5 f. See also League of Nations 'Actes de la neuvième session ordinaire de l'Assemblée, Séances plénières' (1928) League of Nations Official Journal Supplément Spécial No 64 183.

[446] See also Maus (n 37) 18.

[447] League of Nations (n 445) 183. See also the presentation of the resolution in Oda (n 183) 6; Lamm (n 10) 124. But see also the criticism of the Hungarian delegate *Apponyi* who emphasised that for him reservations were 'une maladie' (League of Nations (n 445) 173 (Apponyi)). For the position of the resolution's drafters on subjective reservations see sub-s III B v c of ch 5 at 238.

[448] cp also Maus (n 37) 19; Oda (n 183) 6–7. For the immediate accession of France see League of Nations (n 437) 232. For the competence of the two General Assemblies to shape the Optional Clause see sub-s III A of ch 6 at 310.

with the words 'in all or any of the classes of legal disputes' in Article 36 of the Statute of the Permanent Court.[449] However, that the fact that the deletion of these words in 1945 had no influence in this regard shows that at least in 1945 this justification by the United Kingdom was not necessary anymore.[450] Many states followed the early examples and made reservations. With regard to that state practice and the two resolutions Oda wrote that within ten years after the establishment of the Permanent Court reservations became permissible.[451] However, in the late forties, Vulcan still wrote that the use of reservations by states 'ne prouve rien. Il faudrait pouvoir nous montrer que cette usage n'est non seulement licite, mais au moins inoffensif. Or, il est en même temps illicite et hautement dangereux'.[452]

However, also under the new Statute the making of reservations continued and even aggravated. In 1947 and twice in 1974, also the new General Assembly issued resolutions and encouraged the states to accept, with as few reservations as possible, the compulsory jurisdiction of the Court in accordance with Article 36 of the Statute.[453] Pleading for India in the *Right of Passage* case Waldock in 1957

> pointed out how State practice in the matter of reservations had evolved in a much more complicated way than was or could have been expected. [He] pointed out how this evolution really made it essential to apply to the Optional Clause system principles analogous to those governing reservations to multilateral conventions'.[454]

In line with this evolution of the Optional Clause referred to by Waldock, the general right to make reservations can be considered as being customary law today.[455] At least since the creation of the current Statute states have treated the possibility to make reservations as granted. Their Optional Clause declarations furthermore show that for them there is no minimum of commitment required. The Indian declaration, for example, contains a large number of reservations which even include far reaching ones like the Vandenberg Reservation. These reservations bar almost all applications against India and thereby also almost all applications

---

[449] cp Waldock (n 38) 248 f.

[450] For the first part see sub-s III B iv b 2 of ch 5 at 228.

[451] Oda (n 183) 4–6. See also the separate opinion of Judge S Oda, *ICJ Rep 2000*, para 10.

[452] Vulcan (n 221) 54.

[453] UNGA 'Official Records of the Second Session of the General Assembly, Resolutions' (8.1.1948) UN Doc A/519 104; UNGA 'Review of the role of the International Court of Justice' (12.11.1974) UN Doc A/Res/3232 (XXIX); UNGA 'Peaceful settlement of international disputes' (12.12.1974) UN Doc A/Res/3283 (XXIX).

[454] *Case concerning the Right of Passage over Indian Territory (Portugal v India)* (n 68) (India) 48 (Waldock).

[455] Maus (n 37) 86; Shihata (n 38) 153; Wittmann (n 6) 334–36, 603; critical Thirlway (n 38) 105 f, fn 31.

by India.[456] Other examples are the Optional Clause declaration of the United Kingdom of 1946 which covered only disputes relating to the boundaries of British Honduras and the Egyptian declaration of 1957 which covers only disputes concerning the Suez Canal.[457] Regarding the latter declaration Oda wrote that it may be regarded as the reverse of an Optional Clause declaration.[458] Of course, these three declarations are extreme, but their difference to other declarations is fluent. Regarding the pure quantity of reservations Nigeria, for example, comes close to India and every state having made a single reservation, like the Vandenberg Reservation excludes a huge amount of disputes. State practice seems to know no border in this regard.

b.   The Almost Uncontested and Frequent Use of Reservations Allowing Withdrawals Without Period of Notice

The question is, however, whether state practice likewise supports reservations allowing withdrawal without period of notice. As said above, it can be doubted that the drafters of the Statutes also allowed these as they render the Optional Clause to a certain degree redundant to the ad hoc jurisdiction in Article 36(1) of the Statute.[459]

The first Optional Clause declarations allowing withdrawal without period of notice were the declarations of the United Kingdom and other members of the Commonwealth made in 1929.[460] These should have been valid for a period of ten years and later until notice was given.[461] Such declarations were made with the good purpose to enlarge the commitment.[462] The first declaration allowing withdrawal without period of notice and without an initial period of time was introduced by South Africa in 1940. After it had made a declaration like the other Commonwealth members and the ten year period of that declaration was over, South Africa just made a new declaration which went on until notice was given.[463] The first declaration allowing expressly the introduction of new reservations had been introduced by Portugal in 1955.[464] In the history of the Optional Clause, 52 states have made Optional Clause declarations which provide a right

---

[456] cp C Tomuschat (n 3) para 70.

[457] For the first declaration see UNTS, Volume 1 (1946–1947) 3–5.

[458] Oda (n 183) 8. cp also Maus (n 37) 147.

[459] See sub-s III B iv c 1 of ch 5 at 230.

[460] Oda (n 184) 42, para 35. For the declarations see PCIJ, Series E No 6, 479–82.

[461] PCIJ, Series E No 6, 479–82. See also Kebbon (n 68) 261.

[462] cp Maus (n 37) 36; Vulcan (n 221) 41.

[463] PCIJ, Series E No 16, 334. See also Maus (n 37) 197; Kebbon (n 68) 261; *Military and Paramilitary Activities in and against Nicaragua (Nicaragua v United States of America)* (n 57) (United States of America) para 362.

[464] ICJ Yearbook 1955–1956, 185 f; *Military and Paramilitary Activities in and against Nicaragua (Nicaragua v United States of America)* (n 57) (United States of America) para 353. As this

to withdraw or to amend without a period of notice.[465] Out of the current Optional Clause declarations 46 provide for withdrawals or amendments or both without a period of notice.[466] Accessions without such clauses became few in number.[467] Additionally, at least under the current Statute, states made these reservations even though, or maybe even because, they had been aware of the possibility that it would allow the withdrawal in the face of the dispute. As the United States made their Optional Clause declaration in 1946 it expressly wanted to exclude this possibility. This is why it provided the six month period of notice.[468]

However, no state contested as the United Kingdom introduced the first reservation allowing withdrawal without period of notice.[469] Outside a proceeding before the Court, only Sweden contested the reservation allowing states to amend their declaration without a period of notice which had been introduced by Portugal. However, from the text of the Swedish declaration it becomes clear that it understood the reservation as allowing Portugal to withdraw from a proceeding already pending before the Court.[470] Therefore, its argumentation would have been much more appropriate to challenge a subjective reservation.[471]

India, however, challenged the Portuguese reservation as a reservation allowing the introduction of new reservations without a period of notice in the *Right of Passage* case before the Court. It pleaded that the reservation of Portugal went beyond the flexibility that Article 36(2) of the Statute allows. Such reservations made the whole system instable and finally worthless. India emphasised:

> The unlimited power to vary its obligation claimed by Portugal means that other states are left in a condition of complete uncertainty as to the obligation

---

reservation allowed only the exclusion of one or several groups of disputes Maus inferred that it did not allow to make a Connally Reservation (Maus (n 37) 186). For the distinction between amendments and withdrawals see s I of ch 6 at 275.

[465] See Annex 6. 20 of these declarations provide or provided expressly that the withdrawal or amendment shall be effective when the Secretary-General receives their notice. Nonetheless, also the declarations which provide no period of notice at all can be withdrawn or amended with immediate effect (cp eg Australia in ICJ Yearbook 2000–2001, 117; ICJ Yearbook 2001–2002, 118 and India in ICJ Yearbook 1946–1947, 213 f; ICJ Yearbook 1955–1956, 186 f).

[466] See Annex 6.

[467] cp already Oda (n 183) 19 f, 29.

[468] cp United States of America 'Congressional Record' (1946) 10707 (Report of the Committee on Foreign Relations). See also D'Amato (n 184) 390 f; Morrison (n 57) 56; *Military and Paramilitary Activities in and against Nicaragua (Nicaragua v United States of America)* (n 30) para 125; *Military and Paramilitary Activities in and against Nicaragua (Nicaragua v United States of America)* (Provisional Measures) Oral Proceedings (CR 1984) (Nicaragua) 75 (Brownlie).

[469] Oda (n 184) 42, para 35.

[470] *Case concerning the Right of Passage over Indian Territory (Portugal v India)* (n 139) (Portugal) paras 10–12; *Case concerning the Right of Passage over Indian Territory (Portugal v India)* (n 68) (Portugal) 134 (Bourquin). cp Annex 1 and see the answer of Portugal in Annex 2. See further sub-s III C of ch 4 at 149.

[471] Therefore it will be discussed in the following section.

which, at any given moment, they will be supposed to have accepted under the optional clause vis-à-vis Portugal.[472]

This has, however, been the only reasoning by a state in this regard so far. Having regard to overwhelming affirmative practice which today consists of 46 reservations it can be said that state practice clearly understands the object and purpose as not prohibiting these reservations. As the discussion of the Spanish Optional Clause declaration showed, there might be uncertainty about the reciprocal invocation of reservations,[473] but there is no uncertainty about the admissibility of reservations allowing withdrawal without period of notice. In the *Nicaragua* case the United States even argued, with regard to the Court's judgment in the *Right of Passage* case, that the reservations allowing withdrawals were perfectly accordable with the object and purpose of the Optional Clause.[474] In 1959, Maus still wrote that state practice in this regard seemed to contradict the wording and the purpose of the Optional Clause.[475] Be this concerning the original object and purpose of the Statute as it may, today the states' constant practice has anyway established customary law in this regard.[476]

c. The Decline of Subjective Reservations

Concerning the subjective reservations the practice seems to be different. As Politis presented the draft for the above mentioned resolution for the General Assembly of the League of Nations in 1928, he expressly said that the possibility to make reservations was limited by the fact that, in those days, the reservations were no longer subjective. He emphasised that the reservations allowed were objective and could be assessed by the Court.[477] However, Kebbon wrote that state practice and the lack of objections have rendered these reservations permissible.[478]

Yet, at least today, this position cannot be maintained. In the history of the Optional Clause, only ten states have ever made a Connally Reservation.[479] A subjective reservation concerning national security has been made only by one state.[480] Since 1972 no state has ever made either of

---

[472] *Case concerning the Right of Passage over Indian Territory (Portugal v India)* (n 68) (India) 27–29 (Waldock). See also Whiteman (n 68) 1340.

[473] cp sub-s II C iii b of ch 5 at 189.

[474] *Military and Paramilitary Activities in and against Nicaragua (Nicaragua v United States of America)* (n 57) (United States of America) para 347.

[475] Maus (n 37) 81.

[476] Szafarz (n 10) 64; Wittmann (n 6) 197–99.

[477] League of Nations (n 445) 168 (Politis).

[478] Kebbon (n 68) 265. See also Crawford (Crawford (n 8) 81 f, 85) who, however, applied a kind of mid way between 'permissibility' and 'opposability approach' for Arts 19 and 20 VCLT (see sub-s V A of ch 5 at 264).

[479] cp Alexandrov (n 25) 149; C Stahn, 'Connally Reservation' para 2.

[480] cp Alexandrov, ibid 151, 163; Whiteman (n 68) 1334 (Herter).

these declarations.[481] Many states like the United States have furthermore withdrawn their Optional Clause declaration containing such a reservation. France has even withdrawn its Connally Reservation in 1959 before it withdrew its declaration in 1966.[482] The United Kingdom which was the only state ever with a subjective reservation concerning national security withdrew it in 1958.[483] This could have been triggered by the Secretary-General who addressed the 'new reservations' in 1957 and said that they render illusionary the compulsory jurisdiction. It is clear that he especially meant the Connally Reservations.[484] Today, the only remaining states with a subjective reservation are Liberia, Malawi, Mexico, the Philippines and Sudan. This shows that there has never been a widespread affirmative state practice concerning the Connally Reservations like there has been for the reservations allowing states to withdraw.

Concerning the legal opinion of the states it could, however, be said that the states withdrew their Connally Reservations not because they considered them as illegal but only because they wanted to prevent their reciprocal application.[485] Following this latter point, it could be said that for the states the Connally Reservation is impractical but permissible. Furthermore, also concerning subjective reservations there have been almost no objections. Some authors even wrote that so far no state has objected to a Connally Reservation.[486]

However, as referred to in the previous sub-section, from a material point of view, this is not completely right. It is right that no state has objected to the Connally Reservation as such. But as Sweden objected to the Portuguese reservation allowing it to introduce new reservations without period of notice in 1956, it did so on grounds which related to subjective reservations. According to Sweden Portugal had not accepted the jurisdiction for any dispute and its reservation 'nullifie[d] the obligation intended by the wording of Article 36, paragraph 2, of the Statute where it said that the recognition of the jurisdiction shall be "compulsory *ipso facto*"'. Sweden considered the reservation 'incompatible with a recognition of the "Optional Clause"'.[487] With regard to these arguments by Sweden it can be

---

[481] cp Alexandrov, ibid 149, 151; Kolb (n 6) 504.

[482] Arnold (n 431) 7; de Fumel (n 29) 29; Vignes (n 36) 56, 64; Whiteman (n 68) 1335. For India and Pakistan see Whiteman, ibid 1336.

[483] de Fumel (n 29) 29; Whiteman (n 68) 1334 f. cp also ICJ Yearbook 1959–1960.

[484] cp S Dreyfus, 'Les déclarations souscrites par la France' 269 f.

[485] cp ibid 269; Institut de Droit International, 'Compulsory Jurisdiction of International Courts and Tribunals' (1959) para 2; Ulimubenshi (n 378) 22; Whiteman (n 68) 1309. On the general disadvantage of the reciprocal application of the Connally Reservation see furthermore Alexandrov (n 25) 90; Alexandrov (n 227) 117; D'Amato (n 184) 393; Merrills (n 29) 241; Whiteman, ibid 1295.

[486] Crawford (n 8) 81; Kebbon (n 68) 265; Rosenne and Ronen (n 1) 750; Rotter (n 26) 640.

[487] Annex 1.

said that its objection referred to the Portuguese reservation but implies a perception of the object and purpose of the Optional Clause which rather opposes subjective reservations.[488]

Before the Court India, as referred to in the previous sub-section, addressed the Portuguese reservation primarily as a reservation allowing the introduction of new reservations without period of notice. However, India additionally reasoned the way Sweden did. It did not argue against the Connally Reservation directly but it considered reservations working retroactively impermissible.[489] This argument would be suitable for the Connally Reservation.[490] Portugal endorsed the Indian arguments against subjective reservations to a certain degree and made its case by showing that its reservation did not work retroactively.[491] Additionally, some states even argued expressly against subjective reservations before the Court. In the *Interhandel* case it was Switzerland which argued against the permissibility of the Connally Reservation.[492] According to Switzerland, '[l]e principe même de l'arbitrage obligatoire n'et pas compatible avec l'existence de réserves automatiques *de* ce genre'.[493] In the *Nuclear Tests* cases Australia wrote that 'if, for these reasons, the reservation were to be considered as being, in reality, a subjective or automatic one, the Government of Australia contends ... that it would be null and void'.[494]

Taking into consideration these statements, it can be said that subjective reservations have been much more controversial in states' legal opinions than, for example, reservations allowing withdrawal without period of notice as presented above. Furthermore, as the already quoted statement of Senator Pepper shows, not even the internal protagonists in the United States were sure whether the Connally Reservation which they had created was accordable with the object and purpose of the

---

[488] *Case concerning the Right of Passage over Indian Territory (Portugal v India)* (n 68) (Portugal) 134 (Bourquin). As it has been already referred to above there might have been a misinterpretation of the Portuguese reservation in this regard (cp sub-s III C of ch 4 at 149). It remains a strange fact that Sweden did not object the Connally Reservations which from a legal perspective it would have had likewise reason to do (cp Crawford (n 8) 81).

[489] *Case concerning the Right of Passage over Indian Territory (Portugal v India)* (Preliminary Objections) Memorial (India) para 33; Whiteman (n 68) 1339 f.

[490] cp the presentation in Rotter (n 26) 641.

[491] *Case concerning the Right of Passage over Indian Territory (Portugal v India)* (n 139) (Portugal) para 11; *Case concerning the Right of Passage over Indian Territory (Portugal v India)* (n 68) (Portugal) 132 (Bourquin).

[492] *Interhandel Case (Switzerland v United States of America)* (Preliminary Objections) Observations and Submissions (Switzerland) 408 f, paras 3–5; *Interhandel Case (Switzerland v United States of America)* (Provisional Measures) Oral Proceedings (CR 1957) (Switzerland) 462 f (Guggenheim) against *Interhandel Case (Switzerland v United States of America)* (Provisional Measures) Oral Proceedings (CR 1957) (United States of America) 452 f (Becker) which invoked the reservation. See also Crawford (n 8) 65, fn 4; Ulimubenshi (n 378) 132.

[493] *Interhandel Case (Switzerland v United States of America)* (n 492) para 4.

[494] *Nuclear Tests (Australia v France)* (Jurisdiction and Admissibility) Memorial (Australia) para 310. See also Crawford (n 8) 65, fn 4.

Optional Clause.[495] Still in 1960 they debated this issue in the Senate's Committee on Foreign Relations.[496]

Therefore, state practice regarding subjective reservations provides neither a basis for derogating customary law nor a basis to interpret Article 36 of the Statute as allowing such reservations.[497]

d. Result

All in all it can therefore be said that state practice supports a very generous approach to the object and purpose of the Optional Clause which leaves almost no space to argue that a reservation is impermissible according to Article 19(c) VCLT. The only exceptions are subjective reservations which have been very controversial since their beginning and have not been adopted anymore since 1972.

vi. Jurisprudence on the Permissibility of Reservations

The last question in this regard will be how the two Courts have understood the object and purpose of the Optional Clause.

a. The Position of the Court on this Question in General

Up to now none of the two Courts has ever considered a reservation impermissible.[498] The current Court emphasised the states' freedom to make Optional Clause declarations and the states' freedom to make reservations.[499]

In the already mentioned *Aerial Incident of 1999* case,[500] the Court quoted the resolution of the League of Nations' General Assembly of 1928 and the *travaux préparatoires* of the current Statute. It held that the general freedom to make reservations had been acknowledged by state practice and emphasised its prior findings that states were free to make reservations and that the states were free to define the parameters of their

---

[495] See sub-s III B iii d of ch 5 at 219. See also the statement of the United State Senate's Committee on Foreign Relations in sub-s III B vii of ch 5 at 253. On the other hand Senator Connally and Senator Morse eg argued for the admissibility of the Connally Reservation (United States of America 'Congressional Record' (1946) 10624 (Connally), 10690 (Morse)).

[496] cp Whiteman (n 68) 1311 f (Secretary of State Herter). See also the dissenting opinion of Judge SM Schwebel, *ICJ Rep 1984*, para 65.

[497] For the threshold for derogating customary law see sub-s III D ii of ch 3 at 111.

[498] See also Ende (n 161) 1159; Finke (n 289) 119; Lamm (n 10) 130; Tomuschat (n 3) paras 83, 99; Walter (n 238) para 41. Especially for the Permanent Court see Maus (n 37) 19.

[499] See s I of ch 3 at 86.

[500] See sub-s III A of ch 5 at 201.

Optional Clause declarations. More specifically, the Court also referred to the fact that, since 1929, states had made Commonwealth reservations and that eight states had such reservations at the time of the judgment. The Court came to the result that the Commonwealth reservation was permissible and could be invoked.[501]

These statements of the Court, however, provide no conclusions on whether there are borders to the freedom to make reservations. Of help could be the judges' individual opinions addressing the issue. A rather generous approach was presented by Judge Lauterpacht in the *Norwegian Loans* case. He maintained that states were not free to make subjective reservations but that besides this they could make every commitment no matter how small.[502] In the *Fisheries Jurisdiction* case between Spain and Canada, Judge Kooijmans was more critical of reservations and observed that the unlimited freedom to make them weakened the system instead of strengthening it.[503] In the same case Judge Vereshchetin even maintained:

> A State is not absolutely free to make any reservation or condition it pleases to its optional declaration deposited under Article 36, paragraph 2, of the Statute … Generally, reservations and conditions must not undermine the very raison d'être of the optional clause system.[504]

Also in that *Fisheries Jurisdiction* case, Judge Weeramantry stated: 'There can indeed be reservations which are contrary to the very purpose of the optional clause, and thus invalidate the entire clause'.[505] In the same case, Judge Torres Bernárdez wrote that the freedom to make reservations was very broad but not boundless. For him, the reservations had to conform to the Statute and the Charter and might not 'abuse the good faith and expectations of the other declarant States'.[506] Judge Bedjaoui maintained that reservations were impermissible if their 'purpose or effect' was 'to nullify or distort one or more of the provisions of the Statute or Rules of Court which govern international judicial proceedings'. Furthermore, he considered reservations excluding disputes concerning 'genocide, slavery, piracy, or any other international crime' as impossible. Judge Bedjaoui concluded that a reservation 'must also respect the consistency and the integrity of the optional clause "system"'.[507]

---

[501] *Aerial Incident of 10 August 1999 (Pakistan v India)* (n 225) paras 34–39.

[502] Separate opinion of Judge H Lauterpacht, *ICJ Rep 1957*, 46, 65. cp also the 'contracting in'-approach of Alexandrov (n 25) 124–28.

[503] Separate opinion of Judge PH Kooijmans, *ICJ Rep 1998*, 489.

[504] Dissenting opinion of Judge VS Vereshchetin, *ICJ Rep 1998*, 575 f. Supported by Bernhardt (n 4) 378.

[505] Dissenting opinion of Judge CG Weeramantry, *ICJ Rep 1998*, para 10.

[506] Dissenting opinion of Judge S Torres Bernárdez, *ICJ Rep 1998*, paras 134–39.

[507] Dissenting opinion of Judge M Bedjaoui, *ICJ Rep 1998*, paras 42–44. For his position on subjective reservations and reservations allowing to withdraw without period of notice see the following two sections.

To this extent it seems as if at least some judges within the Court took into consideration that a reservation can be impermissible because it contradicts the objects and purpose of the Optional Clause. The fact that the Court nonetheless did not decide so could mean that it has, so far, considered all reservations accordable with the object and purpose of the Optional Clause. Therefore, it could be said that the Court has accepted all reservations which have appeared so far.[508]

Yet, to answer this question, it is crucial whether the Court raises all issues concerning its jurisdiction *proprio motu* without a state asking it to do so.[509] As mentioned in the previous sub-section, states rarely raised the issue whether a reservation was impermissible. Therefore, if the Court did not address this issue *proprio motu*, the fact that it has never declared a reservation impermissible would have another meaning.[510] In the *Nicaragua* case for example, the Court interpreted and applied the Vandenberg Reservation and did not declare it as being impermissible. On the other hand no party asked the Court to do so.[511]

Gharbi understood Article 36(6) of the Statute as containing a duty for the Court to assess the permissibility of reservations.[512] However, Article 36(6) of the Statute could also be read the other way. According to the paragraph's words the Court only decides upon its jurisdiction when there is a dispute about it.[513] If the defendant raises no objections at all, the Court has jurisdiction due to a *forum prorogatum*.[514] In this situation the Court has no duty to assess the titles of jurisdiction and the reservations attached to them. As Rosenne wrote, 'jurisdiction will be perfected by application of the doctrine of the *forum prorogatum'*.[515]

Similarly, the Court has no duty to address objections to titles of jurisdiction against the will of the involved states. As the Court decided in the *Norwegian Loans* case, if the states involved present an understanding which precludes the objection to the Court's jurisdiction, the Court does

---

[508] cp C Tomuschat (n 3) para 99 with reference to the Court's treatment of the Connally Reservation.

[509] For the fact that the Court raises no titles of jurisdiction *proprio motu* see sub-s II C of ch 1 at 28.

[510] cp the conclusion on the Connally Reservation in Crawford (n 8) 67.

[511] cp *Military and Paramilitary Activities in and against Nicaragua (Nicaragua v United States of America)* (n 30) paras 259–64; *Military and Paramilitary Activities in and against Nicaragua (Nicaragua v United States of America)* (n 57) (United States of America) paras 20–23, 252–322; *Military and Paramilitary Activities in and against Nicaragua (Nicaragua v United States of America)* (n 1) (Nicaragua) 98–101 (Brownlie); *Military and Paramilitary Activities in and against Nicaragua (Nicaragua v United States of America)* (n 6) (United States of America) 148, 199–214 (Norton, Robinson).

[512] Gharbi (n 28) 462.

[513] cp also *Legality of Use of Force (Serbia and Montenegro v Belgium)* (Preliminary Objections) [2004] ICJ Rep 279, 35; Wittmann (n 6) 414 f.

[514] See sub-s I C ii of ch 1 at 15.

[515] Rosenne and Ronen (n 1) 795 f. See also Kolb (n 6) 373 f; Tomuschat (n 3) para 40.

not need to raise it itself.[516] Conversely, Judge Lauterpacht heavily argued for a decision *proprio motu*. For him the parties were entitled to have answers to the legal questions presented and it was also the Court's function to answer open questions of law.[517] He saw no possibility to assume a *forum prorogatum* as Norway had contested the jurisdiction of the Court.[518] Also Judge Guerrero argued for an assessment *proprio motu* as otherwise there was no procedure in which the permissibility of a reservation could be analysed. He pressed the 'nécessité d'avoir une décision judiciaire sur la validité des réserves qui vont au delà de ce qui est permis par l'article 36 du Statut'.[519] Verzijl supported the position of the dissenting judges by emphasising the importance of the question.[520] Conversely the Court focused on the dispute between France and Norway and not on solving the legal question.

This is in line with the Court's later decisions in the *Use of Force* cases and the recent case concerning *Questions relating to the Seizure and Detention of Certain Documents and Data*. In its judgment concerning the *Use of Force* case regarding Belgium, the Court emphasised that '[t]he function of a decision of the Court on its jurisdiction in a particular case is solely to determine whether or not the Court may entertain that case on the merits, and not to engage in a clarification of a controverted issue of a general nature'.[521] In its order on provisional measures in the case concerning *Questions relating to the Seizure and Detention of Certain Documents and Data*, the Court based the order on the Optional Clause declarations of Australia and Timor-Leste. It did not address any matters of jurisdiction as Australia had expressly refrained from raising them at that stage of proceedings.[522]

This approach can be supported with the fact that its jurisdiction is based on the consent of the states.[523] As far as both parties mutually plead before the Court that there is such consent, the Court has not to decide upon the individual sources of jurisdiction themselves.[524]

---

[516] *Case of Certain Norwegian Loans (France v Norway)* (n 38) 27. See also Verzijl (n 83) 601 f.

[517] Separate opinion of Judge H Lauterpacht, *ICJ Rep 1957*, 36; supported by Gharbi (n 28) 462.

[518] Separate opinion of Judge H Lauterpacht, *ICJ Rep 1957*, 60 f.

[519] Dissenting opinion of Judge JG Guerrero, *ICJ Rep 1957*, 69.

[520] Verzijl (n 378) 398 f. cp also the more cautious approach by M Kawano, 'Optional Clause' 431–34.

[521] *Legality of Use of Force (Serbia and Montenegro v Belgium)* (n 513) para 38. See also Rosenne and Ronen (n 1) 536 f.

[522] *Questions relating to the Seizure and Detention of Certain Documents and Data (Timor-Leste v Australia)* (Provisional Measures) [2014] paras 19–21. See also the dissenting opinion of Judge IDF Callinan, paras 18–20, and Australia's statement (*Questions relating to the Seizure and Detention of Certain Documents and Data (Timor-Leste v Australia)* (Provisional Measures) Oral Proceedings (CR 2014/2) (Australia) 21, para 3).

[523] For the latter point see s I of ch 3 at 86 and sub-s II A of ch 4 at 134.

[524] cp also Shihata (n 38) 295; Thirlway (n 6) 601; Tomuschat (n 3) para 30.

This does, however, not answer the question to what extent the Court raises issues *proprio motu* where no such opinion by both states has been expressed. There are several positions on this.[525] In its judgment concerning the *Factory of Chorzów* case the Permanent Court explained that it 'will, in the event of an objection—or when it has automatically to consider the question—only affirm its jurisdiction provided that the force of the arguments militating in favour of it is preponderant'.[526] Shortly afterwards, Judge Huber held in the *Minority School* case that the Court generally had to ascertain *ex officio* the legal foundation of its jurisdiction and based this on the principle *iura novit curia*. Only where the respondent did not raise any objections at all the Court could proceed to the merits. In all other cases in which the Court had to assess a title of jurisdiction the Court had to fully do so.[527] Similarly, Judge McNair held in the *Anglo-Iranian Oil Co* case:

> An international tribunal cannot regard a question of jurisdiction solely as a question *inter partes*. That aspect does not exhaust the matter. The Court itself, acting *proprio motu*, must be satisfied that any State which is brought before it by virtue of such a Declaration has consented to the jurisdiction.[528]

In the *Fisheries Jurisdiction* case between the United Kingdom, Germany and Iceland the Court held:

> [T]he Court, in accordance with its Statute and its settled jurisprudence, must examine *proprio motu* the question of its own jurisdiction to consider the Application of the United Kingdom. Furthermore, in the present case the duty of the Court to make this examination on its own initiative is reinforced by the terms of Article 53 of the Statute of the Court. According to this provision, whenever one of the parties does not appear before the Court, or fails to defend its

---

[525] De Fumel, Kebbon, Maus and Shihata wrote that the Court did not address questions of jurisdiction *propio motu* (de Fumel (n 29) 4; Kebbon (n 68) 265; Maus (n 37) 88, fn 19, 89; Shihata (n 38) 295 f). This is similar to the situation under the human right treaty bodies for the reservations to human rights treaties (cp Walter (n 8) para 130 referring to *Manuel Wackenheim v France* (Communication No 854/1999) (2002) CCPR/C/75/D/854/1999 para 6.2.). But see also Crawford, Lawson, Morrison and Tomuschat who maintained that the Court, at least generally, examined issues of jurisdiction *proprio motu* (Crawford (n 8) 67; Lawson (n 378) 234; Morrison (n 57) 67, fn 29; Tomuschat (n 3) para 30). Thirlway wrote that the Court made an indication in the latter direction (Thirlway (n 6) 602). Szafarz maintained that the Court is obliged to examine its jurisdiction *proprio motu* in cases of Art 53 of the Statute (Szafarz (n 10) 15).
[526] *Case concerning the Factory at Chorzów (Germany v Poland)* (Jurisdiction) PCIJ Series A No 9 3, 32.
[527] Dissenting opinion of Judge M Huber, *PCIJ Series A No 15 1928*, 52–54. As far as Judge Huber even hold that the Permanent Court had to act against the pleadings of the parties it can be said what has already been said above in this section. In such cases the Court does not raise the issue.
[528] Individual opinion of Judge AD McNair, *ICJ Rep 1952*, 116 f. See also Rosenne and Ronen (n 1) 898 f.

case, the Court, before finding upon the merits, must satisfy itself that it has jurisdiction.[529]

This statement allows no clear conclusion on whether the Court acts *proprio motu* in cases not falling under Article 53 of the Statute. On the one hand, according to the Court, Article 53 of the Statute only reinforced the duty of the Court. Therefore, there also was a duty without Article 53 of the Statute. On the other hand, the Court emphasised that it had to satisfy itself whether it had jurisdiction according to Article 53 of the Statute. This suggests that the duty to satisfy itself that it had jurisdiction was based on that article.[530]

In the *Tehran Hostage* case, the Court 'thought it right to examine, *ex officio*, whether its competence to decide the present case, or the admissibility of the present proceedings, might possibly have been affected by the setting up of the Commission announced by the Secretary-General of the United Nations on 20 February 1980'.[531] However, the Court does not seem to have considered the issue discussed as being a question of jurisdiction, as it concluded the paragraph saying that it 'must now proceed ... to determine whether it has jurisdiction to decide the present case'.[532]

In the *Use of Force* cases, the Court wrote:

> The question is whether *as a matter of law* Serbia and Montenegro was entitled to seise the Court as a party to the Statute at the time when it instituted proceedings in these cases. Since that question is independent of the views or wishes of the Parties, even if they were now to have arrived at a shared view on the point, the Court would not have to accept that view as necessarily the correct one.[533]

However, also in this case the mentioned question did not relate to the Court's jurisdiction as provided for in Article 36 of the Statute. The Court introduced the passage just quoted with the words:

> [I]t is the view of the Court that a distinction has to be made between a question of jurisdiction that relates to the consent of a party and the question of the right of a party to appear before the Court under the requirements of the Statute, which is not a matter of consent.[534]

In his last edition on his work on the Court, Rosenne wrote:

> In sum, the instances are so sparse, and the circumstances of each so particular that beyond noting the existence of the right of the Court to raise matters

---

[529] *Fisheries Jurisdiction (United Kingdom of Great Britain and Northern Ireland v Iceland)* (Jurisdiction) [1973] ICJ Rep 3, para 12.

[530] On the question whether Art 53 of the Statute 'reinforces' or constitutes a duty see Rosenne and Ronen (n 1) 858. cp also Szafarz (n 10) 15.

[531] *United States Diplomatic and Consular Staff in Tehran (United States of America v Iran)* (Judgment) [1980] ICJ Rep 3, para 39. See also Tomuschat (n 3) para 30.

[532] *United States Diplomatic and Consular Staff in Tehran (United States of America v Iran)*, ibid para 44.

[533] *Legality of Use of Force (Serbia and Montenegro v Belgium)* (n 513) para 36.

[534] ibid para 36.

of jurisdiction *proprio motu*, no general principles concerning the manner of its exercise can be discerned.[535]

Taking this into consideration, little value can be attached to the fact that the two Courts have so far never declared a reservation being impermissible. It cannot be said for sure that the Courts did not address the admissibility of reservations because they always considered them admissible. It is likewise possible that the Courts did not address the permissibility of the reservations because they did not consider themselves as having the duty to do so. On the other hand it is possible that the judges had considered the permissibility of the reservation and did just not raise the issue as they considered the reservations as valid and therefore without influence on the result of their decision.

b. The Court Accepted Reservations Allowing Withdrawals Without a Period of Notice

As also the parties addressed the issue in the *Right of Passage* case, the Court had to decide about the Portuguese reservation allowing the introduction of new reservations without a period of notice.

The Court acknowledged that such reservations could cause instability but stated that the instability always referred only to the future and not to the present situation. As the Secretary-General informed the other states about new reservations they could always ascertain the current status of the Optional Clause declarations. The instability was similar to the instability caused by the possibility that a new declaration was submitted and was inherent in the Optional Clause system. Just like reservations allowing withdrawals without a period of notice also reservations allowing amending without a period of notice were permissible.[536] This was supported by Oda who emphasised that the group of states which had made a commitment was inherently subject to change. According to Oda the states 'brave the partially unknown' and the underlying instability was part of the system.[537] In the *Nicaragua* case the Court then made clear that a state making an Optional Clause declaration 'may specify how long

---

[535] Rosenne and Ronen (n 1) 901. See also Morrison who wrote that in this regard 'certain aspects remain undefined' (Morrison (n 57) 39). See furthermore Tomuschat who wrote that the Court did not always 'live up to its own standards' when it came to the question whether it addresses question of jurisdiction *proprio motu*. For this conclusion he referred to cases relating to Art 35 of the Statute, too (Tomuschat (n 3) para 30).

[536] *Case concerning the Right of Passage over Indian Territory (Portugal v India)* (n 38) 143 f. For the fact that under the Optional Clause 'amendments' are basically nothing else than partial withdrawals and that therefore reservation allowing amendments are nothing else than reservations allowing withdrawal see s I of ch 6 at 275.

[537] Oda (n 183) 18.

the declaration itself shall remain in force, or what notice (if any) will be required to terminate it'.[538]

Some judges, however, did not share this view. In the *Right of Passage* case Judge Chagla dissented and wrote very clearly that those reservations departed from the inviolable core of the Optional Clause and that they therefore were impermissible. He wrote: 'The Declaration may last 70 years, one year, six months, … [but] the third condition of Portugal is an entirely different kind of reservation'. Judge Chagla referred to authors addressing the decline of the Optional Clause and argued that reservations allowing amending without period of notice rendered the compulsory jurisdiction illusory. For him the minimum of compromise under the Optional Clause was that a state accepts different groups of disputes in the moment the declaration is made. Any further derogation from that minimum was impermissible. At the end Judge Chagla held:

> As the intention of the Optional Clause is to make a State accept the compulsory jurisdiction of the Court, any reservation which frustrates that intention must be held to be opposed to the general purpose of the Optional Clause and therefore invalid.[539]

In the *Fisheries Jurisdiction* case between Canada and Spain Judge Bedjaoui criticised Canada's introduction of a reservation especially for one particular measure in international law. He called this 'some sort of *ad hoc* judicial procedure suiting or benefiting the author of the reservation alone'. However, in his criticism Judge Bedjaoui focused more on the fact that Canada had accepted the compulsory jurisdiction and retained it for a particular allegedly illegal behaviour. He did not address the way in which Canada had introduced its reservation.[540] In the same case Judge Weeramantry emphasised that the rules of the Charter and the Statute are mandatory and that states 'cannot contract out of them by reservations, however framed'.[541] However, by saying this, he made no statement on the permissibility of the reservation in question.

All in all, there seems to be little to support Judge Chagla's position. With regard to the states' approval of reservations allowing withdrawals without a period of notice and the Court's clear jurisprudence, the object and purpose of the Optional Clause has to be understood as allowing these reservations. As Alexandrov wrote: 'The Court appears

---

[538] *Military and Paramilitary Activities in and against Nicaragua (Nicaragua v United States of America)* (n 38) para 59.

[539] Dissenting opinion of Judge MAC Chagla, *ICJ Rep 1957*, 166–68. It has to be emphasised that Judge Chagla distinguished between reservations allowing amendments and those allowing withdrawals. For that issue see s I of ch 6 at 275.

[540] Dissenting opinion of Judge M Bedjaoui, *ICJ Rep 1998*, paras 44 f, 47–59. For the influence of the illegality of the behaviour on the permissibility of the reservation see sub-s III B iii e of ch 5 at 220.

[541] Dissenting opinion of Judge CG Weeramantry, *ICJ Rep 1998*, paras 17–22. See also Kawano (n 520) 424–25.

to have recognized the reality of the increasing number of declarations [which can be terminated immediately upon notice]'.[542] The downsides of this approach, which also Judge Chagla addressed, seem to have been accepted for the sake of universality.

c. The Court has Not Yet Decided on the Connally Reservation
   but Some Judges Have

The last question is how the Court understood the object and purpose of the Optional Clause regarding subjective reservations.

In the case concerning the *Rights of Nationals of the United States of America in Morocco* the Court did not address the United States' Connally Reservation. The United States had only made one preliminary objection which did not relate to its declaration and which it later withdrew to proceed on the merits of the case.[543] The jurisdiction was therefore based on a *forum prorogatum*.[544] As far as Crawford said that the Court and the states relied on Optional Clause declarations and therefore not on a *forum prorogatum*,[545] it can be said that the Court does not raise issues concerning its jurisdiction as far as both states mutually consent.[546] In this respect nothing concerning the permissibility of the Connally Reservation can be inferred from this case.

In the later *Aerial Incident of 1955* case Bulgaria invoked the United States' Connally Reservation and maintained that the incident was a national issue.[547] Before the Court was able to decide upon the reservation the United States withdrew its application.[548] In the *Norwegian Loans* case Norway invoked the French Connally Reservation and France did not challenge its own declaration. Therefore, the Court applied the Connally Reservation and expressly refrained from deciding upon the reservation's permissibility.[549] At the interim stage of the *Interhandel* case, the Court also

---

[542] Alexandrov (n 25) 65.

[543] *Case concerning Rights of Nationals of the United States of America in Morocco (France v United States of America)* Correspondence (United States of America) 424–26, 434. cp also *Case concerning Rights of Nationals of the United States of America in Morocco (France v United States of America)* (Judgment) [1952] ICJ Rep 176, 179 and Ulimubenshi (n 378) 127–29.

[544] See also the separate opinion of Judge H Lauterpacht, *ICJ Rep 1957*, 60; Rosenne and Ronen (n 1) 749, fn 126.

[545] Crawford (n 8) 66.

[546] See sub-s III B vi a of ch 5 at 241.

[547] *Case concerning the Aerial Incident of July 27th, 1955 (Israel v Bulgaria)* (Preliminary Objections) [1959] ICJ Rep 127, 135–42.

[548] *Case concerning the Aerial Incident of July 27th, 1955 (United States of America v Bulgaria)* Correspondence (United States of America) 676 f. See also *Case concerning the Aerial Incident of July 27th, 1955 (United States of America v Bulgaria)* (Order for removal from the list) [1960] ICJ Rep 146, 147.

[549] *Case of Certain Norwegian Loans (France v Norway)* (n 38) 26 f. See also the dissenting opinion of Judge J Basdevant, *ICJ Rep 1957*, 71 f; P Guggenheim, 'Der automatische Vorbehalt' 126. See furthermore above sub-s III B vi a of ch 5 at 241.

refrained from deciding upon the permissibility of the Connally Reservation. It stated that this matter was too complex for the interim stage. It said that both states had made an Optional Clause declaration and expressly reserved the right to decide the issue during the cause of the main hearings.[550] At the later stage, however, the Court declared the application as impermissible for another reason and did not address the permissibility of the Connally Reservation anymore.[551] In the *Nicaragua* case, the United States did not invoke its Connally Reservation and the Court did not decide upon it. It becomes obvious that it is as Rosenne wrote: 'The Court has been able to avoid having to pronounce itself on it'.[552]

Especially Judge Lauterpacht, however, pronounced himself very clearly. In his separate opinion in the *Norwegian Loans* case he did not refer to treaty law but his reasoning is close to what is today Article 19(c) VCLT. He referred to the 'legal principle generally recognized in municipal law according to which a condition, in a contract or any other legal instrument, that is contrary to a fundamental principle of a judicial organization is invalid'. According to Judge Lauterpacht Article 36(2) of the Statute was meant to establish compulsory jurisdiction, which was impossible with the Connally Reservation.[553] He referred to national treaty laws and inferred from there that an obligation could not exist where the debtor could decide upon his obligation. Such an obligation would be nonexistent. For Judge Lauterpacht the same applied for Optional Clause declarations with the Connally Reservation. They were not 'a legal undertaking'.[554] Additionally, Judge Lauterpacht argued that the Connally Reservation interfered with the Court's competence to decide upon its jurisdiction as provided for in Article 36(6) of the Statute. Like reservations which tried to influence the deciding bench, the Connally Reservation was impermissible as reservations could not influence these aspects of the Court. For this argument, Judge Lauterpacht referred to Article 1 of the Statute and Article 92 of the Charter.[555] In the *Interhandel* case he repeated this finding.[556]

---

[550] *Interhandel Case (Switzerland v United States of America)* (Interim Measures of Protection) [1957] ICJ Rep 105, 110 f. See also Holloway (n 184) 687; Whiteman (n 68) 1326, 1331 (Rogers).

[551] *Interhandel Case (Switzerland v United States of America)* (n 68) 26. See furthermore Holloway, ibid 687; Whiteman, ibid 1328, 1332 (Rogers).

[552] Rosenne and Ronen (n 1) 749. See also Crawford (n 8) 67; Kebbon (n 68) 265; Kolb (n 6) 508 f; C Stahn, 'Connally Reservation' para 5; Ulimubenshi (n 378) 131–37. But see also Gross (n 189) 357.

[553] Separate opinion of Judge H Lauterpacht, *ICJ Rep 1957*, 47.

[554] ibid 49–51. See also Lauterpacht's earlier position in Lauterpacht (n 20) 169.

[555] Separate opinion of Judge H Lauterpacht, *ICJ Rep 1957*, 44–48.

[556] Dissenting opinion of Judge H Lauterpacht, *ICJ Rep 1959*, 101–19; supported by RY Jennings, '"Automatic" Reservations' 366: 'brilliant solo forays'. In his opinion on the provisional measures Judge Lauterpacht had not yet decided the question (separate opinion of Judge H Lauterpacht, *ICJ Rep 1957*, 120). See also the presentation in Kawano (n 520) 432–33.

Also in the *Norwegian Loans* case, Judge Guerrero, too, argued against the permissibility of the Connally Reservation. He, too, maintained that the reservation violated both Article 36(2) and (6) of the Statute. He wrote that during the time of the League of Nations it had been possible to allow all reservations as there had been another attitude among the states back then. In 1946 the attitude had changed as the United States made its declaration and introduced new reservations like the Connally Reservation. Jurisdiction based on a declaration with such a reservation could not be compulsory. As the Optional Clause declarations should establish compulsory jurisdiction the reservation was impermissible.[557] In the *Interhandel* case it was furthermore Judge Spender who considered the Connally Reservation as being impermissible as it was 'incompatible with any compulsory legal obligation and with Article 36 (6)'.[558] In the same case the Judges Armand-Ugon and Klaestad, too, considered subjective reservations as impermissible and referred to Article 36(6) of the Statute.[559] Only Judge Koo wanted to apply the Connally Reservation.[560] In the *Nicaragua* case, it was Judge Schwebel who supported Judge Lauterpacht's approach.[561] In the *Fisheries Jurisdiction* case between Spain and Canada it was Judge Bedjaoui who pointed at the incompatibility of subjective reservations and Article 36(6) of the Statute.[562]

In total, it can be held that while the Court has so far never decided upon the permissibility of the Connally Reservation, the individual judges argued very convincingly for an Optional Clause which allows no subjective reservations.

d. Result: The Jurisprudence on the Object and Purpose of the Optional Clause

The Court has acknowledged the states' freedom to make reservations but it cannot be said for sure whether in the Court's perception there are borders to that freedom. When the states asked the Court to decide, it decided and maintained that Commonwealth reservations and reservations allowing

---

[557] Dissenting opinion of Judge JG Guerrero, *ICJ Rep 1957*, 68–70. Similarly, Judge Read held that if the Connally Reservation were to be interpreted as a totally subjective reservation it was 'necessary to conclude that the Declaration ran contrary to Article 36, paragraph 6, of the Statute, and was null and void' (dissenting opinion of Judge JE Read, *ICJ Rep 1957*, 94 f; Jennings, ibid 358).

[558] Separate opinion of Judge PC Spender, *ICJ Rep 1959*, 55–59.

[559] Dissenting opinion of Judge EC Armand-Ugon, *ICJ Rep 1959*, paras 3–7; dissenting opinion of Judge H Klaestad, *ICJ Rep 1959*, 75–78. Supported by Judge P Carry, *ICJ Rep 1959*, 32. For the argument concerning Art 36(6) of the Statute see sub-s III B iv a 1 of ch 5 at 224.

[560] Separate opinion of Judge VK Wellington Koo, *ICJ Rep 1957*, 113 f.

[561] Dissenting opinion of Judge SM Schwebel, *ICJ Rep 1984*, paras 64–66.

[562] Dissenting opinion of Judge M Bedjaoui, *ICJ Rep 1998*, para 44. cp also the dissenting opinion of Judge S Torres Bernárdez, *ICJ Rep 1998*, para 135.

withdrawal without a period of notice were permissible. Concerning the Connally Reservation the Court did not decide yet but individual judges raised the issue and considered the reservation impermissible.

vii. Result: The Object and Purpose of the Optional Clause with Regard to Article 19(c) VCLT

At the beginning of this sub-section several possible approaches to the Optional Clause's object and purpose have been presented. It has been examined to what extent these approaches can be supported or rebutted with Article 36 of the Statute, state practice or the Court's jurisprudence.

The result endorses a perspective which, in 1964, the ILA's Rapporteur Sohn addressed in his 'Report on the Gradual Extension of the Compulsory Jurisdiction of the Court'. He argued that states were reluctant to accept general compulsory jurisdiction because '[a]lmost every State has some skeletons in its closets and might not have to wish to have them exposed before the Court'. Furthermore, he said that states feared the unforeseen consequences resulting from a forgotten subject not covered by a reservation.[563]

The Optional Clause seems to have understood these fears. Its object and purpose is basically universal acceptance. The Optional Clause, as it is especially understood in state practice, welcomes every commitment no matter how small it is. The original Optional Clause of 1920 and 1945 could still have been understood as not allowing reservations which provide for withdrawals without a period of notice. With the later state practice, however, the object and purpose of the Optional Clause has to be understood as allowing these reservations in any case. Apparently the states want an Optional Clause which leaves them the possibility to escape in the face of a dispute or to adjust their Optional Clause declarations quickly according to current policies.

This disassociates the Optional Clause, at least to a certain degree, from the idea that it will provide long-standing and abstract jurisdiction which is in no way related to a particular dispute. However, also with this approach, the Optional Clause is not completely redundant to the ad hoc jurisdiction in Article 36(1) of the Statute as it still provides jurisdiction in cases in which the states do not use their reservations or where a state fails to withdraw before another state files its application.[564] As said above, the Anti Ambush Clauses also provide a certain incentive for states not to withdraw their Optional Clause declarations.[565] Additionally, individual

---

[563] ILA, Report of the Fifty-First Conference, Tokyo 87 (Sohn). See also Lamm (n 10) 126 f.
[564] Similarly already Wittmann (n 6) 199.
[565] cp sub-s III F of ch 3 at 116.

states that want a different Optional Clause with stronger commitment can just exclude states having a reservation allowing withdrawal without a period of notice from the scope of their Optional Clauses.[566]

The situation is, however, different for subjective reservations like the Connally Reservation. With good reason many authors considered subjective reservation as being impermissible.[567] Most of them based their opinion on one or several of the arguments which had also been presented by Judge Lauterpacht in the *Norwegian Loans* or the *Interhandel* case. Even though these arguments did not expressly relate to the object and purpose of the Optional Clause, these arguments can likewise be used to support a certain perception of the object and purpose of the Optional Clause which renders subjective reservations impermissible.[568] Concerning the subjective reservations it can therefore be said what already the United States Senate's Foreign Relations Committee wrote in 1946:

> [A] reservation of the right of decision as to what are matters essentially within domestic jurisdiction would tend to defeat the purposes which it is hoped to achieve by means of the proposed declaration as well as the purpose of Article 36, paragraphs 2 and 6, of the Statute of the Court.[569]

This is also similar to general treaty law. During the drafting of the GPRT it was Simma who similarly said that a reservation may not be shaped later by unilateral interpretation.[570]

C. Result: The Permissibility of Reservations Under the Optional Clause can be Explained with Article 19 VCLT

The result for Article 19(c) VCLT leads to the most important conclusion that also regarding the permissibility of reservations there is nothing in the Optional Clause that cannot be explained with an application of general treaty law. Just as Article 19 VCLT provides, the Optional Clause generally allows the making of reservations. Only in one of the cases of Article 19(a) to (c) VCLT reservations are impermissible. Article 36(3) of the Statute cannot be interpreted as limiting the freedom of states to make reservations according to Article 19(b) VCLT. Article 19(c) VCLT refers to the

---

[566] For more on this see the conclusion at 333.

[567] Anand (n 184) 204–12; de Visscher (n 388) 418–21; Dubisson (n 382) 189; Farmanfarma (n 104) 101, 157; Gharbi (n 28) 455, 498; Jennings (n 556) 361 f, 366; Maus (n 37) 155–57; Verzijl (n 83) 601; Waldock (n 38) 272 f; Yankov (n 26) 594 f.

[568] cp Lauterpacht (n 272) 64 where Lauterpacht himself spoke of the 'purpose of the Optional Clause'.

[569] United States of America 'Congressional Record' (1946) 10707 (Report of the Committee on Foreign Relations). Also quoted in Hudson (n 379) 835.

[570] ILC 'Summary Records of the Meetings of the 53rd Session' (23 April–1 June and 2 July–10 August 2001) UN Doc A/CN.4/SER.A/2001 235, para 30 (Simma).

object and purpose of the treaty in question. The Optional Clause's object and purpose only contradict subjective reservations which are therefore impermissible. There is nothing particular about this flexibility.[571]

IV. THE SEPARABILITY OF OPTIONAL CLAUSE DECLARATIONS AND THEIR RESERVATIONS

Since at least subjective reservations are impermissible the next question of this chapter will be whether they can be separated from their Optional Clause declarations and whether a state could be bound regardless of its reservation. Under the Optional Clause the opinions about this are highly diverse. While some argued that, at least in certain cases, reservations could be separated from Optional Clause declarations,[572] others emphasised that states could not be bound beyond their consent.[573] Nonetheless, this, too, seems to be nothing particular if compared to treaty law.

A. General Treaty Law on Separability and Especially Guideline 4.5.3 GPRT

Under general treaty law there is likewise an ongoing discussion which presents the same two extremes.[574] The provisions of the VCLT provide no answer in this regard.[575]

In its recent guidelines the ILC adopted an intermediate approach. It held: 'As there were logical justifications for both approaches, and as

---

[571] Treaty law theoretically even allows to make all provisions of a treaty open to reservations (compare Tomuschat who wrote that 'it is imaginable, at least in theory, that all provisions of a treaty, without exception, are declared subject to reservations' (Tomuschat (n 43) para 16)).

[572] Dubisson (n 382) 189; dissenting opinion of Judge JG Guerrero, *ICJ Rep 1957*, 70; Pinto (n 353) 54; separate opinion of Judge PC Spender, *ICJ Rep 1959*, 59. See also Verzijl (n 83) 598 considering an impermissible reservation as 'unwritten'.

[573] Crawford (n 8) 68; Jennings (n 556) 362; Rosenne and Ronen (n 1) 741, fn 103. cp also Lauterpacht (n 20) 169: 'contrary to the very purpose of the Optional Clause and as such invalidating its signature'. See also Farmanfarma (n 104) 157; Maus (n 37) 92, 201. At least for the Connally Reservation R Dolzer, 'Connally Reservation' 756.

[574] cp Giegerich (n 8) para 22; Pellet (n 230) para 178 to UNGA 'Fifty-first Session, Report of the Human Rights Committee' (16.9.1996) UN Doc A/51/40 119; United States of America, 'Observations' 423 f and the states' reactions to the draft GPRT of 2010 (ILC 'Reservations to Treaties, Comments and Observations Received from Governments' (15 February 2011) UN Doc A/CN.4/639 31–42; ILC 'Reservations to Treaties, Comments and Observations Received from Governments' (29 March 2011) UN Doc A/CN.4/639/Add.1 44–46).

[575] ILC 'Report of the International Law Commission on the Work of Its 62nd Session' (n 43) 111; Pellet (n 230) para 54; Walter (n 8) para 105.

practice in the matter was ambivalent, the Commission was compelled to engage in progressive development'.[576] Guideline 4.5.3(1) GPRT provides:

> The status of the author of an invalid reservation in relation to a treaty depends on the intention expressed by the reserving State or international organization on whether it intends to be bound by the treaty without the benefit of the reservation or whether it considers that it is not bound by the treaty.[577]

Therefore, at least where a state's consent obviously depends on a reservation that reservation is not separable.[578] A dilemma arises, however, whenever this is not obvious and whenever a state has expressed its intention to accede to a treaty and also its intention not to be bound by the treaty as far as the reservation reaches.[579] If, under the Optional Clause, that state would not be bound at all, it would also have no possibility to file applications against other states in disputes for which it would have otherwise validly consented to. If the state would be bound without the reservations, other states could file an application against that state in disputes for which it had expressly excluded a corresponding obligation. The draft GPRT which the ILC had presented in 2010 contained a list of aspects which could have been taken into consideration to identify the intention of the author of the reservation and which included, for example, the wording of the reservation, the subsequent conduct of the declaring state and object and purpose of the treaty in question.[580] The most recent version of the GPRT does not contain this list anymore,[581] but kept the residual rule that '[u]nless the author of the invalid reservation has expressed a contrary intention or such an intention is otherwise established, it is considered a contracting State or a contracting organization without the benefit of the reservation'.[582]

---

[576] ILC 'Report of the International Law Commission on the Work of Its 62nd Session' (n 43) 22.

[577] ILC 'Report of the International Law Commission on the Work of Its 63rd Session' (n 12) 26. See also the dissenting opinion in the UNCHR's *Kennedy v Trinidad and Tobago* case according to which the reservation in question was crucial for making the declaration and therefore not separable (dissenting opinion of Judges N Ando, PN Bhagwati, E Klein and D Kretzmer, *CCPR/C/67/D/845/1999 1999*, paras 14–17).

[578] cp also Dubisson (n 382) 186, 189; Pinto (n 353) 54. For the Connally Reservation cp Kebbon (n 68) 265.

[579] cp DW Bowett, 'Reservations' 75 f; Walter (n 8) para 114.

[580] ILC 'Report of the International Law Commission on the Work of Its 62nd Session' (n 43) 67.

[581] For the reason for that change cp ILC 'Reservations to Treaties, Comments and Observations Received from Governments' (29 March 2011) UN Doc A/CN.4/639/Add.1 45 f and ILC, 'Oral report by the Chairman of the Working Group on Reservations to Treaties, Mr Marcelo Vázquez Bermúdez' (2011) 9 f.

[582] Guideline 4.5.3(2) GPRT (ILC, 'Oral report by the Chairman of the Working Group on Reservations to Treaties, Mr Marcelo Vázquez Bermúdez' (2011) 9 f; ILC 'Report of the International Law Commission on the Work of Its 63rd Session' (n 12) 26). For a commentary on this presumption see ILC 'Report of the International Law Commission on the Work of Its 63rd Session' (n 12) 537 f, 541, paras 33–40, 49. See also Guideline 4.5.3(3) GPRT which provides: 'Notwithstanding paragraphs 1 and 2, the author of the invalid reservation may express at any time its intention not to be bound by the treaty without the benefit of the reservation'.

Also in this regard the tendency in human rights law, which has already been referred to above,[583] offers no help for the Optional Clause. For human rights treaties there is a strong opinion that reservations are generally separated from the declaration of accession.[584] But again this is based on the particularities of human rights treaties as such,[585] and the particular state practice in this regard.[586] And again, these arguments do not apply to the Optional Clause.[587]

For treaties with compromissory clauses there is little particular practice regarding the issue of separability. Concerning the General Act the Court stated in the *Aegean Sea Shelf* case that there was a 'close and necessary link that always exists between a jurisdictional clause and reservations to it'.[588] Crawford and Ende interpreted this as the Court having outspoken against separability.[589] This one *obiter dictum* seems, however, to be a rather weak argument as the Court's only concern was to interpret a reservation.

---

[583] cp sub-s III B ii of ch 5 at 203.

[584] cp Giegerich (n 8) para 39; Higgins (n 239) xxvi–xxviii; Nowak (n 242) introduction, para 27; Simma (n 239) 670–73; Walter (n 8) paras 117–19. See eg *Belilos v Switzerland* (n 252) para 60 maintained inter alia in *Weber v Switzerland* (n 256) para 38; *Chrysostomos ao v Turkey* (n 259) paras 43–49 and supported by Polakiewicz (n 10) 153 f. See furthermore UNCHR 'General Comment No 24 (52) on issues relating to reservations made upon ratification or accession to the Covenant to the Optional Protocols thereto, or in relation to declarations under article 41 of the Covenant' (n 230) para 18; maintained in *Rawle Kennedy v Trinidad and Tobago* (n 246) paras 6.1–7 and supported by Nowak, ibid introduction, para 30; Stahn (n 243) 614. But see also the dissenting UNCHR's members who did not want to separate the declaration and the reservation when the former depends on the latter (dissenting opinion of Judges N Ando, PN Bhagwati, E Klein and D Kretzmer, CCPR/C/67/D/845/1999 1999, paras 14–16). See furthermore the strong criticism on the UNCHR's position by UNGA 'Fifty-first Session, Report of the Human Rights Committee' (16.9.1996) UN Doc A/51/40 119; United Kingdom, 'Observations' 426, para 14; United States of America, 'Observations' 423 f.

[585] cp Aust (n 43) 130 f; Bauer (n 242) 218, 230 f; C Ovey and RCA White, *ECHR* 455 f. See eg UNCHR 'General Comment No 24 (52) on issues relating to reservations made upon ratification or accession to the Covenant to the Optional Protocols thereto, or in relation to declarations under article 41 of the Covenant' (n 230) para 18; *Loizidou v Turkey* (n 260) paras 90–98.

[586] Under human rights treaties at least some states voiced their opinion about the consequences of their objection and expressed that they considered the other state as bound without the reservation (cp the examples in Aust (n 43) 132; Bauer (n 242) 236–40; Redgwell (n 228) 273–76; Simma (n 239) 666–68; Walter (n 50) paras 33 f).

[587] See also Finke (n 289) 306 f. See furthermore Redgwell who said concerning the *Belilos* case that 'the weight of this precedent must be carefully considered bearing in mind the fact that the Court was relying upon the wording of the European Convention on Human Rights within the context of a 'common European public order', and not simply applying general principles of treaty law' (Redgwell, ibid 266 (footnote omitted)). For state practice under the Optional Clause see the following section.

[588] *Aegean Sea Continental Shelf (Greece v Turkey)* (Jurisdiction) [1978] ICJ Rep 3, para 79.

[589] Crawford (n 8) 68; Ende (n 161) 1156, fn 61. See also the separate opinion of Judge SM Schwebel, *ICJ Rep 1998*, para 10.

B. State Practice and Jurisprudence on Separability Under the Optional Clause

The question arises to what extent the state practice and the jurisprudence under the Optional Clause provide any guidance.

In the *Right of Passage* case Portugal argued that even if its reservation had been impermissible this would not have led to the invalidity of the whole declaration. Portugal emphasised that the reservation did not relate to the dispute before the Court. Furthermore, Portugal held that the reservation was not decisive for its Optional Clause declaration because it had been Portugal's intention to make the declaration to be able to file an application against India. Because of this intention the reservation could be separated from the declaration. To establish this rule Portugal referred to several national laws.[590] For India, Waldock argued that Portugal's reservation did not just touch a procedural issue but went to the roots of the declaration. For him it had been essential for Portugal's Optional Clause declaration and could therefore not be separated from the declaration.[591] In the *Interhandel* case Switzerland presented arguments to say that an Optional Clause declaration with a Connally Reservation contains no obligation but also emphasised that it was certain that the invalid reservation could be separated from the declaration.[592] Clearly for separability has been Australia in the *Nuclear Tests* case as it maintained very clearly that a subjective reservation is null and void but leaves the declaration effective. Australia referred to the individual opinions of some of the ICJ's judges, Article 44(3) VCLT and the fact that the French reservation in question was not essential for the declaration.[593] In the *Aerial Incident of 1999* case India maintained that the Court had decided that Optional Clause declarations cannot be separated from their reservations. India referred to the *Fisheries Jurisdiction* case between Spain and Canada in which the Court had interpreted the Optional Clause declaration and the reservation likewise. It argued that thereby the Court had also decided on the question of separability. Additionally, India referred to the positions of Judge Lauterpacht and Rosenne. The latter had emphasised the unilateral origin of Optional Clause declarations.[594] Pakistan argued against this that the reservation

---

[590] *Case concerning the Right of Passage over Indian Territory (Portugal v India)* (n 68) (Portugal) 145–48 (Bourquin).

[591] *Case concerning the Right of Passage over Indian Territory (Portugal v India)* (n 68) (India) 31 f (Waldock).

[592] *Interhandel Case (Switzerland v United States of America)* (n 492) 408, 411, paras 5, 8. In the oral proceedings Switzerland expressly refrained from deciding this question (*Interhandel Case (Switzerland v United States of America)* (n 492) (Switzerland) 463 (Guggenheim)).

[593] *Nuclear Tests (Australia v France)* (n 494) paras 310–27.

[594] *Aerial Incident of 10 August 1999 (Pakistan v India)* (n 227) paras 67 f referring to S Rosenne, *Practice 1920–1996* 770, fn 91. For India's argument relating to the jurisprudence of the Court and the position of Judge Lauterpacht see below in this section.

in question is 'not so central as to constitute an essential basis of the consent of India'. Because of this, the reservation could be separated from the declaration and leave India bound without it.[595] In the later oral proceedings Elihu Lauterpacht, pleading for Pakistan maintained: 'The concept of severability is fully recognized in treaty law' and referred to Article 44(3) VCLT which concerns the separability of treaties in general. He applied this provision on the Indian Optional Clause declaration and its reservation. Concerning India's reference to the previous jurisprudence of the Court, he argued that the Court's statements did not refer to the question whether reservations can be separated.[596]

It becomes clear that the states' opinion upon the question is divided. With the exception of India which had inter alia emphasised the unilateral origin of the Optional Clause declarations, no state presented an argument which could not have also been made under treaty law. Pakistan even referred expressly to treaty law itself. The question is, however, if arguments against the application of treaty law could be found in the jurisprudence.

In the *Right of Passage* case the Court did not consider the reservation in question as impermissible and therefore refrained from answering the question of separability. It expressly said that it did not have to answer the question whether Portugal's reservation would have been invalid in total.[597] In the *Norwegian Loans*, the *Interhandel* and the *Nicaragua* case the Court had been asked to base its jurisdiction on declarations with the Connally Reservation. The Court nonetheless never decided that a declaration was invalid. In the *Nicaragua* case it even affirmed its jurisdiction based on the Optional Clause.[598] Therefore, it could be said the Court considered the declarations as separable.[599] However, as said above, little can be inferred from the fact that the Court did not address the invalidity of the Optional Clause declarations in question.[600] In the *Norwegian Loans* case the Court expressly left it open whether the Connally Reservation was impermissible.[601] Necessarily, the Court did not proceed to the question whether an impermissible reservation can be separated from an Optional

---

[595] *Aerial Incident of 10 August 1999 (Pakistan v India)* (n 226) para D(1). See also *Aerial Incident of 10 August 1999 (Pakistan v India)* (n 362) (Pakistan) 20 f, para 48 (E Lauterpacht).

[596] ibid 20 f, paras 37–49 (E Lauterpacht). See also Kolb (n 6) 498, 508 applying Art 44(3) VCLT by analogy.

[597] *Case concerning the Right of Passage over Indian Territory (Portugal v India)* (n 38) 144.

[598] *Military and Paramilitary Activities in and against Nicaragua (Nicaragua v United States of America)* (n 38) paras 109 f. In the *Interhandel* case the Court decided that it had at least *prima facie* jurisdiction for provisional measures (cp *Interhandel Case (Switzerland v United States of America)* (n 550) 110 f).

[599] cp Alexandrov (n 25) 84, fn 412.

[600] See sub-s III B vi a of ch 5 at 241.

[601] *Case of Certain Norwegian Loans (France v Norway)* (n 38) 26 f.

Judge Lauterpacht also asked whether according to the will of the declaring state the permissibility of the reservation should have been decisive for the whole declaration. He considered that France had internally justified the reservation with the sovereignty of the state and the protection of its rights under all circumstances. Additionally, he also referred to the fact that India and the Union of South Africa had both withdrawn their declaration to add the Connally Reservation. Due to this importance of the reservation he came to the result that it cannot be separated from the declaration.[611] This result was, however, opposed to that of Judge Guerrero. In a rather short statement without much reasoning he wrote:

> I cannot agree that the Court is without jurisdiction when its lack of jurisdiction is founded on the terms of a unilateral instrument which I consider to be contrary to the spirit and to the letter of the Statute and which, in my view, is, for that reason, null and void.[612]

In the *Interhandel* case, the Judges Armand-Ugon and Klaestad argued that the declaration and the reservations are two elements which can be separated. According to Judge Klaestad the Court was not barred from giving effect to the other parts of the declaration. Referring to the drafting of the declaration and also to the United States later behaviour, Judge Klaestad concluded that it had shown the clear intention to submit a valid Optional Clause declaration.[613] Also Judge Armand-Ugon emphasised that the United States had applied its Optional Clause declaration in other cases and treated it as valid. He came to the conclusion that the reservation was only an attachment which could be separated.[614] Judge Spender emphasised that the reservation in question was essential for the declaration. Even though he argued that it was impermissible to have recourse to the debates in the United States Senate, Judge Spender maintained that without the reservation the declaration would not have been made. He came to the result that the United States had 'never legally submitted to the jurisdiction of the Court'.[615] In the *Nicaragua* case Judge Schwebel referred benevolently to the aforementioned findings of Judge Lauterpacht but left the issue undecided.[616] He waited until the later *Fisheries Jurisdiction* case to decide on the issue. In that case Judge Schwebel maintained that the impermissibility of the Canadian reservation led to the nullity of the Canadian declaration as a whole. He referred to the *Aegean Sea Continental*

---

[611] Separate opinion of Judge H Lauterpacht, *ICJ Rep 1957*, 55–59.

[612] Dissenting opinion of Judge JG Guerrero, *ICJ Rep 1957*, 70. For this opinion see also Jennings (n 556) 362: '[I]t is a pity that Judge Guerrero did not state the reasons which enabled him to reach the … conclusion'.

[613] Dissenting opinion of Judge H Klaestad, *ICJ Rep 1959*, 76–78.

[614] Dissenting opinion of Judge EC Armand-Ugon, *ICJ Rep 1959*, 91, 93 f.

[615] Separate opinion of Judge PC Spender, *ICJ Rep 1959*, 57, 59.

[616] Dissenting opinion of Judge SM Schwebel, *ICJ Rep 1984*, paras 64–66.

Clause declaration. The Court did likewise in the *Interhandel* case in wh
it expressly refrained from deciding 'upon so complex and delicate a qu
tion as the validity of the American reservation'.[602] In the aforementio
Fisheries Jurisdiction case between Spain and Canada, the Court w
that the declarations and reservations have to be read 'as a whole'.[603]
Alexandrov, just like for India later, this meant that the Court has dec
that declarations with impermissible reservations are invalid in tot
However, the position of Pakistan and Weil is more convincing.[605]
context of the words of the Court had been the interpretation of the
of an Optional Clause declaration and not the question of separabilit
very unlikely that the Court, which was so reluctant to address this
before, decided it in a case in which it was not relevant at all.

Lastly, it could again be emphasised that the Permanent Court a
Court both held that their jurisdiction only existed as far as the
had transferred it.[606] However, again it can be said that there is nc
ence between the Optional Clause and other treaties in this rega
that up to now the Court has never made such a statement rel
the question whether reservations and declarations can be separ
Rosenne wrote: 'The question of severability has not been author
decided'.[607]

Individual judges, however, decided the issue. In the *Right c*
case, Judge Chagla emphasised that the reservation allowing
ing without a period of notice was essential in the Portuguese
Clause declaration. For him the separation of an essential re
from its declaration was equivalent to the creation of a new d
which was beyond the Court's competence.[608] In the *Norwegian*
Judge Lauterpacht came to the result that the 'entire French D
of Acceptance must be treated as devoid of legal effect and as
of providing a basis for the jurisdiction of the Court'. To a la
this result has been based on particularities of the Connally I
as a subjective reservation.[609] Also the judge's statements tha
declaration did not have 'the element of legal obligation' a
instrument is not a legal instrument' point in this direction.[6]

---

[602] *Interhandel Case (Switzerland v United States of America)* (n 550) 110 f.
[603] *Fisheries Jurisdiction (Spain v Canada)* (Jurisdiction) [1998] ICJ Rep 432,
[604] Alexandrov (n 227) 96 f.
[605] P Weil, *Écrits* 131, fn 48.
[606] See sub-s III A of ch 4 at 145.
[607] Rosenne and Ronen (n 1) 741, fn 103 supported also by *Aerial Inciden*
(Pakistan v India) (n 362) (Pakistan) 20 f, para 49 (E Lauterpacht). For 1959 :
[608] Dissenting opinion of Judge MAC Chagla, *ICJ Rep 1957*, 168.
[609] cp also Maus (n 37) 155, 157. For these points see furthermore the fc
[610] cp the separate opinion of Judge H Lauterpacht, *ICJ Rep 1957*, 48,
position Lauterpacht already voiced in 1930: Lauterpacht (n 20) 169.

Shelf case and argued that there may be cases in which a reservation may be separated from an Optional Clause declaration or a treaty providing jurisdiction. Concerning the Canadian reservation Judge Schwebel, however, emphasised that Canada had withdrawn its old declaration to introduce the reservation in question. He concluded that when a reservation 'has been treated by the state as an essential one but for which—or without which—the declaration would not have been made' the Court cannot separate them.[617] In the same case but in the other direction Judge Bedjaoui argued for the separability. He started by referring to common sense but then also expressly referred to Article 44(3) VCLT which for him included the *'principle of separability'*. He continued by stating that he could not see 'why a declaration should wholly escape this principle'. For him this principle was also present in the jurisdiction of the Court, on the regional level and in international commercial arbitration.[618] Judge Torres Bernárdez on the other hand held: 'There can be no question of the declaration being automatically invalid. The intention of the declarant State has to be interpreted in light of the circumstances of the case'.[619]

In total, it becomes clear that also among the judges the opinions are not homogenous. However, it can be said that, aside from Judge Guerrero, none had a position which was outside those presented in treaty law. With reference to the intention of the submitting state especially the Judges Lauterpacht, Schwebel and Spender made arguments which are very much in line with what is provided for in the GPRT today.

C. Result

To sum up, under the Optional Clause the issue of separability is as disputed as it is in general treaty law. For both the issue is not yet fully settled.[620] In any case there are no arguments which demand that the reservations to the Optional Clause declarations should be treated differently from those made to other declarations of accession. Also in this regard the relevant guideline of the ILC is based inter alia on the jurisprudence of the Court on the Optional Clause.[621] Corresponding to the ILC's

[617] Separate opinion of Judge SM Schwebel, *ICJ Rep 1998*, paras 7–10.

[618] Dissenting opinion of Judge M Bedjaoui, *ICJ Rep 1998*, paras 60 f referring to the Court's judgments in the *Interhandel* and *Norwegian Loans* case and the ECtHR's judgment in the *Loizidou* case. For an assessment of the former cases see this section. For the problems to draw conclusions from the latter case on the Optional Clause see sub-s III B ii of ch 5 at 203.

[619] Dissenting opinion of Judge S Torres Bernárdez, *ICJ Rep 1998*, paras 140–42. cp also the presentation in M Falkowska, M Bedjaoui and T Leidgens, 'Article 44' para 11.

[620] For treaty law see ILC, 'Oral report by the Chairman of the Working Group on Reservations to Treaties, Mr Marcelo Vázquez Bermúdez' (2011) 10.

[621] ILC 'Report of the International Law Commission on the Work of Its 63rd Session' (n 12) 534, para 23.

approach provided for in that guideline, it can be said that it depends on the intention of the state which had made the reservation whether it can be separated from the Optional Clause declaration.[622]

The problem with this approach might be that it causes insecurity as the current 71 Optional Clause declarations contain no express statements concerning the importance of certain reservations. Ende already suggested that states could settle the issue by making appropriate remarks to their reservations,[623] but the states have not yet adopted that idea. Therefore, only Judge Lauterpacht's way to interpret the will of the submitting state remains.

This holds also for subjective reservations. As it became obvious in the previous sub-section most of the discussion concerning the separability of Optional Clause declarations and reservations focused on the Connally Reservation anyway. Yet, as referred to there, sometimes arguments have been used which relate to that reservation only and which seem to argue against separability. It has been emphasised that the states making such reservations do not accept any obligation at all and that therefore also the whole Optional Clause is necessarily without effect.[624] Against this it could, however, be said the declared will of a state in this case is as ambiguous as it is in other cases where a state makes a declaration with an impermissible reservation. As Rosenne wrote, the state makes a declaration which is a kind of 'mid-way'.[625] On the one hand the state expresses the intention to accede to the Optional Clause and on the other hand it expresses to be bound. As, however, the 'mid-way' does not exist, the question is whether the state would have preferred to go either the full way or not to go at all. This has to be solved through interpretation.[626]

If states are nonetheless reluctant to make an Optional Clause declaration because they do not want to be bound without their reservations in any way,[627] they can make sure that this does not happen by expressing so

---

[622] See also Dubisson (n 382) 189; Pinto (n 353) 54.

[623] Ende (n 161) 1182.

[624] cp Dubisson (n 382) 189; de Fumel (n 29) 24, 30; separate opinion of Judge H Lauterpacht, *ICJ Rep 1957*, 48; Maus (n 37) 155; Verzijl (n 83) 601.

[625] cp sub-s III B iii d of ch 5 at 219.

[626] cp Dubisson (n 382) 189; Gharbi (n 28) 455–57 and the corresponding position of the judges in the previous section. Even though it has already been established that the arguments relating to human rights treaties cannot be transferred to the Optional Clause, the ECtHR's *Loizidou* case might provide an argument which could also be used for Connally Reservations in Optional Clause declarations. In the *Loizidou* case the ECtHR took into consideration that Turkey must have been aware that the permissibility of its reservation was strongly doubted and that Turkey had kept it nonetheless and thereby risked to be bound without it (*Loizidou v Turkey* (n 260) paras 91–95; Frowein (n 38) 406). Having regard to the criticism the Connally Reservation received in state practice and in literature (see above 203), the ECtHR's reasoning could also apply for states which keep their Connally Reservations.

[627] For the importance of the reservations in eg the German Optional Clause declaration cp the reference in n 306 of this ch.

in their declaration. In any case, also in this regard there is no difference between the Optional Clause and other multilateral treaties.

V. THE STATES' OBJECTIONS TO RESERVATIONS (ARTICLE 20 VCLT)

The last sub-section of this chapter will show that objections to other states' reservations have no effect under the Optional Clause. However, there is no difference to treaty law in this regard.

With reference to the ILC's Guideline 2.6.1 GPRT it can be said:

> 'Objection' means a unilateral statement, however phrased or named, made by a State or an international organization in response to a reservation formulated by another State or international organization, whereby the former State or organization purports to preclude the reservation from having its intended effects or otherwise opposes the reservation.[628]

Maus wrote that there was a difference between Optional Clause declarations and multilateral treaties concerning objections. According to him Article 36(4) of the Statute established a procedure where the acceptance of the other states was neither required nor provided for. Furthermore, the control of the declarations was completely up to the Court and also therefore not to the states. When it was up to the Court to decide in the last resort there was no more space to let the states decide upon the issue.[629] In line with this Lamm wrote that reservations made to Optional Clause declarations did not require the consent of other states. States could freely decide upon the scope of their declarations. According to Lamm this was a special feature of the Optional Clause, as under treaty law the states' consent for a reservation was necessary.[630]

The state practice seems to support Maus's and Lamm's finding. Outside a proceeding before the Court so far only Sweden has ever made an objection to a reservation.[631] As referred to above, in 1956, Sweden contested the Portuguese reservation allowing the amendment of the declaration.[632] In the answer Portugal replied that it was the Court which had to decide.[633] Concerning that Portuguese Optional Clause declaration

---

[628] ILC 'Report of the International Law Commission on the Work of Its 63rd Session' (n 12) 11 f.

[629] Maus (n 37) 86, 88 f, 94. cp also O Elias and C Lim, 'Right of Passage Doctrine' 240; Greig (n 91) 210. Where Maus wrote that states could object anytime and even after they had declared a similar reservation (Maus, ibid 92 f), he referred to the invocation of the objective impermissibility of the reservation (for that see the following section).

[630] Lamm (n 10) 130 f.

[631] cp ibid 130; Maus (n 37) 87 fn 11. For the objections relating to a state's right to introduce a new reservation at all see sub-s II C i of ch 6 at 292.

[632] See Annex 1. See sub-ss III B v b and c of ch 5 at 236.

[633] See Annex 2.

it can furthermore be added that the Court applied it in the *Right of Passage* case even though it had just been made a few days before the application had been filed.[634] With regard to what has been said above,[635] it could be argued that, according to treaty law, the Portuguese declaration with the reservation would have had required an Indian acceptance or the lapse of twelve months to enter into force. In line with this Waldock pleaded for India that '[i]n principle, no reservation can be effective against any State without its agreement thereto and in principle the consent of other States must be obtained before they can be bound by a reservation'.[636]

The question is whether the situations under the Optional Clause can nonetheless be explained with treaty law.

A. Objections to Impermissible Reservations

As Sweden objected due to an alleged impermissibility of a reservation,[637] the first question will be to what extent states can object to reservations which are objectively impermissible according to Article 19(c) VCLT.

According to the convincing 'permissibility school' the objective impermissibility of Article 19 VCLT is independent of states' individual reactions.[638] Article 19 VCLT is of no use if its violation would have no consequences independently of the objections provided for Article 20 VCLT.[639] Furthermore, if States were able to accept a reservation which is impermissible according to Article 19 VCLT the integrity of the treaty would be harmed and the prior agreement disrespected.[640] In line with this the ILC held that the 'articles 20 and 21 [do not] answer the question of what effects are produced by a reservation that does not meet the conditions of permissibility set out in article 19'.[641] Guideline 4.5.2(1) GPRT provides therefore: 'The nullity of an invalid reservation does not depend on the objection or the acceptance by a contracting State or a contracting organization',[642] and Guideline 3.3.3 GPRT reads as follows: 'Acceptance

---

[634] cp sub-s II B of ch 1 at 26.

[635] cp sub-s III B ii of ch 3 at 99.

[636] *Case concerning the Right of Passage over Indian Territory (Portugal v India)* (n 68) (India) 49 (Waldock). See also Lamm (n 10) 130.

[637] cp sub-ss III B v b and c of ch 5 at 236.

[638] Aust (n 43) 129 f; Pellet (n 230) Art 19, paras 176, 179 f, 187; Redgwell (n 228) 257–62; Simma (n 239) 663; Walter (n 8) paras 106–08, 110; United Kingdom, 'Observations' 425 f, para 13. For the 'opposability school' see Ruda (n 43) 95.

[639] Bauer (n 242) 211–13; Kühner (n 10) 143; Pellet, ibid para 179; Redgwell ibid 260 f; Walter, ibid para 106.

[640] cp Bauer, ibid 214; Tomuschat (n 43) para 22.

[641] ILC 'Report of the International Law Commission on the Work of Its 62nd Session' (n 43) 111, 114 f.

[642] ILC, 'Oral report by the Chairman of the Working Group on Reservations to Treaties, Mr Marcelo Vázquez Bermúdez' (2011) 8; ILC 'Report of the International Law Commission on the Work of Its 63rd Session' (n 12) 26.

of an impermissible reservation by a contracting State or by a contracting organization shall not affect the impermissibility of the reservation'.[643]

Article 36 of the Statute contains no provision which could lead to a different result for the Optional Clause. Furthermore, there has been almost no state practice in this respect. As said above, up to now only one state has ever objected to a reservation outside a particular dispute before the Court.[644] In this respect there is no reason not to apply general treaty law: The permissibility of a reservation does not depend on other states' reactions.

Nonetheless, states can of course voice their opinions nonetheless as, also according to Guideline 4.5.2(2) GPRT, their objections might be helpful in establishing whether the reservation is permissible under Article 19 VCLT.[645]

B. Individual Objections According to Article 20(4) VCLT

This does, however, not answer the question whether states can object to reservations even though they are permissible.

i. Article 36(6) of the Statute and Individual Objections

Also Article 36(6) of the Statute provides no answer in this regard even though it might empower the Court to decide upon the question whether a reservation is effective.[646] Yet, as referred to in the introduction to this sub-section, some authors argued that the competence of the Court to decide necessarily ruled out the possibility that states object to reservations.[647] Against this it can, however, be said that Article 36(6) of the Statute does not contain the reasons why a reservation could be ineffective. This could be either its impermissibility under Article 19 VCLT or an objection according to Article 20 VCLT.[648] Regarding objections according

---

[643] ILC 'Report of the International Law Commission on the Work of Its 63rd Session' (n 12) 21. For the possibility of collective acceptance cp ILC 'Report of the International Law Commission on the Work of Its 62nd Session' (n 43) 61; ILC 'Reservations to Treaties, Comments and Observations Received from Governments' (29 March 2011) UN Doc A/CN.4/639/Add.1 38 f; ILC 'Reservations to Treaties, Comments and Observations Received from Governments' (15 February 2011) UN Doc A/CN.4/639 16–20, paras 68–86; ILC, 'Oral report by the Chairman of the Working Group on Reservations to Treaties, Mr Marcelo Vázquez Bermúdez' (2011) 7; C Walter, 'Article 20' para 16.

[644] See also Lamm (n 10) 130.

[645] ILC 'Report of the International Law Commission on the Work of Its 63rd Session' (n 12) 26. See also Walter (n 8) paras 110, 131 f.

[646] For that see sub-s V D of ch 5 at 271.

[647] See the references in n 629 of this ch.

[648] For this approach see the previous section ('permissibility school').

to Article 20 VCLT the Court still has to decide whether for example a state has objected in time.

This is also recognised under general treaty law as the ILC has recently emphasised.[649] The Guideline 3.2.4 GPRT provides:

> When a treaty establishes a treaty monitoring body, the competence of that body is without prejudice to the competence of the contracting States or contracting international organizations to assess the permissibility of reservations to that treaty, or to that of dispute settlement bodies competent to interpret or apply the treaty.[650]

ii. Article 20 VCLT Applied to the Optional Clause

The question remains what will be the result if Article 20 VCLT is applied to the Optional Clause.

It can already be ruled out that all states together have to accept a reservation. For this Article 20(2) VCLT provides:

> When it appears from the limited number of the negotiating States and the object and purpose of a treaty that the application of the treaty in its entirety between all the parties is an essential condition of the consent of each one to be bound by the treaty, a reservation requires acceptance by all the parties.[651]

In relation to this it can be said that the Optional Clause aims at universality,[652] and that it is no plurilateral treaty with a limited number of states. Even if the second requirement of Article 20(2) VCLT, the object and purpose of the treaty, is considered as being the decisive one,[653] it can be said that the Optional Clause allows the bilateralisation of the states' relations.[654] Its object and purpose does therefore not require the 'traditional unanimity system' and does not rule out the 'flexible system' of the VCLT.[655] Therefore, states do not have to accept a reservation altogether.

---

[649] ILC 'Report of the Commission to the General Assembly on the Work of Its 49th Session' (n 240) 57: 'The Commission stresses that th[e] competence of the monitoring bodies does not exclude or otherwise affect the traditional modalities of control by the contracting parties ... in accordance with the above-mentioned provisions of the Vienna Conventions of 1969 and 1986'.

[650] ILC 'Report of the International Law Commission on the Work of Its 63rd Session' (n 12) 20.

[651] See also the Guideline 4.1.2 GPRT in ibid 22.

[652] cp sub-ss III B iii a and vii of ch 5 at 213 and 252.

[653] cp ILC 'Documents of the Second Part of the 17th Session and of the 18th Session Including the Reports of the Commission to the General Assembly' (1966) UN Doc A/CN.4/SER.A/1966/Add.1 207, para 19; Kühner (n 10) 162 f; D Müller, 'Article 20' para 80; Ruda (n 43) 186; Walter (n 643) para 27. According to ILC 'Report of the International Law Commission on the Work of Its 62nd Session' (n 43) 122, the number of contracting states is just 'an auxiliary criterion'.

[654] See sub-s II C iv c of ch 5 at 195.

[655] For this object and purpose test see ILC 'Report of the International Law Commission on the Work of Its 62nd Session' (n 43) 122, 132 f; ILC 'Documents of the Second Part of the 17th Session and of the 18th Session Including the Reports of the Commission to the General Assembly' (n 653) 207, para 19; Müller (n 653) para 81; Walter (n 643) paras 28 f.

And the Court also does not have to accept the reservations. As Crawford maintained Article 20(3) VCLT does not apply to the Optional Clause. For him this paragraph does not work for a Court which has to apply principles of law.[656] Leaving this argument of Crawford aside, it can furthermore be doubted that the Optional Clause and the Optional Clause declarations can be considered as 'constituent instruments of an international organization'.[657] Of course, the Optional Clause relates to the competences of the Court as organ of the United Nations, but instruments which establish an international organisation contain obligations which are at least not fully reciprocal.[658] As established above,[659] the Optional Clause is different in this regard. Article 20(3) VCLT does therefore not apply to it.[660]

The reason why states do not object under the Optional Clause could, however, be Article 20(1) VCLT which provides: 'A reservation expressly authorized by a treaty does not require any subsequent acceptance by the other contracting States unless the treaty so provides'. Article 20(4) VCLT adds that states can only object to other states' reservations '[i]n cases not falling under the preceding paragraphs and unless the treaty otherwise provides'.

Also Guideline 4.1.1(1) GPRT provides: 'A reservation expressly authorized by a treaty does not require any subsequent acceptance by the other contracting States and contracting organizations, unless the treaty so provides'.[661] This includes the idea that if a treaty allows reservations expressly the other states have already consented to the reservation and there is no need to protect them.[662] This anticipated acceptance can furthermore not be revoked,[663] and therefore also objections to expressly

---

[656] Crawford (n 8) 79.

[657] For the notion of 'treaties constituting international organizations' cp Müller (n 653) para 85; K Schmalenbach, 'Article 5' para 5. cp also *Legality of the Use by a State of Nuclear Weapons in Armed Conflict* (Advisory Opinion) [1996] ICJ Rep 66, para 19: 'their object is to create new subjects of law endowed with a certain autonomy, to which the parties entrust the task of realizing common goals'.

[658] For the latter cp Müller, ibid para 85.

[659] s II of ch 1 at 22.

[660] It can be said that the Court is established by the Charter and the Statute (Thirlway (n 6) 595). For the separation of Optional Clause and Statute see sub-ss II A i and B i of ch 2 at 47 and 55.

[661] ILC 'Report of the International Law Commission on the Work of Its 63rd Session' (n 12) 22. See also Aust (n 43) 138; *The Effect of Reservations on the Entry Into Force of the American Convention on Human Rights (Arts 74 and 75)* (n 263) paras 35–37 and already Tomuschat (n 43) paras 5, 17.

[662] Villiger (n 222) Art 20, para 4: 'The other parties are considered as having *all* given their consent in advance to the reservation by postulating this in the treaty itself'. cp also Müller (n 653) paras 66, 72; Ruda (n 43) 179 f, 183.

[663] Walter (n 643) para 25 who supports this view with the ILC's guideline 2.8.13 which provides: 'Acceptance of a reservation cannot be withdrawn or amended' (ILC 'Report of the International Law Commission on the Work of Its 63rd Session' (n 12) 16).

allowed reservations are irrelevant.[664] The Guideline 2.6.2 GPRT provides no other result. It provides: 'A State or international organization may formulate an objection to a reservation irrespective of the permissibility of the reservation'.[665] This Guideline shall only ensure that a state is not bound towards a reserving state against its will. It only emphasises that even if a reservation is not prohibited by the treaty or not conflicting with its object and purpose a state may nonetheless object to it. As referred to in the previous sub-section, the impermissibility of a reservation shall be no requirement for objections.[666]

The question is what this means for the Optional Clause. As said above, Article 36(3) of the Statute cannot be interpreted as limiting the possibility to make reservations. The drafters considered the Optional Clause as containing the right to make reservations.[667] Article 20(1) VCLT does, however, not cover reservations which are only 'impliedly' authorised.[668] A general allowance of reservations is not an express allowance of every single reservation. According to the ILC a general allowance of reservations can generally only be considered as a reference to the Vienna regime for reservations.[669] This is, however, a fine line to walk. As the IACtHR held:

> A treaty may expressly authorize one or more specific reservations or reservations in general. If it does the latter, which is what the Court has concluded to be true of the Convention, the resultant reservations, having been thus expressly authorized, need not be treated differently from expressly authorized specific reservations.[670]

In the aforementioned pleading for India in the *Right of Passage* case, Waldock started by saying that under the Optional Clause only the reservations in Article 36(3) of the Statute were expressly allowed. He went on by saying that the practice added some more reservations but not the ones allowing states to amend Optional Clause declarations without period of notice.[671] This leads in the right direction. It is right that Article 36(3) of

---

[664] cp ILC 'Report of the International Law Commission on the Work of Its 62nd Session' (n 43) 76 f, para 9; Müller (n 653) para 73; United Kingdom, 'Observations' 425, para 9.

[665] ILC 'Report of the International Law Commission on the Work of Its 63rd Session' (n 12) 12.

[666] ILC 'Report of the International Law Commission on the Work of Its 62nd Session' (n 43) 76 f, para 9.

[667] See sub-s III A of ch 5 at 200.

[668] ILC 'Report of the International Law Commission on the Work of Its 62nd Session' (n 43) 117, para 3. cp also Müller (n 653) para 67; Ruda (n 43) 183 f; Tomuschat (n 43) paras 17–21.

[669] ILC 'Report of the International Law Commission on the Work of Its 62nd Session' (n 43) 118, para 5. See also Müller, ibid paras 67–72; Walter (n 8) para 70 with reference to *Delimitation of the Continental Shelf between the United Kingdom of Great Britain and Northern Ireland, and the French Republic (United Kingdom v France)* (1977) XVIII RIAA 3, 32 f, para 39.

[670] *The Effect of Reservations on the Entry Into Force of the American Convention on Human Rights (Arts 74 and 75)* (n 263) para 36.

[671] *Case concerning the Right of Passage over Indian Territory (Portugal v India)* (n 68) (India) 49 (Waldock).

the Statute allows only a few particular reservations expressly. According to Article 20(1) VCLT no state can object to those and also Article 36(3) of the Statute provides that these reservations are 'made' and not only 'formulated'.[672] As the later practice added some more reservations the states made no difference between the reservations provided for in Article 36(3) of the Statute and those which had been added later. Just as they did not object to the former reservations they did not object to the latter. It seems as if they made no difference concerning the effect of these reservations. As already said, under the Optional Clause, only one state has ever objected to a reservation due to its content outside a current proceeding. All there has been was a wide consent that basically all reservations under the Optional Clause were allowed and that other states could not react.[673] The fact that this is not represented in the wording of Article 36(2) of the Statute can be explained with the attitude of the drafters of the Statute in 1945. They felt no need to change the Statute as they considered it as being unnecessary to express this opinion which had already been established.[674] This can be considered as 'carelessness in drafting' or a product of 'woolly thinking'.[675] More lenient Maus wrote that during the drafting of the Statute the desire for continuance was higher than the necessity for a greater precision in the wording.[676]

It can therefore well be held that all reservations which are permissible are also reservations falling into the scope of Article 20(1) VCLT. Of course in the wording of Article 36 of the Statute they are not 'expressly authorized' but this can be explained with the said attitude of the drafters in 1945. But even if the Optional Clause is understood as containing only a normal 'unspecified' authorisation, the Optional Clause can at least be considered as providing otherwise in the sense of Article 20(4) VCLT.[677] In both cases the general principles for acceptance and objections, which are enshrined in Article 20(4) VCLT, do not apply.[678] In line with the constant practice under the Optional Clause the states can be understood as having accepted all permissible reservations already beforehand.[679] To say it with the words of the ILC: 'There is no surprise, and the principle of consent is not undermined'.[680]

---

[672] For the difference of the authorisation to 'make' and the authorisation to 'formulate' reservations in this regard see eg Müller (n 653) para 72.

[673] cp Walter (n 8) para 45. cp also Maus (n 37) 86–93; Lamm (n 10) 129, 130 f; Szafarz (n 10) 49.

[674] cp United Nations, *Conference on International Organization, Volume XIII—Commission IV, Judicial Organization* 559.

[675] Verzijl (n 83) 588 f: 'highly possible'.

[676] Maus (n 37) 21.

[677] For the residual character of Art 20 VCLT see also Ruda (n 43) 185.

[678] cp Villiger (n 222) Art 20, paras 3 f, 9; Ruda, ibid 185, 188; Walter (n 643) para 3.

[679] cp also Maus (Maus (n 37) 93 f).

[680] ILC 'Report of the International Law Commission on the Work of Its 62nd Session' (n 43) 120, para 10.

iii. Conclusion

This sub-section showed that also the missing objections under the Optional Clause do not provide a basis to argue that the Optional Clause is no treaty. The Optional Clause is like any other treaty which provides otherwise in the sense of Article 20(4) VCLT or whose reservations fall under Article 20(1) VCLT.[681]

Nonetheless, Waldock's aforementioned pleading in the *Right of Passage* case has a certain merit. As said above, the permissibility of reservations allowing withdrawal without period of notice has, to a certain degree, been established by the state practice following that judgment.[682] It could be argued that at the time Portugal made its declaration and the Court decided its case, the Portuguese reservation did not yet have the same standing as those reservations named in Article 36(3) of the Statute. Therefore, India should have had the possibility to object to the new reservation.[683] That the Court nevertheless relied on the Portuguese Optional Clause declaration can be explained with the fact that the Court considered the Portuguese reservation as already established like the other reservations under the Optional Clause.[684]

C. Result

This sub-section supports to the assumption that all reservations made to Optional Clause declarations are already accepted in the Optional Clause and that states cannot object to them. The only exceptions are impermissible subjective reservations like the Connally Reservation. However, also these do not require objections as they are already ineffective *per se*. This is not different from general treaty law as provided for in Articles 19 and 20 VCLT and the GPRT. Under these articles other treaties, too, can provide that the reservations are already accepted beforehand and that they do not require subsequent individual acceptance by other states.

This does not mean that states cannot enter into a dialogue upon the reservations. The dialogues which have occurred recently in human rights law could be an example for such behaviour.[685] Although under the Optional Clause the states' objections have no legal effect, states could,

---

[681] With regard to the result of chapter three, it is therefore also no problem that Optional Clause declarations enter into force immediately when the Secretary-General receives them and states have no time to object to the reservations (cp sub-s III B ii of ch 3 at 99 and F at 116).

[682] cp sub-s III B v b of ch 5 at 236.

[683] cp *Case concerning the Right of Passage over Indian Territory (Portugal v India)* (n 68) (India) 49 (Waldock). See also Elias and Lim (n 629) 240.

[684] cp sub-s III B vi b of ch 5 at 247.

[685] cp Simma (n 239) 667 f.

for example, nonetheless ask the reserving state to clarify the scope of its reservation or to reconsider it.[686]

D. Excursus: The Body Competent to Decide Upon the Permissibility of Reservations

As it is therefore not up to the states to decide upon the question whether a reservation is permissible, the question arises who else does.

It is at least imaginable that the behaviour of the Sectary-General as depository plays a role in this regard. According to Article 77(1)(d) VCLT a depositary is, however, only competent to examine 'whether the signature or any instrument, notification or communication relating to the treaty is in due and proper form and, if need be, [to bring] the matter to the attention of the State in question'. As also the Court has ruled in the Advisory Opinion on the Genocide Convention, the depositary shall only collect the reservations and the objections and notify the states.[687] Also during the drafting of the VCLT it was been made clear that it shall not be the depositary who decides upon the validity of declarations and reservations.[688] In line with this also the ILC's most recent Guideline 2.1.7(1) GPRT furnishes a depositary only with basically the same standard function as the VCLT already did.[689] For the Optional Clause there is no reason

---

[686] For the possibility to react by shaping the states' own Optional Clause declarations see below in the conclusion at 333.

[687] *Reservations to the Convention on the Prevention and Punishment of the Crime of Genocide* (n 228) 27. cp also F Ouguergouz, S Villalpando and J Morgan-Foster, 'Article 77' para 9.

[688] ILC 'Documents of the 14th Session Including the Report of the Commission to the General Assembly' (1962) UN Doc A/CN.4/SER.A/1962/Add.l 186, paras 4, 6, 7. cp also Ouguergouz, Villalpando and Morgan-Foster, ibid para 16.

[689] Walter (n 8) para 122. cp ILC 'Report of the International Law Commission on the Work of Its 63rd Session' (n 12) 6. The draft guidelines of 2010 still contained a guideline 2.1.8 which had slightly enhanced the position of depositaries and provided:

> Where, in the opinion of the depositary, a reservation is manifestly impermissible, the depositary shall draw the attention of the author of the reservation to what, in the depositary's view, constitutes such [impermissibility]. If the author of the reservation maintains the reservation, the depositary shall communicate the text of the reservation to the signatory States and international organizations and to the contracting States and international organizations and, where appropriate, the competent organ of the international organization concerned, indicating the nature of legal problems raised by the reservation' (ILC 'Report of the International Law Commission on the Work of Its 62nd Session' (n 43) 43).

This had not been considered as pure codification of already existing law but more as 'constructive innovation' (A Pellet and W Schabas, 'Article 23' para 78). It does not appear in the final GPRT anymore (cp ILC 'Report of the International Law Commission on the Work of Its 63rd Session' (n 12) 6 f) since the ILC received only negative feedback from states (ILC 'Reservations to Treaties, Comments and Observations Received from Governments' (29 March 2011) UN Doc A/CN.4/639/Add.1 18–20; ILC, 'Oral report by the Chairman of the Working Group on Reservations to Treaties, Mr Marcelo Vázquez Bermúdez' (2011) 4).

to see this differently. The Secretary-General has no competence to decide on this issue.[690]

This corresponds to the common opinion that it is the Court which decides upon the permissibility of the reservations.[691] Article 36(6) of the Statute clearly includes this answer. It provides: 'In the event of a dispute as to whether the Court has jurisdiction, the matter shall be settled by the decision of the Court'. Throughout the history of the Optional Clause, Article 36(4) of the Statute of the Permanent Court and Article 36(6) of the current Statute have been understood as granting the Court the possibility to decide upon the permissibility of reservations.[692]

Nonetheless, there seems to be a problem with that solution. According to Article 59 of the Statute, a decision of the Court only binds the parties of the case. Therefore, in later cases, other states could emphasise this limitation and demand a different decision. This could lead to contradictive results.[693] Maus solves this problem by simply stating that the decision of the Court 's'impose à toutes les parties du Statut'.[694] These other states, however, are not parties of the proceedings before the Court and cannot present their arguments there. Judge Lauterpacht suggested that other states which had made a reservation like the one contested might join the case under Article 63 of the Statute.[695] As long as this does not happen, Judge Lauterpacht considered the decisions on reservations as just not binding beyond the dispute in question.[696] Following this approach the Optional Clause would be in line with Guideline 3.2.5 GPRT which provides:

> When a dispute settlement body is competent to adopt decisions binding upon the parties to a dispute, and the assessment of the permissibility of a reservation is necessary for the discharge of such competence by that body, such assessment is, as an element of the decision, legally binding upon the parties.[697]

---

[690] See also Maus (n 37) 64; Wittmann (n 6) 147. The same holds true for the registrar of the Court (Maus, ibid 64; Hambro (n 177) 152).

[691] cp Bernhardt (n 4) 371; Farmanfarma (n 104) 28–31, 35 f, 97; de Fumel (n 29) 4; Gallus (n 307) 392; Gharbi (n 28) 462; Kolb (n 6) 497 f; Lamm (n 10) 123; Maus, ibid 17, 86, 94; Rosenne and Ronen (n 1) 741; Szafarz (n 10) 48. At the early days of the Optional Clause Lauterpacht doubted whether Art 36(6) of the Statute applies on the Optional Clause (Lauterpacht (n 20) 152 f).

[692] Maus, ibid 93; Rosenne and Ronen, ibid 741.

[693] cp the separate opinion of Judge H Lauterpacht, *ICJ Rep 1957*, 63 f.

[694] Maus (n 37) 88. See also the United Kingdom's position concerning the CCPR which even seems to favour the determination in judicial proceedings (United Kingdom, 'Observations' 425, para 12).

[695] Separate opinion of Judge H Lauterpacht, *ICJ Rep 1957*, 63 f; separate opinion of Judge H Lauterpacht, *ICJ Rep 1957*, 120.

[696] Separate opinion of Judge H Lauterpacht, *ICJ Rep 1957*, 64. cp also Verzijl (n 378) 398 f, fn 1.

[697] ILC 'Report of the International Law Commission on the Work of Its 63rd Session' (n 12) 20. For the commentary which also refers to the Court see ibid 403.

Be this as it may, there is no reason why there should be a difference between the Optional Clause and other treaties in this regard. It does not matter whether reservations are made to Optional Clause declarations or to accessions to a multilateral treaty with a compromissory clause, the Court decides.[698]

VI. RESULT

As Giegerich and Walter already remarked, the reservations made to Optional Clause declarations raise the same problems as those made to treaties.[699] The problem that the integrity of a multilateral treaty is endangered by reservations and that accessions may be an empty shell is a common problem of multilateral treaties.[700] Walter already found that it is possible to draw 'parallels' between the regime for reservations under the Optional Clause and the general regime for reservations under the VCLT.[701] The arguments in this chapter show that this is true.

It can even be said that there are not only parallels but that the regime for reservations under the Optional Clause is completely in harmony with the law of treaties. The reciprocal application of reservations made to Optional Clause declarations corresponds to Article 21(1) VCLT and the generosity of the Optional Clause regarding the permissibility of reservations can very well be explained with Article 19 VCLT. The missing possibility to object other states' reservations is in line with Article 20 VCLT. There is no phenomenon in this regard which cannot be explained by the application of the VCLT and the GPRT.

---

[698] cp also the separate opinion of Judge H Lauterpacht, *ICJ Rep 1957*, 63 f.

[699] Walter (n 8) para 45; Giegerich (n 8) para 4. cp also Crawford (n 8) 75, 76–83.

[700] cp eg H Neuhold, 'Law-Making' 44 f.

[701] cp Walter (n 8) para 46. Compare also Giegerich who wrote that restrictive statements made to optional clause declarations shall be subject to the same standard as reservations (Giegerich (n 8) para 4) and Kolb who wrote that a reservation to an Optional Clause declaration 'must be subject to the limits applicable under the law of treaties'(Kolb (n 6) 497).

6

Withdrawals and Agreements

T HE LAST CHAPTER will address two questions. The first will be whether states can unilaterally withdraw their Optional Clause declarations and the second will be to what extent they can shape the Optional Clause and Optional Clause declarations mutually.

Tomuschat wrote that Optional Clause declarations formed no multilateral treaty as they did 'not provide the same expectations of stability and reliability since [they] are not placed under the proposition *pacta sunt servanda* or *declaratio est servanda*'.[1] Also for Rosenne one of the main differences between the Optional Clause and treaties was that the Optional Clause declarations 'may be modified or terminated unilaterally'.[2] For Shihata the 'insistence on applying the rules relating to the termination of treaties ... is not always justified'. He maintained that the vague relationship before the seisin of the Court 'could hardly be called a treaty subject to the rules governing the termination of treaties'.[3] According to Szafarz, only the principle of *clausula rebus sic stantibus* and the law of treaties' period of notice from Article 56(2) VCLT (Vienna Convention on the Law of Treaties) were applicable.[4] Judge Oda criticised the majority's decision in the *Nicaragua* case because the majority of the judges had applied treaty law by analogy and also allowed reservations providing for withdrawals without a period of notice.[5] For Judge Oda a treaty allowing states to withdraw without period of notice was no treaty. In a system in which corresponding reservations were common it was more consistent not to apply treaty law at all.[6]

Oellers-Frahm on the other hand emphasised that Optional Clause declarations resulted in relations among the states, too. She questioned whether there really was a difference between the Optional Clause and a treaty concerning withdrawals.[7] Holloway went even further as he held

---

[1] C Tomuschat, 'Article 36 of the Statute' para 71.

[2] S Rosenne and Y Ronen, *Practice 1920–2005* 792. See also R Kolb, *ICJ* 455 f, 463.

[3] IFI Shihata, *Compétence de la Compétence* 167. For the importance of the moment of seisin for the relations under the Optional Clause see s I of ch 1 at 10.

[4] R Szafarz, *Compulsory Jurisdiction* 70–82.

[5] For the latter see sub-s III B vi b of ch 5 at 247.

[6] Separate opinion of Judge S Oda, *ICJ Rep 1984*, 510.

[7] K Oellers-Frahm, 'Der Rücktritt der USA' 566. cp also F Wittmann, *Obligatorium* 193 f, 195.

that the withdrawal of an Optional Clause declaration was governed by the same rules as a withdrawal from a treaty.[8] The following sub-sections will show that there is indeed no difference between the withdrawal from a treaty and the withdrawal from the Optional Clause.

I. PARTIAL WITHDRAWALS AND 'AMENDMENTS' OF OPTIONAL CLAUSE DECLARATIONS

Yet, as a preliminary issue, it is necessary to ask whether a right to withdraw an Optional Clause declaration includes the right to withdraw only partially or whether there is a difference of quality between an 'amendment' and a withdrawal of an Optional Clause declaration.

Some states seem to consider amendments and withdrawals of Optional Clause declarations as being something different. There are declarations distinguishing between the right to add reservations and the right to withdraw. As Portugal introduced the right to amend an Optional Clause declaration by excluding further disputes without a period of notice, it provided a different regime for withdrawals. For these the declaration provided an initial period of one year.[9] In the *Nicaragua* case the United States argued that the introduction of a new reservation by Israel in 1984 had not been based on the Israeli Optional Clause declaration as the declaration only allowed withdrawals.[10] Spain made a distinction in its 1990 declaration and allowed the introduction of new reservations without a period of notice but provided a period of notice of up to six month for withdrawals. Pastor Ridruejo commented on this distinction that the addition of a new reservation was the way to avoid a dispute before the Court in case other states submit a new declaration and Spain had to act within the period of its Anti Ambush Clause.[11] The longer period for withdrawals he explained with the principle of reasonableness and good faith.[12]

In the *Right of Passage* case, India attacked the reservations allowing states to amend their declarations. India argued that a withdrawal

---

[8] K Holloway, *Modern Trends* 671, fn 71. See also E Hambro, 'Compulsory Jurisdiction' 142 f.

[9] ICJ Yearbook 1955–1956, 185 f. cp also CHM Waldock, 'Decline' 275. Compare also the proposals of the Council of Europe to its member states (Council of Europe 'Recommendation of the Committee of Ministers to member states on the acceptance of the jurisdiction of the International Court of Justice' (2008) CM/Rec(2008)8).

[10] *Military and Paramilitary Activities in and against Nicaragua (Nicaragua v United States of America)* (Jurisdiction and Admissibility) Counter-Memorial (United States of America) para 372; *Military and Paramilitary Activities in and against Nicaragua (Nicaragua v United States of America)* (Jurisdiction and Admissibility) Oral Proceedings (CR 1984) (United States of America) 220 (McDougal). See also the separate opinion of Judge RY Jennings, *ICJ Rep 1984*, 552. cp ICJ Yearbook 1983–1984, 57, 70 f.

[11] For more on that possibility see sub-s III F of ch 3 at 116.

[12] JA Pastor Ridruejo, 'The Spanish Declaration' 32.

deprived the withdrawing state of all its possibilities to base its applications on the Optional Clause. The introduction of new reservations offered the opportunity to exclude only the disliked disputes and to maintain the right to file applications concerning other disputes. The reservations allowing states to add new reservations were therefore 'double-faced' as they allowed states to file applications and to evade jurisdiction in cases where the state did not want the Court to decide.[13] Similarly, Judge Chagla held in his later dissenting opinion that reservations allowing withdrawals and reservations allowing states to add new reservations were different. The latter allowed states to pick the disputes for which they end their commitment. Unlike in the case of a withdrawal they still had the opportunity to file applications in the rest of the disputes.[14]

However, the Court clearly referred to the Portuguese reservation as allowing 'partial denunciation' and held that there was no difference to reservations allowing withdrawal without period of notice as they had already appeared in previous declarations before. According to the Court both kinds of reservations led to a similar level of insecurity. The remaining possibility to file applications after an amendment was considered as no 'relevant differential factor'. It was met by the corresponding right of other states to file corresponding applications.[15] The Court thereby followed Portugal which had also considered the possibility to add a new reservation as a possibility to withdraw partially.[16] In the aftermath of this judgment Feydy even wrote that since this judgment it was clear that reservations allowing states to amend their declarations are redundant besides those allowing to withdraw.[17]

This view can be further supported by the decision of the Court in the *Nicaragua* case. In this case the United States argued that its declaration's provision for withdrawals did not apply to amendments. It also referred to the Court's judgment in the *Right of Passage* case where, according to its opinion, the Court had distinguished between amendment and withdrawal.[18] Furthermore, the United States emphasised that, in 1946, reservations allowing states to add reservations had been unknown in the state practice and that the Senate only considered the

[13] *Case concerning the Right of Passage over Indian Territory (Portugal v India)* (Preliminary Objections) Oral Proceedings (CR 1957) (India) 30 (Waldock). cp also the dissenting opinion of Judge MAC Chagla, *ICJ Rep 1957*, 166.

[14] Dissenting opinion of Judge MAC Chagla, ICJ Rep 1957, 167.

[15] *Case concerning the Right of Passage over Indian Territory (Portugal v India)* (Preliminary Objections) [1957] ICJ Rep 125, 144.

[16] *Case concerning the Right of Passage over Indian Territory (Portugal v India)* (Preliminary Objections) Observations and Submissions (Portugal) para 84.

[17] J Feydy, 'La déclaration française' 160.

[18] *Military and Paramilitary Activities in and against Nicaragua (Nicaragua v United States of America)* (Jurisdiction and Admissibility) Counter-Memorial (United States of America) paras 331–36. See also IR Cohn, 'Pre-Seisin Reciprocity' 715.

right to terminate and not the right to 'modify'.[19] The Court, however, made clear that it made no difference whether the United States' act was an amendment or a withdrawal. The rules provided for in the declaration applied to both.[20]

This equation convinces as new reservations and withdrawals have basically the same effect.[21] With both instruments states can likewise evade the jurisdiction of the Court.[22] After a withdrawal a state can furthermore submit a new declaration with a new reservation so that also in this regard the result is basically the same.[23] Such withdrawing and redrafting is common state practice.[24] Moreover, as said above, also for Anti Ambush Clauses it makes no difference whether a state adds a new reservation or whether it reintroduces a declaration with a new reservation. With regard to the object and purpose of the Anti Ambush Clause it does not apply to any of these cases.[25] Furthermore, Israel amended its 1984 declaration by introducing a new reservation even though the declaration only allowed withdrawals.[26]

It becomes clear that the difference between the introduction of new reservations and a complete withdrawal is only one of quantity and not of quality.[27] The introduction of a new reservation is, as the Court maintained, too, nothing else than a partial withdrawal. This means that everything that has to be provided for in a declaration is the right to fully or partially withdraw. If, for example, a state provides that its declaration cannot only be withdrawn but that it also 'reserves the right … either to add to, amend or withdraw any of the foregoing reservations, or any that may hereafter be added',[28] this must be considered as being declared

---

[19] *Military and Paramilitary Activities in and against Nicaragua (Nicaragua v United States of America)* (Jurisdiction and Admissibility) Counter-Memorial (United States of America) para 400, fn 2.

[20] *Military and Paramilitary Activities in and against Nicaragua (Nicaragua v United States of America)* (Jurisdiction and Admissibility) [1984] ICJ Rep 392, para 58. See also the separate opinion of Judge H Mosler, *ICJ Rep 1984*, 465.

[21] cp also S Oda, 'Reservations in the Declarations' 16 f; N Kebbon, 'Optional Clause' 262.

[22] K Oellers-Frahm, 'Obligatorische Gerichtsbarkeit' 250 f.

[23] See also SA Alexandrov, *Declarations* fn 266; Kolb (n 2) 463; B Maus, *Réserves* 185 f; HWA Thirlway, 'Reciprocity' 119. But see Aust (A Aust, 'Termination' paras 52 f) according to whom the withdrawal to make a new reservation seems impermissible.

[24] See the examples of Australia, the United Kingdom and India in Waldock (n 9) 267 f. Further examples can be found in Cohn (n 18) fn 105.

[25] cp sub-s III F of ch 3 at 116.

[26] ICJ Yearbook (n 10) 55, 70 f. See also the already mentioned position of the United States (*Military and Paramilitary Activities in and against Nicaragua (Nicaragua v United States of America)* (Jurisdiction and Admissibility) Counter-Memorial (United States of America) para 372).

[27] And even concerning the quantity there does not need to be a big difference. If for example a state introduces a reservation which excludes all disputes which arose after the year 1700, this would effectively be a complete withdrawal.

[28] cp the 2008 Optional Clause declaration of Germany.

ex abundanti cautela. The 'amendments' mentioned in these declarations seem to have no relevance. If the scope of a reservation is enlarged this can be considered as a partial withdrawal of the declaration, and if the scope of a reservation is reduced this can be considered as a partial withdrawal of the reservation.

All in all, it can hence be said that the law which applies to withdrawals also applies to partial withdrawals and vice versa. All arguments concerning the permissibility of one action also fit for the other and the same holds true for the permissibility of corresponding reservations. For Optional Clause declarations this means that everything states have to provide for in their Optional Clause declarations are reservations allowing states to withdraw because these cover all reductions of the commitment. Furthermore, the enlargement of the commitment is always possible and needs no reservation.[29]

The question remains whether states are nonetheless free to provide different rules for withdrawals and amendments in their declarations as Spain has done in its declaration of 1990. García argued that, according to the ruling of the Court in the *Nicaragua* case, in such cases the rules for withdrawals also apply to the introduction of new reservations.[30] This, however, can be questioned with the reasoning of the Court. The Court basically bound the United States to the wording of their Optional Clause declaration and the trust other states had been able to put in that wording.[31] If states, however, provide differently in their wording they do not violate other states' legitimate expectations. They act according to that wording even though it provides different rules for total and partial withdrawals. Having in mind the expectations of other states, it is therefore appropriate not to transfer the modalities from one provision to the other.

In general, however, especially with regard to state practice under the Optional Clause,[32] it can be said that reservations allowing states to withdraw Optional Clause declarations likewise allow them to 'amend' the declarations. This holds also true for a right to withdraw which is based on Article 56 VCLT or on another state's violation of the Optional Clause.[33]

---

[29] See s IV of ch 3 at 120.

[30] FJ Garcia, *Jurisdicción Obligataria* 310 f.

[31] cp *Military and Paramilitary Activities in and against Nicaragua (Nicaragua v United States of America)* (n 20) paras 59 f, 62.

[32] See the references in n 24 of this ch.

[33] For this and the exception for the principle of *clausula rebus sic stantibus* see sub-s II A i to iv of ch 6 at 281–89.

II. THE RIGHT TO UNILATERALLY WITHDRAW OPTIONAL CLAUSE DECLARATIONS

Regarding the right to unilaterally withdraw Optional Clause declarations, a distinction has to be made between withdrawals based on a reservation and situations in which a corresponding reservation does not exist.

Withdrawals based on a reservation raise no problems. As it has been established above, reservations allowing withdrawals with or without a period of notice are permissible,[34] and states are free to revoke their declaration according to their terms.[35] The often missing period of notice in this regard shows no difference between the Optional Clause and a multilateral treaty. As mentioned above, Oda did not want to apply treaty law to a system with reservations allowing states to withdraw without a period of notice.[36] However, under treaty law it is likewise possible to conclude a treaty which allows withdrawals without a period of notice.[37] And as under treaty law reservations can provide a right to withdraw, too,[38] reservations allowing states to withdraw Optional Clause declarations without a period of notice are nothing out of the ordinary.

Withdrawals which cannot be based on a corresponding reservation are more controversial. Oda wrote that there was no problem in this regard as nowadays all Optional Clause declarations could be withdrawn without a period of notice.[39] Conversely Briggs and Fachiri came to the conclusion that Optional Clause declarations remained in force indefinitely if they did not contain a reservation allowing states to withdraw.[40] Maus argued that declarations which had not been made for a certain period of time could only end according to the law of treaties. For him this meant that the declarations could be amended and withdrawn with the consent of all states which had made an Optional Clause declaration or according to the doctrine of *clausula rebus sic stantibus*.[41] However, according to Rotter the application of the rules for treaties on the Optional Clause declarations in this regard constituted a methodical dilemma with regard to the *sui generis*

---

[34] See sub-ss III B iii c and iv-vii of ch 5 at 216 to 252.

[35] Dissenting opinion of Judge M Bedjaoui, *ICJ Rep 1998*, para 42; F Gharbi, 'Le déclin' 471.

[36] See above the introduction of this chapter at 274.

[37] K Widdows, 'Unilateral Denunciation' 83 f. The ILC's Special Rapporteur Waldock even drafted Art 56(2) VCLT in light of state practice providing treaties which allow withdrawals with immediate effect (cp ILC 'Documents of the 15th Session Including the Report of the Commission to the General Assembly' (1963) UN Doc A/CN.4/SER.A/1963 68 f, para 19 (Waldock); ILC 'Documents of the Second Part of the 17th Session and of the 18th Session Including the Reports of the Commission to the General Assembly' (1966) UN Doc A/CN.4/SER.A/1966/Add.1 251, para 6 (Waldock)).

[38] See sub-s I A of ch 5 at 166.

[39] S Oda, 'From the Bench' 42 f, paras 36 f.

[40] HW Briggs, 'Reservations' 272 f; AP Fachiri, 'Repudiation' 55 f. See also Waldock (n 9) 265.

[41] Maus (n 23) 76. cp also RP Anand, *Compulsory Jurisdiction* 176–80.

character of the Optional Clause.[42] Kooijmans and Rosenne also objected to the applicability of treaty law.[43]

The following assessment of the relevant treaty law, state practice and jurisprudence will show that Optional Clause declarations have been and can be withdrawn according to treaty law.

One approach will already be rejected here without further assessment. It cannot be said that Optional Clause declarations become a part of the accession to the Charter and Statute and that it is therefore only possible to withdraw from all, Charter, Statute and Optional Clause together. Such an approach has been maintained by the Inter-American Court of Human Rights (IACtHR) for the optional clause of Article 62(1) ACHR (American Convention on Human Rights),[44] and has been considered for the optional protocol to the Vienna Convention on Consular Relations (VCCR).[45] This approach of the IACtHR is again based inter alia on the necessary efficiency of the substantial human rights provisions in ACHR and therefore has to be distinguished from the Optional Clause.[46] The same would also hold for the optional protocol to the VCCR. If the accessions to that protocol were bound to the accession to the VCCR it would likewise be a result based on the substantive content of the VCCR.[47] As again no such material content exists for the Optional Clause it cannot be treated like that protocol.[48] Furthermore, as it has already been addressed above,[49] optional clauses generally have to be considered as treaties separate from the major ones.[50] Concerning the withdrawal of accessions this can well be supported with the fact that the optional clause in Article 41(2)(3) CCPR (International Covenant on Civil and Political Rights) even contains a special provision for the withdrawal of optional clause declarations. In this regard it is clearly distinct from the covenant it is attached to.[51] In case of the Optional Clause it is not the clause itself which expressly provides the right to withdraw but the Optional Clause declarations which very commonly do so.[52]

---

[42] M Rotter, 'Art 36 Abs 2 des Statuts' 650, fn 35.

[43] PH Kooijmans, 'Compulsory Jurisdiction' 77; Rosenne and Ronen (n 2) 786 f.

[44] *Constitutional Court v Peru* (Competence) IACtHR Series C No 55 (1999) paras 48–50; *Ivcher Bronstein v Peru* (Competence) IACtHR Series C No 54 (1999) paras 32–54; Oellers-Frahm (n 7) 569–71. See also R Bernhardt, 'Vorbehalte' 375 f where this is treated in the section for treaties. For criticism on this approach see T Christakis, 'Article 56' fn 89.

[45] Oellers-Frahm, ibid 567, 572, 580 f. cp also T Giegerich, 'Article 56 VCLT' paras 44 f.

[46] Oellers-Frahm, ibid 572. cp also *Ivcher Bronstein v Peru* (Competence) (n 44)) paras 35–40.

[47] See Oellers-Frahm, ibid 573–75, 580 f and compare also the Court's reasoning in the *Fisheries Jurisdiction* case between the United Kingdom and Iceland (sub-s II A i of ch 6 below at 281).

[48] See also Oellers-Frahm, ibid 581.

[49] See above sub-s II A i b 1 of ch 2 at 49.

[50] For optional protocols see also Giegerich (n 45) para 45.

[51] cp E Schwelb, 'Measures of Implementation' 848–50. cp also Giegerich, ibid para 45.

[52] For the fact that in general treaty law, too, reservations can contain corresponding provisions see sub-s I A of ch 5 at 166.

A. The Application of Treaty Law to the Optional Clause

In treaty law the principle of *pacta sunt servanda* generally prevails. It is also provided for in Article 26 VCLT which says: 'Every treaty in force is binding upon the parties to it and must be performed by them in good faith'. States can only terminate valid treaties in the case of an exception. Article 42(2)(1) VCLT clearly provides: 'The termination of a treaty, its denunciation or the withdrawal of a party, may take place only as a result of the application of the provisions of the treaty or of the present Convention'.

i. Unilateral Withdrawal with a Period of Notice (Article 56 VCLT)

In line with this Article 56 VCLT establishes the presumption that a party cannot withdraw from a treaty if the treaty contains no corresponding provision.[53] According to Article 56(1)(a) and (b) VCLT the presumption can be rebutted with the intention of the parties or the nature of the treaty. The nature of the treaty can, however, be considered foremost as a means to establish the first requirement, the intention of the parties.[54] It is therefore the latter which is essential here.[55] If from that intention it is inferred that a right to withdraw exists, a withdrawal can be made with a twelve months period of notice (Article 56 (2) VCLT).

It is an open debate whether Article 56 VCLT is fully based on solid customary law.[56] In 1972, in the *Fisheries Jurisdiction* cases of the United Kingdom and Germany against Iceland, for example, the customary basis of Article 56(1)(b) VCLT has been a highly controversial issue.[57] However, in the United Nations Conference on the Law of Treaties the whole article had been adopted with 95 votes to none with six abstentions.[58]

---

[53] Christakis (n 44) para 17. For a stricter approach prior to the VCLT see Fachiri (n 40) 55.

[54] Widdows (n 37) 92 f. cp also ILC 'Documents of the Second Part of the 17th Session and of the 18th Session Including the Reports of the Commission to the General Assembly' (n 37) 250 f; *Fisheries Jurisdiction (Federal Republic of Germany v Iceland)* (Jurisdiction) Memorial (Germany) paras 52–58.

[55] cp ILC 'Documents of the Second Part of the 17th Session and of the 18th Session Including the Reports of the Commission to the General Assembly' (n 37) 250 f and earlier ILC 'Summary Records of the 15th Session' (6 May–12 July 1963) UN Doc A/CN.4/SER.A/1963 103, 105 (Rosenne, Ado). See also Widdows, ibid 111.

[56] cp Christakis (n 44) paras 13–16. See also the dispute concerning Senegal's withdrawal from the Geneva Conventions on the Law of the Sea (cp Widdows, ibid 105 f).

[57] The United Kingdom treated Art 56(1) VCLT as having a complete customary law background (cp *Fisheries Jurisdiction (United Kingdom of Great Britain and Northern Ireland v Iceland)* (Jurisdiction) Oral Proceedings (CR 1973) (United Kingdom) 256–58 (Rawlinson)) while Germany on the other hand strongly opposed this for Art 56(1)(b) VCLT (*Fisheries Jurisdiction (Federal Republic of Germany v Iceland)* (n 54) (Germany) paras 52–58). See also M Fitzmaurice, 'Treaties' para 71; Widdows, ibid 99.

[58] United Nations 'Official Records of the United Nations Conference on the Law of Treaties, Second Session, 9 April–22 May 1969' (1970) A/CONF.39/ll/Add.l 110. cp also Widdows, ibid 93.

In one of his first drafts for the VCLT, Waldock, as Special Rapporteur, suggested providing an implied right to withdraw from certain treaties. Among those were 'treat[ies] of arbitration, conciliation or judicial settlement'.[59] To establish this position he expressly referred to the state practice under the Optional Clause. Even though he regretted it, he came to the result that such treaties and such declarations 'are regarded as essentially of a terminable character'.[60] The whole issue roused heavy argumentation and other members of the ILC (International Law Commission) argued that such a right to withdraw would heavily impair the value of any treaty in question. Three of the members specifically addressed the treaties of arbitration, conciliation or judicial settlement.[61] Verdross furthermore particularly doubted whether state practice under the Optional Clause argued for an implied right to withdraw.[62] Rosenne on the other hand supported the inclusion of treaties of arbitration, conciliation or judicial settlement in the group of treaties with an implied right to terminate. Furthermore, he argued that Optional Clause declarations should not be covered by this provision as they 'were not of quite the same character as arbitration treaties'.[63] However, he was the only one who referred to a difference in this regard.[64]

Especially Ago then suggested dropping the categories as it would be difficult to achieve unanimity for every group.[65] At the end what basically became the current Article 56 VCLT was a compromise between the different views. The ILC maintained Waldock's focus on the intent of parties, but dropped the particular classes of treaties for which the former draft contained a certain presumption for the intent.[66] This solution has been acknowledged for its briefness and clarity.[67] The discussions contain no reference that the change had been made because the treaties of judicial settlement or the Optional Clause should be excluded from the scope of the article. On the other hand the argumentations of Rosenne and Verdross have not been rebutted either.[68] Also the latest commentary of the VCLT contained no reference to that point.[69]

---

[59] ILC 'Documents of the 15th Session Including the Report of the Commission to the General Assembly' (n 37) 64 (Waldock).

[60] ibid 68 (Waldock).

[61] ILC 'Summary Records of the 15th Session' (n 55) 101 f (Amado, Verdross, Bartoš). See also the criticism of Christakis (n 44) paras 62 f. See further ILC 'Summary Records of the 15th Session', ibid 105, 106 (Tunkin, Jiménez de Aréchaga).

[62] ibid 101 f (Verdross).

[63] ibid 103 (Rosenne).

[64] cp ibid 99–107, 239–41.

[65] ibid 104 (Ago). See also ibid 106 (Jiménez de Aréchaga).

[66] ibid 239. See also Widdows (n 37) 88 f.

[67] ILC 'Summary Records of the 15th Session' (n 55) 240 (Lachs).

[68] cp ibid 99–107, 239–41.

[69] ILC 'Documents of the Second Part of the 17th Session and of the 18th Session Including the Reports of the Commission to the General Assembly' (n 37) 250 f.

What became obvious, however, is that the practice under the Optional Clause is the main foundation for treaty law in this area of law. Discussing state practice regarding this aspect of treaty law Widdows wrote that 'the only major incidents involving serious claims of a right unilaterally to denounce a treaty at will are certain cases of unilateral alterations in acceptance of the Optional Clause of the ICJ and PCIJ'.[70] So if the nature of treaties providing the settlement of disputes argues for the right to withdraw, this must also apply for the Optional Clause.

Whether treaties providing the jurisdiction of the Court are generally subject to Article 56(1)(b) VCLT is, however, still an open question.[71] For example, in the aforementioned *Fisheries Jurisdiction* case between the United Kingdom and Iceland, the United Kingdom strongly argued against the assumption that treaties establishing the jurisdiction of the Court 'are to be regarded as intrinsically short-lived and ephemeral'. It emphasised the functions of the Court which would be otherwise undermined.[72] Iceland, on the other hand, emphasised that 'an undertaking for judicial settlement cannot be considered to be of a permanent nature' and unilaterally terminated the corresponding agreement.[73] The Court considered the 'object of the [compromissory] clause when read in the context of the Exchange of Notes' and came to the conclusion that in the absence of any provision the obligation is not of a permanent nature.[74] The Court remarked that instruments which provided general jurisdiction could be subject to an implied right to withdraw. According to the Court this was different for provisions which provided jurisdiction only for 'a concrete kind of dispute which was foreseen and specifically anticipated by the parties'. The Court named the Optional Clause with the instruments providing general jurisdiction but also emphasised that the question of whether such instruments were generally subject to withdrawals was not crucial for the current case. The Court made clear that it did 'not need to examine or pronounce upon the point of principle involved'.[75] All in all,

---

[70] Widdows (n 37) 94 f (footnote omitted). cp also the examples used in Christakis, 'Article 56 (2006)' paras 87–93.

[71] cp Christakis, ibid paras 62 f; Widdows, ibid 98.

[72] *Fisheries Jurisdiction (United Kingdom of Great Britain and Northern Ireland v Iceland)* (n 57) (United Kingdom) 254 (Rawlinson). See also Widdows, ibid 98.

[73] *Fisheries Jurisdiction (United Kingdom of Great Britain and Northern Ireland v Iceland)* Correspondence (Iceland) 374–76. See also Widdows, ibid 97.

[74] *Fisheries Jurisdiction (United Kingdom of Great Britain and Northern Ireland v Iceland)* (Jurisdiction) [1973] ICJ Rep 3, paras 26–29.

[75] ibid para 29. cp also Oellers-Frahm (n 7) 574 f; *Military and Paramilitary Activities in and against Nicaragua (Nicaragua v United States of America)* (Jurisdiction and Admissibility) Counter-Memorial (United States of America) para 410. For the United States' withdrawal from the optional protocol to the VCCR in 2005 see Christakis (n 44) fn 87; Oellers-Frahm, ibid 579–81.

it therefore depends on the Optional Clause itself whether states can withdraw according to Article 56 VCLT.

It similarly depends on the Optional Clause to what extent a right to withdraw based on Article 56 VCLT could be used for partial withdrawals. Article 44(1) VCLT provides:

> A right of a party, provided for in a treaty or arising under article 56, to denounce, withdraw from or suspend the operation of the treaty may be exercised only with respect to the whole treaty unless the treaty otherwise provides or the parties otherwise agree.

The provision is based on Waldock's position that 'the parties to a treaty cannot be supposed to have intended to authorize such partial denunciation or suspension of its provisions unless they have done so expressly in the treaty'.[76] However, it is the treaty's integrity which shall be protected by Article 44 VCLT.[77]

The drafters of the Optional Clause have not considered withdrawals and accordingly they have not expressly authorised partial withdrawals either.[78] However, the drafters provided the choice between different groups of disputes which later became the possibility to shape Optional Clause declarations with all kinds of reservations.[79] With regard to this wide possibility to make reservations and the fact that under the Optional Clause it makes no difference whether a state withdraws partially or whether it withdraws fully and makes a new declaration with a new reservation, the integrity of the Optional Clause declaration and the declarations cannot be harmed by partial withdrawals. Having regard to the object and purpose of Article 44 VCLT, it therefore makes sense to say that, if the Optional Clause allows withdrawals according to Article 56 VCLT, this would also hold true for partial withdrawals.

Concerning the period of notice it can be said that in the first draft of Article 56 VCLT the period of notice had been formulated in vague terms and the drafters only referred to a 'reasonable period' which would have had to be determined in each case with regard to its circumstances and the character of the treaty in question.[80] Waldock preferred a standard period of notice of twelve months and included it in his draft. He considered it to be the usual period in this regard and

---

[76] ILC 'Documents of the 15th Session Including the Report of the Commission to the General Assembly' (n 37) 93, para 11 (Waldock).

[77] cp K Odendahl, 'Article 44' paras 1 f, 10; M Falkowska, M Bedjaoui and T Leidgens, 'Article 44' paras 2, 15. Furthermore, Art 44 VCLT is not considered customary law (Odendahl, ibid para 9).

[78] For more on the drafters' position see sub-s II B of ch 6 at 290.

[79] cp sub-s II B i of ch 5 at 175.

[80] ILC 'Documents of the 9th Session Including the Report of the Commission to the General Assembly' (1957) UN Doc A/CN.4/SER.A/1957/Add.l 22 (Fitzmaurice). See also Widdows (n 37) 85.

wanted to clarify the law by not using a 'reasonable' period of notice.[81] He considered twelve months as sufficient to make arrangements dealing with the new situation.[82] However, at least according to Giegerich this period is only a presumption which can be rebutted with the means of Article 56(1) VCLT.[83] Furthermore, not even today can the twelve month period be regarded as being customary law.[84] Even though the Court referred to Article 56(2) VCLT in the advisory opinion concerning the *Agreement between the WHO and Egypt*, it did not clarify whether it wanted to apply a twelve month period. Basically, the Court again referred to a 'reasonable period of notice'.[85]

ii. Clausula Rebus Sic Stantibus *(Article 62 VCLT)*

Another source for the right to withdraw could be the principle of *clausula rebus sic stantibus*. It is based on the idea that the equilibrium established by a treaty can be deranged by a change of circumstances and that therefore the treaty has to be adjusted. It can even be applied if a treaty is made for a longer duration which has not yet lapsed or if it contains a provision for withdrawals whose requirements are not met.[86]

Article 62(1) VCLT provides:

> A fundamental change of circumstances which has occurred with regard to those existing at the time of the conclusion of a treaty, and which was not foreseen by the parties, may not be invoked as a ground for terminating or withdrawing from the treaty unless ... the existence of those circumstances constituted an essential basis of the consent of the parties to be bound by the treaty; and ... the effect of the change is radically to transform the extent of obligations still to be performed under the treaty.

These words contain five conditions which all have to be met cumulatively.[87] The 'essential basis for the consent of the parties' and the fact that the change had not been foreseen have to be established objectively, taking into consideration the positions of all parties concerned.[88] For the former

---

[81] ILC 'Documents of the 15th Session Including the Report of the Commission to the General Assembly' (n 37) 68 f, para 19 (Waldock). See also the later commentary on the draft articles (ILC 'Documents of the Second Part of the 17th Session and of the 18th Session Including the Reports of the Commission to the General Assembly' (n 37) 251, para 6).

[82] ILC 'Documents of the 15th Session Including the Report of the Commission to the General Assembly' (n 37) 241 (Waldock).

[83] Giegerich (n 45) para 51.

[84] cp Christakis (n 44) para 16; Giegerich, ibid para 53.

[85] *Interpretation of the Agreement of 25 March 1951 between the WHO and Egypt* (Advisory Opinion) [1980] ICJ Rep 73, paras 47–49.

[86] A Aust, *Treaty Law* 262; MN Shaw and C Fournet, 'Article 62' para 16. But see also T Giegerich, 'Article 62 VCLT' paras 7, 28.

[87] Giegerich, ibid para 31.

[88] ibid paras 32 f, 36, 53, 59 f.

requirement this means that the existence of the circumstance must have been decisive for all the parties to accede to the treaty.[89] Furthermore, the Court has established a high threshold for a 'fundamental change of circumstances' and demands that the obligations became 'something essentially different from that originally undertaken'. It therefore denied a corresponding pleading of Iceland in the aforementioned *Fisheries Jurisdiction* case concerning a compromissory clause.[90] The principle of *clausula rebus sic stantibus* has been criticised as, due to its vagueness, it leads to uncertainty.[91] Article 62 VCLT is nonetheless customary law, at least if it is applied restrictively.[92]

The question is, however, what circumstances could change so that a state can withdraw from a treaty providing jurisdiction. It is hard to see what changes of circumstances can justify not settling a dispute with recourse to law if there has been consent in this regard before.[93] García held that such changes are generally possible but also made clear that upcoming procedures before the Court are no such a change in any case.[94] According to Verzijl, the outbreak of war is, at least for third states, no fundamental change in this regard either.[95] The question, however, remains whether an *excès de pouvoir* by the Court could constitute a reason to withdraw.[96] As said above, only the states are parties of the Optional Clause,[97] the Court is therefore more like an external element and part of the circumstances. Be this as it may, in general nothing argues against the application of Article 62 VCLT to the Optional Clause. It is a matter of interpretation whether certain existing circumstances were essential for the states to make their Optional Clause declarations.[98]

Concerning the consequences of a fundamental change of circumstances Article 62(1) VCLT clearly refers to the possibility to invoke the change as a reason to withdraw.[99] Also Article 62(3) VCLT refers to that

---

[89] ibid para 60.

[90] *Fisheries Jurisdiction (United Kingdom of Great Britain and Northern Ireland v Iceland)* (n 74) para 43. cp also M Fitzmaurice, 'Law of Treaties' 194; Oellers-Frahm (n 7) 577.

[91] See eg the short remark of JG Merrills, 'Clause Revisited' 209.

[92] cp *Gabčíkovo-Nagymaros Project (Hungary/Slovakia)* (Judgment) [1997] ICJ Rep 7, para 46; Giegerich (n 86) paras 103 f; W Heintschel von Heinegg, 'Change of Circumstances' paras 25, 52; Oellers-Frahm (n 7) 577; Shaw and Fournet (n 86) para 15.

[93] cp JHW Verzijl, 'Optional Clause' 606 f. See further the reasoning of H Lauterpacht, 'Différends non justiciables' 591.

[94] Garcia (n 30) 303–05.

[95] Verzijl (n 93) 607. Furthermore, he seems to treat the principle more as granting an objection in ongoing proceedings than as a right to amend or withdraw a declaration (ibid 607 f). For the relation of Art 62 VCLT and the outbreak of hostilities in general see Giegerich (n 86) para 37.

[96] cp FO Vicuña, 'Legal Nature' 476 f.

[97] See s II of ch 1 at 22 and cp ch 2 at 39.

[98] For a withdrawal from the Optional Clause in case of an amendment of the Statute see W Karl, 'Article 69' para 40.

[99] But see also the 'procedural safeguards' in sub-s II A iv of ch 6 at 289.

possibility and adds that a state can also suspend the operation of the treaty in question.[100] According to Article 44(3) VCLT, the withdrawal has, however, to be limited to the parts of the Optional Clause declarations effected by the fundamental change of circumstances.[101]

iii. A Withdrawal as a Consequence of a Violation of the Treaty (Article 60 VCLT)

Article 60 VCLT provides the possibility to withdraw when another state breaches its duties under the treaty. Article 60(2) VCLT treats the breach of a multilateral treaty. The principle behind Article 60 VCLT is customary law but it is still an open question whether the details of the article can be considered the same.[102] According to Szafarz the application of this provision to the Optional Clause is more controversial than the application of *clausula rebus sic stantibus*.[103]

Article 60 VCLT allows states to react to material violations of the treaty by other states. According to Article 60(3) VCLT a material breach is either 'a repudiation of the treaty not sanctioned by the present Convention [or] the violation of a provision essential to the accomplishment of the object or purpose of the treaty'. A 'repudiation of the treaty' is fulfilled when a state tries to free itself from the obligations of the treaty without justification.[104] The second alternative of the paragraph additionally covers an insignificant violation of a provision as long as that provision is essential.[105] Under the Optional Clause this could be the case if a state does not accept a proceeding before the Court which is based on the Optional Clause by the applicant.

---

[100] cp Shaw and Fournet (n 86) paras 42 f. According to Giegerich the suspension is mandatory when the change of circumstances is not permanent (Giegerich (n 86) para 95).

[101] For the fulfilments of the requirements of Art 44(3) VCLT compare the arguments presented above at sub-s II C iv c of ch 5 at 195, sub-s II A i of ch 6 at 281 and sub-s III B i of ch 6 at 316. For the procedural safeguards provided by the VCLT see the following sub-s II A iv of ch 6 at 289.

[102] cp T Giegerich, 'Article 60 VCLT' paras 87 f; B Simma and CJ Tams, 'Article 60' paras 8–10. cp also *Legal Consequences for States of the Continued Presence of South Africa in Namibia (South West Africa) notwithstanding Security Council Resolution 276 (1970)* (Advisory Opinion) [1971] ICJ Rep 16, para 95: 'The rules laid down by the Vienna Convention on the Law of Treaties concerning termination of a treaty relationship on account of breach (adopted without a dissenting vote) may in many respects be considered as a codification of existing customary law on the subject'. See also Aust (n 86) 258; *Gabčíkovo-Nagymaros Project (Hungary/Slovakia)* (n 92) para 46.

[103] Szafarz (n 4) 78. See also the position of Wittmann (n 7) 200.

[104] Simma and Tams (n 102) paras 16 f. cp also ILC 'Documents of the Second Part of the 17th Session and of the 18th Session Including the Reports of the Commission to the General Assembly' (n 37) 255, para 9 and furthermore *Legal Consequences for States of the Continued Presence of South Africa in Namibia (South West Africa) notwithstanding Security Council Resolution 276 (1970)* (n 102) para 95: 'disavowed the Mandate'.

[105] Simma and Tams, ibid paras 18 f. But see also the position in Giegerich (n 102) para 32 which is less focused on the wording of the article.

The next question is which states would be entitled to invoke the violation in order to amend or withdraw their declaration. According to Article 60(2)(a) VCLT all other states may take a collective action either regarding the treaty in total or vis-à-vis the violating state. For such an action a unanimous agreement between all the states is necessary.[106] According to Article 60(2)(b) and (c) VCLT individual states can only suspend the treaty vis-à-vis the violating state if they are particularly affected by the breach or if the breach 'radically changes the position of every party with respect to the further performance of its obligations under the treaty'. The possibility for a bilateral action is therefore more limited. For Article 60(2)(b) VCLT the state has to have a special interest in the fulfilment of the obligation which goes beyond those of the other states. This is of particular importance where a multilateral treaty establishes bilateral obligations between the states.[107] The suspension entails the results provided for in Article 72 VCLT.[108] According to Article 44(2) VCLT the state whose rights have been violated can choose whether to withdraw fully or partially.[109]

It argues for an application of Article 60 VCLT to the Optional Clause that the provision for the breach of a treaty is to a large degree based on the principle of reciprocity.[110] According to Article 60(5) VCLT it cannot be applied to human rights treaties because the individuals in one state shall not be affected by human rights violations in a third state.[111] As said above the Optional Clause provides obligations between the states vis-à-vis each other.[112] When one state violates its obligations it has in fact not accepted 'the same obligation'. Furthermore, withdrawals *inter partes* are not contrary to the Optional Clause.[113] In this respect there is no problem with applying Article 60 VCLT when one state does not fulfil its obligations under the Optional Clause.[114] For example, in the aftermath of the *Nicaragua* case this could have resulted in the right of Nicaragua to withdraw its declarations vis-à-vis the United States of America if the latter had not withdrawn its declaration itself.

---

[106] Art 60(2)(a) VCLT. See also Giegerich, ibid para 53; Simma and Tams, ibid para 28.

[107] CJ Tams, 'Article 60' paras 35 f.

[108] See I Cameron, 'Suspension' paras 1–5.

[109] cp Giegerich (n 102) para 50; Odendahl (n 77) para 13; Falkowska, Bedjaoui and Leidgens (n 77) para 36. For the procedural safeguards see Giegerich, ibid paras 35–39; Simma and Tams (n 102) paras 67 f and the following section.

[110] For the latter see Fitzmaurice (n 90) 191; B Simma, 'Reciprocity' para 15. cp also B Simma, 'Community Interest' 350–52.

[111] cp Giegerich (n 102) paras 81, 83.

[112] See s II of ch 1 at 22.

[113] See sub-s II C iv c of ch 5 at 195.

[114] cp also Verzijl (Verzijl (n 93) 607) even though it seems like he does not see this means as a right which can be invoked before the seisin of the court but more as an objection after proceedings have been instituted (see also n 95 of this ch).

iv. The Procedural Provisions of Article 65 to 68 VCLT

The drafters of the VCLT predicted that states might arbitrarily invoke grounds which allow them to withdraw from a treaty. They further predicted that states would disagree on the validity of such actions and therefore they provided procedural safeguards in Articles 65 to 68 VCLT for almost all disputes which might arise regarding Articles 46 to 64 VCLT.[115]

According to Article 65(1) VCLT states have to notify other states of their claim when they invoke a ground for withdrawing from a treaty. Article 65(2) VCLT provides that a state shall then wait for three months before it proceeds as notified. According to Article 65(2) and (3) VCLT other states can object to withdrawals.[116] This procedure is especially important for the invocation of the principle *clausula rebus sic stantibus* according to Article 62 VCLT. According to Giegerich the aim of this procedure is a consensual adjustment of the treaty. The withdrawal shall just be the *ultima ratio*.[117]

Concerning these procedural provisions it is, however, an open question whether or to what extent they can be considered customary law.[118] At least to a certain degree they have been an innovation by the drafters of the VCLT.[119] In any way they are residual rules and treaties can provide otherwise.[120]

v. Result

If the law of treaties is applied, Optional Clause declarations can be withdrawn according to their terms, according to the principle of *clausula rebus sic stantibus* and as consequence of a violation of the Optional Clause by another state. Yet, as also treaty law is not unequivocal in this regard, the question whether the Optional Clause is subject to withdrawals according to Article 56 VCLT requires a deeper consideration of the Optional Clause itself.

---

[115] M Prost, 'Article 65' para 1; H Krieger, 'Article 65' paras 1, 24–26. For the exception of Art 62(2)(a) VCLT see Simma and Tams (n 102) para 68.

[116] According to Hofmann the omission of an objection can have a law creating force (B Hofmann, *Beendigung* 224 f).

[117] Giegerich (n 86) paras 6, 97–100. For the application on Art 60 VCLT see Giegerich (n 102) paras 35–39.

[118] cp Fitzmaurice (n 57) para 12; Krieger (n 115) paras 8 f; Oellers-Frahm (n 7) 578; Prost (n 115) paras 11–15. In relation to Art 62 VCLT cp Giegerich (Giegerich (n 86) para 105) who points at the different jurisprudence in *Gabčíkovo-Nagymaros Project (Hungary/Slovakia)* (n 92) 109 and *A Racke GmbH & Co v Hauptzollamt Mainz* (Case C-162/96) [1998] ECR I-3688 paras 58 f.

[119] cp ILC 'Summary Records of the 15th Session' (n 55) 280, para 54 (Waldock); Krieger, ibid paras 7, 11; Prost, ibid paras 5–7.

[120] Krieger, ibid para 25.

B. Article 36 of the Statute and the Drafters' Attitude in 1920

As the General Secretary of the League of Nations remarked as he faced the first withdrawals, there is no explicit provision in the Statute dealing with withdrawals of Optional Clause declarations.[121]

However, the question is whether nonetheless something can be inferred from the Statute. As said above,[122] in contrast to the ad hoc jurisdiction Article 36(2) of the Statute shall provide compulsory jurisdiction. The right to withdraw without a period of notice moves the Optional Clause much closer to the ad hoc jurisdiction for which Article 36(1) of the Statute already provides. This argues for the assumption that at least the Optional Clause itself allows no withdrawals without a period of notice.

Article 36(3) of the Statute deals with the period of validity of Optional Clause declarations, at least implicitly. That paragraph provides that Optional Clause declarations can be made 'for a certain time'. As mentioned above, Article 36(3) has lost some of its meaning,[123] but it could nonetheless be useful to establish whether the drafters of the Optional Clause 'intended to admit the possibility of denunciation or withdrawal' (Article 56(1)(a) VCLT). Waldock inferred from Article 36(3) of the Statute that an Optional Clause declaration is made for an indefinite period of time if it does not provide that it is made for a certain period of time only.[124] This position has merits to a certain degree. The 'condition of reciprocity' which is also named in that paragraph is certainly a possible reduction of the commitment for the declaring state. From a systematic point of view the same seems to hold for the second possibility provided for in that paragraph. Now if Optional Clause declarations were open to withdrawals without period of notice anyway, states which make their Optional Clause declaration for any 'certain time' would necessarily deepen their commitment.[125] This seems not to fit the conception of Article 36(3) of the Statute as it is understood here. Therefore, the possibility to make Optional Clause declarations for a certain time argues for the assumption that the declarations are not subject to withdrawals according to Article 56 VCLT.

However, during the drafting of the Statute of the Permanent Court the withdrawal of declarations has not been addressed at all. The earlier Article 96(2) of the 1907 Convention for the Pacific Settlement of International Disputes had provided: 'The denunciation shall only have effect in regard to the notifying power and one year after the notification has reached the Netherlands Government'. But, as already addressed for the

---

[121] PCIJ, Series E No 14, 58.
[122] cp sub-s I C iii of ch 1 at 17 and sub-s III B iv c 1 of ch 5 at 230.
[123] cp sub-s III A of ch 5 at 200.
[124] Waldock (n 9) 265.
[125] For the question whether provisions which deepen the commitment can be considered reservations see sub-s I B of ch 5 at 168.

reservations allowing withdrawals without period of notice,[126] it cannot be said for sure what the drafters of the Optional Clause would have provided for, if they had considered the issue. An example of how controversial a discussion on this issue might have been can be seen in the aforementioned 1926 conference of states signatories of the Statute of the Permanent Court. There the matter became important in regard to the Statute of the Permanent Court itself which likewise contained no provision for withdrawals. The Czechoslovakian delegate Osusky immediately made clear that all international conventions like the Statute of the Permanent Court were open to withdrawal if they did not provide otherwise.[127] The other delegates objected without hesitation and a highly controversial discussion arose.[128] At the end the delegates agreed on a particular rule allowing them to withdraw their acceptance of the United States' conditions but did not decide the matter concerning their own right to withdraw.[129]

In this regard it is interesting that in the later treaties providing the jurisdiction of the Court the states have provided rules for withdrawals. According to Article 45(2) of the General Act, for example, the states can withdraw with a period of notice of six months to the end of a five year period. Article 40(1) of the European Convention provides likewise. Article XLI of the Pact of Bogotá provides the possibility to withdraw with a period of notice of one year.

In total, it can be said that it is unlikely that the drafters of the Statutes would have provided a right to withdraw Optional Clause declarations without a period of notice. However, it is unclear whether they really wanted states to be bound indefinitely or would have provided for a right to withdraw with a period of notice.

C. Withdrawals of Optional Clause Declarations in State Practice

As the previous sub-section provided no clear answer on whether Optional Clause declarations without any reservation in this regard can be withdrawn according to Article 56 VCLT, the question of how the states have treated the issue is all the more interesting now.

Greig maintained that also Optional Clause declarations without reservations could be withdrawn without a period of notice and referred inter alia to the state practice.[130] According to Rotter, state practice essentially supported the view that Optional Clause declarations were withdrawable without a period of notice even when they contained no such reservation.[131]

---

[126] See sub-s III B iv b 1 of ch 5 at 227.
[127] League of Nations, 'Minutes of the Conference of States Signatories of the Protocol of Signature of the Statute of the Permanent Court of International Justice' (1926) 12 f (Osusky).
[128] ibid 13 f (Erich, Markovitch, Rolin).
[129] cp ibid 52–64, 77, 83.
[130] DW Greig, 'Confrontation' 179 f.
[131] Rotter (n 42) 650 f.

In 1984, the Judges Jennings and Oda likewise wrote that states in these days generally expected that other states could withdraw their declarations or add new reservations without a period of notice. They based this on prior state practice in which states had withdrawn their declarations without corresponding reservations and in which states had made many Optional Clause declarations providing for withdrawals without periods of notice.

i. Withdrawals Without Reservations and Corresponding Statements

The aspect of state practice which will be analysed below is how states withdrew and how other states reacted to those withdrawals.

a. State Practice Under the Permanent Court

The first Optional Clause declaration that was withdrawn had been made by France. France had signed an Optional Clause declaration in 1924. That declaration was subject to ratification and should have been valid for 15 years.[132] Already in 1929 France made a new declaration which was again subject to ratification and made for a period of only five years. France ratified that declaration in 1931.[133] No objections were raised to that but, as it can also be seen in the General Secretary's reaction, the withdrawal was accepted because the declaration had not yet entered into force.[134]

The first case of a withdrawal of an effective declaration without any provision to do so in the declaration was the withdrawal of the Colombian declaration of 1932. In 1936, Columbia replaced that declaration due to an error in that declaration's wording. Columbia allegedly had forgotten to exclude prior disputes in its declaration. As proof of its original intention it provided the domestic law of 1930.[135] There have been no objections against this 'amendment'.[136]

---

[132] See eg PCIJ, Series E No 4, 418.

[133] See eg PCIJ, Series E No 15, 221.

[134] cp ibid 221, fn 2. For the value of Optional Clause declarations which are subject to ratification see sub-s II B of ch 3 at 89.

[135] PCIJ, Series E No 13, 276 f, 281. For the prior text see eg PCIJ, Series E No 15, 341. Compare *Territorial and Maritime Dispute (Nicaragua v Colombia)* (Preliminary Objections) Memorial (Colombia) 119; ILC 'Documents of the 15th Session Including the Report of the Commission to the General Assembly' (n 37) 68; Oda (n 21) 11 f; *Military and Paramilitary Activities in and against Nicaragua (Nicaragua v United States of America)* (Jurisdiction and Admissibility) Counter-Memorial (United States of America) para 368. As first case one could also consider Costa Rica which had signed an Optional Clause declaration before 28 January 1921. However, Costa Rica did not ratify the protocol of signature for the Statute of the Permanent Court and withdrew from the League of Nations in 1924. For the General-Secretary of the League of Nations this seemed to point to the result that the obligations resulting from the Statute and the Optional Clause had also lapsed (cp eg PCIJ, Series E No 7, 450). Without reference to this previous declaration Costa Rica made a new declaration in 1973. For the Costa Rican withdrawal see also H Wundram, *Fakultativklausel* 18 f.

[136] *Territorial and Maritime Dispute (Nicaragua v Colombia)*, ibid 119; Oda, ibid 11.

In 1938, Paraguay, facing a lawsuit by Bolivia,[137] fully withdrew its declaration without having a corresponding reservation.[138] According to Maus Paraguay based its withdrawal on the assumption that declarations which have not been made for a certain period of time can be withdrawn.[139] However, Paraguay presented reasons for its withdrawal and explained its step inter alia with its withdrawal from the League of Nations.[140] Regarding this explanation, it can better be said that Paraguay based its withdrawal on the principle of *clausula rebus sic stantibus* and not on a general right to withdraw. Even though Paraguay did not expressly refer to the principle, it materially referred to changed circumstances.[141]

Against this withdrawal there have been objections by Bolivia and five other states.[142] Brazil stated that 'it cannot accept such declaration without express reservation'. Sweden wrote that it was up to the Court to decide upon the validity of the withdrawal. Bolivia and Belgium did not specify the reason for their objection. As they could also have argued that the withdrawal of Paraguay did not meet the requirements of a *clausula rebus sic stantibus*,[143] it cannot be said for sure whether they objected only to the current withdrawal or whether they objected to Paraguay's way of withdrawing in general. In any case it can be said that they did not accept withdrawals without a period of notice in general. However, the objection by Czechoslovakia is very helpful. This state argued that in this issue reference should be made to the general rules of international law concerning the withdrawal from international undertakings. The Netherlands did not oppose the withdrawal of the Optional Clause declaration but 'felt obliged to formulate every reservation as regards the right of States to denounce treaties which do not contain a clause to that effect'.[144] Waldock understood these objections as indicating that the issue at hand should be governed by the law of treaties.[145] Against this it can, however, be said that the Netherlands seemed to distinguish between the regime for the Paraguayan declaration and the regime for general treaties.

---

[137] cp PCIJ, Series E No 14, 57 f. See also AN Farmanfarma, *Declarations* 79.

[138] Kolb (n 2) 521; Oellers-Frahm (n 7) 571; Widdows (n 37) 97. cp also PCIJ, Series E No 14, 57.

[139] Maus (n 23) 76. cp also Widdows, ibid 94 f, 97.

[140] PCIJ, Series E No 14, 57. See also Fachiri (n 40) 52–55; Farmanfarma (n 137) 80 f; Oellers-Frahm (n 7) 571. For an assessment of this argument see Farmanfarma, ibid 81–83 who doubted its validity.

[141] Fachiri, ibid 52–55. cp also Farmanfarma, ibid 86. See also Oellers-Frahm (Oellers-Frahm, ibid 572) who doubted the value of this case precedent as support for the opinion that states can immediately withdraw per se.

[142] PCIJ, Series E No 15, 227. See also *Military and Paramilitary Activities in and against Nicaragua (Nicaragua v United States of America)* (Jurisdiction and Admissibility) Counter-Memorial (United States of America) para 369; Widdows (n 37) 88, 97.

[143] cp Fachiri (n 40) 57.

[144] PCIJ, Series E No 15, 227. See also Oellers-Frahm (n 7) 571; Oda (n 21) 11 f.

[145] Waldock (n 9) 263.

In 1939, the United Kingdom and other states of the Commonwealth together with France added a new reservation to their Optional Clause declarations without any period of notice even though their declarations contained a minimum period of validity that had not yet run out. They wanted to exclude disputes which relate to the Second World War.[146] They did not expressly invoke the doctrine of *clausula rebus sic stantibus*. However, their explanations reflected it.[147] The United Kingdom for example maintained expressly that the situation had 'fundamentally changed from that which existed at the time of their signature of the Optional Clause'. It argued that as it had made its Optional Clause declaration in 1929, it had been able to make that declaration without a reservation excluding 'disputes arising out of events occurring during a war' because it had believed in the order established by the League of Nations which included inter alia effective sanctions against aggressor states. For the United Kingdom this order had been set aside and the states ignored their obligations arising under the League of Nations so the United Kingdom considered its new reservations as necessary.[148] France argued similarly and maintained:

> Les conditions, dans lesquelles le Gouvernement français avait adhéré à cette clause se trouvent aujourd'hui profondément modifiées. En particulier, depuis que le système de règlement des conflits internationaux établi par le Pacte de la Société des Nations n'est plus regardé comme liant uniformément et obligatoirement tous les Membres de la Société des Nations, la question de la belligérance et des droits des neutres apparaît sous un aspect entièrement nouveau.[149]

Also here other states objected to the amendments. Switzerland made 'reservations ... regarding the principle which a denunciation effected in such circumstances involves'. Belgium, Brazil, Estonia, the Netherlands, Peru and Siam 'reserved their points of view'. For those objections it could now be said what has already been said for the objections of Bolivia and Belgium to the Paraguayan withdrawal. However, unlike Paraguay the declarations of the states which made a new reservation in 1939 provided that they were still valid for some more time while the Paraguayan declaration provided nothing in this regard. Therefore, it can be said that the objecting states spoke out against withdrawal without a period of notice, but it cannot be said for sure whether they would also have done

---

[146] PCIJ, Series E No 16, 332–40, 341–44.

[147] Alexandrov (n 23) 12; Holloway (n 8) 671, fn 71; ILC 'Summary Records of the 15th Session' (n 55) 101 f (Verdross); Maus (n 23) 77; Waldock (n 9) 264. cp also Kolb (n 2) 521; Wittmann (n 7) 208–13.

[148] PCIJ, Series E No 16, 337–39.

[149] ibid 337. See also S Dreyfus, 'Les déclarations souscrites par la France' 263 f.

so if the declarations in question had provided nothing in this regard at all. Sweden, this time accompanied by Norway, emphasised again the

> fact that, in virtue of Article 36 of the Statute and the declarations relating thereto, it rests with the Court itself to decide questions as to its own jurisdiction and, should the case arise, to pronounce upon the validity and, if necessary, the scope of the acts of denunciation referred to.

However, this time Norway and Sweden additionally made 'reservations as to the legal effect of the above-mentioned acts of denunciation, more particularly as regards disputes not connected with the war'.[150] This latter part at least points towards an application of the principle of *clausula rebus sic stantibus*.

b. El Salvador and Honduras

In 1973, El Salvador substituted its declaration of 1921 without corresponding reservation. It also explained this step with 'present circumstances'. In the case of El Salvador, however, this expression referred to a change in its own domestic political constitution and only 'furthermore' the text of other Optional Clause declarations as external source.[151] Honduras objected in 1974 and held that 'a declaration not containing a time-limit cannot be denounced, modified or broadened unless the right to do so is expressly reserved in the original declaration'. It pointed at the fact that states had objected to the Paraguayan withdrawal and that unilateral withdrawals undermined inter alia the respect for international treaties. Furthermore, Honduras referred to Article 27 VCLT to show that the reference to internal law could have no influence on international obligations and that therefore the El Salvadorian justification of its behaviour was not convincing.[152] El Salvador answered that the 'letter and spirit' of Article 36(2) of the Statute allowed states to make a new declaration 'at any time' and that the old declaration of El Salvador did not bar it from making its first declaration under the new Court. For El Salvador, Optional Clause declarations were a unilateral and free act in which no

---

[150] For all the states' objections see PCIJ, Series E No 16, 333, fn 1; Oda (n 21) 12 f. See furthermore Wittmann (Wittmann (n 7) 208–13) who wrote that there was no fundamental change of circumstances which allowed the introduction of the new reservations. cp also Verzijl (Verzijl (n 93) 593) who denied that the states had a right to withdraw parts of their declarations.

[151] ICJ Yearbook, 1973–1974, 49, 56–58. See also *Military and Paramilitary Activities in and against Nicaragua (Nicaragua v United States of America)* (Jurisdiction and Admissibility) Counter-Memorial (United States of America) para 371; S Rosenne, *Documents* 359–61.

[152] Honduras, 'Objection by Honduras' 345–58. See also Rosenne, ibid 361–64 and *Military and Paramilitary Activities in and against Nicaragua (Nicaragua v United States of America)* (Jurisdiction and Admissibility) Counter-Memorial (United States of America) para 371.

other state could interfere. To support this El Salvador referred to the two Court's jurisprudence in the *Phosphates in Morocco*, the *Anglo-Iranian Oil Co* and the *Norwegian Loans* case.[153] El Salvador further referred to Colombia's introduction of its reservation in 1937 to maintain that the application of the law of treaties on an Optional Clause declaration went beyond the reality of the law and state practice in this regard. Article 27 VCLT was therefore not applicable. Additionally, El Salvador emphasised the unequal position between states which had made a permanent commitment and those which could withdraw according to the terms of their declarations. Concerning the application of *clausula rebus sic stantibus* El Salvador stated that it was of 'no avail' for the states which had made permanent declarations but nonetheless also referred to Rosenne who had written that states having made their Optional Clause declarations in the days of the Permanent Court should also be able to withdraw contemporaneously as there had been changes in the international community.[154]

In total it can be said that while Honduras presented arguments which were close to those which could also have been made under treaty law, El Salvador emphasised the unilateral nature of Optional Clause declarations but used at least one argument which likewise could have been used for a treaty.

c. The United States and Nicaragua

The aforementioned introduction of a new reservation by the United States in 1984 has been much discussed. The United States wanted its new reservation to be effective immediately even though its Optional Clause declaration prescribed a six month period of notice. It argued that the states had shaped a *sui generis* Optional Clause system and introduced the right to withdraw and amend without a period of notice even if the relevant declaration did not contain a corresponding reservation or even stipulated otherwise. For the United States such a right was nothing other than the already recognised right emerging from the corresponding reservations and there was no reason to distinguish declarations with and without such a reservation. The insecurity caused was equal. Similar to El Salvador,

---

[153] For these arguments see ch 2 at 39 and for the judgments especially s IV of ch 2 at 74. El Salvador's position has been taken into consideration in sub-s III A of ch 2 at 69.

[154] El Salvador, 'Declaration' 535–43. See also Rosenne (n 151) 365–69 and *Military and Paramilitary Activities in and against Nicaragua (Nicaragua v United States of America)* (Jurisdiction and Admissibility) Counter-Memorial (United States of America) para 371. El Salvador also referred to Portugal's new declaration of 1955 but, taking into consideration how the Court decided on the range of Art 36(5) of the Statue, the making of the new Portuguese declaration in 1955 can be considered as the making of a new declaration without previous declaration (cp sub-s II B iii of ch 2 at 62). Against the argument that there would be inequality see sub-s II C of ch 5 at 181.

the United States furthermore argued that the denial of such a right was unjust for all those states which had made their declaration at earlier stages of the Optional Clause and had not included a corresponding reservation. Their declarations were frozen. The United States additionally argued that as other states had already withdrawn their declaration without corresponding reservations and the majority of other states had not objected, the right to withdraw without a period of notice could therefore be regarded as established.[155] Furthermore, the United States emphasised that the Court had not yet applied treaty law to Optional Clause declarations and that, even if treaty law applied, it would allow withdrawals from treaties concerning jurisdiction.[156] Lastly, the United States invoked Article 33(1) of the Charter and the free choice of means for dispute settlement to show that the principle of good faith did not contradict its withdrawal either.[157]

Nicaragua on the other hand argued against a right to withdraw Optional Clause declarations without a period of notice and without corresponding reservation. It referred to the 'contractual nature of the legal bond resulting from interlocking declarations' and came to the conclusion that Optional Clause declarations can only be withdrawn according to their own terms or a rule of treaty law. Nicaragua emphasised the principle of good faith as it also appeared in Article 26 VCLT. It argued that, if states were free in making and shaping their Optional Clause declarations, it was justified to bind them to those declarations later. Furthermore, Nicaragua challenged the United States' reference to state practice and maintained that almost all states named by the United States invoked a ground for their withdrawals.[158] At the end the United States abstained from the proceedings and withdrew its declaration later with a six month period of notice.[159]

---

[155] El Salvador, ibid 535–43. See also Rosenne, ibid 365–69 and *Military and Paramilitary Activities in and against Nicaragua (Nicaragua v United States of America)* (Jurisdiction and Admissibility) Counter-Memorial (United States of America) paras 337–401. cp also *Military and Paramilitary Activities in and against Nicaragua (Nicaragua v United States of America)* (n 20) para 53.

[156] *Military and Paramilitary Activities in and against Nicaragua (Nicaragua v United States of America)* (Jurisdiction and Admissibility) Counter-Memorial (United States of America) paras 340, 409 referring to Waldock's proposals as Special Rapporteur presented above in sub-s II A i of ch 6 at 281.

[157] *Military and Paramilitary Activities in and against Nicaragua (Nicaragua v United States of America)* (Jurisdiction and Admissibility) Counter-Memorial (United States of America) para 397.

[158] cp *Military and Paramilitary Activities in and against Nicaragua (Nicaragua v United States of America)* (Jurisdiction and Admissibility) Memorial (Nicaragua) paras 104–38, 142–44; *Military and Paramilitary Activities in and against Nicaragua (Nicaragua v United States of America)* (Provisional Measures) Oral Proceedings (CR 1984) (Nicaragua) 69–77 (Brownlie); *Military and Paramilitary Activities in and against Nicaragua (Nicaragua v United States of America)* (Jurisdiction and Admissibility) Oral Proceedings (CR 1984) (Nicaragua) 57–72 (Brownlie).

[159] *Military and Paramilitary Activities in and against Nicaragua (Nicaragua v United States of America)* Correspondence (United States of America) 408, 422; AC Arend, *Compulsory Jurisdiction* 213. See also E McWhinney, 'Jurisdiction and Justiciability' 84.

What can be inferred from this is that the United States did not consider the withdrawal of Optional Clause declarations to be subject to treaty law while Nicaragua wanted to apply treaty law in this regard and to bind the United States to the wording of its declaration.

d. Honduras and Nicaragua

Another state which faced an application by Nicaragua and added a new reservation to prevent the proceedings was Honduras. It introduced a new Optional Clause declaration in June 1986 even though its Optional Clause declaration of 1960 had been made for 'an indefinite term' and provided no possibility to withdraw. This seems to be completely contrary to what Honduras had maintained vis-à-vis El Salvador in 1974.

In July 1986, one month after the Court had decided upon the merits of the *Nicaragua* case, Nicaragua filed the application against Honduras and wanted to base the application on the Honduran declaration of 1960. It maintained—as Honduras before—that the new Honduran reservations had no effect on the old declaration because Honduras had not been able to introduce them and that in any case the new reservations could not be effective against Nicaragua. To support its position Nicaragua emphasised that the Optional Clause declarations resulted in contractual relations between the states and referred inter alia to the Court's judgment in the *Right of Passage* case. Nicaragua then specifically referred to the position Honduras had previously maintained concerning the new reservation of El Salvador and claimed that Honduras now wanted to do what it had objected to earlier. Nicaragua further argued that, in 1960, Honduras had not had the intention to allow itself to withdraw and that no such right could be deduced from the nature of the Optional Clause declarations. Additionally, Nicaragua maintained that in any case Article 56(2) VCLT had to be applied to the Honduran declaration and that therefore the new reservations had not yet been effective when Nicaragua filed its application.[160]

In the oral proceedings Honduras came back to the Optional Clause in particular and expressly contradicted its earlier position that it had maintained vis-à-vis El Salvador. It wrote that it wanted to make a new declaration in the same way as El Salvador because it had had to accept the objected behaviour of El Salvador in 1973. As the United States before, Honduras maintained that Optional Clause declarations were *sui generis*

---

[160] *Border and Transborder Armed Actions (Nicaragua v Honduras)* (Jurisdiction and Admissibility) Counter-Memorial (Nicaragua) paras 48–104. cp *Border and Transborder Armed Actions (Nicaragua v Honduras)* (Jurisdiction and Admissibility) [1988] ICJ Rep 69, 74. For the *Right of Passage* judgment in this regard see sub-s IV B of ch 2 at 76. In the written proceedings Honduras did not argue against this position of Nicaragua. Instead, Honduras referred to the Pact of Bogotá and maintained that Optional Clause declarations and Art XXXI of the Pact of Bogotá established one single basis of jurisdiction. For that argument see the following sub-s III B of ch 6 at 316.

and that the earlier state practice of Paraguay and of the seven states in 1939 supported the view that Optional Clause declarations were withdrawable. Treaty law could not be applied. As the Honduran declaration of 1960 contained no period of notice and for Honduras preceding state practice supported a right to withdraw without a period of notice, it could likewise withdraw without a period of notice.[161] Nicaragua maintained its position and, represented by Pellet, rebutted Honduras' references to state practice. As Brownlie had already pleaded for Nicaragua in 1984, Pellet showed that in the prior state practice almost all states had invoked a justification for withdrawals without a period of notice.[162]

Regarding the prior case between the United States and Nicaragua, it can be said that Honduras adopted the position of the United States while Nicaragua clarified its position, extending it to declarations which contain no explicit minimum period of notice for withdrawals.

e. Colombia, Costa Rica and Nicaragua

In 2001 interestingly Nicaragua, too, made a new reservation to its Optional Clause declaration even though its declaration did not contain a provision allowing it to amend or to withdraw it. This time it was Costa Rica which objected. On 26 September 2002 both states concluded a moratorium in the Tovar-Caldera Treaty.[163] In October 2002, both states informed the United Nations Secretary-General about this agreement by which Nicaragua maintained the legal status 'existing on today's date' for three years.[164] As Costa Rica filed an application against Nicaragua on 29 September 2005 it referred inter alia to the jurisdiction established under Article 36(2) of the Statute 'by virtue of the operation of ... the declarations of acceptance made respectively by the Republic of Costa Rica dated 20 February 1973 and by the Republic of Nicaragua dated 24 September 1929 ... [and] the Tovar-Caldera Agreement, Alajuela, 26 September 2002'.[165] Costa Rica went on explaining that

> under the Tovar-Caldera Agreement, in consideration of Nicaragua maintaining unchanged for three years the legal status with respect to its declaration

---

[161] *Border and Transborder Armed Actions (Nicaragua v Honduras)* (Jurisdiction and Admissibility) Oral Proceedings (CR 1988) (Honduras) 18–22 (Bowett).

[162] *Border and Transborder Armed Actions (Nicaragua v Honduras)* (n 161) (Nicaragua) 124 (Pellet). See also ibid 84–88 (Chayes).

[163] *Dispute Regarding Navigational and Related Rights (Costa Rica v Nicaragua)* (Judgment) [2009] ICJ Rep 13, paras 27 f; the whole Tovar-Caldera Treaty can be found in UNTS, Volume 2197 (2004) 75–81.

[164] ICJ Yearbook 2002–2003, 127, 156. This communication has also been attached to Nicaragua's Optional Clause declaration on the Court's homepage (see above n 28 of the introduction).

[165] *Dispute Regarding Navigational and Related Rights (Costa Rica v Nicaragua)* Application (Costa Rica) 8, para 2.

of acceptance of this Court, Costa Rica agreed during the same period not to initiate any action 'before the Court nor before any other authority on any matter or protest mentioned in treaties or agreements currently in force between both countries'.[166]

Nicaragua did not object.[167] On 18 November 2011, Costa Rica filed another application against Nicaragua and named Nicaragua's declaration 'as modified 23 October 2001' as a source of jurisdiction for the case concerning *Certain Activities Carried out by Nicaragua in the Border Area*.[168] Concerning the merits of its case Costa Rica invoked a treaty of 1858 and two arbitral awards of 1888 and 1897 even though Nicaragua's new declaration does not apply to 'any matter or claim based on interpretations of treaties or arbitral awards that were signed and ratified or made, respectively, prior to 31 December 1901'.[169] Costa Rica saw this contradiction but emphasised that it also invoked other sources for the merits of the case and presented a note of the Nicaraguan acting Foreign Minister in which Nicaragua had accepted the jurisdiction of the Court in the present case.[170] In line with this Argüello Gómez, representing Nicaragua, directly argued on the merits of the case including, for example, the treaty of 1858 and did not object to the jurisdiction of the Court.[171]

However, Nicaragua did not only have a dispute with Costa Rica but also with Colombia. As referred to above,[172] in this latter constellation it was Colombia which withdrew its Optional Clause declaration. Also this Optional Clause declaration contained no corresponding reservation.[173] Nicaragua filed an application against Colombia on 6 December 2001, only one day after Colombia had submitted its withdrawal.[174] In later proceedings before the Court Colombia presented several arguments to support its position that this withdrawal was valid and immediately effective. As El Salvador in 1973, Colombia referred to a statement made by Rosenne arguing that those states which had made an unlimited

---

[166] ibid 8, para 4.

[167] *Dispute Regarding Navigational and Related Rights (Costa Rica v Nicaragua)* (n 163) para 28; *Dispute Regarding Navigational and Related Rights (Costa Rica v Nicaragua)* Counter-Memorial (Nicaragua) para 3.

[168] *Certain Activities Carried out by Nicaragua in the Border Area (Costa Rica v Nicaragua)* Application (Costa Rica) para 3.

[169] cp *Certain Activities Carried out by Nicaragua in the Border Area (Costa Rica v Nicaragua)* (Provisional Measures) [2011] ICJ Rep 6, paras 1, 8.

[170] *Certain Activities Carried out by Nicaragua in the Border Area (Costa Rica v Nicaragua)* (Provisional Measures) Oral Proceedings (CR 2011/1) (Costa Rica) 55 f (Crawford).

[171] *Certain Activities Carried out by Nicaragua in the Border Area (Costa Rica v Nicaragua)* (Provisional Measures) Oral Proceedings (CR 2011/2) (Nicaragua) 10 f (Argüello Gómez).

[172] cp sub-s III B iii c of ch 5 at 218.

[173] cp *Territorial and Maritime Dispute (Nicaragua v Colombia)* (Preliminary Objections) [2007] ICJ Rep 832, para 122.

[174] *Territorial and Maritime Dispute (Nicaragua v Colombia)* (n 135) 114; *Territorial and Maritime Dispute (Nicaragua v Colombia)* (n 173) para 139.

Optional Clause declaration during the time of the Permanent Court should now be able to amend and withdraw.[175] As said above, because of this reference to the underlying change of circumstances this is very similar to an invocation of the principle of *clausula rebus sic stantibus*. This, however, was not Colombia's only reasoning. It furthermore seemed to understand the Optional Clause as granting a right to amend and withdraw without a period of notice. Colombia emphasised that the Court's contradictory ruling in the *Nicaragua* case was only *obiter dicta* and furthermore highly controversial.[176] Lastly, it pointed at Nicaragua's and Colombia's own state practice of 1937 and 2001 respectively and pressed that in 1937 no state, including Nicaragua, had objected.[177]

Nicaragua answered that unreserved withdrawals and amendments required one year to become effective. It provided its own assessment of the Court's judgments and literature and pointed especially at its own amendment of 2001. It wrote that also its own declaration would have become effective after one year and that this was why it had concluded the treaty with Costa Rica.[178] For Colombia this happened just due to a policy change inside Nicaragua.[179]

f. Conclusions

The first conclusion that can be drawn is that cases in which a state files an application against another state after that state has withdrawn its Optional Clause declaration do not belong into the 'realm of theory' anymore as some authors had maintained in the 1960s.[180]

The second conclusion which may be drawn is that states have the opinion that the principle of *clausula rebus sic stantibus* can be applied to Optional Clause declarations. In particular the introduction of the new reservations by the United Kingdom, the other Commonwealth states and France in 1939 clearly reflects this principle. The Paraguayan withdrawal of 1938 shows at least some similarities. The basic argumentation in these

---

[175] *Territorial and Maritime Dispute (Nicaragua v Colombia)* (n 135) 115 referring to S Rosenne, *Practice 1920–1996* 820.

[176] See sub-s II D of ch 6 at 305 for the position of the Court.

[177] *Territorial and Maritime Dispute (Nicaragua v Colombia)* (n 135)) 115–20; *Territorial and Maritime Dispute (Nicaragua v Colombia)* (Preliminary Objections) Oral Proceedings (CR 2007/16) (Colombia) 48–52 (Schwebel); *Territorial and Maritime Dispute (Nicaragua v Colombia)* (Preliminary Objections) Oral Proceedings (CR 2007/18) (Colombia) 13–15.

[178] *Territorial and Maritime Dispute (Nicaragua v Colombia)* (Preliminary Objections) Written Statement (Nicaragua) 86–105; *Territorial and Maritime Dispute (Nicaragua v Colombia)* (Preliminary Objections) Oral Proceedings (CR 2007/17) (Nicaragua) 47–54 (Brownlie); *Territorial and Maritime Dispute (Nicaragua v Colombia)* (Preliminary Objections) Oral Proceedings (CR 2007/19) (Nicaragua) 15 f (Argüello).

[179] *Territorial and Maritime Dispute (Nicaragua v Colombia)* (Preliminary Objections) Oral Proceedings (CR 2007/18) (Colombia) 14 f (Schwebel).

[180] cp S Rosenne, *Time Factor* 24, 26 and also Shihata (n 3) 167: 'unrealistic'.

cases resembles the material treaty law in this regard so strongly that it is of no big importance that at that time the states did not follow the procedural rules which have been introduced in the VCLT later.[181] As Krieger recently wrote concerning general treaty law, states do not—or not yet—act according to these provisions of the VCLT.[182] The application of the principle *clausula rebus sic stantibus* does, however, not answer the question of whether Optional Clause declarations are treated as accessions to a treaty or purely unilateral declarations because Article 62 VCLT and also Principle 10(2)(c) GPUD (Guiding Principles for Unilateral Declarations) contain a corresponding provision.[183]

However, the fact that almost all states tried to justify their withdrawals without a period of notice leads to the conclusion that the states do not consider the Optional Clause declarations as being withdrawable without period of notice *per se*. If they were, there would have been no necessity for the states to justify their behaviour so strongly. Especially the explanations which the states gave in 1939 are so similar to the rules of law that they cannot be considered as purely political justifications. Furthermore, they amended their Optional Clause declarations only to the extent that the changed circumstances allegedly justified. This also corresponds to an application of the principle *clausula rebus sic stantibus*.[184] As Waldock wrote and Brownlie later pleaded for Nicaragua, it seems as if the states invoked the principle of *clausula rebus sic stantibus* precisely because they considered the introduction of a new reservation as otherwise impossible.[185] The Netherlands, El Salvador, the United States, Honduras and Colombia which argued that Optional Clause declarations were open to withdrawals are in the minority. Furthermore, as far as they based their position on the precedents of 1939, they based it on a wrong conclusion as Waldock and Brownlie showed. Against these states Belgium, Bolivia, Brazil, Czechoslovakia, Estonia, Nicaragua, Paraguay, Peru, Siam, Switzerland, the United Kingdom and the other Commonwealth states of 1939 had the opinion that Optional Clause declarations are not immediately withdrawable. From this perspective state practice argues against a residual right to withdraw Optional Clause declarations.[186]

---

[181] cp sub-s II A ii of ch 6 at 285.

[182] Krieger (n 115) para 9.

[183] For the principles see ILC 'Report of the International Law Commission on the Work of Its 58th Session' (1 May–9 June and 3 July–11 August 2006) UN Doc A/61/10 380.

[184] cp sub-s II A ii of ch 6 at 285.

[185] Waldock (n 9) 265; *Military and Paramilitary Activities in and against Nicaragua (Nicaragua v United States of America)* (Jurisdiction and Admissibility) Oral Proceedings (CR 1984) (Nicaragua) 65 f (Brownlie). cp also *Border and Transborder Armed Actions (Nicaragua v Honduras)* (n 161) (Nicaragua) 124 (Pellet). This was also the reasoning by Verdross (ILC 'Summary Records of the 15th Session' (n 55) 101 f) to which has already been referred to above in sub-s II A i of ch 6 at 281.

[186] See also Kolb (n 2) 521; Waldock (n 9) 265.

Yet, a distinction has to be made between the cases where a declaration has been made for a certain period of time or contained a period of notice for withdrawals and those cases where the declaration contained no provision in this regard at all. For the cases of 1939 it cannot be said for sure whether the states making the new reservations would have likewise referred to the changed circumstances if they had not had to act against the clear wording of the declarations. Similarly it cannot be said for sure whether in that case all the states would have objected as well. The states which have directly or indirectly maintained that declarations which contain no provision cannot be withdrawn immediately were Belgium, Brazil, Czechoslovakia, Nicaragua and Paraguay only. Against them stand the five states already named which argued for immediate withdrawals whether or not the declaration provides otherwise. To this extent state practice provides no clear picture for such a case.

However, it cannot be said for sure whether Paraguay would also have invoked the principle of *clausula rebus sic stantibus* for its withdrawal if it would have had the time to withdraw with a period of notice. Likewise it is not certain whether the states named above would have objected in that case. Furthermore, even Nicaragua, which has constantly opposed a right to withdraw without a period of notice, considered a withdrawal of declaration with a period of notice as valid if the declaration does not provide otherwise.

All in all state practice supports an interpretation of the Optional Clause which allows states to withdraw even if the declaration does not provide so.[187] Although state practice provides no clear result on whether these withdrawals can be without a period of notice, at least withdrawals with a certain period of notice are possible.

ii. Reservations Allowing Withdrawals

The fact that many states made reservations allowing withdrawals without periods of notice does not contradict the result found so far.[188]

According to Judge Oda the fact that these reservations were no longer challenged meant that states not having made such reservations also had the same right to amend their declarations.[189] And as mentioned above, the United States argued similarly in the *Nicaragua* case.[190]

However, state practice could also be interpreted the other way around. It could be said that states make these reservations foremost because they have the legal opinion that otherwise they would not have such

---

[187] So also Kolb (n 2) 521 f.
[188] For that practice see sub-s III B v b of ch 5 at 236.
[189] Separate opinion of Judge S Oda, *ICJ Rep 1984*, 503–10; Oda (n 21) 16–18.
[190] Sub-s II C i c of ch 6 at 296.

a possibility.[191] Under treaty law it has even been argued that where only some treaties contain a right to withdraw the presumption must be that the others have deliberately excluded such a right.[192] This could be also applied to the Optional Clause declarations.

Yet, again it could also be said that states have just made the reservations *ex abundanti cautela* and that under the Optional Clause there have already been some reservations which contained unnecessary repetitions of a rule already existing.[193] Therefore, the fact alone that so many states have made this reservation allows no clear argument on whether states without this reservation, too, can withdraw without a period of notice.[194]

Also the fact that some states have made declarations which provided for a right to withdraw with a period of notice,[195] can be interpreted in both directions. These reservations could have either established a right that otherwise would have not existed at all, or they could likewise have repeated a right which already existed.

iii. Result

As most of those states which withdrew their Optional Clause declarations without a period of notice or added new reservations without a period of notice tried to justify this with the principle of *clausula rebus sic stantibus* and as many states objected even to this position, it can be said that at least the Optional Clause declarations which provide otherwise are not open to immediate withdrawal. For the declarations which do not provide otherwise state practice supports a right to withdraw. However, it cannot be said for sure whether in the opinion of the states such a withdrawal can be made without a period of notice.

Be this as it may even if the Optional Clause allows withdrawals without a period of notice this does not necessarily mean that it is different to treaties as these also can grant such a right.[196] And the states which maintained that treaty law cannot be applied to Optional Clause declarations made no valid arguments to support this position either. As Brownlie and Waldock showed, the states' reference to the cases of Paraguay in 1938 and the cases of the Commonwealth states and France in 1939 was mistaken.

---

[191] See also the similar reasoning in Widdows (n 37) 96.

[192] For example, this was also the reasoning of Castrén and Briggs during the drafting of the VCLT (ILC 'Summary Records of the 15th Session' (n 55) 100, 103) contested by de Luna (ibid 101) who wanted to pay more attention to the particular case. See also Oellers-Frahm (Oellers-Frahm (n 7) 575) who argued that the silence of a treaty alone should not be interpreted as excluding the right to withdraw.

[193] cp Widdows (n 37) 96 and above sub-s III D ii of ch 3 at 111.

[194] For the similar difficulty in general international law see HWA Thirlway, 'Sources' 107.

[195] cp Alexandrov (n 23) 158 f.

[196] See above in the introduction to s II of ch 6 at 279.

D. Jurisprudence on the Right to Withdraw Without Corresponding Reservation

Considering that no certain answer could be derived from the material hitherto examined, the analysis of the Court's jurisprudence on the right to withdraw without corresponding reservation is of particular value.

The first case in which a state filed an application against a state which had withdrawn its declaration or introduced a new reservation was the *Nicaragua* case. There, the Court basically acknowledged an implied right to withdraw and suggested a result which was very similar to an application of Article 56 VCLT. The Court argued that 'the unilateral nature of declarations does not signify that the State making the declaration is free to amend the scope and the contents of its solemn commitments as it pleases'. It therefore bound the United States to the wording of its declaration. It went on by emphasising the principle of good faith but then started to also refer to the power to amend or terminate 'which is inherent in any unilateral act'. The Court ended by saying:

> [T]he right of immediate termination of declarations with indefinite duration is far from established. It appears from the requirements of good faith that they should be treated, by analogy, according to the law of treaties, which requires a reasonable time for withdrawal from or termination of treaties that contain no provision regarding the duration of their validity.[197]

Of course this has been only obiter dicta as the Court already denied the United States to invoke the terms of the Nicaraguan declarations,[198] and the Court had based a lot of its reasoning on the unilateral character of the Optional Clause declarations.[199] But at the end the Court's result was an analogy to treaty law.

The Judges Jennings, Oda and Schwebel dissented. The opinions of the Judges Jennings and Oda which were based on state practice have already been discussed in that context.[200] Judge Schwebel argued that the missing commitment of other states under the Optional Clause had been changed circumstances for the United States which allowed them to withdraw according to the *principle clausula rebus sic stantibus*. Furthermore, he referred to the fact that Optional Clause declarations were drafted unilaterally and not accompanied by negotiations. Judge Schwebel therefore followed the United States' approach to consider Optional Clause declarations as *sui generis* and as subject to an implied right of immediate withdrawal. Additionally, he referred to the drafting of Article 56 VCLT

---

[197] *Military and Paramilitary Activities in and against Nicaragua (Nicaragua v United States of America)* (n 20) paras 59 f, 63. Supported by Szafarz (n 4) 76 f.

[198] cp Merrills (n 91) 208 f.

[199] For the Court's position on the nature of the Optional Clause see s IV of ch 2 at 74.

[200] See above sub-s II C of ch 6 at 291.

and added that also under treaty law the Optional Clause declarations were likewise withdrawable. Especially concerning Nicaragua's Optional Clause declaration Judge Schwebel furthermore followed the already mentioned position by Rosenne that Optional Clause declarations which had been made unconditionally under the Permanent Court could be withdrawn because of the changes which had happened since then.[201]

As addressed above, Judge Schwebel's argument, that the Optional Clause declarations are *sui generis* because they are drafted unilaterally and are not accompanied by negotiations, does not convince.[202] Besides that he made arguments which related either to the principle *clausula rebus sic stantibus* or directly to treaty law. In this aspect Judge Schwebel's position corresponds to that of the Court which, even though only by analogy, applied treaty law.

The close relation between the Optional Clause and treaty law in this regard can be further shown with the fact that commentators of Article 56 VCLT even refer to the Court's judgment in the *Nicaragua* case to show that the article is customary law.[203] Concerning the 'reasonable time' referred to by the Court there have been different proposals from four days to one year.[204] This vague period of time represents an uncertainty which likewise exists in general treaty law and is discussed there along with the period provided for in Article 56(2) VCLT.[205]

But not only literature, the Court itself later also adopted the approach introduced in the *Nicaragua* case. In the *Bakassi Peninsula* case the Court emphasised that in the case of Optional Clause declarations without a corresponding reservation states put legitimate trust into those declarations. A withdrawal of a declaration therefore took an 'accrued right' from another state. Hence, the rules for withdrawal or amendment can be different to those for the submission of the declaration. In this reasoning the Court furthermore reiterated its finding in the *Nicaragua* case.[206]

In the cases involving Colombia, Costa Rica, Honduras and Nicaragua the Court did, unfortunately, not decide upon the issue. In the *Border and Transborder Armed Actions* case between Honduras and Nicaragua the Court held that no valid reservation had been made to the Pact of Bogotá

---

[201] Dissenting opinion of Judge SM Schwebel, *ICJ Rep 1984*, paras 94–106.

[202] See sub-s I A ii of ch 2 at 43. In the *Nuclear Tests* cases Judge Barwick argued that a reservation made to an Optional Clause declaration worked immediately and based this on the fact states voluntarily acceded to the Optional Clause (Dissenting opinion of Judge G Barwick, *ICJ Rep 1974*, 418). For that argument see s I of ch 3 at 86.

[203] See the references in n 21 of the introduction.

[204] Kolb (n 2) 524; Oellers-Frahm (n 22) 260; JJ Quintana, 'The Nicaragua Case' 118; Tomuschat (n 1) para 76. Quintana thereby referred to the time necessary for other states to prepare an application (Quintana, ibid 117 f).

[205] cp Christakis (n 44) paras 14–19.

[206] *Land and Maritime Boundary between Cameroon and Nigeria (Cameroon v Nigeria: Equatorial Guinea intervening)* (Preliminary Objections) [1998] ICJ Rep 275, paras 33 f.

and that thus it has jurisdiction under Article XXXI of that pact. This was why it did not decide on the validity of Honduras' new Optional Clause declaration of 1986.[207] In Nicaragua's and Colombia's *Territorial and Maritime Dispute* the Court mentioned Nicaragua's new reservation as if it had been valid. However, not too much weight can be attached to this because the new reservation was obviously without relevance to that case and the Court did not consider it in depth.[208] Colombia's withdrawal was likewise not really considered by the Court as it already denied the existence of a dispute.[209] In the case concerning the *Navigational and Related Rights* between Nicaragua and Costa Rica the Court referred to the Optional Clause declarations as a source of jurisdiction under Article 36(2) of the Statute. However, also in this case this was of little importance as Nicaragua had raised no objections concerning the jurisdiction.[210] The same holds true for the most recent case concerning *Certain Activities Carried out by Nicaragua in the Border Area* between Nicaragua and Costa Rica in which Nicaragua behaved likewise.[211]

In total, it can be concluded that up to now the Court has never decided on an Optional Clause declaration which had been withdrawn immediately before the proceedings started and where there had been no provision on withdrawals in that declaration at all.[212] However, the Court's position in the *Nicaragua* case as also reiterated in the *Bakassi Peninsula* case supports the idea that Optional Clause declarations are withdrawable with a period of notice. According to Szafarz, 'it may be assumed that in the opinion of the Court a "reasonable" time for termination of a declaration made for an indefinite time is twelve months (see Article 56(2) [VCLT])'.[213]

E. The Legal Value of the Court's Yearbook

As some authors referred not only to the statements of the Court but also to the statements of the two Courts' registries, the latter will also be considered here. The registry of the Court has been confronted with

---

[207] *Border and Transborder Armed Actions (Nicaragua v Honduras)* (Jurisdiction and Admissibility) [1988] ICJ Rep 69, para 36. cp also Merrills (n 91) 208; Szafarz (n 4) 77 f.

[208] *Territorial and Maritime Dispute (Nicaragua v Colombia)* (n 173) para 122.

[209] ibid para 139. Also none of the judges' individual opinions analysed Colombia's withdrawal. Judge Bennouna only called it a withdrawal '*in extremis* (just before Nicaragua's Application was filed)' (dissenting opinion of Judge M Bennouna, *ICJ Rep 2007*, 930).

[210] *Dispute Regarding Navigational and Related Rights (Costa Rica v Nicaragua)* (n 163) paras 27 f.

[211] *Certain Activities Carried out by Nicaragua in the Border Area (Costa Rica v Nicaragua)* (n 169) paras 1, 9, 49–51.

[212] For the situation up to 1995 see Alexandrov (n 23) 60 f.

[213] Szafarz (n 4) 77.

new reservations and withdrawals as it publishes the Optional Clause declarations in the Court's Yearbooks and therefore has to decide whether it continues to publish declarations after they have been withdrawn.

Concerning the withdrawal of Paraguay in 1938 Maus took the publication of the Paraguayan Optional Clause declaration in Courts' Yearbooks into consideration. He considered Paraguay's declaration as still in force and based this not only on the fact that for him the withdrawal seemed to be invalid. He furthermore pointed to the circumstance that Paraguay had not objected to the continued appearance of its declaration in the publication of the registry.[214]

In the case of Paraguay the registry continued to publish the declaration and only added the notice of withdrawal of 1938 and the objections.[215] The registry of the current Court transferred the declaration according to Article 36(5) of the Statute and continued to publish it. Only in 1960 it stopped.[216] As late as the 1950s Waldock inferred from this behaviour that the registry was not sure how to treat such a withdrawal and wanted to let the Court decide.[217] In 1965, Shihata published parts of a letter he had received from the deputy registrar concerning this question. The deputy registrar wrote that, in light of the *Aerial Incident of 1955* and the *Temple of Preah Vihear* case, it might have been 'more misleading' to further publish Paraguay's declaration. He emphasised that legal argument could be advanced for both views concerning the continuance or non-continuance of the declaration.[218] It becomes clear that the registry did not want to decide the question itself. It only wanted to prevent a wrong semblance in any direction. This can also be supported by the text the registry has added to its publication of Optional Clause declarations since 1956. Since then the declarations are introduced with the following words:

> The inclusion of a declaration made by any State should not be regarded as an indication of the view entertained by the Registry or, *a fortiori*, by the Court regarding the nature, scope or validity of the instrument in question'.[219]

From the yearbook 1958/1959 on the registry has additionally made clear that this holds also for the omission of a declaration.[220] Later the registry added that '[t]he fact that a declaration is or is not included in this section,

---

[214] Maus (n 23) 77.

[215] cp PCIJ, Series E No 15, 227; PCIJ, Series E No 16, 359 and ICJ Yearbook 1959–1960, 249.

[216] cp ibid 249 to ICJ Yearbook 1960–1961, 211. See also JG Merrills, 'Optional Clause Today' 93; Oellers-Frahm (n 7) 571; Shihata (n 3) 166 f; *Military and Paramilitary Activities in and against Nicaragua (Nicaragua v United States of America)* (Jurisdiction and Admissibility) Counter-Memorial (United States of America) para 369.

[217] Waldock (n 9) 264.

[218] cp Shihata (n 3) 167, fn 1.

[219] ICJ Yearbook (n 9) 207.

[220] cp ICJ Yearbook (n 216) 192; ICJ Yearbook 1958–1959, 233. cp also ICJ Yearbook 1971–1972, 55; ICJ Yearbook 1980–1981, 49.

is without prejudice to its possible application by the Court in a particular case'.[221] As therefore the publication of a declaration in the Yearbooks has no legal value at all, it seems to follow that this also holds for the reaction or the non-reaction of the states thereto.[222]

F. Result

It becomes clear that the rules for withdrawals under the Optional Clause are essentially those of treaty law. There are no arguments to the contrary. Of course, in its *Nicaragua* case the Court based its judgment on the unilateral character of Optional Clause declarations, but in the end the Court applied treaty law.

State practice supports this impression as many states considered the Optional Clause declarations as not being withdrawable without a period of notice. States which wanted to withdraw without a period of notice tried to invoke the principle *clausula rebus sic stantibus* which is also provided for in Article 62(1) VCLT.

Concerning the application of Article 60 VCLT, there has been hardly any chance for the states to invoke it because generally compliance with the Court's judgments is good,[223] and the United States, for example, already withdrew its Optional Clause declaration itself after the Court's judgment in the *Nicaragua* case. But, as it has been shown above, theoretically the application of this article is possible.

Regarding the application of Article 56 VCLT it has to be said that the Statute of the Court contains at most scarce reference to the intention of the states as they drafted it. Explicitly the drafters voiced no opinion in this regard. Whether the Optional Clause declarations can be withdrawn according to treaty law has been unclear for a long time as the later discussion during the drafting of the VCLT also showed.

With regard to state practice and the Court's jurisprudence a withdrawal is not possible when states provide otherwise in their declaration. Then they are bound to their declarations' wording. Optional Clause declarations which are silent in this regard can be withdrawn. Yet especially with regard to the Court's jurisprudence, it can be said that the Optional Clause declarations have to be withdrawn with a period of notice.[224] Whether or not this is a twelve month period as provided in Article 56(2) VCLT,

---

[221] ICJ Yearbook 1996–1997, 84; ICJ Yearbook (n 164) 121, 127.
[222] This should also hold for cases in which it is doubtful whether a declaration could have been transferred by Art 36(5) of the Statute (but see *Military and Paramilitary Activities in and against Nicaragua (Nicaragua v United States of America)* (n 20) paras 36–38).
[223] AP Llamazon, 'Compliance' 825, 846, 852; C Schulte, *Compliance* 403 f.
[224] cp also Aust (n 23) para 21; Rosenne and Ronen (n 2) 785; Szafarz (n 4) 76 f.

there is no difference between treaty law and the law for the Optional Clause as under treaty law the period of notice is likewise unclear.

All in all, also regarding the possibility to withdraw Optional Clause declarations there is no basis to argue that the Optional Clause is not a treaty. Furthermore, as already mentioned, treaty law is even based on the Optional Clause in this regard. The practice under the Optional Clause has been a major point of reference during the drafting of Article 56 VCLT.[225] And the later Court's jurisprudence on the Optional Clause has been used by commentators, like Christakis and Giegerich, when they assessed the article.[226] This also supports the impression that there is no difference between the Optional Clause and other treaties in this regard at all.[227] With reference to the Court's judgment in the *Nicaragua* case the IACtHR wrote, that 'in order for an optional clause to be unilaterally terminated, the pertinent rules of the law of treaties must be applied'.[228]

III. MUTUAL AMENDMENTS AND AGREEMENTS

After the previous sub-section considered unilateral actions the following sub-section will discuss what states can do when they act together.

A. Amending the Optional Clause Itself

The first question is how Article 36(2) to (4) of the Statute can be amended.

There have already been several suggestions to solve problems or alleged problems of the Optional Clause with an amendment. Debbasch and Gharbi proposed an amendment of the Optional Clause to regulate the right to withdraw and to standardise it for all states.[229] Rosenne suggested for a period of 90 days to pass before a declaration becomes effective.[230] Waldock proposed to amend the Optional Clause so that new declarations

---

[225] cp sub-s II A i of ch 6 at 283.

[226] See the references in n 21 of the introduction.

[227] See already H Lauterpacht and L Oppenheim, *Treatise* 61, fn 2: 'In general, unilateral termination of the obligations of the Optional Clause must be regarded as subject to conditions governing the termination of treaties'. Unnecessary repetitions in Optional Clause declarations are therefore the reservations of Togo and Côte d'Ivoire which provide for them 'the power of denunciation and modification attached to any obligation assumed by a [sovereign] [s]tate in its international relations'.

[228] *Constitutional Court v Peru* (Competence) (n 44) para 52. See also ILC 'Summary Records of the 40th Session' (24 April–29 June 1962) UN Doc A/CN.4/Ser.A/1962 56, para 72 (Liang); J Crawford, *Principles* 727.

[229] C Debbasch, 'La compétence' 258; Gharbi (n 35) 481, 497.

[230] Rosenne and Ronen (n 2) 726, fn 61 (referring to Rosenne's proposal in the ILC which had not been adopted (for the discussion in the ILC see n 81 of this chapter)); supported by Judge CG Weeramantry, *ICJ Rep 1998*, 374; criticised by V Lamm, 'Declarations' 48.

cannot cover disputes which arose in the two years before the submission of the declarations.[231]

i. The Statute, the VCLT and Other Solutions

The first reference for such amendments could be the Statute. Articles 69 and 70 of the Statute provide for '[a]mendments to the present Statute'. According to Article 69 of the Statute in combination with Article 108 of the Charter, such an amendment would require, inter alia, a vote by two thirds of the members of the GA and ratification by all permanent members of the UNSC. 'Amendments to the present Statute' could now be interpreted as also referring to amendments of the named provisions of the Optional Clause.

What is no problem for the Statute might, however, be a problem for the Optional Clause. Under the current Statute the group of states bound by the Statute and the group of members of the General Assembly are generally the same.[232] Therefore, the states voting on the amendments and the states bound by the Statute are also the same. General Assembly Resolution 2520 (XXIV) even ensured that all Member States of the Statute which are not also a member of the United Nations are able to participate in the amendment proceedings in the General Assembly.[233] On the other hand, under the Optional Clause these two groups are not identical. Not all Member States of the General Assembly are bound by the Optional Clause. If Articles 69 and 70 of the Statute applied to the Optional Clause, the latter would be open to an amendment by states which are not parties of it.[234] It is true that the drafters of the Statute referred to the possibility to amend the Statute as they presented the possibility that one day the Court might have compulsory jurisdiction.[235] This, however, would be an amendment of the Statute. It would make the Optional Clause redundant, but it would not touch the obligations among its Member States.

As the amendment of the Optional Clause might change the commitment of the states having made a declaration, this cannot happen without their consent. This has, for example, been clearly pointed out by the dissenting opinions in the *Aerial Incident of 1955* case. The Judges Lauterpacht, Koo and Spender wrote that Article 36(5) of the Statute provided the necessary 'consensual link' for the 'modification' of the Optional

---

[231] Waldock (n 9) 286.
[232] The Statute of the Permanent Court contained no provision for amendments. However, the parties of that Statute amended it with a Protocol of Amendment which became effective in 1936 (cp Karl (n 98) paras 6 f).
[233] cp ibid paras 2, 5, 9, 11 f; MM Whiteman, *Digest* 1467, 1470 f.
[234] See a similar argument for the CCPR in M Nowak, *CCPR Commentary* Art 51, 4.
[235] United Nations, *Conference on International Organization, Volume XIII—Commission IV, Judicial Organization* 57 with reference to Art 70 of the Statute.

Clause declarations in this case.[236] Without its consent Bulgaria's declaration would not have been referred to the Court.[237] According to Judge Goitein, 'not a jot of it could [have] be[en] altered without the consent of Bulgaria'.[238] This is consistent with the rule that multilateral treaties can generally not be amended without the consent of all states if there is no other rule provided.[239]

Just as the rules for withdrawals for an optional clause cannot be transferred to the major treaty,[240] the rules for amendments should not be transferred to the optional clauses either if no corresponding intention of the drafters has been established. Normally, a special regime should be provided to let the states, which are actually bound by the optional clause, decide upon their obligation themselves. This can also be emphasised with Article 11 of the first optional protocol to the CCPR which basically empowers the Member States of the protocol to amend it. As far as the optional protocol or optional clause contains no such rules, general treaty law could apply.

Article 39(1) VCLT contains the general principle that 'A treaty may be amended by agreement between the parties'.[241] Article 40(4) VCLT furthermore provides that '[t]he amending agreement does not bind any State already a party to the treaty which does not become a party to the amending agreement'. 'Parties' in the case of the Optional Clause are all those states which have already made an Optional Clause declaration.[242] According to Article 30(4)(b) VCLT such parties which do not agree to the amendment remain bound vis-à-vis the other states according to the old terms of the Optional Clause. Article 30 VCLT, however, only applies if the earlier treaty has not been terminated according to Article 59 VCLT.[243]

One problem, however, would be that the Optional Clause has been drafted along with the Statute by the General Assembly. It can be said that the General Assembly should therefore also have a possibility to approve

---

[236] cp the joint dissenting opinion of Judges H Lauterpacht, VK Wellington Koo and PC Spender, *ICJ Rep 1959*, 171 and cp also *Case concerning the Aerial Incident of July 27th, 1955 (Israel v Bulgaria)* (Preliminary Objections) [1959] ICJ Rep 127, 136.

[237] cp the joint dissenting opinion of Judges H Lauterpacht, VK Wellington Koo and PC Spender, *ICJ Rep 1959*, 186.

[238] Dissenting opinion of Judge D Goitein, *ICJ Rep 1959*, 198.

[239] K Zemanek, 'Revision' 981.

[240] For Art 41 CCPR see E Schwelb, 'Legislative History' 289. cp also Nowak (n 234) Art 12 First OP, para 1; Schwelb (n 51) 849 f; UNCHR 'General Comment No 26 (61) on issues relating to the continuity of obligations to the International Covenant on Civil and Political Rights' (1997) CCPR/C/21/Rev.1/Add.8/Rev.1 paras 2, 5.

[241] For the customary nature of Art 39 and its alleged focus on bilateral treaties cp K Odendahl, 'Article 39' paras 2, 7 to P Sands, 'Article 39' paras 17–19, 25 f.

[242] cp Art 2(1)(g) VCLT: '"party" means a State which has consented to be bound by the treaty and for which the treaty is in force'. This definition is today commonly accepted and used (P Gautier, 'Article 2' para 48).

[243] Aust (n 86) 258.

or reject amendments.[244] Even though many freedoms are granted to the states regarding the liberty to shape their declarations with reservations, one cannot presume that the General Assembly waived all its control over the Optional Clause. A compromise would be an 'approval by the GA of amendments adopted by the States parties',[245] which would accommodate the competence of the states and the General Assembly. One could consider applying Article 40 VCLT *and* Article 69 of the Statute to ensure the position of the General Assembly and the states parties of the Optional Clause.

Another solution to this issue has already been provided for in Article 51 CCPR and Article 11 of its first optional clause. The former reads as follows:

> Any State Party to the present Covenant may propose an amendment and file it with the Secretary-General of the United Nations. The Secretary-General of the United Nations shall thereupon communicate any proposed amendments to the States Parties to the present Covenant with a request that they notify him whether they favour a conference of States Parties for the purpose of considering and voting upon the proposals. In the event that at least one third of the States Parties favours such a conference, the Secretary-General shall convene the conference under the auspices of the United Nations. Any amendment adopted by a majority of the States Parties present and voting at the conference shall be submitted to the General Assembly of the United Nations for approval ... Amendments shall come into force when they have been approved by the General Assembly of the United Nations and accepted by a two-thirds majority of the States Parties to the present Covenant in accordance with their respective constitutional processes ... When amendments come into force, they shall be binding on those States Parties which have accepted them, other States Parties still being bound by the provisions of the present Covenant and any earlier amendment which they have accepted.[246]

This provision was a compromise between two schools of thought. One had favoured the will of the contracting states while the other had favoured the control of the General Assembly.[247] The CCPR's compromise grants influence to both entities and was repeated later in Article 50 CRC (Convention on the Rights of the Child) and Article 18 of the Optional Protocol to the CEDAW (Convention on the Elimination of All Forms of Discrimination Against Women) of 1999.[248] With regard to the similarities between the situations under the CCPR and the Optional Clause it might

---

[244] See also the similar argument for the CCPR in MJ Bossuyt, *Guide* 770–72; Nowak (n 234) Art 51, para 4.

[245] For the notion see ibid Art 51, para 5.

[246] See also Art 29 CESCR and Art 19 of the Optional Protocol of the CESCR.

[247] cp Bossuyt (n 244) 770–72.

[248] But see also the different solutions in Art 29 of the Convention against Torture, Art 26 CEDAW and Art 23 CERD. These refer either to the General Assembly (CEDAW, CERD) or the states parties (Convention against Torture). For Klabbers the provisions of the CEDAW and similar treaties have just been used to postpone the decision on how to amend these treaties (J Klabbers, 'Amendment' para 2).

be worth considering applying these rules to the Optional Clause by analogy. Against an analogy to Article 51 CCPR it could, however, be said that especially its details are the result of a rather complex drafting procedure with different emphasis on either the General Assembly or the state parties.[249] Nonetheless, the solution evades the problems raised by an application of Article 40 VCLT or Article 69 of the Statute alone.[250]

ii. Amendments of the Optional Clause in Practice

Leaving the introduction of the new Statute in 1945 aside, up to now Article 36 of the Statute has never been explicitly amended.

However, what can be considered as amendments are the changes concerning the regime for reservations and the rules for the entry into force of declarations. As said above it has generally been state practice which has shaped the regime for reservations as the drafters of the Statute of the Permanent Court did not consider the issue. Backed by two resolutions of the General Assembly of the League of Nations states established an ongoing practice of making reservations and in 1945 the drafters of the current Statute therefore considered it as unnecessary to amend the wording of the Optional Clause as they considered the freedom to make reservations as having been established.[251]

The question is to what extent this freedom was established by the General Assembly of the League of Nations. Concerning the last one of the already mentioned resolutions Lamm wrote that it was 'a political declaration without any binding force'.[252] For Maus, too, the interpretation of the Optional Clause by the General Assembly of the League of Nations could have had no binding force because the assembly was not entitled to interpret the Statute of the Permanent Court. Maus argued that that Statute was a separate treaty independent of the Covenant and that the body of Member States of Statute and Covenant were not the same. According to him, only the Permanent Court (according to Article 36(4) of its Statute) and all the Member States of the Statute of the Permanent Court would have been able to make a binding interpretation.[253]

Concerning this argument, however, it can be said that in those days the possibility to amend the Statute of the Permanent Court generally was a controversial issue. In 1926, the delegates of the signatory states of the Statute of the Permanent Court heavily argued on this issue. While,

---

[249] cp Bossuyt (n 244) 770–77; Nowak (n 234) Art 51, paras 3, 6.
[250] Another possibility could be to interpret the ratification requirement of Art 108 of the Charter as referring to the parties of the Optional Clause. For that requirement see Karl (n 98) paras 24–34.
[251] cp sub-s III A and B iv b 2 of ch 5 at 200 and 228.
[252] V Lamm, 'Reservations to Declarations' 124.
[253] Maus (n 23) 19. See also Wittmann (n 7) 324.

for example, the New Zealand delegate Bell considered the signatories of the Statute as incompetent to amend it without the consent of the General Assembly or the Council of the League,[254] the Italian delegate Pilotti emphasised the character of the Statute as an international covenant. Pilotti argued that the Statute 'did not derive its authority from the Assembly of the League of Nations' and that therefore no approval by the assembly was necessary.[255] The Belgian delegate Rolin took into consideration both, the character of the Statute as a convention and the approval it had received by the General Assembly. Unfortunately rather vague, he is reported as having concluded that due to his statements 'both' was necessary.[256] Be this as it may, as the freedom to make reservations has been established not only by the General Assembly of the League of Nations but also by the states making their Optional Clause declarations and the other states which did not object to this, it can be said that there has been at least a certain cooperation between the General Assembly and the Member States of the Optional Clause in this regard.

Yet, this is different concerning the reservations allowing withdrawals without a period of notice and the immediate entry into force of Optional Clause declarations. As mentioned above these two aspects have strongly been shaped by the practice of the Member States of the Optional Clause.[257] There were no corresponding resolutions by a General Assembly for this even though the assembly addressed the Optional Clause and the reservations in 1947 and 1974.[258] However, for the two aspects of the Optional Clause in question it could be said that state practice decided issues which had not been clearly provided for in the Statute,[259] and that therefore the General Assembly did not consider itself as being confronted with a real amendment.

iii. Result

In total, it can be said that clear statements concerning the amendment of the Optional Clause are difficult as up to now there is a dearth of practice in this regard. From a theoretical point of view, the arguments presented

---

[254] League of Nations, 'Minutes of the Conference of States Signatories of the Protocol of Signature of the Statute of the Permanent Court of International Justice' (1926) 55 f (Bell). See also ibid 60 (Latham).
[255] ibid 61 (Pilotti).
[256] ibid 61 (Rolin).
[257] cp sub-s III D of ch 3 at 108 and sub-s III B v b of ch 5 at 236.
[258] UNGA 'Review of the role of the International Court of Justice' (12.11.1974) UN Doc A/Res/3232 (XXIX); UNGA 'Resolution on the International Covenant on Economic, Social and Cultural Rights, the International Covenant on Civil and Political Rights and the Optional Protocol to the International Covenant on Civil and Political Rights' (16.12.1966) UN Doc A/RES/2200 (XXI).
[259] cp sub-s III C of ch 3 at 102 and sub-s III B iv of ch 5 at 224.

support an approach involving both the General Assembly and the Member States of the Optional Clause.

B. The Relationship of Optional Clause Declarations and Agreements

What has been said above, however, only applies to amendments of the Optional Clause itself. Another question is whether a state can withdraw its Optional Clause declaration with the consent of all Member States or maybe just with the consent of some states. In this regard there might be a difference between Optional Clause declarations and the accessions to other treaties.

To answer this question the relation between the obligations arising under the Optional Clause and those arising under other treaties will be taken into consideration, too. The question in this regard is what prevails if two or more states conclude a treaty besides their Optional Clause declarations. This is particularly crucial in cases in which there are reservations attached to one declaration of accession but not to the other.

It was especially Maus who considered this issue. Like Hersch Lauterpacht and Ténékidès,[260] he considered the making of an Optional Clause declaration to be like the conclusion of a treaty. Therefore for him the general principles of concurring acts applied and *lex posterior* and *lex specialis* should generally prevail. Yet, Maus emphasised above all the importance of the intention of the parties and maintained further that the jurisdiction established by the Optional Clause was neither always more general nor always more special.[261] The question is to what extent Maus's position is right.

i. The VCLT's Provisions on Subsequent Treaties Applied on the Optional Clause

To answer this question one has to distinguish first between agreements which only aim at the withdrawal of a state from the Optional Clause and treaties which do not, or at least not only, concern such a withdrawal.

For the agreements aiming at a withdrawal Article 54(b) VCLT could apply. According to that provision a state can withdraw from a treaty 'at any time by consent of all the parties after consultation with the other contracting states'. Such a withdrawal can take place especially if

---

[260] H Lauterpacht, 'British Reservations' 146; CG Ténékidès, 'Les actes concurrents' 729–33. cp also Wittmann (n 7) 275.

[261] Maus (n 23) 119–21. cp also Ténékidès, ibid 734–36, 738–40; Wittmann, ibid 273–82.

otherwise the state had to observe a period of notice for its withdrawal.[262] For the Optional Clause this would mean that a state can withdraw if all other states having made an Optional Clause declaration consent to that withdrawal.[263] Under treaty law, the consent of states which have not yet expressed their consent to be bound and which only might become members of the Optional Clause is not required.[264]

The next question is whether only some of the states could agree to withdraw or suspend their Optional Clause declarations *inter partes*. In the VCLT, Article 41 provides for 'agreements to modify multilateral treaties between certain of the parties only' and Article 58 provides for the 'suspension of the operation of a multilateral treaty by agreement between certain of the parties only'. While the suspensions under Article 58 VCLT can only be maintained 'temporarily',[265] Article 41 VCLT allows permanent modifications between the parties. According to Giegerich and Sinclair the limitation of Article 58 VCLT does not mean that agreements providing withdrawals *inter partes* are prohibited. According to them such agreements can be based on Article 41 VCLT.[266] Article 41(1)(b) VCLT requires for agreements *inter partes* that

the modification in question is not prohibited by the treaty and:

(1) does not affect the enjoyment by the other parties of their rights under the treaty or the performance of their obligations;
(2) does not relate to a provision, derogation from which is incompatible with the effective execution of the object and purpose of the treaty as a whole.

Concerning these requirements it can be said that the Optional Clause does not explicitly prohibit modifications *inter partes*. The withdrawals under the Optional Clause do furthermore 'not affect the enjoyment by the other parties of their rights under the treaty or the performance of their obligations'. The other states' rights and obligations remain untouched if two or a certain group of states agree to reduce the scope of one or several declarations among themselves. The only question that remains is whether the withdrawal would 'relate to a provision, derogation from which is incompatible with the effective execution of the object and purpose of the treaty as a whole'. In this regard the question is whether the object and purpose of the Optional Clause allows for the relations of the states under it to be bilateralised resurfaces.[267] As discussed above, there is no reason why

---

[262] Aust (n 86) 254.
[263] Hambro (n 8) 143; Maus (n 23) 76; Wittmann (n 7) 200.
[264] Maus, ibid 76. For general treaty law cp T Giegerich, 'Article 54 VCLT' paras 37–46 and K Schmalenbach, 'Article 2' paras 46 f.
[265] M Lanfranchi, 'Article 58' paras 37–39; T Giegerich, 'Article 58 VCLT' paras 17 f.
[266] Giegerich, ibid para 16; IM Sinclair, *VCLT* 185.
[267] K Odendahl, 'Article 41' paras 16–18; A Rigaux and others, 'Article 41' paras 35–39. cp also Giegerich, ibid paras 1–3, 35; Simma (n 110) 349.

this should not be possible. Through the huge numbers of reservations the Optional Clause declarations are framed very individually anyway and there are furthermore good reasons why bilateralisation should be possible.[268] Therefore, modifications according to Article 41 VCLT cause no problems under the Optional Clause.[269]

This does, however, not answer the question how to handle treaties like the General Acts or the Pact of Bogotá which do not only concern the withdrawal of one or several states, but provide their own regime for the compulsory jurisdiction of the Court. For such treaties Article 30 VCLT could apply which deals with 'successive treaties relating to the same subject manner'.[270] As the Optional Clause contains no rule for its relation towards other agreements and Article 103 of the Charter does not apply to it,[271] applying Article 30 VCLT and especially Article 30(4)(a) VCLT seems to pose no problem. Combined with Article 30(3) VCLT that paragraph provides that between the Member States of a subsequent treaty the earlier treaty only applies as far as 'its provisions are compatible with those of the later treaty'. The result of these paragraphs are unequal obligations as the other states remain bound to the earlier treaty, which also applies in the relations between the Member States of the old treaty and those of the new treaty. This is sometimes considered undesirable when there is a need for uniformity of obligations.[272] This does not seem to be the case for the Optional Clause where, as pointed out inter alia in this sub-section, the pairs of obligations are unequal anyway.

Concerning Article 30 VCLT however, there is a debate on whether the earlier treaty is the one which has first been adopted or the one which has first entered into force.[273] Be this as it may, according to Rigaux and Simon Article 30(4) VCLT also applies if the multilateral treaty is concluded after the 'limited' treaty.[274] It can be said that the last legislative intention of the states is decisive.[275] The states can especially provide 'conflict clauses' which regulate the conflict between two treaties.[276] Where there are such

---

[268] See sub-s II C iv c of ch 5 at 195.
[269] For the same result see Wittmann (n 7) 185 f. As the requirements are basically the same this means that suspensions according to Art 58(1) VCLT are likewise possible (cp Giegerich (n 265) para 31).
[270] Art 30 VCLT contains residual rules which are also customary law (Aust (n 86) 202).
[271] For Art 103 of the Charter see also Maus (n 23) 120 f; Wittmann (n 7) 280 f. For the same result under the League of Nations see Ténékidès (n 260) 734. For Art 103 of the Charter see further the discussions presented in the two following sections.
[272] Aust (n 86) 200.
[273] cp ibid 204 to EW Vierdag, 'Time of the Conclusion' 92–96, 110. cp also N Matz-Lück, 'Conflicts' para 26; K Odendahl, 'Article 30' para 11.
[274] Rigaux and others (n 267) para 4. cp also Matz-Lück, ibid para 13.
[275] cp also Odendahl (n 273) para 11 and ILC 'Documents of the Second Part of the 17th Session and of the 18th Session Including the Reports of the Commission to the General Assembly' (n 37) 253, para 3.
[276] Matz-Lück (n 273) paras 1–3; Odendahl (n 273) paras 16–21.

clauses the rules of Article 30(3) and (4) VCLT and the incorporated rule of *lex posterior* do not apply.[277]

ii. The States' Conflict Clauses and Their Pleadings in Court

The question is how states have handled this issue under the Optional Clause.

States have been confronted with the issue as they concluded further treaties which provided the jurisdiction of the Court under Article 36(1) of the Statute or which established other means to settle disputes between them. With regard to the latter treaties states frequently made reservations in their Optional Clause declarations which could be understood as conflict clauses. They excluded for example 'disputes in regard to which the parties to the dispute have agreed or shall agree to have recourse to some other method or methods of settlement'. This practice has been started by the Netherlands in 1921 and has been used steadily since then even though sometimes the wording and the scope of the particular reservation varied.[278] According to Alexandrov reservations of this kind have been used 107 times until 1995.[279] Today, 43 out of the 71 current declarations contain a corresponding reservation.[280] With these reservations it was ensured that the other treaties are the only ones regulating the matter in question. They are neither influenced by Optional Clause declarations nor are these applicable besides them. The other treaties are therefore concluding *leges specialis*. An additional reservation was provided by Cambodia, Malta and Mauritius whose declarations do not cover 'disputes relating to any matter excluded from judicial settlement or compulsory arbitration by virtue of any treaty, convention or other international agreement or instrument to which the [state in question] is a party'. Lithuania has submitted a similar reservation. Regarding the transfer of limitations to the Optional Clause declarations Norway provides in its declaration that

> the limitations and exceptions relating to the settlement of disputes pursuant to the provisions of, and the Norwegian declarations applicable at any given time to, the United Nations Convention on the Law of the Sea of 10 December 1982 and the Agreement of 4 December 1995 for the Implementation of the Provisions of the United Nations Convention on the Law of the Sea of 10 December 1982 relating to the Conservation and Management of Straddling Fish Stocks and Highly Migratory Fish Stocks, shall apply to all disputes concerning the law of the sea.

---

[277] Matz-Lück, ibid para 24; Odendahl, ibid para 21.
[278] For the different types of 'conflict clauses' made to the Optional Clause see Maus (n 23) 121–26.
[279] cp Alexandrov (n 23) 145–47.
[280] See Annex 7.

Besides providing 'conflict clauses' in their Optional Clause declarations, states concluded treaties with 'conflict clauses' relating to the Optional Clause. These clauses contained different solutions. Article 35(4) of the European Convention, for example, provides:

> If a High Contracting Party accepts the compulsory jurisdiction of the International Court of Justice under paragraph 2 of Article 36 of the Statute of the said Court, subject to reservations, or amends any such reservations, that High Contracting Party may by a simple declaration, and subject to the provisions of paragraphs 1 and 2 of this article, make the same reservations to this Convention. Such reservations shall not release the High Contracting Party concerned from its obligations under this Convention in respect of disputes relating to facts or situations prior to the date of the declaration by which they are made. Such disputes shall, however, be submitted to the appropriate procedure under the terms of this Convention within a period of one year from the said date.

Article VIII of the Brussels Treaty of Economic, Social and Cultural Collaboration and Collective Self-Defence of 17 March 1948 provides otherwise:

> The High Contracting Parties will, while the present Treaty remains in force, settle all disputes falling within the scope of Article 36, paragraph 2, of the Statute of the International Court of Justice by referring them to the Court, subject only, in the case of each of them, to any reservation already made by that Party when accepting this clause for compulsory jurisdiction to the extent that that Party may maintain the reservation.[281]

It seems as if, without a provision like the latter Article VIII, reservations made to Optional Clause declarations are generally not transferred to later treaties on peaceful dispute settlement.[282] As the United States signed the Pact of Bogotá, it expressly excluded all disputes which were also excluded from its Optional Clause declaration.[283] It felt the need to express this because it was sure that otherwise the pact would cover these disputes.[284] The United States expressed this conviction also in numerous

---

[281] For the practical solutions offered by this article see Pastor Ridruejo (n 12) 22. For further examples of references to the Optional Clause declarations in treaties see MO Hudson, *Permanent Court* 474.

[282] cp also the joint dissenting opinion of Judges CD Onyeama, HC Dillard, E Jiménez de Aréchaga and CHM Waldock, *ICJ Rep 1974*, paras 84, 86.

[283] cp http://www.oas.org/juridico/english/sigs/a-42.html (last visit on 19 January 2015).

[284] cp also *Border and Transborder Armed Actions (Nicaragua v Honduras)* (Jurisdiction and Admissibility) Counter-Memorial (Nicaragua) paras 137–39; joint dissenting opinion of Judges CD Onyeama, HC Dillard, E Jiménez de Aréchaga and CHM Waldock, *ICJ Rep 1974*, para 85. But see Honduras which maintained that the reservation to the Pact of Bogotá was 'superfluous' (*Border and Transborder Armed Actions (Nicaragua v Honduras)* (Jurisdiction and Admissibility) Memorial (Honduras) 75, fn 2). Against this see *Border and Transborder Armed Actions (Nicaragua v Honduras)* (Jurisdiction and Admissibility) [1988] ICJ Rep 69, paras 38–40. For Honduras' reasons see the following section.

other treaties with compromissory clauses in which it either transferred the reservations from its Optional Clause declarations or added an extra Connally Reservation.[285]

In Court, the issue became relevant in the *Electricity Company of Sofia and Bulgaria* case. In the oral proceedings Rolin stated that it was absurd to assume that the two governments had the intention to provide the jurisdiction of the Court a second time when they concluded a treaty in addition to their earlier Optional Clause declarations. For him it was clear that for the time of its validity the 'traité particulier doit prévaloir sur la clause facultative' and concluded:

> Du 3 février 1933—date de la mise en vigueur du traité de 1931—au 3 février 1938, nos relations ont été régies par le traité. Du 3 février 1938 à nos jours, et pour l'avenir, nos relations sont de nouveau régies par la clause facultative. En 1937, si ma manière de voir est exacte, nous étions donc entièrement sous l'empire du traité de 1931, et la situation était la même au mois de janvier 1938.[286]

Altinoff pleaded against this for Bulgaria that it was neither the expressed nor the implied object of the treaty to influence the Optional Clause declarations. The agreement between Bulgaria and Belgium was like the General Act, which left the Optional Clause declarations wholly intact, too. For Altinoff these treaties were furthermore not able to influence Optional Clause declarations anyway. A change of an Optional Clause declaration would influence the rights of other states, too, and therefore the treaties would be *res inter alios acta*. The Optional Clause declarations could furthermore not be influenced *inter partes* in the relation of Belgium and Bulgaria as for Altinoff, '[u]ne notion juridique existe ou elle n'existe pas, mais elle n'existe pas à moitié'.[287]

The situation in which an Optional Clause declaration with a new reservation follows an earlier treaty was a subject in the case concerning the *Appeal Relating to the Jurisdiction of the ICAO Council*. In this situation Bakhtiar suggested on behalf of Pakistan that a reservation made by India to its Optional Clause declaration could also be invoked by Pakistan in a

---

[285] cp WW Bishop Jr and DP Myers, 'Connally-Amendment' 135–45; United States of America, 'Memorandum' 941 f (Hager); Whiteman (n 233) 1314 f.

[286] *Electricity Company of Sofia and Bulgaria (Belgium v Bulgaria)* (Public Sittings and Pleadings) PCIJ Series C No 88 (Belgium) 406 f (Rolin). See also the dissenting opinion of Judge FJ Urrutia Olano, *PCIJ Series A/B No 77 1939*, 102.

[287] *Electricity Company of Sofia and Bulgaria (Belgium v Bulgaria)*, ibid 436 f (Altinoff). See also the dissenting opinion of Judge FJ Urrutia Olano, *PCIJ Series A/B No 77 1939*, 102 and *Military and Paramilitary Activities in and against Nicaragua (Nicaragua v United States of America)* (Provisional Measures) Oral Proceedings (CR 1984) (Nicaragua) 75 (Brownlie). Altinoff further argued that also the relation between the states and the Court would be influenced. Against this it can be said that the Optional Clause declarations provide no obligations towards the Court (see s II of ch 1 at 22).

case which India had based on another treaty.[288] Palkhilvala answered for
India only that the reservation was 'irrelevant to the issues arising here'.[289]

More expressly than Pakistan before, France argued in the *Nuclear Tests*
cases that its reservation excluding 'différends concernant des activités
se rapportant à l a défense nationale' which it had made to its Optional
Clause declaration also applied to its earlier accession to the General Act.
For France Article 36 of the Statute including its Optional Clause declaration and also including the reservation made to that declaration all fell
under Article 103 of the Charter and therefore took precedence over the
General Act. It held that even without Article 103 of the Charter 'on serait
ramené au problème ordinaire d'un traite postérieur portant sur la même
matière qu'un accord antérieure dans les relations entre les mêmes pays'.
France ascertained that normally a state cannot unilaterally influence earlier treaties by making an Optional Clause declaration but that the General
Act was something different.[290] Against this Australia and New Zealand
rightly argued that the reservation made to the Optional Clause declaration was without relevance to France's obligations under the General Act.
They emphasised that the General Act and the Optional Clause were two
different sources of jurisdiction. They referred to the Court's decision in
the *Electricity Company of Sofia and Bulgaria* case and maintained that the
finding there must hold, especially, when an Optional Clause declaration
follows a treaty. The state making the declaration should not be able to
alter the earlier treaty alone.[291] Lastly, Australia added that also Article
103 of the Charter did not change this as it did not cover Optional Clause
declarations.[292]

Regarding Article XXXI of the Pact of Bogotá Honduras and Nicaragua
heavily argued about its relation to the Optional Clause. In the *Border and
Transborder Armed Actions* case Honduras maintained:

> [I]f the jurisdiction of the Court under Article XXXI was a conventional juris-
> diction under Article 36, paragraph 1, of the Statute and quite separate from
> any jurisdiction under the optional clause, based on the two declarations of
> Honduras (1954) and Nicaragua (1929), there was no reason whatever why

[288] *Appeal Relating to the Jurisdiction of the ICAO Council (India v Pakistan)* Oral Proceedings (CR 1972) (Pakistan) 632 f (Bakhtiar). See also *Appeal Relating to the Jurisdiction of the ICAO Council (India v Pakistan)* (Judgment) [1972] ICJ Rep 46, para 15.
[289] *Appeal Relating to the Jurisdiction of the ICAO Council (India v Pakistan)* Oral Proceedings (CR 1972) (India) 688 (Palkhilvala).
[290] *Nuclear Tests (Australia v France)* Correspondence (France) 347–49, 356 f.
[291] *Nuclear Tests (Australia v France)* (Jurisdiction and Admissibility) Memorial (Australia) paras 353–88; *Nuclear Tests (New Zealand v France)* (Jurisdiction and Admissibility) Memorial (New Zealand) paras 177–87.
[292] *Nuclear Tests (Australia v France)* (Jurisdiction and Admissibility) Memorial (Australia) paras 365, 379–86 referring furthermore to the dissenting opinion of Judge J Basdevant, *ICJ Rep 1957*, 75 f. For Art 103 of the Charter see already n 271 of this ch.

a treaty reservation, operating under Article 36, paragraph 1, of the Statute, should have any effect on a consensual jurisdiction established by two valid declarations under Article 36, paragraph 2.[293]

However, Honduras stressed that this was not the case and maintained that the Optional Clause declarations and the Pact of Bogotá were linked and that therefore the reservations of one also applied for the other. Honduras argued that Article XXXI of the pact had been made to establish one means for jurisdiction in total and that it seemed inconsistent to have one set of conditions governing the Honduran acceptance of the jurisdiction of the Court vis-à-vis other States accepting the Optional Clause and a different set of conditions governing the relations between Honduras and the other parties of the Pact of Bogotá. Honduras emphasised that it had communicated its new declaration of 1986 not only to the Secretary-General of the United Nations but also to the General Secretary of the Organization of American State (OAS) and that all reservations basically referred to Honduras' neighbours which had also been members of the pact. From its perception of the Pact of Bogotá Honduras then inferred that '[s]ince the Reservation applied to Article XXXI, it also applied, by virtue of that very fact, to that article's reference provision, namely Article 36, paragraph 2'.[294] Nicaragua on the other hand argued that 'Article XXXI of the Pact of Bogota provides a wholly independent basis of jurisdiction'. To support this position Nicaragua extensively referred to the intention of the drafters of the pact. It emphasised inter alia that the drafters wanted to enforce compulsory jurisdiction among the American states after their efforts at San Francisco had been fruitless. For Nicaragua they wanted to provide an additional source of jurisdiction 'not dependent on and not qualified by any declarations parties may have made under Art 36 (2)'.[295] In the oral proceedings Honduras maintained its understanding of the drafters' intention and referred inter alia to the wording of Article XXXI of the pact. It also emphasised the means of interpretation provided for in Article 31 VCLT and read the article in the context of other provisions of the pact.[296]

---

[293] *Border and Transborder Armed Actions (Nicaragua v Honduras)* (n 284) 55 (footnote omitted).

[294] ibid 55, 57 f, 74–77. See also Jiménez De Aréchaga for whom the Pact of Bogotá 'contractualised' the 'loose relationships' which resulted from the Optional Clause declarations. Between the member states of the pact 'the jurisdictional link … is only that resulting from Art XXXI of the Pact' (E Jiménez De Aréchaga, 'Compulsory Jurisdiction' 356–60). For the fact that the Optional Clause declarations are normal accessions to a treaty and do not result into 'loose relationships' see ch 2 at 39.

[295] *Border and Transborder Armed Actions (Nicaragua v Honduras)* (Jurisdiction and Admissibility) Counter-Memorial (Nicaragua) paras 107–09, 120–40. cp *Border and Transborder Armed Actions (Nicaragua v Honduras)* (Jurisdiction and Admissibility) [1988] ICJ Rep 69, 74.

[296] *Border and Transborder Armed Actions (Nicaragua v Honduras)* (n 161) (Honduras) 48–62 (Dupuy). Against this see *Border and Transborder Armed Actions (Nicaragua v Honduras)* (n 161) (Nicaragua) 84–88 (Chayes).

In the later *Territorial and Maritime Dispute* Nicaragua again referred to the Optional Clause and Article XXXI of the Pact of Bogotá as two different sources of jurisdiction. Colombia did not object to this but held that wherever the Pact of Bogotá applied, it applied exclusively as *lex specialis* as Colombia understood the Court's judgment in *Border and Transborder Armed Actions* case in that way. It added that in the case in question the pact was also *lex posterior* because the two Optional Clause declarations had been made before the pact.[297] Conversely Nicaragua wrote that Colombia misunderstood the Court's judgment and referred again to the intention of the drafters of the pact, which had been to broaden the jurisdiction of the Court and not to restrict it.[298]

In the recent case concerning *Questions relating to the Seizure and Detention of Certain Documents and Data*, Australia emphasised Article 23 of the Timor Sea Treaty. That Article 23 provides inter alia that

> any dispute concerning the interpretation or application of this Treaty shall, as far as possible, be settled by consultation or negotiation. Any dispute which is not settled ... shall, at the request of either Australia or East Timor, be submitted to an arbitral tribunal in accordance with the procedure set out in Annex B.

Crawford pleading for Australia considered this article as '*clausula specialia*' to the Optional Clause and furthermore referred to the conflict clause in Australia's Optional Clause declaration.[299]

Especially the later discussions concerning the Pact of Bogotá show that also in the opinion of the states it depends on the intention of the states whether the Optional Clause and other treaties influence each other or whether they are totally independent. The only exceptions so far came from Bulgaria, represented by Altinoff, who argued that states could not influence their relationship arising from the Optional Clause, as a corresponding agreement would be *res inter alia acta*. But nonetheless even he also emphasised that the states concluding the subsequent treaty had not wanted to influence their earlier Optional Clause declarations.

The fact that the intention of the states is crucial poses no problem in cases where the states clearly pronounce on this issue. In cases involving the 43 Optional Clause declarations referred to above, it is clear that a treaty providing for another means of peaceful dispute settlement is not influenced by the Optional Clause and that the Optional Clause provides no

---

[297] *Territorial and Maritime Dispute (Nicaragua v Colombia)* (n 135) 109–12; *Territorial and Maritime Dispute (Nicaragua v Colombia)* (Preliminary Objections) Oral Proceedings (CR 2007/16) (Colombia) 29–31 (Weil). cp also *Territorial and Maritime Dispute (Nicaragua v Colombia)* (n 173) paras 12–14, 43 f, 121–28.

[298] *Territorial and Maritime Dispute (Nicaragua v Colombia)* (Preliminary Objections) Written Statement (Nicaragua) 137–39; *Territorial and Maritime Dispute (Nicaragua v Colombia)* (Preliminary Objections) Oral Proceedings (CR 2007/17) (Nicaragua) 59 f (Pellet).

[299] *Questions relating to the Seizure and Detention of Certain Documents and Data (Timor-Leste v Australia)* (Provisional Measures) Oral Proceedings (CR 2014/2) (Australia) 43 f (Crawford).

jurisdiction besides it.[300] Furthermore, the reservations in these Optional Clause declarations ensure the scope of the Optional Clause declarations is reduced with subsequent agreements in these relations. A problem arises, however, when the states have not clearly pronounced on the relation of the Optional Clause and the other treaty as it happened in Article XXXI of the Pact of Bogotá.

iii. Jurisprudence: The Courts' Judgments and the Individual Opinions

The most prominent statement by the Courts on this issue came from the Permanent Court in 1939. In the *Electricity Company of Sofia* case it ruled:

> [T]he multiplicity of agreements concluded accepting the compulsory jurisdiction is evidence that the contracting Parties intended to open up new ways of access to the Court rather than to close old ways or to allow them to cancel each other with the ultimate result that no jurisdiction would remain. In concluding the treaty of conciliation, arbitration and judicial settlement, the object of Belgium and Bulgaria was to institute a very complete system of mutual obligations with a view to the pacific settlement of any disputes which might arise between them. There is, however, no justification for holding that in doing so they intended to weaken the obligation which they had previously entered into with a similar purpose.[301]

This statement could be understood as implying that the treaties providing jurisdiction under Article 36(1) of the Statute and the Optional Clause should always be regarded as being separate and independent. Verzijl wrote that according to the Court 'a multiplicity of concurring titles of jurisdiction *must* be interpreted in the sense that the parties wish to extend compulsory jurisdiction rather than to restrict it'.[302] However, another reading of the judgment is more convincing. What the Court referred to was the intention of the states. Only because the states did not intend to weaken the obligation they had previously entered they did not weaken it. There is no reason to assume that states could not have influenced the obligation previously accepted if they had wanted to. In this respect, in the Court's judgment the multiplicity of agreements was just evidence for the intention of the parties.[303]

This also seems to have been the position of the individual judges. Concerning the Optional Clause declarations Judge Urrutia Olano wrote:

> The undertaking could be modified either by extending or restricting the obligations, or by supplementary provisions embodied in some later agreement.... In the present case it is the Treaty, which is a *later law* between the Parties, a

---

[300] cp also Ténékidès (n 260) 725–28.

[301] *Electricity Company of Sofia and Bulgaria (Belgium v Bulgaria)* (Preliminary Objection) PCIJ Series A/B No 77 63, 76.

[302] Verzijl (n 93) 608 (emphasis added).

[303] See also Hudson (n 281) 473 f; Maus (n 23) 118 f; Wittmann (n 7) 276 f and especially the joint dissenting opinion of Judges CD Onyeama, HC Dillard, E Jiménez de Aréchaga and CHM Waldock, *ICJ Rep 1974*, para 88.

special law, the text of which is so perfectly clear that there can be no choice of construction, still less any confusion.[304]

Therefore, according to Judge Urrutia Olano the states could not invoke their Optional Clause reservations during the period in which the treaty prevailed. Judge Hudson wrote that the relation between the text of the treaty and the text of the declarations cannot be disregarded. He inferred from the intention of the states that only the treaty was applicable.[305] According to Judge Van Eysinga states are free to modify the method for their pacific settlement established through the declarations by concluding treaties.[306] Judge Anzilotti, however, maintained that the same facts could not be ruled by two different provisions at the time and as a general principle one provision had to prevail. If the interpretation of a later treaty with a compromissory clause showed that the earlier treaty alone should decide upon the jurisdiction of the Court only the earlier treaty would take precedence.[307] It becomes clear that these judges, too, sought for the intention of the states and assumed that states could modify earlier Optional Clause declarations if they want to.

Concerning Optional Clause declarations following a treaty Judge Basdevant wrote in the *Norwegian Loans* case that it was consistent to let the reservations in Optional Clause declarations prevail over an earlier treaty when the declarations of all states involved contained that reservation. However, he rightly went on by saying that when only one state makes this reservation at a later point this is not sufficient. The reservation attached to the French Optional Clause was therefore not able to influence the earlier treaties concluded by France and Norway.[308] This was also how the Court subsequently decided the *Appeal Relating to the Jurisdiction of the ICAO Council* case. In this case the Court relied on the treaties providing its jurisdiction and did not refer to the Commonwealth reservation India had attached to its Optional Clause later. The Court held: 'In any event, such matters would become material only if it should appear that the Treaties and their jurisdictional clauses did not suffice, and that the Court's jurisdiction must be sought outside them'.[309]

In the *Nuclear Tests* cases the Court did not consider this question because it already denied the existence of a dispute.[310] However, the

---

[304] Dissenting opinion of Judge FJ Urrutia Olano, *PCIJ Series A/B No 77 1939*, 103.

[305] Dissenting opinion of Judge MO Hudson, *PCIJ Series A/B No 77 1939*, 125–32.

[306] Dissenting opinion of Judge WJM Jonkheer van Eysinga, *PCIJ Series A/B No 77 1939*, 109–11.

[307] Separate opinion of Judge D Anzilotti, *PCIJ Series A/B No 77 1939*, 89–93.

[308] Dissenting opinion of Judge J Basdevant, *ICJ Rep 1957*, 75 f. Supported by Alexandrov (n 23) 100; dissenting opinion of Judge F De Castro, *ICJ Rep 1974*, 383 f.

[309] *Appeal Relating to the Jurisdiction of the ICAO Council (India v Pakistan)* (n 288) paras 15, 46.

[310] cp *Nuclear Tests (Australia v France)* (Judgment) [1974] ICJ Rep 253, paras 21–24. See also Alexandrov (n 23) 99.

presentation of the Judges Dillard, Jiménez de Aréchaga, Onyeama and Waldock is very revealing. These judges extensively argued against the transfer of a reservation from a single Optional Clause declaration to the prior General Act. With reference to prior decisions of the Court and the existence of Article 36(5) and Article 37 of the Statute, they emphasised that the Optional Clause and the treaties falling under Article 36(1) of the Statute are different and separate sources of jurisdiction. Also for these judges the earlier consent between the states expressed in the General Act cannot be influenced by a later unilateral action. With reference to the European Convention the Judges wrote that the only exception could come from a clear empowerment in the treaty itself which weakened the commitment entered into and opened it for unilateral changes. They emphasised that 'whenever States [had] desired to establish a link between reservations to jurisdiction under the optional clause and jurisdiction under a treaty, this [had] been done by an express provision to that effect'. Also for the four judges Article 103 of the Charter did not apply. They argued that the obligations in question resulted from the Optional Clause and not from the Charter or the Statute. Furthermore they held that, if Article 103 of the Charter applied to the Optional Clause, it also applied to the treaties falling under Article 36(1) of the Statute.[311] This position of the judges supports the impression that the General Act, too, is generally providing jurisdiction independently of the Optional Clause.[312]

Concerning Article XXXI of the Pact of Bogotá the Court made clear that it also considered these as two different sources providing its jurisdiction. In the judgment on the *Border and Transborder Armed Actions* between Nicaragua and Honduras the Court emphasised that the Pact of Bogotá is

an autonomous commitment, independent of any other which the parties may have undertaken or may undertake by depositing with the United Nations Secretary-General a declaration of acceptance of compulsory jurisdiction under Article 36, paragraphs 2 and 4, of the Statute.

The Court again decided that the relation of the Optional Clause and the other treaty depended on the intention of the states and referred to *travaux préparatoires* of the pact. There it had been maintained that states

---

[311] Joint dissenting opinion of Judges CD Onyeama, HC Dillard, E Jiménez de Aréchaga and CHM Waldock, *ICJ Rep 1974*, paras 77–91. cp also the dissenting opinion of Judge G Barwick, *ICJ Rep 1974*, 416–20. See also Alexandrov, ibid 99–102. For Art 36(5) and Art 37 of the Statute see sub-s II B iii of ch 2 at 62.

[312] JG Merrills, 'General Act' 161. See also Gallus who already held so before and additionally wrote that where the Optional Clause and the General Act both cover the dispute the General Act is subsidiary to the Optional Clause according to its Art 29(2) (Gallus, 'L'acte général' 394 f, see also Ténékidès (n 260) 726). See, however, also Hudson who described the situation resulting from Art 29 of General Act as being 'somewhat uncertain' (Hudson (n 281) 475) and furthermore Judge Oda who maintained that the General Act provides no jurisdiction in addition to the Optional Clause declarations (separate opinion of Judge S Oda, *ICJ Rep 2000*, paras 11–17).

which want to maintain their own reservations attached to their Optional Clauses should repeat them for their accessions to the pact. The Court therefore came to the result that the declaration of Honduras

> cannot in any event restrict the commitment which Honduras entered into by virtue of Article XXXI [of the Pact of Bogotá]. The Honduran argument as to the effect of the reservation to its 1986 Declaration on its commitment under Article XXXI of the Pact therefore cannot be accepted.[313]

In the more recent judgment of 2007 on the *Territorial and Maritime Dispute* between Colombia and Nicaragua the Court again maintained that 'the Pact of Bogotá and the declarations made under the Optional Clause represent two distinct bases of the Court's jurisdiction which are not mutually exclusive'. The Court also stated that the Pact of Bogotá was 'particular' and the Optional Clause 'more general' but also made clear that from its perspective this did not mean that therefore the pact prevailed over the latter. It therefore concluded that the 'limitation imposed by Article VI of the Pact would not be applicable to jurisdiction under the optional clause'.[314] Conversely Judge Abraham wrote that he considered the Pact of Bogotá as having established an exclusive regime for the jurisdiction of the Court and rendered the Optional Clause declarations between the states involved inoperative. For him the Court established a general rule that multiple sources provide jurisdiction additional to each other in its judgment in the *Electricity Company of Sofia* case. Due to the language used in the Pact of Bogotá he considered it as providing otherwise.[315]

iv. Result

Regarding the relation between the Optional Clause and treaties it can be concluded that the law of treaties, state practice and jurisprudence provide one similar picture. It depends on the states' mutual intentions whether they want to influence their earlier obligations.[316] This is easy

---

[313] *Border and Transborder Armed Actions (Nicaragua v Honduras)* (Jurisdiction and Admissibility) [1988] ICJ Rep 69, paras 34–41; supported by Shahabuddeen who even considered the possibility of two parallel declarations under Art 36(2) of the Statute (separate opinion of Judge M Shahabuddeen, *ICJ Rep 1988*, 133–44). But see also the already mentioned (n 218) position of Oda for whom Art XXXI of the Pact of Bogotá itself provides no jurisdiction (separate opinion of Judge S Oda, *ICJ Rep 1988*, paras 1–15).

[314] *Territorial and Maritime Dispute (Nicaragua v Colombia)* (n 173) paras 133, 136 f. See also the dissenting opinion of Judge AS Al-Khasawneh, *ICJ Rep 2007*, para 18; declaration of Judge B Simma, *ICJ Rep 2007*, 897.

[315] Separate opinion of Judge R Abraham, *ICJ Rep 2007*, paras 52–55. See also Judge Parra-Aranguren (declaration of Judge G Parra-Aranguren, *ICJ Rep 2007*, 892) whose position has already been presented above at sub-s III B of ch 2 at 71 and see also Judge Bennouna who left this question undecided (dissenting opinion of Judge M Bennouna, *ICJ Rep 2007*, 929 f).

[316] So already Maus (n 23) 119; Ténékidès (n 260) 725–29, 735, 738–40; Wittmann (n 7) 275–77.

where the states make provisions expressly dealing with the relation of the treaties and later or earlier Optional Clause declarations. They can, for example, state that the reservations made to their accession to an earlier treaty shall also apply to their later Optional Clause declarations or that their reservations made to their earlier Optional Clause declarations shall also apply to the later treaty. What states cannot do is to influence an earlier treaty with a single Optional Clause declaration made later. They can only do so when the earlier treaty like the European Convention allows it. The situation is more difficult with treaties like the Pact of Bogotá, for which the intention of its drafters concerning its relation to the Optional Clause is hard to define. According to the Court Article XXXI of the pact and the Optional Clause are two separate sources of its jurisdiction which do not influence each other.

IV. RESULT

In total it can be said that also concerning the ending or the reduction of a commitment under the Optional Clause there is no difference to treaty law. Like under other multilateral treaties states can generally only withdraw according to the terms of the treaty or, respectively, the terms of a reservation. Besides, they can invoke the principle of *clausula rebus sic stantibus* or withdraw as consequence of a breach of the Optional Clause by another state. Whether states can withdraw with a period of notice even though their declaration provides anything in this regard depends on the intention of the drafters of the Optional Clause. According to the Court, states can withdraw from the Optional Clause with a period of 'reasonable time'. This is very close to Article 56(2) of the Statute and commentators of that article refer to the Court's decision on the Optional Clause to show the article's customary basis in the law of treaties. Moreover, states can withdraw with the consent of all other states having made an Optional Clause declaration or only vis-à-vis a single state with the consent of that state. Whether the Optional Clause and other treaties influence each other depends on the mutual intention of the states concluding the treaty and the *terms* of the Optional Clause declarations.

Conclusion

THE OPTIONAL CLAUSE can very well be considered a treaty. The current work shows that all characteristics of the Optional Clause can be explained with an application of treaty law. In some aspects treaty law is even based on the Optional Clause and in others treaty law and the Optional Clause are at least entangled.

With regard to the obligations arising under the Optional Clause it can be said that these are obligations vis-à-vis other states which arise as soon as an Optional Clause declaration becomes effective. There are no obligations vis-à-vis the Court. The idea that the obligation exists before an application is filed can be based on a comparison to other means providing for the jurisdiction of the Court under Article 36(1) of the Statute. In comparison to the *forum prorogatum* and the ad hoc jurisdiction covered by that paragraph, the Optional Clause in Article 36(2) of the Statute shall generally provide a longstanding and abstract jurisdiction which is not related to a certain dispute. This necessarily requires an obligation which exists before an application is filed. This obligation directly corresponds to a right of the other states, not to any right of the Court, which can be proved not only by the genesis of the Optional Clause but also with a survey of current state practice. States used Optional Clause declarations as an offensive means to be able to file applications themselves. They did not make their declarations to grant a right to the Court. They considered the Optional Clause as providing rights for themselves as it enabled them to sue other states. This can be supported with the opinion of bodies of human rights treaties on the Optional Clause. They emphasised that their optional clauses were different to the one in the Statute of the Court as the latter established reciprocal rights and obligations between the states.

From this point of view it can be inferred that Optional Clause declarations are not purely unilateral declarations. These can only result in obligations for the submitting state. As the declarations under Article 36(2) of the Statute also provide rights for the submitting state, every rule deduced from that characteristic of unilateral declarations cannot be applied to the Optional Clause declarations. They are as unilateral as any other declaration of accession to a multilateral treaty. These, too, are drafted by only one state and are not accompanied by negotiations. This result can be supported by a comparison with other optional clauses. As in their cases the major treaty of the Optional Clause, the Statute, contains no obligation for the states concerning the issue covered by the clause. Parallel to the case of optional protocols, the group of states accepting the clause undertakes a further commitment. Optional Protocols are indisputably considered as treaties. The result that the Optional Clause can be considered a treaty can further be backed by the genesis of the Optional Clause, which points in this direction. The idea for the clause arose from the perceived necessity to draft a second treaty besides the Statute of the Permanent Court, because the Covenant was said to prohibit compulsory jurisdiction directly in the Statute of the Permanent Court. The statements of the Statute's drafters show that they never abandoned this original direction. As state practice does not contradict this result either, there is no reason not to apply treaty law to the Optional Clause as to any other treaty.[1]

Concerning the accession to the Optional Clause it can be said that this accession is a choice which is as free as every other accession to a multilateral treaty. The Optional Clause is not particular in this regard. And, like other accessions Optional Clause declarations do not need to be ratified either. That some states made their accession subject to ratification can happen in the case of other multilateral treaties, too. In those cases the accessions are mere letters of intent which do not yet result in obligations provided for in the treaty. Concerning the entry into force of Optional Clause declarations the Optional Clause is specifically linked to the law of treaties as the corresponding parts of the VCLT are based on the jurisprudence of the Court on the Optional Clause. Under the Optional Clause there have been good reasons to maintain that Optional Clause declarations do not enter into force before other states have received the notice by the Secretary-General provided for in Article 36(4) of the Statute. However, state practice has in any case rendered the Optional Clause declarations as entering into force as soon as the Secretary-General receives them, and this is how the Optional Clause has influenced the law of treaties. Especially with regard to the latter point it cannot be held that an Optional Clause declaration results in a higher insecurity than the accession to other multilateral treaties. Under the Optional Clause states are furthermore able to attach Anti Ambush Clauses to their declarations to protect themselves against states which accept the Optional Clause for ad hoc jurisdiction.

Optional Clause declarations are furthermore not interpreted differently to other declarations of accession. Like in treaty law, general restrictive

---

[1] The result that the Optional Clause is basically a treaty might also hold true for other optional clauses. Just like other accessions to a multilateral treaty their declarations are unilateral. An optional clause is only drafted together with another treaty and combined with it. Besides a certain declaration in principle, there seems to be no legally significant difference (cp E Schwelb, 'Measures of Implementation' 862 and see also Fuchs (E Fuchs, 'Optional Provision') who made no distinction between the different 'optional provisions'). Furthermore, as far as this holds true, it seems to be better to draft optional protocols instead of pressing all treaty provisions including those for reservations, amendments and withdrawals into the paragraphs of one article as it happened in the case of Art 41 CCPR or Art 36(2) to (4) of the Statute.

interpretation can be considered as a phenomenon of the past. It is true that the Court referred to domestic material, like national legislative acts, to interpret Optional Clause declarations, but it has already acted similarly for the interpretation of treaties and reservations made to declarations of accession to a treaty. The rule of *contra proferentem* has not been applied to Optional Clause declarations by the Court, but it is unclear whether the Court would have applied the rule to the accession to another treaty in a similar case. In any case there is no reason to treat Optional Clause declarations differently in this regard. The same holds true for the rule of effectiveness if it is understood as a means to establish the intention of the author of an international act. States making an Optional Clause declaration can be understood as having the intention to accept the jurisdiction of the Court. States making a reservation can be understood as having the intention to exclude that jurisdiction for certain disputes. Like in the case of other instruments it can be assumed that states include no unnecessary words in their declarations. However, the assumption can be rebutted when it can be shown that a state had a reason to do so and acted, for example, only *ex abundanti cautela*. With a view to the International Law Commision (ILC)'s recent Guideline 4.2.6 GPRT (Guide to Practice on Reservations to Treaties) concerning the interpretation of reservations it can even be said that the way to interpret Optional Clause declarations was adopted for all declarations with reservations. It seems as if the whole *sui generis* aspect of the Optional Clause in this regard was nothing more than the fact that under the Optional Clause primarily the declarations of accession and not the Optional Clause itself had to be interpreted.

In relation to reservations made to Optional Clause declarations, much confusion has been caused by the 'principle of reciprocity'. This principle repeats what Article 21 VCLT (Vienna Convention on the Law of Treaties) already provides. According to both, principle and article, reservations work for all parties involved. Under the Optional Clause there is no reason to treat any reservation differently either. Even reservations allowing withdrawals are no exception and every other result would lead to inequality and a race to the bottom regarding the level of commitment in this regard. This cannot be the result the drafters would have wanted as for them reciprocity was important and they would not have departed from that principle without reason. Concerning the permissibility of reservations the Optional Clause is rather generous with the states. Especially state practice shaped an Optional Clause which today allows the making of almost any reservation. In 1945, this was endorsed by the drafters of the current Statute. The only exceptions are subjective reservations whose scope depends on a decision by the submitting state. This generosity of the Optional Clause is, however, no characteristic which distinguishes it from general treaty law. Article 19 VCLT also allows all reservations and only makes exceptions according to Article 19(a) to (c) VCLT. The subjective reservations fall under Article 19(c) VCLT. And also the rules of Article 20 VCLT are not at variance with the practice under the Optional Clause. As states made new reservations they basically considered them as being like those which have been expressly provided for in Article 36(3) of the Statute. Also with regard to the attitude of the drafters of the Statute in 1945 it can thus be said that the Optional Clause provides otherwise in the sense of Article 20(4) VCLT and that therefore no objections are allowed.

Regarding the subject of the last chapter it can be said that Optional Clause declarations can be withdrawn like every other declaration of accession to a multilateral treaty. State practice supports this particularly with regard to the principle *clausula rebus sic stantibus* as provided for in Article 62(1) VCLT. According to state practice and the jurisprudence of the Court the states are furthermore bound to the provisions of their declarations. According to the Court states whose declarations are silent in this regard can withdraw these after a notice and the lapse of 'reasonable time'. Such a period of notice is not required if a state withdraws its Optional Clause declaration or adds a new reservation with the consent of the other states. If states conclude subsequent treaties it is a question of their intention whether they influence their Optional Clause declaration vis-à-vis each other.

In the matter of the imbalances under the Optional Clause as addressed in the introduction it has to be said that they really exist. States can submit Optional Clause declarations to have immediate ad hoc jurisdiction for a certain dispute and states can also make reservations allowing withdrawals without a period of notice to reduce their commitment as soon as a dispute arises which they do not wish to have before the Court. However, the Optional Clause is flexible due to the possibility to make reservations and allows states to adjust the situation under the Optional Clause to their needs. The already established Anti Ambush Clauses are one example which should be applied by more states and there are even more possibilities. For example, if states do not want an Optional Clause from which states can withdraw without a period of notice they can make their declarations with a reservation excluding all states with declarations allowing withdrawals without a period of notice.[2] Of course this would exclude many other declarations at the moment, but it opens the gate for all states which likewise want to extend their commitment. Similarly, it is possible that states exclude *ratione personae* all states with declarations they dislike and so shape their relations under the Optional Clause very much according to their needs.[3] It seems as if all problems of the Optional Clause can be solved by the individual states themselves without amending the Statute itself. Verzijl even voiced the idea that states could introduce a

---

[2] cp A D'Amato, 'Modifying' 390, 392, fn 18; LB Sohn, 'Compulsory Jurisdiction' 10 f.
[3] cp SA Alexandrov, *Declarations* 126 f; R Szafarz, *Compulsory Jurisdiction* 49.

reservation excluding other states which have failed to comply with an earlier judgment of the Court.[4]

The reciprocal application of reservations furthermore ensures that for every step a state makes it also gains an equal amount of disputes in which they can then file an application themselves. Law-abiding states can benefit from the opportunity to file an application against other states and protect themselves against another state's unlawful acts. Likewise, if a state chooses to deepen its commitment by introducing a period of notice to its reservation allowing withdrawals, it will also benefit. Other states can no longer invoke its reservation and the state in question can profit from the similar commitments other states have already made. This allows progression at different rates. While some states only want to accede to the Optional Clause with a right to withdraw without period of notice others can establish a higher level of commitment between them providing a period of notice from which all of them profit alike. If states are reluctant to make an Optional Clause declaration because others have none either,[5] they can use the possibility expressly provided and make their declaration 'on condition of reciprocity on the part of several or certain states' as it was already provided in 1920.[6] The Optional Clause is therefore an ideal and secure means to keep track with the political will of states.

As Gerald Fitzmaurice already wrote in 1976, the Statute and the Optional Clause are anything but dysfunctional. Both are very useful for every state which wants to use them.[7] They only require more political commitment and that states proceed on, respectively re-enter, the path of gradual development that was proclaimed in 1920 and 1945.

---

[4] JHW Verzijl, 'Optional Clause' 607.

[5] cp eg WM Reisman, 'Termination' 95.

[6] cp the proposal for the United States by FL Morrison, 'General Discussion' 157 and WM Reisman, 'General Discussion' 183.

[7] GG Fitzmaurice, 'Enlargement' 472–76. See also ILA, Report of the Fifty-First Conference, Tokyo 41 (Green) and R Kolb, *ICJ* 453: 'The period when doubts were being expressed about the effectiveness of the optional clause ... is long since over' (footnote omitted).

Annexes

1. Annex: The Swedish Letter of 1956

Royal Ministry for   Stockholm.
Foreign Affairs   February 23, 1956.

Sir,

By letter of January 19, 1956 (C.N, 127. 1955, Treaties), you have transmitted for the information of my Government a copy of the Declaration made on behalf of the Government of Portugal by the Portuguese Ambassador in Washington in accordance with paragraph 2 of Article 36 of the Statute of the International Court of Justice, recognizing as compulsory *ipso facto* and without special agreement the jurisdiction of the said Court.

The acceptance of the jurisdiction of the Court has, however, been made subject to i.e. the following condition:

> "(3) The Portuguese Government reserves the right to exclude from the scope of the present declaration, at any time during its validity, any given category or categories of disputes, by notifying the Secretary-General of the United Nations and with effect from the moment of such notification."

The Swedish Government is compelled to state that in its opinion the cited condition in reality signifies that Portugal has not bound itself to accept the jurisdiction of the Court with regard to any dispute or any category of disputes. The condition nullifies the obligation intended by the wording of Article 36, paragraph 2, of the Statute where it is said that the recognition of the jurisdiction of the Court shall be "compulsory *ipso facto*".

For the stated reason, the Swedish Government must consider the cited condition as incompatible with a recognition of the "Optional Clause" of the Statute of the International Court of Justice.

Accept, Sir, the assurances of my highest consideration.

For the Minister:
(Signed) K. F. Almqvist.
Assistant Chief of the Legal Department.

The Honourable Dag Hammarskjold,
Secretary-General to the United Nations,
New York.

(*Case concerning Right of Passage over Indian Territory (Portugal v India)*, Pleadings, vol. 1, 217)

2. Annex: The Portuguese Letter of 1956

UNITED NATIONS

Missao Permanente de Portugal
Junto das Nacoes Unidas
New York,   July 5, 1956.

No. 126

Excellency,

At the request of the Swedish Government, the United Nations conveyed to my Government, by letter of April 19, 1956 (CN.40.1956. Treaties), the translation of a letter from the Ministry of Foreign Affairs of Sweden, dated February 23, 1956, commenting upon the Declaration made by the Portuguese Government under Article 36 (2) of the Statute of the International Court of Justice.

2. The unequivocal wording of sub-paragraph (3) of the Declaration offers no basis for the interpretation put upon this particular proviso by the Swedish Government. As, however, the conclusion drawn by the latter is liable to raise doubts regarding the validity of the Declaration, a correction is essential.

3. In no way, indeed, does sub-paragraph (3) warrant the conclusion that the Portuguese Government would be in a position to withdraw from the jurisdiction of the Court any dispute, or category of disputes, already referred to it, for it expressly states that the reservation would only take effect from the date of its notification to the Secretary-General of the United Nations. The Portuguese Declaration thus produces all the effect provided for by article 36 as regards disputes referred to the Court prior to a possible notification. Hence, the interpretation of the Swedish Government is not in accord with the facts.

4. This material flaw would suffice to enable further comment to be dispensed with. Yet in order to show more clearly the absence of any basis for such doubts as to the validity of the Portuguese Declaration it should be mentioned that the contents of sub-paragraph (3) amount to no more than a form—attenuated be it said—of the reservation which several countries have in the past invoked (without ever having thereby given rise to any objections), of the right to abrogate at any time their declarations of acceptance. In any case, the Court alone is competent to pronounce on the validity of these declarations.

5. The Portuguese Government being anxious that no misunderstanding should subsist in regard to a matter the importance of which is such as to require that it should be dealt with in as precise a manner as possible, I should be grateful if Your Excellency would be so good as to transmit the contents of this letter to those Governments and entities to whom copies of the letter from the Ministry of Foreign Affairs of Sweden, under reference, were sent.

I avail myself of this opportunity to present to Your Excellency the assurances of my highest consideration.

(Signed) Albano NOGUEIRA.
Deputy Permanent Representative and
Chargé d'Affaires *a.i.*

His Excellency Dag Hammarskjold,
Secretary-General of the United Nations,
New York.

(Case concerning Right of Passage over Indian Territory (Portugal v India), Pleadings, vol. 1, 218 *et seq*).

3. Annex: The Shultz Letter

DECLARATION OF THE UNITED STATES OF
AMERICA OF APRIL 6, 1984

I have the honour on behalf of the Government of the United States of America to refer to the declaration of my Government of 26 August 1946 concerning the acceptance by the United States of America of the compulsory jurisdiction of the International Court of Justice, and to state that the aforesaid declaration shall not apply to disputes with any Central American State or arising out of or related to events in Central America, any of which disputes shall be settled in such manner as the parties to them may agree.

Notwithstanding the terms of the aforesaid declaration, this proviso shall take effect immediately and shall remain in force for two years, so as to foster the continuing regional dispute settlement process which seeks a negotiated solution to the interrelated political, economic and security problems of Central America.

(Signed)   George P. Shultz,
Secretary of State of the
United States of America.

(AC Arend, *Compulsory Jurisdiction* 211)

4. Annex: Dictamen 54285 (extract)

Consejo de Estado: Dictámenes

Número de expediente: 54285 (ASUNTOS EXTERIORES)

Referencia: 54285

Procedencia: ASUNTOS EXTERIORES

Asunto: Declaración Unilateral española en aceptación de la jurisdicción obligatoria del Tribunal Internacional de Justicia.

Fecha de Aprobación: 25/1/1990

TEXTO DEL DICTAMEN

La comisión permanente del Consejo de Estado, en sesión celebrada el día de la fecha, emitió, por mayoría, el siguiente dictamen:

"En cumplimiento de Orden de V.E. de 13 de diciembre de 1989 el Consejo de Estado ha examinado el expediente relativo a la Declaración Unilateral española de aceptación de la jurisdicción obligatoria del Tribunal Internacional de Justicia.

De antecedentes resulta que:

1. El artículo 36.2 del Estatuto del Tribunal Internacional de Justicia tiene el siguiente tenor:

   "Los Estados partes en el presente Estatuto podrán declarar en cualquier momento que reconocen como obligatoria "ipso facto" y sin convenio especial, respecto a cualquier otro Estado que acepte la misma obligación, la jurisdicción del Tribunal en todas las controversias de orden jurídico que versen sobre:

   a. La interpretación de un tratado; b. Cualquier cuestión de derecho internacional; c. La existencia de todo hecho que, si fuere establecido, constituiría violación de una obligación internacional; d. La naturaleza o extensión de la reparación que ha de hacerse por el quebrantamiento de una obligación internacional".

   El propio artículo 36 continúa diciendo en su apartado 3 que "la declaración a que se refiere este artículo podrá hacerse incondicionalmente o bajo condición de reciprocidad por parte de varios o determinados Estados, o por determinado tiempo".

   Y el artículo 36.4 dispone que "estas declaraciones serán remitidas para su depósito al Secretario General de las Naciones Unidas, quien transmitirá copias de ellas a las partes en este Estatuto y al Secretario del tribunal".

2. El texto de la proyectada Declaración unilateral española de aceptación de la jurisdicción obligatoria del Tribunal Internacional de Justicia, tal como fue autorizado por el Consejo de Ministros de 13 de octubre de 1989, es el siguiente:

"1. Tengo el honor de declarar en nombre del Gobierno español, que el Reino de España reconoce como obligatoria "ipso facto" y sin necesidad de convenio específico, la jurisdicción del Tribunal Internacional de Justicia, conforme a lo dispuesto en el párrafo 2 del artículo 36 del Estatuto de dicho Tribunal, respecto a cualquier otro Estado que haya aceptado la misma obligación, bajo condición de reciprocidad, en las controversias de orden jurídico no comprendidas en los supuestos y excepciones siguientes:

a) Controversias respecto de las cuales el Reino de España y la otra u otras partes hayan convenido o convengan recurrir a un medio pacífico distinto de arreglo de la controversia.

b) Controversias en las que la otra parte o partes hayan aceptado la jurisdicción obligatoria del Tribunal únicamente en lo que concierne a la controversia de que se trate o para los fines exclusivos de la misma.

c) Controversias en las que la otra parte o partes hayan aceptado la jurisdicción obligatoria del Tribunal con menos de doce meses de antelación a la fecha de presentación de la solicitud escrita incoando el procedimiento correspondiente ante el Tribunal.

d) Controversias surgidas antes de la fecha de remisión de la presente Declaración al Secretario General de las Naciones Unidas para su depósito o relativas a hechos o situaciones acecidos con anterioridad a dicha fecha, aunque dichos hechos o situaciones puedan seguir manifestándose o surtiendo efectos con posterioridad a la misma".

"2. El Reino de España podrá completar, modificar o retirar en cualquier momento, en todo o en parte, las reservas arriba mencionadas, así como cualesquiera otras que pudiese formular en el futuro, mediante notificación dirigida al Secretario General de las Naciones Unidas. Estas modificaciones tendrán efectos a partir de la fecha de su recepción por el Secretario General de las Naciones Unidas".

"3. La presente Declaración, que se remite para su depósito al Secretario General de las Naciones Unidas de conformidad con lo dispuesto en el párrafo 4 del artículo 36 del Estatuto del Tribunal Internacional de Justicia, permanecerá en vigor mientras no sea retirada por el Gobierno español o reemplazada por otra declaración de dicho Gobierno. La retirada de la Declaración tendrá efectos una vez transcurrido un período de seis meses contados a partir de la recepción por el Secretario General de las Naciones Unidas de la notificación correspondientes del Gobierno español".

3. [...]

4. [...]

5. [...]

6. [...]

7. Volvió el expediente a este Consejo el 14 de diciembre de 1989, enca-
bezado por una Orden de V.E. en la que se hacía constar la urgen-
cia de la consulta. Al expediente se había incorporado un informe
de la Asesoría Jurídica Internacional de 17 de julio de 1989. En dicho
informe (que se refiere a otro anterior, que no figura en el expediente)
se señala que "la formulación de la declaración supone para España
la aceptación de nuevas obligaciones convencionales establecidas en
el Estatuto de la Corte. Consiguientemente, (...), los trámites internos
son los señalados en la Constitución y las leyes para los tratados inter-
nacionales". A juicio de la Asesoría informante, la Declaración de que
se trata queda comprendida en los apartados a), c), d) y e) del artículo
94.1 de la Constitución. Junto con el informe se encuentra el proyecto
de Declaración unilateral objeto del presente dictamen.

   I. [...]

  II. [...]

III. También merece un juicio favorable al Consejo de Estado la
redacción del proyecto de Declaración que se le ha sometido. Tal
proyecto revela un cuidadoso estudio de las declaraciones for-
mulados por otros Estados, y en él parece detectarse, entre otras,
la influencia de la declaración británica.

Estima este Alto Cuerpo Consultivo que el apartado 3 de la
Declaración proyectada podría perfeccionarse teniendo en cuenta
algunos de los resultados del debate doctrinal a que dió lugar la
decisión del Tribunal Internacional de Justicia de 26 de noviem-
bre de 1984 en el caso Nicaragua vs. Estados Unidos. Entre otros
problemas, la doctrina que comentó este caso estudió el de los
efectos en el tiempo de la retirada de una declaración formulada
al amparo del artículo 36.2 del Estatuto del Tribunal Internacional
de Justicia. En el caso que se contempla, la retirada de la Declaración proyectada "tendrá efectos una vez transcurrido un período
de seis meses contados a partir de la recepción por el Secretario
General de las Naciones Unidas de la notificación correspondiente del Gobierno español". Pues bien, a la luz del principio de
reciprocidad que inspira el artículo 36 del Estatuto del Tribunal
Internacional de Justicia, cabe preguntarse cuándo comenzará a
producir efectos la retirada de la Declaración española en relación
con un Estado que haya fijado un plazo de preaviso más breve

o que no haya establecido plazo alguno. Aunque no hay contestación definitiva a esta pregunta, se ha dicho con acierto que cualquier regla razonable podrá servir de guía al Tribunal Internacional de Justicia. Una de estas reglas, añadida al final del apartado 3 de la Declaración que se proyecta, podría ser la siguiente:

"La retirada de la Declaración tendrá efectos una vez transcurrido un período de seis meses contados a partir de la recepción por el Secretario General de las Naciones Unidas de la notificación correspondiente del Gobierno español. Sin embargo, respecto a Estados que hubieran establecido un período inferior a seis meses entre la notificación y la producción de efectos de la retirada de su Declaración, la retirada de la Declaración española surtirá efectos una vez transcurrido dicho plazo más breve".

Naturalmente, esta cautela no resuelve todos los problemas que podría plantear el apartado 3 de la Declaración, cuyo estudio no puede agotarse aquí; aunque alguno sea tan importante como el de si [...] puede el plazo razonable de producción de efectos de la retirada de la Declaración española ser inferior a seis meses.

IV.   [...]

Y en virtud de lo expuesto, el Consejo de Estado es de dictamen:

Que la formulación de la Declaración unilateral de aceptación por España de la jurisdicción obligatoria del Tribunal Internacional de Justicia requiere la previa autorización de las Cortes Generales".

V.   E., no obstante, resolverá lo que estime más acertado.

Madrid, 25 de enero de 1990

EL SECRETARIO GENERAL,

EL PRESIDENTE,

EXCMO. SR. MINISTRO DE ASUNTOS EXTERIORES.

(This document was available on the webpage of the Consejo de Estado: http://www.boe.es/aeboe/consultas/bases_datos_ce/doc.php?coleccion=ce&id=0-54285 (visit on 31 May 2012))

Legal Opinion 54285 (extract, translated)

Council of State: Legal Opinions

File number: 54285 (FOREIGN AFFAIRS)

Reference: 54285

Source: FOREIGN AFFAIRS

Subject: Unilateral Spanish Declaration of Acceptance of the Compulsory Jurisdiction of the International Court of Justice

Date of Approval: 25/1/1990

TEXT OF THE LEGAL OPINION

The standing committee of the Council of State, in session on the date named, hereby issues the following legal opinion by majority:

"Pursuant to Your Excellency's Order dated 13 December 1989, the Council of State has examined the file on the Unilateral Spanish Declaration of Acceptance of the Compulsory Jurisdiction of the International Court of Justice.

The following were used as background information:

1. Article 36(2) of the Statute of the International Court of Justice reads as follows:

   "The states parties to the present Statute may at any time declare that they recognize as compulsory "ipso facto" and without special agreement, in relation to any other state accepting the same obligation, the jurisdiction of the Court in all legal disputes concerning:

   a. the interpretation of a treaty; b. any question of international law; c. the existence of any fact which, if established, would constitute a breach of an international obligation; d. the nature or extent of the reparation to be made for the breach of an international obligation".

   Article 36(3) goes on by saying that "the declarations referred to above may be made unconditionally or on condition of reciprocity on the part of several or certain states, or for a certain time".

   And Article 36(4) stipulates that "such declarations shall be deposited with the Secretary-General of the United Nations, who shall transmit copies thereof to the parties to the Statute and to the Registrar of the Court".

2. The text of the planned Unilateral Spanish Declaration of Acceptance of the Compulsory Jurisdiction of the International Court of Justice as authorised by the Council of Ministers on 13 October 1989, reads as follows:

"1. On behalf of the Spanish Government, I have the honour to declare that the Kingdom of Spain accepts as compulsory "ipso facto" and without special agreement, the jurisdiction of the International Court of Justice, in conformity with Article 36, paragraph 2, of the Statute of the Court, in relation to any other State accepting the same obligation, on condition of reciprocity, in legal disputes not included among the following situations and exceptions:

a) Disputes in regard to which the Kingdom of Spain and the other party or parties have agreed or shall agree to have recourse to another method of peaceful settlement of the dispute.
b) Disputes in regard to which the other party or parties have accepted the compulsory jurisdiction of the Court only in relation to or for the purposes of the dispute in question.
c) Disputes in regard to which the other party or parties have accepted the compulsory jurisdiction of the Court less than 12 months prior to the filing of the application bringing the dispute before the Court.
d) Disputes arising prior to the date on which this Declaration was deposited with the Secretary-General of the United Nations or relating to events or situations which occurred prior to that date, even if such events or situations may continue to occur or to have effects thereafter".

"2. The Kingdom of Spain may at any time, by means of a notification addressed to the Secretary-General of the United Nations, complete, amend or withdraw, in whole or in part, the foregoing reservations or any that may hereafter be added. These amendments shall become effective on the date of their receipt by the Secretary-General of the United Nations".

"3. The present Declaration, which is deposited with the Secretary General of the United Nations in conformity with Article 36, paragraph 4, of the Statute of the International Court of Justice, shall remain in force until such time as it has been withdrawn by the Spanish Government or superseded by another declaration by the latter. The withdrawal of the Declaration shall become effective after a period of six months has elapsed from the date of receipt by the Secretary-General of the United Nations of the relevant notification by the Spanish Government".

3. [...]

4. [...]

5. [...]

6. [...]

7. The file returned to this Council on 14 December 1989 with an Order from Your Excellency stating the urgency of the enquiry. A report by the International Legal Department dated 17 July 1989 was incorporated into the file. That report (which refers to another, prior report that is not in the file) indicated that "the wording of the declaration assumes Spain's acceptance of new conventional obligations established in the Statute of the Court. Consequently ..., the internal procedures are those indicated in the Constitution and the laws governing international treaties." At the discretion of the informing Department, the Declaration concerned remains falling under Article 94(1)(a), (c), (d), and (e) of the Constitution. Along with the report, the draft of the Unilateral Declaration is the object of the present Legal Opinion.

   I. [...]

  II. [...]

 III. The formulation of the submitted draft Declaration also deserves a favourable judgment from the Council of State. The project shows careful study of the declarations developed by other States and the influence of, among others, the British declaration is detectable.

     This High Advisory Board believes that Paragraph 3 of the draft Declaration could be improved by taking into consideration some of the outcomes of the doctrinal debate caused by the International Court of Justice's decision of 26 November 1984 in the case of Nicaragua v the United States. Among other problems, the doctrine commenting this case considered the temporal aspects of a withdrawal of a declaration articulated under Article 36(2) of the Statute of the International Court of Justice. In the event that it should be considered, the withdrawal of the draft Declaration "shall become effective after a period of six months has elapsed from the date of receipt by the Secretary-General of the United Nations of the relevant notification by the Spanish Government". However, in consideration of the principle of reciprocity underlying Article 36 of the Statute of the International Court of Justice, one might wonder when the withdrawal of the Spanish Declaration will start to have an impact with respect to a State that has set a shorter period of notice or that has not provided any period of notice at all. While this question has no definitive answer, it has been correctly said that any reasonable rule could be a guideline for the International Court of Justice. One of those rules, added at the end of Section 3 of the planned Declaration, could be the following:

> 'The withdrawal of the Declaration shall become effective after a period of six months has elapsed from the date of receipt by the Secretary-General of the United Nations of the relevant notification by the Spanish Government. However, in respect of States which have established a period of less than six months between notification of the withdrawal of their Declaration and its becoming effective, the withdrawal of the Spanish Declaration shall become effective after such shorter period has elapsed'.

Of course this precaution does not resolve all the problems that may arise from Section 3 of the Declaration, which cannot be analysed in great detail here; although some may be as important as whether [...] the reasonable period for a withdrawal of the Spanish Declaration to become effective can be less than six months.

IV. [...]

And in light of the foregoing, the Council of State is of the opinion:

That the Unilateral Declaration of Acceptance by Spain of the Compulsory Jurisdiction of the International Court of Justice requires the prior authorisation of the Cortes Generales.'

V. Your Excellency, however, will decide what you consider most appropriate.

Madrid, 25 January 1990

SECRETARY GENERAL

PRESIDENT

HIS EXCELLENCY THE MINISTER OF FOREIGN AFFAIRS

5. Annex: Anti Ambush Clauses

States which have made Optional Clause declarations with an Anti Ambush Clause or a similar reservation protecting them against ambushes:

1.	Australia	22 March 2002
2.	Bulgaria	24 June 1992
3.	Cyprus	29 April 1988
		3 September 2002
4.	France	10 July 1959
		20 May 1966
5.	Germany	30 April 2008
6.	Hungary	22 October 1992
7.	India	14 September 1959
		18 September 1974
8.	Israel	28 February 1984
9.	Italy	25 November 2014
10.	Japan	9 July 2007
11.	Lithuania	26 September 2012
12.	Malta	6 December 1966
		2 September 1983
13.	Mauritius	23 September 1968
14.	New Zealand	22 September 1977
15.	Nigeria	30 April 1998
16.	Philippines	18 January 1972
17.	Poland	25 September 1990
		25 March 1996
18.	Portugal	25 February 2005
19.	Slovakia	28 May 2004
20.	Somalia	11 April 1963
21.	Spain	20 October 1990
22.	United Kingdom of Great Britain and Northern Ireland	18 April 1957
		26 November 1958
		27 November 1963
		1 January 1969
		5 July 2004
		31 December 2014

6. Annex: Reservations Allowing States to Amend or Withdraw Without Period of Notice

States which have made Optional Clause declarations with reservations that allow or allowed withdrawals or amendments or both without period of notice (regardless whether they provided an initial period):

1.	Australia	18 August 1930
		21 August 1940
		6 February 1954
		17 March 1975
		22 March 2002
2.	Austria	19 May 1971
3.	Barbados	1 August 1980
4.	Belgium	17 June 1958
5.	Botswana*	16 March 1970
6.	Cambodia	19 November 1957
7.	Cameroon	3 March 1994
8.	Canada	28 July 1930
	Canada*	7 April 1970
		10 September 1985
		10 May 1994
9.	Cyprus*	29 April 1988
		3 September 2002
10.	Democratic Republic of Congo (formerly listed as Zaire)	8 February 1989
11.	El Salvador	26 November 1973
		24 November 1978
12.	France (only 'au cas où le protocole d'arbitrage, de sécurité et de réduction des armements, signé en date de ce jour, deviendrait caduc')	2 October 1924 (never ratified)
	France	1 March 1949
		10 July 1959
	France*	20 May 1966
13.	Gambia	22 June 1966
14.	Germany*	30 April 2008

15.	Greece	10 January 1994
16.	Guinea, Republic of	4 December 1998
17.	Honduras	6 June 1986
18.	India	5 February 1930
		7 March 1940
		9 January 1956
		14 September 1959
		18 September 1974
19.	Iraq	22 September 1938 (never ratified)
20.	Iran (formerly listed as Persia)	2 October 1930
21.	Ireland	15 December 2011
22.	Israel	17 October 1956
23.	Italy*	25 November 2014
24.	Japan	15 November 1958
		9 July 2007
25.	Kenya*	19 April 1965
26.	Latvia	16 February 1935
27.	Lesotho	6 September 2000
28.	Liberia	30 March 1953
29.	Lithuania*	26 September 2012
30.	Madagascar*	2 July 1992
31.	Malawi*	12 December 1966
32.	Malta*	6 December 1966
		23 January 1981
		2 December 1983
33.	Marshall Islands*	24 April 2013
34.	Mauritius*	23 September 1968
35.	Netherlands	5 August 1946
36.	New Zealand	29 March 1930
		8 April 1940
	New Zealand (only 'in light of the results of the Third United Nations Conference on the Law of the Sea in respect of the settlement of disputes')	22 September 1977

37.	Nigeria*	30 April 1998
38.	Norway (only 'in light of the results of the Third United Nations Conference on the Law of the Sea in respect of the settlement of disputes')	2 April 1976
39.	Pakistan	23 May 1957
		13 September 1960
40.	Peru*	7 July 2003
41.	Philippines	12 July 1947
		18 January 1972
42.	Portugal*	19 December 1955
		25 February 2005
43.	Senegal*	2 May 1985
		2 December 1985
44.	Serbia and Montenegro (formerly listed as Yugoslavia)	26 April 1999
45.	Slovakia*	28 May 2004
46.	Somalia*	11 April 1963
47.	Spain	29 October 1990
48.	Sudan	2 January 1958
49.	Swaziland*	26 May 1969
50.	Timor-Leste	21 September 2012
51.	United Kingdom	5 February 1930
	United Kingdom of Great Britain and Northern Ireland	28 February 1940
		2 June 1955
		31 October 1955
		18 April 1957
	United Kingdom of Great Britain and Northern Ireland*	26 November 1958
		27 November 1963
		1 January 1969
		5 July 2004
		31 December 2014

52.	Union of South Africa	7 April 1930
		20 April 1940
		13 September 1955

* These states especially expressed that their amendments or withdrawals or both shall be effective 'from the moment,' 'from the date' or 'on the day' the Secretary-General receives the notification.

The declarations of Togo (25 October 1979) and Côte d'Ivoire (29 August 2001) provide: 'The present declaration has been made for an unlimited period subject to the power of denunciation and modification attached to any obligation assumed by a [sovereign] [s]tate in its international relations'. Similarly, the declaration of Djibouti (2 September 2005) provides: 'The present declaration is made for a period of five years, without prejudice to the right of denunciation and modification which attaches to any commitment undertaken by the state in its international relations'.

7. Annex: Conflict Clauses in Current Optional Clause Declarations

Current Optional Clause declarations with reservations excluding 'disputes in regard to which the parties to the dispute have agreed or shall agree to have recourse to some other method or methods of settlement' and declarations which contain a provision with a similar object and purpose:

1.	Australia	22 March 2002
2.	Austria	19 May 1971
3.	Barbados	1 August 1980
4.	Belgium	17 June 1958
5.	Botswana	16 March 1970
6.	Cambodia	19 September 1957
7.	Canada	10 May 1994
8.	Ivory Coast	29 September 2001
9.	Djibouti	2 September 2005
10.	Estonia	21 October 1991
11.	Gambia	22 June 1966
12.	Germany	30 April 2008
13.	Guinea, Republic of	4 December 1998
14.	Honduras	6 June 1986
15.	Hungary	22 October 1992
16.	India	18 September 1974
17.	Italy	25 November 2014
18.	Japan	9 July 2007
19.	Kenya	19 April 1965
20.	Lesotho	6 September 2000
21.	Liberia	20 March 1952
22.	Lithuania	26 September 2012
23.	Luxembourg	15 September 1930
24.	Madagascar	2 July 1992
25.	Malawi	12 December 1966
26.	Malta	6 September 1983
27.	Marshall Islands	24 April 2013
28.	Mauritius	23 September 1968

29.	Netherlands	1 August 1956
30.	New Zealand	22 September 1977
31.	Nigeria	30 April 1998
32.	Pakistan	13 September 1960
33.	Peru	7 July 2003
34.	Philippines	18 January 1972
35.	Poland	25 March 1996
36.	Portugal	25 February 2005
37.	Senegal	2 December 1985
38.	Slovakia	28 May 2004
39.	Spain	20 October 1990
40.	Sudan	2 January 1958
41.	Suriname	31 August 1987
42.	Swaziland	26 May 1969
43.	United Kingdom of Great Britain and Northern Ireland	31 December 2014

Bibliography

Acquaviva, G and Pocar, F, 'Stare Decisis' in R Wolfrum (ed), *Max Planck Encyclopedia of Public International Law* (Oxford, Oxford University Press, 2012) cited as 'G Acquaviva and F Pocar, Stare Decisis'

Alexandrov, SA, 'Accepting the Compulsory Jurisdiction of the International Court of Justice with Reservations: An Overview of Practice with a Focus on Recent Trends and Cases' (2001) 14 *Leiden Journal of International Law* 89 cited as 'SA Alexandrov, Reservations'

—— *Reservations in Unilateral Declarations Accepting the Compulsory Jurisdiction of the International Court of Justice* (Dordrecht, Martinus Nijhoff Publishers, 1995) cited as 'SA Alexandrov, *Declarations*'

Anand, RP, *Compulsory Jurisdiction of the International Court of Justice* (London, Asia Publishing House, 1961) cited as 'RP Anand, *Compulsory Jurisdiction*'

Arend, AC, *The United States and the Compulsory Jurisdiction of the International Court of Justice*, (Lanham, University Press of America, 1986) cited as 'AC Arend, *Compulsory Jurisdiction*'

Arnold, R, 'Probleme der Fakultativklausel in der Internationalen Gerichtsbarkeit' in H Kipp, F Mayer and A Steinkamm (eds), *Um Recht und Freiheit. Festschrift für Friedrich August Freiherr von der Heydte* (Berlin, Duncker & Humblot, 1977) 3 cited as 'R Arnold, Fakultativklausel'

Aust, A, *Modern Treaty Law and Practice*, 3rd edn (Cambridge, Cambridge University Press, 2013) cited as 'A Aust, *Treaty Law*'

—— 'Treaties, Termination' in R Wolfrum (ed), *Max Planck Encyclopedia of Public International Law* (Oxford, Oxford University Press, 2012) cited as 'A Aust, Termination'

—— 'Vienna Convention on the Law of Treaties (1969)' in R Wolfrum (ed), *Max Planck Encyclopedia of Public International Law* (Oxford, Oxford University Press, 2012) cited as 'A Aust, Vienna Convention'

—— 'Article 24' in O Corten and Pierre Klein (eds), *The Vienna Conventions on the Law of Treaties: A Commentary* (Oxford a.o., Oxford University Press, 2011) cited as 'A Aust, Article 24'

Bauer, M, *Vorbehalte zu Menschenrechtsverträgen* (Munich, 1994) cited as 'M Bauer, *Vorbehalte*'

Behnsen, A, *Das Vorbehaltsrecht völkerrechtlicher Verträge: Vorschlag einer Reform*, Veröffentlichungen des Walther-Schücking-Instituts für Internationales Recht an der Universität Kiel 165 (Berlin, Duncker & Humblot, 2007) cited as 'A Behnsen, *Vorbehaltsrecht*'

Bernhardt, R, 'Vorbehalte bei völkerrechtlichen Verpflichtungserklärungen und die gerichtliche Kontrolle derartiger Vorbehalte' in N Ando, E McWhinney and R Wolfrum (eds), *Liber Amicorum Judge Shigeru Oda* (The Hague, Kluwer Law International, 2002) 369 cited as 'R Bernhardt, Vorbehalte'

—— 'Anmerkungen zur Rechtsfortbildung und Rechtsschöpfung durch internationale Gerichte' in K Ginther, G Hafner, W Lang, H Neuhold and L Sucharipa-Behrmann (eds), *Völkerrecht zwischen normativem Anspruch und politischer Realität: Festschrift für Karl Zemanek* (Berlin, Duncker & Humblot, 1994) 11 cited as 'R Bernhardt, Rechtsfortbildung'

—— 'Das Gegenseitikeitsprinzip in der obligatorischen internationalen Gerichtsbarkeit' in Faculté de droit de l'Université de Genève (ed), *Recueil d'études de droit international en hommage à Paul Guggenheim* (Geneva, Imprimerie de La Tribune, 1968) 615 cited as 'R Bernhardt, Gegenseitigkeitsprinzip'

Bishop Jr, WW and Myers, DP, 'Unwarranted Extension of Connally-Amendment Thinking' (1961) 55 *American Journal of International Law* 135 cited as 'WW Bishop Jr and DP Myers, Connally-Amendment'

Bossuyt, MJ, *Guide to the 'Travaux Préparatoires' of the International Covenant on Civil and Political Rights* (Dordrecht, Martinus Nijhoff Publishers, 1987) cited as 'MJ Bossuyt, *Guide*'

Bothe, M and Klein, E, 'Bericht einer Studiengruppe zur Anerkennung der Gerichtsbarkeit des IGH gemäß Art. 36 Abs. 2 IGH-Statut' (2007) 67 *Zeitschrift für ausländisches öffentliches Recht und Völkerrecht* 825 cited as 'M Bothe and E Klein, Anerkennung der Gerichtsbarkeit'

Bowett, DW, 'Reservations to Non-Restricted Multilateral Treaties' (1976–77) 48 *British Year Book of International Law* 67 cited as 'DW Bowett, Reservations'

Briggs, HW, 'The Incidental Jurisdiction of the International Court of Justice as Compulsory Jurisdiction' in FA Freiherr von der Heydte, I Seidel-Hohenfeldern, S Verosta and K Zemanek (eds), *Völkerrecht und Rechtliches Weltbild, Festschrift für Alfred Verdross* (Wien, Springer-Verlag, 1960) 87 cited as 'HW Briggs, Incidental Jurisdiction'

—— 'Reservations to the Acceptance of Compulsory Jurisdiction of the International Court of Justice' (1958) 93 *Receuil de Cours* 223 cited as 'HW Briggs, Reservations'

Brownlie, I, *Principles of Public International Law*, 7th edn (Oxford, Oxford University Press, 2008) cited as 'I Brownlie, *Principles*'

Buigues, JLI, 'Les déclarations d'acception de la jurisdiction obligatoire de la cour internationale de justice: Leur nature et leur interprétation' (1972) 23 *Österreichische Zeitschrift für öffentliches Recht* 255 cited as 'JLI Buigues, Les déclarations d'acception'

Caddell, R, 'Treaties, Registration and Publication' in R Wolfrum (ed), *Max Planck Encyclopedia of Public International Law* (Oxford, Oxford University Press, 2012) cited as 'R Caddell, Registration'

Caflish, LC, 'The Recent Judgment of the International Court of Justice in the Case Concerning the Aerial Incident of July 27, 1955, and the Interpretation of Article 36 (V) of the Statute of the Court' (1960) 54 *American Journal of International Law* 855 cited as 'LC Caflish, Aerial Incident'

Cahier, P, 'Le comportement des états comme source de droits et des obligations' in Faculté de droit de l'Université de Genève (ed), *Recueil d'études de droit international en hommage à Paul Guggenheim* (Geneva, Imprimerie de La Tribune, 1968) 237 cited as 'P Cahier, Le comportement des états'

Cameron, I, 'Treaties, Suspension' in R Wolfrum (ed), *Max Planck Encyclope-dia of Public International Law* (Oxford, Oxford University Press, 2012) cited as 'I Cameron, Suspension'

Cassese, A, *International Law*, 2nd edn (Oxford, Oxford University Press, 2005) cited as 'A Cassese, *International Law*'

Christakis, T, 'Article 56' in O Corten and P Klein (eds), *The Vienna Conventions on the Law of Treaties: A Commentary* (Oxford, Oxford University Press, 2011) cited as 'T Christakis, Article 56'

—— 'Article 56' in O Corten and P Klein (eds), *Les conventions de Vienne sur le droit des traités* (Bruxelles, Bruylant, 2006) cited as 'T Christakis, Article 56 (2006)'

Cohen-Jonathan, G, 'Human Rights Covenants' in R Bernhardt (ed), *Encyclope-dia of Public International Law* (Amsterdam, Elsevier, 2000 cited as 'G Cohen-Jonathan, Covenants'

Cohn, IR, 'Nicaragua v United States: Pre-Seisin Reciprocity and the Race to The Hague' (1985) 46 *Ohia State Law Journal* 699 cited as 'IR Cohn, Pre-Seisin Reciprocity'

Conac, G, 'L'affaire relative à l'incident aérien du 27 Juillet 1955 entre Israel et la Bulgerie devant la Cour Internationale de Justice' (1960) 64 *Revue générale de droit international public* 711 cited as 'G Conac, L'incident aérien'

Crawford, J, *Brownlie's Principles of Public International Law*, 8th edn (Oxford, Oxford University Press, 2012) cited as 'J Crawford, *Principles*'

—— 'The Legal Effect of Automatic Reservations to the Jurisdiction of the International Court' (1979) 50 *British Year Book of International Law* 63 cited as 'J Crawford, Automatic Reservations'

D'Amato, A, 'General Discussion' in AC Arend (ed), *The United States and the Com-pulsory Jurisdiction of the International Court of Justice* (Lanham, University Press of America, 1986) 119 cited as 'A D'Amato, General Discussion'

—— 'The United States Should Accept, by a New Declaration, the General Compulsory Jurisdiction of the World Court' (1986) 80 *American Journal of Inter-national Law* 331 cited as 'A D'Amato, New Declaration'

—— 'Modifying U.S. Acceptance of the Compulsory Jurisdiction of the World Court' (1985) 79 *American Journal of International Law* 385 cited as 'A D'Amato, Modifying'

Daoudi, R, 'Article 78' in O Corten and P Klein (eds), *The Vienna Conventions on the Law of Treaties: A Commentary* (Oxford, Oxford University Press, 2011) cited as 'R Daoudi, Article 78'

de Fumel, H, *Les réserves dans les déclarations d'acceptation de la Juridiction obligatoire de la Cour International de Justice*, Publications du Centre Européen Universitaire: Collection des mémoires 4 (Nancy-Saint-Nicolas-de-Port, Indoux, 1962) cited as 'H de Fumel, *Les réserves*'

de Visscher, C, 'L'affaire de l'Interhandel devant la Cour Internatiomale de Justice' (1959) 63 *Revue générale de droit international public* 413 cited as 'C de Visscher, Interhandel'

Debbasch, C, 'La compétence "ratione temporis" de la Cour Internationale de Justice dans le système de la clause facultative de juridiction obligatoire' (1960) 64 *Revue générale de droit international public* 230 cited as 'C Debbasch, La compétence'

Decaux, E, *La réciprocité en droit international*, Bibliothèque de droit international 82 (Paris, Librairie Générale de Droit et de Jurisprudence, 1980) cited as 'E Decaux, *Réciprocité*'

Dehaussy, J, 'Les actes juridiques unilatéraux en droit international public: à propos d'une théorie restrictive' (1965) 92 *Journal du droit international* 41 cited as 'J Dehaussy, Actes unilatéraux'

Dolzer, R, 'Connally Reservation' in R Bernhardt (ed), *Encyclopedia of Public International Law* (Amsterdam, Elsevier, 2000) cited as 'R Dolzer, Connally Reservation'

Dopagne, F, 'Article 4' in O Corten and P Klein (eds), *The Vienna Conventions on the Law of Treaties: A Commentary* (Oxford, Oxford University Press, 2011) cited as 'F Dopagne, Article 4'

Dörr, O, 'Article [x]' in O Dörr and K Schmalenbach (eds), *Vienna Convention on the Law of Treaties: A Commentary* (Berlin, Springer, 2012) cited as 'O Dörr, Article [x]'

Dreyfus, S, 'Les déclarations souscrites par la France aux termes de l'article 36 du Statut de la Cour internationale de Justice' (1959) 5 *Annuaire Francais de Droit International* 258 cited as 'S Dreyfus, Les déclarations souscrites par la France'

Dubisson, M, *La cour internationale de justice* (Paris, Librairie Générale de Droit et de Jurisprudence, 1964) cited as 'M Dubisson, *La cour*'

Eick, C, 'Die Anerkennung der obligatorischen Gerichtsbarkeit des Internationalen Gerichtshofs durch Deutschland' (2008) 68 *Zeitschrift für ausländisches öffentliches Recht und Völkerrecht* 763 cited as 'C Eick, Anerkennung'

Elias, O and Lim, C, 'The Right of Passage Doctrine Revisited: An Opportunity Missed' (1999) 12 *Leiden Journal of International Law* 232 cited as 'O Elias and C Lim, Right of Passage Doctrine'

Ende, DJ, 'Reaccepting the Compulsory Jurisdiction of the International Court of Justice: A Proposal for a New United States Declaration' (1986) 61 *Washington Law Review* 1145 cited as 'DJ Ende, Reaccepting the Compulsory Jurisdiction'

Enriques, G, 'L'acceptation sans réciprocité de la juridiction obligatoire de la Cour permanente de Justice internationale' (1932) 13 *Revue de droit international et de législation comparée* 834 cited as 'G Enriques, Acceptation sans réciprocité'

Fachiri, AP, 'Repudiation of the Optional Clause' (1939) 20 *British Year Book of International Law* 52 cited as 'AP Fachiri, Repudiation'

Falkowska, M, Bedjaoui, M and Leidgens, T, 'Article 44' in O Corten and P Klein (eds), *The Vienna Conventions on the Law of Treaties: A Commentary* (Oxford, Oxford University Press, 2011) cited as 'M Falkowska, M Bedjaoui and T Leidgens, Article 44'

Farmanfarma, AN, *The Declarations of the Members Accepting the Compulsory Jurisdiction of the International Court of Justice* (Montreux, Impr Ganguin & Laubscher, 1952) cited as 'AN Farmanfarma, *Declarations*'

Feydy, J, 'La nouvelle déclaration française d'acceptation de la juridiction obligatoire de la Cour international de Justice' (1966) 12 *Annuaire Francais de Droit International* 155 cited as 'J Feydy, La déclaration française'

Fiedler, W, 'Unilateral Acts in International Law' in R Bernhardt (ed), *Encyclopedia of Public International Law* (Amsterdam, Elsevier, 2000) cited as 'W Fiedler, Unilateral Acts'

—— 'Zur Verbindlichkeit einseitiger Versprechen im Völkerrecht' (1976) 19 *German Yearbook of International Law* 35 cited as 'W Fiedler, Einseitige Versprechen'

Finke, J, *Die Parallelität internationaler Streitbeilegungsmechanismen*, Veröffentlichungen des Walther-Schücking-Instituts für Internationales Recht an der Universität Kiel 147 (Berlin, Duncker & Humblot, 2004) cited as 'J Finke, *Streitbeilegungsmechanismen*'

Fitzmaurice, GG, *The Law and Procedure of the International Court of Justice* (Cambridge, Grotius Publications, 1986) cited as 'GG Fitzmaurice, *Law and Procedure*'

—— 'Enlargement of the Contentious Jurisdiction of the Court' in L Gross (ed), *The Future of the International Court of Justice* (New York, Transnational Publishers, 1976) 461 cited as 'GG Fitzmaurice, Enlargement'

—— 'The Law and Procedure of the International Court of Justice, 1951–1954: Questions of Jurisdiction, Competence and Procedure' (1958) 34 *British Year Book of International Law* 1 cited as 'GG Fitzmaurice, Jurisdiction, Competence and Procedure'

—— 'The Law and Procedure of the International Court of Justice 1951–4: Treaty Interpretation and Other Treaty Points' (1957) 33 *British Year Book of International Law* 203 cited as 'GG Fitzmaurice, Treaty Interpretation and Other Treaty Points'

Fitzmaurice, M, 'International Court of Justice, Optional Clause' in R Wolfrum (ed), *The Max Planck Encyclopedia of Public International Law* (Oxford, Oxford University Press, 2012) cited as 'M Fitzmaurice, Optional Clause'

—— 'Treaties' in R Wolfrum (ed), *Max Planck Encyclopedia of Public International Law* (Oxford, Oxford University Press, 2012) cited as 'M Fitzmaurice, Treaties'

—— 'The Practical Working of the Law of Treaties' in MD Evans (ed), *International Law*, 4th edn (Oxford, Oxford University Press, 2014) 166 cited as 'M Fitzmaurice, Law of Treaties'

—— 'The Optional Clause System and the Law of Treaties: Issues of Interpretation in Recent Jurisprudence of the International Court of Justice' (1999) 20 *Australian Year Book of International Law* 127 cited as 'M Fitzmaurice, Interpretation'

Frowein, JA, 'Reciprocity and Restrictions Concerning Different Optional Clauses' in N Ando, E McWhinney and R Wolfrum (eds), *Liber Amicorum Judge Shigeru Oda* (The Hague, Kluwer Law International, 2002) 397 cited as 'JA Frowein, Optional Clauses'

—— 'The International Court of Justice' in R-J Dupuy (ed), *A Handbook on International Organisations*, 2nd edn (The Hague, Kluwer Law International, 1998) 153 cited as 'JA Frowein, International Court'

—— and Peukert, W, *Europäische Menschenrechtskonvention: EMRK-Kommentar*, 3rd edn (Kehl, NP Engel Verlag, 2009) cited as 'JA Frowein and W Peukert, *EMRK-Kommentar, 2009*'

—— and Peukert, W, *Europäische Menschenrechtskonvention: EMRK-Kommentar*, 2nd edn (Kehl, NP Engel Verlag, 1996) cited as 'JA Frowein and W Peukert, *EMRK-Kommentar, 1996*'

Fuchs, E, 'Optional Provision' in R Wolfrum (ed), *Max Planck Encyclopedia of Public International Law* (Oxford, Oxford University Press, 2012) cited as 'E Fuchs, Optional Provision'

Gallus, 'L'acte général a-t-il une réelle utilité?' (1931) 8 *Revue de droit international* 377 cited as 'Gallus, L'acte général'

—— 'L'Acte General d'Arbitrage' (1930) 11 *Revue de droit international et de législation comparée* 190, 413, 878 cited as 'Gallus, L'Acte General'

Garcia, FJ, *La Jurisdicción Obligataria Unilateral del Tribunal Internacional de Justicia. Sus efectos para España* (Madrid, Dykinson, 1999) cited as 'FJ Garcia, *Jurisdicción Obligataria*'

Gautier, P, 'Article 2' in O Corten and P Klein (eds), *The Vienna Conventions on the Law of Treaties: A Commentary* (Oxford, Oxford University Press, 2011) cited as 'P Gautier, Article 2'

Ghandhi, PR, *The Human Rights Committee and the Right of Individual Communication: Law and Practice* (Aldershot, Ashgate Publishing, 1998) cited as 'PR Ghandhi, *Human Rights Committee*'

Gharbi, F, 'Le statut des déclarations d'acceptation de la juridiction obligatoire de la Cour internationale de justice' (2002) 43 *Les Cahiers de Droit* 213 cited as 'F Gharbi, Déclarations d'acceptation'

——— 'Le déclin des déclarations d'acceptation de la juridiction obligatoire de la Cour internationale de justice' (2002) 43 *Les Cahiers de Droit* 433 cited as 'F Gharbi, Le déclin'

Giegerich, T, 'Article 36' in B Simma, D Khan, G Nolte, A Paulus and N Wessendorf (eds), *The Charter of the United Nations: A Commentary*, 3rd edn (Oxford, Oxford University Press, 2012) cited as 'T Giegerich, Article 36 UN Charter'

——— 'Article [x]' in O Dörr and K Schmalenbach (eds), *Vienna Convention on the Law of Treaties: A Commentary* (Berlin, Springer, 2012) cited as 'T Giegerich, Article [x] VCLT'

——— 'Treaties, Multilateral, Reservations to' in R Wolfrum (ed), *Max Planck Encyclopedia of Public International Law* (Oxford, Oxford University Press, 2012) cited as 'T Giegerich, Reservations 2012'

——— 'Treaties; Reservations, Appendum 1998' in R Bernhardt (ed), *Encyclopedia of Public International Law; Encyclopedia of Public International Law* (Amsterdam, Elsevier, 2000) cited as 'T Giegerich, Reservations 1998'

——— 'Vorbehalte zu Menschenrechtsabkommen: Zulässigkeit. Gültigkeit und Prüfungskompetenzen von Vertragsgremien' (1995) 55 *Zeitschrift für ausländisches öffentliches Recht und Völkerrecht* 713 cited as 'T Giegerich, Vorbehalte zu Menschenrechtsabkommen'

Gigante, A, 'The Effect of Unilateral State Acts in International Law' (1969) 2 *NYU Journal of International Law and Politics* 333 cited as 'A Gigante, Unilateral State Acts'

Gordon, E, 'Legal Disputes under Article 36(2) of the Statute' in LF Damrosch (ed), *The International Court of Justice at a Crossroads* (New York, Transnational Publishers, 1987) 183 cited as 'E Gordon, Legal Disputes'

Grabenwarter, C and Pabel, K, *Europäische Menschenrechtskonvention*, 5th edn (München, CH Beck, 2012) cited as 'C Grabenwarter and K Pabel, *EMRK*'

Graf Vitzthum, W, 'Begriff, Geschichte und Rechtsquellen des Völkerrechts' in W Graf Vitzthum and A Proelß (eds), *Völkerrecht*, 6th edn (Berlin, De Gruyter, 2013) 1 cited as 'W Graf Vitzthum, Rechtsquellen'

Greig, DW, 'Nicaragua and the United States: Confrontation over the Jurisdiction of the International Court' (1991) 62 *British Year Book of International Law* 119 cited as 'DW Greig, Confrontation'

Gross, L, 'Compulsory Jurisdiction under the Optional Clause: History and Practice' in LF Damrosch (ed), *The International Court of Justice at a Crossroads* (New York, Transnational Publishers, 1987) 19 cited as 'L Gross, Optional Clause'

—— 'Bulgaria Invokes the Connally Amendment' (1962) 56 *American Journal of International Law* 357 cited as 'L Gross, Connally Amendment'

Guggenheim, P, 'Der so genannte automatische Vorbehalt der inneren Angelegenheit gegenüber der Anerkennung der obligatorischen Gerichtsbarkeit des Internationalen Gerichtshofes in seiner neuesten Gerichtspraxis' in FA Freiherr von der Heydte, I Seidel-Hohenfeldern, S Verosta and K Zemanek (eds), *Völkerrecht und Rechtliches Weltbild: Festschrift für Alfred Verdross* (Wien, Springer-Verlag, 1960) 117 cited as 'P Guggenheim, Der automatische Vorbehalt'

Hafner, G, 'Subsequent Agreements and Practice: Between Interpretation, Informal Modification, and Formal Amendment' in G Nolte (ed), *Treaties and Subsequent Practice* (Oxford, Oxford University Press, 2013) 105 cited as 'G Hafner, Subsequent Agreements and Practice'

Hambro, E, 'The Jurisdiction of the International Court of justice' (1950) 76 *Receuil de Cours* 121 cited as 'E Hambro, The Jurisdiction'

—— 'Some Observations on the Compulsory Jurisdiction of the International Court of Justice' (1948) 25 *British Year Book of International Law* 133 cited as 'E Hambro, Compulsory Jurisdiction'

Heintschel von Heinegg, W, 'Treaties, Fundamental Change of Circumstances' in R Wolfrum (ed), *Max Planck Encyclopedia of Public International Law* (Oxford, Oxford University Press, 2012) cited as 'W Heintschel von Heinegg, Change of Circumstances'

Henckaerts, J, 'Study on Customary International Humanitarian Law: A Contribution to the Understanding and Respect for the Rule of Law in Armed Conflict' (2005) 87 *International Review of the Red Cross* 175 cited as 'J Henckaerts, Customary Humanitarian Law'

Herdegen, M, 'Das "konstruktive Völkerrecht" und seine Grenzen: die Dynamik des Völkerrechts als Methodenfrage' in P-M Dupuy, B Fassbender, MN Shaw and K Sommermann (eds), *Völkerrecht als Wertordnung/Common Values in International Law: Festschrift für Christian Tomuschat* (Kehl, NP Engel Verlag, 2006) 899 cited as 'M Herdegen, Dynamik des Völkerrechts'

Higgins, AP, *British Acceptance of Compulsory Arbitration under the 'Optional Clause' and its Implications* (Cambridge, Heffer, 1929) cited as 'AP Higgins, British Acceptance'

Higgins, R, 'Introduction' in JP Gardner (ed), *From Human Rights as General Norms and a State's Right to Opt Out, Reservations and Objections to Human Rights Conventions* (London, BIICL, 1997) xv cited as 'R Higgins, Introduction'

—— 'The United Nations: Still a Force for Peace' (1989) 52 *Modern Law Review* 1 cited as 'R Higgins, The United Nations'

Hilf, M and Hörmann, S, 'Effektivität – ein Rechtsprinzip?' in P-M Dupuy, B Fassbender, MN Shaw and K Sommermann (eds), *Völkerrecht als Wertordnung/ Common Values in International Law: Festschrift für Christian Tomuschat* (Kehl, NP Engel Verlag, 2006) 913 cited as 'M Hilf and S Hörmann, Effektivität'

Hilpold, P, 'Das Vorbehaltsregime der Wiener Vertragskonventionen' (1996) 34 *Archiv des Völkerrechts* 376 cited as 'P Hilpold, Vorbehaltsregime'

Hoffmeister, F, 'Article [x]' in O Dörr and K Schmalenbach (eds), *Vienna Convention on the Law of Treaties: A Commentary* (Berlin, Springer, 2012) cited as 'F Hoffmeister, Article [x]'

Hofmann, B, *Beendigung menschenrechtlicher Verträge: Rechtliche und faktische Schranken*, Menschenrechtszentrum der Universität Potsdam 32 (Berlin, Berliner Wissenschafts-Verlag, 2009) cited as 'B Hofmann, *Beendigung*'

Holloway, K, *Modern Trends in Treaty Law: Constitutional Law, Reservations and the Three Modes of Legislation* (London, Stevens & Sons, 1967) cited as 'K Holloway, *Modern Trends*'

Horchani, F and Ben Hammadi, Y, 'Article 16' in O Corten and P Klein (eds), *The Vienna Conventions on the Law of Treaties: A Commentary* (Oxford, Oxford University Press, 2011) cited as 'F Horchani and Y Ben Hammadi, Article 16'

Huber, M, 'Gemeinschafts- und Sonderrecht unter Staaten' in *Festschrift für Otto von Gierke* (Weimar, Böhlau, 1911) 817 cited as 'M Huber, Gemeinschaftsrecht'

Hudson, MO, 'The World Court: America's Declaration Accepting Jurisdiction' (1946) 32 *American Bar Association Journal* 832 cited as 'MO Hudson, America's Declaration'

—— 'Twenty-Fourth Year of the World Court' (1946) 40 *American Journal of International Law* 1 cited as 'MO Hudson, Twenty-Fourth Year'

—— *The Permanent Court of International Justice 1920–1942: A Treatise* (New York, MacMillan Company, 1943) cited as 'MO Hudson, *Permanent Court*'

—— *La Cour Permanente de Justice Internationale* (Paris, Pedone, 1936) cited as 'MO Hudson, *Cour Permanente*'

Imbert, P, *Les réserves aux traités multilatéraux. Evolution du droit et de la pratique depuis l'avis consultatif donné par la Cour internationale de Justice le 28 mai 1951*, Revue générale de droit international public 31 (Paris, Pedone, 1978) cited as 'P Imbert, *Les réserves*'

Jennings, RY, 'Recent Cases on "Automatic" Reservations to the Optional Clause' (1958) 7 *International and Comparative Law Quarterly* 349 cited as 'RY Jennings, 'Automatic' Reservations'

Jiménez De Aréchaga, E, 'The Compulsory Jurisdiction of the International Court of Justice Under the Pact of Bogotá and the Optional Clause' in Y Dinštein and M Tabory (eds), *International Law at a Time of Perplexity: Essays in Honour of Shabtai Rosenne* (Dordrecht, Martinus Nijhoff Publishers, 1989) 355 cited as 'E Jiménez De Aréchaga, Compulsory Jurisdiction'

—— 'International Law in the Past Third of a Century' (1978) 159 *Receuil de Cours* 1 cited as 'E Jiménez De Aréchaga, International Law'

Kälin, W, 'Die Vorbehalte der Türkei zu ihrer Erklärung gem. Art 25 EMRK' (1987) 14 *Europäische Grundrechte-Zeitschrift* 421 cited as 'W Kälin, Vorbehalte der Türkei'

Karl, W, 'Article 69' in A Zimmermann, C Tomuschat, K Oellers-Frahm, CJ Tams, M Kashgar and D Diehl (eds), *The Statute of the International Court of Justice—A Commentary*, 2nd edn (Oxford, Oxford University Press, 2012) cited as 'W Karl, Article 69'

Kawano, M, 'The Optional Clause and the Administration of Justice by the Court' in N Ando, E McWhinney and R Wolfrum (eds), *Liber Amicorum Judge Shigeru Oda* (The Hague, Kluwer Law International, 2002) 419 cited as 'M Kawano, Optional Clause'

Kebbon, N, 'The World Court's Compulsory Jurisdiction under the Optional Clause – Past, Present and Future' (1989) 58 *Nordic Journal of International Law* 257 cited as 'N Kebbon, Optional Clause'

Kelsen, H, *The Law of the United Nations: A Critical Analysis of Its Fundamental Problems* (London, Stevens and Sons, 1950) cited as 'H Kelsen, *Fundamental Problems*'
—— and Tucker, RW, *Principles of International Law*, 2nd edn (New York, Holt, 1966) cited as 'H Kelsen and RW Tucker, *Principles*'
Klabbers, J, 'Treaties, Amendment and Revision' in R Wolfrum (ed), *Max Planck Encyclopedia of Public International Law* (Oxford, Oxford University Press, 2012) cited as 'J Klabbers, Amendment'
—— 'Treaties, Object and Purpose' in R Wolfrum (ed), *Max Planck Encyclopedia of Public International Law* (Oxford, Oxford University Press, 2012) cited as 'J Klabbers, Object and Purpose'
—— *An Introduction to International Institutional Law*, 2nd edn (Cambridge, Cambridge University Press, 2009) cited as 'J Klabbers, *Introduction*'
—— *The Concept of Treaty in International Law*, Developments in International Law 22 (The Hague, Kluwer Law International, 1996) cited as 'J Klabbers, *Treaty*'
Kolb, R, *The International Court of Justice* (Oxford, Hart Publishing, 2013) cited as 'R Kolb, *ICJ*'
—— *Interprétation et création du droit international*, Collection de droit international 63 (Brussels, Editions de l'Université de Bruxelles, 2013) cited as 'R Kolb, *Interprétation*'
Kooijmans, PH, 'Who Tolled the Death-Bell for Compulsory Jurisdiction?' in A Bos and H Siblesz (eds), *Realism in Law-Making. Essays on International Law in Honour of Willem Riphagen* (Dordrecht, Martinus Nijhoff Publishers, 1986) 71 cited as 'PH Kooijmans, Compulsory Jurisdiction'
Krieger, H, 'Article 65' in O Dörr and K Schmalenbach (eds), *Vienna Convention on the Law of Treaties: A Commentary* (Berlin, Springer, 2012) cited as 'H Krieger, Article 65'
Kühner, R, *Vorbehalte zu multilateralen völkerrechtlichen Verträgen: Reservations to Multilateral Treaties;* (Berlin, Springer, 1986) cited as 'R Kühner, *Vorbehalte*'
Lamm, V, *Compulsory Jurisdiction in International Law* (Cheltenham, Edward Elgar, 2014) cited as 'V Lamm, Jurisdiction'
—— 'The Multilateral Treaty Reservation Revisited' (2006) 47 *Acta Juridica Hungarica* 331 cited as 'V Lamm, Multilateral Treaty Reservation'
—— 'Some Remarks on Reservations to Declarations of Acceptance' (2006) 47 *Acta Juridica Hungarica* 119 cited as 'V Lamm, Reservations to Declarations'
—— 'Declarations Accepting the Compulsory Jurisdiction of the International Court of Justice' (2004) 45 *Acta Juridica Hungarica* 25 cited as 'V Lamm, Declarations'
—— 'Reciprocity and the Compulsory Jurisdiction of the International Court of Justice' (2003) 44 *Acta Juridica Hungarica* 45 cited as 'V Lamm, Reciprocity'
Lanfranchi, M, 'Article 58' in O Corten and P Klein (eds), *The Vienna Conventions on the Law of Treaties: A Commentary* (Oxford, Oxford University Press, 2011) cited as 'M Lanfranchi, Article 58'
Lauterpacht, H, *The Development of International Law by the International Court* (London, Praeger, 1958) cited as 'H Lauterpacht, *Development*'
—— 'Restrictive Interpretation and the Principle of Effectiveness in the Interpretation of Treaties' (1949) 26 *British Year Book of International Law* 48 cited as 'H Lauterpacht, Interpretation'
—— 'The British Reservations to the Optional Clause' (1930) 10 *Econimica* 137 cited as 'H Lauterpacht, British Reservations'

—— 'La théorie des différends non justiciables en droit international' (1930) 34 *Receuil de Cours* 494 cited as 'H Lauterpacht, Différends non justiciables'

—— and Oppenheim, L, *International Law: A Treatise*, 7th edn (London, Longmans, Green and Co, 1952) cited as 'H Lauterpacht and L Oppenheim, *Treatise*'

Lawson, RC, 'The Problem of the Compulsory Jurisdiction of the World Court' (1952) 46 *American Journal of International Law* 219 cited as 'RC Lawson, Compulsory Jurisdiction'

Leibiger, M, *Die souveränitätsfreundliche Auslegung im Völkerrecht*, Rechtswissenschaft 4128 (Frankfurt am Main, Lang, 2005) cited as 'M Leibiger, *Auslegung*'

Lijnzaad, L, *Reservations to UN-Human Rights Treaties. Ratify and Ruin?* (Dordrecht, Martinus Nijhoff Publishers, 1995) cited as 'L Lijnzaad, *Reservations*'

Lippman, M, 'Human Rights Revisited: The Protection of Human Rights under the International Covenant on Civil and Political Rights' (1979) 26 *Netherlands International Law Review* 221 cited as 'M Lippman, Human Rights Revisited'

Llamazon, AP, 'Jurisdiction and Compliance in Recent Decisions of the International Court of Justice' (2007) 18 *European Journal of International Law* 815 cited as 'AP Llamazon, Compliance'

Lloyd, L, '"A Springboard for the Future": A Historical Examination of Britain's Role in Shaping the Optional Clause of the Permanent Court of International Justice' (1985) 79 *American Journal of International Law* 28 cited as 'L Lloyd, Britain's Role'

Mahiou, A, 'Article 24' in O Corten and P Klein (eds), *Les conventions de Vienne sur le droit des traités* (Bruxelles, Bruylant, 2006) cited as 'A Mahiou, Article 24'

Marchi, J, 'Article 15' in O Corten and P Klein (eds), *The Vienna Conventions on the Law of Treaties: A Commentary* (Oxford, Oxford University Press, 2011) cited as 'J Marchi, Article 15'

Marks, S, 'Three Regional Human Rights Treaties and Their Experience of Reservations' in JP Gardner (ed), *From Human Rights as General Norms and a State's Right to Opt Out, Reservations and Objections to Human Rights Conventions* (London, British Institute of International and Comparative Law, 1997) 35 cited as 'S Marks, Three Treaties'

Matz-Lück, N, 'Treaties, Conflict Clauses' in R Wolfrum (ed), *Max Planck Encyclopedia of Public International Law* (Oxford, Oxford University Press, 2012) cited as 'N Matz-Lück, Conflict Clauses'

—— 'Treaties, Conflicts between' in R Wolfrum (ed), *Max Planck Encyclopedia of Public International Law* (Oxford, Oxford University Press, 2012) cited as 'N Matz-Lück, Conflicts'

Maus, B, *Les réserves dans les déclarations d'acceptation de la juridiction obligatoire de la Cour Internationale de Justice*, Travaux de juridiction internationale 2 (Genève, E Droz, 1959) cited as 'B Maus, *Réserves*'

McDade, PV, 'The Effect of Article 4 of the Vienna Convention on the Law of Treaties 1969' (1986) 35 *International and Comparative Law Quarterly* 499 cited as 'PV McDade, Effect of Article 4'

McWhinney, E, 'Judicial Settlement of Dipsutes, Jurisdiction and Justiciability' (1990) 221 *Receuil de Cours* 9 cited as 'E McWhinney, Jurisdiction and Justiciability'

Merrills, JG, 'The Optional Clause Revisited' (1993) 64 *British Year Book of International Law* 197 cited as 'JG Merrills, Clause Revisited'

—— 'The International Court of Justice and the General Act of 1928' (1980) 39 *Cambridge Law Journal* 137 cited as 'JG Merrills, General Act'

—— 'The Optional Clause Today' (1979) 50 *British Year Book of International Law* 87 cited as 'JG Merrills, Optional Clause Today'

Minagawa, T, 'Operation of Reciprocity under the Optional Clause' (1960) 4 *Japanese Annual of International Law* 32 cited as 'T Minagawa, Reciprocity'

Morrison, FL, 'General Discussion' in AC Arend (ed), *The United States and the Compulsory Jurisdiction of the International Court of Justice* (Lanham, University Press of America, 1986) 119 cited as 'FL Morrison, General Discussion'

—— 'Potential Revisions to the Acceptance of Compulsory Jurisdiction of the International Court of Justice by the United States of America' in AC Arend (ed), *The United States and the Compulsory Jurisdiction of the International Court of Justice* (Lanham, University Press of America, 1986) 29 cited as 'FL Morrison, Potential Revisions'

Müller, D, 'Article 20' in O Corten and P Klein (eds), *The Vienna Conventions on the Law of Treaties: A Commentary* (Oxford, Oxford University Press, 2011) cited as 'D Müller, Article 20'

Myers, DP, 'The Names and Scope of Treaties' (1957) 51 *American Journal of International Law* 574 cited as 'DP Myers, Treaties'

Neuhold, H, 'The Inadequacy of Law-Making by International Treaties: "Soft Law" as an Alternative?' in R Wolfrum and V Röben (eds), *Legitimacy in International Law* (Berlin, Springer, 2005) 39 cited as 'H Neuhold, Law-Making'

Neuman, GL, 'Inter-American Court of Human Rights (IACtHR)' in R Wolfrum (ed), *Max Planck Encyclopedia of Public International Law* (Oxford, Oxford University Press, 2012) cited as 'GL Neuman, IACtHR'

Nolte, G, 'Introductory Report for the ILC Study Group on Treaties over Time' in G Nolte (ed), *Treaties and Subsequent Practice* (Oxford, Oxford University Press, 2013) 169 cited as 'G Nolte, Introductory Report'

Nowak, M, *UN Covenant on Civil and Political Rights: CCPR Commentary*, 2nd edn (Kehl, NP Engel Verlag, 2005) cited as 'M Nowak, *CCPR Commentary*'

Oda, S, 'The International Court of Justice Viewed from the Bench (1976–1993)' (1993) 244 *Receuil de Cours* 9 cited as 'S Oda, From the Bench'

—— 'Reservations in the Declarations of Acceptance of the Optional Clause and the Period of Validity of Those Declarations: The Effect of the Shultz Letter' (1988) 59 *British Year Book of International Law* 1 cited as 'S Oda, Reservations in the Declarations'

Odendahl, K, 'Article [x]' in O Dörr and K Schmalenbach (eds), *Vienna Convention on the Law of Treaties: A Commentary* (Berlin, Springer, 2012) cited as 'K Odendahl, Article [x]'

Oellers-Frahm, K, 'Der Rücktritt der USA vom Fakultativprotokoll der Konsularrechtskonvention' in P-M Dupuy, B Fassbender, MN Shaw and K Sommermann (eds), *Völkerrecht als Wertordnung/Common Values in International Law: Festschrift für Christian Tomuschat* (Kehl, NP Engel Verlag, 2006) 563 cited as 'K Oellers-Frahm, Der Rücktritt der USA'

—— 'Probleme und Grenzen der obligatorischen internationalen Gerichtsbarkeit' (1989) 27 *Archiv des Völkerrechts* 442 cited as 'K Oellers-Frahm, Obligatorische Gerichtsbarkeit'

—— 'Die "obligatorische" Gerichtsbarkeit des Internationalen Gerichtshofs' (1987) 47 *Zeitschrift für ausländisches öffentliches Recht und Völkerrecht* 243 cited as 'K Oellers-Frahm, Obligatorische Gerichtsbarkeit'

Ouguergouz, F, Villalpando, S and Morgan-Foster, J, 'Article 77' in O Corten and P Klein (eds), *The Vienna Conventions on the Law of Treaties: A Commentary* (Oxford, Oxford University Press, 2011) cited as 'F Ouguergouz, S Villalpando and J Morgan-Foster, Article 77'

Ovey, C and White, RCA, *Jacobs and White, The European Convention on Human Rights*, 4th edn (Oxford, Oxford University Press, 2006) cited as 'C Ovey and RCA White, *ECHR*'

Pastor Ridruejo, JA, 'The Spanish Declaration of Acceptance of the Compulsory Jurisdiction of the International Court of Justice' (1991) 1 *Spanish Yearbook of International Law* 19 cited as 'JA Pastor Ridruejo, The Spanish Declaration'

Pellet, A, 'Article 38' in A Zimmermann, C Tomuschat, K Oellers-Frahm, CJ Tams, M Kashgar and D Diehl (eds), *The Statute of the International Court of Justice: A Commentary*, 2nd edn (Oxford, Oxford University Press, 2012) cited as 'A Pellet, Article 38 of the Statute'

—— 'Article [x]' in O Corten and P Klein (eds), *The Vienna Conventions on the Law of Treaties: A Commentary* (Oxford, Oxford University Press, 2011) cited as 'A Pellet, Article [x] VCLT'

—— and Schabas, W, 'Article 23' in O Corten and P Klein (eds), *The Vienna Conventions on the Law of Treaties: A Commentary* (Oxford, Oxford University Press, 2011) cited as 'A Pellet and W Schabas, Article 23'

Perrin, G, 'L' affaire de l'Interhandel' (1959) 16 *Annuaire suisse de droit international* 73 cited as 'G Perrin, Interhandel'

Pinto, R, 'L'affaire de l'Interhandel' (1958) 1 *Journal du droit international* 4 cited as 'R Pinto, Interhandel'

Polakiewicz, J, 'Anmerkung zur Zulässigkeitsentscheidung der Europäischen Kommission für Menschenrechte im Fall Chrysostomos u a/Türkei vom 4 März 1991' (1991) 51 *Zeitschrift für ausländisches öffentliches Recht und Völkerrecht* 145 cited as 'J Polakiewicz, Anmerkung zum Chrysostomos Fall'

Preuss, L, 'Questions Resulting from the Connally Amendment' (1946) 32 *American Bar Association Journal* 660 cited as 'L Preuss, Connally Amendment'

Prost, M, 'Article 65' in O Corten and P Klein (eds), *The Vienna Conventions on the Law of Treaties: A Commentary* (Oxford, Oxford University Press, 2011 cited as 'M Prost, Article 65'

Quintana, JJ, 'The *Nicaragua* Case and the Denunciation of Declarations of Acceptance of the Compulsory Jurisdiction of the International Court of Justice' (1998) 11 *Leiden Journal of International Law* 97 cited as 'JJ Quintana, The Nicaragua Case'

Redgwell, C, 'Universality or Integrity? Some Reflections on Reservations to General Multilateral Treaties' (1993) 64 *British Year Book of International Law* 245 cited as 'C Redgwell, Reservations'

Reisman, WM, 'General Discussion' in AC Arend (ed), *The United States and the Compulsory Jurisdiction of the International Court of Justice* (Lanham, University Press of America, 1986) 119 cited as 'WM Reisman, General Discussion'

—— 'Has the International Court Exceeded its Jurisdiction?' (1986) 80 *American Journal of International Law* 128 cited as 'WM Reisman, Jurisdiction'

—— 'Termination of the United States Declaration under Article 36(2) of the Statute of the International Court' in AC Arend (ed), *The United States and the Compulsory Jurisdiction of the International Court of Justice* (Lanham, University Press of America, 1986) 71 cited as 'WM Reisman, Termination'

Reuter, P, *Introduction to the Law of Treaties (Translated by José Mico and Peter Haggenmacher)*, Publication of the Graduate Institute of International Studies, 2nd edn (London, Kegan Paul International, 1995) cited as 'P Reuter, *Introduction*'

Rigaldies, F, 'Contribution à l'étude de l'acte juridique unilatéral en droit international public' (1980/1981) 15 *Revue Juridique Thémis* 417 cited as 'F Rigaldies, L'acte unilatéral'

Rigaux, A, Simon, D, Spanoudis, J and Weemaels, E, 'Article 41' in O Corten and P Klein (eds), *The Vienna Conventions on the Law of Treaties: A Commentary* (Oxford, Oxford University Press, 2011) cited as 'A Rigaux, D Simon, J Spanoudis and E Weemaels, Article 41'

Roberts, A, 'Power and Persuasion in Investment Treaty Interpretation: The Dual Role of States' (2010) 104 *American Journal of International Law* 179 cited as 'A Roberts, Power and Persuasion'

Rodríguez Cedeño, V and Torres Cazorla, MI, 'Unilateral Acts of States in International Law' in R Wolfrum (ed), *Max Planck Encyclopedia of Public International Law* (Oxford, Oxford University Press, 2012) cited as 'V Rodríguez Cedeño and MI Torres Cazorla, Unilateral Acts'

Rosenne, S, 'Treaties, Conclusion and Entry into Force' in R Bernhardt (ed), *Encyclopedia of Public International Law* (Amsterdam, Elsevier, 2000) cited as 'S Rosenne, Conclusion of Treaties'

—— *The Law and Practice of the International Court, 1920–1996*, 3rd edn (The Hague, Martinus Nijhoff Publishers, 1997) cited as 'S Rosenne, *Practice 1920–1996*'

—— *The Law and Practice of the International Court*, 2nd edn (Dordrecht, Martinus Nijhoff Publishers, 1985) cited as 'S Rosenne, *Law and Practice*'

—— *Documents on the International Court of Justice*, 2nd edn (Leyden, AW Sijthoff, 1979) cited as 'S Rosenne, *Documents*'

—— *The Time Factor in the Jurisdiction of the International Court of Justice* (Leyden, AW Sijthoff, 1960) cited as 'S Rosenne, *Time Factor*'

—— *The International Court of Justice: An Essay in Political and Legal Theory* (Leyden, AW Sijthoff, 1957) cited as 'S Rosenne, *Essay*'

—— and Ronen, Y, *The Law and Practice of the International Court, 1920–2005*, 4th edn (Leiden, Martinus Nijhoff Publishers, 2006) cited as 'S Rosenne and Y Ronen, *Practice 1920–2005*'

Rotter, M, 'Art 36 Abs 2 des Statuts des Internationalen Gerichtshofes: Bestandsaufnahme und Versuch einer öffentlichrechtlichen Deutung' in H Miehsler, E Mock, B Simma and I Tammelo (eds), *Ius Humanitatis: Festschrift zum 90. Geburtstag von Alfred Verdross* (Berlin, Duncker & Humblot, 1980) 631 cited as 'M Rotter, Art 36 Abs 2 des Statuts'

Rousseau, C, *Droit international public*, 5th edn (Paris, Dalloz, 1970) cited as 'C Rousseau, *Droit*'

Rubin, AP, 'The International Legal Effects of Unilateral Declarations' (1977) 71 *American Journal of International Law* 1 cited as 'AP Rubin, Unilateral Declarations'

Ruda, JM, 'Reservations to Treaties' (1975) 146 *Receuil de Cours* 95 cited as 'JM Ruda, Reservations'

Sands, P, 'Article 39' in O Corten and P Klein (eds), *The Vienna Conventions on the Law of Treaties: A Commentary* (Oxford, Oxford University Press, 2011) cited as 'P Sands, Article 39'

—— and Peel, J, *Principles of International Environmental Law*, 3rd edn (Cambridge, Cambridge University Press, 2012) cited as 'P Sands and J Peel, *Principles*'

Schachor-Landau, C, 'The Judgment of the International Court of Justice in the Aerial Incident Case between Israel and Bulgaria' (1959/1960) 8 *Archiv des Völkerrechts* 277 cited as 'C Schachor-Landau, Aerial Incident Case'

Schilling, T, *Internationaler Menschenrechtsschutz: Das Recht der EMRK und des IPbpR*, 2nd edn (Tübingen, Mohr Siebeck, 2010) cited as 'T Schilling, *Menschenrechtsschutz*'

Schmalenbach, K, 'Article [x]' in O Dörr and K Schmalenbach (eds), *Vienna Convention on the Law of Treaties: A Commentary* (Berlin, Springer, 2012) cited as 'K Schmalenbach, Article [x]'

Schmid, K, *Die Rechtsprechung des Ständigen Internationalen Gerichtshofs* (Stuttgart, Ferdinand Enke Verlag, 1932) cited as 'K Schmid, *Rechtsprechung*'

Schmidt, MG, 'Reservations to United Nations Human Rights Treaties—the Case of the Two Covenants' in JP Gardner (ed), *From Human Rights as General Norms and a State's Right to Opt Out, Reservations and Objections to Human Rights Conventions* (London, British Institute of International and Comparative Law, 1997) 20 cited as 'MG Schmidt, Two Covenants'

Schröder, M, 'Verantwortlichkeit, Völkerstrafrecht, Streitbeilegung und Sanktionen' in W Graf Vitzthum and A Proelß (eds), *Völkerrecht*, 6th edn (Berlin, De Gruyter, 2013) 521 cited as 'M Schröder, Streitbeilegung'

Schulte, C, *Compliance with Decisions of the International Court of Justice* (Oxford, Oxford University Press, 2004) cited as 'C Schulte, *Compliance*'

Schwarzenberger, G, *International Law as Applied by International Courts and Tribunals 1*, 3rd edn (London, Stevens, 1957) cited as 'G Schwarzenberger, *International Law*'

Schwebel, SM, 'Reflections on the Role of the International Court of Justice' (1986) 61 *Washington Law Review* 1061 cited as 'SM Schwebel, The Role'

Schwelb, E, 'Notes on the Early Legislative History of the Measures of Implementation of the Human Rights Covenants' in R Cassin (ed), *Problemes des droits de l'homme et de l'unification europeenne: Melanges offerts a Polys Modinos* (Paris, Pedone, 1968) 270 cited as 'E Schwelb, Legislative History'

—— 'Civil and Political Rights: The International Measures of Implementation' (1968) 62 *American Journal of International Law* 827 cited as 'E Schwelb, Measures of Implementation'

Shaw, MN and Fournet, C, 'Article 62' in O Corten and P Klein (eds), *The Vienna Conventions on the Law of Treaties: A Commentary* (Oxford, Oxford University Press, 2011) cited as 'MN Shaw and C Fournet, Article 62'

Shihata, IFI, *The Power of the International Court to Determine Its Own Jurisdiction: Compétence de la Compétence* (The Hague, Martinus Nijhoff Publishers, 1965) cited as 'IFI Shihata, *Compétence de la Compétence*'

Sicault, J, 'Du caractère obligatoire des engagements unilatéraux en droit international public' (1979) 83 *Revue générale de droit international public* 633 cited as 'J Sicault, Engagements unilatéraux'

Simma, B, 'Reciprocity' in R Wolfrum (ed), *Max Planck Encyclopedia of Public International Law* (Oxford, Oxford University Press, 2012) cited as 'B Simma, Reciprocity'

—— 'How Has Article 36 (2) of the ICJ Statute Fared?' in T Giegerich and UE Heinz (eds), *A Wiser Century? Judicial Dispute Settlement, Disarmament and the Laws of War 100 Years after the Second Hague Peace Conference* (Berlin, Duncker & Humblot, 2009) 455 cited as 'B Simma, Article 36 (2) of the ICJ Statute'

——— 'Reservations to Human Rights Treaties – Some Recent Developments' in G Hafner, G Liobl, A Rest, L Sucharipa-Behrmann and K Zemanek (eds), *Liber Amicorum Professor Ignaz Seidl-Hohenveldern* (The Hague, Kluwer Law International, 1998) 659 cited as 'B Simma, Reservations'

——— 'From Bilateralism to Community Interest in International Law' (1994) 250 *Receuil de Cours* 217 cited as 'B Simma, Community Interest'

——— 'Die Erzeugung ungeschriebenen Völkerrechts: Allgemeine Verunsicherung – klärende Beiträge Karl Zemaneks' in K Ginther, G Hafner, W Lang, H Neuhold and L Sucharipa-Behrmann (eds), *Völkerrecht zwischen normativem Anspruch und politischer Realität, Festschrift für Karl Zemanek* (Berlin, Duncker & Humblot, 1994) 95 cited as 'B Simma, Ungeschriebenes Völkerrecht'

——— *Das Reziprozitätselement im Zustandekommen völkerrechtlicher Verträge: Gedanken zu einem Bauprinzip der internationalen Rechtsbeziehungen*, Schriften zum Völkerrecht 23 (Berlin, Duncker & Humblot, 1972) cited as 'B Simma, *Reziprozitätselement*'

——— and Tams, CJ, 'Article 60' in O Corten and P Klein (eds), *The Vienna Conventions on the Law of Treaties: A Commentary* (Oxford, Oxford University Press, 2011) cited as 'B Simma and CJ Tams, Article 60'

Sinclair, IM, *The Vienna Convention on the Law of Treaties*, Melland Schill Monographs in International Law, 2nd edn (Manchester, University Press, 1984) cited as 'IM Sinclair, *VCLT*'

Sohn, LB, 'Compulsory Jurisdiction of the World Court and the United States Position: The Need to Improve the United States Declaration' in AC Arend (ed), *The United States and the Compulsory Jurisdiction of the International Court of Justice* (Lanham, University Press of America, 1986) 3 cited as 'LB Sohn, Compulsory Jurisdiction'

Sorel, J and Eveno, VB, 'Article 31' in O Corten and P Klein (eds), *The Vienna Conventions on the Law of Treaties: A Commentary* (Oxford, Oxford University Press, 2011) cited as 'J Sorel and VB Eveno, Article 31'

Stahn, C, 'Connally Reservation' in R Wolfrum (ed), *Max Planck Encyclopedia of Public International Law* (Oxford, Oxford University Press, 2012) cited as 'C Stahn, Connally Reservation'

——— 'Vorbehalte zu Menschenrechtsverträgen' (2001) 28 *Europäische Grundrechte-Zeitschrift* 607 cited as 'C Stahn, Vorbehalte'

Steinberger, H, 'The International Court of Justice' in H Mosler and R Bernhardt (eds), *Judicial Settlement of International Disputes* (Berlin, Springer, 1974) 193 cited as 'H Steinberger, International Court'

Suy, E, *Les actes juridiques unilatéraux en droit international public* (Paris, Librairie Générale de Droit et de Jurisprudence, 1962) cited as 'E Suy, *Actes unilatéraux*'

Szafarz, R, *The Compulsory Jurisdiction of the International Court of Justice*, Legal Aspects of International Organization 14 (Dordrecht, Martinus Nijhoff Publishers, 1993) cited as 'R Szafarz, *Compulsory Jurisdiction*'

Szurek, S, 'Article 11' in O Corten and P Klein (eds), *The Vienna Conventions on the Law of Treaties: A Commentary* (Oxford, Oxford University Press, 2011) cited as 'S Szurek, Article 11'

Tams, CJ and Zimmermann, A, '"[T]he Federation Shall Accede to Agreements Providing for General, Comprehensive and Compulsory International Arbitration" – The German Optional Clause Declaration of 1 May 2008' (2008)

51 *German Yearbook of International Law* 391 cited as 'CJ Tams and A Zimmermann, German Optional Clause Declaration'

Ténékidès, CG, 'Les actes compromissoires concurrents' (1936) 17 *Revue de droit international et de législation comparée* 719 cited as 'CG Ténékidès, Les actes concurrents'

Thirlway, HWA, 'Compromis' in R Wolfrum (ed), *Max Planck Encyclopedia of Public International Law* (Oxford, Oxford University Press, 2012) cited as 'HWA Thirlway, Compromis'

—— 'The International Court of Justice' in MD Evans (ed), *International Law*, 4th edn (Oxford, Oxford University Press, 2014) 589 cited as 'HWA Thirlway, International Court, 2014'

—— 'The Sources of International Law' in MD Evans (ed), *International Law*, 4th edn (Oxford, Oxford University Press, 2014) 91 cited as 'HWA Thirlway, Sources'

—— 'The International Court of Justice' in MD Evans (ed), *International Law*, 2nd edn (Oxford, Oxford University Press, 2006) 1057 cited as 'HWA Thirlway, International Court, 2006'

—— 'The Law and Procedure of the International Court of Justice 1960–1989' (1989) 60 *British Year Book of International Law* 1 cited as 'HWA Thirlway, Law and Procedure'

—— 'Reciprocity in the Jurisdiction of the International Court' (1984) 15 *Netherlands Yearbook of International Law* 97 cited as 'HWA Thirlway, Reciprocity'

Tomka, P, 'The Special Agreement' in N Ando, E McWhinney and R Wolfrum (eds), *Liber Amicorum Judge Shigeru Oda* (The Hague, Kluwer Law International, 2002) 553 cited as 'P Tomka, Special Agreement'

Tomuschat, C, 'Article 33' in B Simma, D Khan, G Nolte, A Paulus and N Wessendorf (eds), *The Charter of the United Nations: A Commentary*, 3rd edn (Oxford, Oxford University Press, 2012) cited as 'C Tomuschat, Article 33 UN Charter'

—— 'Article 36' in A Zimmermann, C Tomuschat, K Oellers-Frahm, CJ Tams, M Kashgar and D Diehl (eds), *The Statute of the International Court of Justice—A Commentary*, 2nd edn (Oxford, Oxford University Press, 2012) cited as 'C Tomuschat, Article 36 of the Statute'

—— 'International Covenant on Civil and Political Rights (1966)' in R Wolfrum (ed), *Max Planck Encyclopedia of Public International Law* (Oxford, Oxford University Press, 2012) cited as 'C Tomuschat, ICCPR'

—— 'Admissibility and Legal Effect of Reservations to Multilateral Treaties: Comments on Arts 16 and 17 of the ILC's 1966 Draft Articles on the Law of Treaties' (1967) 27 *Zeitschrift für ausländisches öffentliches Recht und Völkerrecht* 463 cited as 'C Tomuschat, Reservations'

Trindade, AAC, 'The Operation of the Inter-American Court of Human Rights' in DJ Harris and S Livingstone (eds), *Inter-American System of Human Rights* (Oxford, Oxford University Press, 2004) 133 cited as 'AAC Trindade, IACtHR'

Úbeda de Torres, A, 'The Optional Contentious Jurisdiction of the Court' in L Burgorgue-Larsen and A Úbeda de Torres (eds), *The Inter-American Court of Human Rights: Case Law and Commentary* (Oxford, Oxford University Press, 2011) 3 cited as 'A Úbeda de Torres, Contentious Jurisdiction'

Ulimubenshi, PC, *L'exception du domaine réservé dans la procédure de la Cour Internationale* (Genève, 2003) cited as 'PC Ulimubenshi, *Domaine réservé*'

Verdross, A, 'Règles générales du droit international de la paix' (1929) 30 *Receuil de Cours* 271 cited as 'A Verdross, Règles générales'

Verzijl, JHW, 'The System of the Optional Clause' (1959) 12 *International Relations* 585 cited as 'JHW Verzijl, Optional Clause'

—— 'Cour internationale de Justice: Affaire relative a certains emprunts norvégiens (France c. Norvège)' (1957) 4 *Netherlands International Law Review* 373 cited as 'JHW Verzijl, Certains emprunts norvégiens'

Vicuña, FO, 'The Legal Nature of the Optional Clause and the Right of a State to Withdraw a Declaration Accepting the Compulsory Jurisdiction of the International Court of Justice' in N Ando, E McWhinney and R Wolfrum (eds), *Liber Amicorum Judge Shigeru Oda* (The Hague, Kluwer Law International, 2002) 463 cited as 'FO Vicuña, Legal Nature'

Vierdag, EW, 'The Time of the "Conclusion" of a Multilateral Treaty: Article 30 of the Vienna Convention on the Law of Treaties and Related Provisions' (1988) 59 *British Year Book of International Law* 75 cited as 'EW Vierdag, Time of the Conclusion'

Vignes, C, 'Observations sur la nouvelle déclaration française d'acceptation de la juridiction obligatoire de la Cour internationale de Justice' (1960) 64 *Revue générale de droit international public* 52 cited as 'C Vignes, La nouvelle déclaration française'

Villiger, ME, *Commentary on the 1969 Vienna Convention on the Law of Treaties* (Leiden, Martinus Nijhoff Publishers, 2009) cited as 'ME Villiger, *Commentary*'

—— *Customary International Law and Treaties: A Manual on the Theory and Practice of the Interrelation of Sources*, Development in International Law 28, 2nd edn (The Hague, Kluwer Law International, 1997) cited as 'ME Villiger, *Customary International Law*'

Vogiatzi, M, 'The Historical Evolution of the Optional Clause' (2002) 2 *Non-State Actors and International Law* 41 cited as 'M Vogiatzi, Historical Evolution'

Vulcan, C, 'La Clause Facultative' (1947–48) 18 *Nordic Journal of International Law* 30 cited as 'C Vulcan, La Clause Facultative'

Waldock, CHM, 'Decline of the Optional Clause' (1955–56) 32 *British Year Book of International Law* 244 cited as 'CHM Waldock, Decline'

Walter, C, 'Article [x]' in O Dörr and K Schmalenbach (eds), *Vienna Convention on the Law of Treaties: A Commentary* (Berlin, Springer, 2012) cited as 'C Walter, Article [x]'

—— '§ 1: Rechtsschutz durch den Internationalen Gerichtshof' in D Ehlers and F Schoch (eds), *Rechtsschutz im Öffentlichen Recht* (Berlin, De Gruyter, 2009) 3 cited as 'C Walter, Rechtsschutz'

Watts, A, 'The International Court and the Continuing Customary International Law of Treaties' in N Ando, E McWhinney and R Wolfrum (eds), *Liber Amicorum Judge Shigeru Oda* (The Hague, Kluwer Law International, 2002) 251 cited as 'A Watts, Customary International Law'

Weil, P, *Écrits de droit international* (Paris, Presses Universitaires de France, 2000) cited as 'P Weil, *Écrits*'

Weiss, EB, 'Reciprocity and the Optional Clause' in LF Damrosch (ed), *The International Court of Justice at a Crossroads* (New York, Transnational Publishers, 1987) 82 cited as 'EB Weiss, Reciprocity'

Wengler, W, *Völkerrecht, Band I*, Enzyklopädie der Rechts- und Staatswissenschaft (Berlin, Springer, 1964) cited as 'W Wengler, *Völkerrecht*'

Whiteman, MM, *Digest of International Law, Volume 12*, Department of State Publication 8586 (Washington DC, US Government Printing Office, 1971) cited as 'MM Whiteman, *Digest*'

Widdows, K, 'The Unilateral Denunciation of Treaties Containing no Denunciation Clause' (1982) 53 *British Year Book of International Law* 83 cited as 'K Widdows, Unilateral Denunciation'

Wilcox, FO, 'The United States Accepts Compulsory Jurisdiction' (1946) 40 *American Journal of International Law* 699 cited as 'FO Wilcox, Compulsory Jurisdiction'

Wittmann, F, *Das Problem des Obligatoriums in der internationalen Gerichtsbarkeit unter besonderer Berücksichtigung von Art 36 Absatz 2 des Statuts des Internationalen Gerichtshofes* (Geisenfeld, Staudt-Druck, 1963) cited as 'F Wittmann, *Obligatorium*'

Wundram, H, *Die Fakultativklausel (Art 36 Abs II und III des Statuts des Ständigen Internationalen Gerichtshofs)* (Wertheim, Bechstein, 1933) cited as 'H Wundram, *Fakultativklausel*'

Yankov, A, 'Les réserves dans les déclarations d'acceptation de la juridiction obligatoire de la Cour internationale de Justice' (1961) *Annuaire de l'Université de Sofia, Faculté de Droit* 586 cited as 'A Yankov, Les réserves'

Zemanek, K, 'Re-examining the Genocide Opinion: Are the Object and Purpose of a Convention Suitable Criteria for Determing the Admissibility of Reservations?' in N Ando, E McWhinney and R Wolfrum (eds), *Liber Amicorum Judge Shigeru Oda* (The Hague, Kluwer Law International, 2002) 335 cited as 'K Zemanek, Object and Purpose'

—— 'Treaties, Revision' in R Bernhardt (ed), *Encyclopedia of Public International Law* (Amsterdam, Elsevier, 2000) cited as 'K Zemanek, Revision'

—— 'Unilateral Acts Revisited' in K Wellens (ed), *Theory and Practice: Essays in Honour of Eric Suy* (The Hague, Martinus Nijhoff Publishers, 1998) 209 cited as 'K Zemanek, Unilateral Acts'

Zimmermann, A, 'Deutschland und die obligatorische Gerichtsbarkeit des Internationalen Gerichtshofs' (2006) 39 *Zeitschrift für Rechtspolitik* 248 cited as 'A Zimmermann, Die obligatorische Gerichtsbarkeit'

Index

Lightning Source UK Ltd.
Milton Keynes UK
UKHW02f0128281117
313470UK00003B/222/P